Meet the
Southern Living® Foods Staff

On these pages we invite you to match the names and faces of the people behind these pages (left to right unless otherwise noted).

(sitting) PEGGY SMITH, *Associate Foods Editor*;
ANDRIA SCOTT HURST, *Foods Editor*
(standing) PATTY M. VANN, *Associate Foods Editor*;
DONNA FLORIO, *Foods Editor*

(sitting) KAYE MABRY ADAMS, *Executive Editor*;
(standing) VICKI POELLNITZ, *Editorial Assistant;*
WANDA T. STEPHENS, *Administrative Assistant*

(sitting) MARGARET MONROE DICKEY, *Test Kitchens Director;* VANESSA A. MCNEIL, *Test Kitchens staff*
(standing) LYDA H. JONES, MARY ALLEN PERRY, JUSTIN CRAFT, JAN MOON, VIE WARSHAW, *Test Kitchens staff*

Assistant Foods Editors:
(front) CYNTHIA BRISCOE
(back) KATE NICHOLSON, SHANNON SLITER SATTERWHITE

Assistant Foods Editors:
(front) SCOTT JONES
(back) ALISON LEWIS, CYBIL A. BROWN, JOY E. ZACHARIA

Photographers and Photo Stylists: (front) TINA CORNETT, CINDY MANNING BARR, CARI SOUTH
(back) WILLIAM DICKEY, CHARLES WALTON IV, BUFFY HARGETT

Lemon-Basil Potato Salad, page 178

Warm Goat Cheese Salad, page 179

Chicken-and-Fruit Salad, page 178

Southern Living®

2001 ANNUAL RECIPES

Oxmoor House®

Library of Congress Catalog Number: 79-88364
ISBN: 0-8487-2453-4
ISSN: 0272-2003

Printed in the United States of America
First printing 2001

WE'RE HERE FOR YOU!

We at Oxmoor House are dedicated to serving you with reliable information that expands your imagination and enriches your life. We welcome your comments and suggestions. Please write us at:

Oxmoor House, Inc.
Editor, *Southern Living*® *Annual Recipes*
2100 Lakeshore Drive
Birmingham, AL 35209

To order additional publications, call 1-205-877-6560.

We Want Your FAVORITE RECIPES!

Southern Living cooks are the best cooks of all, and we want your secrets! Please send your favorite original recipes for main dishes, desserts, and everything in between, along with any hands-on tips and a sentence about why you like each recipe. We can't guarantee we'll print them in a cookbook, but if we do, we'll send you $20 and a free copy of the cookbook. Send each recipe on a separate page with your name, address, and daytime phone number to:

Cookbook Recipes
Oxmoor House
2100 Lakeshore Drive
Birmingham, AL 35209

For more books to enrich your life, visit
oxmoorhouse.com

Southern Living®

Executive Editors: Kaye Mabry Adams, Susan Dosier
Foods Editors: Donna Florio, Andria Scott Hurst
Associate Foods Editors: Peggy Smith, Patty M. Vann
Assistant Foods Editors: Cynthia Briscoe, Cybil A. Brown, Scott Jones, Allison Lewis, Kate Nicholson, Shannon Sliter Satterwhite, Joy E. Zacharia
Test Kitchens Director: Margaret Monroe Dickey
Test Kitchens Staff: Justin B. Craft, Lyda H. Jones, Vanessa A. McNeil, Jan Moon, Mary Allen Perry, Vie Warshaw
Administrative Assistant: Wanda T. Stephens
Editorial Assistant: Vicki Poellnitz
Photography and Color Quality Director: Kenner Patton
Senior Foods Photographer: Charles Walton IV
Photographers: Ralph Anderson, Tina Cornett, William Dickey, Beth Dreiling
Senior Photo Stylists: Cindy Manning Barr, Buffy Hargett
Photo Stylist: Rose Nguyen
Assistant Photo Stylist: Cari South
Photo Librarian: Tracy Duncan
Photo Services: Lisa Powell, Angela S. Titus
Production Manager: Katie Terrell
Production Coordinator: Kathryn Korotky
Production Assistant: Leah Haney

Oxmoor House, Inc.

Editor-in-Chief: Nancy Fitzpatrick Wyatt
Executive Editor: Susan Carlisle Payne
Art Directors: James Boone, Cynthia R. Cooper

Southern Living® *2001 Annual Recipes*

Editor: Catherine Ritter Scholl
Copy Editor: Donna Baldone
Editorial Assistant: Jane Lorberau Gentry
Director, Production and Distribution: Phillip Lee
Books Production Manager: Theresa L. Beste
Production Assistant: Faye Porter Bonner

Contributors

Designer: Carol O. Loria
Indexer: Mary Ann Laurens
Editorial Consultant: Jean Wickstrom Liles

Cover: Divinity Cake, page 270
Page 1: Holiday Beef Tenderloin, page 238; Bean Bundles, page 234; Sweet Potato Biscuits, page 250; Mashed sweet and russet potatoes

CONTENTS

OUR YEAR AT SOUTHERN LIVING.

Dear Friends and Food Lovers,

Greetings to you from the *Southern Living* Foods Staff! This book is like a Christmas card for us, a year-in-review of what we have learned, cooked, and loved about the magazine in 2001. Executive Editor Kaye Adams led the staff through a mouthwatering year and retired this past fall. (Rumors have it that she may be a grandmother soon!) I was delighted when *Southern Living* Editor John Floyd asked me to rejoin the staff and follow in Kaye's footsteps. You may remember me from my tenure at the magazine during my "single" years from 1986-1995. Now, as a wife and mother of two daughters—Lucy, age 5, and Frances, age 4—this book takes on new significance. It's my guidebook for family survival.

"I need food that's flavorful, fast, and in step with my Southern palate."

Just like you, I'm looking for ways to save time and money. I need food that's flavorful, fast, and in step with my Southern palate. Our standing columns are tailor-made to answer those needs. With bites of colorful history and authentic recipes, "Taste of the South" is enormously popular with you, our readers. Of course, I couldn't cook without "What's for Supper?" And "Quick and Easy" and "Living Light" offer the perfect balance of convenience and good nutrition.

This year brings two bonus sections to our cookbook. First, we introduce a new section, "*Southern Living* Favorites" which includes all the great recipes from our first-ever special issue. Next, we feature the recipes from our *Southern Living* Cooking School. You get every tantalizing recipe and advertiser tip from the fall and spring shows. If you missed us on the road, you can relive the food and ideas here.

Finally, don't miss our Menu Index beginning on page 337. This way, you can plan get-togethers at a glance, or get inspiration for your own parties and entertaining. Whatever lifestyle you lead, we hope this book packages the best of *Southern Living* in an easy-to-use format you'll reference again and again.

It's good to be back. Let me hear from you…and send me your best, original recipes! Visit us online at www.southernliving.com (AOL Keyword: Southern Living), and go to www.southernliving.com/food/survey_readerrecipes.asp to e-mail us your recipes. Or mail them to *Southern Living* Foods Editor, P.O. Box 523, Birmingham, AL 35201. Have questions, story ideas? Write me via email at susan_dosier@timeinc.com.

May your kitchen be a place of joy!

Susan Dosier

Susan Dosier
Executive Editor

P.S. Don't miss a chance to win $100,000 in our *Southern Living* $100,000 Cook-Off 2002. Visit www.southernlivingcookoff.com to enter, see the ad in our magazine, or call toll free 1-866-587-3353 for details.

Best Recipes of 2001

Our team of food professionals gathers almost every day to taste-test recipes, and we can't help but pick favorites. Here we share this year's highest-rated recipes.

Baby Blue Salad (page 20) Spicy pecans, sweet strawberries, and tangy blue cheese mingle with salad greens and a classic Balsamic Vinaigrette for a sensational play on flavors.

Beef Tenderloin With Henry Bain Sauce (page 20) Make this crowd-pleasing recipe the centerpiece of a lavish buffet. Served alone with its sauce or sandwiched in a bun, it'll win raves when company comes.

Tangy Green Beans With Pimiento (page 21) Crisp green beans drizzled with a sweet-and-sour dressing and strewn with pimiento make a colorful and tasty side for any entrée.

Homemade Butter Rolls (page 21) The bread basket will take center stage when filled with these buttery yeast rolls that are so versatile you can make them ahead and freeze them.

Grilled Chicken-and-Pesto Clubs (page 22) Roasted red bell peppers and creamy goat cheese update this time-honored sandwich.

Italian Club Sandwich (page 22) The classic club takes on an Italian accent when loaded with salami, mortadella, and provolone.

Corn Waffles (page 24) Whole kernel corn dresses a traditional breakfast favorite for dinner. Slather the golden squares with Cilantro-Lime Butter for a Southwestern kick.

Lime-Peanut Dressing (page 26) Douse a mix of crisp salad greens with this tangy dressing that boasts a burst of citrus and the crunch of nuts.

Hot-Water Cornbread (page 29) These golden, crisp-edged corn cakes welcome a pat of creamy butter. Four variations offer options for any time of day.

Bacon-Cheddar Hot-Water Cornbread (page 29) Try this variation that's flecked with bits of bacon and sharp Cheddar.

Baked Hot-Water Cornbread (page 29) Enjoy the same great taste and texture of the original recipe—no skillet required. Easy oven procedure eliminates some of the hands-on cooking in batches.

Country Ham Hot-Water Cornbread (page 29) Put leftover smoky, salty ham to good use in these crispy cakes.

Southwestern Hot-Water Cornbread (page 29) This zesty variation of the original, filled with jalapeño, cilantro, and Mexican cheese, delivers a fiesta of flavors.

Scalloped Cabbage (page 43) A golden crust caps this creamy side dish that puts several convenience items to good use and still tastes totally homemade.

Vanilla Cream-Filled Éclairs (page 45) A light, flaky pastry encases billowy, vanilla-tinged cream, all topped with a glossy chocolate glaze. Piecrust mix simplifies the pastry preparation in these bakery delicacies.

Banana-Chocolate Éclairs (page 45) Slivers of banana lace the vanilla custard that fills these impressive pastries.

Mocha Éclairs (page 45) A kiss of coffee in the chocolate filling transforms a simple pleasure into an extraordinary extravagance.

Peanut Butter-Chocolate Éclairs (page 45) This divine dessert pairs two popular flavors in a unique pastry treat that will remind you of a favorite childhood candy.

Strawberry Cream Éclairs (page 45) Spring's sweetest berry infuses the delicate cream nestled in the buttery pastry.

Chicken-Fried Steak (page 47) This meat-and-three staple is crispy outside, tender inside, and is best served with plenty of cream gravy and a side of fluffy mashed potatoes.

Chickpea-Chipotle Tostadas (page 54) A grand alternative to typical tacos, this meatless main dish features the smoky essence of chipotle chiles.

Green Chile-Pimiento Cheese (page 61) Green chiles spike the standard sandwich spread with a new attitude and flavor profile.

Lamb Chops With Mint Aioli (page 70) Chef Frank Stitt of Highlands Bar and Grill celebrates spring with tender lamb chops kissed with mint-tinged aioli.

Classic Trout Amandine (page 110) Buttery toasted almonds cap these golden fillets worthy of a special occasion.

Taste of the South

This monthly column quickly became one of our most-read features as we all renewed our commitment to the treasure of old Southern favorites. Check out these recipes rich in tradition.

Hot-Water Cornbread (page 29) Bet you can't eat just one of these hot, crispy pone bread patties.

Chicken-Fried Steak (page 47) Serve these crisp fried gems with gravy, mashed potatoes, and biscuits.

Beignets (page 59) No trip to New Orleans is complete without sampling one, and now you can enjoy them at home, too.

Faidley's Crab Cakes (page 97) Baltimore's famous seafood market shares their secrets for these shapely savory sensations.

Baby Loin Back Ribs (page 106) Enjoy Tennessee's version of the famous 'cue that's first rubbed with dry spices, then drenched with a vinegar sauce during its long, slow grill. Cloak the ribs with a sweet-and-spicy tomato-based sauce just before the feast.

Classic Fried Catfish (page 135) Our just-right cornmeal coating fries up a crunchy texture without a greasy taste.

Tee's Corn Pudding (page 165) Savor an old-fashioned sweet, corn-flecked custard plus a Southwestern variation when corn is freshest in summer.

Pimiento Cheese (page 169) We share secrets to the right kind of cheese, the right kind of grater, and of course, the perfect blend of ingredients.

Pralines (page 201) We put the South's most famous candy through kitchen tests of its most debated variables and ended up with irresistible nuggets of caramel and pecans.

Brunswick Stew (page 219) Its origin causes as much discussion as what ingredients go into the hearty brew.

Chicken and Dumplings (page 231) Tips, techniques, and the definitive recipe for this Southern sensation.

Aunt Kat's Creamy Eggnog (page 287) Indulge in a cup of this rich beverage of spirit and spice. It's a beloved Southern tradition—with or without the bourbon.

Top-Rated Menus

We often create new menus using our most memorable recipes from past years. We retest and update each one in terms of can sizes, cooking trends, and techniques. The result is no-nonsense menus guaranteed to have everyone asking for the recipes.

■ Next time company's coming, try our beef tenderloin temptation for six complete with buttery homemade rolls you can make ahead and freeze (page 20).

■ Our winter brunch for 10 sports a decidedly Southern accent—slivers of baked ham with bourbon glaze tucked inside sweet potato biscuits (page 42).

■ A springtime soup and salad luncheon for eight is so simple you can make all three recipes ahead and chill them overnight (page 72).

■ Our trout amandine supper for six is mostly make ahead. Follow our menu game plan, and supper can be on the table 45 minutes after you walk through the door from work or play (page 110).

■ Treat your family or weekend guests to a casual breakfast for six. Follow our cook's notes, and you'll hardly have more than heating and eating to do the next morning (page 130).

■ A trio of cool summer salads serves six for an outdoor picnic or an indoor respite from the heat (page 178).

■ Fire up the grill for a tropical shrimp entrée, and grill pineapple for dessert à la mode while you enjoy a simple dinner for six (page 195).

■ Come home to comfort food for a family of four with our baked chicken and golden gravy just right for spooning over mashed potatoes. Applesauce Pie keeps dessert comfy, too (page 212).

Living Light

You tell us that not only do you want your meals to taste great but you want them to be healthy, too. We share your concern, and each month we spotlight a different health-related food issue.

♥ Nuts contain mostly the "good" kind of fat, as well as a host of other nutrients. Permission to indulge (page 26)

♥ All kinds of deceptively delicious recipes (page 34)

♥ Salads and sides to lighten up weeknight menus (page 56)

♥ Minced fresh ginger adds a lively kick to lightened food without adding calories or fat (page 92)

♥ Easy and tasty recipes that excite kids about foods that are good for them (page 108)

♥ Recipes that'll make you want to renew your commitment to five a day of fruits and veggies (page 132)

♥ Easy and mouthwatering beef recipes you can feel good about (page 162)

♥ Terrific tacos—shrimp, vegetable, and even beef versions, all under 30% of calories from fat (page 170)

♥ Italian favorites you can enjoy more than ever knowing they're packed with nutritious ingredients and skillfully stripped of their high-fat vices (page 196)

♥ Lunchtime luxuries that'll have you the envy of your coworkers when you bring out the brown bag (page 216)

♥ A lavish Thanksgiving menu for the whole family that'll have everyone feeling good about the annual indulgence (page 254)

♥ A trio of menus comprise a mix-and-match holiday brunch that's sure to dazzle (page 288)

Quick & Easy

No one understands more than we do the need for simple recipes that taste great, because we're all so busy. That's why this monthly column is so popular with our readers. . .and with our staff!

■ Make these pancakes and waffles ahead of time and catch a few extra winks before breakfast (page 24).

■ Pantry staples provide quick side-dish solutions for supper (page 46).

■ A trio of cakes short on preparation but long on flavor (page 58).

■ Turkey tenderloin medaillons cook in a jiffy and taste terrific in these recipes (page 81).

■ A brunch menu for family and friends, complete with a preparation plan that keeps it all simple (page 103).

■ Invited to a covered dish dinner or family reunion? Prepare these snappy side dishes to go (page 127).

■ As quickly as you can cook the noodles, these sauces and dressings can be ready to toss with the pasta (page 164).

■ Bottled salad dressings pack a lot of flavor and streamline these recipes (page 177).

■ Family-pleasing recipes for one-dish meals that'll solve the nightly dinnertime dilemma (page 199).

■ Lean, mean pork chops cook quickly and keep things on the healthy side (page 208).

■ A collection of recipes that make good use of time-saving products from your grocery store. Keep these recipes on hand for your busiest of days (page 257).

■ A tree-trimming party menu that will satisfy the hungry decorating crew and leave you plenty of time to survey their handiwork (page 299).

■ A make-ahead picnic portable enough to take to the lake, beach, or neighborhood park (page 334).

JANUARY

On the Count of Two

A colorful table and Bean-and-Cheese Chimichangas create a south-of-the-border feast. Two, four—no matter how you count, it comes out right. No leftovers.

Certain stages of our lives fit into categories—newlyweds, career couples, baby boomers, and empty nesters. These stages can mean cooking for two.

Preparing a meal for two can be a challenge for a new cook or an experienced one who is now cooking for a couple after years of feeding a family. These recipes are for two servings, but you can double them if company's coming. Another plus—they require mostly staples, a few fresh items, and 15 minutes or less to prepare.

HONEY-GARLIC PORK TENDERLOIN

Prep: 5 minutes
Chill: 1 hour
Grill: 26 minutes

6   tablespoons lemon juice
6   tablespoons honey
2½ tablespoons soy sauce
1½ tablespoons dry sherry or
    chicken broth
3   garlic cloves, pressed
¾   pound pork tenderloin

• **Stir** together first 5 ingredients in a shallow dish or heavy-duty zip-top plastic bag. Remove ½ cup soy sauce mixture, and set aside.
• **Prick** pork several times with a fork; place in remaining soy sauce mixture.
• **Cover** or seal, and chill 1 hour.
• **Remove** pork, discarding marinade.
• **Grill,** covered with grill lid, over medium heat (300° to 350°) 11 to 13 minutes on each side or until a meat thermometer inserted into thickest portion registers 160°, basting with reserved ½ cup soy sauce mixture. **Yield:** 2 servings.

Note: To serve 4, double all ingredients, and proceed as directed.

STIR-FRY PORK AND CASHEWS

Prep: 5 minutes
Cook: 6 minutes

½   pound boneless pork loin, cut into
    ½-inch pieces
3   tablespoons stir-fry sauce
1   tablespoon frozen orange juice
    concentrate, thawed
1½ teaspoons cornstarch
3   tablespoons vegetable oil
½   cup dry-roasted or unsalted cashews
Hot cooked rice
Orange slices (optional)

• **Stir** together first 4 ingredients.
• **Stir-fry** pork mixture in hot oil in a large nonstick skillet 4 to 6 minutes; stir in cashews.
• **Serve** pork and cashew mixture immediately over rice with, if desired, orange slices. **Yield:** 2 servings.

Note: To serve 4, use ⅓ cup stir-fry sauce, ¼ cup vegetable oil, and double all other ingredients. Proceed as directed.

Charlotte Bryant
Greensburg, Kentucky

BEAN-AND-CHEESE CHIMICHANGAS
(pictured on page 39)

Prep: 10 minutes
Fry: 20 minutes

1   (16-ounce) can refried beans
1   cup (4 ounces) shredded Monterey
    Jack cheese
⅓   cup medium salsa
1   tablespoon taco seasoning mix
½   (5-ounce) package yellow rice mix,
    cooked (optional)
5   (10-inch) flour tortillas
2   cups vegetable oil
Shredded lettuce
Toppings: salsa, Easy Guacamole
    (recipe on facing page),
    sour cream
Hominy Olé (recipe on facing page)
    (optional)

• **Stir** together first 4 ingredients. Stir in rice, if desired.
• **Place** ⅓ cup mixture just below center of each tortilla.
• **Fold** opposite sides of tortillas over filling, forming rectangles; secure with wooden picks.
• **Pour** oil into a large skillet, and heat to 325°. Fry chimichangas, in batches, 4 to 5 minutes on each side or until lightly browned.
• **Drain** on paper towels.
• **Remove** wooden picks, and arrange chimichangas on lettuce.
• **Serve** with toppings and Hominy Olé, if desired. **Yield:** 2 servings.

Note: To serve 4 or 6, double all ingredients, and proceed as directed. To bake, place on a baking sheet, and coat both sides of chimichangas with cooking spray. Bake at 425° for 8 minutes; turn and bake 5 more minutes. Remove wooden picks.

Karen C. Greenlee
Lawrenceville, Georgia

CHICKEN MEDITERRANEAN

Tangy feta cheese and piquant kalamata olives enliven chicken in this Greek-inspired dish.

Prep: 8 minutes
Chill: 2 hours
Cook: 15 minutes
Stand: 5 minutes

½ pound skinned and boned chicken breast halves, cut into cubes
4 garlic cloves, minced
2 tablespoons olive oil
1 (14½-ounce) can diced tomatoes, undrained
¼ cup kalamata olives, pitted and chopped
½ teaspoon dried parsley flakes
½ teaspoon dried basil
½ teaspoon dried oregano
⅓ cup crumbled feta cheese
4 ounces penne pasta, cooked

• **Combine** first 3 ingredients in a heavy-duty zip-top plastic bag. Seal and chill 2 hours.
• **Cook** chicken mixture in a large skillet over medium-high heat 8 minutes or until chicken is done.
• **Remove** chicken mixture from skillet.
• **Add** tomatoes and next 4 ingredients to skillet.
• **Reduce** heat, and simmer, stirring often, 7 minutes.
• **Return** chicken to skillet.
• **Sprinkle** with crumbled feta cheese, and remove from heat.
• **Cover** and let stand 5 minutes.
• **Serve** immediately over hot cooked pasta. **Yield:** 2 servings.

Note: To serve 4, use 1 (14½-ounce) can diced tomatoes, undrained, and double all other ingredients. Cook chicken mixture 8 to 10 minutes or until done; remove from skillet. Add tomatoes and next 4 ingredients to skillet. Reduce heat, and simmer, stirring often, 7 to 8 minutes. Proceed as directed.

Theresa Kopajtic
Jarrettsville, Maryland

ROASTED GARLIC-AND-BASIL TOMATO SOUP
(pictured on page 38)

Serve Basil Pesto Toast (see "Side by Side" at right) with this savory soup for a light lunch or satisfying supper.

Prep: 10 minutes
Bake: 15 minutes
Cook: 5 minutes

3 large garlic cloves, slightly flattened
1 (3-ounce) package shallots, peeled and halved
1 tablespoon olive oil
1 (14½-ounce) can Italian-style stewed tomatoes, undrained
1½ cups chicken broth, divided
½ teaspoon hot sauce
½ teaspoon balsamic vinegar
¼ teaspoon salt
⅛ teaspoon freshly ground black pepper
Pinch of ground red pepper
1½ tablespoons minced fresh basil
Basil Pesto Toast (optional)

• **Place** garlic and shallots in an 8-inch square pan lined with aluminum foil; drizzle with oil.
• **Bake** at 450° for 15 minutes, stirring twice; cool.
• **Process** garlic, shallots, tomatoes, ¾ cup chicken broth, and next 5 ingredients in a blender or food processor until smooth, stopping to scrape down sides.
• **Cook** tomato mixture and remaining ¾ cup broth in a medium saucepan over medium heat 5 minutes or until thoroughly heated.
• **Stir** in basil; serve immediately with Basil Pesto Toast, if desired. **Yield:** 2 servings.

Note: To serve 4, double all ingredients. Process half each of garlic, shallots, and tomatoes with 1 cup broth in blender; repeat. Heat tomato mixture and remaining 1 cup broth in a large saucepan for 8 minutes.

Gloria Pleasants
Williamsburg, Virginia

SIDE BY SIDE

Serve these recipes for easy accompaniments with your meals. They're quick to prepare and sure to satisfy.

Basil Pesto Toast
Lightly toast 1 French baguette; cut into thin slices. Spread basil pesto evenly over slices. Sprinkle with crumbled tomato-basil feta cheese. Broil, 3 inches from heat, 1 to 2 minutes or until lightly browned.

Easy Guacamole
Mash 1 large avocado. Stir in 1 small minced garlic clove, 3 tablespoons salsa, 2 teaspoons lime juice, and ¼ teaspoon salt.

Hominy Olé
Stir together 2 (15.5-ounce) cans golden hominy, drained; 1 (12-ounce) jar salsa; 3 cups (12 ounces) shredded sharp Cheddar cheese; and ¼ teaspoon pepper. Spoon into a lightly greased 8-inch square baking dish. Bake at 350° for 30 minutes.

Down-home Chowders

Ward off winter's chill with one of these creamy, hearty chowders.

Today's chowders are a far cry from their humble beginnings. Whether you prepare yours chock-full of chicken, fish, or vegetables, it's sure to warm your spirit on a cold day. Because of their creamy texture, not all chowders freeze well—we don't recommend freezing these recipes.

MEXICAN CHICKEN-CORN CHOWDER

Prep: 20 minutes
Cook: 30 minutes

3 tablespoons butter or margarine
4 skinned and boned chicken breast halves, cut into bite-size pieces (1½ pounds)
1 small onion, chopped
2 garlic cloves, minced
2 cups half-and-half
2 cups shredded Monterey Jack cheese
2 (14¾-ounce) cans cream-style corn
1 (4.5-ounce) can chopped green chiles, undrained
½ teaspoon hot sauce
¼ teaspoon salt
½ to 1 teaspoon ground cumin
2 tablespoons chopped fresh cilantro

• **Melt** butter in a Dutch oven over medium-high heat; add chicken, onion, and garlic, and sauté 10 minutes.
• **Stir** in next 7 ingredients; cook over low heat, stirring often, 15 minutes.
• **Stir** in 2 tablespoons cilantro. **Yield:** 2 quarts.

Ellie Wells
Lakeland, Florida

SO-QUICK SEAFOOD CHOWDER

Prep: 15 minutes
Cook: 15 minutes

12 ounces fresh or frozen orange roughy fillets, thawed
½ (24-ounce) package frozen hash browns with onions and peppers
1 cup water
1 (12-ounce) can evaporated milk
1 (10¾-ounce) can cream of potato soup, undiluted
¼ cup bacon bits
2 teaspoons chopped fresh dill or ¾ teaspoon dried dillweed
¼ teaspoon salt
¼ teaspoon pepper
1 (2-ounce) jar diced pimiento, drained
Garnish: fresh dill sprig

• **Cut** fish fillets into 1-inch pieces.
• **Bring** hash browns and 1 cup water to a boil in a saucepan. Cover, reduce heat, and simmer 5 minutes or until potatoes are tender.
• **Stir** in evaporated milk and next 5 ingredients; return to a boil.
• **Add** fish and pimiento; cover, reduce heat, and simmer 3 to 5 minutes or until fish flakes easily.
• **Garnish,** if desired, and serve chowder immediately. **Yield:** 2 quarts.

Note: For testing purposes only, we used Ore-Ida Potatoes O'Brien and Hormel Real Bacon Bits.

Betty Henry
Willis, Virginia

CHEESY VEGETABLE CHOWDER

A rich cream sauce laden with a pound of cheese forms the base of this hearty chowder.

Prep: 30 minutes
Cook: 35 minutes

1 medium onion, chopped
5 celery ribs, sliced
3 carrots, sliced
1 large potato, cut into ¼-inch cubes
1 garlic clove, minced
3½ cups chicken broth
1 (14½-ounce) can whole kernel corn, rinsed and drained
¼ cup butter or margarine
¼ cup all-purpose flour
2 cups milk
1 (16-ounce) loaf pasteurized prepared cheese product, cubed
1 (2-ounce) jar diced pimiento, undrained
1 tablespoon prepared mustard
¼ teaspoon pepper
⅛ teaspoon paprika
Garnish: celery leaves

• **Bring** first 6 ingredients to a boil in a Dutch oven. Cover, reduce heat, and simmer 20 minutes or until potato is tender. Stir in corn; remove from heat.
• **Melt** butter in a heavy saucepan over low heat. Add flour, and stir until mixture is smooth. Cook, stirring constantly, 1 minute.
• **Stir** in milk and next 5 ingredients.
• **Cook,** stirring constantly, until cheese melts. Gradually stir cheese mixture into vegetable mixture.
• **Cook** over medium heat, stirring constantly, until soup is thoroughly heated. Garnish, if desired, and serve chowder immediately. **Yield:** 2 quarts.

Oatmeal Cookies

Nothing evokes childhood memories more than the wonderful aroma of cookies baking in the oven. Most of the ingredients for these recipes are staples in your pantry or refrigerator. We used regular oats, but quick oats can be used interchangeably.

Try these combinations, and you're sure to find a winner. Your biggest decision will be whether to drink milk, tea, or coffee with these tasty treats.

RAISIN-OATMEAL COOKIES

Prep: 10 minutes
Chill: 8 hours
Bake: 12 minutes per batch

1 cup butter or margarine,
    softened
1 cup sugar
1 cup firmly packed brown sugar
2 large eggs
2 cups self-rising flour
2 teaspoons ground cinnamon
3 cups uncooked regular oats
1 cup raisins
1 cup chopped pecans

• **Beat** first 3 ingredients at medium speed with an electric mixer until fluffy.
• **Add** eggs, beating until blended. Gradually add flour and ground cinnamon, beating at low speed until blended.
• **Stir** in oats, raisins, and pecans. Cover and chill dough 8 hours.
• **Divide** dough into 2 equal portions. Roll each portion into a 12-inch log.
• **Cut** each log into 1-inch-thick slices. Place slices on ungreased baking sheets.
• **Bake** at 400° for 12 minutes or until golden brown; remove to wire racks to cool. **Yield:** 2 dozen.

Lucy Hallmark
Leighton, Alabama

OATMEAL-COCONUT CRISPIES

Prep: 10 minutes
Bake: 10 minutes per batch

½ cup butter or margarine,
    softened
½ cup firmly packed brown sugar
¼ cup sugar
1 large egg
1 cup all-purpose flour
½ teaspoon baking soda
¼ teaspoon baking powder
¼ teaspoon salt
1 cup uncooked regular oats
1 cup crisp rice cereal
½ cup flaked coconut
½ cup chopped pecans

• **Beat** first 3 ingredients at medium speed with an electric mixer until fluffy. Add egg, beating until blended.
• **Add** flour and next 4 ingredients, beating until blended. Stir in rice cereal, coconut, and pecans.
• **Drop** by tablespoonfuls onto lightly greased baking sheets.
• **Bake** at 350° for 10 minutes or until lightly browned; remove to wire racks to cool. **Yield:** 3½ dozen.

Josephine M. Pitts
Pinellas Park, Florida

SPICY OATMEAL COOKIES

Prep: 10 minutes
Bake: 10 minutes per batch

½ cup shortening
1½ cups sugar
½ cup molasses
2 large eggs
1¾ cups all-purpose flour
1 teaspoon baking soda
1 teaspoon salt
1 teaspoon ground cinnamon
2 cups uncooked regular oats
1½ cups raisins
¾ cup chopped pecans (optional)

• **Beat** first 3 ingredients at medium speed with an electric mixer until blended. Add eggs, beating until blended.
• **Combine** flour and next 3 ingredients. Add to shortening mixture, beating until blended. Stir in oats, raisins, and, if desired, pecans.
• **Drop** by heaping teaspoonfuls onto lightly greased baking sheets.
• **Bake** at 350° for 10 minutes or until golden brown; remove to wire racks to cool. **Yield:** 7 dozen.

Chris Bryant
Johnson City, Tennessee

NUTTY OATMEAL-CHOCOLATE CHUNK COOKIES

Nutty Oatmeal-Chocolate Chunk Cookies, with chopped milk chocolate candy bars, won't last long. They're just too tempting.

Prep: 10 minutes
Bake: 8 minutes per batch

2½ cups uncooked regular oats
1 cup butter or margarine,
    softened
1 cup sugar
1 cup firmly packed brown sugar
2 large eggs
1 tablespoon vanilla extract
2 cups all-purpose flour
1 teaspoon baking powder
1 teaspoon baking soda
½ teaspoon salt
3 (1.55-ounce) milk chocolate candy
    bars, chopped
1½ cups chopped pecans

• **Process** oats in a blender or food processor until ground.
• **Beat** butter and sugars at medium speed with an electric mixer until fluffy. Add eggs and vanilla; beat until blended.
• **Combine** ground oats, flour, and next 3 ingredients. Add to butter mixture, beating until blended. Stir in chocolate and pecans.
• **Drop** dough by tablespoonfuls onto ungreased baking sheets.
• **Bake** at 375° for 7 to 8 minutes or until golden brown; remove to wire racks to cool. **Yield:** 6 dozen.

Cyndy Hinton
Franklin, Tennessee

Top-Rated Recipes

Here we share some of the best from 2000.

Thanks to you, Y2K was absolutely delicious. Your wonderful recipes treated us to a year of great food. It's our pleasure to celebrate by sharing these top-rated recipes.

BABY BLUE SALAD

A balsamic vinaigrette skillfully blends the salad greens, sweet fruit, and tangy blue cheese.

Prep: 10 minutes

¾ pound mixed salad greens
Balsamic Vinaigrette
4 ounces blue cheese, crumbled
2 oranges, peeled and cut into
   thin slices
1 pint strawberries, quartered
Sweet-and-Spicy Pecans

• **Toss** greens with Balsamic Vinaigrette and crumbled blue cheese. Place on 6 individual plates.
• **Arrange** orange slices over greens, and sprinkle with strawberries. Top with Sweet-and-Spicy Pecans. **Yield:** 6 servings.

Balsamic Vinaigrette

Prep: 5 minutes

½ cup balsamic vinegar
3 tablespoons Dijon mustard
3 tablespoons honey
2 garlic cloves, minced
2 small shallots, minced
¼ teaspoon salt
¼ teaspoon pepper
1 cup olive oil

• **Whisk** together first 7 ingredients until blended. Gradually whisk in olive oil. **Yield:** 1⅔ cups.

Sweet-and-Spicy Pecans

Prep: 5 minutes
Soak: 10 minutes
Bake: 10 minutes

¼ cup sugar
1 cup warm water
1 cup pecan halves
2 tablespoons sugar
1 tablespoon chili powder
⅛ teaspoon ground red
   pepper

• **Stir** together ¼ cup sugar and 1 cup warm water until sugar dissolves. Add pecan halves; soak 10 minutes. Drain, discarding sugar mixture.
• **Combine** 2 tablespoons sugar, chili powder, and red pepper. Add pecans, tossing to coat. Place on a lightly greased baking sheet.
• **Bake** at 350° for 10 minutes, stirring once. **Yield:** 1 cup.

Chef Franklin Biggs
Homewood, Alabama

BEEF TENDERLOIN WITH HENRY BAIN SAUCE

Henry Bain Sauce originated with the headwaiter at the Pendennis Club in Louisville.

Prep: 10 minutes
Chill: 2 hours
Bake: 35 minutes
Stand: 15 minutes

1 (8-ounce) bottle mango chutney
1 (14-ounce) bottle ketchup
1 (12-ounce) bottle chili sauce
1 (11-ounce) bottle steak sauce
1 (10-ounce) bottle Worcestershire
   sauce
1 teaspoon hot sauce
¼ cup butter or margarine, softened
2 teaspoons salt
1 teaspoon freshly ground pepper
1 (4½- to 5-pound) beef tenderloin,
   trimmed

• **Process** chutney in a blender or food processor until smooth. Add ketchup and next 4 ingredients, and process until blended. Chill at least 2 hours.
• **Stir** together butter, salt, and pepper; rub over tenderloin. Place tenderloin on a lightly greased rack in a jellyroll pan. Fold under 4 to 6 inches of narrow end of tenderloin to fit onto rack.
• **Bake** at 500° for 30 to 35 minutes or to desired degree of doneness. Let stand 15 minutes. Serve tenderloin with sauce. **Yield:** 10 to 12 servings.

Note: For testing purposes only, we used Major Grey's Chutney and A.1. Steak Sauce.

Smoky Mashed Potato Bake

You'd never guess that the richness and creaminess in these potatoes come mostly from fat-free ingredients. Keep it your secret!

Prep: 50 minutes
Bake: 30 minutes

3 garlic cloves, minced
1 teaspoon olive oil
3½ pounds new potatoes, cut into 1-inch pieces
¾ cup (3 ounces) shredded smoked Gouda cheese, divided
1 cup fat-free half-and-half
2 to 3 chipotle peppers in adobo sauce, minced
½ cup light margarine
½ (8-ounce) package fat-free cream cheese, softened
¼ teaspoon salt

• **Sauté** garlic in hot oil in a skillet coated with cooking spray over medium-high heat 2 to 3 minutes or until tender. Set aside.
• **Cook** potato in a Dutch oven in boiling water to cover 30 minutes or until tender; drain.
• **Mash** potato in a large bowl. Stir in garlic, ¼ cup Gouda cheese, half-and-half, and next 4 ingredients until blended.
• **Spoon** mixture into a 13- x 9-inch baking dish coated with cooking spray.
• **Sprinkle** with remaining ½ cup Gouda cheese.
• **Bake** at 350° for 30 minutes or until cheese is melted. **Yield:** 10 servings.

Michelle Zacharia
Omaha, Nebraska

Tangy Green Beans With Pimiento

Crisp bacon complete with the drippings contributes old-fashioned flavor to these green beans.

Prep: 10 minutes
Cook: 20 minutes

1½ pounds green beans, trimmed
3 bacon slices
1 large onion, chopped
3 garlic cloves, minced
1 (2-ounce) jar diced pimiento, drained
¼ cup red wine vinegar
1 teaspoon sugar
½ teaspoon salt
½ teaspoon pepper
½ teaspoon cumin seeds

• **Cook** green beans in boiling water to cover 4 to 5 minutes. Drain and plunge beans into ice water to stop the cooking process; drain and set aside.
• **Cook** bacon in a large skillet until crisp; remove bacon from skillet, and drain on paper towels, reserving 2 tablespoons drippings in skillet. Crumble bacon, and set aside.
• **Sauté** onion and garlic in hot bacon drippings over medium-high heat until tender. Stir in pimiento and next 5 ingredients.
• **Stir** in beans; cover, reduce heat, and simmer 5 minutes. Sprinkle with bacon. **Yield:** 6 servings.

Kitty Pettus
Huntsville, Alabama

Homemade Butter Rolls

Make these rich, buttery rolls ahead and freeze them for future enjoyment.

Prep: 20 minutes
Chill: 8 hours
Rise: 2 hours
Bake: 10 minutes per batch

2 (¼-ounce) envelopes active dry yeast
1 cup sugar, divided
2 cups warm water (100° to 110°)
1 cup butter or margarine, melted
6 large eggs, lightly beaten
1½ teaspoons salt
8½ to 9½ cups all-purpose flour

• **Stir** together yeast, 2 tablespoons sugar, and 2 cups warm water in a 4-cup glass measuring cup; let mixture stand 5 minutes.
• **Stir** together yeast mixture, remaining sugar, and butter in a large bowl. Stir in eggs and salt. Gradually stir in enough flour to make a soft dough. Cover and chill 8 hours.
• **Divide** dough into 4 equal portions. Turn each portion out onto a lightly floured surface; roll into a 12-inch circle.
• **Cut** each circle into 12 wedges. Roll up each wedge, starting at wide end; place on greased baking sheets. (Rolls may be frozen at this point.)
• **Cover** and let rise in a warm place (85°), free from drafts, 2 hours or until doubled in bulk.
• **Bake** at 400° for 10 minutes or until golden. **Yield:** 4 dozen.

Note: If unbaked rolls are frozen, place frozen rolls on ungreased baking sheets. Cover and let rise in a warm place (85°), free from drafts, 2 hours or until doubled in bulk. Bake as directed.

Joyce Metevia
Baton Rouge, Louisiana

Join the Club

Perk up your appetite with clever
variations on this time-honored sandwich.

Sometimes there's nothing like a good sandwich, and the club is one of the best. Traditionally made with sliced chicken, tomato, bacon, and lettuce—all packed snugly within three layers of toast—this double-decker affair became popular at the turn of the last century.

Because sandwiches are universally loved and easy to make, we found a few reader recipes that give the classic club a new look with ingredients such as avocado and flour tortillas. With these updated variations, you'll serve a sandwich that would make even Dagwood Bumstead proud.

ITALIAN CLUB SANDWICH
(pictured on page 38)

Sliced salami and mortadella give this sandwich a delightful and delicious Italian flair.

Prep: 25 minutes
Bake: 6 minutes

½ (16-ounce) Italian bread loaf
¼ cup Italian dressing
⅓ cup shredded Parmesan cheese
½ cup mayonnaise
½ cup mustard
½ pound thinly sliced Genoa salami
½ pound thinly sliced mortadella or bologna
4 (1-ounce) provolone cheese slices
Romaine lettuce leaves
3 plum tomatoes, sliced
8 bacon slices, cooked and cut in half
Garnish: pimiento-stuffed green olives

• **Cut** bread diagonally into 12 (¼-inch-thick) slices; arrange on a baking sheet.

Brush slices evenly with Italian dressing, and sprinkle with Parmesan cheese.
• **Bake** at 375° for 5 to 6 minutes or until lightly toasted.
• **Spread** mayonnaise and mustard on untoasted sides of bread slices.
• **Layer** 4 bread slices, mayonnaise side up, with salami, mortadella, and provolone.
• **Top** with 4 bread slices, mayonnaise side up; layer with lettuce, sliced tomato, and bacon.
• **Top** with remaining 4 bread slices, mayonnaise side down.
• **Cut** sandwiches in half, and secure with wooden picks. Garnish, if desired. **Yield:** 4 servings.

Melody Eustis
Mandeville, Louisiana

GRILLED CHICKEN-AND-PESTO CLUBS

Prep: 40 minutes
Grill: 20 minutes
Stand: 10 minutes

4 skinned and boned chicken breast halves
½ teaspoon salt
½ teaspoon pepper
Homemade Pesto *
12 large whole wheat bread slices, lightly toasted
1 (3-ounce) package goat cheese, crumbled
1 (5.2-ounce) jar roasted red bell peppers, drained and thinly sliced
4 plum tomatoes, sliced
8 bacon slices, cooked and cut in half
2 cups mixed salad greens

• **Sprinkle** chicken evenly with salt and pepper.
• **Grill,** covered with grill lid, over medium-high heat (350° to 400°) 10 minutes on each side or until chicken is done. Let stand 10 minutes; cut into ¼-inch-thick slices.
• **Spread** Homemade Pesto evenly on 1 side of each bread slice.
• **Layer** 4 bread slices, pesto side up, with chicken, goat cheese, and roasted bell pepper slices.
• **Top** with 4 bread slices, pesto side up; layer with tomato, bacon, and salad greens. Top with remaining 4 bread slices, pesto side down.
• **Cut** sandwiches into quarters, and secure with wooden picks. **Yield:** 4 servings.

* Substitute ¾ cup prepared pesto for homemade, if desired.

Homemade Pesto

Prep: 10 minutes

1 cup firmly packed fresh basil leaves
1 cup shredded Parmesan cheese
½ cup pine nuts, toasted
½ cup olive oil
3 garlic cloves

• **Process** all ingredients in a blender or food processor until smooth, stopping occasionally to scrape down sides. **Yield:** ¾ cup.

Marcus Marshall
Alpharetta, Georgia

COBB CLUBS

Prep: 25 minutes

1 cup blue cheese dressing
4 hoagie rolls, split and lightly toasted
¾ pound thinly sliced cooked turkey
4 (1-ounce) sharp Cheddar cheese slices
1 large avocado, thinly sliced
8 bacon slices, cooked
4 plum tomatoes, sliced
3 cups shredded leaf lettuce
¼ cup olive oil vinaigrette

- **Spread** blue cheese dressing on cut sides of each hoagie roll.
- **Layer** bottom halves of rolls evenly with turkey, Cheddar cheese, and next 4 ingredients. Drizzle with vinaigrette. Cover with top halves of rolls. **Yield:** 4 servings.

Note: For testing purposes only, we used Newman's Own Oil & Vinegar.

CLUB WRAPS

The traditional club gets a new look—wrapped in a flour tortilla.

Prep: 25 minutes

½ cup creamy mustard-mayonnaise blend
4 (10-inch) flour tortillas
½ pound thinly sliced smoked turkey
½ pound thinly sliced honey ham
1 cup (4 ounces) shredded smoked provolone or mozzarella cheese
2 cups shredded leaf lettuce
2 medium tomatoes, seeded and chopped
½ small purple onion, diced
8 bacon slices, cooked and crumbled
½ teaspoon salt
½ teaspoon pepper

- **Spread** mustard-mayonnaise blend evenly over 1 side of each tortilla, leaving a ½-inch border.
- **Layer** turkey and next 6 ingredients evenly over tortillas; sprinkle with salt and pepper.
- **Roll up** tortillas; cut in half diagonally, and secure with wooden picks. **Yield:** 4 servings.

Diane Watson
Madison, Tennessee

Sunshine Pies

On a cold, dreary day, Tangerine Chess Pie offers sweet sunshine by the slice. All of your favorite citrus fruits are in great supply right now. Mounds of ruby red grapefruit, juicy oranges, sweet tangerines, and tart lemons and limes dominate the produce section. Give them a squeeze, and turn the refreshing essence into this terrific dessert. When you need a shortcut, you can use cartons of fresh-squeezed juice. Some markets even carry fresh-squeezed tangerine juice. If tangerines aren't your favorite citrus fruit, then try a lemon-lime, orange, or grapefruit pie.

TANGERINE CHESS PIE
(pictured on page 40)

Classic chess pie gets a tangerine twist in this recipe. Also try the lemon-lime, orange, and grapefruit variations; then get ready to sample and smile.

Prep: 12 minutes
Bake: 53 minutes

1 (15-ounce) package refrigerated piecrusts
1½ cups sugar
1 tablespoon all-purpose flour
¼ teaspoon salt
1 tablespoon yellow cornmeal
¼ cup butter or margarine, melted
¼ cup milk
2 teaspoons grated tangerine rind
⅓ cup fresh tangerine juice
1 tablespoon lemon juice
4 large eggs, lightly beaten
Garnishes: sweetened whipped cream, tangerine slices

- **Unfold** piecrusts; stack piecrusts on a lightly floured surface. Roll into 1 (12-inch) circle.

- **Fit** piecrust into a 9-inch pieplate according to package directions; fold edges under, and crimp.
- **Bake** piecrust at 450° for 8 minutes; cool on a wire rack.
- **Whisk** together sugar and next 9 ingredients until blended. Pour into piecrust.
- **Bake** at 350° for 40 to 45 minutes or until center is set, shielding edges of crust with aluminum foil after 20 minutes to prevent excessive browning. Cool on a wire rack. Garnish with whipped cream and tangerine slices, if desired. **Yield:** 1 (9-inch) pie.

Grapefruit Chess Pie: Substitute fresh grapefruit juice and rind for tangerine juice and rind. Garnish with sweetened whipped cream and grapefruit rind or lime rind and lime slices, if desired.

Lemon-Lime Chess Pie *(pictured on page 40):* Substitute fresh lime juice for tangerine juice and 1 teaspoon grated lime rind and 1 teaspoon grated lemon rind for tangerine rind. Garnish pie with sweetened whipped cream, lime and lemon wedges, and grated lime and lemon rind, if desired.

Orange Chess Pie: Substitute fresh orange juice and rind for tangerine juice and rind. Garnish with sweetened whipped cream, orange slices, and orange rind, if desired.

Quick & Easy

Pancakes and waffles can be whipped up for breakfast on the weekend or for a fast weeknight dinner. If you have leftovers, put them in a single layer on a wax paper-lined baking sheet; freeze. When frozen, place in an airtight container, and return to the freezer (they'll keep up to a month). To reheat, broil 6 inches from heat 2 minutes on each side.

BANANA PANCAKES WITH PEANUT BUTTER AND JELLY SYRUPS

Prep: 10 minutes
Cook: 12 minutes

2 cups biscuit mix
1 cup buttermilk
1 cup mashed banana
2 large eggs
½ teaspoon ground cinnamon
3 tablespoons butter or margarine
¾ cup maple syrup
¼ cup reduced-fat creamy peanut butter spread
Strawberry syrup

• **Whisk** together first 5 ingredients in a large bowl just until dry ingredients are moistened.
• **Melt** 1 tablespoon butter on a hot griddle. Pour about ¼ cup batter for each pancake onto griddle. Cook pancakes until tops are covered with bubbles and edges look cooked; turn and cook other side.
• **Repeat** procedure with remaining butter and batter. Whisk together maple syrup and peanut butter until smooth.
• **Serve** pancakes with peanut butter mixture and strawberry syrup. **Yield:** 12 (4-inch) pancakes.

Note: For smaller pancakes, pour 1 tablespoon batter onto hot griddle. Proceed as directed.

Keith McNeil
Houston, Texas

APPLE PANCAKES

Prep: 10 minutes
Cook: 16 minutes

2 cups all-purpose flour
1 teaspoon baking soda
¼ teaspoon salt
¼ cup sugar
2 cups buttermilk
2 large eggs
2 tablespoons butter, melted
1 large Granny Smith apple, peeled and chopped

• **Combine** first 4 ingredients in a large bowl, and make a well in center of mixture.
• **Stir** together buttermilk, eggs, and melted butter. Add to dry ingredients, stirring just until moistened. Fold in chopped apple.
• **Pour** ¼ cup batter for each pancake onto a hot, lightly greased griddle. Cook until tops are covered with bubbles and edges look cooked; turn and cook other side. **Yield:** 16 (4-inch) pancakes.

Gwen Louer
Roswell, Georgia

WAFFLES

Top these crisp and light waffles with ice cream and fresh fruit for a different—and delicious—dessert.

Prep: 5 minutes
Cook: 15 minutes

2 cups biscuit mix
½ cup vegetable oil
2 large eggs
1 cup club soda

• **Stir** together first 3 ingredients in a large bowl; add club soda, stirring until batter is blended.
• **Cook** in a preheated, oiled waffle iron until golden. **Yield:** 10 (4-inch) waffles.

June G. Dixon
Jacksonville, Florida

CORN WAFFLES

Serve these waffles instead of traditional cornbread for a change of pace at dinner.

Prep: 20 minutes
Cook: 15 minutes

1¾ cups self-rising flour
⅓ cup sugar
½ teaspoon salt
3 large eggs, separated
½ cup buttermilk
⅓ cup vegetable oil
1 cup frozen whole kernel corn, thawed
Cilantro-Lime Butter

• **Combine** first 3 ingredients, and make a well in center of dry ingredients.
• **Stir** together egg yolks, buttermilk, vegetable oil, and corn. Add to dry ingredients, stirring just until dry ingredients are moistened.
• **Beat** egg whites at high speed with an electric mixer until stiff peaks form; fold into batter.
• **Cook** in a preheated, oiled waffle iron until golden. Serve with Cilantro-Lime Butter, honey, or maple syrup. **Yield:** 10 (4-inch) waffles.

Cilantro-Lime Butter

Prep: 5 minutes

½ cup butter, softened
1 tablespoon chopped fresh cilantro
1 teaspoon grated lime rind
1 teaspoon fresh lime juice

• **Stir** together all ingredients until blended. **Yield:** ½ cup.

The Inside Story

There are many good reasons to use stuffing in recipes. It imparts both flavor and moisture to lean cuts of pork and beef.

Pragmatic cooks will note that stuffing can easily stretch a meal where meat is in short supply. More whimsical cooks may employ stuffing to add an element of surprise to what might otherwise look like a plain dish.

Whatever your reason for mixing up the flavorful blend, we think that you'll enjoy these creations developed by Lyda Jones, a member of our Test Kitchens staff.

Lyda gives stuffing an inventive and updated taste and look by using the Southern New Year's Day staple—hopping John. The other version she created features mashed potatoes that lend a flavorful filling to flank steak.

While stuffing is usually made with bread cubes or breadcrumbs, the satisfying and easy-to-make concoctions here add loads of flavor and are a smart way to use leftover starches such as mashed potatoes or rice. In addition, both of these entrées can be made in advance, so they come in handy when time is of the essence and you need a touch of elegance on the plate.

And remember, if you have any extra stuffing, it can be cooked separately and served on the side.

PORK ROAST WITH HOPPING JOHN STUFFING

Prep: 30 minutes
Bake: 1 hour

1   small onion, chopped
½   medium-size green bell pepper, chopped
2   tablespoons vegetable oil
1½ cups cooked long-grain rice
1½ cups frozen chopped collard greens, thawed
1   (15-ounce) can black-eyed peas, rinsed and drained
½   cup diced cooked country ham
½   teaspoon sugar
½   teaspoon salt
1   large egg, lightly beaten
1   (2½-pound) boneless pork loin roast

• **Sauté** chopped onion and bell pepper in hot oil in a large skillet over medium-high heat 5 to 7 minutes or until tender. Remove from heat. Add rice and next 5 ingredients; stir in egg. Set stuffing aside.
• **Butterfly** pork loin roast by making a lengthwise cut down center of 1 flat side, cutting to within ½ inch of bottom. From bottom of cut, slice horizontally to ½ inch from left side; repeat procedure to right side.
• **Open** roast, and place between 2 sheets of heavy-duty plastic wrap. Flatten to ½-inch thickness using a meat mallet or rolling pin.
• **Spoon** 1½ cups stuffing evenly over pork loin roast, leaving a ½-inch border. Roll up roast, and tie with string at 1-inch intervals. Place roast, seam side down, in a lightly greased 11- x 7-inch baking dish.

• **Bake** at 375° for 55 to 60 minutes or until a meat thermometer inserted into center registers 160°.
• **Reheat** remaining hopping John, and serve with roast. **Yield:** 6 to 8 servings.

MASHED POTATO-STUFFED FLANK STEAK

Prep: 25 minutes
Cook: 12 minutes
Bake: 40 minutes

¼   pound andouille sausage, chopped
1   tablespoon olive oil
1   small onion, chopped
1   celery rib, chopped
½   teaspoon salt
⅛   teaspoon pepper
2   tablespoons dry white wine or chicken broth
1   small garlic clove, minced
1   cup instant potato flakes
1   cup hot water
2   tablespoons chopped fresh parsley
1½ teaspoons chopped fresh thyme
⅛   teaspoon ground nutmeg
1   (1½-pound) flank steak

• **Cook** sausage in hot oil in a skillet over medium heat 5 minutes or until browned. Remove from skillet; set aside.
• **Sauté** onion and next 3 ingredients in skillet 5 minutes or until tender. Add wine and garlic; cook 2 minutes or until liquid evaporates. Remove from heat.
• **Stir** together potato flakes and 1 cup hot water in a large bowl; stir in sausage, onion mixture, parsley, thyme, and nutmeg.
• **Place** steak between 2 sheets of heavy-duty plastic wrap; flatten to ¼- to ½-inch thickness using a meat mallet or rolling pin.
• **Spread** potato mixture evenly over flank steak, leaving a ½-inch border.
• **Roll up** steak, jellyroll fashion, starting with a long side; secure with string.
• **Place** on a lightly greased rack in a broiling pan.
• **Bake** at 425° for 10 minutes; reduce heat to 375°. Bake 25 to 30 minutes or to desired degree of doneness. **Yield:** 4 to 6 servings.

Living Light

Give yourself permission to try these nut-inspired recipes. Nuts are an excellent source of protein, fiber, and vitamin E, and they can even help in the fight against heart disease.

Several of these recipes get more than 40% of their calories from fat—but please don't panic, folks. Most of that fat comes from nuts, which contain no cholesterol.

Nuts are low in saturated fat and high in monounsaturated and polyunsaturated fats. This combination can reduce the risk of heart disease by lowering LDL (bad) cholesterol and raising HDL (good) cholesterol. A 1% reduction in LDL results in a 2% to 3% decrease in the risk of heart disease. Many nutrition experts agree that we should limit our fat intake to 30% of *total* daily calories (not necessarily individual servings).

Bold and tangy Lime-Peanut Dressing won our highest rating and brightens the flavor of everything from salad greens to fresh vegetables. Round out a meal featuring Almond Chicken with simple sides such as steamed broccoli and couscous tossed with dried cranberries. Go ahead: enjoy and indulge—you're really doing yourself a favor.

LIME-PEANUT DRESSING

Prep: 10 minutes

½ cup lime juice
4 garlic cloves, minced
3 tablespoons sugar
2 tablespoons finely chopped unsalted roasted peanuts
1 tablespoon minced fresh ginger
1 tablespoon chopped fresh cilantro
2 tablespoons fish sauce

• **Stir** together all ingredients until blended.
• **Serve** dressing over mixed salad greens or assorted fresh vegetables. **Yield:** 1 cup.

Adelyne Smith
Dunnville, Kentucky

❤ Per 2-tablespoon serving:
Calories 54 (30% from fat)
Fat 1.8g (sat 0.3g, mono 0.9g, poly 0.6g)
Protein 1.7g Carb 9g Fiber 0.4g
Chol 0mg Iron 0.3mg
Sodium 174mg Calc 9mg

ALMOND CHICKEN

Prep: 15 minutes
Chill: 1 hour
Cook: 25 minutes

⅓ cup lemon juice
3 tablespoons Dijon mustard
2 garlic cloves, minced
1 tablespoon olive oil
½ teaspoon ground white pepper
4 skinned and boned chicken breast halves
1 teaspoon olive oil
2 cups low-sodium fat-free chicken broth
1 teaspoon cornstarch
1 tablespoon water
3 tablespoons orange marmalade
1 tablespoon light margarine
½ teaspoon salt
½ teaspoon freshly ground black pepper
¼ teaspoon dried crushed red pepper
2 tablespoons chopped fresh parsley
¼ cup sliced almonds, toasted

• **Whisk** together first 5 ingredients. Place in a shallow dish, reserving ¼ cup mixture. Add chicken to dish; cover and chill 1 hour. Remove chicken from marinade; discard marinade.
• **Cook** chicken in 1 teaspoon hot oil in a large nonstick skillet over medium-high heat 8 minutes on each side or until done. Remove chicken, reserving drippings in skillet.
• **Add** reserved ¼ cup marinade mixture and chicken broth, stirring to loosen browned bits from bottom of skillet.
• **Stir** together cornstarch and water; add to broth mixture. Bring to a boil; cook, stirring constantly, 1 minute. Stir in marmalade and next 4 ingredients.
• **Return** chicken to skillet, and spoon sauce over chicken. Sprinkle with parsley and almonds. **Yield:** 4 servings.

Mildred Sherrer
Bay City, Texas

❤ Per serving: Calories 264 (43% from fat)
Fat 12.5g (sat 1.6g, mono 7.1g, poly 2.2g)
Protein 28g Carb 7g Fiber 1.1g
Chol 66mg Iron 1.4mg
Sodium 723mg Calc 48mg

CAJUN PECAN PORK

Pecan-crusted pork, with just the right amount of spice, lives up to its name. You'll also enjoy this crunchy breading on boneless chicken breasts.

Prep: 15 minutes
Chill: 1 hour
Bake: 20 minutes

½ cup pecan halves, toasted
½ cup fine, dry breadcrumbs
½ teaspoon paprika
¼ teaspoon salt
¼ teaspoon dried oregano
¼ teaspoon ground red pepper
6 (4-ounce) lean boneless pork loin chops
¼ cup all-purpose flour
½ cup nonfat buttermilk
Vegetable cooking spray

• **Process** first 6 ingredients in a blender or food processor until pecans are finely chopped.
• **Dredge** pork chops in flour. Dip in buttermilk, and dredge in pecan mixture. Cover and chill 1 hour.
• **Arrange** pork on a rack coated with cooking spray. Place rack in a 13- x 9-inch pan. Coat pork evenly with cooking spray.
• **Bake** at 425° for 15 minutes. Turn pork, and coat evenly with cooking spray. Bake 5 more minutes or until done. **Yield:** 6 servings.

Marsha Littrell
Sheffield, Alabama

♥ Per serving: Calories 298 (48% from fat)
Fat 16g (sat 3.6g, mono 7.9g, poly 2.5g)
Protein 27g Carb 13g Fiber 1g
Chol 69mg Iron 2mg
Sodium 264mg Calc 56mg

SMART BITES

Whether noshing on nuts out of hand or savoring the crunch in recipes, here's how popular nuts compare to each other and to butter and cream cheese in terms of fat content.

Per 1-ounce serving	Calories	Total Fat	Sat. Fat	Mono. Fat	Poly. Fat
Almonds	171	14g	1.1g	8.9g	3g
Cashews	163	13g	2.6g	7.7g	2.2g
Macadamias	199	21g	3.1g	16.5g	0.4g
Peanuts	165	14g	1.9g	6.9g	4.4g
Pecans	187	18.3g	1.5g	11.4g	4.5g
Sunflower seeds	160	14g	1.7g	3.6g	8.7g
Walnuts	172	16g	1g	3.6g	10.6g
Butter	216	24.4g	15.2g	7g	1g
Cream cheese	99	9.9g	6.2g	2.8g	0.4g

*Choose fat from nuts, seeds, avocados, and oils such as olive, canola, safflower, and peanut. Cut back on stick butter and margarine. Choose margarines in a squeeze bottle or tub, and try flavored cooking sprays.

MEXICO NUTS

These sweet-hot nuts are the perfect on-the-go snack.

Prep: 10 minutes
Bake: 1 hour, 30 minutes

¾ cup powdered sugar
1 tablespoon cornstarch
1 teaspoon ground cinnamon
¼ teaspoon salt
¼ teaspoon ground cloves
¼ teaspoon ground red pepper
¼ teaspoon ground allspice
1 egg white
2 tablespoons cold water
1 cup pecan halves
Vegetable cooking spray

• **Combine** first 7 ingredients.
• **Whisk** egg white lightly; add 2 tablespoons water, whisking mixture until blended.
• **Dip** pecan halves into egg white mixture. Drain well with a slotted spoon. Dredge pecan halves in sugar mixture.
• **Place** pecans in a single layer on a baking sheet coated with cooking spray. Bake at 250° for 1½ hours. **Yield:** 1 cup.

Judy Carter
Winchester, Tennessee

♥ Per 2-tablespoon serving:
Calories 144 (58% from fat)
Fat 9.3g (sat 0.7g, mono 5.7g, poly 2.3g)
Protein 1.4g Carb 16g Fiber 1g
Chol 0mg Iron 0.4mg
Sodium 80mg Calc 10mg

What's for Supper?

Economical and easy to prepare, sausage

is an everyday family favorite.

Kielbasa and Italian sausage bring instant appeal to the table. Both are convenient to prepare and may be frozen up to two months. A big difference between them is that kielbasa is precooked and Italian sausage must be cooked.

Keep kielbasa on hand in the refrigerator (store up to two weeks) for last-minute meals. Plump Italian sausage links are suitable for frying, grilling, or braising—store in refrigerator no more than two days. Two types are available—hot (spicy) or mild (sweet).

SAUSAGE SUPPER

Prep: 20 minutes
Cook: 12 minutes

1 (19-ounce) package Italian
   sausage
1 large green bell pepper,
   chopped
1 large sweet onion, chopped
2 garlic cloves, minced
1 (14-ounce) jar spaghetti sauce
1 (8-ounce) container soft cream
   cheese
¼ cup dried tomatoes, cut into thin
   strips
2 teaspoons dried Italian seasoning
1 tablespoon balsamic vinegar
   (optional)
1 (16-ounce) package farfalle pasta,
   cooked

• **Remove** casings from sausage, and discard. Brown sausage, bell pepper, onion, and garlic in a large skillet over medium-high heat, stirring until sausage crumbles and is no longer pink and vegetables are tender. Drain.
• **Stir** in spaghetti sauce, next 3 ingredients, and, if desired, vinegar.

• **Cook,** stirring often, until cream cheese melts and mixture is thoroughly heated. Serve sausage mixture over hot pasta. **Yield:** 6 servings.

Ben Moon
Birmingham, Alabama

SKILLET SAUSAGE AND CABBAGE

Kielbasa sausage and chopped cabbage team up for a hearty, flavorful, and filling meal.

Prep: 15 minutes
Cook: 25 minutes

1 (16-ounce) package kielbasa
   sausage, cut into 1-inch
   pieces
1 medium onion, thinly
   sliced
1 green bell pepper, cut into strips
6 cups coarsely chopped
   cabbage
1 cup dry white wine or chicken
   broth
½ teaspoon caraway seeds
½ teaspoon salt
½ teaspoon pepper

• **Sauté** sausage in a large heavy skillet over medium heat until browned; drain on paper towels.
• **Add** onion and bell pepper to skillet, and sauté 2 to 3 minutes.
• **Add** cabbage, and cook, stirring often, 8 minutes.
• **Add** sausage, wine, and remaining ingredients.
• **Reduce** heat to medium-low, and cook 10 minutes or until cabbage is tender. Serve immediately. **Yield:** 4 servings.

EASY CHEESY KIELBASA WITH BEANS

Prep: 10 minutes
Cook: 1 hour

1 pound ground chuck
1 large green bell pepper,
   diced
1 large onion, chopped
1 (16-ounce) package kielbasa
   sausage, thinly sliced
2 (10¾-ounce) cans tomato soup,
   undiluted
1 (14½-ounce) can diced tomatoes,
   undrained
1 (10-ounce) can diced tomato and
   green chiles, undrained
4 (16-ounce) cans pinto beans,
   undrained
4 (15-ounce) cans pork and beans,
   undrained
½ teaspoon salt
½ teaspoon pepper
2 cups (8 ounces) shredded Cheddar
   cheese

• **Cook** first 3 ingredients in a stockpot over medium-high heat, stirring until meat crumbles and is no longer pink. Remove from pot, and drain.
• **Brown** sausage in stockpot; drain and return sausage to pot. Add ground chuck mixture, tomato soup, and next 6 ingredients.
• **Bring** mixture to a boil; reduce heat, and simmer, uncovered, stirring occasionally, 30 minutes. Stir in cheese. **Yield:** 12 servings.

Note: To prepare in a slow cooker, brown ground chuck and sausage as directed. Place ground chuck mixture, sausage, and next 7 ingredients in a 5-quart slow cooker. Cook, covered, at LOW 8 to 10 hours. Stir in cheese just before serving.

Julie Templeton
Earth, Texas

DEEP-DISH PIZZA

A thick crust and meaty sauce ensure that this Italian classic will be a family favorite.

Prep: 50 minutes
Bake: 17 minutes

½ (32-ounce) package frozen bread dough
Cornmeal
9 ounces Italian sausage
1 cup chunky spaghetti sauce or pizza sauce
½ cup sliced fresh mushrooms
⅓ cup sliced ripe olives
1 cup (4 ounces) shredded mozzarella cheese

• **Thaw** bread dough according to package directions.
• **Press** dough into a lightly greased 12-inch deep-dish pizza pan covered with cornmeal. Let dough rise in a warm place (85°), free from drafts, for 30 minutes.
• **Remove** casings from sausage, and discard. Brown sausage in a small skillet over medium heat, stirring until sausage crumbles and is no longer pink. Drain on paper towels.
• **Press** dough down in center, leaving a 1½-inch edge.
• **Bake** dough on lower oven rack at 400° for 5 minutes.
• **Spread** spaghetti sauce in center of crust; sprinkle with sausage, mushrooms, and olives. Top with cheese. Bake 10 to 12 minutes. **Yield:** 1 (12-inch) pizza.

Laura Slavney
Memphis, Tennessee

Taste of the South

Some folks call these flat pancakes "pone bread" or simply hot-water bread. My family calls them something no Sunday dinner should be without.

This old-fashioned bread, with its crisp edges and mealy center, was a special recipe Mom and I cooked together. I had my own kitchen stool that was ready at a moment's notice when she tied her apron strings. I would stir the cornmeal as Mom eyeballed the amount of boiling water needed for a soft consistency. When it was time to fry, she pulled out her cast-iron skillet, a fixture at mealtime, and dropped heaping spoonfuls of dough into sizzling oil (sometimes adding bacon drippings to the oil). The mounds of cornmeal quickly turned into golden nuggets, each with a different shape. Being Mom's left-handed helper allowed me the privilege of devouring the first bite and nibbling the last crumb.

Even today, our family never passes on a basket of hot-water bread, and we make trips to Science Hill Inn in Shelbyville, Kentucky, just for that. The very thought of their hot-water cornbread makes my mouth water.

This came to mind recently when I talked to David Newell, of Trussville, Alabama, who grew up along the Natchez Trace Parkway in Mississippi. He reminisced about how his mama baked hot-water bread with a little oil. "You don't want thin cornmeal batter; the batter should hold its shape when dropped onto the baking sheet," David says. His method eliminates frying in batches, so 12 patties come out piping hot from the oven at the same time. We tried it, and the pile of crispy patties disappeared as quickly as ever. Here we share the traditional fried version, the baked version, and flavor variations.

Take David's suggestions and make large pones for the adults and small ones for the children. "You always need to have one of these in hand when you sit down to a bowl of greens or butter beans," says David. These hot, crispy, golden patties will tempt you to eat more than just one.

Cynthia Ann Briscoe

HOT-WATER CORNBREAD

Prep: 5 minutes
Cook: 18 minutes

2 cups white cornmeal
¼ teaspoon baking powder
1¼ teaspoons salt
1 teaspoon sugar
¼ cup half-and-half
1 tablespoon vegetable oil
1 to 2 cups boiling water
Vegetable oil
Softened butter

• **Combine** first 4 ingredients in a bowl; stir in half-and-half and 1 tablespoon oil. Gradually add boiling water; stir until batter is the consistency of grits.
• **Pour** oil to a depth of ½ inch into a large heavy skillet; place over medium-high heat. Scoop batter into a ¼-cup measure; drop into hot oil, and fry, in batches, 3 minutes on each side or until golden. Drain on paper towels. Serve with softened butter. **Yield:** 1 dozen.

Note: The amount of boiling water needed varies, depending on the type of cornmeal used. Stone-ground (coarsely ground) cornmeal requires more liquid.

Bacon-Cheddar Hot-Water Cornbread: After adding boiling water, stir in 8 slices cooked and crumbled bacon, 1 cup shredded sharp Cheddar cheese, and 4 minced green onions.

Baked Hot-Water Cornbread: Omit skillet procedure. Pour ⅓ cup vegetable oil into a 15- x 10-inch jellyroll pan, spreading to edges. Drop batter as directed onto pan. Bake at 475° for 12 to 15 minutes. Turn and bake 5 more minutes or until golden brown.

Country Ham Hot-Water Cornbread: After adding boiling water, stir in 1 to 2 cups finely chopped cooked country ham.

Southwestern Hot-Water Cornbread: After adding boiling water, stir in 1 jalapeño pepper, seeded and minced; 1 cup shredded Mexican cheese blend; 1 cup frozen whole kernel corn, thawed; and ¼ cup minced fresh cilantro.

From Our Kitchen

A Splash of Citrus

Give a squeeze to release all the juicy goodness of oranges, tangerines, and grapefruits. You can use these fruits to bake the chess pies on page 23, and be sure to keep some of them on hand for snacks.

From January to June is the time to find slightly sweeter grapefruits that are mature and mellow. Some of the grapefruit hybrids such as Oroblancos and Melogolds are much sweeter than other varieties. Pomelo is another tasty grapefruit choice. The pulp can be a little drier, but pomelos are sweet without a bitter aftertaste.

When oranges top your list, choose the right one for the job. Navel oranges are said to be the best for eating—they peel easily, taste sweet and juicy, and have no seeds. Cooking navel oranges can make them bitter, so add them to recipes at the last minute. Extreme cold can also cause bitterness in navel oranges, so don't try to freeze the juice for drinking. To get the most juice from any orange, bring it to room temperature, roll the fruit on the counter with the palm of your hand, and then squeeze.

Several different types of tangerines are widely available; if you see these choices in your market, be sure to try them. Dancy is sweet with an easy zip-off peel, but be ready for lots of seeds. Satsumas are juicy, sweet, and almost seedless. Honey tangerines are a bit larger than others, and the sweet juice makes their bounty of seeds well worth the trouble. Tangelos are a tasty blend of tangerine and pomelo. You'll recognize them by the knot or knob on one end. Tangelos are juicy, tart, and sweet in the same mouthful.

A TASTE OF OLD-FASHIONED GOODNESS

Grace Vick of Little Rock clipped this recipe from our pages more than 20 years ago, and it's still one of her favorites to this day. When she wrote to tell us about the popularity of the dish, we tried it again. We liked Pickled Black-Eyed Peas just the way the recipe ran originally, but we know you'll also like Test Kitchens staffer Jan Moon's fabulous updated version of the classic, Marinated Black-Eyed Peas.

PICKLED BLACK-EYED PEAS

Prep: 15 minutes
Chill: 2 hours

2 (16-ounce) cans black-eyed peas, rinsed and drained
⅔ cup vegetable oil
⅓ cup white wine vinegar
1 small onion, diced
1 garlic clove, minced
½ teaspoon salt
⅛ teaspoon pepper

• **Stir** together all ingredients; cover and chill mixture at least 2 hours. Serve with tortilla chips. **Yield:** 5 cups.

Mrs. Ted M. Robertson
Canton, Texas

Marinated Black-Eyed Peas: Substitute olive oil for vegetable oil and ½ purple onion for onion; increase black pepper to ½ teaspoon. Add 1 (16-ounce) can whole kernel corn, drained; 1 jalapeño pepper, minced; and ½ red bell pepper, chopped. **Yield:** 5½ cups.

Flavor Boosters

Slivers of country ham or smoked turkey pack a punch in soups, stews, and casseroles. If you're storing leftovers from a whole ham or turkey, pack several small heavy-duty zip-top plastic bags with just enough meat to season one recipe. Store these packages in one large heavy-duty zip-top plastic bag in the freezer. You'll have exactly the amount you need for a recipe without prying small portions from a large frozen block.

To enhance steamed vegetables such as broccoli and brussels sprouts, splash them with a bit of flavorful vinegar.

Freezer Rotation

Do you know what's in your freezer? Now's the time to get to the bottom of your food storage. Buying in bulk can be a great money saver, but savings are lost if the food isn't used in a timely manner.

Before you go to the store, go shopping in your freezer. Plan meals around what you have on hand. Any mystery packages—those with no label or date to identify them—should be discarded.

Discard all freezer-burned food. You'll know the food is burned by the pale gray-colored areas on meat or vegetables. Although it's not harmful to you, freezer-burned food tastes awful.

This project won't take long; you'll probably find some lost treasures, and you'll be starting the year well organized. And with the money you just saved, you can buy something for yourself.

Cheap Sides

Rutabagas, parsnips, winter squash, and turnips are the stars of the produce section right now. These rustic vegetables were winter supper basics for our grandparents. Today they're the savvy sides that we've rediscovered. These vegetables are inexpensive, and they lend themselves well to several cooking methods. Roast them, mash them, glaze them individually or in any tasty combination. Bring their rich, earthy flavors to the dinner table for mere pennies.

FEBRUARY

A Southern Twist on Tapas

Spanish-inspired tapas take on Southern flair in this appetizer menu that's filling enough for a meal.

Southern-Style Tapas Party
Serves 6 to 8

Black-Eyed Pea Cakes
White Bean Hummus   Crackers
Sliced cucumber   Olives
Dressed Mini Oyster Po'boys
Peppered Pork With Pecan Biscuits
Mexican beer

Today's new buzzword for appetizers is tapas. And just so we are all in the know, tapas hail from Spain, where lively eateries and bustling taverns offer small portions of food.

"Tapas" comes from a Spanish word that means "to cover." It's believed that the first tapa was a slice of ham served on a saucer atop a sherry glass, allegedly to keep out dust and other nuisances. Different types of tapas have emerged since then.

A great variety of tapas are served throughout Spain, but we thought it would be exciting to concoct some of our own versions sporting a Southern flair. Vanessa McNeil, a member of our Test Kitchens staff, created these wonderful appetizers using some familiar Southern favorites such as black-eyed peas, fried oysters, biscuits, and pecans.

These tasty recipes will inspire you to gather together friends and family to share an assortment of tempting Southern tapas and lasting conversation.

BLACK-EYED PEA CAKES

Using canned black-eyed peas and packaged hush puppy mix makes this recipe a snap to prepare.

Prep: 20 minutes
Chill: 1 hour
Cook: 25 minutes

1 small onion, chopped
1 tablespoon olive oil
2 (15.5-ounce) cans black-eyed peas, rinsed, drained, and divided
1 (8-ounce) container chive-and-onion-flavored cream cheese, softened
1 large egg
½ teaspoon salt
1 teaspoon hot sauce
1 (8-ounce) package hush puppy mix with onion
Olive oil
Toppings: sour cream, green tomato relish

• **Sauté** onion in 1 tablespoon hot oil in a large skillet over medium-high heat until tender.
• **Process** onion, 1 can of peas, and next 4 ingredients in a blender or food processor until mixture is smooth, stopping to scrape down sides.
• **Stir** in hush puppy mix, and gently fold in remaining can of peas.
• **Shape** mixture by 2 tablespoonfuls into 3-inch patties. Place patties on a wax paper-lined baking sheet. Cover and chill 1 hour.
• **Cook** patties, in batches, in 3 tablespoons hot oil, adding oil as needed, in a large skillet over medium heat for 1½ minutes on each side or until patties are golden brown.
• **Drain** patties on paper towels, and keep warm. Serve with desired toppings. **Yield:** 30 appetizer servings.

WHITE BEAN HUMMUS

Prep: 20 minutes
Chill: 1 hour

2 garlic cloves
1 teaspoon chopped fresh rosemary
2 (15.5-ounce) cans great Northern beans, rinsed and drained
3 tablespoons lemon juice
3 tablespoons tahini
¾ teaspoon salt
¼ teaspoon ground red pepper
¼ cup olive oil
Garnish: paprika

• **Pulse** garlic cloves and rosemary in a food processor 3 or 4 times or until minced.
• **Add** beans and next 4 ingredients; process until smooth, stopping to scrape down sides.
• **Pour** olive oil gradually through food chute with processor running; process until mixture is smooth. Cover and chill 1 hour. Garnish, if desired.
• **Serve** with crackers, sliced cucumber, pimiento-stuffed olives, and pitted kalamata olives. **Yield:** 3 cups.

DRESSED MINI OYSTER PO'BOYS

*To save time, purchase
prepared coleslaw.*

Prep: 30 minutes
Fry: 12 minutes

1¼ cups self-rising cornmeal
2 tablespoons Creole seasoning
2 (8-ounce) containers fresh Select
    oysters, drained
Peanut or vegetable oil
1 cup mayonnaise, divided
2 tablespoons white vinegar
2 tablespoons Dijon mustard
1 (10-ounce) package shredded
    cabbage
2 tablespoons ketchup
1 tablespoon prepared horseradish
1 teaspoon Creole seasoning
¾ teaspoon paprika
12 French bread rolls, split and
    toasted
Garnish: lemon wedges

• **Combine** cornmeal and 2 tablespoons Creole seasoning. Dredge oysters in cornmeal mixture.
• **Pour** oil to depth of 1 inch into a Dutch oven; heat to 375°.
• **Fry** oysters, in 3 batches, 3 to 4 minutes or until golden. Drain oysters on paper towels.
• **Stir** together ½ cup mayonnaise, vinegar, and mustard. Stir in shredded cabbage, and set slaw aside.
• **Stir** together remaining ½ cup mayonnaise, ketchup, and next 3 ingredients in a small bowl.
• **Spread** cut sides of French bread rolls with ketchup mixture. Place oysters and slaw evenly on bottom halves of each roll. Cover with tops. Serve po'boys immediately. Garnish, if desired. **Yield:** 4 to 6 servings.

PEPPERED PORK WITH PECAN BISCUITS

Prep: 30 minutes
Stand: 10 minutes
Bake: 50 minutes

1 teaspoon pepper
½ teaspoon salt
1 pound pork tenderloin
1 (¼-ounce) envelope rapid-rise
    yeast
1 tablespoon sugar
¾ cup warm water (100° to 110°)
4 cups biscuit mix
½ cup diced pecans
1 cup buttermilk
¼ cup butter or margarine, melted
2 tablespoons pesto
16 pecan halves
Coarse-grained Dijon mustard

• **Combine** pepper and salt, and rub evenly over tenderloin. Place on a lightly greased rack inside a roasting pan.
• **Bake** at 450° for 20 to 25 minutes or until a meat thermometer inserted into thickest portion registers 160°. Let stand 10 minutes; thinly slice.
• **Combine** yeast, sugar, and ¾ cup warm water in a large bowl; let mixture stand 5 minutes.
• **Add** biscuit mix, diced pecans, and next 3 ingredients to bowl, stirring until dry ingredients are moistened.
• **Turn** dough out onto a lightly floured surface. Pat or roll dough to 1-inch thickness; cut with a 2-inch round cutter.
• **Place** biscuits on a lightly greased baking sheet; place a pecan half in center of each biscuit.
• **Bake** at 425° for 20 to 25 minutes or until lightly browned.
• **Split** biscuits, and serve pork in biscuits with Dijon mustard. **Yield:** 6 to 8 servings.

Timely Treats

If you haven't been giving your family their just desserts, take a look at these two simple recipes. They'll leave a big impression and make everyone feel special, any day of the week.

BUTTERSCOTCH DROPS

Prep: 15 minutes

1 cup (6 ounces) butterscotch
    morsels *
1 cup dry-roasted peanuts
1 cup shoestring potato sticks, broken
    into pieces

• **Melt** morsels in a saucepan over low heat. Stir in peanuts and potato sticks. Drop by teaspoonfuls onto wax paper, and cool completely. **Yield:** 2½ dozen.

* Substitute 1 cup (6 ounces) peanut butter morsels, if desired.

Shirley Embrey
San Antonio, Texas

INDOOR S'MORES

Prep: 15 minutes
Bake: 10 minutes

1 (4.6-ounce) package vanilla
    pudding mix
8 graham cracker sheets (32 crackers)
4 (1.55-ounce) milk chocolate candy bars
¾ cup miniature marshmallows

• **Cook** pudding according to package directions.
• **Arrange** 4 graham cracker sheets in an 8-inch square pan. Top with 2 candy bars and half of pudding. Repeat layers. Sprinkle with miniature marshmallows.
• **Bake** at 350° for 10 minutes or until lightly browned. **Yield:** 6 servings.

Janice Hodges
Scottsboro, Alabama

Living Light

These heart-healthy recipes are deceptively delicious and feature ingredients that are good for you.

Eat to your heart's content. Don't you wish you were cheered on to do just that? We're inviting you to enjoy these recipes because they're delicious, and they contain ingredients, such as fresh fruits and vegetables, beans, red wine, and olive oil, that promote heart health.

Try these great lunch, supper, and dessert recipes. Love layer cakes, but don't dare delight in them except on special occasions? Then you must sample our reduced-fat, lower calorie version of one of *Southern Living* magazine's most celebrated and most delicious desserts—Hummingbird Cake.

LIGHTENED HUMMINGBIRD CAKE

We lowered the fat and calories by substituting applesauce for some of the oil and light cream cheese for regular, and by using less butter, less sugar, and fewer eggs.

Prep: 20 minutes
Bake: 25 minutes

Vegetable cooking spray
3 cups plus 2 teaspoons all-purpose flour, divided
1 teaspoon baking soda
½ teaspoon salt
1¾ cups sugar
1 teaspoon ground cinnamon
2 large eggs
½ cup unsweetened applesauce
3 tablespoons vegetable oil
1¾ cups mashed banana (about 5 to 6)
1½ teaspoons vanilla extract
1 (8-ounce) can crushed pineapple, undrained
Cream Cheese Frosting

• **Coat** 3 (9-inch) round cakepans with cooking spray; sprinkle 2 teaspoons flour evenly into pans, shaking to coat.
• **Combine** remaining 3 cups flour and next 4 ingredients in a large bowl.
• **Stir** together eggs, applesauce, and oil; add to flour mixture, stirring just until dry ingredients are moistened. (Do not beat.) Stir in mashed banana, vanilla, and pineapple. Pour batter evenly into prepared pans.
• **Bake** at 350° for 23 to 25 minutes or until a wooden pick inserted in center comes out clean. Cool layers in pans on wire racks 10 minutes. Remove layers from pans, and cool completely on wire racks.
• **Spread** Cream Cheese Frosting between layers and on top and sides of cake. **Yield:** 20 servings.

♥ Per slice: Calories 407 (21% from fat)
Fat 9.5g (sat 2.9g, mono 3.2g, poly 2.1g)
Protein 4.6g Carb 78g Fiber 1.7g
Chol 33mg Iron 1.3mg
Sodium 184mg Calc 31mg

Original Hummingbird Cake
Per slice: Calories 476 (45% from fat)
Fat 24g (sat 7.6g) Chol 57mg Sodium 191mg

Cream Cheese Frosting

Prep: 5 minutes

1 (8-ounce) package reduced-fat cream cheese (unsoftened)
1 (3-ounce) package cream cheese, softened
1 tablespoon light butter (unsoftened)
6 cups powdered sugar
1 teaspoon vanilla extract
¾ cup chopped pecans, toasted

• **Beat** cream cheeses and light butter at high speed with an electric mixer until creamy. Gradually add powdered sugar, beating at low speed just until smooth. Stir in vanilla and pecans. **Yield:** 3½ cups.

CHICKEN-CRANBERRY WRAPS

Leftover chicken or turkey mingles with ginger-spiced cranberry sauce in these clever sandwich roll-ups.

Prep: 30 minutes

6 (10-inch) fat-free flour tortillas
½ (15-ounce) can whole-berry cranberry sauce
2 tablespoons spicy brown mustard
2 tablespoons minced crystallized ginger
1½ cups chopped cooked chicken or turkey breast
3 green onions, thinly sliced
2 tablespoons chopped pecans, toasted
1 cup shredded lettuce

• **Heat** tortillas according to package directions.
• **Stir** together cranberry sauce, mustard, and ginger. Spread mixture evenly over 1 side of each tortilla. Top with chicken, green onions, pecans, and lettuce; roll up. **Yield:** 6 servings.

Janice Elder
Charlotte, North Carolina

♥ Per serving: Calories 262 (17% from fat)
Fat 4.9g (sat 0.6g, mono 2.5g, poly 1.1g)
Protein 14.7g Carb 40g Fiber 1.7g
Chol 32mg Iron 2.6mg
Sodium 406mg Calc 27mg

BEAN POT LENTILS

Prep: 50 minutes
Bake: 1 hour, 15 minutes

5 cups low-sodium, fat-free chicken broth
1 cup dried lentils
½ medium onion, chopped
2 tablespoons brown sugar
2 tablespoons ketchup
2 tablespoons molasses
1 to 2 tablespoons prepared mustard
2 bacon slices, cooked and diced
Vegetable cooking spray

• **Bring** first 3 ingredients to a boil in a Dutch oven. Cover, reduce heat, and simmer 45 minutes or until lentils are tender.
• **Stir** in brown sugar and next 4 ingredients. Spoon mixture into a 1-quart baking dish coated with cooking spray.
• **Bake,** uncovered, at 325°, stirring occasionally, for 1 hour and 15 minutes. **Yield:** 3 cups.

❤ Per ½ cup: Calories 180 (9% from fat)
Fat 1.8g (sat 0.5g, mono 0.7g, poly 0.3g)
Protein 10.4g Carb 30g Fiber 3.9g
Chol 2mg Iron 3.9mg
Sodium 138mg Calc 66mg

WHITE BEAN-AND-TUNA SALAD

Stuff a whole wheat pita with this refreshing salad for a new way to enjoy tuna and beans.

Prep: 10 minutes

2 tablespoons lemon juice
1 tablespoon olive oil
¼ teaspoon salt
½ teaspoon freshly ground pepper
½ teaspoon dried oregano
1 (20-ounce) can cannellini beans, rinsed and drained
1 (6½-ounce) can solid white tuna in spring water, drained and flaked
4 green onions, thinly sliced
2 tablespoons chopped fresh parsley
Lettuce leaves

• **Stir** together first 5 ingredients. Add beans, tuna, and green onions, tossing gently to coat. Sprinkle with parsley, and serve over lettuce. **Yield:** about 3 servings.

Anna T. Rucker
Norfolk, Virginia

❤ Per serving: Calories 261 (22% from fat)
Fat 6.3g (sat 1.1g, mono 3.8g, poly 1.1g)
Protein 23g Carb 30g Fiber 5.5g
Chol 17mg Iron 3.7mg
Sodium 711mg Calc 113mg

BLUE RIBBON ANGEL FOOD CAKE

This feathery light cake is great alone or with fresh berries.

Prep: 20 minutes
Bake: 35 minutes
Stand: 1 hour

1½ cups sifted cake flour
12 egg whites
1¼ teaspoons cream of tartar
¼ teaspoon salt
1 teaspoon vanilla extract
¼ teaspoon almond extract
1⅓ cups sugar

• **Sift** flour 4 times, and set aside.
• **Beat** egg whites and next 4 ingredients at high speed with an electric mixer until soft peaks form (about 5 minutes). Gradually add sugar, ⅓ cup at a time, beating until blended after each addition.
• **Fold** in flour. Pour batter into an ungreased 10-inch tube pan.
• **Bake** at 375° for 35 minutes. Invert pan onto a wire rack, and let stand 1 hour or until cake is completely cool. Run a knife around cake to loosen edges. **Yield:** 16 servings.

Carrie E. Treichel
Johnson City, Tennessee

❤ Per serving: Calories 111 (1% from fat)
Fat 0.1g Protein 3.3g Carb 24g
Fiber 0g Chol 0mg Iron 0.7mg
Sodium 78mg Calc 3mg

AN APPLE-A-DAY PORK CHOPS

Simple ingredients create a slightly sweet, tangy flavor in these pork chops.

Prep: 15 minutes
Cook: 20 minutes

6 (4-ounce) boneless pork loin chops
Vegetable cooking spray
1 to 1½ tablespoons dried rosemary
½ to ¾ teaspoon salt
½ to ¾ teaspoon freshly ground pepper
1 medium-size Red Delicious apple, peeled and chopped
½ cup golden raisins
½ cup currants
2 teaspoons olive oil
¾ cup Marsala wine or apple cider
Garnishes: rosemary sprig, apple slices

• **Coat** both sides of pork chops evenly with cooking spray.
• **Combine** rosemary, salt, and pepper. Rub mixture evenly on both sides of pork; set aside.
• **Cook** apple, raisins, and currants in hot oil in a large skillet over medium-high heat, stirring often, 5 minutes.
• **Add** ¼ cup wine, stirring constantly, until most liquid is evaporated.
• **Add** remaining wine, and cook 15 minutes or until mixture is thickened.
• **Cook** pork chops in a large skillet coated with cooking spray over medium-high heat 5 minutes on each side or until done. Top with apple mixture. Garnish, if desired. **Yield:** 6 servings.

Mary Grace Ellis
Delmar, Maryland

❤ Per serving: Calories 286 (34% from fat)
Fat 10.9g (sat 3.3g, mono 5g, poly 1.1g)
Protein 24.5g Carb 23g Fiber 1.4g
Chol 68mg Iron 1.9mg
Sodium 276mg Calc 38mg

What's for Supper?

Bring a sampling of the East to your table
with this Asian-inspired menu.

Chinese Night Menu
Serves 4

Shrimp Oriental
Lemon Rice Pilaf
Chinese Cabbage Slaw
Fortune cookies

SHRIMP ORIENTAL
(pictured on facing page)

Prep: 40 minutes
Cook: 10 minutes

2 **pounds unpeeled, large fresh shrimp**
1 **(15½-ounce) can pineapple chunks,**
   undrained
½ **cup sugar**
2 **tablespoons cornstarch**
1 **teaspoon salt**
¼ **cup rice wine vinegar**
2 **tablespoons chili sauce**
⅓ **cup ketchup**
1 **teaspoon soy sauce**
1 **green bell pepper, cubed**
1 **red bell pepper, cubed**
Garnish: green onion slivers

• **Peel** shrimp, and devein, if desired.
Set shrimp aside.
• **Drain** pineapple, reserving juice. Stir
together pineapple juice, sugar, and
next 6 ingredients.
• **Cook** juice mixture in a large skillet or
wok over high heat, stirring constantly,
15 to 30 seconds or until thickened.
• **Add** cubed bell pepper, and cook 3 to
4 minutes. Add pineapple and shrimp.
• **Cover** and cook, stirring often, 3 to 5
minutes or just until shrimp turn pink.

• **Serve** over Lemon Rice Pilaf, if desired.
Garnish, if desired. **Yield:** 4 servings.

Chicken Oriental: Substitute 4 skinned
and boned chicken breast halves, cubed,
for shrimp. Cook until done.

Leigh Ann Finley
Ashburn, Virginia

LEMON RICE PILAF
(pictured on facing page)

Prep: 15 minutes
Cook: 12 minutes

2 **tablespoons butter or margarine**
4 **celery ribs, sliced**
6 **green onions, chopped**
3 **cups hot cooked rice**
2 **tablespoons grated lemon rind**
½ **teaspoon salt**
¼ **teaspoon pepper**

• **Melt** butter in a skillet over medium-
high heat; add celery and onions. Sauté
until celery is tender. Stir in rice and remaining ingredients; cook over low heat
until heated. **Yield:** 6 servings.

Cathy Laudet
Nokomis, Florida

CHINESE CABBAGE SLAW
(pictured on facing page)

Rice wine vinegar and sugar create
a delicate balance between
sweet and sour flavors in this slaw.

Prep: 15 minutes

1 **head bok choy, shredded**
1 **bunch green onions, diced**
2 **tablespoons butter or margarine**
¼ **cup sliced almonds**
¼ **cup sesame seeds**
½ **cup vegetable oil**
¼ **cup sesame oil**
6 **tablespoons rice wine vinegar**
¼ **cup sugar**
1 **teaspoon salt**
1 **teaspoon pepper**

• **Place** bok choy and onions in a bowl.
• **Melt** butter in a skillet. Add almonds
and sesame seeds; sauté over medium-
high heat 5 minutes or until lightly
browned. Drain; cool slightly. Add to bok
choy mixture.
• **Stir** together vegetable and sesame
oils and remaining 4 ingredients. Toss
with bok choy mixture, and serve
immediately. **Yield:** 4 servings.

Tina Fowler
Lubbock, Texas

SUPPER TIPS

■ Don't throw out those shrimp
shells. Place the washed shells
in a saucepan; cover with water,
and bring to a boil. Cover, reduce
heat, and simmer 30 minutes.
Cool shells in liquid; strain and
discard shells. Use liquid as a
base for soups, chowders, and
sauces. Freeze up to 6 months.

■ For a crispier slaw, shred cabbage, cover with ice water, and let
stand 1 hour. Drain and blot dry.
Chill in a zip-top plastic bag.

Shrimp Oriental, Lemon Rice Pilaf,
Chinese Cabbage Slaw, facing page

Italian Club Sandwich, page 22

Roasted Garlic-and-Basil Tomato Soup, page 17

38

Bean-and-Cheese Chimichangas, page 16

Lemon-Lime Chess Pie, page 23

Tangerine Chess Pie, page 23

Quick Pasta Bakes

There's no denying that our busy schedules limit the amount of time we can spend in the kitchen. And when there's a chill in the air, you need recipes that are not only hearty, but simple to prepare.

By combining pasta with basic ingredients from your pantry and refrigerator, these reader recipes are just what the doctor ordered. In fact, we found the freezer-friendly Macaroni-and-Cheese Bake particularly helpful, because you can easily double the recipe and save one casserole for another night.

MACARONI-AND-CHEESE BAKE

Prep: 20 minutes
Bake: 25 minutes

1 cup uncooked elbow macaroni
1 cup (4 ounces) shredded Cheddar cheese
1 medium onion, chopped
1 medium-size green bell pepper, chopped
1 (10¾-ounce) can cream of mushroom soup, undiluted
1 (2-ounce) jar diced pimiento, undrained
½ cup mayonnaise
½ cup milk
2 cups chopped cooked chicken or turkey
½ cup Italian-seasoned breadcrumbs

• **Cook** pasta according to package directions; drain.
• **Stir** together pasta, cheese, and next 7 ingredients. Spoon into a lightly greased 11- x 7-inch baking dish.
• **Bake** at 350° for 15 minutes. Sprinkle with breadcrumbs; bake 10 more minutes or until golden. **Yield:** 6 servings.

Note: Recipe may be doubled. Freeze up to 3 months; thaw in refrigerator, and bake as directed.

Karen Whitehead
Enterprise, Alabama

BAKED LINGUINE WITH MEAT SAUCE

Thick linguine noodles are dressed with a rich meat sauce and melted cheese in this hearty dish.

Prep: 40 minutes
Bake: 30 minutes
Stand: 5 minutes

2 pounds lean ground beef
2 garlic cloves, minced
1 (28-ounce) can crushed tomatoes
1 (8-ounce) can tomato sauce
1 (6-ounce) can tomato paste
1 teaspoon salt
2 teaspoons sugar
8 ounces uncooked linguine
1 (16-ounce) container sour cream
1 (8-ounce) package cream cheese, softened
1 bunch green onions, chopped
2 cups (8 ounces) shredded sharp Cheddar cheese

• **Cook** beef and garlic in a Dutch oven, stirring until beef crumbles and is no longer pink.
• **Stir** in tomatoes and next 4 ingredients; simmer 30 minutes. Set meat sauce aside.
• **Cook** pasta according to package directions; drain. Place pasta in a lightly greased 13- x 9-inch baking dish.
• **Stir** together sour cream, cream cheese, and green onions. Spread over pasta. Top with meat sauce.
• **Bake** at 350° for 20 to 25 minutes or until thoroughly heated. Sprinkle with Cheddar cheese, and bake 5 more minutes or until cheese melts. Let stand 5 minutes. Serve with a salad and bread, if desired. **Yield:** 8 servings.

Note: Substitute no-salt-added tomato products, light sour cream, light cream cheese, and reduced-fat Cheddar cheese, if desired.

Adeline Johnson
Birmingham, Alabama

PASTA ITALIANO

A meaty tomato sauce drenches these cheese-stuffed pasta shells before their quick stint in the oven.

Prep: 30 minutes
Bake: 15 minutes

1 (15-ounce) container ricotta cheese
1 large egg, lightly beaten
2 teaspoons garlic powder
14 jumbo pasta shells, cooked
1 pound lean ground beef
1 medium onion, chopped
2 garlic cloves, pressed
1 (28-ounce) can whole tomatoes, undrained
1 (8-ounce) package sliced fresh mushrooms
1 tablespoon chopped Italian parsley
1 teaspoon salt
1 teaspoon Italian seasoning
1 (15-ounce) can tomato sauce
Grated Parmesan cheese (optional)

• **Stir** together first 3 ingredients. Spoon 2 tablespoonfuls of ricotta mixture into each shell. Arrange shells, stuffed side up, in a lightly greased 11- x 7-inch baking dish. Set aside.
• **Cook** beef, onion, and garlic in a large skillet over medium heat 15 minutes, stirring until beef crumbles and is no longer pink; drain.
• **Stir** in tomatoes and next 4 ingredients; bring to a boil. Cover, reduce heat, and simmer, stirring occasionally, 10 minutes. Stir in tomato sauce; cook 2 minutes. Pour beef mixture over stuffed shells.
• **Bake** at 350° for 15 minutes. Sprinkle with Parmesan cheese, if desired. **Yield:** 6 servings.

Judy Byars
Pittsboro, Mississippi

Top-Rated Menu

This delightful brunch menu offers convenient make-ahead options.

Winter Brunch
Serves 10

Baked Ham With Bourbon Glaze
Almond-Citrus Salad
Sweet Potato Angel Biscuits

Entertaining friends for brunch can be simple and should be fun. This easy menu gives you enough time to enjoy yourself and your guests.

BAKED HAM WITH BOURBON GLAZE

1998 Recipe Hall of Fame

Prep: 10 minutes
Bake: 2 hours, 30 minutes

1 cup honey
½ cup molasses
½ cup bourbon or orange juice
¼ cup orange juice
2 tablespoons Dijon mustard
1 (6- to 8-pound) smoked ham half

• **Microwave** honey and molasses in a 1-quart glass dish at HIGH 1 minute. Whisk to blend. Whisk in bourbon, juice, and mustard.
• **Remove** skin and fat from ham; place ham in a lightly greased 13- x 9-inch pan. Make ¼-inch-deep cuts in ham in a diamond pattern. Pour glaze over ham.
• **Bake** on lower oven rack at 350° for 2 to 2½ hours or until a meat thermometer inserted into thickest portion registers 140°, basting every 15 minutes with glaze.
• **Remove** from pan, reserving drippings. Cover ham, and chill, if desired. Chill reserved drippings.
• **Remove** and discard fat from drippings. Bring drippings to a boil in a small saucepan. Serve warm with ham. **Yield:** 12 to 14 servings.

ALMOND-CITRUS SALAD

1996 Recipe Hall of Fame

Prep: 30 minutes

⅔ cup vegetable oil
2 teaspoons grated grapefruit rind
½ cup fresh grapefruit juice
1 (0.7-ounce) envelope Italian dressing mix
3 grapefruits, peeled and sectioned
4 oranges, peeled and sectioned
1 (6-ounce) package baby spinach
1 (14-ounce) package mixed salad greens
2 celery ribs, sliced
1 green bell pepper, chopped
2 avocados, peeled and sliced (optional)
1 cup Sweet-and-Spicy Almonds

• **Whisk** together first 4 ingredients; cover and chill, if desired.
• **Combine** grapefruit, next 5 ingredients, and, if desired, sliced avocado in a large bowl. Add citrus dressing, tossing to coat. Sprinkle salad with Sweet-and-Spicy Almonds. **Yield:** 10 servings.

Sweet-and-Spicy Almonds

Prep: 5 minutes
Bake: 15 minutes

1 cup sliced almonds or pecan pieces
1 tablespoon butter or margarine, melted
1½ teaspoons sugar
¼ teaspoon ground cumin
¼ teaspoon chili powder
⅛ teaspoon dried crushed red pepper
Pinch of salt

• **Stir** together almonds and butter in a small bowl. Combine sugar and remaining ingredients; sprinkle over almonds, tossing to coat.
• **Spread** almonds on a lightly greased baking sheet. Bake at 325°, stirring occasionally, for 15 minutes. Cool. **Yield:** 1 cup.

SWEET POTATO ANGEL BISCUITS

1993 Recipe Hall of Fame

Prep: 30 minutes
Rise: 20 minutes
Bake: 12 minutes per batch

3 (¼-ounce) envelopes active dry yeast
¾ cup warm water (100° to 110°)
7½ cups all-purpose flour
1 tablespoon baking powder
1 tablespoon salt
1½ cups sugar
1½ cups shortening
3 cups canned mashed sweet potatoes

• **Combine** yeast and ¾ cup warm water in a 2-cup liquid measuring cup; let stand 5 minutes.

- **Stir** together flour and next 3 ingredients in a bowl. Cut in shortening with a pastry blender until mixture is crumbly.
- **Stir** in yeast mixture and mashed sweet potatoes just until blended.
- **Turn** dough out onto a lightly floured surface, and knead until smooth and elastic (about 5 minutes).
- **Place** dough in a well-greased bowl, turning to grease top. Cover and chill 8 hours, if desired.
- **Roll** dough to ½-inch thickness; cut with a 2-inch round cutter. Freeze up to 1 month, if desired. Thaw biscuits; place on ungreased baking sheets. Cover and let rise in a warm place (85°), free from drafts, 20 minutes or until doubled in bulk.
- **Bake** at 400° for 10 to 12 minutes or until lightly browned. **Yield:** 7½ dozen.

Great Gratins

With their golden cheese or crumb coatings, gratin dishes offer a great way to incorporate vegetables into your menus. So shed new light on butternut squash, broccoli, cauliflower, and cabbage by preparing these family-pleasing selections.

POTATO-BUTTERNUT SQUASH-AND-GRUYÈRE GRATIN

Prep: 35 minutes
Bake: 1 hour

5 medium Yukon gold potatoes (about 2½ pounds)
1 large butternut squash (about 2 pounds)
2 tablespoons butter or margarine
1 large sweet onion, chopped
1 teaspoon salt
½ teaspoon pepper
2 cups shredded Gruyère cheese
Cream Sauce

- **Peel** and thinly slice potatoes. Peel, seed, and thinly slice squash.
- **Cook** potato in boiling water to cover in a Dutch oven 5 minutes.
- **Add** squash; cover and cook 3 more minutes. Remove from heat; drain well.
- **Melt** butter in a large skillet; add onion, and sauté 10 to 12 minutes or until golden brown.
- **Layer** half each of potato and squash in a lightly greased 13- x 9-inch baking dish; sprinkle with half each of salt and pepper. Top with half each of onion, cheese, and Cream Sauce. Repeat layers, ending with Cream Sauce.
- **Bake** at 350° for 1 hour or until golden brown. **Yield:** 10 to 12 servings.

Cream Sauce

Prep: 8 minutes

¼ cup butter or margarine
⅓ cup all-purpose flour
2½ cups milk
1 cup dry white wine
¼ teaspoon salt

- **Melt** butter in a heavy saucepan over low heat; whisk in flour until smooth.
- **Cook,** whisking constantly, 1 minute. Gradually whisk in milk and wine.
- **Cook** over medium heat, whisking constantly, until mixture is thickened and bubbly. Stir in salt. **Yield:** 3½ cups.

BROCCOLI-AND-CAULIFLOWER GRATIN

Prep: 15 minutes
Bake: 25 minutes

2 (16-ounce) packages fresh broccoli and cauliflower flowerets
1½ cups reduced-fat mayonnaise
1 cup (4 ounces) shredded reduced-fat Cheddar cheese
1 (3-ounce) package shredded Parmesan cheese
4 green onions, sliced
2 tablespoons Dijon mustard
¼ teaspoon ground red pepper
3 tablespoons Italian-seasoned breadcrumbs

- **Arrange** flowerets in a steamer basket over boiling water. Cover and steam 6 to 8 minutes or until crisp-tender. Drain well.
- **Arrange** flowerets in a lightly greased 2-quart baking dish.
- **Stir** together mayonnaise and next 5 ingredients. Spoon over flowerets. Sprinkle with breadcrumbs.
- **Bake** at 350° for 20 to 25 minutes or until golden. **Yield:** 8 servings.

Katie Moon
Birmingham, Alabama

SCALLOPED CABBAGE

Prep: 10 minutes
Bake: 1 hour

2 cups crushed cornflake cereal
¼ cup butter or margarine, melted
1 (10-ounce) package shredded angel hair cabbage
1 large sweet onion, halved and thinly sliced
½ cup milk
½ cup mayonnaise
1 (10¾-ounce) can cream of celery soup, undiluted
1 cup (4 ounces) shredded sharp Cheddar cheese

- **Stir** together cereal and butter; spoon half of cereal mixture into a lightly greased 11- x 7-inch baking dish. Top with cabbage and onion.
- **Stir** together milk, mayonnaise, and soup. Pour over cabbage. Sprinkle with cheese and remaining cereal mixture.
- **Bake,** covered, at 350° for 1 hour. **Yield:** 6 to 8 servings.

Note: Substitute light butter, fat-free milk, reduced-fat mayonnaise, reduced-fat soup, and reduced-fat cheese, if desired.

Kathy Rhea
Sevierville, Tennessee

Rolls

Whether you're planning breakfast, lunch, or dinner,
we have the perfect roll for you.

OATMEAL DINNER ROLLS

Prep: 15 minutes
Rise: 1 hour, 30 minutes
Bake: 15 minutes

2   cups water
1   cup quick-cooking oats
3   tablespoons butter or margarine
2   (¼-ounce) envelopes active dry yeast
½   cup warm water (100° to 110°)
1   tablespoon sugar
4   cups all-purpose flour
1½ teaspoons salt
⅓   cup firmly packed brown sugar

• **Bring** 2 cups water to a boil; stir in oats and butter. Boil, stirring constantly, 1 minute. Remove from heat; cool to 110°. Stir together yeast, ½ cup warm water, and 1 tablespoon sugar in a 2-cup measuring cup; let stand 5 minutes.
• **Beat** oat mixture, yeast mixture, flour, salt, and brown sugar at medium speed with an electric mixer until smooth.
• **Turn** dough out onto a lightly floured surface; knead until smooth and elastic (about 5 minutes). Place in a well-greased bowl, turning to grease top.
• **Cover** and let rise in a warm place (85°), free from drafts, 1 hour or until dough is doubled in bulk.
• **Punch** dough down, and divide in half; shape each portion into 16 (1½-inch) balls. Place evenly into 2 lightly greased 9- x 1¾-inch round cakepans.
• **Cover** and let rise in a warm place (85°), free from drafts, 30 minutes or until doubled in bulk.
• **Bake** at 375° for 15 minutes or until golden brown. **Yield:** 32 rolls.

Note: Reserve 1 portion of dough for Cinnamon Rolls recipe, if desired.
Carol Barclay
Portland, Texas

CINNAMON ROLLS

Prep: 20 minutes
Rise: 30 minutes
Bake: 25 minutes

½   Oatmeal Dinner Rolls dough (recipe at left)
3   tablespoons butter or margarine, melted
⅓   cup firmly packed brown sugar
1   to 2 teaspoons ground cinnamon
¼   cup chopped pecans
½   cup powdered sugar
2   teaspoons milk

• **Roll** dough on a lightly floured surface into a 14- x 12-inch rectangle; brush with butter.
• **Combine** brown sugar and cinnamon; sprinkle over butter. Top with pecans.
• **Roll up,** jellyroll fashion, starting at a long edge; cut into 1-inch-thick slices.
• **Arrange** in a lightly greased 13- x 9-inch pan. Cover and let rise in a warm place (85°), free from drafts, 30 minutes or until doubled in bulk.
• **Bake** at 375° for 25 minutes or until golden brown. Whisk together powdered sugar and milk; drizzle over warm rolls. **Yield:** 14 rolls.

Herb Rolls: Substitute ½ teaspoon each of freeze-dried chives, dried basil, and dried rosemary for brown sugar and cinnamon, or use 1 teaspoon each of fresh herbs. Add 3 to 4 tablespoons grated Parmesan cheese, if desired. Omit glaze.

Note: Rolls may be chilled overnight after second rising; let stand at room temperature 30 minutes before baking as directed. Or, freeze up to 1 month after second rising; thaw overnight in refrigerator, and let stand at room temperature 30 minutes before baking as directed.

KNEAD TO KNOW

Follow our tips for preparing, kneading, and baking yeast dough. Once you've mastered the techniques, share your expertise with a friend.

■ Make sure yeast is not out of date (package is stamped with an expiration date).

■ Use 1 envelope of yeast for up to 4½ cups flour unless your recipe specifies otherwise.

■ Dissolve yeast in warm water (100° to 110°).

■ Measure all ingredients carefully, including salt. Salt plays a definite role in developing the dough's flavor and controlling the rising rate of the dough.

■ When kneading dough, flatten and fold it toward you, and use the heels of your hands to push the dough away from you with a rolling motion.

■ Rotate dough a quarter turn; repeat the fold, push, and turn steps.

■ Use a little more flour if dough becomes too sticky, always working the flour into the dough.

■ Don't let dough continue to rise beyond the time called for in recipe.

■ Avoid letting the temperature become too high during the dough-rising period; it will kill the yeast. If the temperature is too low, the dough will take longer to rise.

■ For more information on breads, visit the Fleischmann's Web site at www.breadworld.com.

Éclairs Made Simple

With our basic recipes and variations, you can make sublime éclairs in your favorite combination of flavors.

Éclairs are a culinary achievement worthy of the praise they receive. Tender and flaky pastry encasing a sweet cream filling and topped with a glossy chocolate glaze—what's not to love?

Mary Allen Perry, of our Test Kitchens, developed these recipes. The results are easy to make and hard to resist.

Make the components ahead, and assemble them at the last minute—or make and freeze them (without the fruit). Thaw éclairs in the refrigerator overnight or at room temperature 30 minutes.

VANILLA CREAM-FILLED ÉCLAIRS

Using piecrust mix simplifies the tender pastry in these éclairs.

Prep: 30 minutes
Bake: 25 minutes
Chill: 2 hours

1⅓ cups water
1 (11-ounce) package piecrust mix
3 large eggs
2 egg whites
Vanilla Pastry Cream
Chocolate Glaze

• **Bring** 1⅓ cups water to a boil in a 3-quart saucepan over medium-high heat.
• **Stir** in piecrust mix, beating vigorously with a wooden spoon 1 minute or until mixture leaves sides of pan.
• **Place** dough in bowl of a heavy-duty electric stand mixer; cool 5 minutes.
• **Beat** dough at medium speed with electric mixer using paddle attachment.
• **Add** eggs and egg whites, 1 at a time, beating until blended after each addition. (If desired, eggs and egg whites may be added 1 at a time and beaten vigorously with a wooden spoon.)
• **Spoon** dough into a large heavy-duty zip-top plastic bag. (A large pastry bag may also be used.) Cut a 1½-inch opening across 1 corner of the bag. Pipe 4-inch-long strips of dough 2 inches apart onto ungreased baking sheets.
• **Bake** at 425° for 20 to 25 minutes or until puffed and golden. (Do not underbake.) Remove from oven, and cut a small slit in side of each éclair to allow steam to escape. Cool on wire racks.
• **Split** éclairs using a serrated knife, starting at 1 long side without cutting through opposite side. Pull out and discard soft dough inside.
• **Carefully** spoon about ¼ cup Vanilla Pastry Cream into each éclair; close top of each éclair over filling.
• **Top** with Chocolate Glaze. Chill éclairs 2 hours or freeze up to 1 month. **Yield:** 1 dozen.

Banana-Chocolate Éclairs: Follow recipe for Vanilla Cream-Filled Éclairs, adding 3 medium bananas, quartered lengthwise and thinly sliced, to Vanilla Pastry Cream after chilling 4 hours.

Mocha Éclairs: Follow recipe for Vanilla Cream-Filled Éclairs, substituting Coffee Pastry Cream for Vanilla Pastry Cream.

Peanut Butter-Chocolate Éclairs: Follow recipe for Vanilla Cream-Filled Éclairs, substituting Peanut Butter Pastry Cream for Vanilla Pastry Cream.

Strawberry Cream Éclairs: Follow recipe for Vanilla Cream-Filled Éclairs, substituting Grand Marnier Pastry Cream for Vanilla Pastry Cream. Slice 1 quart strawberries; spoon into éclairs before filling with pastry cream.

Top with White Chocolate Glaze; drizzle with Chocolate Glaze.

Note: For testing purposes only, we used Betty Crocker Pie Crust Mix.

Vanilla Pastry Cream

Prep: 5 minutes
Cook: 10 minutes
Chill: 4 hours

2 large eggs
2 egg yolks
½ cup sugar
⅓ cup cornstarch
2 cups half-and-half
2 tablespoons butter, softened
2 teaspoons vanilla extract

• **Whisk** together first 4 ingredients in a 3-quart saucepan. Gradually whisk in half-and-half. Cook over medium heat, whisking constantly, until mixture comes to a boil. Cook 1 minute or until mixture is thickened and bubbly. Remove from heat; whisk in butter and vanilla. Cover and chill 4 hours. **Yield:** 3 cups.

Coffee Pastry Cream: Stir in 1 tablespoon instant coffee granules with half-and-half.

Grand Marnier Pastry Cream: Omit vanilla; stir in 2 tablespoons Grand Marnier or other orange liqueur.

Peanut Butter Pastry Cream: Omit butter; stir in ⅓ cup creamy peanut butter.

Chocolate Glaze

Prep: 5 minutes

1 cup semisweet chocolate morsels
¼ cup whipping cream
2 tablespoons butter, softened

• **Microwave** morsels and whipping cream at HIGH 30 seconds to 1 minute or until melted, stirring twice. Whisk in butter until blended, and spoon immediately over éclairs. **Yield:** 1⅓ cups.

White Chocolate Glaze: Substitute 4 ounces chopped white chocolate for semisweet chocolate morsels.

Quick & Easy

These recipes invite you to keep supper simple—open, pour, and stir.

Pantry staples supply quick solutions when you're in a quandary about what to cook for supper. With only a few fresh ingredients—onions, bell peppers, cheese, and herbs—you can have these dishes on the table without a trip to the grocery store.

CORN-RICE CASSEROLE

Serve with turkey cutlets, a tossed green salad, and garlic bread.

Prep: 25 minutes
Bake: 35 minutes

2 cups uncooked long-grain rice
2 tablespoons butter or margarine
1 green bell pepper, chopped
1 small onion, chopped
1 (15½-ounce) can cream-style corn
1 (11-ounce) can Mexican-style corn, drained
1 (11-ounce) can whole kernel corn, drained
1 (10-ounce) can diced tomato and green chiles, undrained
1 (8-ounce) loaf mild Mexican pasteurized prepared cheese product, cubed
½ teaspoon salt
¼ teaspoon pepper
½ cup (2 ounces) shredded Cheddar cheese

• **Cook** rice according to package directions; set aside.
• **Melt** butter in a large skillet over medium heat. Add bell pepper and onion, and sauté 5 minutes or until tender.
• **Stir** in cooked rice, cream-style corn, and next 6 ingredients. Spoon into a lightly greased 13- x 9-inch baking dish or 2 (8-inch) baking dishes.

• **Bake** at 350° for 30 minutes or until thoroughly heated. Top with shredded cheese; bake 5 minutes or until cheese melts. **Yield:** 10 to 12 servings.

Note: To freeze, line baking dish with plastic wrap or aluminum foil; fill and freeze. Lift frozen casserole from baking dish, and wrap tightly with foil; return to freezer. When ready to serve, remove foil, and place casserole back into serving dish. Thaw in refrigerator overnight. Let stand at room temperature 30 minutes. Bake at 350° for 45 minutes. Top with shredded cheese; bake 5 minutes or until cheese melts.

Janet E. Naquin
Sulphur, Louisiana

BING CHERRY SALAD

Serve with fried chicken, mashed potatoes, steamed green beans, and rolls.

Prep: 20 minutes
Chill: 8 hours

1 (20-ounce) can crushed pineapple in juice, undrained
1 (16½-ounce) can pitted Bing cherries, undrained
1 (12-ounce) can cola soft drink
2 (3-ounce) packages cherry gelatin
1 cup chopped pecans, toasted

• **Drain** pineapple and cherries, reserving juices. Bring juices and cola to a boil in a saucepan over medium-high heat; stir in gelatin. Remove from heat; stir 2 minutes or until gelatin dissolves.
• **Stir** in pineapple, cherries, and pecans; pour into a lightly greased 6½-cup mold. Cover and chill 8 hours. Unmold onto a serving dish. **Yield:** 12 servings.

SWEET BEAN SALAD

Serve with pork chops, rice, and bread.

Prep: 10 minutes
Cook: 5 minutes

1 (19-ounce) can cannellini beans
1 (15½-ounce) can kidney beans
1 (14½-ounce) can French-cut green beans
½ cup sunflower oil
½ cup white vinegar
⅓ to ½ cup sugar
4 teaspoons dried basil
1 teaspoon dry mustard
½ teaspoon salt
1 (16-ounce) can vegetarian baked beans, undrained
1 small onion, chopped

• **Rinse** and drain first 3 ingredients.
• **Cook** oil and next 5 ingredients in a large saucepan over low heat 5 minutes or until sugar dissolves.
• **Stir** in drained beans, vegetarian baked beans, and onion. Serve salad warm or chilled. **Yield:** 6½ cups.

Ruchel Coetzee
Lauderdale-by-the-Sea, Florida

The Comfort of Cider

Richly hued amber cider offers the essence of apples. Each of these treats lets you sample and serve this flavor in a satisfying new fashion.

WARM CITRUS CIDER

Prep: 5 minutes
Cook: 5 minutes

1 orange
1 lemon
1 teaspoon whole cloves
2 quarts apple cider
Cinnamon sticks (optional)

- **Cut** long strips of orange and lemon rind, reserving fruit for other uses. Insert cloves into rind.
- **Cook** rind strips and cider in a Dutch oven over medium heat 5 minutes or until thoroughly heated. (Do not boil.)
- **Serve** cider with cinnamon sticks, if desired. **Yield:** 2 quarts.

Nora Henshaw
Okemah, Oklahoma

SAVORY APPLESAUCE

Prep: 10 minutes
Cook: 20 minutes

3 Granny Smith apples, peeled and coarsely chopped
¼ cup sugar
¼ cup apple cider
4 whole cloves
¼ cup butter or margarine
2 tablespoons prepared horseradish
1 tablespoon lemon juice

- **Bring** first 4 ingredients to a boil in a saucepan; reduce heat, and simmer 15 minutes. Cool slightly; discard cloves.
- **Process** apple mixture in a blender or food processor, in batches, until smooth.
- **Return** to saucepan; stir in butter, horseradish, and lemon juice. Cook over low heat until heated. **Yield:** 1½ cups.

Hoyt Adair
Moulton, Alabama

APPLE PUDDING CAKE

Prep: 10 minutes
Bake: 35 minutes

1½ cups firmly packed brown sugar, divided
1 cup all-purpose flour
2 teaspoons baking powder
¼ teaspoon salt
1 teaspoon ground cinnamon
½ cup milk
2 tablespoons vegetable oil
1 teaspoon vanilla extract
1 large Granny Smith apple, peeled and chopped
1 cup hot apple cider

- **Combine** ¾ cup brown sugar, flour, and next 3 ingredients in a lightly greased 9- x 1¾-inch round cakepan.
- **Stir** together milk, oil, and vanilla; add to sugar mixture, stirring until blended. Stir in apple.
- **Sprinkle** with remaining ¾ cup brown sugar. Pour hot apple cider slowly over batter. Do not stir.
- **Bake** at 350° for 30 to 35 minutes or until a cake layer forms on top. Cool slightly, and serve with ice cream. **Yield:** 6 servings.

Barbara Hughes
Murphy, North Carolina

PORK CHOPS WITH MUSTARD-GLAZED APPLE AND ONION

Prep: 10 minutes
Cook: 30 minutes

4 (½-inch-thick) boneless pork loin chops
1 teaspoon salt
1 teaspoon pepper
2 tablespoons vegetable oil
1 medium onion, halved and thinly sliced
2 garlic cloves, minced
1 large Granny Smith apple, peeled and thinly sliced
½ cup honey mustard
½ cup apple cider
Hot cooked brown rice (optional)

- **Sprinkle** pork chops with salt and pepper. Cook pork chops in hot oil in a large skillet over medium-high heat 2 minutes on each side. Reduce heat to medium, and cook 3 to 5 minutes on each side or until done. Remove from skillet, and keep warm.
- **Sauté** onion and garlic in skillet over medium-high heat 5 minutes or until tender. Add apple, and sauté 5 minutes or until tender.
- **Stir** in honey mustard and apple cider, and cook 5 minutes or until mustard mixture is thoroughly heated.
- **Spoon** mustard mixture over pork chops. Serve with brown rice, if desired. **Yield:** 4 servings.

Barbara Sherrer
Bay City, Texas

Taste of the South

Chicken-fried steak just might be the state entrée of Texas. One taste of this recipe, and you'll see why Texans are proud to call chicken-fried steak their own.

CHICKEN-FRIED STEAK

Prep: 10 minutes
Cook: 30 minutes

¼ teaspoon salt
¼ teaspoon ground black pepper
4 (4-ounce) cube steaks
38 saltine crackers (1 sleeve), crushed
1¼ cups all-purpose flour, divided
½ teaspoon baking powder
2 teaspoons salt, divided
1½ teaspoons freshly ground black pepper, divided
½ teaspoon ground red pepper
4¾ cups milk, divided
2 large eggs
3½ cups peanut oil

- **Sprinkle** ¼ teaspoon salt and ¼ teaspoon pepper over steaks. Set aside.
- **Combine** cracker crumbs, 1 cup flour, baking powder, 1 teaspoon salt, ½ teaspoon black pepper, and red pepper.
- **Whisk** together ¾ cup milk and eggs. Dredge steaks in cracker crumb mixture; dip in milk mixture, and dredge in cracker mixture again.
- **Pour** oil into a 12-inch skillet; heat to 360°. (Do not use a nonstick skillet.) Fry steaks 10 minutes. Turn and fry 4 to 5 more minutes or until golden brown. Remove to a wire rack on a jellyroll pan. Keep steaks warm in a 225° oven. Carefully drain hot oil, reserving cooked bits and 1 tablespoon drippings in skillet.
- **Whisk** together remaining ¼ cup flour, 1 teaspoon salt, 1 teaspoon black pepper, and 4 cups milk. Pour mixture into reserved drippings in skillet; cook over medium-high heat, whisking constantly, 10 to 12 minutes or until thickened. Serve gravy with steaks and mashed potatoes. **Yield:** 4 servings.

Versatile Dried Fruit

Dried fruit is more than just a snack for the health conscious. It adds vibrant color and flavor to many dishes. Try these recipes, and see if you don't agree.

LEMON-RAISIN SPREAD

Prep: 15 minutes
Chill: 1 hour

2 cups raisins
1 cup sugar
½ cup lemon juice
½ cup mayonnaise

• **Process** raisins in a blender or food processor until finely chopped.
• **Cook** sugar and lemon juice in a small saucepan over medium-high heat, stirring until sugar dissolves. Stir in raisins. Cool. Stir in mayonnaise. Cover; chill 1 hour. Serve with assorted crackers or as a sandwich spread. **Yield:** 2 cups.

Brooks Hart
Woodbury, Connecticut

DRIED FRUIT STRUDELS

Prep: 45 minutes
Bake: 30 minutes

¾ cup pitted prunes, coarsely chopped
¾ cup dried apricots, coarsely chopped
½ cup sugar, divided
½ cup orange juice
¼ cup apricot brandy or orange juice
2 teaspoons ground cinnamon
1 teaspoon vanilla extract
1 (6-ounce) package sweetened dried cranberries
½ cup pistachios, coarsely chopped
½ cup toasted walnuts or pecans, coarsely chopped
1 cup apricot preserves
12 frozen phyllo pastry sheets, thawed
½ cup butter, melted

• **Stir** together prunes, apricots, ¼ cup sugar, and next 3 ingredients in a saucepan; bring to a boil over medium-high heat. Reduce heat to low; cook 3 minutes.
• **Process** fruit mixture and vanilla in a food processor until smooth, stopping to scrape down sides. Stir in dried cranberries and next 3 ingredients; set aside.
• **Unfold** phyllo, and cover with a damp towel to prevent pastry from drying out.
• **Stack** 6 phyllo sheets on a flat surface covered with wax paper, brushing each sheet with melted butter.
• **Spoon** half of fruit mixture down short edge of 1 end of phyllo stack, leaving a 1-inch border around edge. Repeat procedure for remaining phyllo and fruit mixture. Fold in long edges 1 inch.
• **Roll up,** starting at short edge nearest filling. Place each, seam side down, in a lightly greased jellyroll pan. Cut ¼-inch-deep diagonal slits, 1 inch apart, across top. Brush with melted butter; sprinkle with remaining ¼ cup sugar.
• **Bake** at 375° for 30 minutes. Cool on a wire rack. **Yield:** 2 (12-inch) strudels.

FRUITY BAKED CHICKEN

Prep: 20 minutes
Bake: 30 minutes

2 (6.2-ounce) packages long-grain and wild rice mix
2 teaspoons salt, divided
⅓ cup all-purpose flour
½ teaspoon pepper
½ teaspoon paprika
6 skinned and boned chicken breast halves
¼ cup vegetable oil
1 large sweet onion, diced
1 (6-ounce) package chopped mixed dried fruit
2 cups chicken broth
½ cup frozen orange juice concentrate, thawed
2 tablespoons grated fresh ginger
1 teaspoon chili-garlic paste
2 teaspoons cornstarch
¼ cup water

• **Prepare** rice mix according to package directions, omitting seasoning packets; add 1 teaspoon salt. Set aside.
• **Combine** flour, pepper, paprika, and remaining 1 teaspoon salt in a large bowl. Dredge chicken in flour mixture.
• **Cook** chicken in hot oil in a skillet over medium heat about 2 minutes on each side. Remove from skillet; set aside. Add onion to skillet; sauté over medium-high heat, stirring often, 5 minutes. Stir in fruit and next 4 ingredients; bring to a boil.
• **Combine** cornstarch and ¼ cup water. Stir into fruit mixture; cook 1 minute.
• **Spoon** rice into a lightly greased 13- x 9-inch baking dish. Place chicken over rice. Spoon fruit mixture over chicken.
• **Bake,** covered, at 350° for 30 minutes. **Yield:** 6 servings.

Mary Jeffreys
Raleigh, North Carolina

Seasonal Sides

Get excited about winter vegetables, and enjoy these inventive creations that showcase the season's best.

STUFFED POTATOES

Prep: 20 minutes
Bake: 10 minutes

4 large baking potatoes, baked
2 cups (8 ounces) shredded colby cheese
8 bacon slices, cooked and crumbled
8 green onions, chopped
2 garlic cloves, pressed
½ cup sour cream
¼ cup butter or margarine, softened
½ teaspoon salt
½ teaspoon pepper

• **Cut** potatoes in half lengthwise; scoop out pulp, leaving shells intact.
• **Mash** pulp, and stir in cheese and remaining 7 ingredients.
• **Spoon** into shells; place on a baking sheet. Bake at 400° for 10 minutes or until cheese melts. **Yield:** 4 servings.

BROCCOLI SLAW

Prep: 10 minutes
Chill: 3 hours

¼ cup cider vinegar
2 tablespoons light brown sugar
½ teaspoon salt
½ cup vegetable oil
1 (16-ounce) package broccoli
    slaw
2 small Rome apples, chopped
½ cup raisins

• **Whisk** together first 3 ingredients in a large bowl; gradually whisk in oil.
• **Add** slaw, apple, and raisins; toss well to coat. Cover; chill 3 hours. **Yield:** 8 cups.

Valerie G. Stutsman
Norfolk, Virginia

CREAMED CABBAGE

Prep: 10 minutes
Cook: 25 minutes

2 tablespoons butter or margarine
40 saltine crackers, crushed
1 large cabbage, shredded
½ cup water
1 teaspoon salt
1 teaspoon pepper
¼ cup butter or margarine
¼ cup all-purpose flour
2 cups milk

• **Melt** 2 tablespoons butter in a skillet over medium heat. Add cracker crumbs; sauté until browned. Remove from skillet; set aside.
• **Bring** cabbage and ½ cup water to a boil in a saucepan. Cover; cook 5 to 7 minutes or until tender. Drain. Stir in salt and pepper; keep warm.
• **Melt** ¼ cup butter in skillet over low heat; whisk in flour until smooth. Cook, whisking constantly, 1 minute. Gradually add milk; cook over medium heat, whisking constantly, until thickened and bubbly. Stir sauce and crackers into cabbage. **Yield:** 8 to 10 servings.

Margaret Bills
Selma, Alabama

CANDIED SWEET POTATOES

Prep: 10 minutes
Stand: 1 hour
Bake: 1 hour, 30 minutes

6 large sweet potatoes, peeled
1 lemon, peeled
1 orange, peeled
¾ cup butter or margarine, melted
2 cups sugar
½ cup orange juice
2 teaspoons ground cinnamon
1 teaspoon vanilla extract (optional)

• **Cut** sweet potatoes, lemon, and orange into ¼-inch-thick slices.
• **Place** potato slices in a lightly greased 13- x 9-inch baking dish. Arrange lemon and orange slices over potato.
• **Stir** together butter, next 3 ingredients, and, if desired, vanilla. Pour over sweet potato mixture; cover and let stand 1 hour.
• **Bake** at 350° for 1 hour and 30 minutes, basting often with pan juices. **Yield:** 8 to 10 servings.

CURRIED CAULIFLOWER BAKE

Prep: 20 minutes
Bake: 30 minutes

1 medium cauliflower *
½ teaspoon salt
1 (10¾-ounce) can cream of chicken soup, undiluted
1 cup (4 ounces) shredded Cheddar cheese
⅓ cup mayonnaise
2 tablespoons butter or margarine, melted
1 teaspoon curry powder
¾ cup fine, dry breadcrumbs

• **Cut** cauliflower into flowerets (about 3 cups). Cook in boiling water to cover with ½ teaspoon salt 10 minutes or until tender; drain.
• **Arrange** cauliflower in a lightly greased 8-inch square baking dish.
• **Stir** together soup and next 4 ingredients; pour over cauliflower.

• **Sprinkle** with breadcrumbs. Bake at 350° for 30 minutes. **Yield:** 6 servings.

* Substitute 1 (16-ounce) package frozen cauliflower, thawed, if desired.

Kimberly A. Cottrell
Bel Air, Maryland

SPINACH-ARTICHOKE CASSEROLE

Prep: 20 minutes
Bake: 30 minutes

2 (10-ounce) packages frozen chopped spinach, thawed
1 (14-ounce) can artichoke hearts
2 tablespoons butter or margarine
2 tablespoons chopped onion
2 tablespoons all-purpose flour
½ cup milk
¾ teaspoon garlic salt
½ teaspoon pepper
1 teaspoon Worcestershire sauce
¾ cup shredded Parmesan cheese

• **Drain** chopped spinach well, reserving ½ cup liquid. Gently press spinach between layers of paper towels. Set aside.
• **Drain** artichoke hearts, discarding liquid, and cut in half.
• **Melt** butter in a 3-quart saucepan over medium-high heat. Add onion; sauté until tender. Add flour; cook, stirring constantly, 1 minute. Stir in reserved spinach liquid and milk; cook, stirring constantly, 2 minutes or until thickened and bubbly.
• **Stir** in spinach, artichoke, garlic salt, pepper, and Worcestershire sauce. Spoon into a lightly greased 1½-quart baking dish. Sprinkle with cheese.
• **Bake** casserole at 350° for 30 minutes. **Yield:** 6 servings.

Spicy Spinach-Artichoke Casserole: Substitute 1 (10-ounce) can diced tomato and green chiles, undrained, for milk and spinach liquid and ¾ cup shredded Monterey Jack cheese with peppers for Parmesan cheese.

From Our Kitchen

Hand Blenders

We always thought the handheld immersion blender was a cute idea, but it was not at the top of our must-have list. However, when members of our Test Kitchens staff tried one, the blender became our new favorite tool. Simply immerse the extended blade into the food, and press the button. There's no need to transfer food in batches to a stand blender. You can puree salad dressings, soups, and sauces in their own containers. You'll find several brands in housewares and kitchen shops with prices starting around $20.

A Little Drop of Flavor

Assistant Foods Editor Scott Jones has found a way to dress up dishes without adding any saturated fat. "I've been using the most unbelievable olive oil for the past few months," says Scott, "and it's just the thing! The olive oil is called Supremo; it's organic and produced in California. The oil comes in a variety of styles, but I prefer their citrus-infused flavors of orange, lime, and lemon—perfect for dressing vegetables. For example, when I steam sliced carrots and green beans, I toss in fresh dill and hit the vegetables with about a tablespoon of orange-infused olive oil. It's unbelievable. The flavors are clean, with no bitter bite from the fruit." For more information about these oils, visit www.supremooil.com, or call toll free 1-877-787-7366.

Proof It

If you think the dry yeast in your pantry might be too old to be active, you can proof it as a test before sacrificing any bread ingredients. Dissolve it in a little warm water (100° to 110°) with a pinch of sugar. Set it aside in a warm place (85°) for 5 to 10 minutes. If the mixture starts to bubble and swell, it's alive and ready to use. If the mixture lies dormant, toss it out, and buy fresh yeast. You should store yeast in a cool, dry place; it also can be refrigerated or frozen. Make sure the yeast is at room temperature before dissolving it, and always discard any dry yeast when the expiration date on its package has passed.

Chef's Cooking Torch

When you're making crème brûlée, a chef's cooking torch can help you caramelize the perfect sugar cap. For that reason alone, it's a great tool to own. However, the torch has a variety of other uses in the kitchen. Follow the manufacturer's instructions to perform these and other tasks.

- Brown baked Alaska and other meringue-topped desserts.

- Melt and brown cheese on French onion soup.

- Glaze fruit tarts and other pastries.

- Blacken tomatoes, onions, and jalapeños for making salsas.

- Blacken peppers to easily remove the skin.

Keep the torch within easy reach; you may discover many more ways it can help streamline your cooking. You'll love how easy it is to operate. If curious children play in the kitchen, you may want to store fuel and torch separately. The torch is available at kitchen shops and ranges from $20 to $40.

TIPS AND TIDBITS

- Jan Moon, of our Test Kitchens staff, suggests that before you use the food processor to mix sticky ingredients, lightly coat the bowl and blades with cooking spray. The quick spritz doesn't alter the recipe, the ingredients don't stick to the bowl and blades, and it makes cleanup much easier.

- Nuts stored in the freezer stay fresher longer. Frozen nuts, however, do take longer to toast than the thawed version. Jan warns, "Don't be tempted to turn up the heat if you're using nuts right from the freezer; just bake them 5 extra minutes at the same temperature."

- Don't mention mistakes in a recipe you're serving to your guests. They won't notice, and they'd rather not know. Keep smiling and accept all of their compliments.

- If you're still not sure about trying couscous, maybe we can change your mind. It's rapidly becoming more popular than rice and other types of pasta. It's fast and easy to prepare, and it brings a wonderful change of pace to your plate. In some cultures, couscous is believed to be a symbol of happiness and abundance. It's one of our pantry staples, and the happiness is a tasty bonus.

MARCH

A Month of Family Suppers

We invite you to gather your family and enjoy four weeks of homemade meals carefully designed to eliminate your menu planning stress.

Let's face it—the task of getting a family-pleasing meal on the table four nights a week can be overwhelming. But that's what we're going to help you accomplish. Here's the deal. These pages, along with our "Living Light" column (pages 56-58), contain recipes for 16 menus with four suppers per week, plus bonus meals you can pull from your freezer in a pinch.

Editorial Assistant Vicki Poellnitz accepted our challenge to test drive the plan—she said it worked perfectly. Vicki reported the cost per week to be about $68.

See "From Our Kitchen" on pages 67-68 for shopping lists and cook's notes. "Living Light" on pages 56-58 features our side dishes. "Quick and Easy" on pages 58-59 includes desserts that will complete your meals (the desserts aren't included in shopping lists or cost per week).

We bet your family will consider this the best month's worth of meals they've had.

BAKED GLAZED HAM

By preparing this ham at the beginning of the month, you'll have enough left over to use in two casserole recipes and two sandwich recipes.

Prep: 10 minutes
Bake: 1 hour, 30 minutes
Stand: 15 minutes

2 **tablespoons sugar**
1 **tablespoon paprika**
1 **tablespoon chili powder**
1 **teaspoon ground cumin**
¾ **teaspoon ground cinnamon**
½ **teaspoon ground cloves**
1 **(8-pound) smoked fully cooked ham half, trimmed**
1 **(12-ounce) can cola soft drink**
1 **(8-ounce) jar plum or apricot preserves**
⅓ **cup orange juice**

• **Combine** first 6 ingredients. Score fat on ham in a diamond pattern. Sprinkle ham with sugar mixture, and place in a lightly greased shallow roasting pan. Pour cola into pan.
• **Bake**, covered, at 325° for 1 hour. Uncover and bake 15 more minutes.
• **Stir** together preserves and orange juice. Spoon ¾ cup glaze over ham, and bake 15 more minutes or until a meat thermometer inserted into thickest portion registers 140°. Let stand 15 minutes before slicing. Serve ham with remaining glaze. **Yield:** 16 servings.

Sharon Walker Howard
Mayfield, Kentucky

CHICKEN-AND-RICE CASSEROLES

Prep: 15 minutes
Bake: 55 minutes

2 **(1¼-pound) roasted chickens**
1 **small onion, minced**
½ **cup light mayonnaise**
2 **(10¾-ounce) cans reduced-sodium, reduced-fat cream of chicken soup, undiluted**
1 **(8-ounce) can sliced water chestnuts, drained and chopped**
1 **(14½-ounce) can low-sodium, fat-free chicken broth**
1 **(6.2-ounce) package long-grain and wild rice mix, cooked**
½ **small green bell pepper, chopped**

• **Remove** chicken from bones, discarding skin and bones. Chop chicken.
• **Stir** together chicken and remaining ingredients.
• **Spoon** evenly into 2 lightly greased 8-inch square baking dishes. Wrap 1 dish in heavy-duty aluminum foil, and freeze for Monday, Week 4.
• **Bake** remaining casserole at 350° for 55 minutes or until thoroughly heated. **Yield:** 4 servings per casserole.

Note: Thaw frozen casserole in refrigerator overnight. Bake at 350° for 55 to 60 minutes.

Merle L. Porter
Pelham, Georgia

HAM-SWISS-AND-ASPARAGUS SANDWICHES
(pictured on page 77)

Prep: 20 minutes
Broil: 1 minute

¾ **pound fresh asparagus**
3 **tablespoons light butter or margarine, softened**
1 **small garlic clove, minced**
4 **(6-inch) French bread loaves, split**
3 **tablespoons light mayonnaise**
8 **Baked Glazed Ham slices**
4 **Swiss cheese slices ***
Green leaf lettuce
3 **plum tomatoes, sliced**

• **Snap** off tough ends of asparagus. Cook in boiling water to cover 3 minutes or until crisp-tender; drain. Plunge into ice water to stop the cooking process; drain and chill.

• **Stir** together butter and garlic.

• **Spread** butter mixture evenly over bottom halves of bread. Spread mayonnaise evenly over top halves of bread.

• **Layer** bottom halves evenly with ham slices, asparagus, and cheese; place on a baking sheet.

• **Broil** 2 inches from heat 1 minute or just until cheese melts. Top evenly with lettuce, tomato, and top half of bread. **Yield:** 4 servings.

★Substitute 6 ounces thinly sliced Brie with rind removed for Swiss cheese slices, if desired.

EGGPLANT PARMESAN

Prep: 35 minutes
Bake: 45 minutes

3 large eggs
3 tablespoons water
¾ cup Italian-seasoned breadcrumbs
2 tablespoons grated Parmesan cheese
1 large eggplant, peeled and cut into ½-inch-thick slices
3 tablespoons olive oil
¼ cup grated Parmesan cheese, divided
1 (8-ounce) package shredded mozzarella cheese, divided
3 cups Pasta Sauce

• **Whisk** together eggs and 3 tablespoons water until blended.

• **Combine** breadcrumbs and 2 tablespoons Parmesan cheese.

• **Dip** eggplant slices into egg mixture; dredge in breadcrumb mixture.

• **Cook** eggplant, in 3 batches, in 1 tablespoon hot oil (per batch) in a large skillet over medium heat 4 minutes on each side or until tender.

• **Arrange** one-third of eggplant in a single layer in a lightly greased 11- x 7-inch baking dish. Sprinkle with 1 tablespoon Parmesan cheese and ½ cup

mozzarella cheese. Repeat layers twice. Spoon 3 cups Pasta Sauce over top.

• **Bake,** covered, at 375° for 35 minutes. Uncover and sprinkle with remaining 1 tablespoon Parmesan cheese and ½ cup mozzarella cheese. Bake 10 more minutes or until cheese melts. **Yield:** 4 to 6 servings.

Joanne Gibbs
High Point, North Carolina

Pasta Sauce

Follow our tips in "From Our Kitchen" (pages 67-68), and make this sauce on Sunday, Week 1.

Prep: 15 minutes
Cook: 2 hours, 10 minutes

2 small onions, chopped
4 garlic cloves, chopped
¼ cup vegetable oil
2 (28-ounce) cans diced tomatoes, undrained
2 (12-ounce) cans tomato paste
8 cups water
¼ cup sugar
2 tablespoons dried Italian seasoning
1 tablespoon salt
1 tablespoon dried basil
2 teaspoons black pepper
1 teaspoon dried crushed red pepper

• **Sauté** onion and garlic in hot oil in a Dutch oven over medium heat 10 minutes or until onion is tender. Stir in diced tomatoes and remaining ingredients. Bring to a boil; reduce heat, and simmer, stirring often, 2 hours.

• **Divide** into recipe portions; set aside 3 cups for Eggplant Parmesan, and freeze remaining portions. **Yield:** 12 cups.

Donna Snider
Woodbridge, Virginia

MENU TIMELINE

WEEK 1

Sunday
Baked Glazed Ham
Thyme-Scented Green Beans With Smoked Almonds (page 57)
Baked potatoes
Rolls

Monday
Chicken-and-Rice Casserole
Steamed zucchini, yellow squash, and carrots
Rolls

Tuesday
Ham-Swiss-and-Asparagus Sandwiches
Coleslaw With Garden Vegetables (page 57)

Wednesday
Eggplant Parmesan
Romaine salad with Oregano-Feta Dressing (page 57)
Garlic bread

WEEK 2

Sunday
Peasant Soup (page 54)
Cornbread

Monday
Chickpea-Chipotle Tostadas (page 54)
Pear Salad With Jícama and Snow Peas (page 56)

Tuesday
Sausage-Ham Breakfast Casserole (page 54)
Orange wedges
Biscuits

Wednesday
Calzones With Pasta Sauce (page 54)
Baby carrots and celery sticks

WEEK 3

Sunday
Chicken Burritos (page 55)
Yellow rice
Shredded iceberg lettuce

Monday
Chickpea Salad (page 55)
Pita bread
Pineapple wedges

Tuesday
Pasta Sauce With Meatballs (page 55)
Green salad with Oregano-Feta Dressing (page 57)
Breadsticks

Wednesday
Creamy Ham Casserole (page 55)
Apples, strawberries, and canned pineapple chunks with Poppy Seed Dressing (page 56)

WEEK 4

Sunday
Red Pepper Hummus Pizza (page 56)
Tossed salad

Monday
Chicken-and-Rice Casserole from the freezer
Steamed frozen, cut green beans
Breadsticks

Tuesday
Tabbouleh Salad (page 57)
Creamy Cucumber Salad (page 56)
Pita triangles

Wednesday
Panhandle Sandwiches (page 56)
Broccoli Salad (page 58)

PEASANT SOUP

Prep: 35 minutes
Cook: 1 hour, 30 minutes

9   baby carrots, sliced
1   large onion, coarsely chopped
2   celery ribs, diced
¼   cup chopped fresh parsley
1   (16-ounce) package kielbasa
      sausage, cut into ¼-inch-thick
      slices *
1   bay leaf
5   (14½-ounce) cans chicken broth,
      divided
½   (10-ounce) package shredded angel
      hair cabbage slaw
2   russet potatoes, peeled and cut into
      ½-inch cubes
½   cup frozen, cut green beans
1   (15-ounce) can kidney beans, rinsed
      and drained
¼   teaspoon dried thyme
½   teaspoon pepper

• **Bring** first 6 ingredients and 4 cans chicken broth to a boil in a stockpot; reduce heat, and simmer 45 minutes.
• **Add** remaining can of broth, slaw, and remaining ingredients; simmer 30 minutes or until vegetables are tender. Remove and discard bay leaf. (Freeze leftover soup up to 1 month.) **Yield:** 2½ quarts.

*Substitute 1 pound coarsely chopped cooked ham for kielbasa, if desired.

Note: You may cook first 6 ingredients and 4 cans chicken broth in a 5-quart slow cooker on LOW for 4 hours. Add remaining can of broth, slaw, and remaining ingredients; cook on HIGH 1 hour.

Abi Gallagher
Pittsburgh, Pennsylvania

CHICKPEA-CHIPOTLE TOSTADAS

Prep: 45 minutes

Vegetable oil
12 corn tortillas
1   medium onion, chopped
½   red bell pepper, chopped
2   garlic cloves, chopped
1   tablespoon olive oil
1½ (15-ounce) cans chickpeas, rinsed
      and drained *
1   cup chicken broth
2   tablespoons chopped fresh cilantro
2   chipotle peppers in adobo sauce,
      minced *
½   teaspoon salt
2   tablespoons fresh lime juice
1   (8-ounce) container sour cream
½   cup salsa verde or green chile
      sauce *
½   head iceberg lettuce, shredded
6   plum tomatoes, chopped
5   ounces reduced-fat feta cheese,
      crumbled

• **Pour** vegetable oil to a depth of 2 inches into a large skillet. Heat to 375°. Fry tortillas, 1 at a time, over medium-high heat 30 seconds on each side or until crisp and lightly browned. Drain and keep warm.
• **Sauté** onion, bell pepper, and garlic in hot olive oil in a large skillet over medium-high heat 5 minutes or until tender. Add chickpeas and next 4 ingredients; bring to a boil. Reduce heat, and simmer 5 minutes.
• **Process** chickpea mixture in a food processor or with a hand blender until smooth. Return mixture to skillet. Simmer, stirring occasionally, until very thick. Stir in lime juice; cook 2 to 3 minutes.
• **Stir** together sour cream and salsa.
• **Spread** chickpea mixture evenly over tortillas. Top evenly with lettuce and tomato. Drizzle with sour cream mixture, and sprinkle with cheese. Serve immediately. **Yield:** 6 servings.

*Substitute 1½ (15-ounce) cans navy beans for chickpeas, if desired. Substitute 2 canned jalapeño peppers and 2 drops of liquid smoke for chipotle peppers, if desired. Substitute ½ cup regular salsa for salsa verde, if desired.

SAUSAGE-HAM BREAKFAST CASSEROLE

Prep: 35 minutes
Chill: 8 hours
Bake: 45 minutes

½   (1-pound) package ground hot pork
      sausage
3   white bread slices
1   (8-ounce) package shredded sharp
      Cheddar cheese, divided
3   large eggs
1   cup milk
1   teaspoon prepared mustard
⅛   teaspoon pepper
2   cups chopped Baked Glazed Ham

• **Cook** sausage in a large skillet over medium-high heat, stirring until sausage crumbles and is no longer pink. Drain well.
• **Arrange** bread slices in a lightly greased 8-inch square baking dish.
• **Sprinkle** sausage over bread. Sprinkle half of cheese over sausage.
• **Whisk** together eggs and next 3 ingredients. Pour over cheese. Sprinkle with ham; top with remaining cheese. Cover and chill 8 hours.
• **Bake** casserole at 350° for 45 minutes. **Yield:** 4 servings.

Beverly Justice
Columbiana, Alabama

CALZONES WITH PASTA SAUCE

Prep: 25 minutes
Bake: 25 minutes

1   cup small-curd cottage cheese
3   tablespoons grated Parmesan
      cheese
1   large egg
1   tablespoon chopped fresh or
      1 teaspoon dried parsley
½   teaspoon garlic powder
1   (3.5-ounce) package pepperoni
      slices, chopped *
4   Monterey Jack cheese slices,
      chopped
2   (10-ounce) cans refrigerated pizza
      crusts
2   cups Pasta Sauce, thawed

- **Stir** together first 5 ingredients until blended. Stir in pepperoni and chopped cheese slices.
- **Divide** each pizza crust into 2 portions. Roll each dough portion into a 7-inch circle.
- **Spoon** ½ cup cottage cheese mixture in center of each circle. Fold dough over filling, pressing edges to seal; place on a lightly greased aluminum foil-lined baking sheet. Prick dough several times with a fork.
- **Bake** at 375° for 20 to 25 minutes or until golden. Let stand 5 minutes. Serve calzones with warm Pasta Sauce. **Yield:** 4 servings.

*Substitute chopped cooked ham for pepperoni slices, if desired.

Jody Gesell
Houston, Texas

CHICKEN BURRITOS

Prep: 25 minutes
Bake: 15 minutes

1 (1¼-pound) roasted chicken
1 (1¼-ounce) envelope taco seasoning mix
1 (16-ounce) can refried beans
6 (8-inch) flour tortillas
1 (8-ounce) package shredded sharp Cheddar cheese
3 plum tomatoes, diced
1 small onion, diced
Salsa verde*

- **Remove** chicken from bones, discarding skin and bones. Chop chicken.
- **Place** chicken and seasoning mix in a large heavy-duty zip-top plastic bag; seal and shake to coat.
- **Spread** beans evenly down center of tortillas. Top with chicken, cheese, tomato, and onion; roll up. Wrap each burrito in foil.
- **Bake** at 350° for 15 minutes. Serve with salsa verde. **Yield:** 4 servings.

*Substitute regular salsa for salsa verde, if desired.

Bobbie Groenewegen
St. Louis, Missouri

CHICKPEA SALAD
(pictured on page 76)

Prep: 25 minutes

3 tablespoons olive oil
2 tablespoons white wine vinegar
½ teaspoon salt
½ teaspoon freshly ground pepper
2 (15-ounce) cans chickpeas, rinsed and drained*
3 green onions, chopped
1 small cucumber, peeled, seeded, and chopped
½ cup kalamata or ripe olives, pitted and chopped
3 plum tomatoes, seeded and chopped
¼ cup chopped fresh parsley
Garnish: shredded Parmesan cheese

- **Whisk** together olive oil, vinegar, salt and pepper.
- **Combine** chickpeas and next 5 ingredients. Add olive oil mixture, tossing to coat. Garnish, if desired. **Yield:** 6 servings.

*Substitute 2 (15-ounce) cans navy beans for chickpeas, if desired.

Beatriz Swirsky
Sunrise, Florida

PASTA SAUCE WITH MEATBALLS

Prep: 5 minutes
Cook: 20 minutes

4 cups Pasta Sauce, thawed
14 frozen cooked meatballs
Hot cooked spaghetti

- **Cook** Pasta Sauce and meatballs in a saucepan over medium heat 15 to 20 minutes or until thoroughly heated. Serve over hot cooked spaghetti. **Yield:** 4 servings.

CREAMY HAM CASSEROLES
(pictured on page 76)

Prep: 20 minutes
Bake: 30 minutes

8 ounces uncooked egg noodles
1 (10¾-ounce) can cream of mushroom soup, undiluted
1 (8-ounce) container chive-and-onion-flavored cream cheese, softened
⅔ cup milk
2 cups chopped Baked Glazed Ham
1½ cups fresh broccoli flowerets
1 (10-ounce) package frozen asparagus, thawed
6 baby carrots, chopped
1 (8-ounce) package shredded mozzarella cheese
1 (4-ounce) package shredded Cheddar cheese
½ cup crushed seasoned croutons

- **Cook** pasta according to package directions; drain.
- **Stir** together soup, cream cheese, and milk in a large bowl. Stir in pasta, ham, and next 3 ingredients. Spoon half of ham mixture into 2 lightly greased 8-inch square baking dishes.
- **Combine** shredded cheeses. Sprinkle half of cheese mixture over casseroles. Spoon remaining ham mixture over cheeses.
- **Combine** remaining cheese mixture with crushed croutons. Sprinkle over casseroles. Wrap 1 casserole in heavy-duty aluminum foil, and freeze up to 1 month.
- **Bake** remaining casserole at 400° for 30 minutes or until lightly browned. **Yield:** 4 servings per casserole.

Note: Thaw frozen casserole in refrigerator overnight. Bake at 400° for 35 to 40 minutes.

Laurabell J. Long
Peru, Indiana

RED PEPPER HUMMUS PIZZA

Prep: 15 minutes
Bake: 10 minutes

1 (15-ounce) can chickpeas, rinsed and drained *
1 (7-ounce) jar roasted red bell peppers, drained and chopped
2 garlic cloves
2 tablespoons olive oil
2 tablespoons fresh lemon juice
½ teaspoon salt
¼ teaspoon pepper
1 (10-ounce) Italian bread shell *
1 (8-ounce) package feta cheese, crumbled
3 plum tomatoes, sliced
¼ cup pitted kalamata or ripe olives, chopped
1 teaspoon dried oregano

• **Process** first 7 ingredients in a blender or food processor until smooth, stopping to scrape down sides.
• **Spread** chickpea mixture over bread shell. Top with feta cheese and remaining ingredients.
• **Bake** at 450° for 10 minutes or until lightly browned. **Yield:** 6 servings.

* Substitute 1 (15-ounce) can navy beans for chickpeas, if desired. Substitute 1 (10-ounce) can refrigerated pizza crust, baked, for bread shell, if desired.

PANHANDLE SANDWICHES

Prep: 15 minutes
Bake: 5 minutes

½ cup light butter or margarine, softened
4 green onions, diced
2 tablespoons prepared mustard
2 teaspoons Worcestershire sauce
4 (6-inch) French bread loaves, split
4 Monterey Jack cheese slices
8 Baked Glazed Ham slices

• **Stir** together first 4 ingredients.
• **Spread** butter mixture evenly over cut sides of bread.
• **Cut** cheese slices in half; place 2 halves evenly on bottom halves of bread. Top with ham slices and tops of bread. Wrap each sandwich in foil.
• **Bake** sandwiches at 350° for 5 minutes or until thoroughly heated and cheese melts. **Yield:** 4 servings.

Note: Sandwiches may be prepared ahead and frozen. Bake at 350° for 40 minutes.

Jean Voan
Shepherd, Texas

Living Light

This month we are devoting the "Living Light" column to vegetables, salads, and dressings to accompany main dishes for "A Month of Family Suppers" (pages 52-56). Although we've relaxed our limit of total fat grams per recipe, we used heart-friendly oils and reduced-fat dairy products to lower saturated fat and cholesterol. Serve these sides with your favorite main dishes, or combine several for a variety of meatless suppers.

POPPY SEED DRESSING

Leftover apricot nectar may be used for chicken or seafood marinades, brushed over pork chops, or simply enjoyed chilled.

Prep: 10 minutes

⅔ cup light sour cream
½ cup apricot or pear nectar
2 tablespoons white wine vinegar
1 tablespoon vegetable oil
1 tablespoon honey
1 teaspoon poppy seeds

• **Whisk** together all ingredients in a bowl. Chill, if desired. Serve with fresh fruit. **Yield:** 1¼ cups.

Anna J. Beyer
Bristol, Tennessee

♥ Per 2 tablespoons: Calories 48 (66% from fat)
Fat 3.5g (sat 1.5g, mono 1g, poly 0.9g)
Protein 0.6g Carb 4g Fiber 0.1g
Chol 6mg Iron 0.1mg
Sodium 7mg Calc 22mg

CREAMY CUCUMBER SALAD

Prep: 20 minutes
Chill: 2 hours

¼ cup nonfat yogurt
1 teaspoon olive oil
½ teaspoon lemon juice
½ teaspoon minced fresh mint
¾ teaspoon salt
¼ teaspoon sugar
⅛ teaspoon pepper
2 cucumbers

• **Stir** together first 7 ingredients until well blended. Peel, seed, and slice cucumbers. Add to yogurt mixture; toss to coat. Cover and chill, stirring occasionally, at least two hours. **Yield:** 4 servings.

Charlotte Bryant
Greensburg, Kentucky

♥ Per serving: Calories 35 (33% from fat)
Fat 1.3g (sat 0.2g, mono 0.8g, poly 0.2g)
Protein 1.7g Carb 5g Fiber 1.2g
Chol 0mg Iron 0.4mg
Sodium 306mg Calc 46mg

PEAR SALAD WITH JÍCAMA AND SNOW PEAS

Prep: 20 minutes

2 cups fresh snow pea pods *
2 ripe pears, peeled
1½ teaspoons fresh lemon juice
½ small jícama, peeled *
2 cups fresh spinach leaves
2 tablespoons balsamic vinegar
1 teaspoon Dijon mustard
1 garlic clove, minced
½ teaspoon pepper
2 tablespoons olive oil
1 to 2 green onions, thinly sliced
1 tablespoon chopped fresh basil
3 tablespoons chopped pecans, toasted

• **Cook** snow peas in boiling water to cover 1 minute; drain. Plunge into ice water to stop the cooking process, and cut lengthwise into ¼-inch strips.
• **Cut** pears into ¼-inch strips; toss with lemon juice. Cut jícama and spinach into thin strips.

- **Whisk** together vinegar and next 3 ingredients. Gradually add oil, whisking until well blended. Stir in green onions and basil. Chill dressing 15 minutes.
- **Combine** vegetable strips and pear strips. Drizzle with dressing, tossing to coat; sprinkle with pecans. Serve immediately. **Yield:** 4 servings.

* Substitute 1 (9-ounce) package frozen snow pea pods for fresh snow peas, if desired. Substitute 1 Red Delicious apple for jícama, if desired.

Kate Stewart Rovner
Plano, Texas

♥ Per serving: Calories 127 (48% from fat)
Fat 6.8g (sat 0.8g, mono 4.5g, poly 0.9g)
Protein 2.5g Carb 16g Fiber 4.6g
Chol 0mg Iron 2mg
Sodium 43mg Calc 53mg

OREGANO-FETA DRESSING

Prep: 10 minutes

3 ounces reduced-fat feta cheese, crumbled *
¼ cup nonfat buttermilk
3 tablespoons fresh lemon juice
1 garlic clove
½ teaspoon dried oregano *
¼ teaspoon freshly ground pepper
2 tablespoons water
2 tablespoons olive oil
¼ small green bell pepper, chopped

- **Process** first 7 ingredients in a food processor until smooth. Gradually add oil in a steady stream; process until smooth. Add bell pepper; pulse 3 seconds. **Yield:** about 1 cup.

* Substitute 3 ounces crumbled feta cheese for reduced-fat cheese, if desired. Substitute 1 teaspoon chopped fresh oregano for dried, if desired.

Charlotte Bryant
Greensburg, Kentucky

♥ Per 2 tablespoons: Calories 60 (77% from fat)
Fat 5.1g (sat 1.4g, mono 3g, poly 0.7g)
Protein 2.6g Carb 1.2g Fiber 0.1g
Chol 4mg Iron 0.1mg
Sodium 158mg Calc 42mg

TABBOULEH SALAD

Prep: 20 minutes
Stand: 30 minutes
Chill: 1 hour

1 cup uncooked bulghur wheat *
1 cup boiling water *
2 medium tomatoes, chopped
4 green onions, thinly sliced
¼ cup minced fresh parsley
¼ to ½ cup chopped fresh mint
½ teaspoon grated lemon rind
⅓ cup fresh lemon juice
3 tablespoons olive oil
½ teaspoon salt
½ teaspoon pepper
Lettuce leaves

- **Place** bulghur in a large bowl, and add boiling water. Cover, and let stand 30 minutes.
- **Stir** in tomato and next 8 ingredients. Cover and chill 1 hour. Spoon over lettuce leaves. **Yield:** 5 cups.

* Substitute 1 cup instant brown rice, cooked, for 1 cup bulghur and 1 cup boiling water, if desired.

♥ Per ½ cup: Calories 97 (43% from fat)
Fat 4.6g (sat 0.7g, mono 3.2g, poly 0.5g)
Protein 2.1g Carb 14g Fiber 3.2g
Chol 0mg Iron 0.7mg
Sodium 124mg Calc 15mg

COLESLAW WITH GARDEN VEGETABLES
(pictured on page 77)

Prep: 20 minutes

¼ red bell pepper
¼ small green bell pepper
¼ purple onion
¼ cup light mayonnaise
¼ cup light sour cream
1 tablespoon sugar
2 tablespoons fresh lemon juice
¾ teaspoon celery seeds
¼ teaspoon salt
⅛ teaspoon pepper
1 (10-ounce) package shredded angel hair cabbage slaw

- **Chop** bell peppers and onion. Reserve remaining red bell pepper for Week 2 and remaining green bell pepper for Oregano-Feta Dressing.
- **Stir** together mayonnaise and next 6 ingredients in a large bowl. Add bell pepper, onion, and slaw, tossing well to coat. Cover and chill. **Yield:** 4 cups.

Ashley Funderburk
Wilmington, North Carolina

♥ Per ½ cup: Calories 51 (55% from fat)
Fat 3.1g (sat 0.6g, mono 0.3g, poly 0.1g)
Protein 1g Carb 6g Fiber 1.1g
Chol 5mg Iron 0.4mg
Sodium 139mg Calc 30mg

THYME-SCENTED GREEN BEANS WITH SMOKED ALMONDS

Prep: 15 minutes
Cook: 10 minutes

1 pound fresh green beans, trimmed
1 tablespoon light butter
1 teaspoon dried thyme *
¼ teaspoon salt
¼ teaspoon pepper
1 tablespoon chopped smoked almonds *

- **Arrange** green beans in a steamer basket over boiling water. Cover and steam 6 minutes or until crisp-tender.
- **Melt** butter in a large skillet over medium heat. Stir in green beans, thyme, salt, and pepper, and cook until thoroughly heated. Sprinkle beans with almonds. **Yield:** 4 servings.

* Substitute 1 to 2 tablespoons chopped fresh thyme for dried thyme, if desired. Substitute 1 tablespoon chopped toasted almonds for smoked almonds, if desired.

Note: Find smoked almonds in the snack section of the supermarket.

Beth Royals
Richmond, Virginia

♥ Per serving: Calories 76 (44% from fat)
Fat 3.7g (sat 2g, mono 0.5g, poly 1g)
Protein 3.1g Carb 10g Fiber 3g
Chol 5mg Iron 3.5mg
Sodium 196mg Calc 80mg

BROCCOLI SALAD

Prep: 15 minutes
Chill: 30 minutes

4 cups chopped fresh broccoli
1 medium-size purple onion, chopped
¼ cup chopped fresh dill
2 tablespoons capers, drained ✳
Dressing
¼ cup chopped pecans, toasted
    (optional) ✳

• **Toss** together first 5 ingredients. Cover and chill 30 minutes. Sprinkle with pecans before serving, if desired. **Yield:** about 5 cups.

✳ Substitute 2 tablespoons chopped green olives for capers, if desired. Substitute ¼ cup pine nuts, toasted, for pecans, if desired.

Dressing

Prep: 3 minutes

⅓ cup balsamic vinegar
¼ cup olive oil
1 garlic clove, minced
½ tablespoon sugar
½ teaspoon salt
¼ teaspoon pepper

• **Whisk** together all ingredients. **Yield:** about ⅔ cup.

♥ Per cup: Calories 149 (73% from fat)
Fat 12g (sat 1.6g, mono 8.5g, poly 1.1g)
Protein 3.3g Carb 11g Fiber 3.1g
Chol 0mg Iron 2.1mg
Sodium 617mg Calc 92mg

Quick & Easy

If you think easy recipes sacrifice great flavor, you're wrong. Texas Cake and Peanut Butter-Fudge Cake are great examples that can be stirred together in 20 minutes, and then baked. It's so tempting to keep munching on them that you may have a hard time getting them in the freezer for later, but they do freeze well.

When you're planning your "Month of Family Suppers" (pages 52-56), consider these cakes for a perfect ending to any evening.

CARROT-RAISIN CAKE

Prep: 15 minutes
Bake: 30 minutes

1½ cups firmly packed light brown
    sugar
½ cup butter or margarine, softened
2 large eggs
1 teaspoon vanilla extract
1½ cups all-purpose flour
½ teaspoon baking soda
½ teaspoon salt
½ cup chopped raisins
1½ cups finely grated carrot
½ cup pecans or walnuts, finely
    chopped

• **Beat** brown sugar and butter at medium speed with an electric mixer until creamy; add eggs and vanilla, beating well.
• **Stir** in flour, baking soda, and salt just until moistened; stir in raisins and carrot. Spread mixture into a lightly greased 13- x 9-inch pan. Sprinkle with pecans.
• **Bake** at 350° for 30 minutes or until a wooden pick inserted in center comes out clean. Cool on a wire rack, and cut into squares. **Yield:** 12 to 15 servings.

Howard Wiener
Spring Hill, Florida

OATMEAL CAKE

Prep: 30 minutes
Stand: 20 minutes
Bake: 30 minutes
Broil: 3 minutes

1½ cups boiling water
1 cup uncooked regular or quick-
    cooking oats
½ cup butter or margarine, softened
1 cup sugar
2½ cups firmly packed brown sugar,
    divided
1 teaspoon ground cinnamon
¼ teaspoon ground nutmeg
1 teaspoon vanilla extract
2 large eggs
1½ cups all-purpose flour
1 teaspoon baking soda
½ teaspoon salt
1½ to 2 cups flaked coconut
1½ cups chopped pecans
⅓ cup butter or margarine, melted
⅓ cup milk

• **Stir** together 1½ cups boiling water and oats; let stand 20 minutes.
• **Beat** ½ cup butter, 1 cup sugar, and 1 cup brown sugar in a large bowl at medium speed with an electric mixer until creamy; add cinnamon and next 3 ingredients, beating well.
• **Stir** in flour, baking soda, and salt just until moistened; beat in oatmeal. Pour into a lightly greased 13- x 9-inch pan.
• **Bake** at 350° for 30 minutes or until a wooden pick inserted in center comes out clean.
• **Combine** remaining 1½ cups brown sugar, coconut, and remaining ingredients in a bowl; spread over warm cake.
• **Broil** 8 inches from heat 2 to 3 minutes or until golden. **Yield:** 12 to 15 servings.

Sherry Higginbotham
Hurricane, West Virginia

TEXAS CAKE

Prep: 20 minutes
Bake: 25 minutes

2 cups sugar
2 cups all-purpose flour
1 teaspoon baking soda
½ teaspoon salt
1 (8-ounce) container sour cream
2 large eggs, lightly beaten
1 cup butter or margarine
1 cup water
¼ cup cocoa
Fudge Frosting

• **Combine** first 4 ingredients in a large bowl; stir in sour cream and eggs.
• **Melt** butter in a heavy saucepan over medium heat. Whisk in 1 cup water and cocoa. Bring to a boil, whisking constantly. Remove from heat. Stir cocoa mixture into flour mixture. Pour into a greased 15- x 10-inch jellyroll pan.
• **Bake** at 325° for 20 to 25 minutes or until a wooden pick inserted in center of cake comes out clean. Spread frosting over warm cake. **Yield:** 24 servings.

Fudge Frosting

Prep: 20 minutes

½ cup butter or margarine
⅓ cup milk
¼ cup cocoa
1 (1-pound) package powdered sugar
1 teaspoon vanilla extract

• **Melt** butter in a saucepan over medium heat. Whisk in milk and cocoa; bring mixture to a boil. Remove from heat. Gradually add sugar, stirring until smooth; stir in vanilla. **Yield:** 3 cups.

Note: To thin frosting, add 1 to 2 tablespoons milk.

Peanut Butter-Fudge Cake: *(pictured on page 75)* Omit sour cream in cake, and substitute 1½ cups creamy peanut butter and ½ cup buttermilk. Continue as directed to prepare cake and Fudge Frosting. Garnish with miniature peanut butter cup candies, halved, if desired.

Beverly McCravy
Smyrna, Georgia

Taste of the South

Warm beignets are a sweet invitation to southern Louisiana, and no trip to New Orleans is complete without one. Where else but the South can you get so actively involved and committed to a doughnut? The word "beignet" is French for "fritter," and in the Crescent City, these concoctions come light, yeasty, and without holes.

Of course, you can buy beignet mixes almost anyplace, but main ingredients are the atmosphere and appreciation of tradition. So if you're craving beignets and New Orleans is not on your itinerary, make some at home.

Beignets are terrific Saturday morning breakfast treats. No special equipment is necessary—a Dutch oven or deep frying pan is all you need. Let the kids help by selecting cutters in fun shapes and by dusting the beignets with powdered sugar. The easiest method is to pour the sugar in a paper bag, place the hot, drained beignets inside, and shake. Be prepared for lots of giggles, clouds of sugar, and a wonderful taste of a special part of the South.

BEIGNETS

Savor this traditional New Orleans pastry in your own home. The dough can even be made ahead.

Prep: 30 minutes
Rise: 1 hour, 30 minutes
Cook: 15 minutes

1 (¼-ounce) envelope active dry yeast
3 tablespoons warm water (100° to 110°)
¾ cup milk
¼ cup sugar
¼ cup shortening
1 teaspoon salt
1 large egg, lightly beaten
3 cups all-purpose flour
2½ to 3 quarts vegetable oil
Powdered sugar

• **Combine** yeast and 3 tablespoons warm water in a large bowl; let mixture stand 5 minutes.
• **Heat** milk in a small saucepan over medium heat. (Do not boil.) Stir in sugar, shortening, and salt. Cool to lukewarm (100° to 110°).
• **Add** milk mixture, egg, and 2 cups flour to yeast mixture, stirring well. Gradually stir in enough remaining flour to make a soft dough.
• **Turn** dough out onto a floured surface; knead 8 to 10 minutes or until dough is smooth and elastic. Place in a well-greased bowl, turning to grease top. Cover and let rise in a warm place (85°), free from drafts, 1 hour or until doubled in bulk.
• **Punch** dough down, and turn it out onto a floured surface. Roll dough into a 12- x 10-inch rectangle; cut into 2-inch squares. Place on a floured surface; cover and let rise in a warm place (85°), free from drafts, 30 minutes or until doubled in bulk.
• **Pour** oil to a depth of 2 to 3 inches into a Dutch oven; heat to 375°. Fry beignets, in batches, 1 minute on each side or until golden. Drain on paper towels; sprinkle with powdered sugar while still hot. **Yield:** 2½ dozen.

Note: To make ahead, turn dough out onto a floured surface; knead 8 to 10 minutes or until smooth and elastic. Place in a well-greased bowl, turning to grease top. Cover and chill overnight. Punch dough down, and follow directions above.

BETTER BEIGNETS

Test Kitchens staffer Justin Craft tried several beignet recipes before he found the perfect one. He suggests maintaining the oil temperature at 375°, and gently lowering (not dropping) the beignets into the oil using a spatula.

Staple Salsas

These versatile condiments add flavor and flair to most any dish.

Preparing fresh salsas during this time of year can be tough. Although fresh ingredients may be a little more expensive, you can still create homemade salsas and sauces with beans, fruit, and other pantry staples. You can even bypass most of the usual chopping. Just open a bag of tortilla chips to dip into our Simple Salsa, or spoon these others onto your plate to jazz up a so-so supper.

TROPICAL SALSA

Flavors of the Caribbean spice this lively salsa.

Prep: 15 minutes
Chill: 30 minutes

1 (20-ounce) can pineapple tidbits
1 cup chopped mango
¼ cup honey-roasted peanuts, chopped
¼ cup flaked coconut, toasted
¼ cup light coconut milk
½ teaspoon grated lime rind
2 tablespoons fresh lime juice
1 teaspoon sugar
¼ teaspoon salt
¼ teaspoon ground ginger
¼ teaspoon ground red pepper

• **Drain** pineapple, reserving juice.
• **Stir** together pineapple, mango, peanuts, and coconut.
• **Stir** together reserved pineapple juice, coconut milk, and next 6 ingredients; add to pineapple mixture, tossing to coat. Chill 30 minutes. **Yield:** 3 cups.

Note: For testing purposes only, we used mango slices in a jar, drained, found in the produce section of supermarkets.

SIMPLE SALSA

Prep: 10 minutes
Chill: 30 minutes

1 (28-ounce) can crushed tomatoes
½ medium onion, diced
1 (4.5-ounce) can chopped green chiles
1 tablespoon sugar
1 tablespoon dried parsley
½ teaspoon salt
½ teaspoon garlic powder
½ teaspoon ground cumin
½ teaspoon freshly ground pepper

• **Stir** together all ingredients. Cover and chill 30 minutes. **Yield:** 4 cups.
Emelia Marx-Carman
Louisville, Kentucky

HORSERADISH RELISH

This creamy relish turns simple roast beef into a robust and elegant dish.

Prep: 15 minutes
Chill: 4 hours

1 (8-ounce) container sour cream
¼ cup prepared horseradish
2 tablespoons red wine vinegar
2½ teaspoons sugar
¼ teaspoon salt
½ teaspoon dry mustard
Dash of coarsely ground pepper
2 (15-ounce) cans cut beets, rinsed, well drained, and diced

• **Stir** together first 7 ingredients. Add beets, stirring gently until blended. Chill at least 4 hours. **Yield:** 4 cups.
Gwen Louer
Roswell, Georgia

BLACK BEAN SALSA WITH CITRUS DRESSING

This chunky, colorful salsa enlivens everything from tortilla chips to grilled shrimp.

Prep: 10 minutes

2 (15-ounce) cans black beans, rinsed and drained
1 (6.1-ounce) can mandarin oranges, drained
½ small purple onion, chopped
1 large green bell pepper, chopped
1 cup frozen whole kernel corn, thawed
1 tablespoon chopped pickled jalapeño pepper
¼ cup vegetable oil
¼ cup red wine vinegar
⅓ to ½ cup orange juice
¼ teaspoon salt

• **Stir** together first 6 ingredients. Whisk oil and next 3 ingredients. Drizzle over bean mixture, and toss. **Yield:** 8 cups.
Karen C. Greenlee
Lawrenceville, Georgia

HOT SPICED APPLESAUCE

Try topping grilled pork chops or chicken with this warm, fruity sauce.

Prep: 5 minutes
Cook: 5 minutes

1 (24-ounce) jar applesauce
1 (8-ounce) can crushed pineapple, drained
½ teaspoon ground cinnamon
⅛ teaspoon ground nutmeg
⅛ teaspoon ground ginger
⅛ teaspoon ground cloves
2 tablespoons rum (optional)

• **Cook** applesauce and pineapple over medium heat 5 minutes. Stir in cinnamon, next 3 ingredients, and, if desired, 2 tablespoons rum. Serve warm. **Yield:** 3 cups.
Debbie E. Ipock
Charlotte, North Carolina

Box Lunches

Take lunch to a new level. Stack your table with beautiful boxes and whimsical containers for a bridal shower, a ladies' luncheon, or any gathering you host.

Purchase an assortment of boxes from a paper-and-party supply store, and then let the fun begin. You can assemble each one (excluding perishable foods) the night before. The day of the party, fill the containers with sandwiches and salads, and then wrap them as you desire. Extralarge, colorful cloth napkins make great wraps that can be used as place mats. Get inspiration and ideas from the photos on pages 74-75.

Combine these delicious recipes with additions of your own for a lively gathering. You'll be free to toss the apron and attend your own party. By the way, cleanup is a snap because all the guests will want to keep their boxes.

SHERRIED CHICKEN-AND-GRAPE SALAD
(pictured on page 75)

Prep: 20 minutes

6 cups chopped cooked chicken
3 cups sliced green grapes
1 cup toasted slivered almonds
2 celery ribs, diced
3 green onions, minced
¾ cup mayonnaise
¼ cup sour cream
2 tablespoons sherry
½ teaspoon seasoned salt
½ teaspoon seasoned pepper

● **Stir** together all ingredients. **Yield:** 6 to 8 servings.

Note: Serve chicken salad in small grapefruit halves with pulp removed (line grapefruit halves with leaf lettuce). Create a handle for the grapefruit with florist wire, florist tape, and small silk flowers. Bend wire to form handle, insert into citrus shell, and decorate.

FRESH PESTO PASTA SALAD
(pictured on page 74)

Prep: 20 minutes

1 (16-ounce) package small shell pasta
⅓ cup red wine vinegar
1 tablespoon sugar
1 teaspoon seasoned pepper
½ teaspoon salt
1 teaspoon Dijon mustard
1 garlic clove, pressed
¾ cup olive oil
1 cup chopped fresh basil
1 (3-ounce) package shredded Parmesan cheese
½ cup toasted pine nuts
Garnishes: gourmet mixed baby salad greens; grape tomatoes; small, yellow pear-shaped tomatoes

● **Prepare** pasta according to package directions; rinse and drain.
● **Whisk** together vinegar and next 5 ingredients. Gradually whisk in olive oil.
● **Add** vinaigrette to pasta. Add basil, cheese, and pine nuts; toss to combine. Garnish, if desired. **Yield:** 8 servings.

GREEN CHILE-PIMIENTO CHEESE

Prep: 15 minutes

2 (8-ounce) blocks extra-sharp Cheddar cheese, shredded
1 (8-ounce) block Monterey Jack cheese with peppers, shredded
1 cup mayonnaise
1 (4.5-ounce) can chopped green chiles
1 (4-ounce) jar diced pimiento, drained
1 medium poblano chile pepper, seeded and minced
¼ small sweet onion, minced
2 teaspoons Worcestershire sauce

● **Stir** together all ingredients in a large bowl. **Yield:** about 6 cups.

Note: Spread ½ cup cheese mixture on 6 to 8 whole grain bread slices; top with bread slices. Trim crusts; cut sandwiches lengthwise into thirds. Reserve remaining pimiento cheese for other uses.

SMOKED TURKEY WRAPS
(pictured on page 74)

Prep: 15 minutes

2 (6.5-ounce) packages garlic-and-herb-flavored cheese, softened
8 (10-inch) whole grain pita wraps or flour tortillas
Caramelized Onions
1½ pounds thinly sliced smoked turkey
16 bacon slices, cooked and crumbled
4 cups loosely packed arugula or gourmet mixed baby salad greens

● **Spread** cheese evenly over pitas; top evenly with Caramelized Onions and remaining ingredients. Roll up, and wrap in parchment paper; chill. Cut in half to serve. **Yield:** 8 servings.

Note: For testing purposes only, we used Alouette Garlic et Herbes Gourmet Spreadable Cheese for garlic-and-herb-flavored cheese.

Caramelized Onions

Prep: 5 minutes
Cook: 20 minutes

2 large sweet onions, diced
1 tablespoon sugar
2 tablespoons olive oil
2 teaspoons balsamic vinegar

● **Cook** onion and sugar in hot oil over medium-high heat, stirring often, 20 minutes or until onion is caramel colored. Stir in vinegar. **Yield:** 2 cups.

PACKAGING TIPS

■ Line glazed flower pots or baskets with decorative dinner napkins to make great serving pieces.

■ Enhance containers with dried flowers and decorative items secured with a glue gun.

March Madness Munchies

*Try these crowd-pleasing recipes
for your game-day get-together.*

As the basketball tournaments heat up, there's no reason to sideline your hungry party-goers. These easy-to-make and easy-to-handle recipes may come in small packages, but they're loaded with flavor—exactly what you need when you're watching the big game.

Limit the time you spend in the kitchen by making the Golden-Baked Mini Reubens the night before and reheating them prior to tip-off. Your guests will be happy, and you'll have plenty of time to cheer on your favorite team.

GOLDEN-BAKED MINI REUBENS

*A platter piled high with these
hearty sandwiches is a winning
game plan.*

*Prep: 20 minutes
Bake: 10 minutes*

½ cup Thousand Island dressing
1 (16-ounce) loaf party rye bread
1 (6-ounce) package Swiss cheese
   slices, halved
12 ounces thinly sliced corned
   beef
1 (16-ounce) can shredded
   sauerkraut, well drained

• **Spread** dressing evenly on 1 side of each bread slice; top half of slices evenly with half of cheese, corned beef, sauerkraut, and remaining cheese. Top with remaining bread slices.
• **Coat** a baking sheet with butter-flavored cooking spray, and arrange sandwiches on baking sheet. Coat bottom of a second baking sheet with cooking spray; place, coated side down, on sandwiches.
• **Bake** at 375° for 8 to 10 minutes or until bread is golden and cheese melts. **Yield:** 20 sandwiches.

Note: To make ahead, place unbaked sandwiches on baking sheets, and freeze until firm; place sandwiches in heavy-duty zip-top plastic bags, and freeze. Bake according to directions at 375° for 15 minutes.

*Michele Baker
Richardson, Texas*

RED-AND-GREEN BRUSCHETTA

*This colorful appetizer with its
tangy Dried Tomato Pesto updates the
familiar Italian offering.*

*Prep: 20 minutes
Bake: 10 minutes
Broil: 13 minutes*

1 French baguette
1 large red bell pepper
Dried Tomato Pesto
½ pound fresh mozzarella, sliced
8 cornichons, thinly sliced lengthwise *

• **Cut** baguette into ½-inch-thick slices; place on a baking sheet.
• **Bake** at 350° for 8 to 10 minutes or until golden; cool.
• **Place** bell pepper on an aluminum foil-lined baking sheet. Broil 5 inches from heat about 5 minutes on each side or until pepper looks blistered.
• **Place** pepper in a heavy-duty zip-top plastic bag; seal and let stand 10 minutes to loosen skin. Peel pepper; discard seeds, and cut pepper into thin strips.
• **Spread** bread slices evenly with Dried Tomato Pesto. Top each with a mozzarella slice. Crisscross a pepper strip and pickle slice over cheese.
• **Broil** 5 inches from heat 2 to 3 minutes or until cheese melts. Serve immediately. **Yield:** 2½ dozen.

*Substitute gherkin-style pickles for cornichons, if desired.

Dried Tomato Pesto

*Prep: 10 minutes
Bake: 5 minutes*

2 tablespoons pine nuts
1 (8-ounce) jar minced dried tomatoes
   in oil, undrained
¼ cup coarsely chopped fresh basil
4 garlic cloves
2 tablespoons olive oil
½ teaspoon salt
⅛ teaspoon pepper

• **Bake** pine nuts in a shallow pan at 350°, stirring occasionally, 5 minutes or until toasted. Cool.
• **Process** pine nuts and remaining ingredients in a blender or food processor until smooth, stopping to scrape down sides. **Yield:** 1 cup.

EASY ENTERTAINING

■ Invite guests to serve themselves and sit where they'd like. (Diehard fans are sure to want a "sideline view" of the game.)

■ Serve beverages from lightweight pitchers for easy, one-handed pouring.

Bountiful Brownies

There's something quite sly and mischievous about brownies. They're stacked on a plate, innocently enough, yet that's when they're the most dangerous. We hear their sweet and chocolaty siren song drawing us near. Overpowered, we're forced to bite into the delicious, chewy confections. No one is safe—young or old. The brownies' attack is indiscriminate.

We certainly couldn't resist, nor could we decide on our all-time favorite—Candy Bar Brownies or Magnolia Cream Cheese Brownies. In the end, we loved each of these recipes so much that we decided to share them both. And as a bonus, we have included Double-Chocolate Brownies, a fabulous reader recipe that also received our highest rating.

It'll be tough not to indulge yourself as soon as these brownies come out of the oven. However, it's important that you allow them to cool completely before cutting. If you're in a hurry, the freezer works particularly well.

CANDY BAR BROWNIES

Prep: 10 minutes
Bake: 30 minutes

4 large eggs, lightly beaten
2 cups sugar
¾ cup butter or margarine, melted
2 teaspoons vanilla extract
1½ cups all-purpose flour
½ teaspoon baking powder
¼ teaspoon salt
⅓ cup cocoa
4 (2.07-ounce) chocolate-coated caramel-peanut nougat bars, coarsely chopped
3 (1.55-ounce) milk chocolate bars, finely chopped

• **Stir** together first 4 ingredients in a large bowl.
• **Combine** flour and next 3 ingredients; stir into sugar mixture. Fold in chopped nougat bars.
• **Spoon** mixture into a greased and floured 13- x 9-inch baking dish, and sprinkle with chopped milk chocolate bars.
• **Bake** at 350° for 30 minutes. Cool and cut into squares. **Yield:** 2½ dozen.

Note: For testing purposes only, we used Snickers bars for nougat bars.

MAGNOLIA CREAM CHEESE BROWNIES

A sweet swirl of cream cheese makes a good thing even better.

Prep: 15 minutes
Bake: 45 minutes

4 (1-ounce) unsweetened chocolate squares
4 (1-ounce) semisweet chocolate squares
⅓ cup butter or margarine
2 (3-ounce) packages cream cheese, softened
¼ cup butter or margarine, softened
2 cups sugar, divided
6 large eggs, divided
1 teaspoon vanilla extract
2 tablespoons all-purpose flour
1½ cups (9 ounces) semisweet chocolate morsels, divided
2 teaspoons vanilla extract
1 cup all-purpose flour
1 teaspoon baking powder
1 teaspoon salt

• **Microwave** first 3 ingredients in a 1-quart glass bowl at HIGH 2 minutes or until melted, stirring once. Cool and set aside.
• **Beat** cream cheese and ¼ cup butter at medium speed with an electric mixer until creamy; gradually add ½ cup sugar, beating well.
• **Add** 2 eggs, 1 at a time, beating until blended. Stir in 1 teaspoon vanilla. Fold in 2 tablespoons flour and ½ cup chocolate morsels; set aside.
• **Beat** remaining 4 eggs in a large bowl at medium speed with an electric mixer.
• **Gradually** add remaining 1½ cups sugar, beating well. Add melted chocolate mixture and 2 teaspoons vanilla; beat mixture until well blended.
• **Combine** 1 cup flour, baking powder, and salt; fold into chocolate batter until blended, and stir in remaining 1 cup chocolate morsels.
• **Reserve** 3 cups chocolate batter; spread remaining batter evenly in a greased 13- x 9-inch pan. Pour cream cheese mixture over batter. Top with reserved 3 cups batter, and swirl mixture with a knife.
• **Bake** at 325° for 40 to 45 minutes. Cool and cut brownies into squares. **Yield:** 1½ dozen.

DOUBLE-CHOCOLATE BROWNIES

Chocoholics beware: Two kinds of chocolate will lure you to try these decadent brownies.

Prep: 10 minutes
Bake: 35 minutes

1 cup butter or margarine, softened
2 cups sugar
4 large eggs
1 cup cocoa
1 teaspoon vanilla extract
1 cup all-purpose flour
1 cup chopped pecans
⅔ cup semisweet chocolate or white chocolate morsels

• **Beat** butter at medium speed with an electric mixer until creamy; gradually add sugar, beating well. Add eggs, 1 at a time, beating just until blended.
• **Add** cocoa and vanilla; beat at low speed 1 minute or until blended. Gradually add flour, beating well.
• **Stir** in pecans and chocolate morsels. Pour batter into a greased 13- x 9-inch baking pan.
• **Bake** at 350° for 30 to 35 minutes. Cool and cut brownies into squares. **Yield:** 2 dozen.

Stacey Attanasio
Los Angeles, California

Java Juices

Savor one of these cool coffee beverages
for a treat that's too hip to pass up.

Readers everywhere, it seems, love the taste of coffee. We received the Café Latte Slush recipe from Jannet Ewing, a missionary in Honduras. Because her kitchen utensils are limited, Jannet sent the following instructions: "Put the frozen contents in a baggie, wrap in a dish cloth, and smash with a clean kitchen river rock." While we chose to use an electric mixer for blending the drink, we think Jannet would approve of the results.

SPICED MOCHA MIX

Prep: 15 minutes

1 cup sugar
¾ cup instant nonfat dry milk powder
¾ cup powdered nondairy coffee creamer
½ cup cocoa
⅓ cup instant coffee granules
½ teaspoon ground allspice
½ teaspoon ground cinnamon
⅛ teaspoon salt

• **Combine** all ingredients in a large bowl. Store in an airtight container. **Yield:** 12 to 15 servings.

Note: For 1 serving, spoon 2½ tablespoons mix into mug. Add 1 cup hot milk or water, stirring until dissolved. Top with marshmallows, if desired.

Carol Scott
Beaver, Pennsylvania

COFFEE SYRUP

Prep: 15 minutes

½ cup water
1 cup sugar
¼ cup instant coffee granules
¼ cup chocolate syrup

• **Bring** water to a boil; add sugar and coffee granules, stirring until dissolved. Stir in chocolate syrup. Store in refrigerator. **Yield:** 1½ cups.

Ice Cream Sundae: Halve 1 banana; top with 2 scoops vanilla ice cream. Combine 3 tablespoons Coffee Syrup and 1 teaspoon orange liqueur; drizzle over ice cream. Top with whipped cream and chopped almonds.

CAFÉ MOCHA LATTE

Prep: 10 minutes

1½ cups half-and-half
2 tablespoons brown sugar
2 cups strong brewed coffee or espresso
¼ cup chocolate syrup
1 teaspoon vanilla extract
¼ cup whiskey (optional)

• **Heat** half-and-half in a saucepan over medium-high heat. (Do not boil.) Remove from heat; stir in brown sugar, next 3 ingredients, and, if desired, whiskey. Serve warm or over ice. **Yield:** 4 cups.

CHILLY COFFEE PUNCH

Prep: 15 minutes
Chill: 45 minutes

¼ cup sugar
6 cups hot brewed coffee
½ gallon vanilla ice cream
½ gallon chocolate ice cream
½ to ¾ cup coffee liqueur
Toppings: whipped cream, chocolate syrup

• **Stir** together sugar and hot coffee until sugar dissolves. Cover and chill mixture 30 to 45 minutes.
• **Spoon** ice creams into a large punch bowl. Pour coffee mixture over ice cream; stir in coffee liqueur. Serve with desired toppings. **Yield:** 23 cups.

Note: For testing purposes only, we used hazelnut-flavored coffee.

Betty J. Nickels
Tampa, Florida

CAFÉ LATTE SLUSH

Coffee drinks are hot, even when they're as cold as this creamy slush.

Prep: 15 minutes
Freeze: 8 hours

½ to ¾ cup sugar
2 cups hot, strong brewed coffee or espresso
2 cups milk or half-and-half, divided ✻
Garnish: chocolate syrup

• **Combine** sugar and hot coffee in a large bowl, stirring until sugar dissolves; stir in 1 cup milk. Cover; freeze 8 hours.
• **Let** thaw slightly in refrigerator; add remaining 1 cup milk. Beat at medium speed with an electric mixer until smooth. Garnish, if desired. Serve immediately. **Yield:** 7 cups.

✻ Substitute fat-free milk or fat-free half-and-half for regular milk or half-and-half, if desired.

Jannet Ewing
La Ceiba, Honduras

Reunions

Texas is home to this group of families

who gather to honor their German heritage.

About 100 of the Christian-Dreibrodt clan meet every year in Texas reminiscing and celebrating their German heritage. Their original homeplace is in Mathis, but so many members now live in Zorn (near New Braunfels) that they rotate between the two cities.

Each family brings a salad or side dish and one dessert. For the entrée, one of the cousins barbecues enough beef and chicken for everyone. Sweets are favorites, and Connie Krause says, "Some of the members go to the dessert table first."

TEXAS PINTO BEANS

Prep: 10 minutes
Stand: 1 hour
Cook: 2 hours

1 (16-ounce) package dried pinto beans
4⅔ cups water
½ small onion, minced
2 garlic cloves, minced
2 bacon slices, cut into 1-inch pieces
1 teaspoon salt
1 medium tomato, diced
4 jalapeño peppers, seeded and
  chopped

• **Place** beans in a Dutch oven; add water 2 inches above beans. Bring to a boil. Boil 1 minute; cover, remove from heat, and let stand 1 hour. Drain.
• **Bring** beans, 4⅔ cups water, and next 4 ingredients to a boil in Dutch oven. Cover, reduce heat, and simmer, stirring occasionally, 1 hour and 30 minutes or until tender. Add tomato and jalapeño pepper, and simmer mixture for 30 more minutes. **Yield:** 6 cups.

Dorothy Schneider
New Braunfels, Texas

BLITZ TORTE

This delicate dessert can be made ahead and stored in the refrigerator overnight.

Prep: 10 minutes
Bake: 30 minutes

Filling
½ cup butter or margarine,
  softened
¾ cup sugar, divided
4 large eggs, separated
¼ cup milk
1 cup all-purpose flour
1 teaspoon baking powder
⅛ teaspoon salt
1 teaspoon vanilla extract
½ cup powdered sugar
1¼ cups coconut, divided
Garnish: fresh strawberries

• **Prepare** Filling, and cool.
• **Beat** butter and ¼ cup sugar at medium speed with an electric mixer until creamy. Add egg yolks and milk, beating until smooth.
• **Combine** flour, baking powder, and salt. Gradually add to butter mixture, beating until blended; stir in vanilla. Pour into 2 well-greased 9-inch round cakepans.
• **Beat** egg whites at medium speed until frothy. Gradually add remaining ½ cup sugar and powdered sugar, beating 3 minutes or until soft peaks form and sugar dissolves. Spread evenly over batter. Sprinkle evenly with coconut.
• **Bake** at 325° for 30 minutes or until meringue is golden. Cool 10 minutes on wire racks. Remove from pans, and cool completely.
• **Spread** Filling over meringue of 1 layer. Top with other layer, meringue side up. Garnish, if desired. **Yield:** 8 servings.

Filling

Prep: 2 minutes
Cook: 5 minutes

½ cup sugar
¼ cup all-purpose flour
1 large egg, lightly beaten
1 cup milk
1 teaspoon vanilla extract

• **Cook** all ingredients in a heavy saucepan over low heat, stirring constantly, 5 minutes or until thickened. Cool completely. **Yield:** 1⅓ cups.

Dorothy Schneider
New Braunfels, Texas

PFEFFERNÜESSE

Pronounced FEHF-fuhr-noos, this cookie is served at Christmastime in many European countries.

Prep: 10 minutes
Bake: 14 minutes per batch

2 tablespoons butter or margarine,
  softened
2 cups sugar
4 teaspoons ground cinnamon
2 teaspoons ground nutmeg
2 teaspoons ground cloves
⅛ teaspoon pepper
4 large eggs
3 cups all-purpose flour
2 teaspoons baking powder
1 cup chopped pecans

• **Beat** butter and sugar at medium speed with an electric mixer until blended. Add cinnamon and next 3 ingredients, beating until blended. Add eggs, flour, and baking powder, beating well. Stir in pecans.
• **Drop** dough by heaping teaspoonfuls onto ungreased baking sheets.
• **Bake** at 350° for 14 minutes. Remove cookies to wire racks to cool. **Yield:** 6½ dozen cookies.

Connie Krause
Leander, Texas

Soup & Sandwich Night

These hot and hearty recipes are an easy suppertime solution.

Nothing warms the soul like a bowl of soup and a satisfying sandwich for a weeknight meal. Either soup can be paired with the pita pockets or with your favorite sandwich. Prepare soups ahead, and freeze them for an easy, relaxing supper.

CHICKEN-SPINACH PITA POCKETS

Prep: 10 minutes
Bake: 16 minutes

2 (6-ounce) skinned and boned chicken breast halves
½ cup plain yogurt
2 tablespoons mayonnaise
1 tablespoon Dijon mustard
¼ teaspoon ground cumin
⅛ teaspoon ground red pepper
½ small cucumber, cubed
2 green onions, chopped
2 cups shredded fresh spinach
4 pita pockets, cut into halves

• **Cook** chicken in an ovenproof non-stick skillet over medium-high heat until brown. Bake at 350° for 10 to 12 minutes or until done. Cool slightly, and thinly slice.
• **Whisk** together yogurt and next 4 ingredients in a large bowl; add chicken, cucumber, green onions, and spinach, tossing to coat.
• **Bake** pita halves at 200° for 3 to 4 minutes. (Do not toast.)
• **Spoon** filling evenly into pita halves. **Yield:** 4 servings.

WILDEST RICE SOUP

This creamy, sophisticated soup gets a convenient boost from canned soup.

Prep: 25 minutes
Cook: 20 minutes

1 (6.2-ounce) package long-grain and wild rice mix
1 pound bacon, diced
2 cups chopped fresh mushrooms
1 large onion, diced
3¾ cups half-and-half
2½ cups chicken broth
2 (10¾-ounce) cans cream of potato soup, undiluted
1 (8-ounce) loaf pasteurized prepared cheese product, cubed

• **Cook** wild rice mix according to package directions, omitting seasoning packet; set aside.
• **Cook** bacon in a Dutch oven until crisp; remove bacon and drain on paper towels, reserving 2 tablespoons drippings in Dutch oven. Sauté mushrooms and onion in drippings until tender; stir in rice, bacon, half-and-half, and remaining ingredients.
• **Cook** soup over medium-low heat, stirring constantly, until soup is thoroughly heated and cheese melts. **Yield:** 10 cups.

Note: Decrease bacon to ¼ pound, reserve 2 teaspoons drippings, and use fat-free half-and-half, fat-free chicken broth, reduced-fat soup, and light cheese product, if desired.

Barbara Isham
Oldsmar, Florida

SPANISH FIESTA SOUP

You'll say "Olé!" after tasting the fiesta of flavors in this spicy soup.

Prep: 25 minutes
Bake: 10 minutes
Cook: 45 minutes

6 (6-inch) corn tortillas
3 garlic cloves, chopped
1 Spanish onion, chopped
1 tablespoon vegetable oil
4 plum tomatoes, peeled and chopped
2 (32-ounce) containers chicken broth
2 tablespoons chopped fresh cilantro
2 bay leaves
2 tablespoons Old Bay seasoning
1½ teaspoons ground cumin
1 teaspoon chili powder
¼ teaspoon salt
¼ teaspoon pepper
Toppings: shredded cooked chicken, shredded Cheddar cheese, chopped avocado

• **Cut** tortillas into ½-inch strips; place on an ungreased baking sheet.
• **Bake** at 350° for 10 minutes or until crisp; remove to a wire rack to cool. Reserve one third of strips.
• **Sauté** garlic and onion in hot oil in a large saucepan over medium-high heat until tender. Add remaining tortilla strips, tomato, and next 6 ingredients; bring to a boil. Reduce heat, and simmer, stirring occasionally, 30 minutes. Remove and discard bay leaves. Cool soup slightly.
• **Process** soup, in batches, in a blender or food processor until smooth, stopping to scrape down sides. Return soup to saucepan, and cook over medium heat, stirring occasionally, until thoroughly heated. Stir in salt and pepper. Serve with desired toppings and reserved tortilla strips. **Yield:** 10 servings.

From Our Kitchen

This month we've tackled our greatest challenge—a plan for four meals per week for a whole month. We selected some of our readers' favorite recipes, developed a few of our own, and coordinated a master game plan. All you need to do is shop using the nonperishable shopping list, pantry list, and weekly lists. Then follow the daily "Cook's Notes." Tip: Vicki Poellnitz, our staffer who tested this plan, says, "Don't discard any leftover items. Almost every item you buy will be used sometime during the month."

Cook's Notes and Shopping Lists

Follow these weekly guides to make the menus and shopping lists work for you and your family.

WEEK 1 COOK'S NOTES

Sunday
- Bake ham and potatoes.
- While ham bakes, prepare Pasta Sauce for Wednesday dinner, and chill.
- Prepare Thyme-Scented Green Beans With Smoked Almonds, and heat rolls.
- After serving ham for supper, cut part of leftover ham into 16 slices. Refrigerate 8 slices to prepare Ham-Swiss-and-Asparagus Sandwiches on Tuesday.
- Prepare Panhandle Sandwiches (for Week 4) with 8 remaining ham slices, and freeze. Reserve remaining Monterey Jack cheese slices for Week 2.
- Chop remaining ham, and package in 2 (2-cup) portions for Sausage-Ham Breakfast Casserole (Week 2) and Creamy Ham Casseroles (Week 3); freeze ham portions.

Monday
- Prepare Chicken-and-Rice Casseroles; bake one, and freeze one for Week 4.
- While casserole bakes, divide Pasta Sauce into portions. Refrigerate 3 cups for Eggplant Parmesan (Week 1). Freeze 2 cups for calzones (Week 2); freeze 4 cups for Pasta Sauce With Meatballs (Week 3). Freeze remaining 3 cups in desired portions to be served as part of next month's bonus meal.
- Cut 2 zucchini, 2 yellow squash, and 9 baby carrots into slices; steam. Heat rolls.

Tuesday
- Prepare Coleslaw With Garden Vegetables, and chill while preparing Ham-Swiss-and-Asparagus Sandwiches.

Wednesday
- Prepare and bake Eggplant Parmesan.
- Prepare Oregano-Feta Dressing, reserving remaining feta cheese for Week 2. Serve half of dressing on half of Romaine lettuce, reserving remaining Romaine lettuce and dressing for Tuesday, Week 3. Heat garlic bread.

WEEK 2 COOK'S NOTES

Sunday
- Prepare Peasant Soup.
- Prepare cornbread mix, and bake.
- Freeze remaining soup for next month's bonus meal.

Monday
- Prepare Chickpea-Chipotle Tostadas using remaining reduced-fat feta.
- Prepare Pear Salad With Jícama and Snow Peas. Reserve remaining iceberg lettuce and remaining spinach for Week 3.
- Prepare Sausage-Ham Breakfast Casserole, and chill overnight.

Tuesday
- Bake Sausage-Ham Breakfast Casserole and biscuits.
- Cut oranges into wedges.
- Thaw 1 (2-cup) portion Pasta Sauce in refrigerator overnight for calzones.

Wednesday
- Prepare and bake calzones.
- Cut celery into sticks to serve with baby carrots.

WEEK 3 COOK'S NOTES

Sunday
- Prepare Chicken Burritos.
- Cook yellow rice, and shred reserved iceberg lettuce from Week 2.

Monday
- Prepare Chickpea Salad.
- Core pineapple, and cut into wedges.
- Serve half of pita bread; refrigerate remaining pita bread for Week 4.
- Thaw 1 (4-cup) portion of Pasta Sauce in refrigerator.

Tuesday
- Cook Pasta Sauce With Meatballs; cook spaghetti.
- Toss remaining Romaine lettuce, remaining spinach, and 1 cup seasoned croutons with reserved Oregano-Feta Dressing.
- Heat half of breadsticks, reserving remaining breadsticks for Week 4.

Wednesday
- Prepare Creamy Ham Casseroles. Bake 1 now, and freeze 1 for next month's bonus meal.
- Prepare Poppy Seed Dressing; chop apples, and toss with strawberries and drained canned pineapple chunks. Serve with dressing.

WEEK 4 COOK'S NOTES

Sunday
- Prepare and bake Red Pepper Hummus Pizza; serve with mixed salad greens, remaining seasoned croutons, and your favorite dressing.
- Thaw Chicken-and-Rice Casserole in the refrigerator.

Monday
- Bake Chicken-and-Rice Casserole.
- Steam remaining frozen cut green beans from Week 2.
- Heat remaining breadsticks.

Tuesday
- Prepare Tabbouleh Salad and Creamy Cucumber Salad.
- Cut remaining pita bread into triangles, and toast.

Wednesday
- Bake frozen Panhandle Sandwiches.
- Prepare Broccoli Salad.

NONPERISHABLE SHOPPING LIST

Gather these items at the beginning of the month to have on hand throughout the weeks.

- 2 (12-ounce) cans tomato paste
- 2 (28-ounce) cans diced tomatoes
- 1 (14½-ounce) can low-sodium, fat-free chicken broth
- 2 (10¾-ounce) cans reduced-sodium, reduced-fat cream of chicken soup
- 1 (10¾-ounce) can cream of mushroom soup
- 6 (14½-ounce) cans chicken broth
- 1 (15-ounce) can kidney beans
- 5 (15-ounce) cans chickpeas (Substitution A)
- 1 (7-ounce) jar roasted red bell peppers
- 1 (16-ounce) can refried beans
- 1 (1¼-ounce) envelope taco seasoning mix
- 1 (10-ounce) jar kalamata olives or ripe olives
- 1 (3.5-ounce) bottle capers (Substitution B)
- 1 (15¼-ounce) can pineapple chunks
- 1 (12-ounce) can apricot or pear nectar
- Grated Parmesan cheese (about ⅔ cup)
- ¾ cup Italian-seasoned breadcrumbs
- 1 cup light mayonnaise
- 1 (16-ounce) bottle salsa verde (Substitution C)
- 1 (7-ounce) jar chipotle peppers in adobo sauce (Substitution D)
- 8 ounces spaghetti

8 ounces egg noodles
1 cup bulghur wheat (Substitution E)
1 (10-ounce) package yellow rice mix
1 (6.2-ounce) package long-grain and wild
   rice mix
1 (6-ounce) package cornbread mix
1 tablespoon chopped smoked almonds
   (Substitution F)
1 (6-ounce) package seasoned croutons
1 (8-ounce) can sliced water chestnuts
¼ cup plus 3 tablespoons chopped pecans
1 (12-ounce) can cola soft drink
1 (8-ounce) jar plum or apricot preserves

PANTRY SHOPPING LIST

Balsamic vinegar
Bay leaf (1)
Celery seeds (¾ teaspoon)
Chili powder (1 tablespoon)
Dijon mustard
Dried basil (1 tablespoon)
Dried crushed red pepper (1 teaspoon)
Dried Italian seasoning (2 tablespoons)
Dried oregano (1½ teaspoons)
Dried thyme (1¼ teaspoons)
Garlic powder (½ teaspoon)
Ground cinnamon (¾ teaspoon)
Ground cloves (½ teaspoon)
Ground cumin (1 teaspoon)
Honey
Olive oil
Paprika (1 tablespoon)
Poppy seeds (1 teaspoon)
Prepared mustard
Salad dressing
Salt and pepper
Sugar
Vegetable cooking spray
Vegetable oil
White wine vinegar
Worcestershire sauce

WEEK 1 SHOPPING LIST

Produce
1 purple onion
1 pound fresh green beans
4 baking potatoes
3 small onions
1 bunch green onions
1 small green bell pepper
1 red bell pepper
2 zucchini
2 yellow squash
1 large eggplant
1 large head Romaine lettuce
¾ pound fresh asparagus
1 (10-ounce) package shredded angel hair
   cabbage slaw
3 plum tomatoes
1 (1-pound) package baby carrots
1 large head garlic
1 head green leaf lettuce
2 lemons

General
8 dinner rolls
8 (6-inch) French bread loaves
1 (16-ounce) package garlic bread
Refrigerated Section
Eggs (7)
1 (8-ounce) container light sour cream
Light butter (¾ cup)
1 (8-ounce) package reduced-fat feta
   cheese (Substitution G)
1 (6-ounce) package Monterey Jack cheese
   slices (8)
1 (8-ounce) package shredded mozzarella
   cheese
¼ cup nonfat buttermilk
1 (6-ounce) package Swiss cheese slices
⅓ cup orange juice
Meat Section
1 (8-pound) smoked fully cooked ham half
2 (1¼-pound) roasted chickens

WEEK 2 SHOPPING LIST

Produce
1 medium onion
1 large onion
1 bunch celery
1 bunch fresh parsley
1 bunch fresh cilantro
1 (10-ounce) package shredded angel hair
   cabbage slaw
2 russet potatoes
1 head iceberg lettuce
6 plum tomatoes
2 cups fresh snow pea pods (Substitution H)
1 (10-ounce) package fresh spinach
1 jícama (Substitution I)
Fresh basil
4 oranges
1 lemon
1 lime
2 ripe pears
General
3 white bread slices
Refrigerated Section
12 corn tortillas
1 (8-ounce) container sour cream
1 (8-ounce) package shredded sharp
   Cheddar cheese
1 (12-ounce) container small curd cottage
   cheese
2⅓ cups milk
2 (10-ounce) cans refrigerated pizza
   crusts
Meat Section
1 (16-ounce) package kielbasa sausage
½ (1-pound) package ground hot pork
   sausage
1 (3.5-ounce) package pepperoni slices
Frozen Section
1 (16-ounce) package frozen, cut green
   beans
1 (12-ounce) package frozen country-style
   biscuits

WEEK 3 SHOPPING LIST

Produce
6 plum tomatoes
1 small onion
1 small cucumber
1 bunch fresh broccoli (1½ cups flowerets)
1 whole fresh pineapple
1 quart fresh strawberries
2 Red Delicious apples
General
1 (12-ounce) package pita bread rounds
1 (15-ounce) package breadsticks
1 teaspoon poppy seeds
Refrigerated Section
1 (8-ounce) package shredded mozzarella
   cheese
1 (4-ounce) package shredded Cheddar
   cheese
1 (8-ounce) package shredded sharp
   Cheddar cheese
1 (8-ounce) container chive-and-onion-
   flavored cream cheese
6 (8-inch) flour tortillas
⅔ cup milk
Meat Section
1 (1¼-pound) roasted chicken
Frozen Section
1 (32-ounce) package frozen meatballs
1 (10-ounce) package frozen asparagus

WEEK 4 SHOPPING LIST

Produce
3 plum tomatoes
2 medium tomatoes
1 medium-size purple onion
2 cucumbers
Fresh dill
Fresh mint
4 lemons
1 (12-ounce) package mixed salad greens
1 bunch fresh broccoli (4 cups)
General
1 (10-ounce) package Italian bread shell
   (Substitution J)
Refrigerated Section
1 (8-ounce) package feta cheese
¼ cup nonfat yogurt

Substitution Chart

A: 5 (15-ounce) cans navy beans
B: 1 small jar green olives
C: 1 (16-ounce) bottle salsa
D: 1 can jalapeño peppers plus 2 drops
   liquid smoke
E: 1 cup uncooked instant brown rice
F: 1 tablespoon chopped almonds, toasted
G: 1 (8-ounce) package feta cheese
H: 1 (9-ounce) package frozen snow pea pods
I: 1 Red Delicious apple
J: 1 (10-ounce) can refrigerated pizza crust

APRIL

A Spring Celebration With Frank Stitt

This chef finds pleasure in cooking simple meals for friends.

Spring Celebration Menu

Serves 6 to 8

Tapenade
Fresh vegetables   Baguette slices
Lamb Chops With Mint Aioli
New Potato Gratin With Lima Beans and Egg
Steamed asparagus
Strawberry Tart

On a dazzling day, chef and restaurateur Frank Stitt is busy in his home kitchen preparing a feast for friends. His movements are sure as he chops vegetables and browns lamb in a huge skillet. The smells are intoxicating, and the owner of Highlands Bar and Grill, Bottega, and Chez Fonfon in Birmingham is relaxed and charming. The host is obviously in his element.

The large room with its galley kitchen is dominated by a country French table, an armoire that houses linen and crystal, and a well-furnished wine rack. "It's not a typical modern, efficient kitchen," Frank says, "but it's filled with things I love that have character, personality, and history." But efficiency was important in designing the workspace. "The key thing for me was to be able to pivot from the refrigerator to the work area to the cook surface. But I wanted to be with our guests, too. It's only natural—the kitchen is where everyone hangs out. Here they can stand around the bar, sit at the counter, or help cook."

Frank comes by his hospitality honestly. "My mother was an incredible cook, with such a sense of generosity and providing for other people—she was the patron saint of graciousness. She always loved to pull out our nice china and linen. It was beautiful, but not affected or fancy—it was sharing the moment and the good things of life," recalls Frank.

His own gatherings are generally intimate with 8 to 12 friends. "I often tend to share special wines, which I can do with smaller groups." He prefers menus prepared from the very finest ingredients. "Even if the meal is just roast beef with horseradish and fried potatoes, it can be great. You don't have to have a ton of different things for it to be a wonderful meal."

Clearly, entertaining offers Frank a great deal more than just the enjoyment of good food and wine. "It's very spiritual to me to be at the table with friends, loved ones, and family," he muses. "I love to say grace. To break bread and share food is kind of like a sacrament to me. So I like to make being at the table very special."

TAPENADE

Be sure to use full-flavored olives in this appetizer for the best results.

Prep: 10 minutes

1 (6-ounce) jar pitted kalamata olives (about 1½ cups)
1 tablespoon drained capers
1 tablespoon sherry vinegar★
1 teaspoon lemon juice
1 small garlic clove
¼ teaspoon freshly ground pepper
1 teaspoon rum (optional)
3 tablespoons extra virgin olive oil

• **Pulse** first 6 ingredients and, if desired, rum in a blender or food processor 3 or 4 times. Gradually add olive oil, and pulse 3 or 4 times or until mixture forms a coarse paste, stopping to scrape down sides. Serve with fresh raw vegetables and toasted French baguette slices. **Yield:** 1 cup.

★ Substitute white wine vinegar for sherry vinegar, if desired.

LAMB CHOPS WITH MINT AIOLI

Prep: 15 minutes
Bake: 40 minutes

6 garlic cloves, minced
2 teaspoons dried summer savory
1 teaspoon salt
1 teaspoon pepper
16 (2-inch-thick) lamb chops
1 tablespoon olive oil
Mint Aioli
Garnish: fresh mint sprigs

• **Combine** first 4 ingredients, and rub evenly into both sides of lamb chops.
• **Brown** chops in hot oil in a nonstick skillet over medium-high heat 2 to 3 minutes on each side. Arrange on a lightly greased rack in a broiler pan.
• **Bake** chops at 350° for 35 to 40 minutes or until a meat thermometer inserted into thickest portion registers 145° (medium rare). Serve with aioli. Garnish, if desired. **Yield:** 6 to 8 servings.

Mint Aioli

Prep: 5 minutes

1 cup mayonnaise
¼ cup coarsely chopped fresh mint
4 garlic cloves, minced
1 teaspoon grated lemon rind
2 tablespoons fresh lemon juice
½ teaspoon salt
½ teaspoon pepper

• **Process** all ingredients in a blender or food processor until smooth, stopping to scrape down sides. **Yield:** 1¼ cups.

NEW POTATO GRATIN WITH LIMA BEANS AND EGG

Prep: 40 minutes
Bake: 10 minutes

6 small new potatoes, thinly
    sliced
½ cup frozen large lima beans,
    thawed
3 stale French bread slices
¼ cup (1 ounce) shredded Gruyère
    cheese
¼ cup (1 ounce) shredded Parmesan
    cheese
3 hard-cooked eggs, quartered
½ teaspoon salt
½ teaspoon pepper
½ cup whipping cream

• **Cook** potato slices in boiling, salted water to cover 13 minutes. Add beans, and cook 2 more minutes. Remove from heat; drain well.
• **Pulse** bread slices in a blender or food processor 8 or 10 times or until bread is crumbly.
• **Place** potato slices and lima beans in a greased 10-inch deep-dish pieplate; sprinkle with half of Gruyère and half of Parmesan. Top evenly with egg; sprinkle with remaining cheese, salt, and pepper. Pour cream around inside edge of pieplate; sprinkle evenly with breadcrumbs.
• **Bake** at 475° for 10 minutes or until lightly browned. **Yield:** 6 to 8 servings.

STRAWBERRY TART
(pictured on page 80)

Prep: 20 minutes
Chill: 5 hours
Bake: 18 minutes

1½ cups all-purpose flour
½ teaspoon salt
⅓ cup sugar
⅓ cup cold butter or margarine,
    cut up
2 tablespoons cold shortening
3 tablespoons cold water
½ cup sugar
¼ cup cornstarch
2 cups half-and-half
5 egg yolks
1 teaspoon rose water or orange-
    flower water (optional)
3 tablespoons butter or margarine
1 teaspoon vanilla extract
1 quart fresh strawberries, sliced
Garnish: fresh mint sprig

• **Pulse** first 3 ingredients in a blender or food processor 3 or 4 times or until combined.
• **Add** ⅓ cup butter and shortening; pulse 5 or 6 times or until crumbly. With blender or processor running, gradually add 3 tablespoons water, and process until dough forms a ball and leaves sides of bowl, adding more water if necessary. Wrap dough in plastic wrap, and chill 1 hour.
• **Roll** dough to ⅛-inch thickness on a lightly floured surface. Press into bottom and up sides of a 9-inch tart pan. Line dough with parchment paper; fill with pie weights or dried beans.
• **Bake** at 425° for 15 minutes. Remove weights and parchment paper, and bake 3 more minutes.
• **Combine** ½ cup sugar and cornstarch in a medium saucepan.
• **Whisk** together half-and-half, egg yolks, and, if desired, rose water. Gradually whisk half-and-half mixture into sugar mixture in saucepan over medium heat. Bring to a boil; cook, whisking constantly, 1 minute. Remove from heat.
• **Stir** in 3 tablespoons butter and vanilla; cover and chill 4 hours. Spoon into pastry shell; top with strawberry slices. Serve immediately. Garnish, if desired. **Yield:** 1 (9-inch) tart.

WINE PICKS

Enjoy these wine-friendly recipes with recommendations from our resident wine expert, Assistant Foods Editor Scott Jones.

■ **Tapenade**–Most full-flavored appetizers go hand-in-hand with the palate-cleansing properties of sparkling wine. Look for more full-bodied styles of brut, and even brut rosé, which receives a boost from the addition of a small amount of red wine, a wonderful complement to the tapenade.

■ **Lamb Chops With Mint Aioli**–Lamb chops can handle more full-bodied wines such as French Bordeaux, which are largely comprised of the grapes Merlot and Cabernet Sauvignon. Keep in mind that French wines are labeled by place name; for this particular recipe, you'll probably want to stick with wines from the Saint-Julien region of Bordeaux. Wines from America and Australia are labeled according to grape type, meaning the words "Merlot" or "Cabernet Sauvignon" will actually appear on the label.

■ **Strawberry Tart**–The general rule when pairing wines with desserts is that the wine should be sweeter than the dessert. By following this guideline, you'll be able to enjoy the flavors of both the wine and the dessert. For this recipe, sweet wines made with the Muscat grape are in order.

Top-Rated Menu

Invite friends to enjoy a springtime lunch celebrating the season's fresh flavors.

Spring Luncheon Menu
Serves 8

Wild Rice-Chicken Salad
Cream of Pimiento Soup
Orange-Pecan Scones

Spring is the perfect time to have lunch with friends. This simple menu serves eight, but it can easily be halved for a smaller party. For a quick dessert, serve fresh fruit and ice cream. The hardest thing may be finding a day when everyone is free.

WILD RICE-CHICKEN SALAD
(pictured on facing page)

1999 Recipe Hall of Fame

Prep: 40 minutes
Chill: 8 hours

2   (6.2-ounce) packages long-grain and wild rice mix
2   (6-ounce) jars marinated artichoke quarters, undrained
4   cups chopped cooked chicken
1   medium-size red bell pepper, chopped
2   celery ribs, thinly sliced
5   green onions, chopped
1   (2.25-ounce) can sliced ripe olives, drained
1   cup mayonnaise
1½ teaspoons curry powder
Leaf lettuce

• **Cook** rice mix according to package directions.
• **Drain** artichoke quarters, reserving ½ cup liquid. Stir together rice, artichoke, chicken, and next 4 ingredients.
• **Stir** together artichoke liquid, mayonnaise, and curry powder; toss with rice mixture. Cover and chill 8 hours. Serve on leaf lettuce. **Yield:** 8 servings.

CREAM OF PIMIENTO SOUP
(pictured on facing page)

1996 Recipe Hall of Fame

Prep: 10 minutes
Chill: 8 hours
Cook: 20 minutes

2   (4-ounce) jars diced pimiento, undrained
¼   cup butter or margarine
⅓   cup all-purpose flour
2   (14½-ounce) cans chicken broth
3   cups half-and-half
1   tablespoon grated onion
1   teaspoon salt
½   teaspoon hot sauce
Garnish: chopped fresh chives

• **Process** pimiento in a blender or food processor until smooth, stopping to scrape down sides; set aside.
• **Melt** butter in a heavy saucepan over low heat; add flour, and stir until mixture is smooth. Cook, stirring constantly, 1 minute.
• **Add** chicken broth and half-and-half gradually to flour mixture; cook over medium heat, stirring constantly, until mixture is thickened and bubbly.
• **Stir** in reserved pimiento puree, onion, salt, and hot sauce; cook over low heat, stirring constantly, until thoroughly heated. Cover and chill 8 hours.
• **Cook** soup over medium heat 8 to 10 minutes or until thoroughly heated. Garnish, if desired. **Yield:** 8 cups.

ORANGE-PECAN SCONES
(pictured on facing page)

1994 Recipe Hall of Fame

Prep: 10 minutes
Bake: 14 minutes

2   cups self-rising flour
½   cup sugar
2   teaspoons grated orange rind
⅓   cup butter or margarine
½   cup chopped pecans
½   cup buttermilk
¼   cup fresh orange juice
1   teaspoon vanilla extract
Sugar

• **Combine** first 3 ingredients. Cut butter into flour mixture with a pastry blender until crumbly; add pecans and next 3 ingredients, stirring just until dry ingredients are moistened.
• **Turn** dough out onto a lightly floured surface; knead 3 or 4 times.
• **Divide** dough in half; pat each portion into a 7-inch circle, and place on a lightly greased baking sheet. Cut each circle into 8 wedges; sprinkle with sugar.
• **Bake** at 425° for 12 to 14 minutes or until golden brown. **Yield:** 16 scones.

Note: Freeze scones up to 1 month. Thaw in refrigerator 8 hours. Bake at 350° for 10 minutes or until thoroughly heated.

Cream of Pimiento Soup, Wild Rice-Chicken Salad,
Orange-Pecan Scones, facing page

Smoked Turkey Wraps, page 61

*Fresh Pesto Pasta
Salad, page 61*

Sherried Chicken-and-Grape Salad, page 61

Peanut Butter-Fudge Cake, page 59

Chickpea Salad, page 55

Creamy Ham Casserole, page 55

Ham-Swiss-and-Asparagus Sandwiches, page 52;
Coleslaw With Garden Vegetables, page 57

Layered Southwestern Salad, page 97

Sesame-Crusted Turkey Mignons, page 81

Faidley's Crab Cakes, page 97

Strawberry Tart, page 71

Quick & Easy

You can serve turkey year-round by purchasing tenderloins available in your grocery's meat section.

As the weather warms and outdoor activities increase, it's hard to put nutritious meals on your table. Let us help you out (of the kitchen) with some speedy turkey tenderloin recipes. Although tenderloins have been around for several years, Lynda Sarkisian of Seneca, South Carolina, introduced us to turkey mignons, small medaillons sliced from the tenderloin. We hope you'll be as pleased with this new product as we are. Just be sure not to overcook them, or they will be dry.

SESAME-CRUSTED TURKEY MIGNONS
(pictured on page 79)

Prep: 20 minutes
Broil: 24 minutes

½ cup sesame seeds, toasted
¼ cup olive oil
1 garlic clove, minced
1 tablespoon chopped fresh chives
1 tablespoon soy sauce
2 teaspoons lemon juice
1 teaspoon grated fresh ginger
½ teaspoon sesame oil
2 (11-ounce) packages turkey mignons*
Creamy Wine Sauce
Hot cooked noodles
Garnishes: lemon slices and parsley

• **Stir** together first 8 ingredients; dredge turkey in sesame seed mixture. Place on a greased rack in a broiler pan.
• **Broil** 5½ inches from heat 12 minutes on each side or until done. Serve with wine sauce over hot cooked noodles. Garnish, if desired. **Yield:** 4 servings.

*Substitute 2 turkey tenderloins, cut in half, for turkey mignons, if desired.

Creamy Wine Sauce

Prep: 5 minutes
Cook: 15 minutes

1 cup fruity white wine*
2 teaspoons lemon juice
¼ cup whipping cream
2 tablespoons soy sauce
⅓ cup butter or margarine

• **Bring** wine and lemon juice to a boil over medium-high heat. Boil 6 to 8 minutes or until mixture is reduced by half. Whisk in cream. Cook 3 to 4 minutes, whisking constantly, until thickened.
• **Reduce** heat to simmer, and whisk in soy sauce and butter until butter is melted. **Yield:** about ¾ cup.

*Substitute white grape juice for wine, if desired.

Note: For testing purposes only, we used Liebfraumilch for wine.
Lynda Sarkisian
Seneca, South Carolina

PARMESAN TURKEY CUTLETS

A golden Parmesan crust encases these tender cutlets.

Prep: 25 minutes
Cook: 4 minutes

⅔ cup Italian-seasoned breadcrumbs
⅔ cup grated Parmesan cheese
1 teaspoon paprika
½ teaspoon pepper
2 turkey tenderloins (about 1½ pounds)
Vegetable cooking spray
¼ cup olive oil
Lemon wedges

• **Combine** first 4 ingredients; set aside.
• **Cut** tenderloins into 1-inch-thick slices. Place slices between 2 sheets of heavy-duty plastic wrap, and flatten to ¼-inch thickness, using a meat mallet or rolling pin.
• **Coat** both sides of turkey with cooking spray, and dredge in breadcrumb mixture.
• **Cook** half of turkey slices in 2 tablespoons hot olive oil in a large nonstick skillet over medium-high heat 1 minute on each side or until done. Repeat procedure with remaining turkey and hot oil. Serve with lemon wedges. **Yield:** 4 to 6 servings.
Roberta Duffy
Alexandria, Virginia

EASY TURKEY TENDERLOIN RECIPES

Sautéed Turkey Tenders:
Sprinkle 2 turkey tenderloins with salt and pepper. Cook in 2 tablespoons hot olive oil in a large skillet over medium-high heat 5 minutes on each side or until browned. Add 1 cup dry white wine or chicken broth; reduce heat to medium, and cook 10 to 15 more minutes or until done.

Baked Turkey Tenders:
Line a lightly greased 13- x 9-inch pan with 1 small onion, sliced; 2 carrots, sliced; and 3 celery ribs, sliced. Top with 2 turkey tenderloins, and sprinkle with salt and pepper. Cover tightly with aluminum foil, and bake at 375° for 40 to 45 minutes or until done.

Ready in a Flash

Once you get your skillet sizzling with a little butter or oil, you can cook any of these flavorful entrées in 25 minutes or less.

If you're looking for a piece of equipment that gets you out of the kitchen in a hurry, a heavy skillet can be your weapon in the battle of meal preparation.

For these quick recipes, we used a simple cooking method called searing that seals in the juices and flavor of meat or fish. Pat meat as dry as possible, and then place it in a sizzling skillet. Don't turn meat until a rich brown crust has formed—then brown the other side. With our side dish suggestions, you can have an entire meal on the table in no time flat.

HONEY-PECAN PORK CHOPS

Accompany this dish with a fresh apple salad, steamed green beans, and rolls.

Prep: 15 minutes
Cook: 15 minutes

4 (¼-inch-thick) bone-in pork loin chops
¼ cup all-purpose flour
1 tablespoon butter or margarine
¼ cup honey
¼ cup chopped pecans
½ teaspoon Greek seasoning
¼ teaspoon ground red pepper

• **Dredge** pork chops in flour.
• **Melt** butter in a skillet over high heat; add pork chops, and cook 4 minutes on each side or until browned. Remove and drain on paper towels; keep warm.
• **Stir** together honey and remaining ingredients; add to skillet. Reduce heat to medium-low; cook, covered, 7 minutes.
• **Serve** with sauce. **Yield:** 4 servings.

La Juan Coward
Jasper, Texas

SIMPLE PEPPER STEAK

Turn this dish into a hearty meal with hot cooked rice or noodles and a spinach salad.

Prep: 25 minutes
Cook: 25 minutes

¼ cup cornstarch, divided
½ teaspoon ground ginger
1 (10½-ounce) can beef broth
2 tablespoons soy sauce
½ teaspoon dried crushed red pepper (optional)
½ teaspoon salt
½ teaspoon pepper
1 pound boneless top sirloin steak, cut into thin slices
1 tablespoon vegetable oil
2 teaspoons sesame oil
1 garlic clove, pressed
1 green bell pepper, sliced
1 medium onion, sliced
Hot cooked rice

• **Whisk** together 2 tablespoons cornstarch, ginger, beef broth, soy sauce, and, if desired, red pepper; set aside.
• **Combine** remaining 2 tablespoons cornstarch, salt, and pepper; dredge steak in mixture.
• **Heat** vegetable oil and sesame oil in a large skillet over high heat 3 minutes; add steak and garlic, and sauté 4 minutes or until browned.
• **Add** bell pepper and onion; sauté 8 minutes or until tender. Stir in broth mixture; reduce heat, and simmer 3 to 5 minutes or until thickened. Serve over hot cooked rice. **Yield:** 6 servings.

Elizabeth Ann Duncan
Arden, North Carolina

ZESTY SEARED CHICKEN

Sautéed green beans with red bell pepper strips make a colorful accompaniment with this dish.

Prep: 30 minutes
Chill: 30 minutes
Cook: 14 minutes

¼ cup firmly packed brown sugar
2 garlic cloves, minced
1½ teaspoons ground cumin
1½ teaspoons ground coriander
½ teaspoon salt
½ teaspoon pepper
¼ teaspoon dried crushed red pepper
1 teaspoon grated fresh ginger
¼ cup lemon juice
¼ cup soy sauce
4 skinned and boned chicken breast halves
2 tablespoons vegetable oil
Hot cooked couscous
Garnish: chopped green onions

• **Combine** first 10 ingredients in a shallow dish or large heavy-duty zip-top plastic bag; add chicken. Cover or seal, and chill 30 minutes, turning chicken occasionally.
• **Remove** chicken from marinade, discarding marinade.
• **Cook** chicken in hot oil in a large skillet over high heat 4 minutes. Reduce heat to medium-low; turn and cook 10 minutes or until done. Serve with hot cooked couscous. Garnish, if desired. **Yield:** 4 servings.

Delana W. Pearce
Lakeland, Florida

RED SNAPPER WITH LEMON SAUCE

Create a satisfying meal by serving this fish with steamed fresh broccoli and rice pilaf.

Prep: 20 minutes
Cook: 15 minutes

½ cup milk
1 large egg
2 (6- to 7-ounce) red snapper fillets
¼ teaspoon salt
¼ teaspoon freshly ground pepper, divided
¼ cup all-purpose flour
½ cup fine, dry breadcrumbs
3 tablespoons butter or margarine, divided
2 ounces cream cheese
¼ cup (1 ounce) shredded fontina cheese *
1 tablespoon lemon rind
2 tablespoons fresh lemon juice

• **Whisk** together milk and egg.
• **Sprinkle** fillets with salt and ⅛ teaspoon pepper. Dredge fillets in flour; dip in milk mixture, and dredge in breadcrumbs.
• **Melt** 1 tablespoon butter in a large skillet over medium heat; add fish, and cook 2 to 3 minutes on each side or until fish flakes with a fork. Remove fillets, and drain on paper towels; keep warm.
• **Wipe** skillet clean, and melt remaining 2 tablespoons butter over medium-low heat. Add remaining ⅛ teaspoon pepper, cream cheese, and remaining ingredients, stirring until smooth. Pour sauce over fillets. **Yield:** 2 servings.

* Substitute baby Swiss cheese for fontina cheese, if desired.

Elizabeth Langston
Memphis, Tennessee

PASTA WITH SHRIMP SCAMPI

Serve a crisp green salad and crusty garlic bread to round out this easy pasta dish.

Prep: 30 minutes
Cook: 10 minutes

1½ pounds unpeeled, medium-size fresh shrimp
1 to 2 tablespoons chopped chipotle peppers in adobo sauce
2 garlic cloves, minced
2 tablespoons olive oil
¼ cup dry white wine or chicken broth
1 tablespoon Dijon mustard
1 tablespoon Worcestershire sauce
¾ cup butter or margarine, melted
½ teaspoon salt
2 tablespoons fresh lemon juice
1 pound spaghettini or fettuccine, cooked
½ cup chopped fresh Italian parsley
½ cup shredded Parmesan cheese

• **Peel** shrimp, and devein, if desired.
• **Sauté** peppers and garlic in hot oil in a large skillet over medium-high heat until thoroughly heated.
• **Add** shrimp, and cook, stirring constantly, 2 to 3 minutes or just until shrimp turn pink. Remove shrimp, and set aside.
• **Stir** in white wine, mustard, and Worcestershire sauce; cook over high heat 3 to 4 minutes.
• **Return** shrimp to skillet. Stir in butter, salt, and lemon juice; cook 1 to 2 minutes or until combined and thoroughly heated.
• **Place** pasta in a large serving dish; toss with shrimp mixture and parsley. Sprinkle with Parmesan cheese. **Yield:** 4 servings.

Deborah Mele
Tampa, Florida

Cook's Corner

It's time to enjoy the warm weather and prepare cooler and simpler meals. Don't forget about entertaining with friends; it can be a success without much fuss. You'll find ideas for these scenarios and more in the brochures mentioned below.

Fast & Flavorful: What a Pear! Canned pears are the perfect solution for families on the go. Their natural sweetness and real fruit flavor make them a nutritious and convenient pantry staple. Delicious pear recipes include snacks, appetizers, entrées, and desserts. Look for kid-friendly tips and recipes that teach basic cooking skills. To receive a brochure, send a self-addressed, stamped, business-size envelope to Pacific Northwest Canned Pear Service, Dept. SLA, 105 South 18th Street, Suite 205, Yakima, WA 98901, or visit www.pnwcannedpears.com.

Whole Health Grapes help you achieve a healthy lifestyle year-round. Picnic season is upon us, and grapes are the perfect addition to a box lunch. Freeze grapes to use as edible ice cubes in cold beverages, or stir a few into frozen yogurt. This booklet offers tasty choices for salads, entrées, and beverages and includes nutritional analysis. For a booklet, write to California Table Grape Commission, 392 West Fallbrook, Suite 101, Fresno, CA 93711-6150. For additional information and recipes, visit www.tablegrape.com.

Rice Bowl Cuisine The cuisine of Southeast Asia is a popular trend with today's families. Limit the number of ingredients and the preparation time when you serve meals in a bowl. Traditional Asian foods consisting of noodles, meats, vegetables, and broth are served on a bed of hot rice. Each dish offers a variety of unique tastes, colors, and textures. Most meals can be assembled in the time it takes to cook the rice. For a selection of rice bowl recipes, call 1-800-226-9522, or write to Riviana Kitchens, P.O. Box 1323, Houston, TX 77251.

Pass the Sides

Vegetable Stuffing, Carrot Soufflé, and Green Beans in Tomato Sauce are flavored to perfection.

Passover can be a difficult holiday for cooking even though food is such a major part of the tradition. Most people tend to prepare the same foods year after year, but we're offering new side dishes that will delight cooks (even those of you who aren't cooking for Passover). All these recipes will be welcomed at your table.

VEGETABLE STUFFING

Prep: 25 minutes
Bake: 45 minutes

1 cup butter or margarine
1 large sweet onion, diced
2 carrots, grated
2 celery ribs, diced
2 garlic cloves, minced
3 cups crushed egg matzo
1 teaspoon salt
¼ teaspoon pepper
⅛ to ¼ teaspoon poultry seasoning
2 large eggs, lightly beaten
Garnish: parsley sprig

• **Melt** butter in a large skillet over medium-high heat; add onion, carrot, celery, and garlic, and sauté 5 to 6 minutes or until tender. Stir in matzo and next 3 ingredients; let cool.
• **Add** beaten eggs, stirring mixture until well blended.
• **Shape** mixture into a 12-inch roll on a piece of heavy-duty aluminum foil. Fold sides of foil loosely over roll; fold ends over, and crimp to seal. Place on a 15- x 10-inch jellyroll pan.
• **Bake** at 350° for 45 minutes. Unwrap and cut hot stuffing into ½-inch-thick slices. Garnish, if desired. Serve immediately. **Yield:** 8 to 10 servings.

Julie Stein
Birmingham, Alabama

CARROT SOUFFLÉ

Prep: 45 minutes
Bake: 55 minutes

2 pounds fresh carrots, sliced *
6 large eggs
1 cup sugar, divided
⅓ cup matzo meal
¾ cup butter or margarine, melted and divided
¼ teaspoon salt
⅛ teaspoon ground nutmeg
2 teaspoons vanilla extract
1 cup chopped walnuts

• **Cook** carrot in water to cover in a large saucepan over medium-high heat 20 to 25 minutes or until very tender; drain well.
• **Process** carrot and eggs in a blender or food processor until smooth, stopping to scrape down sides.
• **Add** ⅔ cup sugar, matzo meal, ½ cup butter, salt, nutmeg, and vanilla; process until smooth. Pour mixture into a lightly greased 13- x 9-inch baking dish.
• **Bake** at 350° for 40 to 45 minutes or until set. Combine remaining ⅓ cup sugar, ¼ cup butter, and walnuts. Top soufflé with mixture; bake 5 to 10 more minutes. **Yield:** 8 to 10 servings.

*Substitute 1 (2-pound) package sliced frozen carrots for fresh carrots, if desired. Cook according to package directions; drain well.

Jenifer Rotenstreich
Birmingham, Alabama

GREEN BEANS IN TOMATO SAUCE

Prep: 10 minutes
Cook: 25 minutes

1 pound fresh green beans, trimmed *
1 small sweet onion, chopped
1 large garlic clove, minced
2 tablespoons olive oil
1 (8-ounce) can tomato sauce
1 tablespoon sugar
½ to ¾ teaspoon salt
½ teaspoon freshly ground pepper
1 tablespoon red wine vinegar
1 tablespoon chopped fresh parsley

• **Cook** green beans in boiling water to cover 5 to 10 minutes or to desired degree of doneness; drain and set aside.
• **Sauté** onion and garlic in hot oil in a large skillet over medium-high heat 5 minutes or until onion is tender.
• **Add** tomato sauce and sugar; cook, stirring often, 5 minutes. Add green beans, salt, pepper, and vinegar; cook 5 minutes. Sprinkle with parsley, and serve immediately. **Yield:** 4 servings.

*Substitute 1 pound frozen whole green beans for fresh green beans, if desired. Cook according to package directions; drain well.

PASSOVER PRIMER

Passover is a Jewish holiday occurring in late March or April and lasting for eight days. The Seder is the ceremonial dinner held on the first night or first two nights of the holiday. Nothing containing a leavening agent (including leavened bread) is eaten during this holiday to recall the flat bread that the Jews ate during their exodus from Egypt when they could not wait for their bread to rise.

Precious Pineapple

Pineapple doesn't receive as much attention as it should. This tropical beauty is usually purchased to eat fresh or to use in recipes for desserts or salads. Actually, pineapple is very versatile because it's one of the few fruits that retains its shape when heated. Try grilling, broiling, stir-frying, or sautéing pineapple, and then taste its fabulous flavors. Pick up a fresh one, and enjoy these innovative recipes.

PINEAPPLE-TURKEY SANDWICH

Prep: 20 minutes
Cook: 15 minutes

1 fresh pineapple, cored
2 tablespoons butter or margarine
½ teaspoon salt
½ teaspoon pepper
1 (8-ounce) container chive-and-onion-flavored cream cheese, softened
2 (8-ounce) French bread loaves, split lengthwise
1 pound sliced turkey
1 (8-ounce) package Swiss cheese slices

• **Cut** pineapple into ½-inch-thick slices; cut slices in half.
• **Melt** butter in a skillet over medium heat; add pineapple, and sauté 5 minutes. Sprinkle with salt and pepper.
• **Spread** cream cheese evenly on each bread half. Layer bottom bread halves evenly with pineapple, turkey, and Swiss cheese; top with remaining bread halves.
• **Cook** sandwiches on a lightly greased griddle over medium heat 5 minutes on each side or until bread is toasted and Swiss cheese melts. Cut sandwiches into thirds. **Yield:** 6 sandwiches.

Note: For testing purposes only, we used 1 (16-ounce) package Pepperidge Farm Twin French loaves.

PINEAPPLE GAZPACHO

Prep: 25 minutes
Chill: 2 hours

1 medium-size fresh pineapple, cored and cut into chunks
2 medium cucumbers, peeled, seeded, and quartered
1 yellow bell pepper, chopped
1 (48-ounce) can pineapple juice
¼ cup rice vinegar
1 tablespoon salt
1 to 2 teaspoons hot sauce
1 red bell pepper, diced
1 green bell pepper, diced
¼ cup chopped fresh cilantro

• **Process** first 7 ingredients in a blender or food processor, in batches, until minced, stopping to scrape down sides.
• **Stir** together pineapple mixture, diced bell pepper, and cilantro in a bowl. Cover and chill 2 hours. **Yield:** 3 quarts.

PINEAPPLE FLAN

Prep: 20 minutes
Bake: 55 minutes
Cool: 30 minutes
Chill: 2 hours

2 cups pineapple juice
½ cup sugar
1 (14-ounce) can sweetened condensed milk
1 cup whipping cream
3 large eggs
3 egg yolks
1 teaspoon vanilla extract
1 cup finely chopped fresh pineapple
Garnish: dried pineapple

• **Cook** pineapple juice in a saucepan over medium-high heat 20 minutes or until reduced to ½ cup; set aside.
• **Sprinkle** sugar in an 8-inch round cakepan; place over medium heat, and cook, shaking pan constantly, until sugar melts and turns a light golden brown. Remove from heat.
• **Process** reduced pineapple juice, condensed milk, and next 4 ingredients in a blender until smooth, stopping to scrape down sides; stir in pineapple. Pour custard over caramelized sugar in pan. Cover with aluminum foil; place in a roasting pan. Add hot water to roasting pan to a depth of 1 inch.
• **Bake** at 350° for 50 to 55 minutes or until a knife inserted in center comes out clean. Remove cakepan from water, and uncover; cool flan in cakepan on a wire rack 30 minutes. Cover and chill 2 hours.
• **Run** a knife around edge of flan to loosen; invert onto a serving plate. Garnish, if desired. **Yield:** 6 servings.

PINEAPPLE POINTERS

Picking Pineapple

■ Choose pineapples that are slightly soft to the touch with a strong golden-brown color and no sign of green.

■ A ripe pineapple should have a slightly sweet smell. The leaves should be crisp and green.

■ Fresh pineapple is available year-round with its peak season being from March to July.

Preparing Pineapple

Step 1: Cut the leaves off the top of the pineapple. Then cut about 1 inch from each end.

Step 2: Using a sharp knife, slice down about ½ inch into the skin. This should remove the woody eyes. Continue until the pineapple is peeled.

Step 3: Cut the pineapple into quarters. While holding each pineapple quarter firmly, slice away the core.

Step 4: Cut the pineapple into wedges as needed for recipes.

What's for Supper?

Get a jump start on a weekday supper—cook Mary's Roast Beef on the weekend, or put your slow cooker to work during the week. This flavorful roast is a popular meal at Mary Simmons' house. We created a plan for the leftovers: Beef and Vegetables served over grits squares for later in the week. Roast is better if left unsliced before storing. It can be refrigerated up to five days or frozen up to three months.

MARY'S ROAST BEEF

Reserve 1 pound of cooked roast and 1 cup of gravy for Beef and Vegetables.

Prep: 30 minutes
Cook: 2½ hours

1 (3-pound) beef sirloin tip roast
2 tablespoons vegetable oil
1 medium onion, chopped
2 garlic cloves, minced
2½ cups brewed coffee
2½ cups water, divided
2 beef bouillon cubes
1 teaspoon salt
2 teaspoons dried basil
½ teaspoon coarsely ground pepper
½ cup all-purpose flour

• **Brown** all sides of roast in hot oil in a large Dutch oven 8 minutes. Remove roast; set aside.
• **Add** onion and garlic to pan; sauté 5 minutes or until tender. Stir in coffee, 2 cups water, and next 4 ingredients.
• **Return** roast to Dutch oven; bring to a boil. Reduce heat, and simmer, covered, 2½ hours or until done. Transfer roast to a serving platter, reserving drippings in Dutch oven; keep roast warm.
• **Whisk** together remaining ½ cup water and flour; whisk into drippings. Cook, whisking constantly, over medium heat until slightly thickened. Pour gravy over roast. **Yield:** 6 to 8 servings.

Slow Cooker Roast Beef: Cut roast in half, and place both halves in a 4½-quart slow cooker. Add onion; 1 garlic clove, minced; 1 cup brewed coffee; ½ cup water; 1 bouillon cube; and next 3 ingredients. Cover and cook on LOW 6 to 7 hours or until tender. Transfer roast to a serving platter; measure drippings, and pour into a saucepan. Whisk together ¼ cup water and 1 tablespoon flour for every cup of drippings. Whisk mixture into drippings. Proceed with recipe as directed.

Pressure Cooker Roast Beef: Brown roast in hot oil with onion and garlic in a 6-quart pressure cooker. Combine coffee, 2 cups water, bouillon, and next 3 ingredients; pour over roast. Cover with lid, and seal securely; place pressure control over vent tube. Cook over high heat until pressure control rocks back and forth quickly. Reduce heat until pressure control rocks occasionally; cook 40 minutes. Remove from heat, run cold water over cooker to reduce pressure. Carefully remove lid. Proceed with recipe as directed.

Mary A. Simmons
West Jefferson, North Carolina

BEEF AND VEGETABLES

Ginger adds a peppery yet slightly sweet taste to these leftovers.

Prep: 20 minutes
Cook: 15 minutes

1 medium onion, chopped
1 garlic clove, pressed
1 tablespoon olive oil
½ red bell pepper, cut into 1-inch pieces
½ green bell pepper, cut into 1-inch pieces
1 (8-ounce) package sliced fresh mushrooms
1 pound reserved roast beef, sliced (see Mary's Roast Beef at left)
1 cup reserved gravy
½ teaspoon ground ginger (optional)
Chili-Cheese Grits Squares (recipe at right)

• **Sauté** onion and garlic in hot oil in a large nonstick skillet over medium-high heat 3 minutes or until tender. Add bell pepper, and cook 2 minutes; add mushrooms, and cook 3 minutes.
• **Stir** in roast, gravy, and, if desired, ginger; cook until heated. Serve with Chili-Cheese Grits Squares. **Yield:** 4 servings.

CHILI-CHEESE GRITS

Serve half of grits with Mary's Roast Beef and gravy. Then turn the remaining half into grits squares to serve with Beef and Vegetables.

Prep: 15 minutes
Bake: 1 hour

1 cup regular grits
2 cups (8 ounces) shredded sharp Cheddar cheese
½ cup butter or margarine, softened
1 (4.5-ounce) can chopped green chiles
1 garlic clove, pressed
2 large eggs, lightly beaten
½ teaspoon Worcestershire sauce

• **Cook** grits according to package directions. Stir in cheese and remaining ingredients. Spoon into a lightly greased 13- x 9-inch baking dish.
• **Bake,** uncovered, at 350° for 1 hour or until set. **Yield:** 8 servings.

Della Taylor
Jonesboro, Tennessee

Chili-Cheese Grits Squares: Chill remaining half of grits. Cut into squares, and broil 5 inches from heat 1 minute on each side or until golden. Serve with Beef and Vegetables.

"Divine" Dishes

These recipes will add unique and delicious flavors—

as well as cultural diversity—to your family's palate.

To Orthodox Christians, for whom Easter is the most important religious holiday, food serves as an integral part of religious ceremony. We've asked two readers, one a member of All Saints of America Orthodox Church in DeQueen, Arkansas, and another originally from the Republic of Georgia, now living in America in Avondale Estates, Georgia, to share their favorite Easter recipes. Perhaps the most recognizable food item is kulich (KOO-lihch), a lightly sweetened bread. Baked in a coffee can, kulich has a shape meant to resemble the domes of Russia's Orthodox churches.

KULICH

After being iced, the bread is topped with raisins to form the letters "XB," meaning "Christ has risen."

Prep: 25 minutes
Rise: 1 hour, 45 minutes
Bake: 45 minutes

¼ cup golden raisins
1 (¼-ounce) envelope active dry
    yeast
¼ cup warm water (100° to 110°)
1½ teaspoons vanilla extract, divided
¼ cup sugar
½ teaspoon salt
2 teaspoons grated lemon rind
2 teaspoons brandy or rum
¾ cup warm milk (100° to 110°)
¼ cup butter or margarine, melted
2 large eggs
3 cups all-purpose flour
¼ cup blanched almonds, chopped
¼ cup dried orange peel
1 cup powdered sugar
1 tablespoon milk
½ cup raisins

• **Place** ¼ cup golden raisins in a bowl, and cover with boiling water. Let stand 15 minutes. Drain and pat dry; set aside.
• **Combine** yeast and ¼ cup warm water in a large mixing bowl; let stand 5 minutes.
• **Add** 1 teaspoon vanilla, sugar, and next 6 ingredients to yeast mixture; beat at medium speed with an electric mixer until well blended. Gradually stir in enough flour to make a soft dough.
• **Turn** dough out onto a well-floured surface, and knead until dough is smooth and elastic (about 10 minutes). Place in a well-greased bowl, turning to grease top.
• **Cover** and let rise in a warm place (85°), free from drafts, 1 hour or until doubled in bulk.
• **Punch** dough down; turn out onto a well-floured surface. Press dough flat, and work golden raisins, almonds, and orange peel evenly into dough.
• **Shape** dough into a ball; press, seam side down, into a greased 2-pound coffee can, filling half of can.
• **Cover** with wax paper; let rise in a warm place (85°), free from drafts, 30 to 45 minutes or just until dough reaches top of can. (Do not let rise above top.)
• **Bake** at 375° for 40 to 45 minutes or until a long wooden pick inserted in center comes out clean. Remove from can, and place on a serving plate.
• **Stir** together remaining ½ teaspoon vanilla, powdered sugar, and milk until blended; spread over warm bread. Press ½ cup raisins into top of bread, forming initials "XB." **Yield:** 8 to 10 servings.

Note: To make 2 smaller loaves, divide dough in half; place into 2 (1-pound) coffee cans. Proceed with recipe as directed. For testing purposes only, we used Spice Islands Orange Peel.

Paraskeva Brooks
DeQueen, Arkansas

GEORGIAN EGGPLANT WITH WALNUTS

Prep: 30 minutes
Stand: 1 hour
Cook: 15 minutes

1 to 2 eggplants, cut into 24
    (¼-inch-thick) slices
1 tablespoon salt
1 small onion, chopped
3 garlic cloves, chopped
1 tablespoon olive oil
1 cup diced walnuts
1 teaspoon curry powder
1 to 2 teaspoons ground cloves
¾ cup chopped fresh cilantro
½ cup chopped fresh parsley
⅛ teaspoon salt
¼ teaspoon pepper
3 tablespoons water
1½ tablespoons red wine vinegar
Vegetable oil

• **Sprinkle** eggplant slices evenly with 1 tablespoon salt; let stand 1 hour. Rinse and pat dry with paper towels.
• **Sauté** onion and garlic in hot olive oil in a saucepan over medium heat 5 minutes or until tender.
• **Stir** in walnuts, curry, and ground cloves, and cook, stirring constantly, 1 minute. Remove walnut mixture from heat; stir in cilantro and next 5 ingredients. Set aside.
• **Pour** vegetable oil to a depth of 2 inches into a Dutch oven; heat to 375°. Fry eggplant, in batches, 3 to 5 minutes or until golden; drain on paper towels.
• **Top** each eggplant slice with walnut mixture, and fold in half. Lightly coat each half with walnut mixture. **Yield:** 8 servings.

Irakli Beridze
Avondale Estates, Georgia

Let's Do Brunch

Invite some friends over for
relaxing conversation and a flavorful spread.

Weekend Brunch Menu
Serves 6

Quiche Lorraine
Spiced Mixed Fruit
Hot Cross Buns
Bellini

QUICHE LORRAINE

Filled with crunchy bits of bacon and melted Swiss cheese, this quiche tempts the taste buds any time of day.

Prep: 30 minutes
Bake: 47 minutes
Stand: 10 minutes

½ **(15-ounce) package refrigerated piecrusts**
8 **bacon slices, cut into ½-inch pieces**
4 **green onions, chopped**
2 **cups (8 ounces) shredded Swiss cheese, divided**
6 **large eggs**
1 **cup whipping cream**
½ **teaspoon salt**
⅛ **teaspoon ground red pepper**
⅛ **teaspoon ground white pepper**
⅛ **teaspoon ground nutmeg**

• **Fit** piecrust into a 9-inch pieplate according to package directions; fold edges under, and crimp.
• **Bake** at 400° for 7 minutes; remove from oven.
• **Cook** bacon pieces in a large skillet until crisp; drain on paper towels.

Sprinkle bacon, green onions, and 1 cup cheese into prepared crust.
• **Whisk** together eggs and next 4 ingredients; pour into crust, and sprinkle with remaining 1 cup cheese and nutmeg.
• **Bake** at 350° for 35 to 40 minutes or until set. Let stand 10 minutes. **Yield:** 1 (9-inch) quiche.

SPICED MIXED FRUIT

Prep: 30 minutes
Cook: 20 minutes

1 **cup sugar**
1 **cup water**
1 **cup dry white wine**
2 **whole cloves**
1 **(2-inch) cinnamon stick**
½ **teaspoon vanilla extract**
6 **navel oranges**
3 **grapefruits**
3 **bananas**

• **Bring** first 5 ingredients to a boil in a saucepan. Reduce heat to low, and simmer, stirring occasionally, 15 minutes. Stir in vanilla. Cool syrup. Discard cloves and cinnamon stick.

• **Peel** and section oranges and grapefruits, and place in a large bowl. Gently stir in syrup. Cover and chill mixture, if desired. Slice bananas, and stir in just before serving. **Yield:** 6 to 8 servings.

Nan Rowe
Pagosa Springs, Colorado

HOT CROSS BUNS

Prep: 30 minutes
Rise: 3 hours, 15 minutes
Bake: 25 minutes

2 **(¼-ounce) envelopes active dry yeast**
½ **cup warm water (100° to 110°)**
1 **cup warm milk (100° to 110°)**
½ **cup butter, softened**
½ **cup sugar**
½ **teaspoon salt**
3 **large eggs**
1½ **teaspoons vanilla extract**
5 **cups all-purpose flour**
1½ **teaspoons ground cinnamon**
1 **cup raisins**
Sugar Glaze

• **Combine** yeast and ½ cup warm water in a large mixing bowl, and let stand 5 minutes. Add warm milk and next 5 ingredients. Beat at medium speed with an electric mixer until blended.
• **Combine** flour and cinnamon, and gradually add to yeast mixture. Beat at medium speed 2 minutes. Stir in raisins.
• **Place** dough in a well-greased bowl, turning to grease top. Cover and let rise in a warm place (85°), free from drafts, 2 hours or until doubled in bulk.
• **Punch** dough down; cover and let rise in a warm place (85°), free from drafts, 30 minutes.
• **Turn** dough out onto a well-floured surface, and roll to ½-inch thickness. Cut with a 2-inch round cutter.
• **Place** on a lightly greased 15- x 10-inch jellyroll pan. Cover and let rise in a warm place (85°), free from drafts, 45 minutes or until doubled in bulk.
• **Bake,** uncovered, at 350° for 20 to 25 minutes or until lightly browned. Let cool 10 minutes. Pipe Sugar Glaze over rolls in an "X" shape. **Yield:** 4 dozen.

Sugar Glaze

Prep: 5 minutes

1 cup powdered sugar
1½ tablespoons milk
½ teaspoon vanilla extract

• **Whisk** together all ingredients until smooth. **Yield:** ½ cup.

Melanie Smith
Brentwood, Tennessee

BELLINI

Named for the painter Giovanni Bellini, this famous cocktail was created in the thirties at Harry's Bar in Venice, Italy.

Prep: 10 minutes

1 (16-ounce) bottle peach nectar, chilled
1 (750-milliliter) bottle sparkling wine, chilled
Garnish: fresh raspberries

• **Fill** each of 6 champagne flutes with 2 ounces of peach nectar and 4 ounces of sparkling wine. Garnish, if desired. Serve immediately. **Yield:** 6 servings.

Note: For testing purposes only, we used the sweet Italian sparkling wine prosecco.

New Potatoes

Spring delivers an array of new potatoes into grocery store bins. These irregularly shaped potatoes are known for their thin, waxy skins, and they're ideal for tossing with fresh seasonal vegetables or for pan roasting. Just remember to choose potatoes that are uniform in size to make cooking easier.

HERB-ROASTED POTATOES

Prep: 15 minutes
Bake: 30 minutes

12 small new potatoes (about 2 pounds), cut into wedges
¼ cup olive oil
2 garlic cloves, pressed
1 teaspoon salt
1 teaspoon ground cumin
½ teaspoon paprika
¼ teaspoon dried oregano
⅛ teaspoon ground red pepper

• **Toss** together all ingredients in a large bowl; spread mixture evenly into a lightly greased, aluminum foil-lined 13- x 9-inch baking dish.
• **Bake** at 425° for 30 minutes or until tender. **Yield:** 6 to 8 servings.

Roma Millice
Keller, Texas

POTATOES AND GREEN BEANS WITH LEMON-DILL SAUCE

For this recipe, toss potatoes together with fresh ingredients, and leave on the skin—it adds color and nutrients.

Prep: 20 minutes
Cook: 28 minutes

2 cups water, divided
1 extra-large vegetable bouillon cube
2 tablespoons all-purpose flour
2 pounds small new potatoes, quartered
½ pound fresh green beans, trimmed
½ teaspoon pepper
¼ teaspoon dried dillweed
2 tablespoons lemon juice

• **Bring** 1¾ cups water and bouillon cube to a boil in a large skillet, stirring until cube dissolves; cool slightly.
• **Whisk** flour gradually into remaining ¼ cup water; add to broth, and cook over medium-high heat, whisking constantly, 2 minutes or until mixture is slightly thickened.
• **Reduce** heat to medium; add potato, and cook, covered, 15 minutes. Add green beans, and cook, covered, 8 minutes or until crisp-tender. Stir in pepper, dillweed, and lemon juice. Serve immediately. **Yield:** 4 servings.

Note: For testing purposes only, we used Knorr Vegetarian Vegetable Bouillon.

Joan H. Ranzini
Waynesboro, Virginia

CHEESY JALAPEÑO NEW POTATOES

Prep: 35 minutes
Bake: 30 minutes

8 small new potatoes (about 1½ pounds)
¼ cup butter or margarine
1 tablespoon all-purpose flour
1 cup milk
1 (8-ounce) loaf Mexican-style pasteurized prepared cheese product, cubed
2 garlic cloves, pressed
¼ teaspoon salt
⅛ teaspoon pepper
1 (2-ounce) jar diced pimiento, undrained
½ large green bell pepper, chopped

• **Cook** potatoes in boiling water to cover in a large saucepan 20 minutes or until tender; drain. Cool and cut into thin slices; set aside.
• **Melt** butter in a saucepan over low heat; whisk in flour until smooth. Cook, whisking constantly, 1 minute. Gradually whisk in milk; cook over medium heat, whisking constantly, until mixture is slightly thickened and bubbly. Remove mixture from heat; add cheese and next 3 ingredients, stirring until cheese melts.
• **Layer** potato slices, pimiento, and bell pepper in a lightly greased 8-inch square baking dish; top evenly with cheese mixture.
• **Bake** at 350° for 30 minutes. **Yield:** 6 servings.

Beverly Ellis
Bolton, Mississippi

Easter Elegance

In Eclectic, Alabama, spring arrives with a flourish at Kay Wallace's "An Afternoon in Your Bonnet" party.

I started it as a way to introduce my 5-month-old granddaughter, Mary Grace, to my friends," Kay explains. Despite the fact that Mary Grace became ill and missed her own "coming out" party, the event was such a success that Kay continued the day-before-Easter tradition.

"People in the South don't wear hats anymore," Kay says, "so now everyone has a year to look for their hats. It's a dress-up event that mostly ladies attend, but there are lots of little girls, too."

Kay makes much of the food herself, supplementing the delightful menu with purchased petits fours, tiny tarts, and cakes decorated like hats. Her sister-in-law, Cheryl Farrow, makes the Hat Cookies to repeat the day's theme. Savory appetizers complement the tasty sweets, and no one goes away hungry.

DRIED BEEF DIP

Prep: 25 minutes

2 (8-ounce) packages cream cheese, softened
1 (8-ounce) container soft cream cheese
½ (16-ounce) bottle Ranch-style dressing
1 small onion, grated
2 (2.25-ounce) jars dried beef, chopped
1 cabbage
Assorted crackers
Toasted chopped pecans (optional)

• **Beat** first 4 ingredients until blended; stir in beef. Serve in a hollowed cabbage with crackers. Sprinkle with pecans, if desired. **Yield:** about 4 cups.
Kay Wallace
Eclectic, Alabama

PRALINES

A crisp bite and creamy texture distinguish these sugary, pecan-studded candies.

Prep: 20 minutes
Cook: 12 minutes
Stand: 30 minutes

3 cups firmly packed light brown sugar
1 cup whipping cream
2 tablespoons light corn syrup
¼ teaspoon salt
¼ cup butter or margarine
2 cups chopped pecans
1 teaspoon vanilla extract

• **Bring** first 4 ingredients to a boil in a 3-quart saucepan over medium heat, stirring mixture constantly. Cook, stirring occasionally, 6 to 8 minutes, or until a candy thermometer registers 236° (soft ball stage).
• **Remove** mixture from heat, and add butter. (Do not stir.) Let stand until candy thermometer reaches 150°. Stir in pecans and vanilla, using a wooden spoon, and stir constantly until candy begins to thicken.
• **Drop** by heaping teaspoonfuls, working rapidly, onto wax paper. Let stand until firm. **Yield:** 2½ dozen.
Kay Wallace
Eclectic, Alabama

LEMON BUTTER COOKIES

These dainty cookies have a delicate lemon flavor.

Prep: 40 minutes
Bake: 15 minutes per batch

2 cups butter, softened
1 cup powdered sugar
3 cups all-purpose flour
1 teaspoon lemon extract
1 teaspoon grated lemon rind (optional)

• **Beat** butter until creamy; gradually add powdered sugar, beating well. Add flour, 1 cup at a time, beating well after each addition. Stir in lemon extract and, if desired, lemon rind.
• **Form** dough into desired shapes using a cookie press, and place onto parchment paper-lined baking sheets.
• **Bake** at 325° for 12 to 15 minutes. Cool on wire racks. **Yield:** 8 dozen.
Cheryl Farrow
Montgomery, Alabama

DATE BALLS

Toasted pecans and rice cereal add crunch to these chewy goodies.

Prep: 25 minutes
Cook: 18 minutes

½ cup butter or margarine, softened
1 cup sugar
1 (10-ounce) package chopped dates
1 large egg, lightly beaten
1 cup chopped pecans, toasted
1 teaspoon vanilla extract
4 cups crisp rice cereal
Powdered sugar

• **Combine** first 4 ingredients in a saucepan; cook over low heat 6 to 8 minutes, stirring constantly, until sugar dissolves. Add pecans, and cook, stirring constantly, 10 minutes.
• **Remove** from heat, and stir in vanilla. Stir in cereal, and cool slightly.
• **Shape** mixture into 1½-inch balls; roll in powdered sugar. **Yield:** 4 dozen.
Kay Wallace
Eclectic, Alabama

HAT COOKIES

Prep: 2 hours
Bake: 14 minutes

¾ cup butter, softened
1 cup sugar
1 large egg
1 teaspoon almond extract
2½ cups all-purpose flour
½ teaspoon baking soda
½ teaspoon salt
Decorator Frosting

• **Beat** butter and sugar until creamy. Add egg and almond extract, beating well.
• **Combine** flour, soda, and salt; add to butter mixture, beating well. Divide dough in half; cover and chill 1 hour.
• **Roll** half of dough to ⅛-inch thickness on a lightly floured surface. Cut out 36 cookies using a 2½-inch round cutter. Place cookies 1 inch apart on parchment paper-lined baking sheets.
• **Bake** at 375° for 6 to 8 minutes; let cookies stand on baking sheets 5 minutes. Cool completely on wire racks.
• **Roll** remaining dough to ⅛-inch thickness on a lightly floured surface. Cut out 36 cookies using a 1¼-inch round cutter. Place cookies 1 inch apart on parchment paper-lined baking sheets.
• **Bake** at 375° for 4 to 6 minutes; let stand on baking sheets 5 minutes. Cool completely on wire racks.
• **Assemble** cookies by placing 1 small cookie in center of 1 large cookie. Decorate with Decorator Frosting to resemble hats; let dry. **Yield:** 3 dozen.

Decorator Frosting

Prep: 5 minutes

2 tablespoons butter, softened
2¼ cups powdered sugar
2 to 3 tablespoons whipping cream
¼ teaspoon vanilla extract

• **Beat** butter until creamy. Add powdered sugar alternately with whipping cream until blended. Stir in vanilla. **Yield:** about 1 cup.

Cheryl Farrow
Montgomery, Alabama

Sweet Baby Cakes

What do children think of these little cakes?
Just look at the gleam in their eyes.

Petite cakes, cut into whimsical shapes, sparkle with colored sugar and candies. Telia Johnson and Jan Moon of our Test Kitchens created these party delights with their short ingredient list and doable preparation. Although most ingredients can be found in your pantry, visit your grocery's baking aisle to gather cake mix, vanilla icing, candy coating, and decorations.

Little hands are perfect for helping press out cookie-cutter shapes. For ease in cutting, freeze the cake for 10 to 15 minutes, and save leftover pieces for a trifle. When it comes to icing, don't panic. Our secret—a container of vanilla frosting combined with vanilla candy coating. Apply the finishing touches by using your favorite candies, sugar crystals, and more.

SPRING'S LITTLE CAKES

Who'd ever guess these cute petits fours come from a pound cake mix and canned frosting?

Prep: 1 hour
Bake: 25 minutes

1 (16-ounce) package pound cake mix
½ teaspoon almond extract
1 (16-ounce) container ready-to-spread vanilla frosting
2 (2-ounce) squares vanilla candy coating
Decorations: red string licorice, jelly beans, candy cake decorations, assorted sugar crystals, chewy spearmint leaves, chewy fruit snack rolls, candy sprinkles, candy-coated chewy tarts, miniature chewy tarts

• **Prepare** cake batter according to package directions. Stir in extract; pour almond batter into a greased and floured 13- x 9-inch pan.
• **Bake** at 350° for 20 to 25 minutes or until a wooden pick inserted in center comes out clean. Cool in pan on a wire rack 10 minutes; remove from pan, and cool completely on wire rack.
• **Microwave** frosting in a glass bowl at HIGH 30 seconds or until melted. Microwave candy coating in a glass bowl at HIGH 30 seconds or until melted; stir into frosting until blended. Reheat frosting as needed to keep it a good consistency for coating cake squares.
• **Cut** cake into desired shapes using 3- to 4-inch cutters. Dip into warm frosting; place on rack. Smooth sides with spatula, if needed. Let stand 5 minutes. Decorate cakes as desired. **Yield:** 6 cakes.

Note: For testing purposes only, we used Betty Crocker Pound Cake Mix, Betty Crocker Candy Cake Decorations, Betty Crocker Decor Selects Sugar Crystals, Nestlé Chewy Sprees, and Nestlé Chewy Sweet Tart Minis. Decorate cakes with candy sprinkles and sugar crystals while frosting is wet.

Living Light

Ginger enlivens lighter fare by imparting bold flavor without adding calories or fat.

Ginger is one of the few spices that delivers great flavor in both sweet and savory dishes. Once considered an exotic ingredient in Asian or Indian recipes, this knobby-looking root, whether fresh, ground, crystallized (also called candied), or pickled, can now be found in most supermarkets as well as in Asian grocery stores. Fresh ginger adds a peppery kick to dishes such as Grilled Sweet-and-Sour Scallops, while giving Roasted Gingered Sweet Potatoes a piquant aroma.

TANGY GINGER SLAW

Prep: 20 minutes
Chill: 1 hour

1 (10-ounce) package finely shredded cabbage
2 carrots, finely shredded
4 radishes, finely shredded
½ small sweet onion, minced
1 to 2 garlic cloves, minced
¼ cup white balsamic vinegar
1 tablespoon fresh lime juice
1 teaspoon grated fresh ginger
1 teaspoon sesame seeds, toasted
2 teaspoons sesame oil
¼ teaspoon dried crushed red pepper
¼ teaspoon salt

• **Stir** together all ingredients in a large bowl. Cover and chill 1 hour. **Yield:** 6 cups.

♥ Per cup: Calories 45 (36% from fat)
Fat 2g (sat 0.3g, mono 0.7g, poly 0.8g)
Protein 1.1g Carb 6.9g Fiber 2.1g
Chol 0mg Iron 0.5mg
Sodium 116mg Calc 37mg

ROASTED GINGERED SWEET POTATOES

A toasty topping of coconut, fresh ginger, and brown sugar adds taste and texture to these sweet potatoes.

Prep: 15 minutes
Bake: 55 minutes

2 large sweet potatoes, peeled and cut into wedges
2 tablespoons olive oil
¼ cup flaked coconut
2 tablespoons minced fresh ginger
2 tablespoons brown sugar
1 garlic clove, minced
½ teaspoon salt
¼ teaspoon ground red pepper

• **Toss** together sweet potato and olive oil; arrange potato in an aluminum foil-lined 15- x 10-inch jellyroll pan.
• **Bake** at 450° for 10 minutes. Reduce heat to 350°; bake 35 to 40 minutes.
• **Combine** flaked coconut and next 5 ingredients. Spread mixture onto a baking sheet, and bake at 350° for 5 minutes or until golden. Sprinkle sweet potato with coconut mixture. **Yield:** 4 servings.

♥ Per serving: Calories 186 (41% from fat)
Fat 8.4g (sat 2.3g, mono 5.1g, poly 0.6g)
Protein 1.7g Carb 27g Fiber 3g
Chol 0mg Iron 0.6mg
Sodium 316mg Calc 30mg

GRILLED SWEET-AND-SOUR SCALLOPS

Prep: 10 minutes
Chill: 30 minutes
Grill: 6 minutes

¼ cup rice wine
1 tablespoon grated fresh ginger
1½ pounds sea scallops, drained
¼ cup firmly packed brown sugar
¼ cup ketchup
¼ cup chicken broth
2 tablespoons rice vinegar
2 tablespoons soy sauce
1 teaspoon cornstarch
1 teaspoon sesame oil
2 garlic cloves, minced
¼ to ½ teaspoon ground red pepper (optional)
Hot cooked rice
Fresh parsley, chopped
Garnish: green onion strips

• **Stir** together rice wine and grated fresh ginger.
• **Place** scallops in a shallow dish or heavy-duty zip-top plastic bag. Add wine mixture; cover or seal, and chill 30 minutes, turning once.
• **Soak** 6 (12-inch) wooden skewers in warm water 30 minutes. Drain.
• **Bring** brown sugar, next 7 ingredients, and, if desired, red pepper to a boil in a saucepan over medium heat, stirring constantly. Boil 1 minute; remove from heat, and set aside.
• **Remove** scallops from marinade, discarding marinade. Thread scallops ½-inch apart onto skewers.
• **Grill,** covered with grill lid, over medium heat (300° to 350°) 2 to 3 minutes on each side.
• **Brush** scallops with brown sugar sauce, and serve immediately with remaining sauce. Serve scallops over hot cooked rice with chopped fresh parsley. Garnish, if desired. **Yield:** 6 servings.

Linda Marco
Chapel Hill, North Carolina

♥ Per serving: Calories 162 (9.9% from fat)
Fat 1.7g (sat 0.2g, mono 0.4g, poly 0.7g)
Protein 19.5g Carb 16g Fiber 0.2g
Chol 37mg Iron 0.7mg
Sodium 477mg Calc 41mg

Party Punches

Quench your craving for refreshing party drinks with easy-to-prepare spirited and alcohol-free recipes.

You've probably sipped many a cupful of that ubiquitous fruity-fizzy party punch. Although most of us enjoy its familiar flavor, sometimes we thirst for something a little off the beaten path. Expand your party picks with these beverages. With only a few ingredients, they're a snap to make and will complement both savory and sweet treats.

TANGY MARGARITAS

Prep: 10 minutes

1 (12-ounce) can frozen limeade
   concentrate, undiluted
1 teaspoon grated orange rind
⅓ cup fresh orange juice
1 teaspoon grated lime rind
2 tablespoons fresh lime juice
¾ cup tequila
14 ice cubes (about 2¼ cups)
Lime wedges
Coarse salt
Garnishes: lemon and lime wedges

• **Process** first 6 ingredients in a blender until smooth. Gradually add ice, processing until smooth.
• **Rub** lime wedges over rims of stemmed glasses. Place coarse salt in a saucer, and spin rim of each glass in salt. Pour margaritas into salt-rimmed glasses; serve immediately. Garnish, if desired. **Yield:** 5 cups.

Note: Margaritas may be made ahead and frozen. Let stand 5 minutes, and stir before serving.

Tracy R. Hall
Birmingham, Alabama

CRANBERRY COOLER

This fizzy, wine-spiked cooler gets its ruby-red hue from cranberry juice concentrate.

Prep: 10 minutes

3 cups seltzer water, chilled
2 cups dry white or rosé wine, chilled
1 (12-ounce) can frozen cranberry
   juice drink concentrate, thawed
   and undiluted
1 tablespoon lemon juice

• **Stir** together all ingredients; serve over ice. **Yield:** 6½ cups.

Bonnie Phillips
Weaverville, North Carolina

ALMOND TEA

Vanilla and almond extracts add subtle flavor to this Southern favorite.

Prep: 10 minutes

2 cups sugar
6 cups water, divided
1 cup lemon juice
3 tablespoons instant tea
2 tablespoons vanilla extract
2 teaspoons almond extract

• **Bring** sugar and 2 cups water to a boil in a large saucepan; boil mixture 2 minutes. Add lemon juice and next 3 ingredients, stirring well. Cool.
• **Pour** syrup into a pitcher. Stir in remaining 4 cups water. Serve tea over ice. **Yield:** 2 quarts.

Carol S. Noble
Burgaw, North Carolina

LOADED LEMONADE

Tequila, sweet and sour mix, and orange liqueur transform this summer sipper into an adult's-only ade.

Prep: 5 minutes
Chill: 2 hours

½ cup fresh orange juice
½ cup sweet and sour mix
½ cup tequila
½ cup orange liqueur
2 cups lemon-lime soft drink

• **Stir** together first 4 ingredients; chill 2 hours. Stir in soft drink, and serve over ice. **Yield:** 4 cups.

Note: For testing purposes only, we used Finest Call Sweet & Sour mix found in the beverage section of most supermarkets.

Frank Fitzgerald
Cheneyville, Louisiana

BANANA PUNCH

Prep: 20 minutes
Freeze: 8 hours
Stand: 2 hours

5 cups water
3½ cups sugar
1¼ cups fresh orange juice
¾ cup fresh lemon juice
1 (46-ounce) can pineapple
   juice
5 bananas, mashed
2 quarts ginger ale

• **Bring** 5 cups water and sugar to a boil in a large saucepan; reduce heat, and simmer 3 minutes, stirring constantly. Remove from heat; cool completely.
• **Stir** together sugar mixture, orange juice, and next 3 ingredients; freeze 8 hours. Remove from freezer, and let stand at room temperature 2 hours. Pour into a punch bowl, and add ginger ale. **Yield:** 1 gallon.

Dottie B. Miller
Jonesborough, Tennessee

Green Onions

This vegetable tends to be an afterthought when it comes to cooking. However, its versatility shouldn't be overlooked. Here, we showcase green onions in entrée and side dish recipes. All of our selections are simple to prepare and offer a variety of delicious and distinctive flavors.

CREAMY CHICKEN ENCHILADAS

Prep: 30 minutes
Bake: 40 minutes
Stand: 15 minutes

2 (10-ounce) cans diced tomato and green chiles, undrained
2 cups chopped cooked chicken
1 (8-ounce) package cream cheese, softened
5 green onions, chopped
1 (8-ounce) container sour cream
8 (12-inch) flour tortillas
1 cup (4 ounces) shredded Cheddar or Monterey Jack cheese

• **Stir** together ¼ cup diced tomato and green chiles, chicken, cream cheese, and green onions. Stir together remaining diced tomato and green chiles and sour cream; set aside.
• **Microwave** tortillas at HIGH 15 seconds or until warm.
• **Arrange** chicken mixture evenly down center of tortillas; roll up, and place, seam side down, in a lightly greased 13- x 9-inch baking dish.
• **Bake,** covered, at 350° for 30 minutes. Pour sour cream mixture over enchiladas; top with cheese. Bake 10 more minutes; let stand 15 minutes. **Yield:** 4 to 6 servings.

Kathe Cox
Spring, Texas

COLORFUL POTATO SALAD

Prep: 40 minutes

1 pound small red potatoes
1½ tablespoons white wine vinegar
1 tablespoon Dijon mustard
½ teaspoon salt
3 tablespoons olive oil
¼ cup diced red bell pepper
2 green onions, thinly sliced

• **Cook** potatoes in a large saucepan in boiling water to cover 25 to 30 minutes or until tender; drain and cool. Cut into thin slices.
• **Whisk** together vinegar, mustard, and salt in a bowl. Whisk in oil until blended. Add potato, bell pepper, and onions, tossing gently to coat. **Yield:** 4 servings.
Charlotte Pierce
Greensburg, Kentucky

MONGOLIAN BEEF

Prep: 30 minutes
Cook: 27 minutes

2 tablespoons cornstarch
¼ cup lite soy sauce
2 tablespoons dark sesame oil
2 tablespoons hoisin sauce
1 (14½-ounce) can chicken broth
3 tablespoons vegetable oil, divided
2 pounds boneless top sirloin, cut into thin slices
2 bunches green onions, cut diagonally into 1½-inch slices
Hot cooked rice

• **Stir** together first 5 ingredients until mixture is smooth.
• **Heat** 1½ tablespoons vegetable oil in a large skillet or wok over medium-high heat 2 minutes. Add beef, in batches, and stir-fry 8 minutes or until no longer pink. Remove from skillet; set aside.
• **Pour** remaining 1½ tablespoons vegetable oil in skillet; heat 2 minutes. Add green onions, and stir-fry 5 minutes or until tender.
• **Add** beef and cornstarch mixture to skillet, stirring constantly 1 minute or until mixture is thickened. Serve immediately over rice. **Yield:** 4 servings.

CHUTNEY-ONION CHEESE SPREAD

Prep: 5 minutes

2 (8-ounce) packages cream cheese, softened
½ cup mango chutney
⅓ cup chopped green onions
⅓ cup coarsely chopped dry-roasted peanuts (optional)

• **Spread** cream cheese into a 6-inch circle on a serving plate. Spread chutney over cream cheese. Sprinkle with green onions and, if desired, peanuts. Serve immediately, or cover and chill up to 1 hour. Serve with assorted crackers. **Yield:** 3 cups.

CHICKEN WITH GRILLED GREEN ONIONS

Prep: 30 minutes
Chill: 30 minutes
Grill: 22 minutes

1 teaspoon salt
½ teaspoon pepper
2 tablespoons olive oil
2 tablespoons grated lime rind
3 tablespoons fresh lime juice
4 bunches green onions
4 skinned and boned chicken breast halves

• **Process** first 5 ingredients in a blender or food processor until smooth.
• **Place** green onions in a shallow dish or heavy-duty zip-top plastic bag; pour lime juice mixture over green onions. Cover or seal, and chill 30 minutes, turning occasionally.
• **Remove** green onions from marinade, reserving marinade; set aside.
• **Grill** chicken, covered with grill lid, over medium-high heat (350° to 400°) 6 minutes on each side or until done, basting frequently with reserved marinade.
• **Grill** green onions, covered with grill lid, over medium-high heat 3 to 5 minutes on each side or until browned. Serve green onions with grilled chicken. **Yield:** 4 servings.

STIR-FRY SHRIMP

Green onions, sesame oil, and ground ginger add robust flavors to this dish.

Prep: 30 minutes
Cook: 15 minutes

1 pound unpeeled, medium-size fresh shrimp
3 tablespoons cornstarch, divided
1 garlic clove, pressed
¼ teaspoon ground red pepper
3 tablespoons soy sauce, divided
3 tablespoons sesame or vegetable oil, divided
1 (14½-ounce) can chicken broth
½ teaspoon ground ginger
1 red bell pepper, cut into thin strips
1 green bell pepper, cut into thin strips
1 bunch green onions, cut into ½-inch slices
Hot cooked ramen noodles or angel hair pasta

• **Peel** shrimp, and devein, if desired.
• **Combine** shrimp, 1 tablespoon cornstarch, garlic, red pepper, 1 tablespoon soy sauce, and 1 tablespoon oil; let stand 5 minutes.
• **Whisk** together in a bowl remaining 2 tablespoons cornstarch, remaining 2 tablespoons soy sauce, chicken broth, and ginger; set aside.
• **Heat** remaining 2 tablespoons oil in a large skillet or wok over medium-high heat 2 minutes. Add bell pepper strips, and stir-fry 4 minutes or until tender. Add green onions; stir-fry 2 minutes. Remove from skillet.
• **Add** shrimp mixture to skillet; stir-fry 3 minutes. Reduce heat to low, and add vegetables and chicken broth mixture. Stir-fry 3 minutes or until thickened and bubbly. Serve over hot cooked noodles. **Yield:** 4 servings.

An Authentic Crawfish Boil

If you're familiar with crawfish boils, then you probably understand their importance as a culinary and social rite of spring in Louisiana. They bid a warm welcome to sunshine and an official goodbye to all things wintry and gray.

However, if you're not, we've asked Andrew Jaeger, owner of Andrew Jaeger's House of Seafood in New Orleans, to reveal the finer points of cooking up these freshwater crustaceans. His father, Charlie Jaeger, was one of the first businessmen to bring live crawfish into New Orleans on a large scale. Andrew also shares his family's secret Crawfish Boil recipe.

"Each person has their own special way of doing things, but there are two important rules to remember when boiling crawfish. First, you only want to use live ones, so throw out those that don't move. Second, as far as the actual cooking goes, it's really a little boil and a lot of soak," says Andrew. Overboiling crawfish makes them mushy, which is why the soaking stage is so critical. He continues, "This allows the seasonings to gently seep into the shells. The longer you allow them to soak, the more flavorful and spicy they become."

CRAWFISH BOIL

Prep: 1 hour
Cook: 55 minutes
Stand: 30 minutes

1½ gallons water
10 bay leaves
1 cup salt
¾ cup ground red pepper
¼ cup whole allspice
2 tablespoons mustard seeds
1 tablespoon coriander seeds
1 tablespoon dill seeds
1 tablespoon red pepper flakes
1 tablespoon black peppercorns
1 teaspoon whole cloves
4 celery ribs, quartered
3 medium-size onions, halved
3 garlic bulbs, halved crosswise
5 pounds crawfish

• **Bring** 1½ gallons water to a boil in a 19-quart stockpot over high heat. Add bay leaves and next 12 ingredients to water. Return to a rolling boil.
• **Reduce** heat to medium, and cook, uncovered, 30 minutes.
• **Add** crawfish. Bring to a rolling boil over high heat; cook 5 minutes.
• **Remove** stockpot from heat; let stand 30 minutes. (For spicier crawfish, let stand 45 minutes.)
• **Drain** crawfish. Serve on large platters or newspaper. **Yield:** 5 pounds.

Andrew Jaeger
New Orleans, Louisiana

CRAWFISH EATIN' 101

For those unfamiliar with the "art" of eating crawfish, Andrew offers this quick primer on dealing with these delicious little crustaceans.

■ Begin by snapping apart the head and the tail.

■ If you're not a fan of the head, toss it aside, and then peel the tail by working your thumbs down the sides of the hard shell to release the sweet meat.

■ For the true crawfish lover, the renowned sucking of the head gives full access to a fiery concoction of spices and fat.

Loving Layered Salads

Enjoy these traditional and contemporary recipes for layered salads. Then you can have a field day inventing some of your own.

Remember layered salads? There's certainly no shortage of versions. Because of their creative design potential and convenience, the possibilities are endless.

LAYERED BLT SALAD

Another type of lettuce, such as Red Leaf, would also work great in this salad version of the popular sandwich.

Prep: 20 minutes
Chill: 2 hours

1 (8-ounce) container sour cream
1 cup mayonnaise
1 tablespoon lemon juice
1 teaspoon dried basil
½ teaspoon salt
½ teaspoon pepper
¼ teaspoon garlic powder
1 large head iceberg lettuce, torn (about 4 cups)
1 (32-ounce) package thick bacon slices, cooked and crumbled
6 plum tomatoes, thinly sliced
3 cups large croutons

• **Stir** together first 7 ingredients until well blended.
• **Layer** lettuce, bacon, and tomato in a 13- x 9-inch dish. Spread mayonnaise mixture evenly over tomato, sealing to edge of dish. Cover and chill at least 2 hours. Sprinkle with croutons; serve immediately. **Yield:** 8 servings.

OLD-FASHIONED LAYERED SALAD

Prep: 15 minutes
Chill: 8 hours

1 cup mayonnaise
1 cup salad dressing
1 tablespoon milk
1 teaspoon dry mustard
½ teaspoon salt
½ teaspoon pepper
1 head Romaine or iceberg lettuce, coarsely chopped
2 cups (8 ounces) shredded Swiss cheese
1 (10-ounce) package frozen peas, thawed
1 medium-size purple onion, diced
6 hard-cooked eggs, chopped
1½ cups chopped smoked turkey or crumbled cooked bacon
1 large cucumber, seeded and chopped (optional)

• **Stir** together first 6 ingredients.
• **Layer** half each of lettuce, next 5 ingredients, and, if desired, cucumber in a bowl. Spread half of dressing over top; repeat layers. Cover and chill 8 hours. **Yield:** 8 servings.

Note: For testing purposes only, we used Miracle Whip Salad Dressing.

Amanda Whitsel
Hull, Georgia

LAYERED VEGETABLE SALAD WITH PARMESAN DRESSING

Prep: 10 minutes
Chill: 8 hours

1 (8-ounce) package sliced fresh mushrooms
2 cups broccoli flowerets, chopped
1 (10-ounce) package shredded carrot
5 small yellow squash, sliced
2 large red bell peppers, cut into 1-inch pieces
2 green onions, sliced (optional)
Parmesan Dressing

• **Layer** half each of first 5 ingredients and, if desired, green onions in a 3-quart glass bowl.
• **Spread** half of Parmesan Dressing over top, and repeat layers. Cover and chill salad 8 hours. **Yield:** 8 to 10 servings.

Parmesan Dressing

Prep: 5 minutes

¾ cup grated Parmesan cheese
½ cup sour cream
½ cup mayonnaise
¼ cup Italian dressing with balsamic vinegar
¼ teaspoon cracked pepper

• **Whisk** together all ingredients until smooth. **Yield:** about 2 cups.

Ann Peck
Fort Worth, Texas

THE LAYERED LOOK

■ Use a glass bowl or other see-through container to show off the colorful layers.

■ Fresh, crisp vegetables are necessary to handle the weight of the other ingredients.

LAYERED SOUTHWESTERN SALAD
(pictured on page 78)

Black beans, corn, and cilantro give this colorful salad a Tex-Mex twist.

Prep: 15 minutes

⅓ cup chopped fresh cilantro
½ cup lime juice
½ cup olive oil
½ cup sour cream
1 teaspoon sugar
½ teaspoon salt
½ teaspoon pepper
1 (16-ounce) package Romaine lettuce, shredded
5 plum tomatoes, chopped
1 (15-ounce) can black beans, rinsed and drained
1 small purple onion, chopped
1 (8-ounce) package shredded Mexican 4-cheese blend
1 (15-ounce) can whole kernel corn with red and green peppers, drained
1 (6-ounce) can sliced ripe olives, drained
2 cups crushed tortilla chips
Garnish: fresh cilantro leaves

• **Process** first 7 ingredients in a blender or food processor until smooth, stopping to scrape down sides.
• **Layer** Romaine lettuce and next 7 ingredients in a 3-quart glass bowl. Pour vinaigrette over salad just before serving, and gently toss. Garnish, if desired, and serve immediately. **Yield:** 8 to 10 servings.

Taste of the South

Crab cakes, it seems, are on restaurant menus everywhere from the East Coast to Kansas. Simpler eating establishments pay homage to the delicate crab flavor by serving their cakes plain or with a basic sauce. Upscale chefs serve them with a variety of accompaniments including pineapple salsa, tomato concassée, grainy mustard sauce, or fennel coleslaw.

Nancy Devine is the third generation of her family to operate Faidley's Seafood market in Baltimore's Lexington Market. She sells three different grades of crab cakes that she makes by hand. "We make a big one [an award-winning, top-of-the-line version] that's 6½ to 7 ounces that uses jumbo lump and saltines," she says. "It's more moist than the other two. We use backfin [regular] crabmeat in the smaller one, which is 4 to 5 ounces. It looks like a fish cake." The third cake uses body crabmeat and is even smaller.

Nancy is particular about the crabmeat and other ingredients. "I don't want to mask the crab with onion, peppers, and all these flavors. So I just use a little binder [she says crackers produce lighter cakes than breadcrumbs], mayonnaise, and a few seasonings. That way the crab flavor comes through." She cautions that the essence of a great cake is keeping the lump crabmeat intact. "You can only work with so much jumbo lump at a time so as not to break it up. I just weep when I see people throw jumbo lump in a bowl and stir it with a fork."

FAIDLEY'S CRAB CAKES
(pictured on page 79)

If you prefer a spicier crab cake, add finely chopped bell pepper, onion, and Old Bay seasoning to taste.

Prep: 15 minutes
Chill: 1 hour
Fry: 16 minutes

½ cup mayonnaise
1 large egg, lightly beaten
1 tablespoon Dijon mustard
1 tablespoon Worcestershire sauce
½ teaspoon hot sauce
1 pound fresh lump crabmeat, drained
1 cup crushed saltines (about 20 crackers)
1 quart vegetable oil
Tartar sauce (optional)
Lemon wedges (optional)

• **Stir** together first 5 ingredients, and fold in crabmeat and saltines. Let stand 3 minutes.
• **Shape** mixture into 8 patties. Place on a wax paper-lined baking sheet; cover and chill 1 hour.
• **Fry** crab cakes, in batches, in hot oil in a large skillet over medium-high heat 3 to 4 minutes on each side or until golden. Drain on paper towels. If desired, serve crab cakes with tartar sauce and lemon wedges. **Yield:** 8 servings.

Note: To sauté crab cakes, cook in 3 tablespoons butter or oil in a large nonstick skillet 3 to 4 minutes on each side or until golden.

Nancy Devine
Faidley's Seafood
Baltimore, Maryland

THE CRAB CAKE RULES

Start with absolutely fresh crab, preferably jumbo lump. Add an egg or some mayonnaise to moisten the meat; season to taste. Use your hands to gently add in just enough cracker crumbs or breadcrumbs to bind the mixture; form into cakes. Place cakes on a baking sheet; chill at least an hour before sautéing or deep-frying. Cook until slightly crusty and golden.

From Our Kitchen

Cooking Lessons From New Cooks

We talked with three new cooks about their experiences in the kitchen and found them to be a wealth of information. Some things that most of us take for granted can present daily challenges to anyone who is just getting started. Here's their advice for success in the kitchen.

■ Read every recipe thoroughly before you shop.
■ Make your grocery list while reading the recipes, checking amounts of ingredients. This way you won't buy two cans of something when you need only one or vice versa.
■ Make sure that you have the necessary utensils for all of the recipes you've chosen. There is nothing worse than finding out too late that something must be grated, and you don't have a grater.
■ Get to know your oven. Just because you set the dial to 350° doesn't mean that's the internal temperature of the appliance. Calibrate it first using an oven thermometer.
■ Set up spaces for storing produce. Remove everything from those produce plastic bags right away. Fill a basket on your countertop with potatoes, winter squash, rutabagas, and turnips. Be sure to put onions, shallots, and garlic in a different basket from vegetables.
■ Separate the produce to be refrigerated. If you have two crisper bins, use one for fruits and one for vegetables. By doing so, you'll know what you have, and nothing gets buried and forgotten.
■ Learn to do multiple tasks. While the stew simmers, prepare the salad dressing or set the table.
■ Try flavored canned broths to enhance simple recipes.

Canned Beans

Look at all the options of canned beans on the grocer's aisle. Not only are they healthy choices for instant side dishes, they're wonderful bases for appetizer spreads and dips. Canned beans are soft and easy to mash or puree. Simply rinse the beans under cold water, and drain. Then mash with a fork or potato masher or give them a spin in the blender or food processor. Add broth and herbs to taste.

Tips & Tidbits

■ The coldest place in the refrigerator is the back part of the bottom shelf.
■ The hottest spots in the oven are in the back and the racks closest to the top and bottom.
■ An easy way to get the taste of zest without the bother of actually performing the task is to drop the whole thoroughly washed lemon or lime into a soup, stew, or steeping beverage. When the flavor is just right, remove the fruit and reserve it for juice.
■ Add that last piece of cream cheese to scrambled eggs, hot grits, or mashed potatoes.
■ Select lamb for your spring celebration using the following guidelines: Baby lamb should be pale pink, and regular lamb should be pinkish-red. Both should have a fine-grained texture and creamy white fat. Store it in the coldest part of the refrigerator up to three days. Thick bone-in chops deliver more succulent flavor than thin boneless ones. Lamb cooked medium rare is tender and more flavorful. It will be dry and tough if overcooked.

Can I Freeze It?

The number one set of questions from cooks everywhere is, "Can I freeze it? Do I cook, then freeze, or freeze, then cook?" Stick to these general rules for the best texture and flavor.

Cook and freeze stews, casseroles, sauces, and pastries up to three months. Fully cooked dishes will lose moisture when frozen, so slightly under cook casseroles such as lasagna or macaroni and cheese. Do not thaw these before reheating. You can also steam frozen vegetables without thawing them. Baked cake layers, breads, and cookies freeze very well; keep these goodies in the freezer for two to three months. Remember that all foods need to be frozen in airtight containers to prevent freezer burn.

Here's a list of some items that don't freeze well.
■ Hard-cooked egg whites
■ Aspics and gelatins
■ Raw salad ingredients
■ Cream pies
■ Potatoes and rice (frozen in a liquid such as soup or stew)
■ Plain, cooked meats (without any gravy or sauce)

WHEN PAN SIZES DIFFER

If a recipe calls for a pan you don't have, you've got options. But remember, when you change pan sizes, you may need to adjust the baking time and oven temperature.

■ A 7-inch pie pan holds half as much as a 9-inch pan.
■ An 8-inch skillet holds half as many chops as a 10-inch skillet.
■ An 8-inch ring mold holds half as much as a 9½-inch mold.
■ A 2-inch muffin cup holds half as much as a 3-inch muffin cup.

If your pan makes the contents deeper, it will take longer to cook. So increase the cooking time a little, and lower the temperature slightly. If your pan makes the contents more shallow, shorten the time and lower the temperature a little.

MAY

Fiesta in Lucinda's Garden

A gracious invitation to an extraordinary place

Growing up in El Paso, Texas, Lucinda Hutson was exposed to food and culture with a decidedly "border" flair. Today her Austin kitchen comes alive with the smells, flavors, and spirit of the Southwestern and Mexican cultures she holds so dear. And her gusto for entertaining is exemplified in her recipes adapted from her book, *The Herb Garden Cookbook: The Complete Gardening and Gourmet Guide.* "When I entertain, it's usually in the garden, so I try to keep things simple, relying on bold flavors and garnishes to be festive, colorful, and fun," she explains.

Garden Party
Serves 4

Garden Sangría
Basil-Cheese Torta
Toasted baguette slices
Garlic-and-Rosemary Shrimp

GARDEN SANGRÍA
(pictured on page 115)

Prep: 10 minutes
Chill: 8 hours

1 gallon dry white wine
2 cups brandy
1 cup orange liqueur
4 oranges, sliced
1 bunch fresh mint leaves
1 (1-liter) bottle club soda, chilled *
1 quart whole strawberries
2 lemons, thinly sliced
2 limes, thinly sliced
Garnishes: fresh mint sprigs,
    strawberries, red seedless grapes,
    orange and lime wedges

• **Combine** first 5 ingredients in a large container; cover and chill 8 hours.
• **Add** club soda and next 3 ingredients just before serving. Serve over ice, and garnish, if desired. **Yield:** 1½ gallons.

*Substitute ginger ale for club soda, if desired.

BASIL-CHEESE TORTA
(pictured on page 115)

This colorful appetizer makes a beautiful presentation and a delicious garden-party treat.

Prep: 40 minutes
Chill: 8 hours

1 (8-ounce) package cream cheese,
    softened
1 (4-ounce) package feta cheese
2 tablespoons butter or margarine,
    softened
Lucinda's Garden Pesto
2 (6-ounce) packages provolone
    cheese slices
Roasted Red Pepper Salsa, divided
¼ cup chopped pine nuts, toasted
Garnishes: chopped fresh basil, fresh
    basil sprigs, pine nuts

• **Process** first 3 ingredients in a blender or food processor until smooth, stopping to scrape down sides. Stir in Lucinda's Garden Pesto, blending well.
• **Line** an 8- x 4-inch loafpan with plastic wrap, allowing 1 inch to hang over on each side.

• **Arrange** one-third of cheese slices on bottom and up sides of pan. Layer evenly with half of pesto mixture, ⅓ cup Roasted Red Pepper Salsa, 2 tablespoons pine nuts, and half of remaining cheese slices. Repeat layers, ending with cheese slices, gently pressing each layer. Fold cheese slices toward center. Cover and chill 8 hours.
• **Invert** torta onto a serving platter. Top with ⅓ cup salsa; garnish, if desired. Serve with remaining salsa and toasted French baguette slices. **Yield:** 12 servings.

Lucinda's Garden Pesto

Prep: 10 minutes

3 cups fresh basil leaves
4 to 6 garlic cloves
½ cup pine nuts, walnuts, or pecans
¾ cup shredded Parmesan cheese
2 to 3 tablespoons shredded Romano
    cheese
⅔ cup olive oil

• **Process** basil and garlic in a food processor until chopped. Add pine nuts and cheeses, and process until blended, stopping to scrape down sides. With processor running, pour oil through food chute in a slow, steady stream; process until smooth. Chill up to 5 days, if desired. **Yield:** 1 cup.

Roasted Red Pepper Salsa

Prep: 20 minutes
Bake: 12 minutes

4 red bell peppers
1 tablespoon olive oil
½ cup dried tomatoes *
3 tablespoons chopped fresh basil
1 tablespoon balsamic vinegar
2 to 3 garlic cloves, minced
½ teaspoon salt
½ teaspoon fresh rosemary, finely
    chopped
¼ teaspoon ground red pepper

• **Bake** peppers on an aluminum foil-lined baking sheet at 500° for 12 minutes or until peppers look blistered, turning once.
• **Place** peppers in a heavy-duty zip-top plastic bag; seal and let stand 10

minutes to loosen skins. Peel peppers; remove and discard seeds. Coarsely chop peppers. Drizzle with 1 tablespoon olive oil; set aside.

• **Pour** boiling water to cover over dried tomatoes. Let stand 3 minutes; drain and coarsely chop.

• **Stir** together bell pepper, tomato, basil, and remaining ingredients. Cover; chill up to 2 days, if desired. **Yield:** 2 cups.

∗Substitute ⅓ cup dried tomatoes in oil for dried tomatoes, if desired. Drain tomatoes well, pressing between layers of paper towels.

GARLIC-AND-ROSEMARY SHRIMP
(pictured on page 114)

Prep: 20 minutes
Cook: 10 minutes

1 pound unpeeled, medium-size fresh shrimp
2 tablespoons butter or margarine
¼ cup extra-virgin olive oil
1 large garlic bulb
½ cup dry white wine
2 tablespoons white wine vinegar
1 tablespoon lemon juice
3 dried red chile peppers
3 bay leaves
1 teaspoon salt
2 tablespoons chopped fresh rosemary
1 teaspoon dried oregano
½ teaspoon dried crushed red pepper
Garnishes: lemon slices, red chile peppers, fresh rosemary sprigs

• **Peel** shrimp, leaving tails on; devein, if desired, and set aside.

• **Melt** butter with oil in a skillet over medium-high heat. Cut garlic in half crosswise; separate and peel cloves. Add to butter mixture; sauté 2 minutes.

• **Stir** in wine and next 8 ingredients; cook, stirring constantly, 1 minute or until thoroughly heated.

• **Add** shrimp; cook 5 to 6 minutes or just until shrimp turn pink. Garnish, if desired. **Yield:** 4 servings.

Note: If serving over pasta, remove bay leaves.

New Ways With Radishes

Many folks pass radishes by because of bad memories of bitter, limp, spongy discs. Give this year-round vegetable a second look with these fresh recipes.

RADISH BUTTER

This recipe is adapted from Butter Beans to Blackberries: Recipes From the Southern Garden *(North Point Press, 1999).*

Prep: 10 minutes

4 medium radishes, minced
¼ cup butter, softened
1½ teaspoons lemon juice (optional)

• **Stir** together radish, butter, and, if desired, lemon juice. Serve with crackers or fresh vegetables. **Yield:** ⅓ cup.

Radish-and-Chive Butter: Stir in 1 tablespoon chopped fresh chives.

CHILLED RADISH TOSS

Prep: 20 minutes
Chill: 2 hours

½ cup plain yogurt
1 tablespoon cider vinegar
1 tablespoon mayonnaise
1 tablespoon chopped fresh tarragon
1 teaspoon freshly ground pepper
20 to 24 radishes, sliced
3 celery ribs, sliced
1 small cucumber, peeled, seeded, and chopped

• **Stir** together first 5 ingredients. Add radish, celery, and cucumber; toss. Cover and chill. **Yield:** 4 to 6 servings.
Charlotte Bryant
Greensburg, Kentucky

RADISH-VEGETABLE SALAD WITH PARMESAN DRESSING

Prep: 15 minutes
Chill: 2 hours

4 cups broccoli flowerets
24 radishes, sliced
2 cups frozen sweet green peas, thawed
2 to 3 celery ribs, sliced
1 small green bell pepper, chopped
1 small red bell pepper, chopped
1 small yellow bell pepper, chopped
Parmesan Dressing

• **Combine** first 7 ingredients in a large bowl. Pour Parmesan Dressing over vegetables, tossing gently to coat. Cover and chill 2 hours. **Yield:** 6 to 8 servings.

Parmesan Dressing

Prep: 5 minutes

⅔ cup mayonnaise
⅓ cup grated Parmesan cheese
¼ cup buttermilk
2 tablespoons chopped fresh dill or
    2 teaspoons dried dillweed
1 teaspoon salt
½ teaspoon garlic powder
½ teaspoon onion powder
¼ teaspoon pepper

• **Stir** together all ingredients until well blended. **Yield:** about 1 cup.
Jeri K. Cruse
St. Cloud, Florida

ORIENTAL RADISHES

Prep: 5 minutes
Chill: 8 hours

2 tablespoons white vinegar
1½ tablespoons soy sauce
20 radishes, sliced
1 large green bell pepper, chopped

• **Stir** together vinegar and soy sauce. Add sliced radish and chopped bell pepper. Cover and chill 8 hours, stirring occasionally. **Yield:** 4½ cups.
Della Taylor
Jonesborough, Tennessee

Cooking With Mustard

Mustard, the darling of condiments, lends a flavorful kick to sauces, salads, and marinades.

If you ask your spouse to pick up a jar of mustard at the supermarket, you may want to be a little more precise. Buying prepared mustard isn't what it used to be. Today, you could probably spend 20 minutes trying to decide which type to toss in your cart. Whether coarse-grained, Creole, Dijon, Chinese, or mild American style, there's no limit to mustard's potential in savory dishes.

Experiment with a new flavor to add pizzazz to meat or vegetable marinades. Stir some into pasta dishes or tuna, shrimp, or egg salads. Use it as the base for zesty dressings. You can always liven up a tired meat loaf or burger recipe with a bold Dijon or spicy Chinese blend. We think you'll find that these recipes definitely cut the mustard.

MUSTARD VINAIGRETTE

Prep: 5 minutes

2 tablespoons coarse-grained Dijon
    mustard
¾ cup vegetable oil
¼ cup white vinegar
½ teaspoon sesame oil *
¼ teaspoon freshly ground pepper

• **Whisk** together all ingredients, and serve with mixed salad greens. **Yield:** 1⅓ cups.

★See "From Our Kitchen" on page 118 for the recipe.

Charlotte Bryant
Greensburg, Kentucky

MUSTARD SAUCE

Fresh ingredients and tangy mustard create a flavorful sauce for pasta.

Prep: 15 minutes

1 tablespoon butter or margarine
2 garlic cloves, minced
½ cup whipping cream
¼ cup water
2 egg yolks
1 tablespoon sugar
2 tablespoons cider vinegar
2 tablespoons prepared mustard
1 teaspoon salt
Hot cooked pasta
Chopped fresh parsley (optional)

• **Melt** butter in a large skillet over medium-high heat; add garlic, and sauté 2 to 3 minutes.
• **Whisk** together whipping cream and next 6 ingredients. Add to skillet; cook, stirring constantly, 2 to 3 minutes or until thickened. Toss with pasta. Sprinkle with parsley, if desired. **Yield:** 1 cup.

Note: For testing purposes only, we used French's classic yellow mustard.

Charlotte Bryant
Greensburg, Kentucky

TURKEY DIJON WITH GARDEN VEGETABLES

Prep: 30 minutes
Cook: 25 minutes

2 pounds turkey tenderloins
1 large red bell pepper
6 green onions
4 garlic cloves
3 medium-size yellow squash
3 medium zucchini
4 ears corn
1¼ cups Italian-seasoned
    breadcrumbs
½ cup minced walnuts
2 large eggs
2 tablespoons Dijon mustard
½ cup walnut oil, divided *
¾ teaspoon salt
½ teaspoon freshly ground pepper
⅓ cup chopped fresh chives

• **Cut** turkey into ½-inch-thick slices. Cut bell pepper into ¼-inch strips; slice green onions, and mince garlic. Coarsely chop squash and zucchini; cut corn from cob.
• **Combine** breadcrumbs and walnuts in a shallow dish.
• **Whisk** together eggs and mustard. Dip turkey into egg mixture, and dredge in breadcrumb mixture; set aside.
• **Sauté** bell pepper, green onions, and garlic in 2 tablespoons oil in a large skillet over medium-high heat 2 minutes. Add squash, zucchini, and corn; sauté 5 minutes. Stir in salt, pepper, and chives; transfer to a serving dish, and keep warm.
• **Wipe** skillet clean with a paper towel. Heat 2 tablespoons oil in skillet over medium-high heat; add one-third of turkey, and cook 3 minutes on each side or until golden. Drain. Repeat procedure twice with remaining turkey and oil. Serve over vegetables. **Yield:** 8 servings.

★See "From Our Kitchen" on page 118 for the recipe.

Quick & Easy

Welcome guests with a simple and satisfying brunch.

Morning Menu
Serves 6

Cheesy Asparagus Pie
Easy Cheddar Biscuits or Blueberry muffins
Orange-Cranberry Cocktail

It takes a little more than an hour from start to finish to make this tasty brunch menu. Here's the plan—stir up Orange-Cranberry Cocktail, and let it chill while you prepare the pie. Pop the pie into the oven about 40 minutes before guests arrive. Mix Easy Cheddar Biscuits, increase oven temperature when you remove pie from oven, and place biscuits in the oven as soon as temperature is correct. As the biscuits bake, greet friends with a welcoming smile and the assurance that they're in for a hot, delicious meal.

CHEESY ASPARAGUS PIE

Prep: 25 minutes
Bake: 39 minutes
Stand: 15 minutes

1½ pounds fresh asparagus
1 (15-ounce) package refrigerated
    piecrusts
1 tablespoon butter or margarine
1 large sweet onion, diced
2 tablespoons Dijon mustard
1 (8-ounce) package shredded colby-
    Monterey Jack cheese blend
1½ cups half-and-half
2 large eggs
¼ teaspoon salt
¼ teaspoon freshly ground pepper

• **Snap** off tough ends of asparagus (trimmed to about 5 inches). Cook in boiling water to cover 30 seconds; drain. Plunge asparagus into ice water to stop the cooking process, and drain. Reserve 9 spears; set aside. Coarsely chop remaining asparagus; set aside.
• **Unfold** piecrusts; stack on a lightly floured surface, and roll into a 14-inch circle. Fit piecrust into an 11-inch tart pan, trimming excess dough. Line piecrust with foil, and fill with pie weights or dried beans. Place tart pan on a baking sheet.
• **Bake** at 425° for 12 minutes; remove weights and foil. Bake 2 more minutes. Cool on a wire rack.
• **Melt** butter in a skillet over medium-high heat. Add onion, and sauté 5 minutes or until tender. Set aside.
• **Brush** bottom and sides of crust with mustard. Sprinkle with half of cheese, chopped asparagus, onion, and remaining cheese. Arrange reserved asparagus spears over cheese.
• **Whisk** together half-and-half and remaining ingredients. Pour mixture evenly over asparagus.
• **Bake** at 375° for 25 minutes or until set and golden brown. Let stand 15 minutes. **Yield:** 6 to 8 servings.

EASY CHEDDAR BISCUITS

Prep: 20 minutes
Bake: 10 minutes

1½ cups all-purpose flour
1 tablespoon baking powder
½ teaspoon salt
1 tablespoon sugar
1 cup (4 ounces) shredded sharp
    Cheddar cheese
⅓ cup shortening
½ cup milk

• **Pulse** first 4 ingredients in a food processor 4 or 5 times or until dry ingredients are thoroughly combined.
• **Add** shredded Cheddar cheese and shortening, and pulse 4 or 5 times or until mixture is crumbly. With processor running, gradually add milk, and process until dough forms a ball and leaves sides of bowl.
• **Turn** dough out onto a lightly floured surface; shape into a ball.
• **Pat** or roll dough to ½-inch thickness; cut with a 2-inch round cutter, and place on baking sheets.
• **Bake** biscuits at 425° for 10 minutes or until golden. **Yield:** 1½ dozen.

Heidi Kinsella
Wilmington, Delaware

ORANGE-CRANBERRY COCKTAIL

Prep: 10 minutes
Chill: 1 hour

¼ cup sugar
1 cup cranberry juice
1 (6-ounce) can frozen orange juice
    concentrate, thawed and undiluted
3 cups club soda, chilled

• **Combine** first 3 ingredients in a pitcher, stirring until sugar dissolves. Cover and chill 1 hour. Stir in club soda just before serving. Serve cocktail over ice. **Yield:** 5 cups.

Room Service for Mom

Award her tireless efforts with a meal prepared with love.

Mother's Day Menu
Serves 4

Citrus Salad With
Sweet-and-Sour Dressing

Shrimp Enchiladas

Three-Ingredient Orange Sherbet

Skip the restaurant on Mother's Day, and serve this feast at home. Find Mom a comfortable chair, and let her know the kitchen is off-limits. See "Helping Hands" (opposite page) for a list of easy tasks for children so that everyone can get into the act.

Begin preparations for the meal by making Three-Ingredient Orange Sherbet. While the sherbet is freezing, mix together the ingredients for Sweet-and-Sour Dressing. Next start the Shrimp Enchiladas. (If you don't mind spending a little more money to save time, substitute 1 pound peeled, cooked shrimp for 1½ pounds unpeeled, medium-size shrimp.) Put the enchiladas in to bake, and then whip up the Citrus Salad. (Purchase packaged torn Romaine and jars of grapefruit and orange sections from the produce section of your grocery to save even more time.)

Add a final touch of love to the festivities, and here's a tip for your effort: Mothers don't expect perfection.

CITRUS SALAD WITH SWEET-AND-SOUR DRESSING

Prep: 20 minutes
Chill: 1 hour

3 tablespoons sugar
1 teaspoon salt
¼ teaspoon onion powder
¼ teaspoon paprika
⅛ teaspoon pepper
½ cup vegetable oil
⅓ cup white vinegar
4 cups torn Romaine lettuce
2 pink grapefruits, peeled and sectioned
2 oranges, peeled and sectioned
½ small purple onion, thinly sliced

• **Whisk** together first 7 ingredients; chill 1 hour.
• **Arrange** lettuce evenly on 4 salad plates. Top evenly with grapefruit and orange sections and sliced onion. Drizzle with dressing. **Yield:** 4 servings.

Linda L. Shaffer
Milton, Pennsylvania

SHRIMP ENCHILADAS

Prep: 20 minutes
Bake: 30 minutes

6 cups water
1½ pounds unpeeled, medium-size fresh shrimp ∗
1 (10¾-ounce) can cream of shrimp soup, undiluted
1 (10¾-ounce) can cream of onion soup, undiluted
1 cup picante sauce
1 (8-ounce) package cream cheese, softened ∗
½ cup sour cream
2 cups (8 ounces) shredded Monterey Jack cheese, divided ∗
9 green onions, chopped
1 (4.5-ounce) can chopped green chiles
10 (6-inch) flour tortillas ∗
Garnish: chopped fresh cilantro

• **Bring** 6 cups water to a boil; add shrimp, and cook 3 to 5 minutes or just until shrimp turn pink. Drain and rinse with cold water.
• **Peel** shrimp, and devein, if desired. Coarsely chop shrimp, and set aside.
• **Combine** soups and picante sauce in a saucepan over medium-high heat, stirring often until thoroughly heated. Spoon 1 cup mixture into bottom of a lightly greased 13- x 9-inch baking dish. Reserve remaining mixture; keep warm.
• **Beat** cream cheese and sour cream at medium speed with an electric mixer until smooth; stir in shrimp, 1 cup Monterey Jack, green onions, and chiles.
• **Heat** tortillas according to package directions. Spoon 3 to 4 tablespoons shrimp mixture down center of each tortilla. Roll up tortillas, and place, seam side down, in baking dish.
• **Pour** remaining soup mixture over enchiladas; top with remaining 1 cup Monterey Jack cheese.
• **Bake** at 350° for 30 minutes. Garnish, if desired. **Yield:** 4 to 6 servings.

∗Substitute 2 cups chopped cooked chicken for shrimp, if desired. Substitute reduced-fat cream cheese, Monterey Jack cheese, and flour tortillas for regular cheeses and flour tortillas.

Vicky Van der Naillen
Nashville, Tennessee

THREE-INGREDIENT ORANGE SHERBET

This cool, creamy confection is a cinch to prepare and is ready to enjoy in just a couple of hours. Try any (or all) of the variations, and pick your favorite flavor.

Prep: 15 minutes
Freeze: 45 minutes
Stand: 1 hour

1 (15½-ounce) can crushed pineapple, undrained
1 (2-liter) bottle orange soft drink, chilled
1 (14-ounce) can sweetened condensed milk
Garnish: orange rind strips

• **Stir** together first 3 ingredients in a large bowl, and pour into freezer container of a 5-quart electric freezer. Freeze mixture according to manufacturer's instructions.

• **Pack** electric freezer with additional ice and rock salt, and let sherbet stand 1 hour before serving. Scoop sherbet into bowls, and garnish, if desired. **Yield:** about 3 quarts.

Three-Ingredient Blackberry Sherbet: Substitute frozen blackberries for crushed pineapple and grape soft drink for orange soft drink.

Three-Ingredient Peach Sherbet: Substitute frozen peaches for crushed pineapple and peach soft drink for orange soft drink.

Three-Ingredient Strawberry Sherbet: Substitute 1 (16-ounce) package frozen sliced strawberries for crushed pineapple and strawberry soft drink for orange soft drink.

Camille Crist
Wildwood, Missouri

Family Affair

The Bullock family from Parmele, North Carolina, definitely knows how to host a reunion. Their gathering, which started as a backyard picnic in 1977, has evolved into an activity-filled three-day event. Enjoy these treasured recipes from the Bullocks' family cookbook.

SWEET POTATO CAKES

Prep: 7 minutes
Bake: 55 minutes

2 cups sugar
1 cup vegetable oil
4 large eggs
1 (14½-ounce) can mashed sweet potatoes
2¼ cups all-purpose flour
2 teaspoons baking soda
1 teaspoon baking powder
½ teaspoon salt
2 teaspoons ground cinnamon
1 teaspoon pumpkin pie spice
1 cup chopped pecans
1 teaspoon vanilla extract
Powdered sugar

• **Beat** sugar and oil at medium speed with an electric mixer until blended. Add eggs, 1 at a time, beating after each addition. Add sweet potatoes; beat well.
• **Combine** flour and next 5 ingredients. Gradually add to sweet potato mixture; beat 2 minutes. Stir in pecans and vanilla. Pour into 2 greased and floured 9- x 5-inch loafpans.
• **Bake** at 350° for 55 minutes or until a long wooden pick inserted in center comes out clean. Cool cakes in pans on wire racks 10 minutes. Remove from pans; cool on wire racks. Sprinkle cakes with powdered sugar. **Yield:** 2 loaves.

Jenny Stroman
Philadelphia, Pennsylvania

HELPING HANDS

Little hands want to help prepare the special meal. Assign the following duties, taking each child's age into consideration.

- Peel shrimp.

- Stir together soups and picante sauce for enchiladas.

- Heat tortillas in the microwave.

- Spoon shrimp mixture down center of tortillas.

- Sprinkle cheese evenly over enchiladas.

- Prepare dressing for citrus salad.

- Arrange salad ingredients on dinner plates.

- Stir together ingredients for orange sherbet.

- Help prepare mother's tray.

- Deliver tray with love, hugs, and kisses.

RICE JARDIN

Prep: 8 minutes
Cook: 20 minutes

3 **tablespoons butter or margarine**
3 **medium zucchini, sliced**
1 **medium onion, chopped**
1 **(8¾-ounce) can whole kernel corn,**
  drained
1 **(10-ounce) can diced tomato and**
  green chiles
3 **cups cooked rice**
1½ **teaspoons salt**
¼ **teaspoon dried oregano**
¼ **teaspoon pepper**
¼ **teaspoon ground coriander (optional)**

• **Melt** butter in a Dutch oven over medium-high heat. Add zucchini and onion; sauté 5 minutes or until tender. Stir in corn, next 5 ingredients, and, if desired, coriander. Cover; cook over low heat 15 minutes. **Yield:** 4 to 6 servings.
Sheila Linton
Philadelphia, Pennsylvania

FRUIT PUNCH

Prep: 7 minutes
Stand: 30 minutes
Chill: 8 hours

1 **cup loosely packed fresh mint leaves**
2 **cups hot water**
2½ **cups sugar**
2 **cups water**
1½ **cups lemon juice**
½ **cup lime juice**
1 **pint fresh strawberries, quartered**
2 **(46-ounce) cans pineapple juice,**
  chilled
3 **cups orange juice, chilled**
1 **(1-liter) bottle ginger ale**

• **Stir** together mint and 2 cups hot water; let stand 25 to 30 minutes. Pour through a wire-mesh strainer into a 2-quart container, discarding mint.
• **Stir** in sugar and next 3 ingredients. Chill 8 hours. Stir in strawberries and remaining ingredients just before serving. Serve over ice. **Yield:** 7 quarts.
Ernestine M. Williams
Philadelphia, Pennsylvania

Taste of the South

Folks in the South are passionate about barbecue. Whatever the cooking style, rubs, marinades, and sauces are the base for balanced barbecue. The key is a good seasoning rub applied and then allowed to sit. When you add just the right sauce, the experience becomes exceptional.

When it comes to sauces, you can travel from the East Coast to Texas and taste four distinct kinds. Tennessee and most of Texas claim bragging rights for their thick tomato-based sauces. North Carolina is known for pungent vinegar-pepper-based and ketchup-based sauces. South Carolina boasts all of these types plus a mustard-based one.

So turn up the heat, and enjoy this recipe—it's what many Tennesseans call their best barbecue.

BABY LOIN BACK RIBS

Prep: 20 minutes
Chill: 3 hours
Grill: 2 hours, 30 minutes

2 **slabs baby loin back ribs (about 4**
  pounds)
3 **tablespoons Dry Spices**
1 **cup Basting Sauce**
1 **cup Sweet Sauce**

• **Place** ribs in a large, shallow pan. Rub Dry Spices evenly over ribs. Cover and chill 3 hours.
• **Prepare** a hot fire by piling charcoal or lava rocks on one side of grill, leaving other side empty. (For gas grill, light only one side.) Place food rack on grill. Arrange ribs over unlit side.
• **Grill** ribs, covered with grill lid, over medium heat (300° to 350°) for 2 to 2½ hours, basting every 30 minutes with Basting Sauce and turning occasionally. Brush ribs with Sweet Sauce the last 30 minutes. **Yield:** 3 to 4 servings.

Note: Use remaining Dry Spices as a rub on pork or chicken.

Dry Spices

Prep: 5 minutes

3 **tablespoons paprika**
2 **teaspoons seasoned salt**
2 **teaspoons garlic powder**
2 **teaspoons ground black pepper**
1 **teaspoon dry mustard**
1 **teaspoon ground oregano**
1 **teaspoon ground red pepper**
½ **teaspoon chili powder**

• **Combine** all ingredients in a small bowl. **Yield:** 6½ tablespoons.

Basting Sauce

Prep: 5 minutes
Stand: 8 hours

¼ **cup firmly packed brown sugar**
1½ **tablespoons Dry Spices**
2 **cups red wine vinegar**
2 **cups water**
¼ **cup Worcestershire sauce**
½ **teaspoon hot sauce**
1 **small bay leaf**

• **Stir** together all ingredients; let stand 8 hours. Remove bay leaf. (Sauce is for basting only.) **Yield:** 4½ cups.

Sweet Sauce

Prep: 10 minutes
Cook: 30 minutes

1 **cup ketchup**
1 **cup red wine vinegar**
1 **(8-ounce) can tomato sauce**
½ **cup spicy honey mustard**
½ **cup Worcestershire sauce**
¼ **cup butter or margarine**
2 **tablespoons brown sugar**
2 **tablespoons hot sauce**
1 **tablespoon seasoned salt**
1 **tablespoon paprika**
1 **tablespoon lemon juice**
1½ **teaspoons garlic powder**
⅛ **teaspoon chili powder**
⅛ **teaspoon ground red pepper**
⅛ **teaspoon ground black pepper**

• **Bring** all ingredients to a boil. Reduce heat; simmer, stirring occasionally, 30 minutes. **Yield:** 1 quart.

A Leg Up

With a ready supply of chicken and these terrific recipes, you're set for an enticing—and economical—meal.

BENNE SEED CHICKEN

Benne seeds (sesame seeds) add nutty goodness to this dish.

Prep: 10 minutes
Chill: 2 hours
Bake: 40 minutes

4 chicken leg-thigh quarters (about 2 pounds), separated
1 onion, quartered
2 garlic cloves
1 (1-inch) piece peeled fresh ginger
2 tablespoons sugar
2 teaspoons salt
2 teaspoons ground coriander
1 teaspoon dried crushed red pepper
3 tablespoons lemon juice
3 tablespoons soy sauce
2 tablespoons sesame oil ★
½ cup benne seeds
Garnish: lemon slices

• **Place** chicken in a shallow dish or large heavy-duty zip-top plastic bag.
• **Process** onion and next 9 ingredients in a blender or food processor until smooth, stopping to scrape down sides; pour over chicken. Cover or seal, and chill 2 hours.
• **Remove** chicken from marinade, discarding marinade. Place chicken in a lightly greased shallow roasting pan. Sprinkle with benne seeds.
• **Bake** at 375° for 20 minutes on each side or until done. Garnish, if desired. **Yield:** 4 servings.

★See "From Our Kitchen" on page 118 for the recipe.

Vikki D. Sturm
Rossville, Georgia

PEANUT-ROASTED CHICKEN

Honey-roasted peanuts contribute crunch to the moist, tender chicken.

Prep: 15 minutes
Chill: 30 minutes
Bake: 45 minutes

4 chicken leg-thigh quarters (about 2 pounds), separated
½ cup creamy peanut butter
2 tablespoons soy sauce
2 tablespoons honey
1 tablespoon grated lemon rind
1 tablespoon fresh lemon juice
1 (3-ounce) package honey-roasted peanuts
½ cup fine, dry breadcrumbs
2 garlic cloves, minced
1 teaspoon salt
¼ teaspoon ground red pepper

• **Place** chicken in a shallow dish or large heavy-duty zip-top plastic bag.
• **Stir** together peanut butter and next 4 ingredients. Pour mixture over chicken; cover or seal, and chill 30 minutes, turning occasionally. Remove chicken from marinade, discarding marinade.
• **Process** peanuts and remaining ingredients in a blender until mixture is crumbly. Place crumbs in a heavy-duty zip-top plastic bag; add chicken, and seal. Shake to coat. Place chicken in a lightly greased 13- x 9-inch baking dish.
• **Bake** at 375° for 45 minutes or until done. **Yield:** 4 servings.

Frances Benthin
Scio, Oregon

BEER-SMOTHERED CHICKEN

A rich, creamy sauce bathes juicy leg-thigh quarters.

Prep: 15 minutes
Cook: 1 hour, 20 minutes

4 chicken leg-thigh quarters (about 2 pounds), separated
½ cup all-purpose flour
2 garlic cloves, minced
¼ cup vegetable oil
1 small onion, diced
½ medium-size green bell pepper, diced
2 (12-ounce) bottles nonalcoholic beer
1 (6-ounce) jar sliced mushrooms, drained
¼ cup lite soy sauce
1 (10¾-ounce) can cream of celery soup, undiluted
1 cup whipping cream
Hot cooked rice

• **Place** chicken in a large heavy-duty zip-top plastic bag; add flour, and seal. Shake to coat.
• **Sauté** garlic in hot oil in a large skillet. Add chicken, and fry, in batches, 5 minutes on each side or until golden brown. Remove chicken, reserving drippings in skillet. Sauté onion and bell pepper in drippings 5 minutes or until tender; add chicken, beer, mushrooms, and soy sauce.
• **Cook** over medium heat for 30 minutes. Stir in soup, and cook, stirring occasionally, 30 more minutes. Add whipping cream; cook until thoroughly heated. Let stand 5 minutes. Serve over hot cooked rice. **Yield:** 4 servings.

Phy Bresse
Lumberton, North Carolina

Living Light

These easy and tasty recipes will get the kids

in the kitchen—to cook and to eat.

To quit eating junk food is no easy feat once you've established this not-so-great habit. That's why it's so important to offer your kids lots of fresh fruits, vegetables, and grains while they're young. The best way to get children excited about nutritious foods is to be a good role model. Sitting down for meals as a family is a great way to share proper food choices. Encourage kids to sample a variety of foods. These simple recipes allow little ones to help in the kitchen without turning it upside down. Our suggestions are lower in fat and calories than many of your kids' favorite foods, but you won't see any turned-up noses.

TURKEY FAJITAS

Prep: 15 minutes
Cook: 4 hours

3 turkey tenderloins (about 2 pounds)
1 (1¼-ounce) envelope taco
   seasoning
1 celery rib, chopped
1 onion, chopped
1 (14½-ounce) can mild diced tomato
   and green chiles, undrained
1 cup (4 ounces) reduced-fat shredded
   Cheddar cheese
8 (7½-inch) flour tortillas
Toppings: shredded lettuce, light sour
   cream, sliced olives, chopped
   tomato

• **Cut** turkey into 2½-inch strips. Place in a heavy-duty zip-top plastic bag. Add taco seasoning; seal and shake to coat.
• **Place** turkey, celery, and onion in a 2½-quart slow cooker. Stir in diced tomato and green chiles. Cover and cook at HIGH 4 hours. Stir in cheese.

• **Warm** tortillas. Spoon turkey mixture in center of each tortilla. Top with desired toppings, and roll up. **Yield:** 8 servings.

Teresa Hubbard
Russellville, Alabama

♥ Per serving: Calories 328 (13% from fat)
Fat 4.8g (sat 1.5g, mono 1.8g, poly 0.7g)
Protein 36g Carb 33g Fiber 1g
Chol 73mg Iron 2.6mg
Sodium 1,008mg Calc 185mg

FRUIT SALSA WITH CINNAMON CRISPS

Introduce your kids to healthy dipping
with this sweet snack.

Prep: 35 minutes
Bake: 8 minutes

1 pint fresh strawberries, chopped
1 large banana, chopped
1 Red Delicious apple, chopped
1 kiwifruit, peeled and chopped
¼ cup fresh lemon juice
¼ cup sugar
¼ teaspoon ground nutmeg
1¼ teaspoons ground cinnamon,
   divided
4 (7½-inch) flour tortillas
Vegetable cooking spray
2 tablespoons sugar

• **Combine** first 4 ingredients. Stir together lemon juice, ¼ cup sugar, nutmeg, and ½ teaspoon cinnamon; toss with fruit. Chill.
• **Cut** each tortilla into eighths. Arrange pieces on baking sheets. Lightly coat with cooking spray. Combine remaining ¾ teaspoon cinnamon and 2 tablespoons sugar. Sprinkle over tortilla chips.

• **Bake** at 350° for 6 to 8 minutes or until lightly browned. Serve with fruit salsa. **Yield:** 4 servings.

Susan K. Wright
Ithaca, New York

♥ Per serving: Calories 310 (11% from fat)
Fat 3.8g (sat 0.8g, mono 1.5g, poly 0.7g)
Protein 5.6g Carb 67g Fiber 4g
Chol 0mg Iron 1.6mg
Sodium 168mg Calc 122mg

CREAMY BEEF-AND-PASTA SAUCE DIP

Prep: 10 minutes
Cook: 17 minutes

1 pound extra-lean ground beef
½ onion, chopped
Vegetable cooking spray
1 (26-ounce) jar low-fat pasta sauce
1 (8-ounce) package reduced-fat
   cream cheese
¼ teaspoon garlic powder
½ teaspoon chili powder
2 tablespoons grated Parmesan
   cheese

• **Cook** ground beef and onion in a large skillet coated with cooking spray until beef crumbles and is no longer pink. Remove beef mixture from skillet, and drain well; wipe skillet with a paper towel.
• **Add** pasta sauce and next 3 ingredients to skillet; cook over low heat 5 minutes or until thoroughly heated. Stir in beef mixture. Sprinkle with Parmesan cheese. Serve warm with baked tortilla chips, carrots, or celery sticks. **Yield:** 5 cups.

Bobbie J. Napper
Tomball, Texas

♥ Per ½ cup: Calories 149 (45% from fat)
Fat 7.5g (sat 4g, mono 2.6g, poly 0.3g)
Protein 11.2g Carb 9g Fiber 1.4g
Chol 26mg Iron 1.8mg
Sodium 345mg Calc 71mg

FUN FRUIT DIPS

Take your pick of these sweet dips, and serve with fresh fruit, vanilla wafers, or gingersnaps.

Strawberry Dip

Prep: 15 minutes

1 cup plain nonfat yogurt
3 tablespoons strawberry cream cheese
½ cup powdered sugar
1 cup fresh strawberries, chopped

• **Process** first 3 ingredients in a blender or food processor until smooth. Stir in strawberries. **Yield:** 2¼ cups.

♥ Per ¼ cup: Calories 55 (26% from fat)
Fat 1.6g (sat 1g) Protein 1.4g
Carb 10g Fiber 0.4g
Chol 5.6mg Iron 0mg
Sodium 42mg Calc 39mg

Apple-Berry Dip

Prep: 10 minutes

1 cup fresh strawberries
½ cup powdered sugar
1 cup unsweetened applesauce

• **Mash** strawberries with sugar. Stir in applesauce; chill. **Yield:** 1½ cups.

♥ Per ¼ cup: Calories 57 (0% from fat)
Fat 0g Protein 0.2g
Carb 15g Fiber 1g
Chol 0mg Iron 0.1mg
Sodium 1mg Calc 5mg

Peanut Butter Dip

Prep: 10 minutes

1 cup plain nonfat yogurt
½ cup powdered sugar
¼ cup creamy reduced-fat peanut butter

• **Stir** together all ingredients until smooth. **Yield:** 1⅓ cups.

Carol S. Noble
Burgaw, North Carolina

♥ Per 3 tablespoons: Calories 88 (31% from fat)
Fat 3g (sat 0.6g, mono 1.6g, poly 0.9g)
Protein 4g Carb 13g Fiber 0.6g
Chol 0.7mg Iron 0.2mg
Sodium 96mg Calc 47mg

VEGGIE ROLLUP

This calcium-rich rollup will tone bones and teeth.

Prep: 10 minutes

2 tablespoons reduced-fat cream cheese
2 teaspoons light mayonnaise
⅛ teaspoon dillseeds
⅛ teaspoon dried parsley flakes
Dash of garlic powder
Dash of dried basil
1 small carrot, diced
1 small celery rib, diced
1 (7½-inch) flour tortilla

• **Stir** together first 6 ingredients. Stir in carrot and celery. Spread on 1 side of tortilla. Roll up, and wrap in plastic wrap; chill. Unwrap and slice. **Yield:** 1 rollup.

Shaylee Erdelbrock
Castle Rock, Washington

♥ Per rollup: Calories 292 (37% from fat)
Fat 12g (sat 4.5g, mono 2.9g, poly 0.7g)
Protein 9g Carb 38g Fiber 2.8g
Chol 20mg Iron 1.8mg
Sodium 492mg Calc 173mg

SMART BITES

■ Kids need to eat breakfast every day. They will be more creative and alert, and they'll perform better in school. Cereal with milk, yogurt and fruit; an English muffin with low-fat cheese and juice; a tortilla with a scrambled egg and juice; or peanut butter toast with milk are all good choices.

■ Keep their hearts healthy and weight under control by treating them to fun and nutritious snacks such as part-skim mozzarella cheese sticks with low-fat animal crackers, low-fat yogurt cups, or frozen yogurt pops. Keep easy-to-grab fruits and veggies around, such as frozen seedless grapes, sliced oranges, bananas, unsweetened applesauce or fruit cocktail cups, and baby carrots. While juice is nutritious, it has about 120 calories per cup. So, give 'em water and a fun straw, or dilute juices with seltzer water for a bubbly thirst quencher.

■ Limit TV and computer time (two hours or less per day), and offer snacks such as low-fat popcorn, frozen pops, or veggies with low-fat dip. Involve kids in activities—walking the dog, in-line skating, bicycling, jogging, and even dancing in the living room are great for the entire family.

■ Set a good example by serving yourself a little of everything prepared, and encourage tasting. Preparing a wholesome meal every night is difficult enough without having to cater to each child's palate. If children refuse to eat some items, be patient—not pushy. Keep reintroducing foods; they'll probably grow to like some of them.

Top-Rated Menu

*Present this gracious meal and rich dessert
to your guests for a delightful evening.*

Supper With Style
Serves 6

Classic Trout Amandine
Grilled Asparagus Salad With Orange Vinaigrette
Steamed couscous   Bakery rolls
Rich Black-and-White Pudding

Working ahead will make it easy for you to prepare this meal, even though your friends and family are sure to believe that you've been slaving in the kitchen all day. If you're having a larger gathering, this menu can be doubled to serve 12.

CLASSIC TROUT AMANDINE

1996 Recipe Hall of Fame

*Prep: 20 minutes
Chill: 2 hours
Cook: 25 minutes*

2 cups milk
2 teaspoons salt, divided
¼ teaspoon hot sauce
6 (8- to 10-ounce) trout fillets
¾ cup all-purpose flour
½ teaspoon pepper
1¼ cups butter or margarine, divided
1 tablespoon olive oil
¾ cup sliced almonds
2 tablespoons lemon juice
2 teaspoons Worcestershire sauce
¼ cup chopped fresh parsley
Hot cooked couscous with chopped
    parsley and red bell pepper

• **Stir** together milk, 1 teaspoon salt, and hot sauce in a 13- x 9-inch baking dish; add fillets, turning to coat. Cover and chill 2 hours.
• **Combine** flour and ½ teaspoon pepper in a shallow dish.
• **Melt** ¼ cup butter in a large skillet over medium heat; add oil. Remove fillets from marinade, discarding marinade. Dredge fillets in flour mixture. Add to skillet; cook 2 minutes on each side or until golden. Remove to a serving platter; keep warm.
• **Combine** remaining 1 cup butter and almonds in a saucepan, and cook over medium heat until lightly browned.
• **Stir** in lemon juice, Worcestershire sauce, and remaining 1 teaspoon salt; cook 2 minutes. Remove from heat, and stir in chopped parsley; pour over fillets. Serve immediately over couscous. **Yield:** 6 servings.

Note: Prepare fillets and sauce up to 45 minutes before serving. Heat oven to 250°; turn oven off. Place fillets in warm oven. Cook sauce over low heat until warm, and drizzle over fillets just before serving.

GRILLED ASPARAGUS SALAD WITH ORANGE VINAIGRETTE

1999 Recipe Hall of Fame

*Prep: 35 minutes
Chill: 1 hour
Grill: 10 minutes*

1½ pounds fresh asparagus
1½ tablespoons grated orange rind
⅓ cup fresh orange juice
½ cup olive oil
⅓ cup balsamic vinegar
2 teaspoons Dijon mustard
¾ teaspoon salt
½ teaspoon pepper
1½ pounds mixed gourmet salad
    greens
6 bacon slices, cooked and crumbled
    (optional)
Garnish: orange rind strips

• **Snap** off tough ends of asparagus; place in a shallow dish.
• **Whisk** together grated orange rind and next 6 ingredients. Pour one-third of vinaigrette over asparagus; cover and chill 1 hour. Drain. Set aside remaining vinaigrette.
• **Grill** asparagus, covered with grill lid, over medium-high heat (350° to 400°) 8 to 10 minutes or until crisp-tender, and let cool.
• **Combine** greens, remaining vinaigrette, and, if desired, bacon; place evenly on 6 salad plates. Arrange asparagus over salad. Garnish, if desired. **Yield:** 6 servings.

MENU GAME PLAN

Prepare the pudding up to 2 days ahead. The day before, whisk the vinaigrette, wash the salad greens, cook the bacon, and grill the asparagus. Then 45 minutes before serving, prepare the trout, and keep it warm according to directions at left.

RICH BLACK-AND-WHITE PUDDING

Chocolate and vanilla unite in this silky, satisfying pudding—a decadent and impressive finale.

1998 Recipe Hall of Fame

Prep: 20 minutes
Bake: 55 minutes
Chill: 8 hours

3½ cups whipping cream, divided
5 (1-ounce) semisweet chocolate
    squares
6 egg yolks
½ cup sugar
1 teaspoon vanilla extract
3 tablespoons sugar
Grated semisweet chocolate

● **Cook** ½ cup whipping cream and chocolate squares in a heavy saucepan over low heat, stirring constantly, until chocolate melts and mixture is smooth. Pour into a large bowl. Set aside.
● **Whisk** together 2 cups whipping cream, yolks, ½ cup sugar, and vanilla in a bowl until sugar dissolves and mixture is smooth.
● **Whisk** 1 cup egg mixture into chocolate mixture until smooth. Cover and chill remaining egg mixture. Pour chocolate mixture into 6 (8-ounce) custard cups; place cups in a 13- x 9-inch pan. Add hot water to pan to a depth of ½ inch.
● **Bake** at 325° for 30 minutes or until almost set. (Center will be soft.) Slowly pour remaining egg mixture evenly over custards; bake 20 to 25 more minutes or until set. Cool custards in water in pan on a wire rack. Remove from pan; cover and chill at least 8 hours.
● **Beat** remaining 1 cup whipping cream at high speed with an electric mixer until foamy; gradually add 3 tablespoons sugar, beating until stiff peaks form. Top custards with whipped cream; sprinkle with grated chocolate. **Yield:** 6 servings.

What's for Supper?

If your family is weary of the same ho-hum meat and potatoes, enjoy a creative vegetable menu. Try our tasty twist on macaroni-and-cheese with Veggie Mac-and-Cheese, and feed your Italian craving by sampling Eggplant Italian Style.

VEGGIE MAC-AND-CHEESE

Prep: 30 minutes
Bake: 35 minutes

8 ounces uncooked elbow macaroni
1 cup chopped fresh broccoli
1 cup diced yellow squash
½ cup diced carrot
1 small purple onion, diced
2 garlic cloves, minced
2 teaspoons olive oil
1 (7-ounce) jar roasted red bell
    peppers, drained and diced
1 (16-ounce) container ricotta cheese
1 (12-ounce) can evaporated milk
1 tablespoon Dijon mustard
1 teaspoon salt
1 teaspoon freshly ground pepper
2 large eggs, lightly beaten
3 plum tomatoes, sliced
⅓ cup Italian-seasoned breadcrumbs
½ cup (2 ounces) shredded Romano
    cheese

● **Cook** macaroni in a Dutch oven according to package directions; drain and set aside.
● **Sauté** broccoli and next 4 ingredients in hot oil in Dutch oven over medium heat 3 to 4 minutes or until tender. Remove from heat; add macaroni, bell pepper, and next 5 ingredients, stirring until blended. Stir in beaten eggs.
● **Pour** into a lightly greased 13- x 9-inch baking dish. Top with tomato slices; sprinkle with breadcrumbs and Romano cheese. Bake, covered, at 350° for 15 minutes; uncover and bake 20 more minutes or until golden. Serve warm. **Yield:** 6 to 8 servings.

Jenni Dise
Phoenix, Arizona

GARLIC GREEN BEANS

Prep: 10 minutes
Cook: 10 minutes

4 garlic cloves, minced
3 tablespoons olive oil
2 pounds fresh green beans, trimmed
½ cup chicken broth
1 teaspoon sugar
1¼ teaspoons salt
¼ teaspoon pepper

● **Sauté** garlic in hot oil in a large skillet over medium-high heat; add beans, tossing to coat.
● **Add** broth and remaining ingredients. Cover, reduce heat, and simmer 10 minutes or until green beans are crisp-tender. **Yield:** 4 to 6 servings.

Stacye Dages
Hendersonville, North Carolina

EGGPLANT ITALIAN STYLE

Prep: 15 minutes
Cook: 16 minutes

1 large eggplant
3 large eggs, lightly beaten
1½ cups Italian-seasoned
    breadcrumbs
Olive oil
¼ cup grated Parmesan or Romano
    cheese

● **Cut** eggplant crosswise into ⅛-inch-thick slices.
● **Dip** eggplant slices in egg, and dredge in breadcrumbs.
● **Pour** oil to a depth of ⅛ inch in a heavy skillet. Fry eggplant in hot oil, in batches, 1 to 2 minutes on each side or until golden. Drain on paper towels, and keep warm.
● **Arrange** eggplant on a serving dish; sprinkle evenly with cheese, and serve immediately. **Yield:** 4 to 6 servings.

Samuel Balsano
Gamaiel, Arkansas

Sensational Sugar Snaps

Get ready to enjoy this deliciously sweet and crunchy vegetable.

Sugar snap peas are one of spring's most delicious and adaptable vegetables. Whether raw or lightly cooked, these bright green pods complement salads, stir-fries, and dips. We also discovered that they're quite tasty when pickled. And like snow peas, you can enjoy the entire pod. Their sweetness and crunchy texture make sugar snap peas a vegetable your kids will actually eat without coaxing.

If you're a sugar snap purist, simply cook the pods in boiling water for two to three minutes, and then plunge into ice water to stop the cooking process (do not overcook). Toss with a touch of butter, and, if desired, add some grated lemon rind and chopped red bell pepper for a colorful side dish. If you're searching for fresh ways to prepare them, give our great recipes a try. These dishes all use entire pods, but like other edible podded peas (such as sweet green peas), they can be shelled and eaten.

SUGAR SNAP PEAS AND GOAT CHEESE

Prep: 25 minutes

1 pound fresh sugar snap peas
2 shallots, minced
1 tablespoon olive oil
8 ounces grape tomatoes
2 to 3 tablespoons chopped fresh basil
1 (3-ounce) goat cheese log, crumbled
1 teaspoon salt
½ teaspoon freshly ground pepper

• **Cook** peas in boiling water to cover 2 minutes; drain. Plunge into ice water to stop the cooking process; drain.

• **Sauté** shallots in hot oil in a large skillet until tender. Add peas, and cook until thoroughly heated.
• **Place** mixture in a bowl. Add tomatoes and remaining ingredients; toss gently. Serve immediately. **Yield:** 4 servings.

PICKLED SUGAR SNAP PEAS

Prep: 40 minutes

2 (3½-inch) cinnamon sticks
1 to 2 teaspoons whole cloves
2½ cups white vinegar
2½ cups water
½ cup sugar
1 tablespoon pickling salt
¼ to ½ teaspoon ground red pepper
2 pounds fresh sugar snap peas
4 to 6 garlic cloves, thinly sliced

• **Place** cinnamon sticks and whole cloves in a 4-inch square of cheesecloth, and tie with string.
• **Bring** vinegar and next 4 ingredients to a boil in a saucepan, stirring often; add spice bag. Remove saucepan from heat; cool. Remove spice bag.
• **Pack** peas and garlic evenly in hot jars. Pour cooled vinegar mixture evenly over pea mixture, filling to ½ inch from top. Remove air bubbles, and wipe jar rims. Cover at once with metal lids and screw-on bands.
• **Process** in a boiling-water bath 20 minutes. **Yield:** 2 quarts.

Note: To store in refrigerator up to 3 months, omit boiling-water bath.

SOUTHERN-STYLE COBB SALAD
(pictured on facing page)

Sugar snap peas add a bright, fresh touch to this main-dish salad.

Prep: 30 minutes

½ to 1 pound fresh sugar snap peas
2 heads iceberg lettuce
3 hard-cooked eggs
4 plum tomatoes
1 large avocado
1 bunch fresh watercress, torn
2 skinned and boned chicken breast halves, cooked and sliced
12 bacon slices, cooked and crumbled
Blue Cheese-Buttermilk Dressing
Freshly ground pepper
Garnish: edible flowers

• **Cook** peas in boiling water to cover 2 to 3 minutes; drain. Plunge into ice water to stop the cooking process; drain and set aside.
• **Cut** iceberg lettuce into 6 wedges. Coarsely chop eggs. Remove and discard pulp from tomatoes, and cut into thin strips. Dice avocado.
• **Arrange** watercress evenly on 6 salad plates. Top with peas, chopped eggs, avocado, chicken, and tomato strips; sprinkle with bacon. Place a lettuce wedge on each plate. Drizzle with Blue Cheese-Buttermilk Dressing; sprinkle with pepper. Garnish, if desired. **Yield:** 6 servings.

Blue Cheese-Buttermilk Dressing

Prep: 5 minutes

1 (4-ounce) package crumbled blue cheese
1 cup nonfat buttermilk
½ to ⅔ cup reduced-fat mayonnaise
3 to 4 tablespoons lemon juice
1 garlic clove, minced

• **Stir** together all ingredients in a bowl. Serve over salad. **Yield:** 1¾ cups.

Southern-Style Cobb Salad, facing page

Garlic-and-Rosemary Shrimp, page 101

Basil-Cheese Torta, page 100

Garden Sangria, page 100

115

Bread Pudding With Blueberry-Lemon Sauce, facing page

Lemon-Basil Butter Cookies, facing page

Lemon-Kissed Sweets

These recipes have a perfect balance of tart and sweet for fabulous desserts. So pucker up for pure pleasure.

BREAD PUDDING WITH BLUEBERRY-LEMON SAUCE
(pictured on facing page)

Prep: 20 minutes
Bake: 45 minutes

1½ cups sugar
4 large eggs
2 cups whipping cream
2 cups milk
1 tablespoon grated lemon rind
½ teaspoon ground nutmeg
1 teaspoon vanilla extract
1 (16-ounce) loaf stale French bread, cut into 2-inch cubes
1 cup fresh or frozen blueberries
Blueberry-Lemon Sauce
Whipped cream (optional)

• **Beat** sugar and eggs at medium speed with an electric mixer until fluffy. Add whipping cream and next 4 ingredients, beating until blended. Fold in bread cubes and blueberries, and pour into a lightly greased 13- x 9-inch pan. Let stand 10 minutes.
• **Bake** at 375° for 40 to 45 minutes. Cool in pan on a wire rack 5 minutes. Serve with Blueberry-Lemon Sauce and, if desired, whipped cream. **Yield:** 8 servings.

Blueberry-Lemon Sauce

Prep: 5 minutes
Cook: 7 minutes

1 teaspoon grated lemon rind
⅓ cup fresh lemon juice
½ cup sugar
1 tablespoon cornstarch
1½ cups fresh or frozen blueberries

• **Bring** first 4 ingredients to a boil in a saucepan over medium heat, stirring constantly. Reduce heat; add blueberries, and simmer, stirring constantly, 3 to 5 minutes or until thickened. **Yield:** 1½ cups.

Mrs. Michael Dryden
Pollock, Louisiana

LEMON-BASIL BUTTER COOKIES
(pictured on facing page)

You'll love these delicately sweet cookies. Lemon brightens the flavor of the basil.

Prep: 20 minutes
Bake: 10 minutes per batch

1 cup fresh lemon-basil leaves *
1¾ cups sugar, divided
1 pound butter, softened
¼ cup lemon juice
1 large egg
6 cups all-purpose flour
Garnishes: lemon-basil sprig, lemon wedges

• **Process** lemon-basil leaves and ¼ cup sugar in a food processor until blended.
• **Beat** butter at medium speed with an electric mixer until creamy; gradually add remaining 1½ cups sugar, beating well. Add ¼ cup lemon juice and egg, beating until blended. Gradually add flour and basil mixture, beating until blended.
• **Shape** dough into 1-inch balls, and place 2 inches apart on lightly greased baking sheets. Flatten slightly with bottom of a glass dipped in sugar.
• **Bake** at 350° for 8 to 10 minutes or until lightly browned. Cool cookies on wire racks. Garnish, if desired. **Yield:** 6½ dozen.

*Substitute plain fresh basil leaves for lemon-basil leaves, if desired.

LEMON SOUR CREAM POUND CAKE

A large heavy-duty mixer is the secret to this one-step mixing method.

Prep: 10 minutes
Bake: 1 hour, 30 minutes

3 cups sugar
3 cups all-purpose flour
¼ teaspoon salt
¼ teaspoon baking soda
1 cup butter, softened
1 (8-ounce) container sour cream
6 large eggs
2 tablespoons lemon juice
½ teaspoon vanilla extract
Lemon Glaze

• **Place** first 9 ingredients in a 4-quart mixing bowl (in that order). Beat at low speed with a heavy-duty mixer 1 minute, stopping to scrape down sides. Beat at medium speed 2 minutes. Spoon batter into a greased and floured 10-inch tube pan.
• **Bake** at 325° for 1 hour and 30 minutes or until a long wooden pick inserted in center comes out clean. Cool cake in pan on a wire rack 10 minutes; remove from pan, and cool on wire rack. Drizzle evenly with Lemon Glaze. **Yield:** 1 (10-inch) cake.

Note: For testing purposes only, we used a KitchenAid mixer.

Lemon Glaze

Prep: 5 minutes

1 cup powdered sugar
2 tablespoons fresh lemon juice
½ teaspoon vanilla extract
1 teaspoon grated lemon rind (optional)

• **Stir** together first 3 ingredients and, if desired, lemon rind until glaze is smooth. **Yield:** about ⅓ cup.

Bettie Jo Sightler
West Columbia, South Carolina

From Our Kitchen

Tips and Tidbits

▪ When using chocolate morsels from a large container, measure them by volume. For example: 6 ounces equals 1 cup and 12 ounces equals 2 cups.

▪ If your fried tomatoes go soggy right out of the pan, we have a solution for your next batch. Before breading the slices, try sprinkling them with salt and draining them between paper towels for 10 to 15 minutes to remove excess moisture. This will help the breading or batter adhere for a crispy coating. Fry slices in enough oil to cover them. Don't crowd the fryer. (It lowers the temperature of the oil and makes the tomatoes greasy.) Drain slices on a wire rack or in a frying basket—not directly on paper towels. The heat from the slices touching the paper will steam (and soften) the coating.

▪ Stuffed peppers hold their shape when you cook them in a large muffin tin.

▪ As the weather gets hot, keep an ice chest in the trunk of your car to hold refrigerated or frozen foods until you get home from the grocery store.

▪ Sandy Snyder of Lynchburg, Tennessee, found another use for her chef's cooking torch (see February's "From Our Kitchen," page 50). "It is simply the best for thawing frozen locks—something we've had too much of this year in Lynchburg," she says.

Poppin Pork Skins

Assistant Foods Editor Scott Jones introduced us to a new microwave snack—Poppin Pork Skins. It's the same principle as popcorn, but these look like brown plastic chips in a pint-size container. In the microwave, the tough squares puff into crispy pillows of good pork flavor. Sprinkle with hot sauce, and enjoy while warm. The best part is they're not deep-fried. To order, contact County Fair Foods at (817) 265-0094. You'll get two 10-ounce cartons for $10 plus shipping.

Mix to Match

Don't skip a recipe because you're missing an herb or spice blend. You probably have everything you need on hand. Label and store these blends in airtight containers.

▪ **Poultry seasoning:** Combine 4 teaspoons each of dried sage, dried thyme, and dried marjoram.

▪ **Italian seasoning:** Combine 4 teaspoons each of dried oregano, dried marjoram, and dried basil, and 2 teaspoons rubbed sage.

▪ **Apple pie spice:** Combine ½ teaspoon ground cinnamon, ¼ teaspoon ground nutmeg, and ⅛ teaspoon ground cardamom.

▪ **Curry powder:** Combine ¼ cup ground coriander, 2 tablespoons ground cumin, 2 tablespoons ground turmeric, and 1 tablespoon ground ginger.

Fresh Fixings

▪ Pencil-thin asparagus spears have the reputation of being the best, but thick asparagus spears are wonderful too. It's not size that determines their flavor and texture—it's freshness. Select firm, bright-green spears with tight tips. Store them in a zip-top plastic bag in the refrigerator. Plan to use asparagus within two or three days. However, if bottoms get dry and tough, bend each spear near the cut end to snap off any tough, fibrous parts. A vegetable peeler also works well to remove tough exteriors.

▪ Rhubarb is at its peak and begging to become tonight's dessert. Enjoy it right away in a rhubarb pie, and buy extra to freeze for later. Simply cut the stalks into 1- to 2-inch chunks, and freeze in a heavy-duty zip-top plastic bag up to 8 months.

▪ Strawberries are a great buy right now. Enjoy all the fresh ones you can, but don't try to stock them. Save space in your freezer by using packaged frozen strawberries when you need them. Available year-round at a good price, they're great for cooking and making sauces.

▪ Use leftover sprigs of fresh herbs as small, fragrant bouquets for your table.

▪ To keep cauliflower from turning dark as it cooks, add 1 cup of milk or 1 tablespoon of lemon juice to the water.

SESAME AND WALNUT OILS: MAKE YOUR OWN

Sometimes neither an ingredient nor a substitute can be found in your local grocery store. We learned that could be the case with sesame oil and walnut oil. If you omit either from a recipe, the character of the dish is changed. But what do you do when they're not available? Justin Craft of our Test Kitchens staff came to the rescue and developed these recipes.

Walnut Oil: Lightly toast 2½ ounces of walnuts. Process the nuts in a blender or food processor until diced. Transfer to a small jar, and add ½ cup canola oil. Seal and shake jar; let stand at room temperature 24 hours. Strain, squeezing through a double thickness of cheesecloth. Return to jar; seal and refrigerate no more than three days. You'll have a scant ⅓ cup, just enough for most recipes, with no waste. For a recipe using walnut oil, see Turkey Dijon With Garden Vegetables on page 102.

Sesame Oil: Substitute 3 tablespoons lightly toasted sesame seeds for walnuts, and proceed as above. For recipes using sesame oil, try Benne Seed Chicken on page 107 and Mustard Vinaigrette on page 102.

JUNE

Two Chefs, One South

Their backgrounds couldn't be more different, yet these two chefs share a common love of Southern ingredients and flavors. In Kentucky, Anoosh Shariat embraces a culture far from his Iranian roots, and Louisiana native Jan Birnbaum demonstrates Southern flair in California.

Whether you're a Louisiana native cooking in California's wine country or an Iranian-born chef living in Louisville, a few things are certain: Southern food sells, it shouts flavor, and it mingles with any other traditions you toss its way.

"The flavors of the world combine in our dishes," says Anoosh Shariat of Shariat's in Louisville. "When I moved here, I learned about wonderful regional specialties such as bourbon, Bibb lettuce, black walnuts, and burgoo. It was like, 'Hey, it's open season; I can experiment.'"

Though he'd cooked Italian, Tex-Mex, and French in his trek from Iran to Germany to Texas, the Persian influence of his mother's kitchen lingers with him today in the Bluegrass State. Business partner and wife Sharron encourages Anoosh to merge her North Carolina traditions, the regional bounty of their new home, and his Persian passion for fresh herbs and spices. "It's kind of magical here—I can implement some of the flavors of my heritage with some of the Southern flavors I've come to love," he says.

The result is recipes such as Kentucky Bibb Salad With Fried Green Tomatoes and Rose Vinaigrette. "I wanted to add a dimension to traditional fried green tomatoes," he explains. "So I used classic Persian flavorings like cumin and mint, which you don't often find together in Southern food, and paired them with green tomatoes." It's a combination you'll want to try in your own kitchen.

Jan Birnbaum, Baton Rouge-bred and New Orleans-trained, didn't set out to open Napa Valley's token Southern restaurant. However, when he turned his imagination free in his own kitchen at Catahoula Restaurant & Saloon in Calistoga, California (after successful stints at Paul Prudhomme's K-Paul's Louisiana Kitchen and Campton Place in San Francisco), the South danced its way onto the menu—never to stray.

"I must answer the question, 'Are you really from New Orleans?' about 14 times a night," says the former LSU engineering major. "Once they hear that, everything's okay. Now I'm bringing Southern favorites like catfish and grits to Napa. And with the grits, all I do is add a little extra love (translation: cream and butter) and some redeye gravy."

Jan shares his recipe for Collard Green Risotto and Pot Liquor, a blending of his Southern experience and the cross-country cooking that followed. "Pot liquor is one of those things that 80% of the world doesn't know about, but it sounds like greatness and like something your mama made and was the best thing you ever had." When you taste it, you're sure to agree.

STUFFED CHICKEN BREASTS WITH SWEET-AND-SOUR TOMATO SAUCE

Chicken breasts stuffed with fresh thyme, country ham, and chopped apple gain international appeal with Anoosh's Persian-inspired sauce.

Prep: 20 minutes
Cook: 1 hour

1 small onion, chopped
4 tablespoons olive oil, divided
1 cup chopped walnuts
2 garlic cloves, chopped
2 tablespoons tomato paste
¼ cup firmly packed brown sugar
2 cups chicken broth
¼ cup balsamic vinegar
1 teaspoon salt
½ teaspoon pepper
½ teaspoon saffron
6 skinned and boned chicken breast halves
1 McIntosh apple, chopped
1 cup cooked country ham, chopped
1 teaspoon chopped fresh thyme
Garnishes: fresh thyme and basil sprigs

• **Sauté** onion in 2 tablespoons hot olive oil in a large nonstick skillet over medium-high heat 8 to 10 minutes or until tender. Add walnuts and garlic; cook, stirring constantly, 2 minutes. Stir in tomato paste, and cook, stirring often, 5 minutes.

• **Add** brown sugar and next 5 ingredients. Reduce heat, and simmer, stirring often, 30 minutes or until thickened; cool slightly.

• **Pulse** mixture in a blender or food processor 3 or 4 times or until smooth; keep warm.

• **Place** chicken between 2 sheets of heavy-duty plastic wrap, and flatten to ¼-inch thickness using a meat mallet or rolling pin.

• **Toss** together apple, ham, and thyme. Spoon 1 heaping tablespoon of apple mixture onto each chicken breast; roll up, securing with wooden picks.

• **Heat** remaining 2 tablespoons olive oil in a large nonstick skillet over medium heat; add chicken, and cook 2 minutes on each side. Reduce heat; cover and cook 7 to 10 minutes or until done. Drizzle with sauce. Garnish, if desired. **Yield:** 6 servings.

Anoosh Shariat
Shariat's
Louisville, Kentucky

KENTUCKY BIBB SALAD WITH FRIED GREEN TOMATOES

Tart and juicy fried green tomatoes are served on a bed of tender Bibb lettuce and topped with fragrant Rose Vinaigrette.

Prep: 20 minutes
Cook: 8 minutes per batch

½ cup cornmeal
1 teaspoon dried mint
1 teaspoon ground cumin
½ teaspoon salt
½ cup buttermilk
3 large green tomatoes, cut into
    ¼-inch-thick slices
Vegetable or peanut oil
2 large heads Bibb lettuce, rinsed
    and torn
½ cup toasted walnuts
Rose Vinaigrette

• **Whisk** together first 5 ingredients in a bowl until smooth; dip tomato slices evenly in batter.
• **Pour** oil to a depth of 2 inches into a large heavy skillet. Fry tomato slices, in batches, in hot oil over medium-high heat 4 minutes on each side or until slices are golden.
• **Arrange** lettuce evenly on 6 plates; top each with 2 tomato slices. Sprinkle evenly with walnuts; drizzle with Rose Vinaigrette. **Yield:** 6 servings.

Rose Vinaigrette

Prep: 10 minutes

3 large shallots, finely chopped
¼ teaspoon salt
1 tablespoon honey
⅓ cup red wine vinegar
2 teaspoons rose water (optional)
⅓ cup vegetable oil
3 tablespoons walnut oil *

• **Stir** together first 4 ingredients and, if desired, rose water; whisk in oils. **Yield:** ¾ cup.

* Substitute 3 tablespoons vegetable oil for walnut oil, if desired.

Note: For extra-crispy fried tomatoes, dip in batter twice.

Anoosh Shariat
Shariat's
Louisville, Kentucky

COLLARD GREEN RISOTTO AND POT LIQUOR

Creamy risotto gets a clever and delicious Southern twist with the addition of collard greens.

Prep: 15 minutes
Cook: 1 hour

1 tablespoon olive oil
3 bacon slices, cut into ½-inch pieces
1 large onion, chopped
2 garlic cloves, chopped
1 pound fresh collard greens, cut into
    2-inch pieces
¼ teaspoon salt
¼ teaspoon pepper
3 cups chicken broth
¼ cup molasses
2 tablespoons butter or margarine
Risotto

• **Heat** oil in a Dutch oven; add bacon, and cook until crisp. Add onion, and sauté 5 to 7 minutes or until tender. Add garlic; sauté 1 minute.
• **Stir** in collard greens, salt, and pepper; sauté over medium heat 5 minutes or until greens wilt. Stir in chicken broth. Reduce heat to medium-low; cover and cook mixture 45 minutes or until greens are tender.
• **Pour** greens mixture through a wire-mesh strainer into a container, reserving greens and pot liquor. Whisk molasses and butter into pot liquor.
• **Stir** greens into Risotto.
• **Place** 1 cup Collard Green Risotto in each of 6 bowls. Ladle pot liquor mixture evenly on top. Serve immediately. **Yield:** 6 servings.

Risotto

Prep: 10 minutes
Cook: 1 hour

½ cup butter or margarine
1 medium onion, chopped
2¼ cups uncooked Arborio rice
2 garlic cloves, chopped
2 cups dry white wine *
2 bay leaves
5½ cups hot chicken broth, divided
¼ teaspoon salt
¼ teaspoon pepper
⅛ teaspoon hot sauce

• **Melt** butter in a Dutch oven over medium-high heat; add onion, and sauté 5 to 7 minutes or until tender.
• **Stir** in rice and garlic; sauté 2 minutes. Reduce heat to medium; add wine and bay leaves. Cook 5 minutes or until liquid is reduced by half.
• **Add** 1 cup chicken broth, salt, pepper, and hot sauce; cook, stirring often, until liquid is absorbed.
• **Repeat** procedure with remaining broth, ½ cup at a time. (Cooking time is about 45 minutes.) Remove and discard bay leaves. **Yield:** 6 servings.

* Substitute 1 cup chicken broth for white wine, if desired.

Jan Birnbaum
Catahoula Restaurant & Saloon
Calistoga, California

FOOD AND WINE

Assistant Foods Editor Scott Jones, our resident wine expert, recommends these food and wine pairings.

■ Stuffed Chicken Breasts With Sweet-and-Sour Tomato Sauce–Chardonnay or Viognier

■ Collard Green Risotto and Pot Liquor–Pinot Noir

Peppercorns Aplenty

Ground or cracked, this seasoning spices up any recipe.

Sprinkle on flavor or stir in color and heat with this well-known ingredient. Pepper—having captured the hearts of many Southern cooks—has great merit due to its numerous varieties. Do some experimenting to find the perfect pepper-corn that suits your family's taste.

For maximum freshness and flavor, store whole dried peppercorns in a cool, dark place for about a year. Store ground pepper for about four months.

If you need cracked peppercorns, use a rolling pin or meat mallet. Check kitchen departments or gourmet stores for pepper mills to grind peppercorns. There is a wide price range; however, spending a bit more will be beneficial in the long run.

So, round up your peppercorn of choice, and enjoy these recipes.

PEPPERY LEMON VINAIGRETTE

Crisp greens and fresh asparagus are the perfect complement to this tangy vinaigrette.

Prep: 5 minutes

1 teaspoon grated lemon rind
3 tablespoons fresh lemon juice
2 teaspoons assorted freshly ground peppercorns
½ teaspoon salt
½ cup olive oil

• **Process** first 4 ingredients in a blender or food processor until blended. With blender or processor running, add oil in a slow, steady stream; process until smooth. Chill until ready to serve. Serve over salad greens and vegetables, if desired. **Yield:** ½ cup.

Adelyne Smith
Dunnville, Kentucky

PORK TENDERLOIN WITH VEGETABLES

Prep: 15 minutes
Bake: 40 minutes
Cook: 5 minutes

2 fennel bulbs
3 large portobello mushroom caps
1 (1¾- to 2-pound) package pork tenderloins, trimmed
¼ cup olive oil, divided
½ tablespoon salt
3 tablespoons coarsely ground black peppercorns, divided
1 pint whipping cream
½ cup dry sherry

• **Trim** base from fennel bulbs; cut bulbs into fourths, discarding fronds. Cut mushroom caps in half.
• **Brown** tenderloins in 2 tablespoons hot oil in a large skillet over medium-high heat 4 to 5 minutes on each side.
• **Place** pork in a shallow roasting pan; sprinkle with salt and 1½ tablespoons pepper. Top with fennel and mush-rooms; drizzle with remaining 2 table-spoons oil.
• **Bake** at 475° for 35 to 40 minutes or until a meat thermometer inserted into thickest portion registers 160°. Transfer to a serving platter.
• **Cook** whipping cream, sherry, and re-maining 1½ tablespoons pepper in a saucepan over low heat, stirring mixture constantly, until thoroughly heated; serve over pork and vegetables. **Yield:** 4 servings.

Charlie Risien
San Antonio, Texas

PEPPERED RIB-EYE ROAST

An assertive marinade infuses this roast with bold flavors.

Prep: 15 minutes
Chill: 8 hours
Bake: 2 hours, 15 minutes
Cook: 3 minutes

1 cup soy sauce
¾ cup red wine vinegar
1 tablespoon tomato paste
3 garlic cloves, minced
1 teaspoon paprika
½ cup assorted coarsely ground peppercorns
½ teaspoon ground cardamom
1 (5- to 6-pound) rib-eye roast, trimmed
¼ cup water
1½ tablespoons cornstarch
Sautéed sliced mushrooms (optional)

• **Stir** together first 5 ingredients.
• **Combine** peppercorns and ground cardamom; press into roast. Place roast in a shallow dish; pour marinade over roast. Cover and chill 8 hours, turning roast occasionally.
• **Remove** roast from marinade, reserv-ing 1 cup marinade. Wrap roast in alu-minum foil, sealing well; place in a shallow roasting pan.
• **Bake** at 300° for 2 hours or until done. Remove from oven; unwrap foil, and drain, reserving juices. Increase oven temperature to 350°; return roast to pan, and bake 15 minutes.
• **Combine** ¼ cup water and cornstarch in a saucepan, stirring until mixture is smooth. Stir in reserved juices and re-served 1 cup marinade.
• **Bring** to a boil over medium heat, stir-ring constantly; boil, stirring constantly, 1 minute. Stir in sautéed mushrooms, if desired. Serve with roast. **Yield:** 10 to 12 servings.

Sandra F. Alsup
Knoxville, Tennessee

Wedding Shower

When friends gather to honor a bride to be, bright flowers and delicious food are the order of the day. It's easy to host such a party with style and grace. Let ribbons and blossoms lead the way to easy-does-it entertaining.

Use tightly clustered bouquets of fresh flowers as both decorations and party favors, and serve our dainty Parmesan Cheese Bites—perfect for both an afternoon tea and a casual luncheon.

HOT RELISH

Prep: 1 hour, 5 minutes
Cook: 45 minutes

6 large red tomatoes
6 large green tomatoes
3 large onions
1 large red bell pepper
2 cups sugar
3 cups white vinegar (5% acidity)
⅓ cup black peppercorns, cracked
2 to 3 jalapeño peppers, finely chopped
2 tablespoons salt
1 tablespoon ground pepper

• **Chop** first 4 ingredients coarsely. Pulse in a food processor 2 or 3 times or until chopped; drain.
• **Combine** tomato mixture, sugar, and remaining ingredients in a saucepan; bring to a boil over medium-low heat, stirring constantly. Reduce heat, and simmer, stirring often, 45 minutes.
• **Pack** mixture into hot jars, filling to ½ inch from top. Remove air bubbles; wipe jar rims. Cover at once with metal lids, and screw on bands.
• **Process** in boiling-water bath 5 minutes. **Yield:** 10 (12-ounce) jars.
Nora Henshaw
Okemah, Oklahoma

PEPPERED CHEESE SPREAD

This spread boasts a combination of crunchy, sweet, and spicy peppercorns covering smooth cheese and a surprise ingredient—canned tomatoes.

Prep: 20 minutes
Chill: 8 hours

1 (14½-ounce) can whole tomatoes, well drained and chopped
1 (8-ounce) container soft cream cheese
2 cups (8 ounces) shredded sharp Cheddar cheese
½ cup butter or margarine, softened
1 small onion, finely chopped
2 garlic cloves, pressed
½ teaspoon salt
⅛ to ¼ teaspoon ground pepper
Coarsely cracked black, green, and pink peppercorns

• **Stir** together first 8 ingredients, and shape into a log. Roll in coarsely cracked peppercorns. Cover and chill 8 hours. Serve spread with crackers. **Yield:** 8 to 10 appetizer servings.
Pam Thornes
Cape Charles, Virginia

PARMESAN CHEESE BITES

Prep: 20 minutes
Chill: 8 hours
Bake: 15 minutes

1 cup all-purpose flour
⅔ cup grated Parmesan cheese
¼ teaspoon ground red pepper
½ cup butter or margarine, cut up
2 tablespoons milk

• **Pulse** first 4 ingredients in a food processor until blended.
• **Shape** dough into 2 (4-inch) logs. Wrap in plastic wrap, and place in an airtight container. Chill 8 hours. (Freeze up to 3 weeks, if desired; thaw in refrigerator overnight.)
• **Cut** dough into ¼-inch-thick slices, and place on a lightly greased baking sheet. Brush with milk.
• **Bake** at 350° for 12 to 15 minutes or until lightly browned. **Yield:** about 2½ dozen.

Note: Baked cheese bites can be frozen up to 3 weeks. Thaw at room temperature 2 hours before serving.

Sunday Spread

Homemade with love, fried chicken and pizza are a natural combination at this family's get-together.

Sunday afternoons in Helena, Arkansas, three generations of the St. Columbia family share an after-Mass Italian meal—with a few Southern accents. Joe and Joyce St. Columbia, their children, and their grandchildren agree that gathering around the table is family time, and nothing is more important. Joe and Joyce are third-generation Arkansans, but their Sicilian ancestry defines them.

"Our grandfathers came from the same village in Sicily—Cefalu," Joe says. He explains that many men from the village immigrated to this Delta town, lured by the promise of work and a hospitable climate. (While some traditionalists define the Delta as starting at Memphis and ending at Vicksburg, the state of Arkansas lists 27 of its counties as part of the region.) Joe and Joyce's families passed down deep traditions. "My father taught me that God comes first, and then family heritage," Joe says. "I strongly emphasized those values with my children."

Joyce focuses on another aspect of their Sicilian culture—great food. She turns out dishes learned from her grandmother, among them *pasta fritto* (cheese-stuffed fried pie) and homemade sausage. Growing up in Arkansas meant that Southern favorites also found their way into her repertoire. "My mother-in-law had a woman who cooked for her who taught me to make dishes like sweet potato pie and black-eyed peas," she says. "Cooking for family and friends is my way of showing love. When you watch them eating something you made and see the satisfaction on their faces, it fulfills everything. Even if you gave me a lot of money, I'd never be any happier than seeing people enjoy my food."

SICILIAN-STYLE CAPONATA

Serve this sweet-tart eggplant salad with rustic bread for an authentic Sicilian appetizer.

Prep: 25 minutes
Cook: 35 minutes
Cool: 1 hour

2 medium eggplants
½ cup olive oil
2 small onions, diced
3 tablespoons tomato sauce
2 celery ribs, diced
¼ cup capers
6 pitted green olives, chopped
6 pitted black olives, chopped
2 tablespoons sugar
2 tablespoons white vinegar
½ teaspoon salt
½ teaspoon pepper
Garnish: fresh oregano sprigs

• **Peel** and dice eggplants. Sauté in hot oil in a Dutch oven over medium-high heat 5 minutes; remove eggplant from pan, and set aside.
• **Add** onion to pan; sauté 5 minutes or until tender. Add tomato sauce and celery; cook 5 minutes or until celery is tender.
• **Return** eggplant to pan; stir in capers and next 6 ingredients. Reduce heat, and simmer, stirring often, 20 minutes. Let cool 1 hour. Garnish, if desired, and serve with rustic bread slices. **Yield:** 5 cups.

Note: Caponata may be stored in refrigerator up to 1 week.

ITALIAN TOMATO SALAD

Prep: 20 minutes
Chill: 8 hours

3 large tomatoes, chopped or sliced ∗
1 small purple onion, thinly sliced (optional)
1 tablespoon minced fresh basil
1 tablespoon minced fresh oregano
1 garlic clove, minced
¼ teaspoon salt
⅛ teaspoon pepper
3 tablespoons olive oil
3 tablespoons red wine vinegar
¼ cup crumbled Gorgonzola cheese
Garnish: croutons

• **Combine** tomato and, if desired, onion in a large bowl.
• **Combine** basil and next 6 ingredients; add to tomato mixture, tossing to coat. Sprinkle with cheese. Chill 8 hours. Garnish, if desired. **Yield:** 4½ cups.

∗ Substitute 6 plum tomatoes for 3 large tomatoes, if desired.

ITALIAN COTTAGE CHEESE

Prep: 15 minutes
Stand: 30 minutes
Chill: 8 hours

8 cups milk
½ cup whipping cream (optional)
2 cups buttermilk
½ teaspoon salt

• **Heat** milk and, if desired, whipping cream in a saucepan over medium heat to 190°. (Do not boil.) Add buttermilk, stirring until large curds form.
• **Line** a colander with several layers of cheesecloth or a coffee filter, and pour mixture into colander. Let stand 20 to 30 minutes to drain. Press cheese mixture slightly to remove remaining liquid.
• **Invert** cottage cheese onto a serving dish; sprinkle with salt. Cover and chill 8 hours. Serve with fresh fruit, if desired. **Yield:** 1½ cups.

SICILIAN PIZZA

Add your favorite toppings to suit your family's taste.

Prep: 30 minutes
Rise: 1 hour, 45 minutes
Bake: 35 minutes

4 cups all-purpose flour, divided
1 (¼-ounce) envelope active dry yeast
2½ teaspoons salt, divided
1½ cups warm water (100° to 110°)
2 tablespoons vegetable oil
1 small onion, chopped
1 garlic clove, minced
2 tablespoons olive oil
1 (14½-ounce) can diced tomatoes
1 (6-ounce) can tomato paste
½ teaspoon sugar
1½ teaspoons dried basil
1½ teaspoons dried oregano
½ teaspoon dried rosemary
⅛ teaspoon pepper
Toppings: chopped onion, green or red bell pepper rings, shredded mozzarella cheese, shredded Parmesan cheese, shredded fresh basil
Garnish: fresh rosemary sprigs

• **Combine** 2 cups flour, yeast, and 1½ teaspoons salt in a large mixing bowl; stir in 1½ cups warm water and vegetable oil.
• **Beat** at low speed with an electric mixer for 1 to 2 minutes, and beat at high speed 3 minutes. Gradually stir in enough remaining flour to make dough stiff.
• **Turn** dough out onto a well-floured surface, and knead until smooth and elastic (about 5 minutes). Place in a well-greased bowl, turning to grease top.
• **Cover** and let rise in a warm place (85°), free from drafts, 1 hour or until doubled in bulk.
• **Punch** dough down, and press onto a lightly greased 12-inch round pizza pan or into a 15- x 10-inch jellyroll pan.
• **Cover** and let rise in a warm place, free from drafts, 45 minutes or until doubled in bulk.
• **Sauté** onion and garlic in hot olive oil in a large skillet over medium-high heat until tender. Add remaining 1 teaspoon salt, tomatoes, and next 6 ingredients.

• **Bring** to a boil; cook, covered, over medium heat 10 minutes. Spoon sauce over dough.
• **Bake** at 475° for 20 minutes. Sprinkle evenly with desired toppings; bake 10 to 15 more minutes. Garnish, if desired. **Yield:** 1 (12-inch) round pizza.

Note: For thinner crust, divide dough in half; press onto 2 (12-inch) round pizza pans. Proceed with recipe as directed. Traditionally, Joyce makes this recipe in a rectangular shape.

PICNIC FRIED CHICKEN

Enjoy this picnic must-have hot or cold—it's the ideal finger food.

Prep: 20 minutes
Cook: 20 minutes per batch

2 (2-pound) whole chickens, cut up
2 cups milk
1 large egg
2 cups all-purpose flour
2 tablespoons salt
2 teaspoons pepper
3 cups shortening
2 teaspoons salt

• **Rinse** chicken with cold water; pat dry, and set aside.
• **Whisk** together milk and egg in a bowl. Combine flour, 2 tablespoons salt, and pepper in a heavy-duty zip-top plastic bag.
• **Dip** 2 chicken pieces in milk mixture. Place in plastic bag; seal and shake to coat. Remove chicken; repeat procedure with remaining pieces.
• **Melt** shortening in a Dutch oven over medium heat; heat to 350°. Fry chicken, in batches, 10 minutes on each side or until done and golden brown. Drain on paper towels. Sprinkle evenly with 2 teaspoons salt. **Yield:** 6 servings.

CASSATA

Prep: 20 minutes
Freeze: 10 hours
Stand: 30 minutes

½ gallon Neapolitan ice cream, slightly softened
1 (16-ounce) jar maraschino cherries
1 (15½-ounce) can crushed pineapple
1 cup chopped pecans, toasted
1 teaspoon vanilla extract
2 cups whipping cream, divided
2 tablespoons sugar, divided
Chocolate fudge sauce
Garnishes: whole cherries, chopped pecans

• **Spread** a ½-inch-thick layer of ice cream into bottom and up sides of a plastic wrap-lined 2-quart bowl. Cover and freeze 2 hours.
• **Drain** cherries and pineapple; chop cherries. Pat fruit dry with paper towels.
• **Combine** fruit, 1 cup pecans, and vanilla, tossing to coat.
• **Beat** 1 cup whipping cream and 1 tablespoon sugar at high speed with an electric mixer until stiff peaks form. Fold in fruit mixture, and spread evenly over ice cream layer. Cover and freeze 8 hours.
• **Remove** from freezer; let stand 20 minutes. Invert Cassata onto a cold serving dish, and let stand 10 more minutes.
• **Beat** remaining 1 cup whipping cream and remaining 1 tablespoon sugar until stiff peaks form. Drizzle Cassata with chocolate sauce; dollop with whipped cream. Garnish, if desired, and serve immediately. **Yield:** 8 servings.

Note: If preparing ahead, remove Cassata from bowl, and return to freezer until ready to serve. Let stand 30 minutes before serving. Top with chocolate sauce and whipped cream; garnish, if desired.

Doughnuts for Dad

Undecided about a gift for Dad?
Try a sweet treat that the whole family will enjoy.

Forget about the usual shirt and tie for Father's Day. Instead, surprise Dad with homemade doughnuts. Make this gift special by letting everyone join in.

Doughnuts are best served hot, but no matter how you present them, Dad will be all smiles after biting into these sugary delights.

RAISED DOUGHNUTS

Prep: 15 minutes
Stand: 50 minutes
Cook: 2 minutes per batch

1 cup warm water (100° to 110°)
1 (¼-ounce) envelope active dry yeast
3 tablespoons sugar
3 cups all-purpose flour
1 teaspoon salt
⅓ cup shortening, melted
1 large egg, lightly beaten
Vegetable oil
1 cup powdered sugar

• **Stir** together first 3 ingredients in a large glass bowl; let stand 5 minutes.
• **Stir** in flour and next 3 ingredients until blended.
• **Pat** or roll dough to ⅛-inch thickness; cut with a 2½-inch round cutter. Let stand 45 minutes.
• **Pour** oil to a depth of 2 inches into a Dutch oven; heat to 375°. Fry doughnuts, in batches, 1 minute on each side or until golden. Remove with a slotted spoon; drain on paper towels.
• **Roll** doughnuts in powdered sugar. **Yield:** 2 dozen.

Carrie E. Treichel
Johnson City, Tennessee

QUICK DOUGHNUTS AND DOUGHNUT HOLES

Prep: 5 minutes
Cook: 1 minute per batch

1 (11-ounce) can buttermilk biscuits
1 quart vegetable oil
1 cup sugar
1 tablespoon ground cinnamon
Chocolate Glaze (optional)

• **Separate** biscuits, and place them on a flat surface.
• **Cut** a hole from center of each biscuit with an apple corer, and reserve dough balls.
• **Pour** oil into a Dutch oven; heat to 350°. Fry doughnuts, in batches, 30 seconds on each side or until golden. Repeat procedure with dough balls. Remove with a slotted spoon, and drain on paper towels.
• **Combine** sugar and cinnamon. Roll doughnuts and doughnut holes evenly in sugar mixture, or, if desired, dip in Chocolate Glaze. **Yield:** 10 doughnuts and 10 doughnut holes.

A. L. Cook
Clinton, Maryland

Chocolate Glaze

Prep: 5 minutes

¼ cup half-and-half
1 cup semisweet chocolate morsels
½ cup powdered sugar

• **Microwave** half-and-half in a small glass bowl at HIGH 1 minute or until hot. Add chocolate morsels, stirring until smooth. Stir in powdered sugar. **Yield:** ¾ cup.

CINNAMON PUFFS

Prep: 5 minutes
Cook: 5 minutes per batch

3¼ cups vegetable oil, divided
½ cup sugar, divided
1 large egg
1¾ cups all-purpose flour
1 tablespoon baking powder
½ teaspoon salt
1 teaspoon ground nutmeg
¾ cup whipping cream
1 teaspoon ground cinnamon

• **Beat** ¼ cup oil, ¼ cup sugar, and egg in a large mixing bowl at medium speed with an electric mixer until blended.
• **Combine** flour and next 3 ingredients; add to sugar mixture alternately with whipping cream, beginning and ending with flour mixture. Beat at low speed until blended after each addition.
• **Pour** remaining 3 cups oil into a heavy saucepan; heat to 325° to 350°.
• **Drop** dough by tablespoonfuls into hot oil, and fry, in batches, 4 to 5 minutes or until golden. Remove with a slotted spoon; drain on paper towels.
• **Stir** together remaining ¼ cup sugar and cinnamon; sprinkle evenly over puffs. **Yield:** 3 dozen.

Jodie McCoy
Tulsa, Oklahoma

DOUGHNUT DETAILS

■ Use a deep-fat thermometer to make sure the oil temperature is correct. If the oil isn't hot enough, the doughnuts will be greasy; too hot, they'll burn.

■ Coat doughnuts with granulated sugar while warm. Dip in powdered sugar or glaze after cooling.

■ Place granulated sugar in a paper bag. Add 1 or 2 doughnuts at a time; shake gently.

Quick & Easy

*Prepare these snappy side dishes to savor
anytime with family and friends.*

Need something exciting to take to picnics, reunions, and church gatherings that is not only tasty but can also be made in advance? All of these recipes, except the baked beans, chill for several hours. The beans can be prepared a day ahead, covered, and refrigerated. After baking, wrap the container in newspaper to help retain the heat; then head outside to relish the gathering.

Pasta Salad

Prep: 35 minutes

1 pound uncooked fusille
¼ cup white wine vinegar
2 tablespoons chopped fresh parsley
1½ teaspoons dried Italian seasoning
1 teaspoon salt
½ teaspoon garlic powder
½ teaspoon pepper
¾ cup olive oil
1 cup grated Parmesan cheese
⅓ cup diced onion
1 (4-ounce) jar chopped pimiento,
   drained
1 (2¼-ounce) can sliced ripe olives,
   drained

• **Cook** pasta according to package directions; drain.
• **Whisk** together vinegar and next 5 ingredients in a large bowl. Add olive oil in a slow, steady stream, whisking constantly until blended. Add pasta, cheese, and remaining ingredients, tossing to coat. Serve immediately, or cover and chill 8 hours. **Yield:** 10 cups.

*Katrina Robinson
Birmingham, Alabama*

Marinated Veggies

*Prep: 30 minutes
Chill: 8 hours*

1 (15.5-ounce) can red kidney beans,
   rinsed and drained
1 (14-ounce) can artichoke hearts,
   drained and cut into fourths
1 (8-ounce) can cut green beans,
   rinsed and drained
1 (4.5-ounce) jar sliced mushrooms,
   drained
1 cup pitted ripe olives
3 celery ribs, sliced
½ onion, cut into rings
Dressing
¼ cup chopped fresh parsley
2 tablespoons capers

• **Combine** first 7 ingredients in a large bowl; add Dressing, tossing to coat. Cover and chill 8 hours. Sprinkle with parsley and capers just before serving. **Yield:** 6 cups.

Dressing

Prep: 5 minutes

½ cup olive oil
¼ cup tarragon vinegar
1 tablespoon fines herbes
1¼ teaspoons salt
1 teaspoon sugar
¼ teaspoon hot pepper sauce

• **Whisk** together all ingredients in a small bowl. **Yield:** ¾ cup.

*Gayle Millican
Rowlett, Texas*

Cucumber-and-Tomato Salad

*Make the most of bountiful summer
produce with this fresh salad.*

*Prep: 15 minutes
Chill: 3 hours*

2 cucumbers
1 large tomato
1 small green bell pepper
1 small purple onion
⅓ cup vegetable oil
3 tablespoons sugar
3 tablespoons red wine vinegar
¾ teaspoon salt
⅛ teaspoon pepper

• **Cut** cucumbers and tomato in half. Remove seeds. Chop cucumber, tomato, bell pepper, and onion.
• **Whisk** together oil and next 4 ingredients in a large bowl until sugar dissolves. Add cucumber mixture, tossing to coat. Cover and chill salad 3 hours. **Yield:** 2 cups.

*Nancy Matthews
Grayson, Georgia*

Baked Beans

*Prep: 10 minutes
Bake: 45 minutes*

4 bacon slices
1 (28-ounce) can pork and beans,
   drained
1 small onion, diced
¼ cup firmly packed brown sugar
¼ cup sorghum
¼ cup ketchup
1 teaspoon Worcestershire sauce
½ teaspoon dry mustard

• **Cook** bacon in a large skillet over medium-high heat 3 to 4 minutes.
• **Stir** together pork and beans and next 6 ingredients in a lightly greased 1-quart baking dish. Top mixture with bacon slices.
• **Bake** at 350° for 45 minutes. **Yield:** 4 to 6 servings.

*Carla Seagle Schneider
Virginia Beach, Virginia*

Friends, Food, Fun

A group of bridge-playing ladies share their recipes for all three.

About four times a year Betsy Shroat, Pat Hagedorn, Susie Sams, Ouida Hawkins, and Kathy Vanderbilt—also known as the Florida Five—gather for a few days of bridge playing, cooking, eating, and laughter. At the end of each visit, one receives the coveted title of "Bridge Queen" (crown and all).

The group began in Tampa, where they joined once a week to play bridge and to enjoy lunch prepared by that week's hostess. While most have moved away, they still converge for "Bridgefest."

We hope you enjoy this sampling of recipes from the Florida Five. Their motto is keep friendships, play bridge, eat good food, and enjoy life.

BALSAMIC PORK CHOPS

Prep: 5 minutes
Cook: 18 minutes

5 (½-inch-thick) boneless pork loin
   chops
1¼ teaspoons lemon-herb seasoning
2½ tablespoons all-purpose flour
1 tablespoon olive oil
⅔ cup balsamic vinegar
½ cup chicken broth

• **Sprinkle** pork evenly with seasoning and flour. Cook pork in hot oil in a skillet over medium-high heat 3 to 4 minutes on each side or until lightly browned. Remove from skillet; keep warm.
• **Add** vinegar and broth to skillet, stirring to loosen particles from bottom. Cook, stirring often, over medium-high heat 5 minutes or until slightly thickened. Spoon sauce over pork, and serve immediately. **Yield:** 5 servings.

Kathy Vanderbilt
Ponte Vedra Beach, Florida

CHILLED ROASTED PEPPER AND TOMATO SOUP

Turn up the heat on this cool soup by adding jalapeño peppers and using spicy vegetable juice.

Prep: 30 minutes

3 medium-size red bell peppers
2½ cups vegetable juice
2 garlic cloves, chopped
2 tablespoons vegetable oil
2 tablespoons cider vinegar
¼ teaspoon salt
¼ teaspoon freshly ground pepper
1 large avocado, chopped
1 cucumber, seeded and chopped
¼ purple onion, chopped
2 tablespoons chopped fresh cilantro
1 jalapeño pepper, seeded and minced
   (optional)
Lime wedges (optional)

• **Broil** peppers on an aluminum foil-lined baking sheet 5 inches from heat about 5 minutes on each side or until peppers look blistered.
• **Place** peppers in a heavy-duty zip-top plastic bag; seal and let stand 10 minutes to loosen skins. Peel peppers, and remove and discard seeds.
• **Process** peppers, vegetable juice, and next 5 ingredients in a blender or food processor until smooth; chill. Serve with avocado, next 3 ingredients, and, if desired, minced jalapeño and lime wedges. **Yield:** 4 cups.

Note: For testing purposes only, we used V-8 juice for vegetable juice.

Ouida Hawkins
Tampa, Florida

CHICKEN LINGUINE

Prep: 45 minutes
Bake: 30 minutes

8 ounces uncooked linguine
2 tablespoons light butter, divided
4 skinned and boned chicken breast
   halves
½ cup dry sherry
½ cup water
1 small onion, diced
1 (8-ounce) package fresh sliced
   mushrooms
⅔ cup all-purpose flour
2 cups fat-free chicken broth,
   divided
1 (8-ounce) container reduced-fat
   sour cream
1 cup (4 ounces) shredded reduced-fat
   Monterey Jack cheese
½ cup freshly grated Parmesan
   cheese, divided
½ teaspoon freshly ground pepper
½ cup fine, dry breadcrumbs

• **Cook** pasta according to package directions, omitting salt and fat. Set aside.
• **Melt** 1 tablespoon light butter in a large skillet over medium-high heat. Add chicken, and cook 2 minutes on each side or until lightly browned. Stir in sherry and ½ cup water. Cover, reduce heat to low, and simmer 20 minutes or until done. Drain, reserving liquid. Cut chicken into 1-inch pieces; set aside.
• **Melt** remaining 1 tablespoon light butter in skillet. Sauté onion and mushrooms over medium-high heat 5 minutes or until tender.
• **Stir** together flour and ½ cup broth. Add reserved liquid, flour mixture, and remaining 1½ cups broth to skillet. Cook, stirring often, over medium-high heat until thickened. Remove from heat. Stir in reserved pasta, reserved chicken, sour cream, Monterey Jack cheese, ¼ cup Parmesan, and pepper.
• **Spoon** mixture into a lightly greased 13- x 9-inch baking dish. Sprinkle with remaining ¼ cup Parmesan cheese and breadcrumbs.
• **Bake** at 350° for 30 minutes or until thoroughly heated. **Yield:** 8 servings.

Susie Sams
Punta Gorda, Florida

BOK CHOY SALAD

Prep: 15 minutes
Bake: 10 minutes

2 (3-ounce) packages ramen noodle
    soup mix
½ cup sunflower seeds
3 tablespoons slivered almonds, chopped
½ cup sugar
¼ cup olive oil
¼ cup cider vinegar
2 tablespoons soy sauce
1 bok choy, shredded
6 green onions, chopped

• **Remove** flavor packets from soup mix; reserve for another use.
• **Crumble** noodles. Combine noodles, sunflower seeds, and almonds. Spread on a 15- x 10-inch jellyroll pan.
• **Bake** at 350° for 8 to 10 minutes or until golden brown; set aside.
• **Bring** sugar and next 3 ingredients to a boil in a saucepan over medium heat. Remove from heat; cool.
• **Place** bok choy and green onions in a bowl. Drizzle with sugar mixture. Add noodle mixture, tossing well. Serve immediately. **Yield:** 6 to 8 servings.

Pat Hagedorn
Marco Island, Florida

FUDGE PIE
(pictured on page 155)

A scoop of vanilla ice cream and a drizzle of chocolate syrup make this moist and decadent pie irresistible.

Prep: 12 minutes
Bake: 40 minutes

¾ cup butter or margarine
3 (1-ounce) unsweetened chocolate
    squares
3 large eggs
1½ cups sugar
¾ cup all-purpose flour
1 teaspoon vanilla extract
¾ cup chopped pecans, toasted and
    divided
Toppings: vanilla ice cream and
    chocolate syrup

• **Cook** butter and chocolate in a small saucepan over low heat, stirring often until melted.
• **Beat** eggs at medium speed with an electric mixer 5 minutes. Gradually add sugar, beating until blended. Gradually add chocolate mixture, flour, and vanilla, beating until blended. Stir in ½ cup pecans.
• **Pour** mixture into a lightly greased 9-inch pieplate.
• **Bake** at 350° for 35 to 40 minutes or until center is firm. Cool. Top each serving with vanilla ice cream and chocolate syrup; sprinkle with remaining ¼ cup chopped pecans. **Yield:** 1 (9-inch) pie.

Betsy Shroat
Hartford, Connecticut

Up in Smoke

Assistant Foods Editor Kate Nicholson's husband, John, loves to be outside next to his smoker or grill. His many years of practice bring fabulous results. Smoked Turkey Breast received our Test Kitchens' highest marks, and his Smoked Boston Butt garnered our second highest rating.

SMOKED TURKEY BREAST

Prep: 10 minutes
Soak: 1 hour
Smoke: 6 hours

Hickory wood chunks
1 tablespoon salt
1 tablespoon garlic powder
1 tablespoon dried rosemary
1 tablespoon pepper
1 (5-pound) bone-in turkey breast

• **Soak** wood chunks in water 1 hour.
• **Combine** salt and next 3 ingredients; rub mixture over turkey breast.
• **Prepare** charcoal fire in smoker; let burn 15 to 20 minutes.
• **Drain** wood chunks, and place on coals. Place water pan in smoker; add water to depth of fill line. Place turkey in center of lower food rack.
• **Cook**, covered, 5 to 6 hours or until a meat thermometer inserted into thickest portion registers 170°, adding additional water to depth of fill line, if necessary. Remove from smoker, and let stand 10 minutes before slicing. **Yield:** 6 to 8 servings.

SMOKED BOSTON BUTT

To take the chill off the roast, John says to let it stand at room temperature for 30 minutes before cooking.

Prep: 15 minutes
Chill: 8 hours
Soak: 1 hour
Smoke: 8 hours

1 (10-ounce) bottle teriyaki sauce
1 cup honey
½ cup cider vinegar
2 tablespoons pepper
2 tablespoons garlic powder
1 teaspoon dried crushed red pepper
1 (6-pound) Boston butt pork roast
Hickory wood chunks

• **Combine** first 6 ingredients in a shallow dish or large heavy-duty zip-top plastic bag. Cut deep slits in roast using a paring knife; add roast to marinade. Cover or seal, and chill 8 hours, turning occasionally.
• **Soak** wood chunks in water 1 hour.
• **Prepare** charcoal fire in smoker; let burn 15 to 20 minutes.
• **Drain** wood chunks, and place on coals. Place water pan in smoker; add water to depth of fill line. Place roast in center of lower food rack.
• **Cook**, covered, 6 to 8 hours or until a meat thermometer inserted into thickest portion registers 165°, adding additional water, if necessary. Remove from smoker; cool slightly. Chop or shred; serve with barbecue sauce. **Yield:** 6 to 8 servings.

Top-Rated Menu

Weekend guests will want to return for another visit after they've been treated to this eye-opening breakfast. The "Cook's Notes" we've provided share make-ahead tips to give you a good start on a relaxing day.

Casual Breakfast Menu
Serves 6

Maple Coffee
Breakfast Casserole
Hot Tomato Grits
Grand Oranges
Blueberry-Streusel Muffins

MAPLE COFFEE

1997 Recipe Hall of Fame

Maple syrup lends a sweet note to your morning cup of coffee.

Prep: 10 minutes

2 cups half-and-half
¾ to 1 cup maple syrup
3 cups strong brewed coffee

• **Cook** half-and-half and maple syrup in a saucepan over medium heat until thoroughly heated. (Do not boil.) Stir in coffee. **Yield:** 6 cups.

Note: To lighten recipe, use fat-free half-and-half, and reduce maple syrup to ⅔ cup.

BREAKFAST CASSEROLE

1999 Recipe Hall of Fame

Spicy sausage, fluffy eggs, and melted cheese make this dish a family favorite.

Prep: 15 minutes
Chill: 8 hours
Stand: 35 minutes
Bake: 45 minutes

1 pound ground pork sausage ★
10 white sandwich bread slices, cubed (6 cups)
2 cups (8 ounces) shredded sharp Cheddar cheese
6 large eggs
2 cups milk
1 teaspoon salt
1 teaspoon dry mustard
¼ teaspoon Worcestershire sauce

• **Cook** sausage in a skillet over medium heat, stirring until it crumbles and is no longer pink; drain well.

• **Place** bread cubes in a lightly greased 13- x 9-inch baking dish; sprinkle bread evenly with cheese, and top with sausage.
• **Whisk** together eggs and remaining ingredients; pour evenly over sausage mixture. Cover and chill casserole for 8 hours. Let stand at room temperature 30 minutes.
• **Bake** at 350° for 45 minutes or until set. Let stand 5 minutes before serving. **Yield:** 6 to 8 servings.

★ Substitute 2 cups cubed cooked ham for sausage, if desired.

HOT TOMATO GRITS

1995 Recipe Hall of Fame

Prep: 10 minutes
Cook: 30 minutes
Stand: 5 minutes

2 bacon slices, chopped
2 (14½-ounce) cans chicken broth
½ teaspoon salt
1 cup quick-cooking grits
2 large tomatoes, peeled and chopped
2 tablespoons canned chopped green chiles
1 cup (4 ounces) shredded Cheddar cheese

• **Cook** bacon in a heavy saucepan until crisp, reserving drippings in pan. Gradually add broth and salt; bring to a boil.
• **Stir** in grits, tomato, and chiles; return to a boil, stirring often. Reduce heat; simmer, stirring often, 15 to 20 minutes.
• **Stir** in cheese; cover and let stand 5 minutes or until cheese melts. **Yield:** 6 servings.

Note: To decrease fat and calories, drain bacon on paper towels, discarding drippings; substitute reduced-fat sharp Cheddar cheese for regular.

GRAND ORANGES

1993 Recipe Hall of Fame

A jar of marmalade and a splash of liqueur transform orange sections into an elegant fruit dish.

Prep: 35 minutes
Chill: 8 hours

½   cup sugar
1   (12-ounce) jar orange marmalade
¼   cup orange liqueur
16   large navel oranges, peeled and
        sectioned
Garnish: orange rind strips

• **Cook** sugar and orange marmalade in a small saucepan over medium heat until sugar dissolves; allow mixture to cool slightly.
• **Stir** together sugar mixture, orange liqueur, and orange sections. Cover and chill 8 hours. Garnish, if desired. **Yield:** 6 servings.

COOK'S NOTES

Up to one month before:
Prepare muffins, and freeze.

The day before:
Prepare oranges, and chill.
Thaw muffins. Prepare casserole, and chill.

1½ hours before:
Let breakfast casserole stand at room temperature 30 minutes.

45 minutes before:
Bake breakfast casserole.
Prepare grits. Heat muffins.
Prepare coffee.

BLUEBERRY-STREUSEL MUFFINS

1996 Recipe Hall of Fame

These tender muffins are studded with plump blueberries and topped with a buttery almond streusel.

Prep: 15 minutes
Bake: 20 minutes

¼   cup slivered almonds
¼   cup firmly packed brown sugar
3   tablespoons all-purpose flour,
        divided
2   tablespoons butter or margarine
½   cup uncooked regular oats
2   cups all-purpose flour
½   cup sugar
2   teaspoons baking powder
¼   teaspoon baking soda
¼   teaspoon salt
2   teaspoons grated lemon rind
¾   cup buttermilk
¼   cup vegetable oil
1   large egg
1½   cups fresh or frozen
        blueberries

• **Pulse** almonds 2 or 3 times in a blender or food processor until chopped. Add brown sugar and 1 tablespoon flour; process 5 seconds. Add butter; pulse 5 or 6 times or until mixture is crumbly. Stir in oats; set aside.
• **Combine** 2 cups flour and next 5 ingredients in a large bowl; make a well in center of mixture.
• **Whisk** together buttermilk, oil, and egg; add to flour mixture, stirring just until moistened.
• **Toss** blueberries with remaining 2 tablespoons flour, and gently fold into batter. Spoon batter into greased muffin pans, filling two-thirds full; sprinkle batter with oat mixture.
• **Bake** at 400° for 15 to 20 minutes or until golden brown. Remove immediately from pans, and cool on wire racks. **Yield:** 1 dozen.

Note: Freeze muffins up to 1 month.

Pound Cake

Scented geraniums may be the ultimate plant for all seasons. With dainty flowers and fragrant, lovely leaves, these sturdy plants grace the garden in summer, then move willingly indoors for winter. A word of caution—once you have one, you'll be hooked on all the perfumed possibilities.

Use lemon geranium leaves to add a hint of lemon to this classic recipe.

LEMON GERANIUM POUND CAKE

Prep: 25 minutes
Bake: 1 hour, 20 minutes

4   to 6 large fresh lemon geranium
        leaves
Vegetable oil
1   cup butter or margarine,
        softened
3   cups sugar
6   large eggs
3   cups all-purpose flour
½   teaspoon salt
¼   teaspoon baking soda
1   (8-ounce) container sour cream
2   teaspoons vanilla extract
Garnish: fresh lemon geranium leaves

• **Brush** both sides of leaves with oil. Arrange leaves, dull side up, around the sides of a greased and floured 10-inch tube pan; set aside.
• **Beat** butter at medium speed with an electric mixer until creamy; gradually add sugar, beating well. Add eggs, 1 at a time, beating until blended after each.
• **Combine** flour, salt, and baking soda; add to butter mixture alternately with sour cream, beginning and ending with flour mixture. Beat at low speed until blended after each addition. Stir in vanilla. Spoon batter into prepared pan.
• **Bake** at 325° for 1 hour and 20 minutes or until a wooden pick inserted in center comes out clean. Cool in pan on a wire rack 15 minutes. Remove cake from pan. Garnish, if desired. **Yield:** 1 (10-inch) cake.

Living Light

Let fresh fruits and vegetables play the starring role at breakfast, lunch, and supper.

This month we're challenging you to make an important commitment—to eat five servings of fruits and vegetables a day. Although many of us are familiar with their pivotal role in maintaining a healthy weight and heart as well as in preventing various types of cancer, some of us aren't eating enough of them. The good news is that a serving is smaller than you think.

A great way to fit in your five a day is by eating fruits or veggies at every meal and snack. Enjoy this great mix of recipes that shine thanks to fabulous produce.

ROASTED BROCCOLI AND CAULIFLOWER

Prep: 10 minutes
Bake: 25 minutes

2 cups broccoli flowerets
2 cups cauliflower flowerets
5 garlic cloves, peeled and halved
1 tablespoon olive oil
1 teaspoon salt
½ teaspoon freshly ground pepper
1 tablespoon grated Parmesan cheese

• **Place** first 3 ingredients in a baking pan. Drizzle with oil, and toss.
• **Bake** at 450°, stirring occasionally, 20 to 25 minutes or until lightly browned. Sprinkle with salt, pepper, and cheese, tossing to coat. **Yield:** 4 servings.

Nora Henshaw
Okemah, Oklahoma

♥ Per serving: Calories 67 (57% from fat)
Fat 4.2g (sat 0.8g, mono 2.9g, poly 0.5g)
Protein 3g Carb 6g Fiber 2.4g
Chol 1.2mg Iron 0.7mg
Sodium 636mg Calc 58mg

VEGETABLE KABOBS

Prep: 45 minutes
Stand: 1 hour
Grill: 17 minutes

2 (8-ounce) cans tomato sauce
2 tablespoons olive oil
4 garlic cloves, minced
1 tablespoon chopped fresh or dried rosemary
1 teaspoon sugar
½ teaspoon salt
½ teaspoon freshly ground pepper
1 small eggplant
1 red bell pepper
1 green bell pepper
1 large onion
2 zucchini
2 yellow squash
1 (8-ounce) package whole fresh mushrooms

• **Stir** together first 7 ingredients in a 13- x 9-inch baking dish; set aside.
• **Cut** eggplant into 1-inch cubes. Cut bell peppers into 1½-inch pieces. Cut onion into 8 wedges. Cut zucchini and yellow squash into ½-inch-thick slices.
• **Thread** vegetables onto 6 (10-inch) skewers; place in sauce mixture, turning to coat. Cover and let stand 1 hour.
• **Remove** kabobs from marinade, reserving marinade.
• **Grill,** covered with grill lid, over medium heat (300° to 350°) 12 to 17 minutes; turn occasionally and baste with reserved marinade. **Yield:** 4 main-dish servings.

♥ Per serving: Calories 223 (31% from fat)
Fat 7.7g (sat 1g, mono 5g, poly 0.9g)
Protein 8g Carb 36g Fiber 10.8g
Chol 0mg Iron 6.4mg
Sodium 878mg Calc 95mg

VEGGIE BREAD BOWL

Poppy seed rolls filled with fresh vegetables and feta cheese make a hearty brunch dish.

Prep: 15 minutes
Cook: 12 minutes

4 poppy seed crusty rolls (about 1.7 ounces each)
1 small sweet onion, chopped
1 small zucchini, chopped
½ medium-size red bell pepper, chopped
½ cup chopped fresh mushrooms
½ teaspoon freshly ground pepper
Butter-flavored cooking spray
2 cups egg substitute
3 ounces fat-free cream cheese, diced
½ cup (2 ounces) crumbled reduced-fat feta cheese
1 to 2 teaspoons minced fresh dill (optional)

• **Cut** off tops of rolls, reserving tops. Hollow out rolls, leaving a ¼-inch shell in each.
• **Sauté** onion and next 4 ingredients in a large skillet coated with cooking spray over medium-high heat 5 to 7 minutes or until tender. Remove from pan; set aside.
• **Heat** skillet coated with cooking spray over medium heat; add egg substitute and cream cheese. Cook, without stirring, until eggs begin to set on bottom.
• **Draw** a spatula across bottom of skillet to form large curds. Continue cooking until eggs are thickened and moist (do not stir constantly). Remove from heat.
• **Spoon** evenly into rolls. Top evenly with onion mixture and feta cheese. Sprinkle with dill, if desired. Replace tops of rolls. Serve with sliced cantaloupe, if desired. **Yield:** 4 servings.

♥ Per serving: Calories 284 (17% from fat)
Fat 5.4g (sat 1.3g) Protein 24g
Carb 34g Fiber 1.3g
Chol 9mg Iron 4.9mg
Sodium 822mg Calc 157mg

Avocado Citrus Salad

Prep: 30 minutes

3 tablespoons cider vinegar
2 tablespoons vegetable oil
1 tablespoon sugar
¼ teaspoon salt
8 cups torn salad greens
2 oranges, peeled and sectioned
1 large grapefruit, peeled and sectioned
1 pear, peeled and thinly sliced
2 ripe avocados, peeled and sliced
1 cup seedless green grapes
2 tablespoons chopped walnuts, toasted (optional)

• **Whisk** together first 4 ingredients.
• **Place** greens in a large bowl. Add orange sections and next 4 ingredients. Drizzle with dressing, tossing gently to coat. Sprinkle with walnuts, if desired. Serve immediately. **Yield:** 6 servings.

Ellie Wells
Lakeland, Florida

❤ Per serving: Calories 355 (35% from fat)
Fat 14g (sat 2g, mono 7.6g, poly 3g)
Protein 4g Carb 34g Fiber 11g
Chol 0mg Iron 1.5mg
Sodium 109mg Calc 71mg

Yummy Breakfast Drink

Prep: 10 minutes

1 medium banana, sliced and frozen
1 cup strawberries, halved and frozen
¼ cup orange juice concentrate, undiluted
1½ cups fat-free milk
¼ teaspoon almond extract

• **Process** all ingredients in a blender until smooth, stopping to scrape down sides. Serve immediately. **Yield:** 3 cups.

Suzan L. Wiener
Spring Hill, Florida

❤ Per cup: Calories 136 (3% from fat)
Fat 0.4g (sat 0g, poly 0.1g)
Protein 5.8g Carb 28g Fiber 2.3g
Chol 2.5mg Iron 0.4mg
Sodium 67mg Calc 167mg

SMART BITES

What's a serving?
■ 1 cup raw leafy vegetables (lettuce, spinach, greens)

■ ½ cup cooked vegetables (green beans, squash, turnips)

■ ½ cup cooked dry beans or peas (lentils, black-eyed peas, pinto beans)

■ 1 medium piece of fruit (apple, banana, pear, orange)

■ 1 cup fresh fruit (cantaloupe, strawberries, grapes) or ½ cup canned fruit (pineapple, peaches)

■ ¾ cup (6 ounces) 100% fruit or vegetable juice (pineapple juice, orange juice, vegetable juice cocktail)

■ ¼ cup dried fruit (raisins, dried plums, mixed dried fruit)

How can I get in five servings a day?
■ Drink a glass of 100% fruit or vegetable juice with breakfast, after a workout, or instead of a soft drink with lunch or supper.

■ Add veggies such as bell peppers, mushrooms, celery, carrots, and a variety of beans to create a satisfying chili.

■ Prepare fruit salad on the weekend to enjoy for several days (add apples, pears, or bananas just before eating). Offer your kids fresh fruit salad in a fun bowl or cup instead of cookies. Be a good role model. If they see you enjoying sweet, fresh fruit, they will too. What's not to love?

■ Treat your family to a colorful macaroni and cheese by adding frozen vegetable medleys such as a broccoli, carrot, and cauliflower mixture. Add to boiling pasta during the last three to five minutes of cooking. Drain and add remaining ingredients. It's a great way to disguise vegetables in a favorite dish.

■ Process one fresh fruit in the blender (mango, blueberries, raspberries, or blueberries); put puree in a squeeze bottle, and let your kids paint on dessert plates or use to decorate pancakes, waffles, angel food cake, or peanut butter toast. They will never guess it's good for them.

■ Combine prewashed salad greens with crunchy broccoli slaw mix for a quick and terrific salad. Jazz it up with presliced mushrooms, grape or cherry tomatoes, canned baby corn, and sliced water chestnuts. Serve with a tangy vinaigrette. Best of all, there's no chopping.

■ Kids can become fruit and veggie advocates when they are part of a project. Let them sprinkle raisins or berries in their yogurt or ice cream. Have them place a variety of vegetables on skewers, and teach them how to season and grill them (supervised, of course).

■ For more great tips on reaching your five a day, visit www.5aday.com. Also check out www.aboutproduce.com for an excellent resource on fruits and vegetables.

Spicy Bites

A dash of Tex-Mex flavor creates
bold beginnings for fun-filled gatherings.

Give your next fiesta a lively start with our tasty beyond-the-border-inspired appetizers. These fuss-free recipes guarantee casual entertaining with ease. You'll spend less time in the kitchen with the help of convenience items, such as pre-seasoned chicken strips and won ton wrappers. You can even fill and freeze our Taco Teasers ahead, and then fry them just before serving.

And if things get a little too fiery, cool off with a tall glass of limeade, or, if you prefer, a refreshing margarita or cold Mexican beer.

SHRIMP-AND-CHEESE APPETIZER

Prep: 15 minutes

¼ pound unpeeled, medium-size fresh shrimp, cooked
¾ to 1 cup salsa
2 teaspoons chopped fresh cilantro
1 (8-ounce) package cream cheese, softened
1 green onion, chopped
Tortilla chips

• **Peel** shrimp, and devein, if desired; chop shrimp.
• **Stir** together salsa and cilantro; spoon mixture over cream cheese. Top with shrimp, and sprinkle with green onion. Serve with tortilla chips. **Yield:** 4 to 6 appetizer servings.

Note: You can purchase cooked, peeled shrimp from the seafood department of your supermarket.

TACO TEASERS

Serve these appetizers with your favorite salsa and sour cream, or try them with spicy Tex-Mex Mayonnaise.

Prep: 40 minutes
Cook: 35 minutes

1 pound ground beef
1 small onion, chopped
¼ cup chopped green bell pepper
¼ cup water
1 (1¼-ounce) envelope taco seasoning mix
1 cup (4 ounces) shredded Monterey Jack or Cheddar cheese
40 won ton wrappers
Vegetable oil

• **Cook** first 3 ingredients in a large nonstick skillet, stirring until beef crumbles and is no longer pink. Drain and return beef mixture to skillet. Add ¼ cup water and taco seasoning.
• **Simmer** 3 to 4 minutes or until liquid evaporates. Remove from heat, and stir in cheese.
• **Spoon** 1 level tablespoon of mixture onto center of each won ton wrapper.
• **Moisten** won ton wrapper edges with water. Bring corners together, pressing to seal.
• **Pour** oil to a depth of 2 inches into a Dutch oven; heat to 365°. Fry filled won tons, in batches, 2 minutes on each side or until golden. Drain on wire racks over paper towels. **Yield:** 40 appetizer servings.

Note: Store uncooked appetizers in an airtight container in freezer up to 1 month. Fry, unthawed, in hot oil 2½ minutes on each side or until golden.

Donna Nystrom
Boulder, Wyoming

SPICY CASHEWS

Prep: 5 minutes
Cook: 5 minutes

¼ cup butter or margarine
¼ cup vegetable oil
2 (7-ounce) jars dry-roasted cashews
½ teaspoon salt
¼ to ½ teaspoon ground red pepper
½ teaspoon chili powder

• **Melt** butter with oil in a large skillet over medium heat; add cashews, and cook 3 to 5 minutes or until browned. Remove cashews, and drain on paper towels; place in a bowl.
• **Combine** salt, ground red pepper, and chili powder in a small bowl. Sprinkle over warm cashews, tossing to coat. **Yield:** 3 cups.

Jean Voan
Shepherd, Texas

TEX-MEX MAYONNAISE

A dollop of this mayonnaise adds zesty flavor to sandwiches, raw vegetables, or even grilled burgers.

Prep: 15 minutes
Chill: 3 hours

1 cup mayonnaise
2 tablespoons ketchup
2 tablespoons lime juice
2 tablespoons milk
2 to 3 teaspoons chili powder
1 teaspoon ground red pepper
½ teaspoon onion powder
½ teaspoon garlic powder
½ teaspoon hot sauce
½ teaspoon Worcestershire sauce
¼ teaspoon lemon pepper

• **Combine** all ingredients in a bowl. Cover and chill at least 3 hours. **Yield:** 1¼ cups.

Anne Stokes-Krusen
Nashville, Tennessee

SOUTHWESTERN ROLLUPS

For neater slices, avoid overfilling the tortillas, and roll tightly. Before serving, cut the rollups on the diagonal.

Prep: 25 minutes
Cook: 7 minutes
Chill: 30 minutes

1 (10-ounce) package frozen chopped spinach, thawed
1 (1-ounce) envelope fajita seasoning mix
½ cup chicken broth or water
3 (6-ounce) packages refrigerated Southwestern-flavored chicken breast strips, chopped
1 (15-ounce) can black beans, rinsed and drained
1 (11-ounce) can yellow corn with red and green bell peppers, drained
2 cups (8 ounces) shredded Monterey Jack cheese with peppers
6 (10-inch) flour tortillas
Salsa

• **Combine** spinach and fajita seasoning in a large nonstick skillet; add broth. Cook over medium heat, stirring often, 5 minutes. Stir in chicken and next 3 ingredients; simmer until cheese melts.
• **Spread** 1 cup chicken mixture on 1 side of each tortilla, leaving a ½-inch border around edges.
• **Roll** up tortillas tightly, and wrap in plastic wrap. Chill 30 minutes.
• **Unwrap** rollups, and cut into slices. Serve with salsa. **Yield:** 8 to 10 appetizer servings.

Note: For testing purposes only, we used refrigerated Louis Rich Carving Board Southwestern-flavored Chicken Breast Strips.

Terri Groover
Augusta, Georgia

Taste of the South

Members of our Foods staff have a tough time arriving at a consensus when it comes to the Southern delicacy of fried catfish. These words seem to evoke a flood of personal memories.

In searching for the perfect fried catfish recipe, we tried a variety of techniques, from soaking catfish overnight to combining the best ingredients from several different recipes. The more we sampled, the more we realized that it's hard not to go back to what you know or grew up eating.

Ed Scott, a retired catfish farmer from Drew, Mississippi, recalls that the rise of farm-raised catfish helped save the Delta during the decline of farming in the 1970s. Now available year-round at grocery seafood counters and in the freezer section, farm-raised catfish delivers a mild flavor and a firm texture that's perfect for anything from panfrying to grilling. Our Test Kitchens found 4- to 6-ounce, thin-cut fillets easy to manage in the skillet, and they curl up when cooked, giving great eye appeal. It's enough to make your mouth water in anticipation of that first bite. (If you purchase frozen fillets, place them in a colander with a pan underneath, and thaw in the refrigerator overnight; otherwise, keep them in the coldest part of your refrigerator, and use within two days.)

Still, all opinions aside, when we whipped up our Classic Fried Catfish recipe, it didn't stay on the table long. We relished it hot from the skillet and even continued munching at room temperature till only crumbs remained. And what made it so popular? Test Kitchens staffer Lyda Jones had the answer. "The cornmeal offers a crunchy texture without a greasy taste." With a recipe this easy, how can you not prepare it? Enhance these crispy fillets with your favorite side dishes. Our choice for sides included hush puppies, baked beans, and coleslaw. As for condiments, Ed Scott says, "The number one item for catfish is hot sauce." For us, though, a dab of ketchup and tartar sauce and a squeeze of lemon were also high on the list.

CLASSIC FRIED CATFISH

Prep: 15 minutes
Cook: 6 minutes per batch

¾ cup yellow cornmeal
¼ cup all-purpose flour
2 teaspoons salt
1 teaspoon ground red pepper
¼ teaspoon garlic powder
6 (4- to 6-ounce) farm-raised catfish fillets
¼ teaspoon salt
Vegetable oil

• **Combine** first 5 ingredients in a large shallow dish. Sprinkle fish with ¼ teaspoon salt; dredge in cornmeal mixture, coating evenly.
• **Pour** oil to a depth of 1½ inches into a deep cast-iron skillet; heat to 350°. Fry fish, in batches, 5 to 6 minutes or until golden; drain on paper towels. **Yield:** 6 servings.

LYDA'S FRYING TIPS

■ Remove excess moisture from fish before dredging.
■ Keep one hand clean for dredging and the other hand available for frying.
■ Use a large Dutch oven or deep cast-iron skillet to keep the hot oil from popping out.
■ Don't overcrowd the skillet; fry, in batches, two fillets at a time. Bring remaining oil back to the proper temperature before frying the next batch.
■ Remove fish from skillet with a wide, slotted, curved spoon.
■ To keep warm, place fried fish on a wire rack with an aluminum foil-lined pan underneath; place in a 250° oven. For a crisp texture, do not cover fillets.
■ For more information, visit the catfish Web site at www.catfishinstitute.com.

What's for Supper?

Ground beef comes to the dinner bell's rescue.

Easy to prepare, quick to cook, and economical to use—these are just some of the advantages of ground beef. It also tastes great, and its versatility provides a variety of menu options.

Another plus is you can keep ground beef on hand. Refrigerate uncooked ground beef up to two days, or freeze in the original packaging up to two weeks. Shape into individual patties or flatten into a 1-inch-thick layer for quicker freezing and thawing. To store, wrap in aluminum foil, plastic wrap, or freezer paper; freeze up to three months. If you don't like squishing the meat with your hands, put the ingredients in a large zip-top plastic bag; seal bag, and then squeeze the mixture until well blended.

For these recipes, use the type of ground beef that fits your budget.

GARDEN HERB BURGERS

Brush potato wedges with a flavored oil before grilling with burgers.

Prep: 15 minutes
Grill: 12 minutes

1 pound ground beef
3 tablespoons chopped fresh parsley
2 tablespoons chopped fresh chives
1 tablespoon chopped fresh basil
1 garlic clove, minced
1 teaspoon salt
1 teaspoon chopped fresh oregano
½ teaspoon chopped fresh or dried rosemary
½ teaspoon pepper
Toppings: lettuce, yellow tomato slices, purple onion slices
4 large crusty French rolls, split
Grilled potato wedges

• **Combine** first 9 ingredients; shape into 4 patties.

• **Grill,** covered with grill lid, over medium-high heat (350° to 400°) 5 to 6 minutes on each side or until beef is no longer pink. Place desired toppings on bottom half of rolls; add patties and roll tops. Serve with potato wedges. **Yield:** 4 burgers.

Amy Parmar
Virginia Beach, Virginia

BARBECUE BEEF SANDWICHES

This is a great way to stretch a pound of ground beef. Serve with coleslaw, corn on the cob, and plenty of napkins.

Prep: 10 minutes
Cook: 16 minutes

1 pound ground beef
1 medium onion, chopped
1 (12-ounce) bottle chili sauce
1 cup ketchup
1 tablespoon sugar
1 tablespoon dry mustard
1 tablespoon prepared mustard
1 tablespoon Worcestershire sauce
1 tablespoon white vinegar
1 teaspoon celery seeds
8 hamburger buns

• **Cook** beef and onion in a large skillet over medium-high heat 5 to 6 minutes, stirring until meat crumbles and is no longer pink. Drain and return to skillet.
• **Stir** in chili sauce and next 7 ingredients; cook over medium-high heat, stirring often, 8 to 10 minutes. Serve on buns. **Yield:** 8 servings.

Sherrie Ziegler-Phillips
Hampstead, Maryland

MARMALADE-GLAZED BEEF PATTIES

Add sautéed squash medley and rolls to round out this entrée.

Prep: 10 minutes
Broil: 22 minutes

1 pound ground beef
1 large egg
½ cup fine, dry breadcrumbs
2 tablespoons prepared horseradish
½ teaspoon salt
1 (8-ounce) can water chestnuts, drained and diced
⅔ cup orange marmalade
½ cup water
⅓ cup soy sauce
2 tablespoons lemon juice
1 garlic clove, pressed
Hot cooked rice

• **Combine** first 6 ingredients; shape into 4 patties.
• **Cook** patties in a large nonstick skillet over medium-high heat 2 minutes on each side or until browned; remove from skillet.
• **Add** orange marmalade and next 4 ingredients to skillet. Bring to a boil over medium heat; cook, stirring constantly, 6 minutes. Add patties; reduce heat to low, and simmer 10 minutes. Serve over rice. **Yield:** 4 servings.

Marmalade-Glazed Meatballs: Shape beef mixture into 1-inch balls; place on a rack in a broiler pan, and broil 5½ inches from heat 5 minutes or until no longer pink. Place in a chafing dish. Bring marmalade and next 4 ingredients to a boil in a saucepan over medium heat; cook, stirring constantly, 6 minutes. Pour over meatballs. **Yield:** about 3½ dozen.

Clarissa McConnell
Orlando, Florida

Perk It Up With Pimientos

A familiar jar of pimientos gives these recipes a burst of color and flavor.

Look in anyone's refrigerator door, and you're likely to find a little jar of pimientos. While we often associate them with Cheddar cheese, don't stop there with these mild red peppers (similar in taste to sweet red bell peppers). Add them to pasta recipes, salsas, and even pot roast. Sprinkle the peppers into omelets, cornbread batter, burgers, meat loaf, and bean salads. If you enjoy the subtle, sweet flavor of pimientos, try these pleasing recipes.

PEPPERED PIMIENTO CHEESE

Prep: 10 minutes
Chill: 8 hours

½ (8-ounce) package cream cheese, softened*
¼ cup mayonnaise*
1 garlic clove, minced
1 teaspoon sweet pickle relish, drained
2 cups (8 ounces) shredded sharp Cheddar cheese*
1 (4-ounce) jar diced pimiento, drained
½ (4.5-ounce) can chopped green chiles
¼ cup chopped pecans, toasted

• **Beat** first 4 ingredients until smooth. Stir in Cheddar cheese and remaining ingredients. Cover; chill up to 8 hours. Serve with crackers. **Yield:** 2¼ cups.

*Substitute reduced-fat cream cheese, light mayonnaise, and reduced-fat sharp Cheddar cheese, if desired.

Alma Carey
Sarasota, Florida

ZUCCHINI-AND-CORN SKILLET

Fresh basil brightens the flavors in this colorful dish.

Prep: 10 minutes
Cook: 10 minutes

3 small zucchini
1 tablespoon butter or margarine
1 tablespoon vegetable oil
1 to 2 garlic cloves, minced
1 (15½-ounce) can whole kernel corn, drained*
1 (2-ounce) jar diced pimiento, drained
1 teaspoon salt
¾ teaspoon lemon pepper
½ cup (2 ounces) shredded mozzarella cheese
2 tablespoons chopped fresh basil

• **Cut** each zucchini lengthwise into quarters. Thinly slice quarters.
• **Melt** butter with vegetable oil in a large skillet over medium-high heat; add zucchini and garlic, and sauté 3 to 4 minutes.
• **Add** corn and next 3 ingredients; cook, stirring often, 2 to 3 minutes or until zucchini is tender. Sprinkle with cheese and basil; heat until cheese melts. **Yield:** 6 servings.

*Substitute 2 cups fresh corn kernels (about 4 ears), if desired.

Lilann Hunter Taylor
Savannah, Georgia

CREAMY PORK CHOPS WITH MUSHROOMS

Fresh vegetables and a can of soup enhance these saucy chops.

Prep: 20 minutes
Cook: 1 hour

6 to 8 (½-inch-thick) boneless pork loin chops
½ teaspoon salt
1½ teaspoons lemon pepper
¼ cup all-purpose flour
2 tablespoons olive oil
1 cup sliced fresh mushrooms
½ small green bell pepper, diced
1 (10¾-ounce) can cream of mushroom soup, undiluted
1 (4-ounce) jar diced pimiento, undrained
Hot cooked rice (optional)

• **Sprinkle** pork chops evenly with salt and lemon pepper; dredge in flour.
• **Cook** pork in hot oil in a large skillet over medium-high heat 2 to 3 minutes on each side or until browned. Remove pork, and drain on paper towels, reserving drippings in skillet.
• **Add** sliced mushrooms and bell pepper to skillet, and sauté over medium heat 5 minutes or until tender. Return pork to skillet; spoon soup over pork, and sprinkle with pimiento. Reduce heat to low. Cook, covered, 45 minutes to 1 hour or until pork is tender. Serve with hot cooked rice, if desired. **Yield:** 6 servings.

From Our Kitchen

Tips and Tidbits

■ It's National Dairy Month and a good time to take advantage of the products in the ever-expanding dairy case. Many varieties of shredded cheese combinations make it easy to add flavor to steamed vegetables, grits, or mashed potatoes. To soothe burning taste buds after eating spicy foods, drink milk instead of water. A spoonful of sour cream has the same cooling effect.

■ It's not necessary to peel away the outside rinds of cheeses such as Brie—they're edible. However, you will need to remove and discard the *waxed* covering from cheeses such as Gouda and Edam.

■ When a recipe calls for brandy, good substitutes are apple cider, peach syrup, or apricot syrup.

■ White grape juice or ginger ale works well to replace white wine in many recipes.

Safety Reminders for Transporting Food

■ Store perishables in refrigerator or iced-down cooler. Food that must be chilled should not be out longer than 2 hours.

■ Store hot items wrapped in foil and then newspaper in a separate cooler from cold items. These should not be out at room temperature longer than 2 hours.

■ Plastic bags and containers with lids that seal are great for storing food.

■ Place your cooler in the shade, and keep the lid closed to maintain low temperatures.

■ Travel with your cooler inside the car rather than packing it in the hot trunk.

Super Salt

With a shake, sprinkle, or pinch of salt, food flavors come to life. But before you reach for the salt, you have some choices to make. Do you want iodized or plain, sea or kosher? No matter which is your favorite or how you choose to store and measure it, salt is an indispensable pantry staple.

■ Sea salt is evaporated from sea water. It is sometimes called *sel gris* or gray salt because of its color, and it comes in small and large grains.

■ Coarse salt stays in place and doesn't melt fast, which makes it terrific to sprinkle on pretzels, corn on the cob, and bread loaves (just before baking).

■ Kosher salt is free of additives, and its large, irregular crystals taste about half as salty as regular table salt. Assistant Foods Editor Cybil Brown cooks with kosher salt. "I think the flavor is better," she says, "and that makes the foods taste richer.

Iodized salt seems to have a slower reaction time with foods, making it easy for me to oversalt a recipe."

■ Table salt, a ground and refined rock salt, is available with or without added iodine. Salt is iodized to combat iodine deficiency, which can cause serious health problems and developmental delays.

■ Rock salt (not as refined as the others) looks like large, dull-gray, irregular-size crystals. It's not usually eaten; use rock salt to freeze ice cream, add some to the ice bed for an oyster bar, or sprinkle a handful into a tub of sodas (the beverages will stay cold longer with less ice).

■ Suzanne Rudisill of North Augusta, South Carolina, recycles her empty baking powder container for measuring salt. She slides the measuring spoon against the lip of the container for accurate amounts, and the excess salt falls back inside rather than on the counter or floor.

SHRIMP BUTLER

This item is not a must for everybody, but if you clean several pounds of shrimp at a time, it's for you. Yes, we were skeptical about the timesaving value of the Shrimp Butler, which deveins one shrimp at a time. However, after deveining 5 pounds of shrimp in 10 minutes, we believed its claims. The process is quick *and* clean. Simply place any size headless shrimp—one at a time—in the hopper, and turn the handle. The butler splits the shell and removes the vein in one motion, and clean, shell-on shrimp exit the machine.

The process makes removing the shells a speedy task too. They peel right off because they're already cut. You'll love this new gadget ($39.95) whether you're cleaning 2 pounds or 20 pounds of shrimp. For more information call (407) 324-3101 or (toll free) 1-866-837-2821, or visit www.shellmaster.net.

JULY

Sharing the Fruits of Fellowship

This rural Southern parish serves its neighbors in a number of exceptional ways.

The sun has been up only for a few hours, and already there's no escaping summer's sweltering heat and thick humidity. While the mosquitoes may still be sleeping off a night's work, the climate leaves no doubt you're in the South. Most of us would balk at the idea of spending even one minute in these conditions doing anything, let alone harvesting green tomatoes and picking blueberries—but not Reverend Dorsey Walker. There's work to be done and families to be served.

Altruism is a way of life at the Upper Sand Mountain Parish in Sylvania, Alabama. For 28 years, Reverend Walker (who prefers to be called Dorsey) has set the example by directing the parish's effort to offer food, clothing, shelter, and emergency care to low-income families throughout Alabama.

None of this, however, is possible without the tremendous dedication of volunteers who serve on the Mission Service Teams. Gathering from around the country for one-week trips, team members tend the community gardens, work in the parish's Better Way Cannery, and participate in other activities. "These folks find real meaning, purpose, and value in what they're doing. Whether it's packing bags of groceries in the food pantry or driving nails into one of our Better Way Heart and Hand homes, people are involved in things that have tangible consequences to the community," says Dorsey.

B.J. Owen has worked with students in the cannery for the past three summers. The West Chester, Pennsylvania, native always had a garden growing up, so only the heat is new to her. The same cannot be said for many of the youthful team members. "The majority of the kids are from urban areas," notes B.J., "so some of them see vegetables in an actual garden for the first time. But the real amazement comes when we carry the morning's harvest over to the cannery and make jams and relishes with it that afternoon."

Indeed, later that day, just down the road from the fields, an excited buzz flows from an old renovated church, now home to the Better Way Cannery. Inside the austere cement-block building, team members outfitted in red aprons busily silk corn and chop carrots for vegetable soup to be distributed in the parish's food pantry. Others ladle freshly cooked Green Tomato-Blueberry Jam into jars to be sold at the Better Way Clothing Shoppe.

Dorsey hopes that this unique and delicious jam, along with several other green tomato-based products, will help pave the way to the cannery's—and ultimately the parish's—financial independence. The long-term goal is simple: Self-sufficiency means even more funds can be channeled to families in need. "We're more excited about the things to come than the things that have transpired," says Dorsey. "Because of the wonderful support base of marvelous people in congregations around the country, we can do almost anything we can dream of."

The realization of this dream may be just around the corner. This past summer, with the help of a federal grant and hardworking volunteers, the line of specialty products (including marmalade, relish, and pickles) was finally launched under the Sand Mountain's Finest label. The parish kindly shared these wonderful recipes with us so you, too, will be able to enjoy the products that continue to touch the lives of so many.

GREEN TOMATO-BLUEBERRY JAM

Prep: 35 minutes
Cook: 10 minutes
Process: 10 minutes

5 cups fresh blueberries, stemmed ✱
4 large green tomatoes, coarsely chopped (about 4 pounds)
1½ cups water
5 cups sugar
3 (1.75-ounce) packages fruit pectin
¼ cup lemon juice
2 teaspoons ground cinnamon
½ teaspoon ground nutmeg

● **Pulse** blueberries and chopped tomato in a blender or food processor 3 or 4 times or until mixture is almost smooth.
● **Cook** blueberry mixture, 1½ cups water, and sugar in a Dutch oven over medium heat, stirring constantly, until sugar dissolves.
● **Stir** in fruit pectin and remaining ingredients. Bring to a boil; cook, stirring constantly, 5 minutes or until mixture thickens.
● **Pour** hot mixture into hot jars, filling to ¼ inch from top. Remove air bubbles; wipe jar rims. Cover at once with metal lids, and screw on bands.
● **Process** in boiling-water bath 10 minutes. **Yield:** 5 pints.

✱Substitute 5 cups frozen blueberries, thawed, if desired.

Note: For testing purposes only, we used Sure-Jell Fruit Pectin.

GREEN TOMATO MARMALADE

Prep: 40 minutes
Cook: 4 hours
Process: 10 minutes

1 cup water
2 oranges, thinly sliced
1 lemon, thinly sliced
6 large green tomatoes, chopped (about 4 pounds)
4 cups sugar
½ teaspoon salt

• **Cook** first 3 ingredients in a Dutch oven over medium heat 17 to 20 minutes or until fruit is tender. Add tomato and remaining ingredients, stirring until sugar dissolves.

• **Bring** to a boil, stirring constantly; reduce heat, and simmer, stirring occasionally, 3 hours and 30 minutes or until mixture thickens.

• **Pour** hot mixture into hot jars, filling to ¼ inch from top. Remove air bubbles; wipe jar rims. Cover at once with metal lids, and screw on bands.

• **Process** in boiling-water bath 10 minutes. **Yield:** 3 pints.

GREEN TOMATO PICKLES

Prep: 45 minutes
Stand: 6 hours
Cook: 30 minutes
Process: 10 minutes

5   pounds green tomatoes, chopped
1   large onion, chopped
2   tablespoons pickling salt
1½ cups firmly packed brown sugar
2   cups cider vinegar (5% acidity)
2   teaspoons mustard seeds
2   teaspoons whole allspice
2   teaspoons celery seeds
1½ teaspoons whole cloves
3   cups water

• **Sprinkle** tomato and onion with pickling salt; let stand 4 to 6 hours. Drain and pat dry with paper towels; set aside.

• **Combine** brown sugar and vinegar in a Dutch oven; cook over medium heat, stirring constantly, until sugar dissolves.

• **Place** mustard seeds and next 3 ingredients on a 6-inch square of cheesecloth; tie with string. Add spice bag, tomato, onion, and 3 cups water to vinegar mixture.

• **Bring** to a boil, stirring constantly; reduce heat, and simmer, stirring occasionally, 25 minutes or until tomato and onion are tender. Remove and discard spice bag.

• **Pour** hot mixture into hot jars, filling to ½ inch from top. Remove air bubbles; wipe jar rims. Cover at once with metal lids, and screw on bands.

• **Process** in boiling-water bath 10 minutes. **Yield:** 7 pints.

GREEN TOMATO PIE FILLING

This delicious recipe also makes a great condiment served with roasted meat.

Prep: 1 hour
Cook: 2 hours, 30 minutes
Process: 15 minutes

17 medium-size green tomatoes, chopped (about 6¾ pounds)
10 medium Granny Smith apples, peeled and chopped (about 4¾ pounds)
1   (15-ounce) package raisins
1   (15-ounce) package golden raisins
2½ cups sugar
2½ cups firmly packed brown sugar
2   cups water
½   cup cider vinegar (5% acidity)
2   tablespoons grated orange rind
2   tablespoons grated lemon rind
1   cup fresh lemon juice
1   tablespoon ground cinnamon
1   teaspoon ground nutmeg
1   teaspoon ground cloves

• **Combine** all ingredients in a Dutch oven; simmer over medium-low heat, stirring often, 2 hours and 30 minutes or until tomato and apple are tender and liquid thickens.

• **Pour** hot mixture into hot jars, filling to ½ inch from top. Remove air bubbles; wipe jar rims. Cover at once with metal lids, and screw on bands.

• **Process** in boiling-water bath 15 minutes. **Yield:** 6 quarts.

Green Tomato Pie: Roll each refrigerated piecrust from 1 (15-ounce) package into ⅛-inch thickness. Press 1 piecrust into a 9-inch pieplate; fold edges under, and crimp. Spoon 4½ cups Green Tomato Pie Filling into piecrust, and dot with 2 tablespoons butter. Cut remaining piecrust into ½-inch strips; arrange in a lattice design over filling. Sprinkle evenly with 2 tablespoons sugar. Bake pie at 425° for 10 minutes; reduce oven temperature to 350°, and bake 30 minutes or until golden.

Sweet Melons

How do people enjoy summer's melons? Alabamian Tina Cornett told us that she waits for July's sweetest treat, the 'Ambrosia' cantaloupe, which she covers with freshly ground black pepper. Texan Vanessa McNeil prefers honeydew eaten with a squeeze of fresh lime. Another special version is to make a simple syrup (combine equal parts of water and sugar; bring to a boil, flavor with mint, and refrigerate) and drizzle it over fresh melon *(pictured on page 149)*.

So, whether you enjoy them fresh cut and unadorned or accompanied with unusual ingredients, be sure to pick up some melons during their peak season.

SUMMER RIPENESS

Let your senses guide you in selecting flavorful melons.

Cantaloupe
■ Shake melon, and listen for rattle of seeds.
■ Pick one with a soft stem end and a smooth round scar.
■ Look for a light-yellow ridged or smooth outer shell.

Honeydew
■ Gently press blossom end; it should yield slightly.
■ Look for a cream-colored shell with a waxy feel.
■ Five-pound melons tend to have the best flavor.
■ Sniff for a sweet aroma.

Watermelon
■ Thump outer rind for a dull, hollow sound.
■ Look for a white or yellow underside color.
■ Choose one with a dark brown curl on stem end.

Summer Suppers.

*Summertime means outdoor activities with family and friends.
These terrific recipes will turn even weeknight gatherings
into celebrations.*

Independence Day Picnic

On the Fourth of July, our nation celebrates in a big way. From backyard barbecues to the megagathering on The Mall in Washington, D.C., we come together to share our pride of place, patriotism, and love of a good party.

Wherever you plan to be, you'll need food. Use this menu to adorn your picnic blanket with a delicious but doable meal. Make the coleslaw, potato salad, grilled vegetable salad, pie, brownies, and lemonade on July 3. Roll the sandwiches the morning of the picnic, or bring the ingredients with you, and let each person make his or her own.

Be sure all the food is cold before it goes into the cooler. Stock the cooler well with gel packs or heavy-duty zip-top plastic bags filled with ice (don't forget extra ice for the drinks). Once you've claimed your picnic spot, relax and raise a birthday toast. Take a nap on the grass, wave the flag, slice a watermelon. Then wait for the sun to slide below the trees so the fireworks can begin. They'll be a fitting end to a wonderfully festive day.

PHILLY FIRECRACKERS

*Prep: 20 minutes
Chill: 8 hours*

½ cup sour cream*
½ cup mayonnaise*
1 green onion, chopped
2 tablespoons prepared horseradish
½ teaspoon salt
½ teaspoon pepper
8 (12-inch) flour tortillas
1 pound roast beef, cut into 24 thin slices
2 (6-ounce) packages deli-style sharp Cheddar cheese slices (optional)
2 cups shredded iceberg lettuce

• **Stir** together first 6 ingredients. Spread evenly on one side of each tortilla; top with 3 beef slices and, if desired, 2 cheese slices. Sprinkle evenly with lettuce.
• **Roll** up tortillas tightly; wrap in parchment paper or plastic wrap. Chill 8 hours. **Yield:** 8 servings.

*Substitute ½ cup light sour cream and ½ cup light mayonnaise, if desired.

Note: For testing purposes only, we used Sargento Deli Style Sharp Cheddar Cheese slices.

NEW POTATO SALAD
(pictured on page 151)

*Prep: 15 minutes
Cook: 30 minutes
Chill: 8 hours*

4 pounds new potatoes
¼ cup white vinegar
2 garlic cloves
1 teaspoon sugar
½ teaspoon salt
½ teaspoon pepper
¾ cup olive oil
2 tablespoons chopped fresh basil
2 pints grape tomatoes*
⅓ cup chopped purple onion
8 bacon slices, cooked and crumbled

• **Cook** potatoes in boiling water to cover 25 to 30 minutes or just until tender; drain and cool. Cut potatoes in half, and set aside.
• **Process** vinegar and next 4 ingredients in a blender, stopping to scrape down sides. Turn blender on high, and gradually add oil in a slow, steady stream. Stir in chopped basil.
• **Place** potato, tomatoes, and onion in a large bowl. Drizzle with dressing; toss gently. Cover and chill 8 hours. Top with crumbled bacon just before serving. **Yield:** 8 servings.

*Substitute 2 large tomatoes, seeded and chopped, if desired.

Summer Suppers

CREAMY DILL SLAW
(pictured on pages 150-151)

Prep: 10 minutes
Chill: 8 hours

4   green onions, sliced
1   (8-ounce) container sour cream*
1   cup mayonnaise*
2   tablespoons sugar
2   tablespoons chopped fresh dill
2   tablespoons white vinegar
1   teaspoon salt
½   teaspoon pepper
1   (16-ounce) package shredded coleslaw mix
1   (10-ounce) package finely shredded cabbage
Garnish: chopped fresh dill

• **Stir** together first 8 ingredients until mixture is blended; stir in coleslaw mix and cabbage. Cover and chill 8 hours. Garnish, if desired. **Yield:** 8 servings.

*Substitute 1 (8-ounce) container light sour cream and 1 cup light mayonnaise, if desired.

GRILLED MARINATED VEGETABLE SALAD
(pictured on pages 150-151)

Prep: 35 minutes
Grill: 14 minutes
Chill: 8 hours

4   tablespoons olive oil, divided
3   tablespoons honey
2   tablespoons balsamic vinegar
1   teaspoon salt
½   teaspoon pepper
3   large yellow squash
3   large zucchini
2   medium-size green bell peppers
2   medium-size red bell peppers
2   medium-size orange bell peppers
2   medium-size yellow bell peppers
1   pound fresh green beans

• **Stir** together 1 tablespoon oil, honey, and next 3 ingredients until blended. Set aside.

• **Slice** squash and zucchini; cut bell peppers into 1-inch pieces. Trim green beans. Toss squash, zucchini, and bell pepper with 2 tablespoons oil. Toss beans with remaining 1 tablespoon oil.
• **Grill** squash, zucchini, and bell pepper in a grill wok, covered with grill lid, over medium-high heat (350° to 400°), stirring occasionally, 5 to 7 minutes or until vegetables are tender. Remove from wok.
• **Grill** green beans in grill wok, covered with grill lid, over medium-high heat, stirring occasionally, 5 to 7 minutes or until tender.
• **Toss** vegetables with honey mixture; cover and chill. **Yield:** 8 to 10 servings.

CHOCOLATE-GLAZED BROWNIES

Prep: 30 minutes
Bake: 30 minutes
Stand: 5 minutes

1   cup sugar
⅔   cup butter or margarine
¼   cup water
4   cups semisweet chocolate morsels, divided
1   teaspoon vanilla extract
1½   cups all-purpose flour
½   teaspoon baking soda
½   teaspoon salt
4   large eggs
1   cup chopped pecans, toasted

• **Cook** first 3 ingredients in a large saucepan over high heat, stirring constantly, until sugar melts. Add 2 cups chocolate morsels and vanilla extract, stirring until mixture is smooth. Let cool 15 minutes.
• **Add** flour, baking soda, and salt to cooled chocolate mixture, stirring until blended; stir in eggs and chopped pecans until blended. Spread brownie batter into a greased and floured 13- x 9-inch pan.
• **Bake** at 325° for 30 minutes. Sprinkle remaining 2 cups chocolate morsels evenly over warm brownies; let stand 5 minutes to soften. Spread over top. Cool on a wire rack. **Yield:** 18 brownies.

GRANNY SMITH APPLE PIE
(pictured on page 151)

Prep: 30 minutes
Bake: 50 minutes

1½   (15-ounce) packages refrigerated piecrusts, divided
6   medium Granny Smith apples, peeled and sliced
1½   tablespoons lemon juice
¾   cup brown sugar
½   cup sugar
⅓   cup all-purpose flour
1   teaspoon ground cinnamon
½   teaspoon ground nutmeg

• **Stack** 2 piecrusts; gently roll or press together. Fit pastry into a 9-inch deep-dish pieplate. Toss together apple and lemon juice in a bowl. Combine brown sugar and next 4 ingredients. Sprinkle over apple mixture; toss to coat. Spoon into prepared piecrust.
• **Roll** remaining piecrust to press out fold lines; place over filling. Fold edges under, and crimp; cut slits in top for steam to escape.
• **Bake** at 450° for 15 minutes. Reduce oven temperature to 350°, and bake 35 minutes. **Yield:** 1 (9-inch) pie.

HOMEMADE LEMONADE
(pictured on pages 150-151)

Prep: 20 minutes
Chill: 8 hours

1½   cups sugar
½   cup boiling water
2   teaspoons grated lemon rind
1½   cups fresh lemon juice
5   cups cold water
Garnish: lemon slices

• **Stir** together sugar and ½ cup boiling water until sugar dissolves. Stir in rind, juice, and 5 cups cold water. Chill 8 hours. Garnish, if desired. **Yield:** 8 cups.

Limeade: Substitute 2 teaspoons grated lime rind for lemon rind and 1½ cups fresh lime juice for lemon juice.

Dining With Flair

This cooking teacher and former caterer

shares a sensational menu.

When Betty Sims of Decatur, Alabama, entertains, her friends know the food will be wonderful and the setting lovely—she is a former caterer.

Now Betty teaches cooking classes and loves to entertain. Try this menu adapted from her cookbook, *Southern Scrumptious: How To Cater Your Own Party,* the next time you have a dinner party.

Dinner Party Menu
Serves 6

Portobello Mushroom Burgers
Artichoke-Rice Salad
Chocolate Chubbies

PORTOBELLO MUSHROOM BURGERS

Prep: 20 minutes
Soak: 30 minutes
Grill: 10 minutes

1½ cups mesquite wood chips
⅓ cup olive oil
1 tablespoon minced garlic
1 medium-size purple onion, cut into 6 slices
6 large portobello mushroom caps
6 hamburger buns, split
1 cup light mayonnaise
⅓ cup chopped fresh basil
2 tablespoons Dijon mustard
1 teaspoon lemon juice
½ teaspoon salt
½ teaspoon pepper
6 Romaine lettuce leaves
2 tomatoes, cut into 6 slices each

• **Soak** wood chips in water at least 30 minutes; drain.
• **Prepare** a charcoal fire on grill, and scatter wood chips over hot coals.
• **Whisk** together oil and garlic; brush on both sides of onion and mushrooms.
• **Grill** onion and mushrooms, covered with grill lid, over medium-high heat (350° to 400°) 4 minutes on each side or until tender. Grill bun halves, cut sides down, 2 minutes or until lightly browned.
• **Stir** together mayonnaise and next 5 ingredients. Layer 6 bottom bun halves evenly with lettuce, onion, mushrooms, mayonnaise mixture, and 2 tomato slices; top with remaining bun halves. **Yield:** 6 servings.

ARTICHOKE-RICE SALAD

Prep: 10 minutes
Cook: 20 minutes
Chill: 2 hours

1 (14½-ounce) can chicken broth
1 cup uncooked long-grain rice
1 (12-ounce) jar marinated artichoke hearts, drained and cut into quarters
2 green onions, chopped
8 pimiento-stuffed olives, sliced
½ cup light mayonnaise
½ teaspoon curry powder
1 (8-ounce) can sliced water chestnuts, drained (optional)

• **Bring** chicken broth and rice to a boil in a saucepan over medium heat. Cover, reduce heat, and simmer 20 minutes or until tender. Cool slightly.
• **Stir** together rice, artichoke, next 4 ingredients, and, if desired, water chestnuts; cover and chill at least 2 hours. **Yield:** 6 to 8 servings.

CHOCOLATE CHUBBIES

Chock-full of chocolate and nuts, these cookies round out any summertime meal.

Prep: 20 minutes
Bake: 15 minutes per batch

6 (1-ounce) semisweet chocolate squares, chopped
2 (1-ounce) unsweetened chocolate squares, chopped
⅓ cup butter
3 large eggs
1 cup sugar
¼ cup all-purpose flour
½ teaspoon baking powder
⅛ teaspoon salt
2 cups (12 ounces) semisweet chocolate morsels
2 cups coarsely chopped pecans
2 cups coarsely chopped walnuts

• **Combine** first 3 ingredients in a heavy saucepan; cook, stirring often, over low heat until chocolate melts. Remove from heat; cool slightly.
• **Beat** eggs and sugar at medium speed with an electric mixer until smooth; add chocolate mixture, beating well.
• **Combine** flour, baking powder, and salt; add to chocolate mixture, stirring just until dry ingredients are moistened. Fold in chocolate morsels, pecans, and walnuts.
• **Drop** batter by tablespoonfuls 2 inches apart onto lightly greased baking sheets.
• **Bake** at 325° for 12 to 15 minutes or until done. Cool cookies on baking sheets 1 minute. Remove to wire racks; cool. **Yield:** 3½ dozen.

Summer Suppers

Escape to the Shore

Tom and Beverly Burdette of Atlanta enjoy summer visits to their forties-era beach house on St. Simons Island, Georgia. "It's a family gathering spot with many memories, and it's like a second home to our two children, Britt and Shay," says Beverly.

So if you're in the mood to nibble, do what they do: Indulge in Cheesy Baked Vidalia Onions or Crab Cakes Our Way with a glass of Chardonnay.

SHRIMP-CHEESE SOUP

Prep: 15 minutes
Cook: 30 minutes

1 pound unpeeled, jumbo fresh shrimp
1 tablespoon butter
2 tablespoons olive oil
1 medium onion, minced
1 to 2 garlic cloves, minced
1 cup dry white wine
1 (8-ounce) bottle clam juice
4 tomatoes, peeled and chopped
1 teaspoon salt
¾ teaspoon dried oregano
½ teaspoon freshly ground pepper
1 (4-ounce) package feta cheese, crumbled*
¼ cup chopped fresh parsley

• **Peel** shrimp, and devein, if desired. Set aside.
• **Melt** butter with oil in a Dutch oven over medium heat. Add onion and garlic; sauté 5 minutes, stirring constantly.
• **Add** wine and next 5 ingredients; bring to a boil. Reduce heat, and simmer 10 minutes or until thickened.
• **Stir** in cheese, and simmer 10 minutes. Add shrimp, and cook 3 to 5 minutes or just until shrimp turn pink. Stir in parsley. **Yield:** 6 cups.

✱ Substitute 1 (3-ounce) log goat cheese, crumbled, if desired.

CRAB CAKES OUR WAY

The spicy Rémoulade sauce enhances the mild, delicate crab cakes.

Prep: 20 minutes
Cook: 10 minutes

1 pound fresh crabmeat
6 to 8 saltine crackers, finely crushed
½ cup mayonnaise
1 large egg, lightly beaten
1 tablespoon minced fresh parsley
1½ teaspoons Old Bay seasoning
½ teaspoon dry mustard
½ teaspoon pepper
½ teaspoon Worcestershire sauce
2 tablespoons butter or margarine
Red Pepper Rémoulade Sauce

• **Drain** and flake crabmeat, removing any bits of shell.
• **Combine** crushed crackers and next 7 ingredients; gently fold crabmeat into mixture. Shape into 6 thin patties.
• **Melt** butter in a skillet over medium heat. Add crab cakes; cook 4 to 5 minutes on each side or until golden. Drain on paper towels. Serve with Red Pepper Rémoulade Sauce. **Yield:** 6 cakes.

Red Pepper Rémoulade Sauce

Prep: 5 minutes
Chill: 30 minutes

1 (7-ounce) jar roasted red bell peppers, drained
1 cup mayonnaise
¼ cup chopped fresh parsley
¼ cup dill pickle relish
1 green onion, minced
1 tablespoon grated lemon rind
1½ to 2 tablespoons grated fresh or prepared horseradish
1 tablespoon drained capers
¼ teaspoon salt
¼ teaspoon pepper

• **Process** bell peppers and mayonnaise in a blender or food processor until smooth, stopping to scrape down sides. Add parsley and remaining ingredients; process until almost smooth. Chill 30 minutes. **Yield:** 2 cups.

CHEESY BAKED VIDALIA ONIONS

Prep: 30 minutes
Bake: 1 hour, 15 minutes
Broil: 2 minutes

4 small Vidalia onions
2 tablespoons chicken broth
2 tablespoons dry white wine
2 tablespoons Worcestershire sauce
½ teaspoon hot sauce
1 tablespoon seasoning blend
½ teaspoon garlic salt
½ teaspoon lemon pepper
4 tablespoons butter or margarine
4 ounces Jarlsberg cheese, cut into pieces*

• **Peel** onions, and cut a thin slice from bottom of each one, forming a base for onions to stand on. Scoop out a shallow hole in top of each onion.
• **Place** each onion on a 12-inch square of heavy-duty aluminum foil; wrap sides of each one, forming a basin for liquid. Allow some overhang of foil, leaving tops of onions exposed.
• **Stir** together broth and next 3 ingredients; drizzle evenly over onions. Stir together seasoning blend, garlic salt, and lemon pepper. Sprinkle onions evenly with seasoning mixture. Top each onion with 1 tablespoon butter.
• **Press** foil edges together; gently twist to seal. Place on a baking sheet.
• **Bake** onions at 400° for 1 hour and 15 minutes. Gently unseal foil edges, leaving onions and liquid in foil cups. Top onions evenly with cheese.
• **Broil** 5½ inches from heat 1 to 2 minutes or until cheese melts. Serve immediately. **Yield:** 4 servings.

✱ Substitute Swiss cheese, Monterey Jack cheese with peppers, or fontina cheese for Jarlsberg cheese, if desired.

Note: For testing purposes only, we used Morton Nature's Seasons Seasoning Blend for seasoning blend.

Weekends on the Water

On most weekends from Memorial Day to Labor Day, you'll find George and Lynn O'Connor, of Little Rock, Arkansas, out on Lake Ouachita in their 75-foot-long houseboat. An easy menu allows them time to enjoy company and be the perfect hosts.

As the sun slowly slides behind the mountains, George drops anchor in a secluded spot, lights the grill, and starts cooking Smoked Nachos. While guests munch on nachos, he grills the chicken. Lynn stays busy in the galley putting the finishing touches on their meal. Don't you wish you were with them? Nothing beats the food, except being with friends and enjoying the great outdoors. Whether they're entertaining family or friends on their boat or at home, the O'Connors share fabulous recipes. Here are some of their favorites.

MUSTARD BREAD

Prep: 15 minutes
Bake: 35 minutes

½ cup butter or margarine, softened
3 tablespoons horseradish mustard
4 green onions, chopped
1 to 2 tablespoons poppy seeds
1 (16-ounce) French or Italian bread loaf
6 bacon slices, cooked and crumbled
2 (6-ounce) packages Swiss cheese slices

• **Stir** together first 4 ingredients until well blended.
• **Slice** bread in half lengthwise; spread butter mixture evenly on cut side of bottom half. Sprinkle with bacon; top with cheese. Replace top bread half; wrap in aluminum foil.
• **Bake** at 350° for 30 to 35 minutes or until bread is thoroughly heated. **Yield:** 6 to 8 servings.

GREEK RICE PILAF

Prep: 15 minutes
Bake: 45 minutes

¼ cup butter or margarine
3 cups uncooked quick rice
1 bunch celery, chopped
1 medium onion, chopped
2 (10½-ounce) cans beef consommé
¼ cup chopped fresh parsley
½ teaspoon salt
½ teaspoon pepper
4 bay leaves
Garnish: sliced green onions

• **Melt** butter in a large skillet over medium-high heat; add rice, celery, and onion, and sauté 5 minutes or until vegetables are tender.
• **Stir** in consommé and next 4 ingredients. Pour mixture into a lightly greased 13- x 9-inch baking dish.
• **Bake,** covered, at 350° for 45 minutes or until rice is done. Remove bay leaves. Garnish, if desired. **Yield:** 6 to 8 servings.

Note: For testing purposes only, we used Minute Rice.

SWAMP BREEZE

This potent potable is sure to relax and refresh you on a hot summer day.

Prep: 15 minutes

1 (6-ounce) can frozen limeade concentrate
1 cup spiced rum
¾ cup dark rum
⅓ cup orange liqueur
Ice cubes
2 to 3 fresh mint sprigs
Garnish: fresh mint sprigs

• **Process** first 4 ingredients in a blender until smooth. Add ice to 5-cup level; process until smooth. Add mint; process until smooth. Garnish with additional mint, if desired. **Yield:** 5 cups.

SMOKED NACHOS

Prep: 10 minutes
Grill: 20 minutes

1 (9-ounce) package tortilla chips
3 cups (12 ounces) shredded Cheddar-Jack-American cheese blend
½ cup sliced fresh or canned jalapeño peppers

• **Spread** chips in a lightly greased aluminum foil-lined 13- x 9-inch pan; sprinkle with cheese and jalapeños. Place pan on food rack, and grill, covered with grill lid, over low heat (less than 300°) 15 to 20 minutes. **Yield:** 6 to 8 servings.

GRILLED CHICKEN WITH BASTING SAUCE

Prep: 15 minutes
Grill: 45 minutes

¼ cup butter or margarine
2 tablespoons red wine vinegar
2 tablespoons Worcestershire sauce
1 tablespoon sugar
1½ teaspoons lemon juice
1 garlic clove, chopped
½ teaspoon dried crushed red pepper
½ teaspoon coarsely ground black pepper
8 bone-in chicken breast halves
1 teaspoon salt
½ teaspoon black pepper

• **Cook** first 8 ingredients in a saucepan over medium-low heat, stirring occasionally, until butter melts; set aside.
• **Sprinkle** chicken evenly with salt and black pepper.
• **Grill** chicken, covered with grill lid, over medium-high heat (350° to 400°) 40 to 45 minutes or until done, turning occasionally and basting with sauce the last 10 minutes. **Yield:** 8 servings.

Carolina Barbecue: Eastern vs. Western

Southerners are passionate about barbecue,
and North Carolinians are no exception.

Backyard Barbecue
Serves 6

Smoked Pork Shoulder

Cider Vinegar Barbecue Sauce   Peppery Vinegar Sauce

Brunswick Stew

Creamy Sweet Coleslaw

Hush Puppies

A tantalizing smell rising from Bob and Ruthie Garner's backyard in Burlington, North Carolina, is a sign that Bob is performing one of his favorite tasks—barbecuing. Bob likes to use the best of eastern and western Carolina-style barbecue. Eastern Carolinians serve pork with a vinegar sauce, while folks in the western half of the state add tomato to the sauce.

The long, slow barbecuing method using smoldering charcoal and wood works well for large pieces of meat. Bob keeps an auxiliary fire going, and live coals are added to the main fire as needed.

At the end of the day, the Garners' guests enjoy a plate filled with pork, stew, coleslaw, and hush puppies. "These dishes have delighted the palates of Tar Heels for generations," Bob writes in his book *North Carolina Barbecue: Flavored by Time.* "Learning to prepare them has been a lot like learning to cook barbecue—a satisfying way of participating in our collective experience as North Carolinians."

SMOKED PORK SHOULDER

Follow our "Slow-Barbecuing Tips" at right to achieve optimum results for this recipe. Choose your favorite style of sauce—vinegar- or tomato-based—to serve with the smoky, flavorful meat.

Prep: 30 minutes
Chill: 30 minutes
Cook: 5 hours, 30 minutes

1 **(5- to 6-pound) pork shoulder or Boston butt pork roast**
2 **teaspoons salt**
10 **pounds hardwood charcoal, divided**
Hickory wood chunks

• **Sprinkle** pork with salt; cover and chill 30 minutes.
• **Prepare** charcoal fire with half of charcoal in grill; let burn 15 to 20 minutes or until covered with gray ash.

• **Push** coals evenly into piles on both sides of grill. Carefully place 2 hickory chunks on top of each pile, and place food rack on grill. Place pork, meaty side down, on rack directly in center of grill. Cover with lid, leaving ventilation holes completely open.
• **Prepare** an additional charcoal fire with 12 briquets in an auxiliary grill or fire bucket; let burn 30 minutes or until covered with gray ash. Carefully add 6 briquets to each pile in smoker, and place 2 more hickory chunks on each pile. Repeat procedure every 30 minutes.
• **Cook,** covered, 5 hours and 30 minutes or until meat thermometer inserted into thickest portion registers at least 165°, turning once the last 2 hours. (Cooking the pork to 165° makes the meat easier to remove from the bone.)
• **Remove** pork; cool slightly. Chop and serve with Cider Vinegar Barbecue Sauce or Peppery Vinegar Sauce (recipes on following page). **Yield:** 6 servings.

SLOW-BARBECUING TIPS

■ Resist peeking. This slows down the cooking process.

■ Build an auxiliary fire in a bucket, charcoal chimney starter, or extra grill.

■ Add coals and wood chunks to maintain the temperature.

■ Place additional briquets on already burning coals in small piles on either side of the grill.

■ Wear heavy-duty rubber gloves to squeeze hot cooked pork with both hands. (Meat should be done if you feel it give beneath your fingers and a meat thermometer registers 165°.)

Summer Suppers

CIDER VINEGAR BARBECUE SAUCE

This sauce is often referred to as Lexington-Style Dip, but there are many variations. Most folks can't resist adding their own touch.

Prep: 10 minutes
Cook: 7 minutes

1½ cups cider vinegar
⅓ cup firmly packed brown sugar
¼ cup ketchup
1 tablespoon hot sauce
1 teaspoon browning and seasoning
     sauce
½ teaspoon salt
½ teaspoon onion powder
½ teaspoon pepper
½ teaspoon Worcestershire sauce

• **Stir** together all ingredients in a medium saucepan; cook over medium heat, stirring constantly, 7 minutes or until sugar dissolves. Cover and chill sauce until ready to serve. Serve with Smoked Pork Shoulder (recipe on previous page). **Yield:** 2 cups.

Note: For testing purposes only, we used Texas Pete Hot Sauce and Kitchen Bouquet Browning & Seasoning Sauce.

PEPPERY VINEGAR SAUCE

Prep: 5 minutes

1 quart cider vinegar
1 tablespoon dried crushed red
     pepper
1 tablespoon salt
1½ teaspoons pepper

• **Stir** together all ingredients, blending well. Serve sauce with Smoked Pork Shoulder (recipe on previous page). **Yield:** 4 cups.

BRUNSWICK STEW
(pictured on page 152)

This hearty stew originated in Brunswick County, Virginia, in 1828 and has devoted fans throughout the South.

Prep: 30 minutes
Cook: 6 hours

2 quarts water
1 (3½-pound) whole chicken,
     cut up
1 (15-ounce) can baby lima beans,
     undrained
1 (8-ounce) can baby lima beans,
     undrained
2 (28-ounce) cans whole tomatoes,
     undrained and chopped
1 (16-ounce) package frozen baby
     lima beans
3 medium potatoes, peeled and diced
1 large yellow onion, diced
2 (15-ounce) cans cream-style corn
¼ cup sugar
¼ cup butter or margarine
1 tablespoon salt
1 teaspoon pepper
2 teaspoons hot sauce

• **Bring** 2 quarts water and chicken to a boil in a Dutch oven; reduce heat, and simmer 40 minutes or until tender. Remove chicken; set aside. Reserve 3 cups broth in Dutch oven. (Reserve remaining broth for other uses.)
• **Pour** canned lima beans and liquid through a wire-mesh strainer into Dutch oven, reserving beans; add tomato to Dutch oven.
• **Bring** to a boil over medium-high heat; cook, stirring often, 40 minutes or until liquid is reduced by one-third.
• **Skin,** bone, and shred chicken. Mash reserved beans with a potato masher.
• **Add** chicken, mashed and frozen beans, potato, and onion to Dutch oven. Cook over low heat, stirring often, 3 hours and 30 minutes.
• **Stir** in corn and remaining ingredients; cook over low heat, stirring often, 1 hour. **Yield:** 3½ quarts.

CREAMY SWEET COLESLAW
(pictured on page 152)

Prep: 20 minutes
Chill: 1 hour

1 medium cabbage, shredded ＊
1½ cups mayonnaise
¾ cup sweet salad cube pickles
⅓ cup sugar
⅓ cup prepared mustard
1 tablespoon celery seeds
2 tablespoons cider vinegar
1½ teaspoons salt
⅛ teaspoon pepper

• **Stir** together all ingredients in a bowl. Cover; chill 1 hour. **Yield:** 8 servings.

＊Substitute 8 cups coleslaw mix for cabbage, if desired.

HUSH PUPPIES
(pictured on page 152)

Bacon drippings add extra flavor to these Hush Puppies.

Prep: 15 minutes
Cook: 6 minutes per batch

1½ cups self-rising white cornmeal
½ cup all-purpose flour
½ teaspoon baking powder
1 small onion, diced (optional) ＊
1½ teaspoons sugar
1 cup plus 2 tablespoons buttermilk
1 tablespoon bacon drippings
Vegetable oil

• **Combine** first 5 ingredients in a bowl; make a well in center of mixture.
• **Add** buttermilk and bacon drippings to dry ingredients, stirring just until dry ingredients are moistened.
• **Pour** oil to a depth of 2 inches into a Dutch oven; heat to 350°. Drop batter by tablespoonfuls into oil; fry, in batches, 3 minutes on each side or until golden. Drain on paper towels. **Yield:** 2 dozen.

＊Substitute ½ teaspoon onion powder for onion, if desired.

Sweet Melons, page 141

Homemade Lemonade, page 143

Creamy Dill Slaw, page 143

Grilled Marinated Vegetable Salad, page 143

Clockwise from front: Granny Smith Apple Pie, Grilled Marinated Vegetable Salad, Homemade Lemonade, Creamy Dill Slaw, page 143; New Potato Salad, page 142

Brunswick Stew, Creamy Sweet Coleslaw, Hush Puppies, page 148

Tee's Corn Pudding, page 165

Bow Tie Pasta, page 164

153

Clockwise from right:
Gazpacho, page 157;
Couscous With Peas and
Feta, Grilled Snapper
With Orange-Almond Sauce,
Charred Tomato Salad,
Grilled Corn With
Jalapeño-Lime Butter,
page 158

Fudge Pie, page 129

Crispy Peanut Squares,
Luscious Lemon Bars,
Layered Apricot Bars,
page 161

Catching and Cooking

After these women take to the sea, their husbands take to the kitchen and make short work of their wives' catch of the day.

Fresh Catch Menu
Serves 6

Gazpacho
Grilled Snapper With Orange-Almond Sauce
Grilled Corn With Jalapeño-Lime Butter
Couscous With Peas and Feta
Charred Tomato Salad
Lemon icebox pie
White wine

When Brenda Nunnery and Ann Dent want to get away from it all, they gather some girlfriends, hire a charter boat, and head out into the Gulf of Mexico.

Brenda, who has been fishing since she was 4 or 5 years old, reports that their group of six women generally goes out several times a year. But she and Ann, now co-owners of Cuvée Beach, a restaurant and wine bar in Destin, Florida, are confined to dry land most of the time.

"This is the first time Ann and I have gone out this summer," Brenda says, gesturing to their ample catch. "We did a lot better than we expected in a four-hour trip!" After a tiring day on the high seas, the two are happy to hand cooking duty over to husbands Phillip Nunnery and Bill Dent.

The couples have been friends for nine years, sharing a love of great food and fine wines. They used to cook together every Sunday, an activity that led to opening the restaurant. Now, they say, it is a rare luxury when they can all relax together at one time.

Both men are "great grill cooks" and wine aficionados, who actually help select the labels sold at the restaurant. Ann says that Bill also does most of the cooking at home. "Our youngest son is 4 years old," she says. "Bill took over the cooking when he was an infant, and I've been happy ever since."

Phillip and Bill share these mouth-watering recipes for a fantastic midsummer menu. Try them at home and enjoy your own celebration with good friends and wonderful food.

GAZPACHO
(pictured on page 154)

Start the meal with a bowl of this cool, tomatoey soup.

Prep: 20 minutes
Chill: 8 hours

8 large tomatoes
2 cucumbers
1 large green bell pepper
1 large yellow bell pepper
1 small purple onion
1 jalapeño pepper, seeded
1 large garlic clove
1 (32-ounce) bottle vegetable juice
⅓ cup red wine vinegar
1 tablespoon grated lemon rind
¼ cup fresh lemon juice
2 teaspoons salt
1 teaspoon paprika
2 to 3 teaspoons hot sauce
Toppings: sour cream, avocado slices, croutons, boiled shrimp, chopped fresh cilantro, chopped fresh mint
Garnishes: green and yellow baby tomatoes, fresh basil sprigs

• **Peel** tomatoes and cucumbers. Cut tomatoes, cucumbers, bell peppers, and onion into quarters. Remove and discard cucumber and bell pepper seeds.
• **Process** vegetables, jalapeño pepper, and garlic in a blender or food processor until almost smooth, stopping to scrape down sides. Transfer mixture to a large bowl, and stir in vegetable juice and next 6 ingredients. Cover and chill, stirring often, 8 hours. Serve with toppings, if desired. Garnish, if desired. **Yield:** 12½ cups.

Summer Suppers

GRILLED SNAPPER WITH ORANGE-ALMOND SAUCE
(pictured on page 154)

Prep: 20 minutes
Grill: 12 minutes

6 (8-ounce) snapper or grouper fillets
2 tablespoons olive oil
1 teaspoon coarse-grain sea salt
1 teaspoon freshly ground pepper
4 fresh thyme sprigs ✱
½ cup butter
½ cup sliced almonds
½ to 1 tablespoon grated orange rind
Garnishes: orange wedges, thyme
   sprigs ✱

• **Rub** fish fillets with oil. Sprinkle evenly with salt and pepper.
• **Arrange** thyme sprigs on hot charcoal or lava rocks on grill. Coat food rack with vegetable cooking spray; place on grill over high heat (400° to 500°). Place fish on rack; grill 5 to 6 minutes on each side or until fish flakes with a fork.
• **Melt** butter in a saucepan over medium-high heat; add almonds, and sauté 5 minutes or until butter is brown. Remove from heat. Stir in orange rind. Pour sauce over fish. Garnish, if desired. **Yield:** 6 servings.

✱Substitute orange thyme for thyme sprigs, if desired.

GRILLED CORN WITH JALAPEÑO-LIME BUTTER
(pictured on page 154)

Prep: 25 minutes
Chill: 1 hour
Grill: 20 minutes

½ cup butter, softened
2 jalapeño peppers, seeded and
   minced
2 tablespoons grated lime rind
1 teaspoon fresh lime juice
6 ears fresh corn
1 tablespoon olive oil
2 teaspoons kosher salt
1 teaspoon freshly ground pepper

• **Combine** first 4 ingredients, and shape into a 6-inch log; wrap in wax paper, and chill 1 hour.
• **Rub** corn with olive oil; sprinkle evenly with salt and pepper.
• **Grill** corn, covered with grill lid, over high heat (400° to 500°), turning often, 15 to 20 minutes or until tender. Serve with flavored butter. **Yield:** 6 servings.

COUSCOUS WITH PEAS AND FETA
(pictured on page 154)

Toasty pine nuts and tangy feta give this cool side dish plenty of personality.

Prep: 30 minutes
Chill: 2 hours

1½ cups water
1 cup uncooked couscous
¼ cup olive oil
1 teaspoon grated lemon rind
1 tablespoon fresh lemon juice
¾ teaspoon kosher salt
⅛ teaspoon ground red pepper
¾ cup frozen sweet green peas,
   thawed
¼ purple onion, thinly sliced
½ cup crumbled feta cheese
¼ cup chopped fresh mint
2 tablespoons pine nuts, toasted

• **Bring** 1½ cups water to a boil in a saucepan over high heat. Remove from heat, and stir in couscous; let stand 10 minutes. Transfer to a large bowl.
• **Stir** together olive oil, lemon rind, and next 3 ingredients; add to couscous, stirring with a fork.
• **Toss** peas, sliced onion, crumbled feta, and chopped mint gently into couscous; cover and chill at least 2 hours. Stir in pine nuts just before serving. **Yield:** 6 servings.

CHARRED TOMATO SALAD
(pictured on page 154)

Prep: 20 minutes
Cook: 20 minutes
Stand: 1 hour

8 large tomatoes
2 tablespoons olive oil
⅓ cup sliced fresh basil
½ cup olive oil
3 tablespoons red wine vinegar
1 teaspoon kosher salt
½ teaspoon freshly ground pepper
Garnish: fresh basil leaves

• **Cut** tomatoes into quarters; remove and discard seeds. Pat dry, and brush each side evenly with 2 tablespoons olive oil.
• **Cook** tomato quarters, in batches, in a hot cast-iron skillet over high heat 1½ to 2 minutes on each side or until blackened. Remove from skillet, and cool, reserving juice from skillet.
• **Toss** tomato with reserved juice, basil, and next 4 ingredients in a large bowl. Cover and let stand, stirring occasionally, 1 hour. Garnish, if desired. **Yield:** 6 to 8 servings.

Meal With a View

Dave and Judy Juergens loved the Virginia location of their weekend getaway so much that they made it their permanent residence. "We built this house as our place to entertain," says Dave. "Nestled in the valley at Wintergreen Resort, it's the perfect spot for our casual approach to dining with a fabulous view."

Whether they gather on the patio or at a scenic spot, Dave usually prepares the food. "I love to cook for our friends," he says. "We always have great times together." So try some of Dave's easy recipes—they're just right for most casual gatherings.

Summer Suppers

ROAST LEG OF LAMB

Slather leftover lamb slices with Special Mustard Sauce for quick and tasty sandwiches.

Prep: 10 minutes
Bake: 1 hour, 5 minutes
Stand: 20 minutes

¼ cup white vinegar
1½ teaspoons salt
1 teaspoon pepper
1 teaspoon dry mustard
1 (4- to 5-pound) leg of lamb, trimmed

• **Stir** together first 4 ingredients in a small bowl. Rub mixture over lamb, and place in a shallow roasting pan.
• **Bake** lamb at 425° for 45 minutes; reduce oven temperature to 375°, and bake 20 minutes or until a meat thermometer inserted into thickest portion registers 155°. Let lamb stand for 20 minutes before serving. **Yield:** 8 to 10 servings.

SPECIAL MUSTARD SAUCE

Prep: 10 minutes
Cook: 25 minutes

½ cup butter or margarine
2 beef bouillon cubes
3 egg yolks, lightly beaten
½ cup sugar
½ cup prepared mustard
¼ cup cider vinegar
1 teaspoon salt

• **Combine** butter and bouillon cubes in top of a double boiler. Place over simmering water, and cook, whisking constantly, until butter melts and bouillon cubes dissolve. Gradually whisk in beaten egg yolks. Add sugar and remaining ingredients; cook, whisking often, 20 minutes. Cover and chill. **Yield:** 1½ cups.

GRILLED BRATWURST

Prep: 10 minutes
Grill: 15 minutes
Cook: 20 minutes

6 bratwurst links (about 1½ pounds)
2 tablespoons butter or margarine
2 large onions, thinly sliced
1 medium-size green bell pepper, cut into thin strips
1 medium-size red bell pepper, cut into thin strips
2 (12-ounce) bottles beer (do not use dark)
2 teaspoons salt-free seasoning blend
6 hoagie rolls, split

• **Grill** bratwurst, covered with grill lid, over medium-high heat (350° to 400°) for 10 to 15 minutes or until thoroughly cooked, turning once.
• **Melt** butter in a large skillet over medium heat; add onion and bell pepper strips, and sauté until tender.
• **Stir** in beer and seasoning blend; add sausage, and simmer mixture for 20 minutes.
• **Place** 1 bratwurst link in each roll, and top evenly with vegetable mixture. Serve with Special Mustard Sauce (recipe at left). **Yield:** 6 servings.

Note: For testing purposes only, we used Mrs. Dash Original Blend.

TOSSED SPINACH SALAD

Prep: 20 minutes

1 (10-ounce) package fresh spinach*
1 medium-size purple onion, thinly sliced
2 hard-cooked eggs, chopped
1 cup garlic-seasoned croutons
2 tablespoons grated Parmesan cheese
Dressing

• **Toss** first 5 ingredients in a large bowl; serve with Dressing. **Yield:** 6 servings.

Dressing

Prep: 10 minutes

¼ cup lemon olive oil
3 tablespoons lemon juice
1 tablespoon red wine vinegar
1 teaspoon Dijon mustard
½ teaspoon salt
¼ teaspoon freshly ground pepper
6 ounces Canadian bacon, cut into thin strips

• **Whisk** together first 6 ingredients. Add Canadian bacon just before serving. **Yield:** ½ cup.

*Substitute 1 (10-ounce) package salad greens for spinach, if desired.

Note: For testing purposes only, we used Stutz Limonato California Extra Virgin Lemon and Olive Oil.

FRESH ASPARAGUS SALAD

Prep: 10 minutes
Cook: 3 minutes

2 pounds fresh asparagus
¼ cup olive oil
2 tablespoons balsamic vinegar
1 tablespoon lemon juice
2 teaspoons chopped fresh chives
1 teaspoon Dijon mustard
¼ teaspoon salt
¼ teaspoon pepper
1 shallot, chopped (optional)
1 hard-cooked egg, chopped (optional)

• **Snap** off tough ends of asparagus. Cook in boiling salted water to cover 2 to 3 minutes or until crisp-tender, and drain. Plunge asparagus into ice water to stop the cooking process; drain and set aside.
• **Whisk** together oil, next 6 ingredients, and, if desired, shallot.
• **Drizzle** asparagus with vinaigrette, and sprinkle with chopped egg, if desired. **Yield:** 6 servings.

Summer Suppers

Firemen Turn Up the Heat

In 1997, former Houston Oilers quarterback Dante "Dan" Pastorini was searching for a place to escape the hustle and bustle of Houston. He found what he was looking for in the rural and picturesque town of Chappell Hill, Texas.

Eager to immerse himself in the community, Dan joined the Chappell Hill Volunteer Fire Department.

Dan and the other volunteers enjoy cooking together, both for recreation and to raise money for the fire department. "We're totally self-sufficient, so we have quite a few fund-raisers throughout the year. These give us a chance to showcase our cooking and barbecuing skills," Dan says with a grin.

ITALIAN MEAT SAUCE

Prep: 35 minutes
Cook: 3 hours

1 pound ground pork *
1 pound ground beef
1 medium onion, diced
2 celery ribs, diced
2 small carrots, diced
3 garlic cloves, minced
1 teaspoon salt
1 teaspoon pepper
1 (8-ounce) package sliced fresh mushrooms
2 (15-ounce) cans tomato sauce
1 (14½-ounce) can beef broth
1 (10¾-ounce) can tomato puree
1 (6-ounce) can Italian-style tomato paste
1 tablespoon chopped fresh thyme
1 tablespoon chopped fresh oregano
1 tablespoon chopped fresh basil
1 (20-ounce) package refrigerated cheese-filled ravioli, cooked

• **Cook** first 8 ingredients in a Dutch oven over medium heat; stir until meat crumbles and is no longer pink. Drain.
• **Stir** in mushrooms and next 6 ingredients; simmer 3 hours. Stir in 1 tablespoon basil just before serving; serve over ravioli. **Yield:** 10 cups.

✳ Substitute 1 pound ground beef for ground pork, if desired.

Dan Pastorini
Chappell Hill, Texas

GUMBO

Prep: 30 minutes
Cook: 1 hour
Stand: 10 minutes

2 pounds unpeeled, large fresh shrimp
¼ cup vegetable oil
¼ cup all-purpose flour
1 medium onion, chopped
1 medium-size green bell pepper, chopped
1 (32-ounce) container chicken broth
3 garlic cloves, diced
1 teaspoon salt
1 teaspoon black pepper
½ teaspoon ground red pepper
4 green onions, chopped
1 to 2 teaspoons filé powder
Hot cooked rice
French bread

• **Peel** shrimp; devein, if desired. Set aside. Cook oil and flour in a Dutch oven over medium heat, whisking roux constantly until roux is dark caramel-colored (about 12 minutes).
• **Reduce** heat to low; add onion and bell pepper. Sauté 5 minutes or until tender.
• **Add** broth gradually, stirring until blended. Stir in garlic and next 3 ingredients; cover and simmer, stirring occasionally, 30 minutes. Add shrimp and green onions; cook, covered, 10 minutes or just until shrimp turn pink.
• **Remove** from heat; stir in filé powder. Let stand 10 minutes; serve over rice with French bread. **Yield:** 8 cups.

John Gunn
Chappell Hill, Texas

TEXAS CAVIAR

Prep: 30 minutes
Chill: 8 hours

2 medium tomatoes, seeded and chopped
1 medium-size red bell pepper, chopped
1 bunch green onions, chopped
2 garlic cloves, minced
1 (15.8-ounce) can black-eyed peas, rinsed and drained
1 (15.5-ounce) can white hominy, rinsed and drained
1 (8-ounce) jar medium picante sauce
½ cup chopped fresh cilantro
3 tablespoons lime juice
½ teaspoon salt

• **Stir** together all ingredients. Cover; chill, stirring occasionally, 8 hours. Serve with tortilla chips. **Yield:** 6 cups.

Dan Pastorini
Chappell Hill, Texas

SQUASH DRESSING

Prep: 15 minutes
Cook: 30 minutes
Bake: 50 minutes

5 medium-size yellow squash, sliced (1¾ pounds)
1 medium onion, chopped
1 large egg, lightly beaten
1 (6-ounce) package Mexican-style cornbread mix
1 (8¼-ounce) can cream-style corn
½ cup chunky picante sauce
2 tablespoons butter, softened
¼ teaspoon salt
⅛ teaspoon pepper

• **Boil** squash and onion in water to cover in a Dutch oven 30 minutes or until squash is tender; drain and lightly mash squash with a fork. Add egg and remaining ingredients; stir until blended.
• **Spoon** into a lightly greased 1½-quart baking dish. Bake at 350° for 50 minutes or until set. **Yield:** 4 to 6 servings.

Ken Burnette
Chappell Hill, Texas

Cookies by the Pan

Relish the rich taste of Crispy Peanut Squares, Luscious Lemon Bars, and Layered Apricot Bars.

Quick-to-mix bar cookies make great desserts and snacks, but there's a secret to perfecting these easy treats. After preparing the batter, spread it evenly in the correct-size pan—using a smaller pan makes gummy cookies, while a larger pan produces dry ones. After baking, most cookies should be cooled completely in the pan on a wire rack before cutting.

LUSCIOUS LEMON BARS
(pictured on page 156)

Prep: 15 minutes
Bake: 50 minutes

2¼ cups all-purpose flour, divided
½ cup powdered sugar
1 cup butter or margarine, softened
4 large eggs
2 cups sugar
⅓ cup lemon juice
½ teaspoon baking powder
Powdered sugar

• **Combine** 2 cups flour and ½ cup powdered sugar.
• **Cut** butter into flour mixture with a pastry blender until crumbly. Firmly press mixture into a lightly greased 13- x 9-inch pan.
• **Bake** at 350° for 20 to 25 minutes or until lightly browned.
• **Whisk** eggs in a large bowl; whisk in 2 cups sugar and lemon juice. Combine remaining ¼ cup flour and baking powder; whisk into egg mixture. Pour batter over crust.
• **Bake** at 350° for 25 minutes or until set. Let cool completely on a wire rack. Cut into bars, and sprinkle evenly with additional powdered sugar. **Yield:** 2½ dozen.

LAYERED APRICOT BARS
(pictured on page 156)

Prep: 25 minutes
Bake: 1 hour, 5 minutes

1 (6-ounce) package dried apricots
½ cup butter or margarine, softened
¼ cup sugar
1⅓ cups all-purpose flour, divided
2 large eggs
¾ cup firmly packed brown sugar
½ teaspoon baking powder
¼ teaspoon salt
½ cup chopped walnuts
1 teaspoon vanilla extract
Powdered sugar

• **Bring** apricots and water to cover to a boil in a small saucepan. Reduce heat, and simmer, uncovered, 15 minutes or until tender. Drain and coarsely chop apricots; set aside.
• **Beat** butter at medium speed with an electric mixer until creamy; gradually add ¼ cup sugar, beating well. Stir in 1 cup flour, and press mixture into a lightly greased aluminum foil-lined 9-inch square pan.
• **Bake** at 350° for 15 to 20 minutes or until lightly browned.
• **Beat** eggs at medium speed until thick and pale; gradually add brown sugar, beating well. Add remaining ⅓ cup flour, baking powder, and salt, beating well. Stir in chopped apricot, walnuts, and vanilla, and spread mixture evenly over crust.
• **Bake** at 325° for 45 minutes. Let cool completely in pan. Cut into bars, and sprinkle with powdered sugar. **Yield:** 1½ dozen.

CRISPY PEANUT SQUARES
(pictured on page 156)

You don't have to heat up the kitchen to enjoy these peanutty treats. Use your microwave to make these no-bake bars.

Prep: 10 minutes
Chill: 1 hour

1 cup sugar
1 cup light corn syrup
1 cup creamy peanut butter
1 teaspoon vanilla extract
6 cups crisp rice cereal squares
1 cup peanuts

• **Combine** first 3 ingredients in a glass bowl; microwave at HIGH 3 to 4 minutes or until melted, stirring once. Stir in vanilla.
• **Fold** in 6 cups cereal and peanuts. Spread mixture into a lightly greased 13- x 9-inch pan. Cover and chill 1 hour or until set; cut into small squares. **Yield:** 4 dozen.

CLEVER CUTTING

■ To make cutting bar cookies easier, line a baking pan with aluminum foil, allowing several inches to extend over sides; lightly grease foil. Spread batter in pan; bake and cool. Lift from pan using foil; press foil sides down, and cut cookies into desired size and shape.

■ For diamond-shaped bar cookies, cut diagonally in one direction and straight across in the other direction. The yield will be slightly less, but you'll have great little tidbits for nibbling later.

Living Light

Lean and healthy dishes made with—surprise—beef.

Since when can you enjoy beef in a heart-healthy diet? Since we have learned that moderate amounts fit well within the dietary recommendations of the American Heart Association. These mouthwatering beef recipes are not only good but also good for you.

CURRIED BEEF STIR-FRY

Prep: 15 minutes
Cook: 10 minutes

1 pound boneless top sirloin steak, thinly sliced
1 onion, chopped
2 garlic cloves, minced
2 teaspoons olive oil
3 cups cooked brown rice
1½ teaspoons grated fresh ginger
1½ teaspoons curry powder
½ teaspoon salt
½ teaspoon ground red pepper
2 medium apples, coarsely chopped
½ cup apple juice
2 tablespoons slivered almonds, toasted (optional)

• **Sauté** first 3 ingredients in hot oil in a large nonstick skillet over medium-high heat 5 to 7 minutes or until onion is tender. Stir in cooked rice and next 4 ingredients.
• **Stir** in apple and apple juice; cook, stirring often, until thoroughly heated. Sprinkle with almonds, if desired. **Yield:** 6 servings.

Mildred Sherrer
Bay City, Texas

❤ Per serving: Calories 283 (22% from fat)
Fat 6.8g (sat 1.5g, mono 3.6g, poly 0.9g)
Protein 20g Carb 36g Fiber 4.5g
Chol 46mg Iron 3mg
Sodium 245mg Calc 35mg

SUMMER MEAT LOAF

Freshly grated carrot and zucchini give this meat loaf terrific flavor and moisture.

Prep: 20 minutes
Bake: 50 minutes

1½ pounds extra-lean ground beef
1 cup Italian-seasoned breadcrumbs
1 carrot, peeled and grated
1 small zucchini, grated
½ onion, chopped
2 garlic cloves, minced
¼ cup low-sodium fat-free beef or chicken broth
¼ cup egg substitute
¼ cup ketchup
1 tablespoon chopped fresh or 1 teaspoon dried basil
1 tablespoon Dijon mustard
½ teaspoon salt
½ teaspoon freshly ground pepper
Vegetable cooking spray

• **Combine** first 13 ingredients, and shape into a 9- x 4-inch loaf. Place on an aluminum foil-lined jellyroll pan coated with cooking spray.
• **Bake** at 375° for 45 to 50 minutes or until beef is no longer pink. **Yield:** 6 servings.

Lisa Helm
Monticello, Florida

❤ Per serving: Calories 302 (36% from fat)
Fat 12g (sat 4g, mono 4.6g, poly 0.7g)
Protein 28g Carb 20g Fiber 2g
Chol 41mg Iron 3.7mg
Sodium 985mg Calc 76mg

LONDON BROIL SANDWICHES WITH YOGURT-CUCUMBER SAUCE

Prep: 15 minutes
Chill: 8 hours
Grill: 14 minutes
Stand: 5 minutes

1½ pounds London broil (about ¾ inch thick)
2 garlic cloves, minced
⅓ cup fresh lemon juice
1 tablespoon Greek seasoning
1 tablespoon olive oil
1 (8-ounce) container plain nonfat yogurt
1 large cucumber, peeled, seeded, and chopped
1 tablespoon fresh lemon juice
½ teaspoon dried dillweed
6 pita bread rounds
Shredded lettuce
1 large tomato, diced
Garnishes: fresh dill, lemon wedges, cucumber slices

• **Place** beef between 2 sheets of heavy-duty plastic wrap, and flatten to ½-inch thickness using a meat mallet or rolling pin.
• **Combine** garlic and next 3 ingredients in a shallow dish or large heavy-duty zip-top plastic bag, and add beef. Cover or seal, and chill 8 hours. Remove beef from marinade, and discard marinade.
• **Stir** together yogurt and next 3 ingredients. Set aside.
• **Grill** beef, covered with grill lid, over medium-high heat (350° to 400°) 7 minutes on each side or to desired degree of doneness. Let stand 5 minutes. Cut into thin slices.
• **Place** beef evenly down center of warm pita rounds. Top with yogurt mixture, lettuce, and tomato, and roll up. Garnish, if desired, and serve immediately. **Yield:** 6 servings.

Susan H. Price
Greensboro, North Carolina

❤ Per serving: Calories 402 (29% from fat)
Fat 13g (sat 4.3g, mono 5.5g, poly 1.3g)
Protein 31g Carb 43g Fiber 5.6g
Chol 57mg Iron 4.4mg
Sodium 518mg Calc 79mg

What's for Supper?

Take advantage of the cool night air to serve this classic meal in the great outdoors.

Visit a nearby park and have supper outside. Your family and friends will enjoy the change of scenery as much as the food. This menu can be prepared ahead and chilled thoroughly before being packed in a cooler.

Picnic in the Park
Serves 8

Mom's Fried Chicken
Potato Salad
Broccoli-Grape Salad
Pink Lemonade

MOM'S FRIED CHICKEN

Prep: 10 minutes
Chill: 1 hour
Cook: 16 minutes per batch

3 quarts water
4 teaspoons salt, divided
1 (3½- to 4-pound) package chicken pieces, skinned
1 large egg
1 cup water
1 cup all-purpose flour
1 teaspoon garlic powder
2 teaspoons pepper
1 quart vegetable oil

• **Combine** 3 quarts water and 3 teaspoons salt in a large bowl, and add chicken. Cover and chill 1 hour. Drain chicken, and rinse with cold water; pat dry.
• **Whisk** together egg and 1 cup water.
• **Combine** remaining 1 teaspoon salt, flour, garlic powder, and pepper in a heavy-duty zip-top plastic bag. Dip 2 chicken pieces in egg mixture. Place pieces in bag; seal and shake to coat. Remove and repeat procedure with remaining pieces.
• **Heat** oil to 360° in a Dutch oven. Fry chicken, in batches, 16 minutes or until golden, turning twice. Drain on paper towels. **Yield:** 8 servings.

A.L. Cook
Clinton, Maryland

POTATO SALAD

Prep: 20 minutes
Cook: 30 minutes
Chill: 1 hour

5 pounds small red potatoes
12 hard-cooked eggs, separated
2 cups mayonnaise
¼ cup sweet pickle juice or relish
2 tablespoons prepared mustard
1½ teaspoons salt
¾ teaspoon pepper
Garnish: paprika

• **Peel** potatoes, if desired, and cut into pieces. Cook in boiling water to cover in a Dutch oven 30 minutes or until tender; drain and cool.
• **Chop** egg whites.
• **Mash** yolks with a fork in a large bowl; stir in mayonnaise and next 4 ingredients until blended. Add potato and chopped egg whites, tossing gently to coat. Cover and chill 1 hour. Garnish, if desired. **Yield:** 10 to 12 servings.

Kathleen Hebert
Franklin, Louisiana

BROCCOLI-GRAPE SALAD

For transporting, pack bacon and almonds separately in zip-top plastic bags to keep each ingredient crunchy.

Prep: 25 minutes
Chill: 3 hours

1 cup mayonnaise
½ cup sugar
1 teaspoon white vinegar
1 (16-ounce) package broccoli flowerets
2 cups seedless green grapes
3 celery ribs, sliced
8 bacon slices, cooked and crumbled
1 (2-ounce) package slivered almonds, toasted

• **Stir** together first 3 ingredients in a large bowl; add broccoli, grapes, and celery, tossing gently to coat. Cover and chill 3 hours.
• **Sprinkle** with bacon and almonds just before serving. Serve with a slotted spoon. **Yield:** 6 cups.

Margaret A. Mahoney
Ogden, Iowa

PINK LEMONADE

Prep: 15 minutes
Chill: 2 hours

1 cup sugar
10 cups water
1 cup lemon juice
¼ cup grenadine
½ pint fresh raspberries or strawberries (optional)

• **Cook** sugar and 1 cup water in a saucepan, stirring constantly, until sugar dissolves. Cool; pour into a large container. Stir in remaining 9 cups water, lemon juice, grenadine, and, if desired, raspberries. Chill 2 hours. **Yield:** 3 quarts.

Laura Morris
Bunnell, Florida

Quick & Easy

Short on prep time but long on flavor, these sauces and dressings can all be prepared in 15 minutes or less.

CHICKEN PICANTE PASTA

Picante sauce and green chiles add zing to the creamy sauce in this hearty dish.

Prep: 10 minutes

1 cup picante sauce
½ cup light sour cream
½ cup light cream cheese, softened
¼ teaspoon ground cumin
3 cups chopped cooked chicken
8 ounces penne pasta, cooked
1 (4.5-ounce) can chopped green chiles
3 small green onions, chopped

• **Stir** together first 4 ingredients in a large bowl. Add chopped chicken and remaining ingredients, tossing gently to coat. Serve pasta chilled or heated. **Yield:** 6 servings.

Jo Latino
Dallas, Texas

SPINACH ALFREDO FETTUCCINE

Prep: 10 minutes
Cook: 5 minutes

1 (10-ounce) package frozen creamed spinach, thawed
1 (10-ounce) container refrigerated Alfredo sauce
½ cup grated Parmesan cheese, divided
1 teaspoon dried basil
½ teaspoon pepper
8 ounces fettuccine, cooked
2 green onions, chopped

• **Cook** spinach and Alfredo sauce in a saucepan over medium heat, stirring constantly until mixture is thoroughly heated. Stir in ¼ cup cheese, basil, and pepper. Serve over pasta, and top with remaining cheese and green onions. **Yield:** 4 servings.

Note: For testing purposes only, we used Contadina Alfredo Sauce.

PASTA WITH SHRIMP

Prep: 15 minutes
Cook: 20 minutes

3 cups water
1 pound unpeeled, large fresh shrimp
1 teaspoon Creole seasoning
1 pound fresh asparagus
8 ounces uncooked spaghetti
1½ cups basil leaves
½ cup olive oil
⅓ cup lemon juice
3 garlic cloves
2 teaspoons salt
¼ teaspoon black pepper
¼ teaspoon dried crushed red pepper

• **Bring** 3 cups water to a boil; add shrimp and seasoning, and cook 3 minutes or just until shrimp turn pink. Drain; rinse with cold water. Peel shrimp; devein, if desired. Set aside. Snap off tough ends of asparagus; cut asparagus into 2-inch pieces. Cook spaghetti according to package directions; add asparagus the last 5 minutes. Drain, rinse, and set aside.
• **Process** basil and next 5 ingredients in a blender or food processor until smooth, stopping to scrape down sides.
• **Combine** shrimp, pasta, and asparagus in a bowl; drizzle with dressing. Toss gently to coat. Sprinkle with red pepper. **Yield:** 3 to 4 servings.

Barbara Wagner
Gainesville, Florida

BOW TIE PASTA
(pictured on page 153)

Try the herb-infused dressing served with sliced tomatoes or tossed with mixed salad greens.

Prep: 15 minutes
Chill: 2 hours

8 ounces bow tie pasta, cooked
½ green bell pepper, diced
½ red bell pepper, diced
⅓ cup crumbled feta cheese
1 celery rib, thinly sliced
12 kalamata olives, pitted and quartered
½ teaspoon salt
¼ teaspoon pepper
¼ cup Pasta Salad Dressing
Garnishes: fresh basil sprigs, tomato wedges

• **Toss** together first 9 ingredients; add more dressing as desired. Cover and chill at least 2 hours. Garnish, if desired. **Yield:** 6 servings.

Pasta Salad Dressing

Prep: 5 minutes

¼ cup balsamic vinegar
¼ cup vegetable oil
¼ cup olive oil
1 tablespoon chopped fresh parsley
1 green onion, thinly sliced
1 garlic clove, minced
1 teaspoon lemon juice
½ teaspoon dried basil
½ teaspoon dried tarragon
¼ teaspoon salt

• **Whisk** together all ingredients in a small bowl until blended. Serve any remaining dressing over salad greens. **Yield:** 1 cup.

Chicken-and-Bow Tie Pasta: Add 2 cups chopped cooked chicken to Bow Tie Pasta.

Catherine David
Moscow, Texas

Ways With Okra

Nothing compares to the crisp delights of fresh fried okra or the soul-satisfying savor of steaming gumbo.

Look for okra with firm green pods no more than 4 inches long. To test for tenderness, touch tops of pods with the tip of a knife, which should easily pierce the skin. If not, okra should be discarded. Okra is best stored for no more than three days in the refrigerator.

OKRA GUMBO FREEZER MIX

Prep: 45 minutes
Bake: 2 hours

5   **pounds fresh okra, sliced**
6   **medium onions, chopped**
4   **celery ribs, chopped**
2   **green bell peppers, chopped**
2   **garlic cloves, minced**
1   **(15-ounce) can tomato sauce**
4   **bay leaves**
1   **tablespoon salt**
1   **tablespoon pepper**

• **Combine** all ingredients; spoon into 2 (13- x 9-inch) pans. Cover with foil. Bake at 300° for 2 hours; stir after 1 hour. Cool completely; spoon into 4 (1-pint) containers, and freeze up to 4 months. **Yield:** 4 pints.

Okra Gumbo

Prep: 20 minutes
Cook: 1 hour, 20 minutes

1   **pound unpeeled, medium-size fresh shrimp**
1   **pint Okra Gumbo Freezer Mix**
1   **(32-ounce) container chicken broth**
1   **(14½-ounce) can diced tomatoes**
¼   **teaspoon pepper**
3   **cups hot cooked rice**

• **Peel** shrimp; devein, if desired. Set aside. Bring Okra Gumbo Freezer Mix and next 3 ingredients to a boil in a Dutch oven over medium heat, stirring often. Cover, and reduce heat. Simmer, stirring occasionally, 1 hour and 10 minutes.
• **Add** shrimp; cook 10 minutes or just until shrimp turn pink. Discard bay leaves; serve over rice. **Yield:** 4 servings.
Evelyn Appelbee
Henderson, Texas

CRUNCHY FRIED OKRA

Go ahead and double the recipe—there's never enough of these crispy, golden morsels.

Prep: 20 minutes
Cook: 6 minutes

1½ **cups buttermilk**
1   **large egg**
2   **cups saltine cracker crumbs (2 sleeves)**
1½ **cups all-purpose flour**
1   **teaspoon salt**
1   **pound fresh okra, cut in half lengthwise**
Peanut oil

• **Stir** together buttermilk and egg. Combine cracker crumbs, flour, and salt. Dip okra pieces in buttermilk mixture; dredge in cracker crumb mixture.
• **Pour** oil to a depth of 2 inches into a Dutch oven or cast-iron skillet; heat to 375°. Fry okra, in 3 batches, 2 minutes or until golden, turning once. Drain on paper towels. **Yield:** 4 to 6 servings.
Harry Adams
Augusta, Georgia

Taste of the South

Serve golden, sweet corn pudding the next time you're looking for a side dish that offers old-fashioned Southern appeal.

Kathy Nash Cary, of Lilly's Restaurant in Louisville, shares a version of the creamy, corn-flecked custard. Kathy's maternal grandmother, Tee, first taught her mother, Sissy, to prepare this classic dish. We've streamlined Tee's recipe a bit, but the flavor still boasts the same goodness.

TEE'S CORN PUDDING
(pictured on page 153)

Prep: 15 minutes
Bake: 45 minutes
Stand: 5 minutes

¼   **cup sugar**
3   **tablespoons all-purpose flour**
2   **teaspoons baking powder**
1½ **teaspoons salt**
6   **large eggs**
2   **cups whipping cream**
½   **cup butter or margarine, melted**
6   **cups fresh corn kernels (about 12 ears) ✱**

• **Combine** first 4 ingredients.
• **Whisk** together eggs, cream, and butter. Gradually add sugar mixture, whisking until smooth; stir in corn. Pour into a lightly greased 13- x 9-inch baking dish.
• **Bake** at 350° for 45 minutes or until golden brown and set. Let stand 5 minutes. **Yield:** 8 servings.

✱Substitute 6 cups frozen whole kernel corn or canned shoepeg corn, drained, for fresh corn kernels, if desired.

Note: For testing purposes only, we used 'Silver Queen' corn.

Southwestern Corn Pudding: Stir in 1 (4.5-ounce) can drained chopped green chiles and ¼ teaspoon ground cumin.

From Our Kitchen

Tips and Tidbits

■ Now is the prime time for fresh blueberries, so look for a U-pick farm in your area. Store the fruit in airtight containers in the refrigerator up to five days. Remember not to wash the berries until you're ready to eat them or use them in a recipe. If you're lucky enough to have more than you can eat in five days, freeze the rest. Place unwashed berries in a single layer on a baking sheet. Place the baking sheet in the freezer. Transfer the frozen berries into airtight containers, and store them in the freezer up to five months.

■ Chipotle peppers are actually dried, smoked jalapeño chiles. You can find them dried in the produce section. When recipes call for chipotle peppers in adobo sauce, you'll find these on the shelves with the canned chiles. Adobo is a thick sauce containing herbs, vinegar, and chiles. Chipotles in adobo sauce add wonderful flavor to meat loaf, taco meat, or hamburgers. They'll soon become a staple in your pantry.

■ Cathryn Matthes, Executive Chef at Hilton Head Health Institute, keeps a large bowl near her food preparation area to save steps and time. As she peels and chops fruits and vegetables, she puts all the discards in the bowl. This eliminates repeated trips to the trash can or the garbage disposal. Gardeners can put the trimmings to good use by tossing them into the compost pile.

■ Is your refrigerator the right temperature? It should be no lower than 35°F and no higher than 40°F. The freezer compartment should register minus 5°F to 0°F. If your freezer is set too low, it's wasting energy; if the temperatures are too high, you risk food safety problems. A refrigerator or freezer that is too cold can also destroy the taste and texture of some fruits and vegetables. Periodically clean the front grill and condenser coils on your refrigerator with a brush or vacuum for best cooling and energy efficiency. When cleaning the coils, unplug the unit first.

■ Next time you stay in a hotel, be sure to take home those sealed shower caps to use in your kitchen. The plastic caps come in handy to cover containers for storing leftovers in the refrigerator or protecting picnic foods from pests. They also provide the right fit for cut melon halves; just slip one over a honeydew or cantaloupe to keep it fresh.

■ July is National Baked Bean month. Would you believe that Americans eat about 400 million pounds of baked beans a year? Whether you prefer canned or dry, serve baked beans this summer, and celebrate the benefits of this nutrient-rich food. For more information visit www.americanbean.org.

Coffee Coolers

If you're crazy for coffee even in summer heat, two of our readers found a way to enjoy it and stay cool too. Use fresh-brewed, double-strength, dark-roast coffee in iced drinks to ensure plenty of flavor and aroma when diluted.

LOW-FAT CAPPUCCINO COOLER

Prep: 5 minutes

1½ cups brewed coffee, chilled
1½ cups low-fat chocolate ice cream
¼ cup chocolate syrup
Reduced-fat frozen whipped topping, thawed (optional)

● **Process** first 3 ingredients in a blender until smooth. Serve immediately over crushed ice. Top with whipped topping, if desired. **Yield:** 3 cups.

Dottie B. Miller
Jonesborough, Tennessee

CHOCOLATE ICED COFFEE

To keep the drink from diluting, freeze leftover coffee and half-and-half in ice cube trays to use in place of ice.

Prep: 15 minutes
Chill: 2 hours

3½ cups water
1 cup ground coffee
2 tablespoons sugar
¾ teaspoon ground cinnamon
2 cups half-and-half
⅓ cup chocolate syrup

● **Bring** 3½ cups water and coffee to a boil in a saucepan, and remove from heat. Let stand 10 minutes.
● **Pour** mixture through a fine wire-mesh strainer into a bowl, discarding coffee grounds.
● **Stir** sugar and cinnamon into coffee until sugar dissolves; cool. Stir in half-and-half and syrup; chill 2 hours. Serve over ice. **Yield:** 2 quarts.

Sandi Pichon
Slidell, Louisiana

PRETTY PRODUCE

New and unusual produce is usually worth a try. 'Burgundy' okra looks pretty and tastes good too. Unlike the green type, these pods remain tender up to 7 and 8 inches long. Use it in the same recipes as you would green okra. This okra magically turns green when cooked.

White eggplants look like jumbo-size eggs. They have a firmer flesh and contain a little less water than the traditional type. Work with these the same way you would the purple variety, but you'll want to peel them because the skin can be thicker and a bit tough. Use white eggplant when you need a firm-textured vegetable, as it holds its shape regardless of the cooking method.

AUGUST

Smoked for Flavor

From main dish to unusual sides,
let the wood chips do the work.

Smoking makes for take-it-easy cooking. Smoke from the wood chips wraps food in a blanket, sealing in the natural juices. It's an easy process, but it isn't quick. You'll get tender meats and vegetables, but don't stop there: Fill your grill with shrimp, cheese, and pecans too. If you don't have a smoker, your grill with a lid and a pan of water works well. The liquid in the water pan keeps foods moist. To achieve that wood-smoked flavor, purchase hickory and mesquite chips found near the charcoal in most grocery stores.

If you can't get outside, there's a stove-top unit available. Some smoke may escape during cooking, so open the windows. Small items and thin cuts of meat work best for this method.

STOVE-TOP SMOKED SHRIMP

These are great peel-and-eat appetizers.
They also give shrimp cocktail and
shrimp salad a terrific flavor boost.

Prep: 10 minutes
Cook: 10 minutes

1 cup finely ground hickory wood chips
3 pounds unpeeled, large fresh shrimp
3 tablespoons olive oil
½ teaspoon salt
¼ teaspoon freshly ground pepper

• **Place** wood chips into center of stove-top smoking pan. Insert drip pan and food rack.
• **Toss** shrimp with remaining ingredients. Arrange shrimp on food rack; cover with smoker lid.
• **Cook** shrimp over medium heat 10 minutes or just until shrimp turn pink. **Yield:** 3 pounds.

SMOKY PECANS

Prep: 30 minutes
Cook: 1 hour

Hickory wood chips
2 pounds pecan halves
½ cup butter or margarine, melted
1 teaspoon salt

• **Soak** wood chips in water at least 30 minutes.
• **Prepare** charcoal fire in smoker; let burn 15 to 20 minutes.
• **Drain** chips, and place on coals. Place water pan in smoker; add water to depth of fill line.
• **Stir** together pecans, butter, and salt in a 24- x 12-inch pan. Place on upper food rack; cover with smoker lid.
• **Cook** 1 hour or until golden, stirring once after 30 minutes. **Yield:** 2 pounds.

Note: Use a baking pan that fits your grill if the 24- x 12-inch baking pan is too large.

Richard Powell
Enid, Oklahoma

EASY SMOKED CHEDDAR

Prep: 30 minutes
Cook: 2 hours

Hickory wood chips
2 (16-ounce) blocks Cheddar cheese
Vegetable cooking spray
Cheesecloth

• **Soak** wood chips in water at least 30 minutes.
• **Prepare** charcoal fire in smoker; let burn 15 to 20 minutes.

• **Place** 1 cheese block on top of the other; coat with cooking spray. Place lengthwise in center of a 24-inch piece of cheesecloth. Tightly wrap cheesecloth around stacked cheese. Place wrapped cheese crosswise in center of another 24-inch piece cheesecloth; tightly wrap.
• **Drain** chips, and place on coals. Place water pan in smoker; add water to depth of fill line. Place wrapped cheese, seam side down, on upper food rack; cover with smoker lid.
• **Cook** cheese 2 hours. **Yield:** 2 (16-ounce) blocks.

Gerry N. Brown
Conyers, Georgia

CHICKEN WITH WHITE BARBECUE SAUCE

Prep: 30 minutes
Chill: 8 hours
Cook: 2 hours

1 cup mayonnaise
½ cup white vinegar
1 tablespoon lemon juice
1 teaspoon salt
1 teaspoon pepper
Hickory wood chips
2 (2½-pound) whole chickens
1 teaspoon salt
1 teaspoon pepper
2 lemons, cut in half

• **Stir** together first 5 ingredients; cover and chill 8 hours.
• **Soak** wood chips in water at least 30 minutes.
• **Prepare** charcoal fire in smoker; let burn 15 to 20 minutes.
• **Rinse** chickens, and pat dry. Sprinkle each chicken with ½ teaspoon salt and ½ teaspoon pepper. Place 2 lemon halves into the cavity of each chicken.
• **Drain** chips; place on coals. Place water pan in smoker, and add water to depth of fill line. Place chickens on lower food rack, and cover with smoker lid.
• **Cook** 1 hour and 30 minutes to 2 hours or until a meat thermometer inserted into thickest portion registers 180°. Serve chicken with sauce. **Yield:** 8 servings.

SMOKED BRISKET

Prep: 30 minutes
Cook: 3 hours, 30 minutes

Hickory wood chips
2 tablespoons dried rosemary
2 tablespoons paprika
2 tablespoons pepper
2 tablespoons dried garlic flakes
1 teaspoon salt
1 (7-pound) untrimmed beef brisket
Barbecue sauce
Hamburger buns
Pickles
Garnish: fresh rosemary sprigs

• **Soak** wood chips in water at least 30 minutes.
• **Prepare** charcoal fire in smoker; let burn 15 to 20 minutes.
• **Combine** rosemary and next 4 ingredients; rub on brisket.
• **Drain** wood chips, and place on coals. Place water pan in smoker; add water to depth of fill line. Place brisket on lower food rack; cover with smoker lid.
• **Cook** 3 hours and 30 minutes or until meat thermometer inserted into thickest portion registers 155°. Slice and serve with barbecue sauce, buns, and pickles. Garnish, if desired. **Yield:** 8 servings.

SMOKED CORN

Thyme and butter seep through the kernels of the sweet, smoky corn.

Prep: 40 minutes
Cook: 40 minutes
Stand: 10 minutes

Hickory wood chips
½ cup butter, softened
2 tablespoons chopped fresh thyme
8 ears fresh corn with husks

• **Soak** wood chips in water at least 30 minutes.
• **Prepare** charcoal fire in smoker; let burn 15 to 20 minutes.
• **Stir** together butter and thyme.
• **Remove** heavy outer husks from corn; pull back inner husks. Remove and discard silks. Rub corn with butter mixture. Pull husks back over corn.
• **Drain** chips, and place on coals. Place water pan in smoker; add water to depth of fill line. Place corn on upper food rack; cover with smoker lid.
• **Cook** 30 to 40 minutes. Remove from smoker, and let stand 10 minutes. Pull husks back, and serve. **Yield:** 8 ears corn.

Taste of the South

Barbecue, catfish, and grits—all examples of true Southern culinary icons. Enter pimiento cheese. A cookbook containing one true recipe, let alone the many regional variations, is almost impossible to find; favorite recipes survive by way of oral tradition.

In our search for the definitive blend, we asked Mary Allen Perry of our Test Kitchens to share her recipe. She drew upon childhood memories to record this fabulous formula. So you should feel confident with this terrific version and its variations.

Mary Allen's tip: Use a box grater to achieve both coarse-grated and finely shredded cheese. (For more information, see "From Our Kitchen" on page 182.)

PIMIENTO CHEESE

Prep: 15 minutes

1½ cups mayonnaise
1 (4-ounce) jar diced pimiento, drained
1 teaspoon Worcestershire sauce
1 teaspoon finely grated onion
¼ teaspoon ground red pepper
1 (8-ounce) block extra-sharp Cheddar cheese, finely shredded
1 (8-ounce) block sharp Cheddar cheese, shredded

• **Stir** together first 5 ingredients in a large bowl; stir in cheeses. Store in refrigerator up to 1 week. **Yield:** 4 cups.

Jalapeño Pimiento Cheese: Add 2 seeded and minced jalapeño peppers.

Cream Cheese-and-Olive Pimiento Cheese: Reduce mayonnaise to ¾ cup. Stir together first 5 ingredients, 1 (8-ounce) package softened cream cheese, and 1 (5¾-ounce) jar drained sliced salad olives. Proceed with recipe as directed.

Pecan Pimiento Cheese: Stir in ¾ cup toasted chopped pecans.

SMOKE SIGNALS

■ Soak your favorite wood chips in water at least 30 minutes before using. (The wet wood will smoke slowly; dry wood will flame and quickly burn out.) Hickory and mesquite are the most popular in our region, but apple, cherry, and pecan chips impart great flavor, too.

■ Add wine, broth, or fresh herbs to the water pan for more flavor.

■ Electric, gas, and charcoal smokers work equally well.

■ If you're using a charcoal grill, arrange the hot coals and wood chips on one side. (For a gas grill, light only one side.) Position a small pan of water on the unlit side. Place the food rack on the grill; arrange food over the water pan. Close the lid, leaving a small vent open to keep the coals alive.

■ Use an instant-read thermometer to check for doneness of smoked foods. Don't depend on appearance alone. When the proper internal temperature is reached, the outside of large pieces of meat may be quite dark; the interior may appear slightly red or pink, but it's perfectly safe. Smoked meats retain some of their internal pink color.

Living Light

Soft tacos are basically small fajitas without the tableside sizzle. Warmed flour or corn tortillas can be filled with a variety of delicious and nutritious ingredients. Seasoned lean meats, seafood, and vegetables are terrific in tortillas. Just wrap them up with some peppers, spices, and cheese, and you've got supper in a flash. We offer these easy-to-prepare soft tacos with tasty new fillings.

SKILLET VEGGIE TACOS

Prep: 15 minutes
Cook: 20 minutes

2 **red bell peppers, coarsely chopped**
1 **medium onion, chopped**
1 **cup sliced fresh mushrooms**
1 **to 2 jalapeño peppers, seeded and chopped**
2 **garlic cloves, minced**
2 **teaspoons olive oil**
1½ **teaspoons ground cumin**
1 **teaspoon dried oregano**
¾ **cup sweet white wine**
1 **(15-ounce) can pinto beans, rinsed and drained**
2 **cups chopped fresh spinach**
12 **(8-inch) fat-free flour tortillas, warmed**
½ **cup crumbled reduced-fat feta cheese (optional)**

• **Sauté** first 5 ingredients in hot oil in a skillet over medium-high heat 5 minutes or until vegetables are tender. Add cumin and oregano; sauté 2 minutes.
• **Stir** in wine; reduce heat, and simmer 10 minutes or until liquid is reduced by half. Add beans, and cook until thoroughly heated. Add spinach; cook 2 minutes or until spinach wilts. Serve in warm tortillas with cheese, if desired. **Yield:** 12 servings.

♥ Per serving: Calories 200 (10% from fat)
Fat 2.3g (sat 1g, mono 0.6g, poly 0.1g)
Protein 8g Carb 34g Fiber 5g
Chol 3mg Iron 1.2mg
Sodium 419mg Calc 59mg

SHRIMP TACOS WITH SPICY CREAM SAUCE

Chili powder, cumin, and red pepper add zing to the cool cream sauce.

Prep: 20 minutes
Chill: 15 minutes
Cook: 10 minutes

1 **(16-ounce) container nonfat sour cream**
2 **teaspoons chili powder, divided**
1 **teaspoon ground cumin, divided**
¾ **teaspoon ground red pepper, divided**
¾ **teaspoon salt, divided**
¼ **teaspoon ground cinnamon**
½ **cup water**
1 **pound unpeeled, medium-size fresh shrimp**
3 **tablespoons orange juice**
2 **garlic cloves, minced**
2 **teaspoons olive oil**
1 **avocado, chopped**
8 **(8-inch) corn tortillas, warmed**

• **Whisk** together sour cream, 1 teaspoon chili powder, ½ teaspoon cumin, ½ teaspoon red pepper, ¼ teaspoon salt, and cinnamon. Add ½ cup water, stirring until smooth. Cover and chill until ready to serve.
• **Peel** shrimp, and devein, if desired; chop. Combine remaining 1 teaspoon chili powder, ½ teaspoon cumin, ¼ teaspoon red pepper, and ½ teaspoon salt in a shallow dish or heavy-duty zip-top plastic bag; add orange juice and shrimp, turning to coat. Cover or seal, and chill 15 minutes. Remove shrimp from marinade, discarding marinade.
• **Sauté** garlic in hot oil in a large skillet over medium-high heat 2 to 3 minutes. Add shrimp, and cook 5 minutes or just until shrimp turn pink. Serve with sour cream mixture and avocado in warm tortillas. **Yield:** 8 servings.

♥ Per serving: Calories 212 (26% from fat)
Fat 6.2g (sat 1g, mono 3.6g, poly 1.1g)
Protein 13g Carb 26g Fiber 3g
Chol 72mg Iron 2mg
Sodium 391mg Calc 140mg

JERK STEAK TACOS

Jerk seasoning, a blend of spices that originated in the Caribbean, gives this spicy dish its name and its flavor.

Prep: 20 minutes
Chill: 8 hours
Grill: 29 minutes
Stand: 10 minutes

4 **green onions, coarsely chopped**
1 **garlic clove**
1 **jalapeño pepper, seeded**
1 **tablespoon ground allspice**
1 **teaspoon dried thyme**
½ **teaspoon ground nutmeg**
½ **teaspoon ground red pepper**
2 **tablespoons lime juice**
1 **to 1½ pounds flank steak**
1 **bunch green onions**
4 **large tomatoes**
Vegetable cooking spray
¼ **teaspoon salt**
8 **(8-inch) flour tortillas, warmed**

• **Process** first 8 ingredients in a blender or food processor until smooth, stopping to scrape down sides. Spread seasoning mixture evenly over steak; cover and chill 8 hours.
• **Grill** steak, covered with grill lid, over medium-high heat (350° to 400°) 6 to 7 minutes on each side or to desired degree of doneness. Let stand 10 minutes; cut into thin slices.
• **Coat** 1 bunch green onions and tomatoes evenly with cooking spray; sprinkle with salt.
• **Grill,** covered with grill lid, over medium-high heat 10 to 15 minutes, turning occasionally. Coarsely chop vegetables. Serve with steak in warm tortillas. **Yield:** 8 servings.

Judy Carter
Winchester, Tennessee

♥ Per serving: Calories 232 (26% from fat)
Fat 6.6g (sat 2g, mono 1.8g, poly 0.3g)
Protein 16g Carb 29g Fiber 2.5g
Chol 29mg Iron 3.2mg
Sodium 399mg Calc 89mg

What's for Supper?

Why not consider a hearty sandwich for dinner? Each of these recipes can be prepared in 15 minutes or less.

Sandwiches are not just for lunch. And eating one with a knife and fork adds a bit of refinement to the handheld standby. We've taken three sandwich recipes and served them open-faced. Instead of the customary sandwich bread, these versions utilize some delicious alternatives. The rustic bread in Open-Faced Summer Sandwiches can be found in the bakery section of your local grocery store.

Any of these would pair nicely with a simple green salad or fruit salad for a complete meal. You'll find that having a sandwich for supper has been elevated to a whole new level.

OPEN-FACED MONTE CRISTO SANDWICHES

A dusting of powdered sugar distinguishes this time-honored sandwich.

Prep: 15 minutes
Broil: 3 minutes

2 large eggs
½ cup milk
½ teaspoon salt
¼ teaspoon pepper
4 (1-inch-thick) white bread slices
2 tablespoons butter or margarine
4 tablespoons strawberry jam or red currant jelly
4 ounces thinly sliced cooked turkey or chicken
4 ounces thinly sliced smoked cooked ham
8 (¾-ounce) Swiss cheese slices
Powdered sugar (optional)

• **Whisk** together first 4 ingredients in a shallow dish. Dip both sides of bread slices in egg mixture.

• **Melt** butter in a large skillet; add bread slices, and cook 2 to 3 minutes on each side or until golden brown.

• **Spread** 1 tablespoon strawberry jam on 1 side of each bread slice; top evenly with turkey, ham, and cheese. Place on a baking sheet.

• **Broil** 5 inches from heat 2 to 3 minutes or until cheese is melted. Sprinkle with powdered sugar, if desired. Serve immediately. **Yield:** 4 servings.

OPEN-FACED CRAB MELTS

Prep: 10 minutes
Broil: 3 minutes

1 pound fresh lump crabmeat, drained *
¼ to ⅓ cup mayonnaise
½ teaspoon salt
¼ teaspoon pepper
¼ teaspoon sugar
3 English muffins, split and toasted
1 cup (4 ounces) shredded sharp Cheddar cheese

• **Stir** together first 5 ingredients. Spread mixture evenly over cut sides of muffin halves; sprinkle evenly with cheese.

• **Broil** 5 inches from heat 2 to 3 minutes or until cheese is melted. Serve immediately. **Yield:** 6 servings.

*Substitute 2 (6-ounce) cans lump crabmeat or 2 (6-ounce) cans solid white tuna in spring water, drained, if desired.

*Carol S. Noble
Burgaw, North Carolina*

OPEN-FACED SUMMER SANDWICHES

Pesto, mayonnaise, and sweet onion slices update the classic tomato sandwich.

Prep: 10 minutes
Grill: 26 minutes

2 large tomatoes, cut into ½-inch-thick slices
1 teaspoon salt
½ teaspoon pepper
4 (1- to 1½-inch-thick) rustic bread slices *
¼ cup olive oil
2 large sweet onions, cut into ½-inch-thick slices
½ cup mayonnaise
3 tablespoons pesto
1 cup sliced ripe olives
2½ tablespoons chopped fresh mint (optional)

• **Sprinkle** tomato slices evenly with salt and pepper; set aside.

• **Brush** both sides of bread slices with olive oil.

• **Grill** bread, without grill lid, over medium heat (300° to 350°) 2 to 3 minutes on each side or until lightly browned.

• **Grill** onion, covered with grill lid, over high heat (400° to 500°) 8 to 10 minutes on each side or until tender and browned.

• **Stir** together mayonnaise and pesto; spread evenly on 1 side of each bread slice. Top evenly with tomato and onion slices; sprinkle with olives. Sprinkle with mint, if desired. **Yield:** 4 servings.

*Substitute 4 (1-inch-thick) French bread slices, if desired.

*Adelyne Smith
Dunnville, Kentucky*

Way Cool Cupcakes

Who says you can't have your cake and ice cream too?

This summer, treat your family and friends to the unbeatable combination of ice cream and cake or cookies. Pair these respected companions in cupcake fashion for a fun and unique dessert. Their unconventional style, great taste, and charm will delight kids and adults alike. As an added bonus, they can be made ahead and stored in an airtight container in your freezer up to two weeks, so these cool concoctions are ready when you are.

LEMON-BLUEBERRY ICE-CREAM CUPCAKES

Prep: 20 minutes
Freeze: 8 hours

24 lemon cookies, coarsely crushed
1 (21-ounce) can blueberry fruit filling
1 (14-ounce) can sweetened condensed milk
1 (6-ounce) can frozen lemonade concentrate, thawed and undiluted
1 (8-ounce) container frozen whipped topping, thawed
Multicolored candies and sprinkles

• **Place** 12 foil baking cups into muffin pans; sprinkle crushed cookies evenly into cups. Spoon 2 teaspoons fruit filling over cookies in each cup, reserving remaining fruit filling for another use.
• **Fold** condensed milk and lemonade concentrate into whipped topping, and spoon over fruit filling in prepared baking cups. Freeze 8 hours or until firm. Top with candies and sprinkles just before serving. **Yield:** 12 cupcakes.

Note: For testing purposes only, we used Keebler Lemon Coolers cookies.

MINT-CHOCOLATE CHIP ICE-CREAM CUPCAKES

Ice cream, liqueur, and candy provide more than just a hint of mint in these cool, chocolaty cupcakes.

Prep: 20 minutes
Bake: 25 minutes
Freeze: 8 hours

1 (19.8-ounce) package fudge brownie mix
½ cup water
½ cup vegetable oil
3 large eggs
½ gallon mint-chocolate chip ice cream, softened
1 (8-ounce) container frozen whipped topping, thawed
2 to 3 tablespoons green crème de menthe (optional)
½ (4.67-ounce) package chocolate mints

• **Stir** together first 4 ingredients until blended. Place 12 foil baking cups into muffin pans; spoon batter into cups.
• **Bake** at 350° for 20 to 25 minutes. (A wooden pick inserted in center does not come out clean.) Cool in pans on wire racks 10 minutes; remove from pans, and cool completely on wire racks.
• **Return** baking cups to muffin pans, and spoon ice cream evenly over each brownie. Freeze 8 hours or until firm.
• **Stir** together whipped topping and, if desired, liqueur. Dollop evenly over ice cream. Freeze until ready to serve.
• **Pull** a vegetable peeler down sides of mints, making tiny curls; sprinkle curls over cupcakes just before serving. **Yield:** 12 cupcakes.

Note: For testing purposes only, we used Andes Creme De Menthe Thins for chocolate mints.

CHOCOLATE-BRICKLE ICE-CREAM CUPCAKES

Indulging in one of these frozen delights is like enjoying a miniature hot fudge sundae.

Prep: 15 minutes
Freeze: 9 hours

1 (12-ounce) loaf pound cake
1 (7.5-ounce) package almond brickle chips, divided
½ cup chopped pecans, toasted
2 pints chocolate mocha-fudge ice cream, softened
1 (8-ounce) container frozen whipped topping, thawed
½ (11.5-ounce) jar hot fudge sauce

• **Cut** cake in half horizontally. Cut each cake half into 6 (2-inch) circles, using a 2-inch round cutter. Reserve remaining cake for another use. Place 12 foil baking cups into muffin pans; place 1 cake round in each cup.
• **Stir** ½ cup almond brickle chips and toasted pecans into ice cream. Freeze 1 hour or until almost firm.
• **Spoon** ice cream evenly over each cake round, filling to top of baking cup and mounding slightly. Dollop evenly with whipped topping. Freeze 8 hours or until firm.
• **Microwave** fudge sauce at HIGH 30 seconds; drizzle over cupcakes, and sprinkle with remaining almond brickle chips just before serving. **Yield:** 12 cupcakes.

Note: For testing purposes only, we used Heath Bits O' Brickle for almond brickle chips; you can find them near the chocolate morsels in your local supermarket.

Banana Pudding Ice-Cream Cupcakes

Place muffin pans over ice in a roasting pan to keep the ice cream from melting when broiling the meringue.

Prep: 25 minutes
Broil: 2 minutes
Freeze: 9 hours

12 vanilla wafers, coarsely crushed
2 medium-size ripe bananas, mashed
2 teaspoons lemon juice
4 cups vanilla ice cream, softened
½ cup frozen whipped topping, thawed
1 tablespoon meringue powder
¼ cup cold water
6 tablespoons sugar

• **Place** 12 foil baking cups into muffin pans; sprinkle crushed wafers evenly into cups.
• **Stir** together banana and lemon juice; stir mixture into ice cream. Gently fold in whipped topping. (Do not blend completely.) Freeze 1 hour or until almost firm.
• **Spoon** ice cream mixture evenly into prepared baking cups. Freeze 8 hours.
• **Stir** together meringue powder, ¼ cup cold water, and 3 tablespoons sugar. Beat at high speed with an electric mixer 5 minutes. Gradually add remaining 3 tablespoons sugar, beating mixture at high speed for 5 minutes or until stiff peaks form.
• **Spread** 2 tablespoons meringue (working rapidly) over frozen cupcakes in pans, sealing to edge of foil liner. Fill a roasting pan with ice, and place muffin pans over ice.
• **Broil** 5½ inches from heat 2 minutes or until meringue is golden. Remove cupcakes from pans, and serve immediately, or refreeze, if desired. **Yield:** 12 cupcakes.

Elizabeth Taliaferro
Birmingham, Alabama

Frosty Shakes

For many, shakes and malts in dazzling colors, oozing over the sides of frosted glasses, symbolize relief from summer's heat. An all-time favorite after-school snack: homemade chocolate- and berry-flavored shakes. We've enhanced those old-fashioned treats with fresh fruits, flavored yogurts, and buttermilk. We also included some healthy options. Children and adults can't resist these chilly coolers, so add a straw and sip away.

Three-Fruit Yogurt Shake

If you can't find pretty blueberries and peaches in your area, substitute packages of frozen fruit—no thawing required.

Prep: 10 minutes

2 cups low-fat vanilla yogurt
1 cup fresh blueberries, frozen
1 cup fresh peach slices, frozen
1 (8-ounce) can unsweetened pineapple chunks, drained and frozen

• **Process** all ingredients in a blender until smooth, stopping to scrape down sides. Serve immediately. **Yield:** 5 cups.

Chocolate-Yogurt Malt

Prep: 5 minutes

4 cups low-fat frozen vanilla yogurt
1 cup chocolate 1% low-fat milk
¼ cup chocolate-flavored instant malted milk

• **Process** all ingredients in a blender until smooth, stopping to scrape down sides. Serve immediately. **Yield:** 5 cups.

Note: For testing purposes only, we used Ovaltine for chocolate-flavored instant malted milk.

Double Strawberry-Banana Shake

A double dose of strawberries gives this fruity shake its pleasing pink hue.

Prep: 10 minutes

2 cups strawberries, sliced and frozen
2 large ripe bananas, sliced and frozen
1 pint strawberry ice cream
2 cups milk
1 teaspoon vanilla extract

• **Process** all ingredients in a blender until smooth, stopping to scrape down sides. Serve immediately. **Yield:** 8 cups.

Light Double Strawberry-Banana Shake: Substitute fat-free frozen strawberry yogurt and fat-free milk. Proceed with recipe as directed, and serve immediately.

Jean Voan
Shepherd, Texas

Pineapple-Buttermilk Shake

The tang of buttermilk balances the sweetness of pineapple in this chilly cooler.

Prep: 10 minutes

1 (8-ounce) can unsweetened pineapple chunks, drained and frozen
1 quart vanilla ice cream
½ cup firmly packed brown sugar
2 cups buttermilk

• **Process** all ingredients in a blender until smooth, stopping to scrape down sides. Serve immediately. **Yield:** 6 cups.

Light Pineapple-Buttermilk Shake: Substitute low-fat vanilla ice cream and fat-free buttermilk, and reduce brown sugar to ⅓ cup. Proceed with recipe as directed, and serve immediately.

Marie Davis
Charlotte, North Carolina

Entertaining Made Easy

Try this winning menu for your next gathering.

Entertaining Menu
Serves 10

Fruit Spritzer
Fiery Salsa with blue corn chips
Grilled Pork Tenderloins With Rosemary Pesto
Wild Rice-and-Kidney Bean Salad
Broccoli-and-Squash Casserole

Editorial Assistant Vicki Poellnitz and her husband, Hank, love to entertain. And with family and friends living nearby, this is a regular occurrence. "Hank and I are pretty laid-back when it comes to having people over, and we always have more than enough food, so if extra people show up, it's no problem. The more the merrier," says Vicki.

However, don't confuse this easygoing attitude with a lack of attention to details—quite the contrary. Vicki has a real flair for cooking and serving dishes with style, which is evident in her delicious recipes and beautiful presentations.

And what does Vicki do when extra guests show up and she's running low on serving pieces? "I always keep nice paper products on hand. I look for them on sale and choose colors that match my dishes. I've also used wine glasses to serve ice cream because I was out of bowls," she says. Vicki's motto: Be prepared, and improvise when necessary.

FRUIT SPRITZER

Prep: 10 minutes

1 cup frozen raspberries
2 tablespoons powdered sugar
3 cups orange juice
1 cup vodka*
½ cup Key lime juice
1 (16-ounce) bottle ginger ale, chilled

• **Process** first 5 ingredients in a blender until smooth. Pour mixture into a large pitcher; stir in ginger ale. Chill and serve over ice. **Yield:** about 6 cups.

*Substitute 1 cup each of orange juice and ginger ale for 1 cup vodka, if desired.

FIERY SALSA

Prep: 15 minutes
Cook: 20 minutes

2 large onions, thinly sliced
4 garlic cloves, minced
2 tablespoons vegetable oil
1 (28-ounce) can diced tomatoes, undrained
½ jalapeño pepper, seeded and minced
1 teaspoon chopped canned chipotle peppers in adobo sauce
2 teaspoons adobo sauce (from canned chipotle peppers)
½ cup frozen whole kernel corn
¼ teaspoon salt
¼ cup chopped fresh cilantro
2 tablespoons lime juice

• **Sauté** onion and garlic in hot oil in a large saucepan over medium-high heat 5 minutes or until tender. Add tomatoes and next 3 ingredients. Bring to a boil. Reduce heat to medium-low; cook, covered, 10 minutes, stirring occasionally.
• **Process** 1 cup tomato mixture in blender until smooth, stopping to scrape down sides; return to saucepan.
• **Stir** in corn and salt; cook 3 minutes or until thoroughly heated. Stir in cilantro and lime juice. Serve with blue corn chips. **Yield:** 3 cups.

Note: Spice flavor increases when chilled overnight.

GRILLED PORK TENDERLOINS WITH ROSEMARY PESTO

Rosemary replaces traditional basil in the fragrant pesto that flavors the tender pork.

Prep: 30 minutes
Grill: 1 hour, 30 minutes

6 to 10 fresh rosemary sprigs
¼ cup chopped walnuts
2 tablespoons Creole mustard
3 garlic cloves, chopped
½ cup olive oil, divided
4 (½- to ¾-pound) pork tenderloins
⅛ teaspoon salt
⅛ teaspoon pepper
Garnish: fresh rosemary sprigs

- **Remove** leaves from rosemary sprigs, and measure ¾ cup leaves. Soak rosemary stems in water; set aside.
- **Process** rosemary leaves, walnuts, mustard, and garlic in a food processor until smooth, stopping to scrape down sides. With processor running, pour ¼ cup oil through food chute in a slow stream; process until smooth. Set pesto aside.
- **Place** tenderloins between 2 sheets of heavy-duty plastic wrap, and flatten to ½- to ¾-inch thickness, using a meat mallet or rolling pin. Spread pesto evenly over top of 2 tenderloins; place remaining tenderloins on top, and tie tenderloin pairs together with kitchen string. Rub remaining oil over pork; sprinkle with salt and pepper.
- **Prepare** a hot fire by piling charcoal on 1 side of grill, leaving other side empty. (For gas grills, light only 1 side.) Remove rosemary stems from water, and place on hot coals. Place food rack on grill, and place pork tenderloins over unlit side.
- **Grill,** covered with grill lid, 1 hour and 30 minutes or until a meat thermometer inserted into thickest portion registers 160°. Let stand 10 minutes. Garnish, if desired. **Yield:** 10 to 12 servings.

WILD RICE-AND-KIDNEY BEAN SALAD

Prep: 35 minutes
Chill: 2 hours

1 (6-ounce) package long-grain and wild rice mix
1 cup chicken broth
1 cup orange juice
⅓ cup water
2 (16-ounce) cans kidney beans, rinsed and drained
3 large hard-cooked eggs, peeled and diced
1 large onion, minced
½ cup mayonnaise
¼ teaspoon salt
¼ teaspoon pepper
⅛ teaspoon ground red pepper
½ cup sliced almonds, toasted
Garnish: chopped fresh parsley

- **Cook** rice according to package directions, using chicken broth, orange juice, and ⅓ cup water for liquid.
- **Stir** beans and next 6 ingredients into rice. Cover and chill 2 hours; top with almonds just before serving. Garnish, if desired. **Yield:** 8 to 10 servings.

BROCCOLI-AND-SQUASH CASSEROLE

Ample amounts of broccoli and squash fill this crowd-pleasing casserole.

Prep: 30 minutes
Bake: 25 minutes

2 pounds fresh broccoli florets, cut into bite-size pieces
2 pounds yellow squash, sliced
2 small onions, chopped
4 tablespoons butter or margarine
2 large eggs, lightly beaten
1 cup mayonnaise
4 cups (16 ounces) shredded Cheddar cheese
¼ teaspoon pepper
3 cups fine, dry breadcrumbs

- **Arrange** broccoli in a large steamer basket over boiling water. Cover and steam 5 to 8 minutes or until crisp-tender; remove from basket. Add squash and onion to basket, and repeat procedure.
- **Combine** squash, onion, and butter in a large bowl; mash. Stir in broccoli, eggs, and next 3 ingredients; spoon into 2 lightly greased 2-quart baking dishes. Sprinkle evenly with breadcrumbs.
- **Bake** at 350° for 20 to 25 minutes or until golden. **Yield:** 8 to 12 servings.

Chop and Stir

Turn up the heat, and stir chopped chicken and vegetables in a wok for a terrific meal. A large skillet works just as well. Take this easy recipe from the page to the table in just 35 minutes.

CHICKEN-VEGETABLE STIR-FRY

Prep: 25 minutes
Cook: 10 minutes

4 skinned and boned chicken breast halves
1 medium-size sweet onion
1 green bell pepper
1 red bell pepper
3 carrots
3 green onions
1 (10½-ounce) can chicken broth, undiluted
¼ cup soy sauce
1 to 2 tablespoons chili-garlic paste
2 tablespoons cornstarch
1 tablespoon brown sugar
1 tablespoon grated fresh ginger
2 tablespoons dark sesame oil
Hot cooked rice
Garnish: green onions

- **Cut** chicken into ¼-inch-thick strips; cut sweet onion in half, and cut halves into slices. Cut bell peppers into ¼-inch-thick strips, and cut carrots and green onions diagonally into slices. Set aside.
- **Whisk** together broth and next 5 ingredients until smooth.
- **Heat** sesame oil in a wok or large skillet at medium-high heat 2 minutes. Add chicken, and stir-fry 3 to 5 minutes or until lightly browned. Add vegetables, and stir-fry 3 to 4 minutes. Add broth mixture, and stir-fry 1 minute or until thickened. Serve over rice. Garnish, if desired. **Yield:** 4 to 6 servings.

Cool and Creamy Soups

Take a break from the kitchen and the heat with these chilled no-cook summer soups.

Chilled soups can provide a cooling respite from summer's sultry heat. They make a great start to a light meal or a main course when they're served with a crisp green salad and warm rolls. Best of all, these creamy creations don't require a bit of cooking, and they can be prepared in 15 minutes or less. Chill them at least two hours to bring out the best flavor. If you prefer more texture, you can puree the soup mixture until it's partially smooth, or toss in some diced vegetables to garnish and to add a little crunch to the dish. Serve these recipes in well-chilled bowls to help keep them cold longer.

CREAMY AVOCADO SOUP

Prep: 15 minutes
Chill: 3 hours

3 avocados, quartered
½ cup coarsely chopped fresh cilantro
¼ cup coarsely chopped onion
¼ cup coarsely chopped green onions
¼ cup coarsely chopped fresh parsley
1 to 3 tablespoons lime juice
1 teaspoon chili powder
1 teaspoon salt
¼ teaspoon pepper
¼ teaspoon ground cumin
¼ to ½ teaspoon hot sauce
1 (32-ounce) container chicken broth
1 (16-ounce) container sour cream*

• **Process** avocado in a blender or food processor until mixture is smooth, stopping to scrape down sides. Add chopped cilantro and next 9 ingredients, and process until mixture is smooth, stopping to scrape down sides. Pour into a large bowl; stir in chicken broth and sour cream. Cover and chill 3 hours. **Yield:** 8 cups.

*Substitute 1 (16-ounce) container light sour cream, if desired.

Sheryl Davidson
Atlanta, Georgia

FIESTA CITRUS SOUP

Prep: 15 minutes
Chill: 4 hours

1 large grapefruit
2 large oranges
1 cup chopped plum tomato
½ cup chopped green bell pepper
¼ cup chopped English cucumber*
¼ cup chopped tomatillos
2 tablespoons chopped purple onion
2 tablespoons chopped fresh cilantro
2 garlic cloves, minced
½ cup reduced-sodium tomato juice
¼ cup low-sodium fat-free chicken broth
2 tablespoons lime juice
1 teaspoon hot sauce

• **Peel,** section, and seed grapefruit and oranges. Coarsely chop sections, and place in a bowl.
• **Add** chopped tomato and remaining ingredients; cover and chill mixture 4 hours. **Yield:** 4 cups.

*Substitute ¼ cup peeled, seeded, and chopped cucumber, if desired.

CUCUMBER-DILL SOUP

Prep: 10 minutes
Chill: 2 hours

2 cucumbers, peeled, seeded, and coarsely chopped
1 green onion, coarsely chopped
1 tablespoon lemon juice
1 (16-ounce) container sour cream*
1 cup half-and-half*
1 tablespoon minced fresh dill
1 teaspoon salt
¼ teaspoon pepper
⅛ teaspoon hot sauce
Garnish: fresh dill sprigs

• **Process** first 3 ingredients in a blender or food processor until smooth, stopping to scrape down sides. Pour into a large bowl; stir in sour cream and next 5 ingredients. Cover and chill 2 hours. Garnish, if desired. **Yield:** 4 cups.

*Substitute 1 (16-ounce) container light sour cream and 1 cup fat-free half-and-half, if desired.

WATERCRESS SOUP

Prep: 15 minutes
Chill: 8 hours

2 cups chicken broth
1½ cups loosely packed watercress leaves
2 cucumbers, peeled, seeded, and chopped
1 green bell pepper, chopped
4 green onions, chopped
3 tablespoons chopped fresh dill
¼ cup light mayonnaise
¼ cup light sour cream
2 tablespoons sugar
3 tablespoons white wine vinegar
1 teaspoon salt
½ teaspoon pepper

• **Process** first 6 ingredients in a blender or food processor until mixture is smooth, stopping to scrape down sides. Add mayonnaise, sour cream, and remaining ingredients; process until blended. Cover and chill 8 hours. **Yield:** 6 cups.

GAZPACHO BLANCO

Prep: 15 minutes
Chill: 2 hours

3 small cucumbers, peeled, seeded, and chopped
1 garlic clove, pressed
2 cups chicken broth
1 (16-ounce) container sour cream✻
1 (8-ounce) container plain low-fat yogurt
3 tablespoons white vinegar
½ teaspoon salt
¼ teaspoon pepper
Toppings: diced tomato, sliced green onions, chopped fresh parsley

• **Process** cucumber, garlic, and 1 cup broth in a blender or food processor until smooth, stopping to scrape down sides. Pour into a bowl; stir in remaining 1 cup broth, sour cream, and next 4 ingredients. Cover and chill at least 2 hours. Sprinkle with desired toppings. **Yield:** 9 cups.

✻ Substitute 1 (16-ounce) container light sour cream, if desired.

Lee Small
Dallas, Texas

Quick & Easy

When you open your refrigerator, are you almost attacked by all those partially used bottles of salad dressings in the door? If so, we can help you clean out your refrigerator and create some tasty dishes in one sweep.

You've probably tried Italian dressing as a quick, familiar marinade for meats or vegetables, but there are plenty of other possibilities. These recipes make salad dressings dual purpose by using them in innovative ways, adding zest to entrées and flavor to greens. We promise your family will agree with us that they are all keepers.

SESAME PORK

Linda likes to use these ingredients in kabobs, but to save time, we grilled them in a basket.

Prep: 25 minutes
Chill: 3 hours
Grill: 28 minutes

½ cup soy sauce
½ cup Russian dressing
2 tablespoons sesame seeds
3 tablespoons lemon juice
½ teaspoon ground ginger
½ teaspoon garlic powder
½ (1½-pound) package pork tenderloins, cut into 1-inch cubes
2 yellow summer squash
2 small onions
1 green bell pepper
1 (15-ounce) can pineapple spears, drained
Saffron rice (optional)
Garnish: sliced green onions

• **Combine** first 6 ingredients; remove ½ cup mixture, and chill.
• **Place** pork in a shallow dish or heavy-duty zip-top plastic bag; pour remaining sesame mixture over pork. Cover or seal, and chill 3 hours.
• **Cut** squash into ½-inch slices, onions into quarters, and bell pepper and pineapple into 1-inch pieces. Arrange vegetables in a grill basket, and set pineapple aside.
• **Grill** vegetables over medium-high heat (350° to 400°) 15 to 20 minutes, turning occasionally and basting with half of reserved sesame mixture. Remove vegetables from grill basket.
• **Remove** pork from marinade, discarding marinade. Arrange pineapple and pork in grill basket.
• **Grill** over medium-high heat 4 minutes on each side, basting with remaining sesame mixture.
• **Toss** together vegetables, pork, and pineapple. Serve mixture over saffron rice, if desired. Garnish, if desired. **Yield:** 4 servings.

Linda C. Joynes
Virginia Beach, Virginia

CORN-AND-FIELD PEA DIP

Zesty Italian dressing adds its signature zip to this chunky, colorful dip.

Prep: 10 minutes
Chill: 8 hours

2 (15.8-ounce) cans field peas with snaps, rinsed and drained
2 (11-ounce) cans white shoepeg corn, drained
2 (10-ounce) cans diced tomato and green chiles
1 (14½-ounce) can diced tomatoes
5 green onions, diced
1 (16-ounce) bottle zesty Italian dressing
2 garlic cloves, minced
1 tablespoon finely chopped fresh parsley

• **Stir** together all ingredients. Cover and chill 8 hours. Drain before serving. Serve with corn chips. **Yield:** 8 cups.

PARMESAN-TURKEY-RANCH ROLLUPS

Ranch dressing, always a favorite, teams with turkey, tomato, and lettuce for a quick, satisfying sandwich.

Prep: 10 minutes

¾ cup Ranch dressing
8 (6- to 7-inch) flour tortillas
½ cup grated Parmesan cheese
4 green onions, diced
1 medium tomato, seeded and diced
2 cups chopped iceberg lettuce
12 ounces thinly sliced deli turkey

• **Spread** dressing evenly on 1 side of each tortilla. Sprinkle evenly with Parmesan cheese, green onions, and tomato. Top with lettuce and turkey. Roll up tortillas; secure with wooden picks. **Yield:** 8 rollups.

Linda H. Sutton
Winston-Salem, North Carolina

Top-Rated Menu

Enjoy the warmth of summer by serving this cool salad plate outside. There are some last minute preparations to make, so ask your friends to help toss the salads while you sauté the goat cheese. Add crunchy breadsticks and tall glasses of iced tea to complete this colorful, delicious meal.

Salad Sampler
Serves 6

Chicken-and-Fruit Salad
Lemon-Basil Potato Salad
Warm Goat Cheese Salad
Breadsticks   Iced tea

CHICKEN-AND-FRUIT SALAD
(pictured on page 4)

1996 Recipe Hall of Fame

Prep: 40 minutes
Chill: 8 hours
Grill: 12 minutes

¾ cup orange marmalade
3 tablespoons soy sauce
3 tablespoons lemon juice
1½ tablespoons chopped fresh ginger
6 skinned and boned chicken breast halves
1 cored fresh pineapple
1 large jícama (optional)
Vegetable cooking spray
2 cups fresh strawberry halves
1 cup fresh raspberries
Orange-Raspberry Vinaigrette
Lettuce leaves

• **Combine** first 4 ingredients; remove ¼ cup marmalade mixture, and chill.
• **Place** chicken in a shallow dish or heavy-duty zip-top plastic bag; pour remaining marmalade mixture over chicken. Cover or seal, and chill 8 hours, turning occasionally.
• **Cut** pineapple into spears; peel jícama, if desired, and cut into ½-inch slices.
• **Place** pineapple and jícama in a shallow dish or heavy-duty zip-top plastic bag; pour ¼ cup reserved marmalade mixture over pineapple mixture. Cover or seal, and chill 8 hours.
• **Remove** chicken from marinade, discarding marinade; drain pineapple mixture. Coat chicken and pineapple mixture with cooking spray.
• **Grill** chicken, covered with grill lid, over medium-high heat (350° to 400°) 5 to 6 minutes on each side or until done. Grill pineapple and jícama 2 to 3 minutes on each side.
• **Cut** chicken and jícama into thin strips; cut pineapple into bite-size pieces.
• **Combine** chicken, jícama, pineapple, strawberry halves, and raspberries; toss gently with Orange-Raspberry Vinaigrette. Serve over lettuce leaves. **Yield:** 6 servings.

Orange-Raspberry Vinaigrette

Prep: 10 minutes

½ cup orange marmalade
¼ cup raspberry vinegar
1 medium jalapeño pepper, seeded and minced
2 tablespoons finely chopped fresh cilantro
2 tablespoons olive oil

• **Whisk** together all ingredients in a small bowl. **Yield:** 1 cup.

LEMON-BASIL POTATO SALAD
(pictured on page 4)

1997 Recipe Hall of Fame

Prep: 20 minutes
Bake: 25 minutes

2½ pounds small Yukon gold potatoes, cut into eighths *
Vegetable cooking spray
¼ cup lemon juice
4 garlic cloves, minced
¾ cup chopped fresh basil
1 tablespoon Dijon mustard
1 teaspoon salt
½ teaspoon freshly ground pepper
⅔ cup olive oil
½ medium-size purple onion, chopped
1 (10-ounce) package fresh spinach, cut into thin strips
10 thick bacon slices, cooked and crumbled

• **Arrange** potato evenly on a lightly greased 15- x 10-inch jellyroll pan; coat potato with cooking spray.
• **Bake** at 475°, stirring occasionally, 20 to 25 minutes or until tender and golden.
• **Whisk** together lemon juice and next 5 ingredients; whisk in oil in a slow,

steady stream. Gently toss potato and onion with ½ cup vinaigrette.

● **Arrange** spinach evenly in 6 bowls, and drizzle with remaining vinaigrette. Top with potato mixture; sprinkle with bacon. **Yield:** 6 servings.

＊Substitute 2½ pounds small new potatoes, if desired.

WARM GOAT CHEESE SALAD
(pictured on page 4)

Warm, creamy goat cheese rounds elevate this salad's status to superb.

1997 Recipe Hall of Fame

Prep: 20 minutes
Chill: 2 hours

½ **cup olive oil**
⅓ **cup lemon juice**
1 **tablespoon diced green onions**
1½ **teaspoons Dijon mustard**
½ **cup Italian-seasoned breadcrumbs**
1½ **tablespoons grated Parmesan cheese**
1½ **tablespoons sesame seeds**
3 **(4-ounce) goat cheese logs**
1 **large egg, lightly beaten**
3 **tablespoons butter or margarine**
6 **cups torn mixed salad greens**
12 **pitted ripe olives, sliced**

● **Combine** first 4 ingredients; set aside.
● **Combine** breadcrumbs, Parmesan cheese, and sesame seeds.
● **Cut** each goat cheese log into 4 slices. Dip in egg, and dredge in breadcrumb mixture. Cover and chill 2 hours.
● **Melt** butter in a large skillet over medium-high heat. Add goat cheese, and fry 1 to 2 minutes on each side or until browned; drain on paper towels.
● **Toss** mixed greens with dressing; add olives, and top with warm goat cheese. **Yield:** 6 servings.

COOK'S NOTES

The day before
■ Prepare dressings for all salads.

■ Marinate chicken.

■ Marinate pineapple and jícama.

■ Wash salad greens.

■ Cut spinach into strips.

2 hours before
■ Dredge goat cheese in coating, and chill.

■ Grill pineapple, jícama, and chicken; cut as directed. Toss with vinaigrette, and chill.

■ Cut strawberries in half.

45 minutes before
■ Cook bacon.

■ Roast potato; toss with onion and ½ cup vinaigrette.

15 minutes before
■ Sauté goat cheese rounds, and arrange them on prepared greens as directed.

■ Toss together chicken mixture, strawberry halves, and raspberries; arrange on lettuce.

■ Arrange spinach in bowls; complete potato salad as directed.

New-Style Squash

If you think the only varieties of summer squash are zucchini, yellow crookneck, and straightneck, do we have great news for you. Now is the time to scour farm stands and markets—if you're not already growing them in your own garden—for all the summer squash selections.

Regardless of the type, these thin-skinned squash require much less cooking time than their hard-shelled winter cousins. When selecting summer squash, remember that a small size generally translates into a more tender product.

SQUASH PUPPIES

Prep: 20 minutes
Cook: 6 minutes per batch

¾ **cup self-rising cornmeal**
¼ **cup all-purpose flour**
½ **teaspoon salt**
¼ **teaspoon black pepper**
⅛ **teaspoon ground red pepper**
6 **medium-size yellow squash, cooked and mashed ＊**
½ **cup buttermilk**
1 **small onion, minced**
1 **large egg**
Vegetable oil
½ **teaspoon salt**

● **Combine** first 5 ingredients in a bowl.
● **Stir** together squash and next 3 ingredients; add to cornmeal mixture, stirring until blended.
● **Pour** oil to a depth of ½ inch into a deep cast-iron skillet; heat to 350°. Drop batter by tablespoonfuls, in batches, into oil; fry 3 minutes on each side or until golden brown. Drain on paper towels; sprinkle evenly with ½ teaspoon salt. **Yield:** 20 squash puppies.

＊Substitute 6 medium-size zucchini or 'Zephyr' squash for the yellow squash, if desired.

Virginia Harvey
Bella Vista, Arkansas

BASIL SUMMER SQUASH

Prep: 15 minutes
Cook: 15 minutes

¼ cup chicken broth
1 pound pattypan or 'Peter Pan'
   squash, cut in half★
1 small Vidalia onion, chopped
¼ cup butter or margarine
1 tablespoon sugar
1 garlic clove, chopped
½ teaspoon Creole seasoning
½ teaspoon salt
¼ teaspoon pepper
1 to 2 tablespoons chopped fresh basil

● **Bring** broth to a boil in a large skillet. Reduce heat to low; add squash and next 5 ingredients. Cook, covered, 10 to 12 minutes or until squash is tender and liquid evaporates. Stir in salt, pepper, and basil. **Yield:** 6 servings.

★Substitute 2 pounds yellow squash, if desired. Reduce cooking time by 2 minutes.

Linda LaCombe Thabet
Cottonport, Louisiana

CREOLE SQUASH

Prep: 10 minutes
Cook: 32 minutes

5 bacon slices, chopped
1 large onion, chopped
1½ pounds pattypan or 'Peter Pan'
   squash, chopped★
½ cup chopped tomato
1 teaspoon Creole seasoning
⅛ teaspoon salt
¼ teaspoon pepper

● **Cook** bacon in a skillet over medium heat 5 minutes; add onion, and cook 7 minutes or until lightly browned. Add squash and remaining ingredients; cover and simmer 20 minutes or until squash is tender. **Yield:** 4 to 6 servings.

★Substitute 1½ pounds yellow squash, if desired.

Suzan Wiener
Spring Hill, Florida

Green Beans & Herbs

New twists on an old favorite, snapped or whole

BASIC STEAMED GREEN BEANS

Prep: 10 minutes
Cook: 12 minutes

1 pound fresh green beans
1 cup water
1 teaspoon salt

● **Bring** all ingredients to a boil in a Dutch oven. Cover and simmer 10 to 12 minutes or until desired degree of doneness. Drain and serve hot, or rinse with cold water. **Yield:** 4 servings.

GINGER-ROASTED GREEN BEANS

Prep: 15 minutes
Bake: 20 minutes

2 tablespoons olive oil
1 teaspoon salt
1 teaspoon sesame oil
1 garlic clove, sliced
¼ teaspoon chopped fresh thyme
1 pound fresh green beans
1 tablespoon grated fresh ginger

● **Combine** first 5 ingredients in a jelly-roll pan, and add green beans, tossing to coat.
● **Bake** at 400°, stirring occasionally, for 20 minutes or until beans are crisp-tender. Toss in ginger. **Yield:** 6 servings.

GREEN BEAN ALFREDO WITH CHEESE RAVIOLI

Mix sautéed green beans, cheese ravioli, and rosemary-tinged cream sauce for a simple-to-prepare Alfredo entrée.

Prep: 20 minutes
Cook: 23 minutes

1 (1-pound) package frozen cheese-
   filled ravioli
3 tablespoons butter or margarine
1 pound fresh green beans
2 garlic cloves, pressed
½ teaspoon chopped fresh
   rosemary
1½ cups whipping cream
¾ cup dry white wine or chicken
   broth
¾ teaspoon freshly ground pepper
¼ cup shredded Parmesan cheese
Garnish: fresh rosemary sprigs

● **Cook** pasta according to package directions; drain and keep warm.
● **Melt** butter in a large nonstick skillet over medium-high heat; add green beans, garlic, and rosemary, and sauté 6 minutes or until beans are crisp-tender. Remove mixture, and set aside.
● **Add** whipping cream to skillet, and bring to a boil, stirring constantly. Cook, stirring constantly, 10 minutes.
● **Return** green bean mixture to skillet; add wine and pepper, and cook 5 minutes. Stir in 2 tablespoons cheese. Serve over ravioli, and sprinkle evenly with remaining 2 tablespoons cheese. Garnish, if desired. **Yield:** 6 servings.

PESTO GREEN BEANS

If you're short on time or ingredients, you can substitute ¼ cup refrigerated pesto for homemade.

Prep: 25 minutes

1 cup packed basil leaves
½ cup chopped pecans, toasted
¼ cup olive oil
3 tablespoons lemon juice
2 garlic cloves
1 teaspoon salt
1 pound fresh green beans, trimmed
   and steamed

• **Process** basil, ¼ cup pecans, olive oil, and next 3 ingredients in a blender or food processor until smooth, stopping to scrape down sides. Remove ½ cup pesto, and reserve for other uses. Toss hot green beans with remaining pesto; sprinkle with remaining ¼ cup pecans. **Yield:** 6 servings.

Note: Spoon leftover pesto into an airtight container; refrigerate up to 2 weeks, or freeze up to 3 months.

LEMON-DILL GREEN BEANS

Lemon, dill, and feta cheese combine to tastefully flavor fresh green beans.

Prep: 10 minutes
Chill: 1 hour

3 tablespoons chopped fresh dill
2 tablespoons olive oil
1 teaspoon salt
1 teaspoon grated lemon rind
⅓ cup fresh lemon juice
1 pound fresh green beans,
   steamed
1 (4-ounce) package crumbled
   feta cheese
Garnishes: lemon slices, fresh dill sprigs

• **Whisk** together first 5 ingredients in a large bowl; add green beans, tossing gently to coat. Cover and chill 1 hour. Sprinkle with cheese before serving. Garnish, if desired. **Yield:** 4 servings.

GREEN BEAN-POTATO SALAD

Prep: 20 minutes
Cook: 20 minutes
Chill: 2 hours

2 pounds red potatoes
1 pound fresh green beans
¼ cup red wine vinegar
4 green onions, sliced
2 tablespoons chopped fresh tarragon
2 tablespoons Dijon mustard
2 tablespoons olive oil
2 teaspoons salt
1 teaspoon pepper

• **Combine** potatoes and water to cover in a large saucepan; bring to a boil over medium heat, and cook 13 minutes. Add green beans, and cook 7 minutes or until potatoes are tender. Drain and rinse with cold water. Cut each potato into 8 wedges.
• **Whisk** together vinegar and remaining 6 ingredients in a large bowl; add potato wedges and green beans, tossing gently to coat. Cover and chill 2 hours. **Yield:** 8 servings.

GREEN BEAN SALAD IN TOMATOES
(pictured on page 189)

Cilantro lends a Southwestern flair to this salad. Leave the tips on tender beans for a striking presentation.

Prep: 30 minutes
Stand: 30 minutes

1 red bell pepper, sliced
¼ cup chopped fresh cilantro
¼ cup olive oil
3 green onions, sliced
3 tablespoons red wine vinegar
1 garlic clove, pressed
1 teaspoon ground cumin
½ teaspoon salt
¼ teaspoon pepper
1 (15-ounce) can black beans, rinsed
   and drained
¾ pound small fresh green beans,
   steamed
6 large firm tomatoes
Garnish: fresh cilantro sprigs

• **Combine** first 9 ingredients in a shallow dish or a heavy-duty zip-top plastic bag; add black beans and green beans. Cover or seal, and let mixture stand 30 minutes.
• **Cut** a ¼-inch slice from top of each tomato; scoop out and discard pulp, leaving tomato shells intact. Invert tomato shells, and drain on paper towels.
• **Place** each shell on a salad plate. Spoon ¼ cup bean mixture into each tomato shell; spoon remaining mixture evenly on plates around shells. Garnish, if desired. **Yield:** 6 servings.

GREEN GROWS THE BEAN

■ There are two general types of green beans (also known as snap beans). **Bush beans** come in both round and flat varieties, are basically stringless, and are very tender. They grow on bushes, making them easy to harvest commercially. **Pole beans,** resembling runner beans, grow on vines trained on trellises or fences. Pole beans also come in round and flat varieties. Most have strings, but a couple of types are stringless. Because pole beans are labor-intensive to grow and must be picked by hand, they often cost more and are not as widely available.

■ Choose bush beans for their tender, quick-cooking qualities, and pole beans for long, slow-cooking dishes. We used stringless beans for all of our recipes; if you purchase beans with strings, be sure to remove them before cooking for best results.

From Our Kitchen

Tips and Tidbits

■ Keep a large container of seeded watermelon cubes in the refrigerator for a refreshing, anytime snack.

■ Thanks to Gourmet House's Gourmet Grains, you can add wild rice to your list of speedy supper choices. Their quick-cooking wild rice goes from package to table in five minutes. You get the same great texture and nutty flavor as if it cooked for an hour. Look for "Quick Cooking" on the tan box. It's become one of our pantry staples.

■ When you need to speed up all or part of a recipe that requires refrigeration, do a rapid chill. Jan Moon of our Test Kitchens wraps cake layers in plastic wrap while they're still warm. She then places them in the freezer. In no time the layers are chilled enough for frosting. Large quantities of hot food should be cooled before storing. To chill food quickly, place containers of soups, stews, and sauces in a sink filled with ice.

■ Freeze punch, iced tea, or juice in ice cube trays, and use the cubes to chill beverages without diluting them.

Five a Day Fun

Associate Foods Editor Peggy Smith suggests getting the kids involved with Dole Food Company's 5 A Day Adventures CD-ROM. Using the program, youngsters can create fun family adventures through songs and games. They also can take virtual trips to different places such as Adventure Theater where they'll see animated fruits and vegetables, Fit Kid Park to learn all about fitness, the Salad Factory to find out how to make salads that are high in vitamins, and Creative Kitchen for nutritious recipes. To order send $14.95 to: Dole Food Company, 5 A Day Adventures, 100 Hegenberger Road, Suite 100, Oakland, CA 94621. Visit the Web site for additional information at www.dole5aday.com.

SHRIMP COCKTAIL

In July 2000 *Southern Living* Editor John Floyd asked readers to send in their favorite shrimp cocktail sauce recipes. He got a lot of tasty renditions, but a call from his friend Virginia Spencer was one of the most enjoyable responses. She said that her husband, Bill, made the best cocktail sauce that John would ever taste. Politely John said to have Bill send it and let our Test Kitchens decide. Guess what? The pros thought that, of all the recipes we received, those from Bill; Jim Goodrich of Enid, Oklahoma; and Belle Fields of Columbia, South Carolina, rated tops. So boil some shrimp, try these sauces, and let us know your favorite. And Virginia is right. Bill's recipe is fabulous.

SHRIMP SAUCE
Prep: 5 minutes

6 tablespoons prepared horseradish
6 tablespoons ketchup

● **Stir** together horseradish and ketchup. Cover and chill until ready to serve. **Yield:** ¾ cup.
Belle S. Fields
Columbia, South Carolina

SHRIMP COCKTAIL SAUCE
Prep: 5 minutes

½ cup mayonnaise
½ cup ketchup
½ cup chili sauce
2⅓ tablespoons lemon juice
1 tablespoon lime juice
2 teaspoons prepared horseradish
½ to 1 teaspoon hot sauce

● **Stir** together all ingredients until blended. Cover and chill until ready to serve. **Yield:** 1¾ cups.
William M. Spencer III
Birmingham, Alabama

GRANDPA JIM'S SHRIMP SAUCE
Prep: 5 minutes

½ cup chili sauce
⅓ cup prepared horseradish
⅓ cup ketchup
2 tablespoons lemon juice
1½ teaspoons Worcestershire sauce
½ to 1 teaspoon hot sauce
¼ teaspoon salt
¼ teaspoon pepper

● **Stir** together all ingredients until blended. Cover and chill until ready to serve. **Yield:** 1⅓ cups.

Grandpa Jim's Salad Dressing: Stir together equal parts of mayonnaise and Grandpa Jim's Shrimp Sauce. Serve over salad greens tossed with peeled boiled shrimp, sliced onion, diced celery, and diced hard-cooked eggs, if desired.
Jim Goodrich
Enid, Oklahoma

Pizza Stone

Recently, Foods Editor Andria Hurst made the best pizza she's ever had. It was the same recipe that she's always used, but this time she baked it on a pizza stone. The crust was crisp and tender while the toppings were moist and bubbly. It was evenly baked in less time than usual, with no spillovers in the oven. The stone is terrific for baking bread, cookies, biscuits, tortillas, and rolls. You'll love the results when you cook frozen or ready-made pizza. Remember to place the stone on the middle oven rack. Most kitchen shops carry pizza stones starting as low as $10.

Grater Textures

Mary Allen Perry of our Test Kitchens staff makes perfect pimiento cheese. She says the trick is in the combination of textures that comes from her box grater. Each side grates a different size, so you really taste the flavor of the individual cheeses in her terrific spread. For Mary Allen's recipe, see "Taste of the South" on page 169.

September

Treasured Apples

Indulge yourself with these five simple and scrumptious apple recipes.

What comes to mind when you think about apples? Everyone's taste buds tingle for favorite flavor combinations—crisp apple slices dipped in creamy peanut butter, hot apple pie, homemade applesauce.

So, with thousands of apple selections and even more ways to eat them, how do you choose a few recipes to represent this illustrious fruit? It wasn't easy—but we harvested some we think you'll enjoy.

ORANGE-GINGER ROASTED APPLES

Prep: 15 minutes
Bake: 1 hour

4 medium Braeburn apples *
½ cup honey
¼ cup fresh orange juice
1 tablespoon lime juice
1 teaspoon grated orange rind
1 teaspoon grated fresh ginger
Toppings: yogurt, granola

• **Remove** cores from apples, leaving a ½-inch core on bottom of each. Place apples in a lightly greased 8-inch square baking dish.
• **Stir** together honey and next 4 ingredients. Drizzle mixture over apples, filling apple centers.
• **Bake,** covered, at 400° for 15 minutes. Uncover and bake 30 to 45 minutes or until apples are tender, basting every 15 minutes with drippings. Serve with desired toppings. **Yield:** 4 servings.

* Substitute McIntosh, Golden Delicious, or Fuji apples, if desired.

APPLE-ALMOND STUFFING
(pictured on page 191)

Enjoy this savory stuffing with baked or grilled pork chops.

Prep: 30 minutes
Bake: 45 minutes

½ cup butter or margarine
3 celery ribs, diced
1 medium onion, diced
2 large Granny Smith apples, coarsely chopped
24 white bread slices, cubed
1½ cups chicken broth
1 cup almonds, chopped and toasted
¼ cup almond liqueur *
2 tablespoons chopped fresh parsley
1 tablespoon fresh sage sprigs
1½ teaspoons poultry seasoning
1 teaspoon salt
¼ to ½ teaspoon pepper
Garnish: chopped fresh sage

• **Melt** butter in a Dutch oven over medium heat. Add celery and onion; sauté 5 minutes or until tender. Add apple; cook, stirring often, 5 minutes. Remove from heat.
• **Add** bread and next 8 ingredients to Dutch oven, tossing gently to combine. Spoon into a lightly greased 13- x 9-inch baking dish.
• **Bake,** covered, at 325° for 35 minutes. Uncover and bake 10 more minutes or until golden. Serve with baked or grilled pork chops, if desired. Garnish, if desired. **Yield:** 8 cups.

* Substitute 2 teaspoons almond extract for ¼ cup almond liqueur, if desired.

Betty J. Nichols
Eugene, Oregon

APPLE FRITTERS WITH LEMON SAUCE
(pictured on pages 190-191)

These golden fritters render sweet and tangy flavor in one small package.

Prep: 25 minutes
Cook: 4 minutes per batch

1½ cups all-purpose flour
⅛ teaspoon salt
1¼ teaspoons baking powder
1 large egg
2 tablespoons butter or margarine, melted
3 Mutsu or Crispin apples, peeled and diced *
Peanut or vegetable oil
Powdered sugar
Lemon Sauce

• **Pulse** first 5 ingredients in a food processor 5 times or until crumbly. Spoon mixture into a large bowl. Stir in diced apple. Shape mixture into 1½-inch balls.
• **Pour** oil to a depth of 3 inches into a Dutch oven; heat to 350°. Fry fritters, in batches, 1 to 2 minutes on each side or until golden. Drain on paper towels. Sprinkle fritters evenly with powdered sugar; serve with Lemon Sauce. **Yield:** 22 fritters.

* Substitute 3 McIntosh apples, if desired.

Lemon Sauce

Prep: 5 minutes
Cook: 15 minutes

1 cup sugar
2 tablespoons all-purpose flour
1 large egg, lightly beaten
1 tablespoon butter or margarine
3 tablespoons lemon juice

• **Cook** all ingredients in a saucepan over medium heat, whisking constantly, until thickened. **Yield:** 1 cup.

CHUNKY APPLE CAKE WITH CREAM CHEESE FROSTING

(pictured on pages 190-191)

The batter for this moist spice cake will be thick, but resist the temptation to add more liquid.

Prep: 25 minutes
Bake: 45 minutes

½ cup butter, melted
2 cups sugar
2 large eggs
1 teaspoon vanilla extract
2 cups all-purpose flour
1 teaspoon baking soda
1 teaspoon salt
2 teaspoons ground cinnamon
4 Granny Smith apples, peeled and sliced
1 cup chopped walnuts, toasted
Cream Cheese Frosting
Chopped walnuts, toasted (optional)

• **Stir** together first 4 ingredients in a large bowl until blended.
• **Combine** flour and next 3 ingredients; add to butter mixture, stirring until blended. Stir in apple and 1 cup walnuts. Spread into a greased 13- x 9-inch pan.
• **Bake** at 350° for 45 minutes or until a wooden pick inserted in center comes out clean. Cool completely in pan on a wire rack. Spread with Cream Cheese Frosting; sprinkle with walnuts, if desired. **Yield:** 12 to 15 servings.

Cream Cheese Frosting

Prep: 10 minutes

1 (8-ounce) package cream cheese, softened
3 tablespoons butter or margarine, softened
1½ cups powdered sugar
⅛ teaspoon salt
1 teaspoon vanilla extract

• **Beat** cream cheese and butter at medium speed with an electric mixer until creamy. Gradually add sugar and salt, beating until blended. Stir in vanilla. **Yield:** 1⅔ cups.

Helen Mack
Fontana, California

QUICK APPLE DUMPLINGS

(pictured on page 191)

Refrigerated piecrusts make quick work of these pastry-wrapped desserts. They're perfect for a weeknight supper or elegant meal.

Prep: 25 minutes
Bake: 45 minutes

1½ cups sugar
2 cups water
½ teaspoon ground cinnamon, divided
½ teaspoon ground nutmeg, divided
¼ cup butter or margarine
⅔ cup sugar
2 (15-ounce) packages refrigerated piecrusts
8 medium Braeburn apples, peeled and cored*
3 tablespoons butter or margarine, cut up
Vanilla ice cream (optional)

• **Bring** 1½ cups sugar, 2 cups water, ¼ teaspoon cinnamon, and ¼ teaspoon nutmeg to a boil in a saucepan over medium-high heat, stirring constantly; reduce heat, and simmer, stirring occasionally, 10 minutes. Remove from heat, and stir in ¼ cup butter. Set syrup aside.
• **Combine** ⅔ cup sugar, remaining ¼ teaspoon cinnamon, and remaining ¼ teaspoon nutmeg.
• **Cut** piecrusts in half, and roll into 8-inch circles. Place 1 apple in center of each circle. Sprinkle each evenly with sugar mixture; dot evenly with 3 tablespoons butter.
• **Fold** dough over apples, pinching to seal. Place in a lightly greased 13- x 9-inch baking dish. Drizzle with syrup.
• **Bake** at 375° for 40 to 45 minutes. Serve with vanilla ice cream, if desired. **Yield:** 8 servings.

*Substitute Golden Delicious or Granny Smith apples, if desired.

Debbie Leibham
Cypress, Texas

Easy Italian Classic

Wishing you could pay a visit to your favorite Italian restaurant? In lieu of a trip across town and a hit to your wallet, try this flavorful pasta bake. Our recipe calls for rotini, but ziti or even elbow macaroni would be a fine substitute. Although the ingredient list looks long, you probably already have most items on hand. Add a salad and bread, and dinner can be on the table in a little more than an hour. All that will be missing is a candle in a Chianti bottle and a red-checked tablecloth.

BAKED ROTINI

Prep: 10 minutes
Cook: 30 minutes
Bake: 35 minutes

1 pound ground beef
1 small onion, chopped
1 small green bell pepper, chopped
1 (28-ounce) can crushed tomatoes
1 (6-ounce) can tomato paste
1 (4.5-ounce) jar sliced mushrooms, undrained
1 teaspoon salt
½ teaspoon dried basil
¼ teaspoon garlic powder
¼ teaspoon dried oregano
¼ teaspoon dried crushed red pepper
8 ounces rotini, cooked
3 cups (12 ounces) shredded mozzarella cheese

• **Cook** first 3 ingredients in a large skillet over medium heat, stirring until beef crumbles and is no longer pink; drain and return to skillet.
• **Stir** in crushed tomatoes and next 7 ingredients; bring to a boil. Reduce heat, and simmer, stirring occasionally, 20 minutes. Stir in rotini and cheese. Spoon into a lightly greased 13- x 9-inch baking dish.
• **Bake** at 350° for 35 minutes. **Yield:** 8 servings.

Eugenia W. Bell
Lexington, Kentucky

Party in El Paso

This Texan specializes in Southwestern flavors, and his favorite place to entertain is his own garden.

Backyard Fiesta
Serves 8

Rio Grande Limeade
Roasted Poblano Chile Con Queso
Adobo Grilled Pork Tacos With Cucumber-Radish Salsa
Grilled Chicken Tortas Marinated Olives
Margarita-Key Lime Pie With Gingersnap Crust

Park Kerr's passion for chiles—from smoky chipotles to mild Anaheims—fuels the selection of salsas and hot stuff at his El Paso Chile Company, a thriving mail-order business.

This true love of hot stuff surfaces in his cooking and entertaining. He delivers big flavors, not just scorching heat. So bring the Southwest to your backyard with a few of Park's favorite recipes.

RIO GRANDE LIMEADE

Prep: 10 minutes
Chill: 8 hours

2 (12-ounce) cans frozen limeade
   concentrate, thawed
3 cups tequila
3 cups water
2 cups orange liqueur
1 cup fresh lime juice
Garnish: lime slices

• **Stir** together first 5 ingredients. Chill 8 hours. Serve over ice, and garnish, if desired. **Yield:** 3 quarts.

ROASTED POBLANO CHILE CON QUESO

Prep: 20 minutes
Grill: 7 minutes
Stand: 10 minutes
Cook: 10 minutes

3 fresh poblano peppers
2 fresh red Anaheim peppers
1 large onion, minced
2 garlic cloves, minced
2 tablespoons olive oil
2 cups (8 ounces) shredded Monterey
   Jack cheese
1 (8-ounce) loaf pasteurized prepared
   cheese product, cubed
½ cup half-and-half
Tortilla chips

• **Grill** poblano and Anaheim peppers, without grill lid, over medium-high heat (350° to 400°) 5 to 7 minutes or until peppers look blistered, turning peppers often.
• **Place** peppers in a heavy-duty zip-top plastic bag; seal and let stand 10 minutes to loosen skins. Peel peppers; remove and discard seeds. Slice peppers into thin strips.

• **Sauté** onion and garlic in hot oil in a large skillet over medium-high heat. Add pepper strips, and cook 2 minutes or until tender; reduce heat to low. Add cheeses and half-and-half, stirring until cheese is melted. Serve warm with tortilla chips. **Yield:** 3½ cups.

Note: For testing purposes only, we used Velveeta for cheese product.

ADOBO GRILLED PORK TACOS WITH CUCUMBER-RADISH SALSA

Prep: 15 minutes
Stand: 30 minutes
Marinate: 30 minutes
Grill: 20 minutes

1 (2-ounce) package dried mild New
   Mexico chiles
2 teaspoons cumin seeds
1 tablespoon dried oregano
3 garlic cloves
2 tablespoons cider vinegar
1 teaspoon sugar
¼ teaspoon salt
¼ teaspoon ground red pepper
2 (¾-pound) pork tenderloins
1 (8-ounce) container sour cream
Cucumber-Radish Salsa
24 corn or flour tortillas,
   warmed

• **Slice** chiles in half lengthwise. Remove and discard stems and seeds. Place chiles in a bowl, and add boiling water to cover. Let stand 20 minutes or until chiles are softened. Drain chiles, reserving liquid.
• **Cook** cumin seeds in a skillet over medium heat 30 seconds. Add oregano, and cook, stirring constantly, 30 seconds or until cumin is toasted.
• **Process** cumin mixture, soaked chiles, 1 cup reserved liquid, garlic, and next 4 ingredients in a blender or food processor until smooth, adding more reserved liquid if needed.
• **Place** pork in a shallow dish or heavy-duty zip-top plastic bag. Pour half of chile mixture over meat. Cover or seal, and chill 30 minutes. Remove pork from marinade, discarding marinade.

• **Stir** together sour cream and ½ cup Cucumber-Radish Salsa; cover and chill until ready to serve.

• **Grill** pork, covered with grill lid, over medium-high heat (350° to 400°), turning occasionally and basting with reserved chile mixture, 20 minutes or until a meat thermometer inserted into thickest portion registers 160°. Remove from grill; let stand 10 minutes. Coarsely chop pork. Serve in tortillas with remaining Cucumber-Radish Salsa and sour cream mixture. **Yield:** 24 servings.

Cucumber-Radish Salsa

Prep: 10 minutes

2 cucumbers, peeled, seeded, and chopped
1 (6-ounce) package radishes, grated
1 small onion, minced
2 tablespoons chopped fresh cilantro
¼ cup lime juice
½ teaspoon salt
¼ teaspoon ground red pepper

• **Stir** together all ingredients. Cover and chill, if desired. **Yield:** 3 cups.

GRILLED CHICKEN TORTAS

Prep: 45 minutes
Chill: 1 hour
Grill: 17 minutes

4 large skinned and boned chicken breast halves
1 (16-ounce) container refrigerated hot chile salsa
¼ cup tequila
2 tablespoons chopped fresh cilantro
2 tablespoons lime juice
3 poblano peppers
¼ teaspoon salt
1 (16-ounce) can refried beans or black beans
1 tablespoon olive oil
8 (6-inch) crusty sandwich rolls, split
3 avocados, peeled and mashed
2 cups (8 ounces) shredded Monterey Jack cheese

• **Place** chicken between 2 sheets of heavy-duty plastic wrap, and flatten to ¼-inch thickness using a meat mallet or rolling pin.

• **Stir** together salsa and next 3 ingredients. Remove 1 cup mixture, and set aside remaining mixture.

• **Place** chicken in a shallow dish or heavy-duty zip-top plastic bag; pour 1 cup salsa mixture over chicken. Cover or seal, and chill 1 hour, turning occasionally. Remove chicken from marinade, discarding marinade.

• **Grill** peppers, covered with grill lid, over medium-high heat (350° to 400°) 5 to 7 minutes, turning often, until peppers look blistered.

• **Place** peppers in a heavy-duty zip-top plastic bag; seal and let stand 10 minutes to loosen skins. Peel peppers; remove and discard seeds. Cut peppers into thin strips; set aside.

• **Grill** chicken, covered with grill lid, over medium-high heat (350° to 400°) about 5 minutes on each side or until done. Cool slightly. Cut into thin slices, and sprinkle evenly with salt.

• **Stir** together beans and olive oil in a 1-quart glass bowl, and microwave at HIGH 2 minutes or until thoroughly heated, stirring once.

• **Spread** beans evenly over bottom halves of rolls. Spread avocado over top halves of rolls. Top bottom halves evenly with chicken, pepper strips, cheese, and top halves of rolls. Serve with reserved salsa mixture. **Yield:** 8 servings.

MARINATED OLIVES

Prep: 20 minutes
Chill: 8 hours

1 pound drained kalamata olives
12 pimiento-stuffed green olives, drained
12 pickled serrano or jalapeño peppers
¼ cup tequila
¼ cup lime juice
2 tablespoons orange liqueur
¼ cup minced fresh cilantro
1 teaspoon coarsely grated orange rind

• **Stir** together all ingredients. Chill 8 hours. **Yield:** 8 servings.

MARGARITA-KEY LIME PIE WITH GINGERSNAP CRUST

This cool, creamy pie is a refreshing and lively end to a spicy meal.

Prep: 25 minutes
Cool: 2 hours
Freeze: 2 hours
Stand: 20 minutes

4 large eggs
½ cup fresh lime juice
¼ cup orange liqueur
¼ cup tequila
2 (14-ounce) cans sweetened condensed milk
2 teaspoons grated lime rind
2 cups whipping cream
Gingersnap Crust
Garnishes: lime rind curls, sweetened whipped cream

• **Combine** first 5 ingredients in a heavy saucepan over medium heat, stirring often, 20 minutes or until temperature reaches 165°; remove from heat. Stir in lime rind; cool completely.

• **Beat** whipping cream at high speed with an electric mixer until soft peaks form. Fold into egg mixture. Spoon into Gingersnap Crust.

• **Freeze** 2 hours or until firm. Let stand 20 minutes before cutting. Garnish, if desired. **Yield:** 1 (9-inch) pie.

Gingersnap Crust

Prep: 15 minutes
Bake: 8 minutes

¾ cup flaked coconut, toasted
18 gingersnap cookies, crumbled
3 tablespoons unsalted butter, melted

• **Stir** together all ingredients. Press into bottom and up sides of a 9-inch pieplate.

• **Bake** at 350° for 8 minutes. Cool on a wire rack. **Yield:** 1 (9-inch) crust.

What's for Supper?

Stir-frying solves the supper question in the blink of an eye.

Stir-frying is one of the quickest ways to prepare a meal. Meat or seafood and vegetables are cut into pieces, and then cooked rapidly in hot oil. Any large, deep skillet will do for cooking. Don't crowd the pan, and keep the food moving. You won't have time to chop while something cooks, so prepare everything before you begin. Store the chopped ingredients in zip-top plastic bags in the refrigerator. Then you'll have a meal in minutes with little cleanup.

CASHEW CHICKEN

Prep: 20 minutes
Chill: 1 hour
Cook: 15 minutes

2 cups chicken broth, divided
¼ cup cornstarch, divided
¼ cup soy sauce, divided
3 to 4 chicken breast halves, cubed
    (about 1½ pounds) *
2 tablespoons vegetable oil
1½ cups broccoli florets
3 medium carrots, thinly sliced
1 medium onion, sliced
½ cup frozen sweet green peas,
    thawed
Hot cooked rice
½ cup cashews

• **Combine** ½ cup broth, 2 tablespoons cornstarch, and 2 tablespoons soy sauce in a shallow dish or heavy-duty zip-top plastic bag; add chicken. Cover or seal, and chill 1 hour.
• **Remove** chicken from marinade, discarding marinade.
• **Heat** oil in a large nonstick skillet or wok over medium-high heat 2 minutes. Add chicken; stir-fry 3 minutes or until lightly browned. Add vegetables; stir-fry 3 minutes. Add 1 cup broth; bring to a boil. Reduce heat, and simmer 2 to 5 minutes or until vegetables are crisp-tender.
• **Stir** together remaining ½ cup broth, 2 tablespoons cornstarch, and 2 tablespoons soy sauce. Add to chicken mixture; stir-fry 1 minute or until thickened. Serve over rice, and sprinkle with cashews. **Yield:** 4 servings.

* Substitute 1 pound pork tenderloin, cut into thin strips, for chicken, if desired.

Kathy London
Murphy, North Carolina

SESAME NOODLES

Prep: 15 minutes
Cook: 5 minutes

¼ cup lite soy sauce
3 tablespoons tahini
2 tablespoons water
4 teaspoons rice vinegar
2 garlic cloves
2 teaspoons sugar
2 teaspoons grated fresh ginger
¼ teaspoon ground red pepper
2 tablespoons sesame oil
2 green onions, minced
½ pound unpeeled, medium-size
    fresh shrimp
1 tablespoon vegetable oil
1 (5-ounce) package Japanese curly
    noodles, cooked

• **Process** first 8 ingredients in a food processor until smooth, stopping to scrape down sides. With food processor running, pour sesame oil through food chute in a slow, steady stream; process until sauce is smooth. Stir in minced green onions.
• **Peel** shrimp, and devein, if desired.
• **Heat** vegetable oil in a large nonstick skillet or wok over medium-high heat 1 minute; add shrimp, and stir-fry 2 to 3 minutes or just until shrimp turn pink.
• **Add** sauce and hot cooked noodles, tossing to coat. **Yield:** 4 servings.

Note: For testing purposes only, we used KA-ME Japanese Curly Noodles.
Vicki Kahl
Columbia, South Carolina

TEX-MEX FAJITAS

Prep: 25 minutes
Chill: 1 hour
Cook: 10 minutes

½ pound boneless top sirloin steak
2 tablespoons seasoned rice vinegar
½ teaspoon chili powder
1 tablespoon olive oil
¾ teaspoon fajita seasoning
1 large green bell pepper, cut into
    thin strips
1 large red bell pepper, cut into
    thin strips
1 small onion, thinly sliced
1 large tomato, chopped
4 (8-inch) flour tortillas
Salsa

• **Cut** beef diagonally across the grain into thin strips.
• **Combine** vinegar and chili powder in a shallow dish or large heavy-duty zip-top plastic bag; add beef. Cover or seal, and chill 1 hour, turning occasionally.
• **Remove** beef from marinade, discarding marinade.
• **Heat** oil in a nonstick skillet or wok at medium-high heat 2 minutes. Add beef and fajita seasoning; stir-fry 2 minutes or until beef is lightly browned. Remove from skillet; drain on paper towels.
• **Add** bell pepper strips and onion; stir-fry 4 minutes. Return beef to skillet; stir-fry 2 minutes. Add tomato, and cook until thoroughly heated. Serve with tortillas and salsa. **Yield:** 4 servings.
Anna J. Beyer
Bristol, Tennessee

Green Bean Salad in Tomatoes, page 181

Chunky Apple Cake With Cream Cheese Frosting, page 185

Apple Fritters With Lemon Sauce, page 184

190

*Chunky Apple Cake
With Cream Cheese
Frosting, page 185*

*Apple Fritters With Lemon Sauce,
page 184*

Quick Apple Dumplings, page 185

*Baked pork chops with
Apple-Almond Stuffing,
page 184*

Braised Short Ribs, facing page

Braising and Broiling

Try these two easy solutions when you don't have a lot of time to spend in the kitchen.

When it comes to preparing your family's weeknight meals, speed and ease are important considerations. Braising and broiling offer both—only in very different ways.

Braising refers to cooking meat or vegetables in a small amount of liquid in an ovenproof container with a tight-fitting lid. Tough, inexpensive cuts of meat are transformed into something fall-off-the-bone tender with little effort (think pot roast).

Broiling is essentially grilling in the oven with the heat element located above the meat. It doesn't have a tenderizing effect like braising, so it's best used with naturally tender cuts. Broiled meats tend to take on a smoky, somewhat charred flavor.

BEST CUTS FOR BEST RESULTS

BROILING
Beef: tenderloin steaks
Pork: chops, loin cutlets
Chicken: breasts
Fish: fillets, steaks

BRAISING
Beef: short ribs, bottom round, eye of round, chuck
Pork: picnic shoulder, Boston butt
Chicken: thighs, legs
Lamb: shanks, leg of lamb
Veal: shanks

BRAISED RED CABBAGE

Prep: 20 minutes
Bake: 1 hour, 15 minutes

1 medium onion, chopped
1 Granny Smith apple, diced
3 tablespoons bacon drippings or olive oil
1 cup water
¼ cup dry red wine (optional)
¼ cup red wine vinegar
¼ cup red currant jelly
2 tablespoons sugar
½ teaspoon salt
½ teaspoon ground cinnamon
½ teaspoon pepper
¼ teaspoon ground cloves
1 medium-size red cabbage, shredded
½ teaspoon cornstarch
1 teaspoon water
Garnish: chopped cooked bacon

• **Sauté** onion and apple in hot bacon drippings in a skillet over medium-low heat 5 minutes or until onion is tender.
• **Add** 1 cup water, wine, if desired, and next 7 ingredients; bring to a boil. Add cabbage, and tightly cover.
• **Bake** at 350° for 1 hour and 15 minutes or until cabbage and apple are tender. Return skillet to stove top.
• **Stir** together ½ teaspoon cornstarch and 1 teaspoon water; add to cabbage mixture, and bring to a boil. Boil, stirring constantly, 1 minute or until thickened. Garnish, if desired. **Yield:** 6 to 8 servings.

BRAISED SHORT RIBS
(pictured on facing page)

Prep: 35 minutes
Chill: 6 hours
Bake: 3 hours
Cook: 15 minutes

2¼ cups dry red wine, divided
2¼ cups beef broth, divided
2 garlic cloves, chopped
1 teaspoon ground allspice
½ teaspoon ground ginger
4 pounds beef short ribs, trimmed and cut in half
1 teaspoon salt
1 teaspoon pepper
½ cup all-purpose flour
3 tablespoons olive oil
1 carrot, chopped
½ onion, chopped
1 celery rib, chopped
2 tablespoons tomato paste
Roasted red potatoes
Garnish: chopped fresh parsley

• **Combine** ¼ cup wine, ¼ cup broth, garlic, allspice, and ginger in a large shallow dish; add ribs, turning to coat. Cover and chill ribs 4 to 6 hours, turning occasionally.
• **Remove** ribs from marinade, reserving marinade. Sprinkle ribs with salt and pepper; dredge in flour.
• **Cook** ribs, in batches, in hot oil in a Dutch oven over medium-high heat 15 minutes or until browned. Remove ribs, and set aside.
• **Reduce** heat to medium; add carrot, onion, and celery, and sauté 7 minutes or until browned. Add tomato paste; cook, stirring constantly, 3 minutes.
• **Return** ribs to pan. Stir in reserved marinade and remaining 2 cups wine and 2 cups broth; bring mixture to a boil, and tightly cover.
• **Bake** at 300° for 3 hours. Remove ribs from pan.
• **Skim** fat from sauce and discard; simmer sauce 12 to 15 minutes or until reduced by half. Serve with ribs over roasted potatoes. Garnish, if desired. **Yield:** 6 servings.

Mildred Bickley
Bristol, Virginia

BROILED LAMB CHOPS WITH SOUTHWESTERN BUTTER

Prep: 25 minutes
Chill: 2 hours
Broil: 11 minutes

¼ cup olive oil or vegetable oil
2 garlic cloves, chopped
1 tablespoon dried or 2 teaspoons chopped fresh thyme
1½ to 2 tablespoons paprika
18 (2- to 3-ounce) lamb rib chops ✱
1 teaspoon salt
1 teaspoon pepper
Southwestern Butter
Garnish: fresh thyme sprigs

• **Combine** first 4 ingredients in a large shallow dish or large heavy-duty zip-top plastic bag; add lamb chops, turning to coat. Cover or seal, and chill 2 hours.
• **Remove** lamb chops from marinade, discarding marinade. Sprinkle evenly with salt and pepper. Place on a lightly greased aluminum foil-lined rack in a broiler pan.
• **Broil** 3 inches from heat 5 minutes on each side or to desired degree of doneness. Top each lamb chop with a slice of Southwestern Butter; broil 30 more seconds. Serve immediately. Garnish, if desired. **Yield:** 6 servings.

✱ Substitute 12 loin chops for rib chops, if desired. Broil 3 more minutes on each side or to desired degree of doneness.

Southwestern Butter

Prep: 5 minutes
Chill: 6 hours

1 cup unsalted butter, softened
1½ teaspoons chili powder
¼ teaspoon ground cumin
1 teaspoon ground red pepper
1 teaspoon dried oregano
1 teaspoon Worcestershire sauce
⅛ teaspoon garlic powder
⅛ teaspoon onion powder

• **Stir** together all ingredients, and shape into a log, using parchment paper or wax paper. Chill 4 to 6 hours. **Yield:** 1 cup.

Creamy Dips

Preparing for a get-together couldn't be easier if you use one of these dip recipes from Laura Morris of Bunnell, Florida. They each take 20 minutes or less to prepare and should be made ahead. Blue Cheese Dip and Bacon-Cheese Dip offer a bonus: Add a little milk to them to create two great salad dressings.

SHRIMP DIP

Prep: 20 minutes
Chill: 8 hours

½ pound unpeeled, medium-size fresh shrimp, cooked
1 (8-ounce) container sour cream
1 (3-ounce) package cream cheese, softened
2 tablespoons lemon juice
1 (0.7-ounce) package Italian dressing mix
⅛ teaspoon hot sauce

• **Peel** and chop shrimp.
• **Stir** together sour cream and remaining 4 ingredients in a large bowl; stir in shrimp. Cover and chill 8 hours. Serve with celery or carrot sticks, potato chips, or crackers. **Yield:** 2 cups.

BLUE CHEESE DIP

Thin this creamy, tangy dip with a little milk for a delightfully robust salad dressing.

Prep: 10 minutes
Chill: 2 hours

1 (8-ounce) package cream cheese, cubed
3 tablespoons dry white wine or buttermilk
2 tablespoons sour cream
1 (4-ounce) package crumbled blue cheese

• **Process** first 3 ingredients and half of blue cheese in a blender or food processor until smooth, stopping to scrape down sides. Stir in remaining blue cheese. Cover and chill dip 2 hours. Serve with apple or pear slices. **Yield:** 1½ cups.

BACON-CHEESE DIP

Prep: 20 minutes
Chill: 2 hours

½ cup sour cream
1 (4-ounce) package crumbled blue cheese
1 (3-ounce) package cream cheese, softened
⅛ teaspoon hot sauce
2 tablespoons diced onion
4 bacon slices, cooked and crumbled

• **Process** first 5 ingredients in a blender or food processor until smooth, stopping to scrape down sides. Stir in half of bacon. Cover and chill 2 hours. Sprinkle with remaining bacon. Serve with crackers, raw vegetables, or potato chips. **Yield:** 1½ cups.

CLAM DIP

Prep: 10 minutes
Chill: 2 hours

1 (10-ounce) package frozen chopped spinach, thawed and well drained
1 (8-ounce) package cream cheese, softened
1 cup mayonnaise
2 (0.9-ounce) packages dry vegetable soup mix
1 (10-ounce) can chopped clams
1 (16-ounce) round sourdough loaf, cut into cubes

• **Combine** first 5 ingredients in a large bowl. Cover and chill 2 hours.
• **Serve** with bread cubes and raw vegetables. **Yield:** 3 cups.

Top-Rated Menu

Summer may well be over, but there's still time to grill. Cook both the main dish and the pineapple for dessert over the coals. You'll find unusual ingredients such as chili-garlic paste in your super-market's international foods section.

Grilling With Flair

Serves 6

Grilled Shrimp With Tropical Fruit Sauce

Crispy Asian Slaw

Grilled Pineapple With Vanilla-Cinnamon Ice Cream

GRILLED SHRIMP WITH TROPICAL FRUIT SAUCE

1997 Recipe Hall of Fame

Prep: 20 minutes
Cook: 50 minutes
Chill: 1 hour
Grill: 8 minutes

2   pounds unpeeled, large fresh shrimp
1   (33.8-ounce) jar peach nectar
¼   cup fresh lime juice, divided
2   tablespoons dark sesame oil
1   tablespoon grated fresh ginger
½   teaspoon salt
4   plum tomatoes, seeded and diced
2   papayas or mangoes, peeled and cubed *
3   green onions, sliced
¼   cup minced fresh cilantro
½   to 1 teaspoon chili-garlic paste
Hot cooked rice

• **Peel** shrimp, and devein, if desired; set aside.

• **Bring** nectar to a boil in a medium saucepan; boil 45 minutes or until reduced to 1 cup. Stir in 2 tablespoons lime juice and next 3 ingredients. Remove from heat, and cool.
• **Pour** half of nectar mixture in a large shallow dish or heavy-duty zip-top plastic bag; add shrimp. Cover or seal, and chill 1 hour.
• **Remove** shrimp from marinade, discarding marinade.
• **Grill,** in 2 batches, in a grill basket over medium-high heat (350° to 400°) 3 to 4 minutes or until shrimp turn pink.
• **Add** remaining 2 tablespoons lime juice, tomato, and next 4 ingredients to remaining nectar mixture. Cook over medium heat until thoroughly heated. Stir in shrimp; serve over rice. **Yield:** 6 servings.

* Substitute 1 pineapple, chopped, for papaya, if desired.

Note: Select unblemished papayas or mangoes that yield slightly to pressure. If underripe, place in a paper bag at room temperature to speed up the process.

CRISPY ASIAN SLAW

1997 Recipe Hall of Fame

Prep: 20 minutes
Bake: 5 minutes

1   (3-ounce) package ramen noodle soup mix
1   tablespoon sesame seeds
2   pounds napa cabbage
1   small carrot
4   ounces fresh snow pea pods
Sesame Vinaigrette

• **Remove** flavor packet from soup mix, and reserve for another use; crumble noodles. Place noodles and sesame seeds on a baking sheet.
• **Bake** at 350°, stirring occasionally, 4 to 5 minutes or until toasted.
• **Cut** cabbage, carrot, and snow peas into thin strips; place in a bowl. Drizzle with Sesame Vinaigrette, tossing gently to coat. Sprinkle with noodles and sesame seeds. **Yield:** 6 servings.

Sesame Vinaigrette

Prep: 10 minutes

¼   cup rice vinegar
¼   cup dark sesame oil
3   tablespoons chunky peanut butter
2   tablespoons lime juice
1   tablespoon honey
1   teaspoon grated fresh ginger
¼   teaspoon dried crushed red pepper

• **Whisk** together all ingredients. **Yield:** about 1 cup.

GRILLED PINEAPPLE WITH VANILLA-CINNAMON ICE CREAM

2000 Recipe Hall of Fame

Prep: 15 minutes
Grill: 14 minutes

1   pineapple
3   tablespoons brown sugar
½   teaspoon ground cinnamon
1   tablespoon grated fresh ginger
Vanilla-Cinnamon Ice Cream

• **Skin** pineapple; remove and discard pineapple core. Cut pineapple lengthwise into halves.
• **Combine** brown sugar, cinnamon, and ginger; rub evenly over pineapple.
• **Coat** a food rack with cooking spray; place on grill over medium-high heat (350° to 400°). Place pineapple on rack.
• **Grill,** covered with grill lid, 5 to 7 minutes on each side. Remove pineapple from grill; cut into ¼-inch-thick slices. Serve with Vanilla-Cinnamon Ice Cream. **Yield:** 6 servings.

Vanilla-Cinnamon Ice Cream

Prep: 10 minutes
Freeze: 1 hour

1   quart vanilla ice cream, softened
¼   cup milk
2   tablespoons brown sugar
¼   teaspoon ground cinnamon

• **Stir** together all ingredients. Freeze 1 hour. **Yield:** about 4 cups.

Living Light

*Sample a menu of delicious Italian favorites
including a terrific grand finale.*

Light Italian Fare
Serves 6 to 8

Cheesy Spinach Lasagna
Roasted Tomato-and-Pepper Salad
Parmesan Crisps
Two-Layered Ice-Cream Freeze

We love sharing light, tasty recipes. Sometimes, though, we create a menu that's hearty enough for anyone who simply enjoys a delectable meal—we think this is one of them.

Italian dishes are often reserved for special occasions. But you can easily replace high-fat sausage and beef with vegetables in classic dishes. Button and portobello mushrooms have a meaty texture but add almost no fat. Low-calorie spinach, zucchini, and carrots are fiber rich and impart wonderful flavor.

If you must have meat, try our Cheesy Spinach Lasagna with Canadian bacon (naturally low in fat). Think of Italian dishes as comfort foods but also health foods when packed with nutritious ingredients such as these.

CHEESY SPINACH LASAGNA

*To reduce sodium,
omit Canadian bacon and salt.*

Prep: 20 minutes
Bake: 35 minutes
Stand: 5 minutes

9 uncooked lasagna noodles
2 cups (8 ounces) shredded part-skim
    mozzarella cheese, divided
1 (16-ounce) container fat-free ricotta
    cheese
1 (10-ounce) package frozen chopped
    spinach, thawed and well drained
½ cup grated Parmesan cheese
1 teaspoon dried Italian seasoning
½ teaspoon garlic powder
¼ teaspoon salt
1 (3-ounce) package Canadian bacon,
    chopped
½ small onion, diced
Vegetable cooking spray
1 (26-ounce) jar low-fat pasta sauce

• **Cook** pasta according to package directions; set aside.
• **Stir** together 1½ cups mozzarella cheese, ricotta cheese, and next 5 ingredients in a bowl.
• **Sauté** chopped Canadian bacon and diced onion in a skillet coated with cooking spray over medium heat 5 to 6 minutes or until onion is tender. Stir into cheese mixture.
• **Spread** ½ cup pasta sauce on bottom of an 11- x 7-inch baking dish coated with cooking spray. Layer with 3 noodles and ½ cup pasta sauce; top with half of cheese mixture. Repeat layers once, ending with remaining cheese mixture. Top with remaining 3 noodles and remaining pasta sauce.
• **Bake** at 350° for 30 minutes. Sprinkle with remaining ½ cup mozzarella cheese; bake 5 more minutes or until cheese melts. Let stand 5 minutes. **Yield:** 8 servings.

Note: Freeze individual portions as desired. To reheat, bake, covered, at 300° for 1 hour.

Shannon Gaudin
Shreveport, Louisiana

♥ Per serving: Calories 295 (22% from fat)
Fat 7.3g (sat 4.3g, mono 2.2g, poly 0.5g)
Protein 24g   Carb 33g   Fiber 3.6g
Chol 42mg   Iron 2.9mg
Sodium 799mg   Calc 504mg

ROASTED TOMATO-AND-PEPPER SALAD

Prep: 15 minutes
Broil: 30 minutes

6 large plum tomatoes
Vegetable cooking spray
1 yellow bell pepper
1 green bell pepper
1 red bell pepper
1 medium-size purple onion, cut into
    eighths
1 tablespoon olive oil
1 tablespoon balsamic vinegar
1 garlic clove, minced
½ teaspoon salt
½ teaspoon dried oregano
½ teaspoon freshly ground pepper
¼ cup sliced fresh basil

• **Cut** tomatoes into ¼-inch-thick slices. Arrange on an aluminum foil-lined baking sheet coated with cooking spray.

- **Broil** 5 minutes on each side; set tomato aside.
- **Cut** bell peppers in half lengthwise; remove and discard seeds.
- **Arrange** peppers (cut sides down) and onion on a foil-lined baking sheet coated with cooking spray.
- **Broil** 5 inches from heat 8 to 10 minutes on each side or until peppers look blistered. Remove peppers, and broil onion 3 more minutes, if necessary.
- **Place** peppers in a heavy-duty zip-top plastic bag; seal and let stand 10 minutes to loosen skins. Peel peppers; cut into thin strips.
- **Whisk** together oil and next 5 ingredients in a large bowl; add vegetables, tossing to coat. Sprinkle with basil. **Yield:** 6 servings.

Per serving: Calories 61 (38% from fat)
Fat 2.6g (sat 0.4g, mono 1.8g, poly 0.3g)
Protein 1.4g Carb 9g Fiber 2.3g
Chol 0mg Iron 0.8mg
Sodium 201mg Calc 28mg

PARMESAN CRISPS

Prep: 15 minutes
Bake: 8 minutes

1½ cups (6 ounces) finely shredded Parmesan cheese
Vegetable cooking spray

- **Sprinkle** about 1 tablespoon Parmesan cheese, forming a 2-inch round, on an aluminum-foil lined baking sheet coated with cooking spray. Repeat with remaining cheese, leaving 1 inch between rounds.
- **Bake** at 350° for 8 minutes or until lightly browned. Quickly remove cheese wafers from baking sheet with a spatula. Cool on a wire rack. Store in an airtight container. **Yield:** 2 dozen.

Demetra Economos Anas
Potomac, Maryland

Per 2 crisps: Calories 118 (59% from fat)
Fat 7.7g (sat 5g, mono 2.5g, poly 0.2g)
Protein 11g Carb 1g Fiber 0g
Chol 21mg Iron 0.3mg
Sodium 481mg Calc 355mg

TWO-LAYERED ICE-CREAM FREEZE

In this version of spumoni, an Italian ice-cream dessert, use our Vanilla Meringue Cookies recipe or store-bought meringue cookies. A ruby-hued raspberry sauce accompanies this frosty treat.

Prep: 30 minutes
Freeze: 3 hours, 30 minutes

2 cups no-sugar-added, fat-free vanilla ice cream, softened
1 (16-ounce) container fat-free frozen whipped topping, thawed and divided
1 teaspoon almond extract
10 Vanilla Meringue Cookies, crushed
2 cups no-sugar-added, fat-free chocolate fudge ice cream, softened
1½ cups fresh or frozen raspberries, thawed
¼ cup sugar
1 tablespoon lemon juice

- **Stir** together softened vanilla ice cream, ½ cup whipped topping, and almond extract. Spoon mixture into a plastic wrap-lined 2-quart glass bowl, and freeze 15 minutes or until mixture is set.
- **Stir** together 1½ cups whipped topping and cookie crumbs; spread evenly over vanilla ice-cream mixture. Freeze 15 minutes.
- **Stir** together softened chocolate fudge ice cream and ½ cup whipped topping. Spread over cookie crumb mixture. Cover and freeze 3 hours or until firm.
- **Process** raspberries in a blender or food processor until smooth. Pour through a fine wire-mesh strainer into a small saucepan, pressing pulp with a wooden spoon; discard seeds.
- **Bring** raspberry puree, sugar, and lemon juice to a boil, stirring constantly; cook, stirring constantly, 2 minutes or until sauce is thickened.
- **Remove** ice-cream mixture from freezer. Dip glass bowl in warm water 15 seconds. Invert onto a serving dish,

discarding plastic wrap. Cut ice cream into wedges, and serve with raspberry sauce and, if desired, remaining whipped topping. **Yield:** 8 servings.

Note: For testing purposes only, we used Edy's No Sugar Added Fat Free ice creams.

Per serving: Calories 261 (0% from fat)
Fat 0g Protein 4.2g Carb 57g
Fiber 2g Chol 0mg Iron 0.3mg
Sodium 130mg Calc 66mg

Vanilla Meringue Cookies

Prep: 15 minutes
Bake: 2 hours
Stand: 8 hours

3 egg whites
¼ teaspoon cream of tartar
⅛ teaspoon salt
1¼ teaspoons vanilla extract
½ cup superfine sugar

- **Beat** first 4 ingredients at high speed with an electric mixer until foamy.
- **Add** sugar, 1 tablespoon at a time, beating until stiff peaks form and sugar dissolves.
- **Spoon** mixture into 36 (1¼-inch) mounds onto parchment paper-lined baking sheets.
- **Bake** at 200° for 2 hours; turn oven off. Let meringues stand in closed oven with light on for 8 hours. **Yield:** 3 dozen.

Cool Bean Salads

Versatile bean salads boast the flavors
of the South as well as the Mediterranean.

For a change of pace from the usual leafy salad, offer a chilled bean one instead. Start with canned beans, and add flavorful herbs and vegetables. Toss in a vinaigrette, and you'll have a super main course or side dish to accompany your entrée.

Our quick recipes are easy on the budget. Make the salads at least one hour before serving to allow the flavors to blend thoroughly.

BEAN-AND-FENNEL SALAD

Prep: 20 minutes
Chill: 1 hour

6 tablespoons olive oil
3 tablespoons white wine vinegar
¾ teaspoon coarsely ground
    pepper
½ teaspoon salt
½ teaspoon dried thyme
½ teaspoon dried crushed red pepper
2 (15.5-ounce) cans chickpeas, rinsed
    and drained*
2 medium fennel bulbs, thinly sliced
3 garlic cloves, minced
½ cup crumbled Gorgonzola cheese*
¼ cup minced fresh Italian parsley
Garnish: fresh fennel fronds

• **Whisk** together first 6 ingredients in a bowl; add beans, fennel, and garlic, tossing gently to coat. Sprinkle with cheese and parsley. Cover and chill at least 1 hour. Garnish, if desired. **Yield:** 6 to 8 servings.

*Substitute 2 (15-ounce) cans navy beans and ½ cup crumbled blue cheese for chickpeas and Gorgonzola, if desired.
Julie DeMatteo
Clementon, New Jersey

BLACK-EYED PEA-AND-SWEET POTATO SALAD

Prep: 20 minutes
Cook: 25 minutes
Chill: 1 hour

2 medium-size sweet potatoes,
    peeled and cubed
1 purple onion, quartered and
    thinly sliced
1 tablespoon vegetable oil
2 garlic cloves, minced
1 teaspoon dried basil
1 teaspoon dried thyme
½ teaspoon ground cumin
½ teaspoon ground coriander
⅓ cup lime juice
½ cup mango chutney
3 (15.8-ounce) cans black-eyed peas,
    rinsed and drained
½ cup chopped fresh Italian parsley
1 teaspoon salt
1 teaspoon pepper

• **Bring** potato and water to cover to a boil in a large saucepan over medium heat. Cook 15 minutes or until potato is tender. Drain and set potato aside.
• **Sauté** onion in hot oil in saucepan over medium heat 4 minutes or until tender. Add garlic and next 4 ingredients. Cook, stirring constantly, 1 to 2 minutes.
• **Stir** together lime juice and chutney in a large bowl; add potato, onion mixture, peas, and remaining ingredients, tossing gently to coat. Cover and chill at least 1 hour. **Yield:** 6 to 8 servings.
Caroline Kennedy
Lighthouse Point, Florida

BLACK BEAN SALAD

Prep: 20 minutes
Chill: 1 hour

2 tablespoons orange juice
2 tablespoons lemon juice
2 teaspoons olive oil
½ teaspoon salt
½ teaspoon ground cumin
½ teaspoon hot sauce
2 (15-ounce) cans black beans, rinsed
    and drained
1 cup cooked long-grain white rice
3 plum tomatoes, seeded and chopped
1 red bell pepper, chopped
½ green bell pepper, chopped
½ small purple onion, chopped
2 green onions, sliced
1 celery rib, diced

• **Whisk** together first 6 ingredients in a bowl; add beans and remaining ingredients, tossing gently to coat. Cover; chill at least 1 hour. **Yield:** 6 to 8 servings.
Cyndy Hinton
Franklin, Tennessee

CONFETTI BEAN SALAD

Prep: 15 minutes
Chill: 1 hour

¼ cup olive oil
3 tablespoons lemon juice
½ teaspoon salt
½ teaspoon pepper
1 (15.5-ounce) can cannellini beans,
    rinsed and drained
1 medium-size red bell pepper, cut into
    thin strips
½ medium onion, finely chopped
1 small carrot, thinly sliced
1 celery rib, thinly sliced
¼ cup chopped fresh parsley
¼ cup crumbled feta cheese (optional)

• **Whisk** together first 4 ingredients in a large bowl; add beans and next 5 ingredients, tossing gently to coat. Cover and chill at least 1 hour. Sprinkle with feta cheese, if desired. **Yield:** 4 servings.
Mary Pappas
Richmond, Virginia

Quick & Easy

Deciding what to make for dinner is half the battle with nightly meals. Here's help.

It's an age-old dilemma: Your family wants delicious home-cooked meals, and you want easy dishes that come from your pantry and refrigerator. What's a cook to do? We can solve both requests with these recipes. They'll have you serving supper in less than an hour, allowing your family to have a great meal and spend more time together. While the entrée is cooking, prepare a salad or other side dish, and set the table. See? This dinner is a breeze.

BEEF CASSEROLE

This casserole will become a favorite for both large and small appetites. Serve with a tossed green salad.

Prep: 15 minutes
Bake: 35 minutes
Stand: 10 minutes

2 (8-ounce) cans crescent rolls, divided
1½ pounds ground beef
½ small onion, minced
2 cups (8 ounces) shredded Cheddar cheese
½ cup water
½ cup chili sauce
2 tablespoons taco seasoning
1 tablespoon Worcestershire sauce
½ teaspoon garlic salt
½ teaspoon pepper
Toppings: sour cream, salsa

• **Unroll** 1 can crescent rolls, and press into a lightly greased 13- x 9-inch pan.
• **Bake** at 375° for 10 minutes or until lightly browned.
• **Cook** ground beef and onion in a large skillet, stirring until beef crumbles and is no longer pink. Drain. Stir in cheese and next 6 ingredients; spoon over crust.
• **Unroll** remaining can of crescent rolls, and shape into a rectangle, pressing perforations to seal; cut into ½-inch strips. Arrange strips in a lattice design over beef mixture.
• **Bake** at 375° for 25 minutes or until golden. Let casserole stand 10 minutes. Serve with sour cream and salsa, if desired. **Yield:** 6 servings.

Carol Taylor
Milan, Georgia

CHEESY MEXICAN CHICKEN

Serve with shredded lettuce and guacamole.

Prep: 10 minutes
Cook: 26 minutes
Bake: 25 minutes

2 tablespoons butter or margarine
1 (6.4-ounce) package Mexican-style rice-and-pasta mix
1 medium-size green bell pepper, chopped
1 small onion, chopped
2¼ cups water
2 (14½-ounce) cans Mexican-style stewed tomatoes, undrained
2 cups chopped cooked chicken
1 cup (4 ounces) shredded Monterey Jack or Cheddar cheese

• **Melt** butter in a large ovenproof skillet over medium heat; add rice mix, reserving seasoning packet. Stir in bell pepper and onion, and sauté 6 minutes or until rice mix is lightly browned.
• **Stir** in 2¼ cups water and seasoning packet. Bring to a boil; cover, reduce heat, and simmer 15 to 20 minutes or until rice is tender. Let stand 3 minutes. Stir in tomatoes and chicken.
• **Bake** at 350° for 20 minutes; sprinkle with shredded cheese, and bake 5 more minutes or until thoroughly heated. **Yield:** 6 servings.

Note: For testing purposes only, we used Mexican Style Rice-A-Roni.

Lynda Kenan-Kidwell
Independence, Missouri

SAUSAGE-POTATO PIZZA

Prep: 10 minutes
Bake: 30 minutes

2 cups biscuit mix
½ cup water
1 pound ground pork sausage
1 to 1½ cups frozen hash browns, thawed
1 cup (4 ounces) shredded Cheddar cheese
3 large eggs
2 tablespoons milk
⅛ teaspoon pepper

• **Stir** together biscuit mix and ½ cup water until dough forms.
• **Turn** dough out onto a lightly floured surface; knead 4 or 5 times. Pat into a 12-inch circle on a lightly greased baking sheet.
• **Cook** sausage in a large skillet, stirring until meat crumbles and is no longer pink; drain well.
• **Layer** dough evenly with sausage, hash browns, and cheese. Whisk together eggs, milk, and pepper; pour mixture evenly over cheese.
• **Bake** at 400° for 30 minutes or until golden. **Yield:** 6 servings.

Note: To make ahead, prepare dough as directed; layer with sausage, hash browns, and cheese. Cover and chill 8 hours. Add egg mixture, and bake at 400° for 35 minutes or until golden.

Eloise Patrick
Sunnyvale, Texas

Grab It and Go Breakfast

Treat yourself to a good breakfast even when you're in a hurry.

The morning routine of getting yourself and the children out the door can be taxing to say the least. Some days there's not even time for cereal. On those mornings, you'll be glad for these recipes.

CARROT-ZUCCHINI MUFFINS

Prep: 10 minutes
Bake: 20 minutes

1 cup all-purpose flour
1 cup whole wheat flour
½ cup sugar
1 teaspoon baking powder
1 teaspoon ground cinnamon
½ teaspoon salt
½ teaspoon baking soda
1 large egg, lightly beaten
¾ cup orange juice
¼ cup butter or margarine, melted
2 medium carrots, shredded
1 medium zucchini, shredded

• **Combine** first 7 ingredients in a large bowl; make a well in center of mixture.
• **Stir** together egg, orange juice, and butter; add to dry ingredients, stirring just until moistened. Fold in carrot and zucchini. Spoon into greased muffin pans, filling two-thirds full.
• **Bake** at 400° for 20 minutes. Remove from pans immediately, and cool on wire racks. **Yield:** 1 dozen.

Note: Freeze in an airtight container up to 3 months. To reheat, wrap each muffin in a damp paper towel; microwave at HIGH 40 seconds or until warm.
Valerie G. Stutsman
Norfolk, Virginia

TOASTED CREAM CHEESE-AND-APPLE POCKETS

Get the day off to a good start with these eye-opening breakfast treats.

Prep: 25 minutes
Bake: 10 minutes

34 fresh whole wheat bread slices
1 (8-ounce) package reduced-fat cream cheese, softened
1 Golden Delicious apple, peeled and diced
¼ cup powdered sugar
¼ teaspoon ground cinnamon, divided
1 tablespoon butter or margarine, melted
2 tablespoons sugar

• **Cut** out centers of each bread slice with a 3-inch round cutter; reserve scraps for another use. Place half of bread rounds on a lightly greased baking sheet.
• **Stir** together cream cheese, apple, powdered sugar, and ⅛ teaspoon cinnamon until blended. Spoon 1 tablespoon apple mixture onto center of each bread round on baking sheet; top with remaining bread rounds. Crimp edges with a fork to seal; brush tops with butter.
• **Stir** together remaining ⅛ teaspoon cinnamon and 2 tablespoons sugar; sprinkle over tops.
• **Bake** at 400° for 8 to 10 minutes or until golden. **Yield:** 17 pockets.

Note: Store in an airtight container in freezer. To reheat, wrap each pocket in a damp paper towel; microwave at HIGH 1 minute or until thoroughly heated.

BERRY BLUE SHAKE

Prep: 5 minutes

2 cups frozen blueberries
1 banana
½ (8-ounce) container blueberry or strawberry yogurt
½ cup orange juice
1 strawberry (optional)

• **Process** first 4 ingredients in a blender until smooth, stopping to scrape down sides. Pour into a chilled glass; top with strawberry, if desired. **Yield:** 1 serving.
Bradley Horneffer
Simpsonville, South Carolina

RUSH HOUR REMEDIES

Busy-day breakfasts are sometimes eaten while you're stalled in traffic or waiting to drop the children off at school. Here are some additional ideas to make your mornings easier.

■ Stock up on disposable plastic containers with lids, packaged knife-fork-and-spoon sets, and plastic cups with lids and straws. Keep packets of moist towelettes in the glove box, along with plastic grocery bags to use for trash.

■ A granola sundae offers nutrition and convenience; layer vanilla yogurt, granola, and chopped apple in a plastic container.

■ Spread a flour tortilla with peanut butter, and then roll it around a banana.

■ Roll cheese slices in a tortilla, and microwave for 20 seconds or just until the cheese melts. Wrap in plastic or foil, and you're out the door.

Taste of the South

Few confections are so readily identified with the South as pralines—irresistible nuggets made of caramel and pecans. Whether you pronounce it "PRAY-leen" or "PRAH-leen," your taste buds will love this candy's rich flavor.

Different Southern cooks swear by a variety of recipes—with or without brown sugar or baking soda; with evaporated milk, buttermilk, or half-and-half; and dropped large or small. We tasted them all before determining our favorite recipe, a combination of white and brown sugars with evaporated milk.

Pralines aren't difficult to make, but they can be tricky. The requirements are plenty of stirring, patience, and careful attention. Two big questions usually come up during preparation: when to remove the candy mixture from the heat, and when to stop beating and start spooning it. (You're allowed to enlist an extra set of hands at this stage.)

If the mixture gets too hot, the candy will be dry and crumbly. If it isn't cooked long enough, the mixture will be runny and sticky.

One trick we learned after making several batches in our Test Kitchens: Use a candy thermometer for the best temperature reading—it will take out most of the guesswork. We like to use two thermometers for accuracy.

Beat the mixture with a wooden spoon just until it begins to thicken. You'll feel the mixture become heavier, and its color will become lighter. Often the last few pralines that you spoon will be thicker and less perfectly shaped than the first, but they'll still be just as good. The candy tastes best if eaten within a day or two; pralines become sugary and gritty with age. Be sure to store them in an airtight container for best results (a metal tin or other container with a tight-fitting lid works well).

If your pralines don't turn out right the first time, don't despair. Simply create a new dessert. Fold them into softened vanilla ice cream. Or, if they're too soft, scrape up the mixture, chill it, and roll it into 1-inch balls. Then dip the balls into melted chocolate to make truffles. If the candy mixture hardens in the pot, break it into pieces, and sprinkle it over a hot apple pie, cheesecake, or ice cream.

Practice helps. So does a candy thermometer. Keep one handy to make these Southern delicacies.

PRALINES

Prep: 10 minutes
Cook: 30 minutes

1½ cups sugar
1½ cups firmly packed brown sugar
1 cup evaporated milk
¼ cup butter or margarine
2 cups pecan halves, toasted
1 teaspoon vanilla extract

• **Bring** sugars and milk to a boil in a Dutch oven, stirring often. Cook over medium heat, stirring often, 11 minutes or until a candy thermometer registers 228° (thread stage).
• **Stir** in butter and pecans, and cook, stirring constantly, until candy thermometer registers 232°.
• **Remove** from heat; stir in vanilla. Beat with a wooden spoon 1 to 2 minutes or just until mixture begins to thicken. Quickly drop by heaping tablespoonfuls onto buttered wax paper or parchment paper; let stand until firm. **Yield:** about 2½ dozen.

Cupcakes

These miniature versions of the classic Southern caramel cake are sure to please and worth the extra effort.

BROWN SUGAR-FROSTED CUPCAKES

We generously frosted 2 dozen cupcakes with Brown Sugar Frosting. Freeze any extra unfrosted cupcakes.

Prep: 30 minutes
Bake: 20 minutes

1 cup shortening
2 cups sugar
4 large eggs
3 cups cake flour
2½ teaspoons baking powder
½ teaspoon salt
1 cup milk
1 teaspoon almond extract
1 teaspoon vanilla extract
Brown Sugar Frosting

• **Beat** shortening at medium speed with an electric mixer until fluffy; gradually add sugar, beating well. Add eggs, 1 at a time, beating well after each addition.
• **Combine** flour, baking powder, and salt; add to shortening mixture alternately with milk, beginning and ending with flour mixture. Beat at low speed until blended after each addition. Stir in extracts. Spoon batter into paper-lined muffin pans, filling them half full.
• **Bake** at 375° for 20 minutes. Remove and cool on wire racks. Spread with Brown Sugar Frosting. **Yield:** 3 dozen.

Brown Sugar Frosting

Prep: 5 minutes
Cook: 13 minutes

½ cup butter or margarine
1 cup firmly packed dark brown sugar
¼ cup dark corn syrup
2 teaspoons cream of tartar
3 cups sifted powdered sugar
3 tablespoons whipping cream
2 teaspoons vanilla extract

• **Melt** butter in a saucepan over medium-high heat. Stir in brown sugar, corn syrup, and cream of tartar; bring to a boil. Boil 5 minutes. (Do not stir.) Remove from heat; stir in powdered sugar, whipping cream, and vanilla. Beat at medium speed with an electric mixer 2 minutes. Frost cupcakes immediately. **Yield:** 2 cups.

From Our Kitchen

Hot and Spicy Peppers

"Party in El Paso" on page 186 celebrates hot and spicy chiles. To prepare for your own gathering, look for fresh chile peppers in the produce section of the supermarket. Roast mild Anaheims—long green chiles—to add to cheese sauces or salsas. Moderately warm dark green poblanos are great for stuffing. Jalapeño peppers generally range from hot to very hot while round cherry peppers yield mild to medium heat. Serranos and habaneros are very hot, so be sure to use them cautiously. Check out the dried chiles too. They're easy to rehydrate, or they can be crushed and sparingly stirred into dishes. Remember dried chiles may deliver a bit more heat than their fresh counterparts.

Wear rubber gloves when you're working with the hot ones to eliminate possible burns to skin. And be careful to keep your hands away from your face until they've been thoroughly washed.

Although not all chile peppers are flaming hot, serve sour cream or yogurt as a cooling condiment alongside dishes that might pack extra heat. For a taste of Park Kerr's salsas, sauces, and peppers, call the El Paso Chile Company at 1-888-472-5727 for a catalog, or visit www.elpasochile.com.

Tips and Tidbits

■ Fresh bread was the topic of several e-mail messages we've received, so we did some checking. Because bread is delivered fresh five days a week to grocery stores, it can be hard to judge freshness. Here's our method: Bread wrappers have color-coded twist ties and plastic clips to indicate the delivery day. Learn the color codes for your area, and you won't have to squeeze to find which loaf of bread is the freshest.

MUSHROOMS

Mushrooms add earthy goodness to recipes or can stand alone as a side dish. White button, brown cremino, and portobello are the most popular cultivated types. Shiitake, morel, oyster, porcino, enoki, and chanterelle are the favorite wild varieties.

Remove any plastic wrap immediately. Store mushrooms, unwashed, in a paper bag in the refrigerator, and use within three days. Don't peel or wash; clean with a mushroom brush or damp paper towels just before cooking. Discard tough or shriveled stems.

For better flavor, sauté mushrooms before adding to a recipe. Use a hot skillet and a small amount of butter or oil. Don't crowd the skillet, or they'll steam and become watery.

Dried mushrooms are ready to add to a dish after they've had a 30-minute to 1-hour soak in warm water; use the soaking liquid in place of water in the recipe for added taste.

■ Apples will stay fresh longer if they're not touching each other in a bowl.

■ Turn jars of tahini (sesame seed paste) and fresh ground peanut butter upside down every once in a while to allow the oil to redistribute itself throughout the mixture.

■ Don't throw away stale tortillas. They can be cut into strips or triangles, and then baked or fried for soup toppings or salsa scoops.

■ When a recipe calls for chopped celery, try this method. Keeping the stalk intact, start at the top, and slice across all the ribs until you've chopped the desired amount. This way you'll chop just enough without leftover pieces that usually get thrown away.

■ Take advantage of the convenient breads in the dairy case—crescent rolls, breadsticks, pizza crusts, and biscuits. They're hearty ways to top casseroles or wrap around leftovers.

■ Now that you're cooking outside, get additional tips from the Dial-A-Chef Grilling Hotline. A team of prominent chefs offers their favorite ways to prepare simple, tasty recipes. Ming Tsai, host of the Food Network's *East Meets West* show; Bruce Auden, chef/owner of Biga on the Banks in San Antonio; Traci Des Jardins, chef/owner of Jardinière in San Francisco; and Michael Leviton, chef/owner of Lumière in West Newton, Massachusetts, are all just a phone call away. The hot line is open 24 hours a day, 7 days a week at 1-888-723-4468, or visit www.dialachef.com.

Cooking for a Picky Eater

Bianca Priest-Varner, culinary school student and newlywed, wants to share her love of food with her husband. His list of dislikes makes it hard. "I try to sneak in a new meal or ingredient about once every other week," says Bianca. "I can only introduce one thing at a time or he immediately hates it. I can't forget the time I served him pork chops with a peach and balsamic vinegar glaze. He's not a big fan of pork chops anyway, so the sauce just made it worse. But when I served that sauce with chicken, he liked it."

Try this method to introduce something new to your family. Make only one new dish at a time, not the entire menu. Talk about it at the table. Respect your family's dislikes, but don't eliminate something you love simply because they don't.

OCTOBER

Ghosts and Goblins Come Knocking

Bone Crackers

Prep: 20 minutes
Bake: 30 minutes

2 (13.5-ounce) packages 9-inch
   flour tortillas
½ cup butter or margarine,
   melted
¼ teaspoon garlic salt

• **Cut** tortillas with a 3½-inch bone-shaped cutter, and place on baking sheets.
• **Stir** together butter and garlic salt; brush mixture on tortillas.
• **Bake** at 250° for 30 minutes or until crisp. **Yield:** 60 crackers.

Note: Flour tortillas may be cut into bone shapes using kitchen shears.

Spooktacular Halloween Party
Serves 8

Goblin Dip With Bone Crackers
Trash Mix
Witches' Brew Chicken Soup
Cheesy Witches' Brooms   Candy Apples

The chills and thrills of October 31 bring family and friends together to share the Halloween spirit with creative costumes and whimsical touches.

GOBLIN DIP WITH BONE CRACKERS

Guests will love scooping up this chunky dip with clever, crunchy Bone Crackers.

Prep: 10 minutes
Cook: 15 minutes

1 (16-ounce) can chili without
   beans
1 (16-ounce) can refried beans
1 (8-ounce) package cream
   cheese
1 (8-ounce) jar chunky pico de
   gallo
1 (4.5-ounce) can chopped
   green chiles,
   undrained
½ teaspoon ground cumin
Toppings: shredded Cheddar or
   Monterey Jack cheese with
   peppers, chopped black olives,
   sliced green onions
Bone Crackers

• **Cook** first 6 ingredients in a heavy saucepan over low heat, stirring often, 15 minutes or until cream cheese is melted.
• **Sprinkle** with desired toppings, and serve warm with Bone Crackers. **Yield:** 6 cups.

TRASH MIX

Prep: 5 minutes

1 (16-ounce) package candy corn
1 (15-ounce) package pretzel
   nibblers
1 (12-ounce) package caramel
   popcorn and peanuts
1 (15-ounce) package banana chips
1 (15-ounce) package candy-coated
   chocolate pieces
1 (15-ounce) package dried mango
1 (15-ounce) package dried
   pineapple
1 (10-ounce) package toffee pretzels
1 (6-ounce) package sweetened dried
   cranberries
1 (6-ounce) package worm-shaped
   chewy candy

• **Stir** together all ingredients. Store in an airtight container. **Yield:** 16 cups.

Note: For testing purposes only, we used pretzel Nuggets, Crunch 'n Munch, M&M's, and Craisins.

HALLOWEEN DECOR

These little fellows add the right touch of whimsy to your Halloween decor.

SHRUNKEN HEADS

Prep: 45 minutes
Stand: 1 week

8 small Granny Smith
   apples, peeled
1 cup lemon juice
1 tablespoon salt
Red licorice, cut into short lengths

• **Core** apples; carve face features.
• **Combine** lemon juice and salt. Add apples; toss to coat. Let stand 1 minute. Drain; let stand at room temperature 1 week. Add licorice for hair. **Yield:** 8 heads.

WITCHES' BREW CHICKEN SOUP

Scare up a devilishly good time with this warming soup.

Prep: 15 minutes
Cook: 40 minutes

1 tablespoon butter or
    margarine
4 skinned and boned chicken breast
    halves, chopped
1 large onion, chopped
3 carrots, chopped
2 garlic cloves, minced
2 (14-ounce) cans low-sodium
    chicken broth
1 tablespoon chicken bouillon
    granules
1 teaspoon ground cumin
¼ teaspoon ground red pepper
3 (16-ounce) cans great Northern
    beans, rinsed, drained, and
    divided
1 (4.5-ounce) can chopped green
    chiles
2 tablespoons all-purpose flour
½ cup milk
¼ cup chopped fresh cilantro
Toppings: shredded Cheddar
    cheese, sour cream, sliced
    green onions, cooked and
    crumbled bacon

• **Melt** butter in a large Dutch oven over medium-high heat; add chicken and next 3 ingredients, and sauté 10 minutes. Stir in chicken broth and next 3 ingredients.
• **Bring** to a boil; reduce heat, and simmer, stirring occasionally, 20 minutes. Stir in 2 cans of beans and chiles.
• **Mash** remaining can of beans in a small bowl. Whisk together flour and milk, and stir into beans. Gradually add bean mixture to soup mixture, stirring constantly. Cook 10 minutes or until thickened. Remove from heat, and stir in cilantro. Serve with desired toppings. **Yield:** 12 cups.

PARTY PERFECT

Choose a party theme. Plan your menu and make a checklist. Getting organized is the key to successful entertaining.
Etch or print handmade invitations on construction or handmade papers.
Make your gathering easy by keeping the decorations and food simple.
Explore fall foliage; let it set the tone with bales of hay and cornstalks.
Light the inside of carved pumpkins and gourds with candles or use cordless battery-powered candles.
Embellish the driveway, sidewalk, windowsills, door knocker, lamppost, and front porch with odd-size pumpkins, vines, and gourds.
Backs of chairs can be as fun to dress up as the table. Attach natural swags or vines to the chair backs with twine.
Round up flashlights and lanterns to use in the dark. Tape a spooky stencil over a flashlight bulb to create mysterious shadows.
Arrange one or two large displays to greet guests as they arrive. Include fall produce, gourds, nuts, mums, and dried leaves around the base of the arrangement. Cast-iron kettles make creative pots for plants.
Transform a garage, loft, or recreation room into a barn setting.
Let the child in you shine through while you're bobbing for apples and sharing ghost tales.
Enjoy your company. When you relax they'll have a good time, too.

CHEESY WITCHES' BROOMS

Children and adults alike will "sweep" their bowls clean with these tasty breadsticks.

Prep: 15 minutes
Bake: 12 minutes

2 (11-ounce) packages cornbread
    twists or breadsticks
½ cup shredded Parmesan cheese

• **Separate** cornbread twists, and place on a baking sheet. Flatten 1 end of dough, and cut dough into small strips to resemble a broom. Sprinkle cut end with cheese.
• **Bake** brooms at 375° for 10 to 12 minutes or until lightly browned. **Yield:** 16 servings.

CANDY APPLES

Prep: 40 minutes

8 wooden craft sticks
8 medium Gala apples
2 (6.5-ounce) packages caramel
    apple wraps
1 (16-ounce) chocolate bar
16 ounces vanilla bark coating
Orange paste food coloring
Toppings: colored sprinkles, chopped
    peanuts, black writing gel

• **Insert** craft sticks into apples. Cover each apple with 1 caramel wrap.
• **Microwave** at HIGH 15 to 20 seconds. Cool. Melt chocolate bar in a small saucepan over low heat.
• **Dip** each apple into chocolate; let dry.
• **Melt** vanilla bark coating in a saucepan over low heat; stir in food coloring.
• **Dip** or drizzle each apple with vanilla coating mixture. Decorate with desired toppings, and let dry. **Yield:** 8 apples.

Note: For testing purposes only, we used a Ghirardelli chocolate bar.

PECANS
A Southern Favorite

Enliven both sweet and savory dishes with the distinctive flavor of pecans.

We may not be able to agree on the official pronunciation, but we can certainly agree that few things announce the arrival of fall in the South more clearly than pecans. A simple bowlful of these freshly shelled nuts is a mouthwatering beacon for gathering friends and family. However, it's in the kitchen that pecans are elevated to something truly special. So be sure to get a head start on the season with our selection of delicious recipes, all highlighting the many talents of this crunchy Southern gem.

SPICY PECANS
(pictured on pages 226-227)

Enjoy these toasty nuts by the handful or in the savory cornbread stuffing on opposite page.

Prep: 5 minutes
Bake: 8 minutes

2 tablespoons brown sugar
2 tablespoons orange juice concentrate
1½ tablespoons butter or margarine
½ teaspoon salt
½ teaspoon chili powder
¼ teaspoon pepper
1½ cups coarsely chopped pecans

• **Cook** first 6 ingredients in a skillet over medium-high heat, stirring until brown sugar dissolves. Remove from heat, and stir in pecans. Transfer to a lightly greased baking sheet.
• **Bake** at 350° for 8 minutes or until toasted. Cool and store in an airtight container. **Yield:** 1½ cups.

PECAN-PIE MUFFINS
(pictured on pages 226-227)

Serve these moist, tender muffins as a sweet start to the day, or as an afternoon snack. Bake an extra batch to freeze or give to a friend.

Prep: 5 minutes
Bake: 25 minutes

1 cup chopped pecans
1 cup firmly packed brown sugar
½ cup all-purpose flour
2 large eggs
½ cup butter or margarine, melted

• **Combine** first 3 ingredients in a large bowl; make a well in center of mixture.
• **Beat** eggs until foamy. Stir together eggs and butter; add to dry ingredients, stirring just until moistened.
• **Place** foil baking cups in muffin pans, and coat with cooking spray; spoon batter into cups, filling two-thirds full.
• **Bake** at 350° for 20 to 25 minutes or until done. Remove from pans immediately, and cool on wire racks. **Yield:** 9 muffins.

Ellie Wells
Lakeland, Florida

PECAN POPOVERS

Prep: 10 minutes
Bake: 40 minutes

½ cup butter or margarine, softened
2 tablespoons honey
4 large eggs
2 cups milk
3 tablespoons butter or margarine, melted
2 cups all-purpose flour
½ teaspoon salt
⅓ cup finely chopped pecans

• **Stir** together ½ cup butter and honey; cover and chill until ready to serve.
• **Whisk** together eggs, milk, and melted butter in a large bowl; add flour and salt, stirring until smooth. Stir in pecans.
• **Spoon** batter into 8 (6-ounce) greased custard cups, filling half full; place on a baking sheet.
• **Bake** at 400° for 40 minutes or until firm. Immediately prick popovers with a fork to release steam. Serve immediately with honey butter. **Yield:** 8 popovers.

Betty Rabe
Plano, Texas

CORNISH HENS WITH SPICY PECAN-CORNBREAD STUFFING
(pictured on page 227)

Prep: 15 minutes
Bake: 55 minutes

Spicy Pecan-Cornbread Stuffing
8 (1- to 1½-pound) Cornish hens
Melted butter or margarine

• **Spoon** about 1 cup Spicy Pecan-Cornbread Stuffing into each hen; close opening with skewers. Place hens, breast side up, in a roasting pan. Brush with butter.
• **Bake,** covered, at 450° for 5 minutes. Reduce heat to 350°, and bake 50 more minutes or until a meat thermometer inserted into stuffing registers 165°. Remove skewers, and serve. **Yield:** 8 servings.

Spicy Pecan-Cornbread Stuffing

Prep: 20 minutes
Bake: 40 minutes
Cook: 8 minutes

10 bacon slices
1⅓ cups yellow cornmeal
1⅓ cups all-purpose flour
2 teaspoons baking powder
1 teaspoon garlic powder
¾ teaspoon baking soda
½ teaspoon salt
½ to 2 cups chicken broth
2 large eggs
2 tablespoons butter or margarine, melted
1½ cups Spicy Pecans (recipe on opposite page)
1 large onion, diced
2 tablespoons vegetable oil
3 celery ribs, diced
1 red bell pepper, chopped
¾ cup diced mushrooms
2 teaspoons dried thyme
2 teaspoons dried sage
3 to 4 large eggs, lightly beaten

● **Cook** bacon in a 9-inch cast-iron skillet until crisp; remove bacon, and drain on paper towels, reserving 2 tablespoons drippings in skillet. Keep skillet warm. Crumble bacon, and set aside.
● **Combine** cornmeal and next 5 ingredients in a large bowl.
● **Whisk** together broth, 2 eggs, and butter; add to dry ingredients, stirring just until moistened. Pour mixture into hot skillet with drippings.
● **Bake** at 400° for 25 minutes or until golden around edges. Crumble cornbread onto a baking sheet; reduce oven temperature to 350°, and bake, stirring occasionally, 15 minutes or until lightly toasted. Transfer cornbread to a large bowl, and stir in crumbled bacon and Spicy Pecans.
● **Sauté** diced onion in hot oil in a large skillet over medium-high heat 5 minutes or until tender. Add diced celery, chopped bell pepper, and diced mushrooms, and cook 3 minutes; stir in thyme and sage. Stir vegetable mixture into cornbread mixture; stir in lightly beaten eggs. **Yield:** 8 cups.

ORANGE-PECAN BISCOTTI

(pictured on page 226)

Dunk these twice-baked treats into a cup of your favorite flavored coffee.

Prep: 10 minutes
Freeze: 30 minutes
Bake: 55 minutes

4 large eggs
1 cup sugar
1½ tablespoons grated orange rind
2 tablespoons vegetable oil
1 teaspoon vanilla extract
1 teaspoon almond extract
3⅓ cups all-purpose flour
2 teaspoons baking powder
1 cup chopped pecans

● **Beat** eggs and sugar at high speed with an electric mixer 5 minutes or until foamy. Add orange rind, oil, and extracts, beating until blended.
● **Combine** flour and baking powder; add to sugar mixture, beating well. Fold in pecans. Cover and freeze 30 minutes or until firm.
● **Divide** dough in half; shape each portion into an 8- x 5-inch log on a lightly greased baking sheet.
● **Bake** at 325° for 25 minutes or until firm. Cool on baking sheet 5 minutes. Remove to wire racks to cool.
● **Cut** each log diagonally into ½-inch slices with a serrated knife. Place on greased baking sheets.
● **Bake** at 325° for 15 minutes. Turn cookies over, and bake 15 more minutes. Remove cookies to wire racks to cool. **Yield:** 2 dozen.

Nell Lutz
Athens, Alabama

Cook's Corner

These brochures showcase a variety of recipes and quick tips to help you with family meal planning or entertaining during the busy holiday season ahead.

Bread: A Great Choice, Any Way You Slice It!

Bread recipes for the entire family are waiting for you in this brochure. You'll find bread history, facts, nutrition information, and family serving ideas. Post this educational guide on your refrigerator so the food pyramid and 22 bites of bread trivia are at your fingertips. For the latest information on how this staple helps prevent birth defects and heart disease, send a self-addressed, stamped envelope to Bread Brochure/VK, 2405 Grand Ave., Ste. 700, Kansas City, MO 64108.

Carapelli Olive Oil:

This brochure describes a variety of olive oils perfect for all cooking styles throughout the year. Let the experts help you discover the many benefits of cooking with olive oils in everything from appetizers to dinner entrées. Or dress up simple meals without cooking by drizzling with oil for that perfect taste. Twenty-four tips help you incorporate these oils into daily meals. For your free booklet call Carapelli Consumer Information toll-free at 1-877-287-5678.

Creative Cooking With Couscous:

This tender grain offers a quick alternative to rice and potatoes. Couscous has a light, fluffy texture that goes well with main dishes or becomes a nice base for stews, soups, and salads. Serve it as an easy side dish with a variety of seasonings or some stir-in ingredients. Included in this brochure are some quick tips and recipes with nutritional information. To receive your free copy call 1-800-822-7423, or visit their Web site at www.neareast.com.

Quick & Easy

Versatile pork chops allow you to have

a savory meal in minutes.

A lean revolution has hit the meat counter, giving pork a new reputation. A 3.5-ounce serving of a pan-fried pork chop has about half the saturated fat and 40% less cholesterol than the same amount of pan-fried top sirloin.

CREAMY PORK CHOPS

Prep: 5 minutes
Cook: 17 minutes

¼ cup all-purpose flour
¾ teaspoon salt, divided
½ teaspoon pepper
8 pork breakfast chops
2 tablespoons vegetable oil
¼ cup white vinegar
1 (8-ounce) container sour cream
2 tablespoons sugar
⅛ teaspoon ground cloves
2 bay leaves
1 tablespoon chopped fresh parsley (optional)

• **Combine** flour, ½ teaspoon salt, and pepper. Dredge pork breakfast chops in flour mixture.
• **Cook** pork chops in hot oil in a large skillet over high heat 5 minutes on each side or until golden. Remove pork chops from skillet.
• **Add** vinegar, and cook 2 minutes, stirring to loosen particles from bottom of skillet. Stir in remaining ¼ teaspoon salt, sour cream, and next 3 ingredients; simmer 5 minutes. Remove and discard bay leaves; pour sauce over pork chops. Sprinkle with parsley, if desired. **Yield:** 4 to 6 servings.

Nancy Brock
Huntsville, Alabama

BALSAMIC PORK CHOPS

Fresh rosemary adds an herbal note to this satisfying entrée that can be prepared in only 30 minutes.

Prep: 10 minutes
Cook: 20 minutes

1 (6.2-ounce) package fast-cooking long-grain and wild rice mix
3 tablespoons all-purpose flour
1 teaspoon chopped fresh rosemary
½ teaspoon salt
½ teaspoon pepper
6 (¾-inch-thick) boneless pork chops
2 tablespoons butter or margarine
2 tablespoons olive oil
2 garlic cloves, pressed
1 (14½-ounce) can chicken broth
⅓ cup balsamic vinegar
Garnish: fresh rosemary sprigs

• **Cook** rice according to package directions; keep warm.
• **Combine** flour, 1 teaspoon rosemary, salt, and pepper. Dredge pork chops in flour mixture.
• **Melt** butter with oil in a large skillet over medium-high heat; add garlic, and sauté 1 minute. Add pork chops, and cook 4 minutes on each side or until golden. Remove pork chops.
• **Add** broth and vinegar, stirring to loosen particles from bottom of skillet. Cook 6 minutes or until liquid is reduced by half. Add pork chops, and cook 5 minutes or until done. Serve over rice. Garnish, if desired. **Yield:** 6 servings.

Hetty Vrinds
Houston, Texas

SMOKED PORK CHOPS WITH JALAPEÑO-CHERRY SAUCE

The simple, spicy-sweet sauce enhances the smoky pork and requires only three ingredients.

Prep: 10 minutes
Grill: 12 minutes

6 (1-inch-thick) boneless smoked pork chops
1 (14-ounce) can dark, sweet pitted cherries
1 cup jalapeño jelly
½ teaspoon ground coriander

• **Grill** pork chops, covered with grill lid, over medium-high heat (350° to 400°) 5 to 6 minutes on each side or until done. Transfer to a serving dish.
• **Bring** cherries, jalapeño jelly, and coriander to a boil in a saucepan, stirring constantly. Pour over pork chops. **Yield:** 6 servings.

Merna Hanson
Hastings, Nebraska

PRETZEL PORK CHOPS

Prep: 15 minutes
Cook: 10 minutes

6 (½-inch-thick) boneless pork chops, trimmed
¼ cup mayonnaise
½ teaspoon garlic powder
½ cup crushed pretzels
2 teaspoons butter or margarine
¼ teaspoon dried sage

• **Place** pork chops between 2 sheets of heavy-duty plastic wrap, and flatten to ¼-inch thickness, using a meat mallet or rolling pin.
• **Stir** together mayonnaise and garlic powder. Dip pork in mayonnaise mixture; dredge in crushed pretzels.
• **Melt** butter in a large nonstick skillet over medium heat. Add pork chops; sprinkle with sage. Cook 4 to 5 minutes on each side or until done. **Yield:** 6 servings.

Vikki D. Sturm
Rossville, Georgia

Hot Fish in a Flash

Serving fish at your next meal is easier

than you might think.

Some folks think that selecting and preparing fish takes special skills and lots of time. Nothing could be further from the truth. Fact is, naturally tender fish cooks up in minutes and requires few additional ingredients for great results. Here's a good example: Patricia Pick of McLean, Virginia, simply coats salmon fillets with pesto, and then broils or grills them.

All these recipes take no more than 10 minutes to prepare. And today, fresh and frozen fish choices are better than ever. Go forward fearlessly and enjoy the wonderful taste of fish right in your very own home.

SPICY CATFISH

Try this quick entrée as an alternative to frying this popular freshwater fish.

Prep: 5 minutes
Cook: 8 minutes

¼ teaspoon salt
¼ teaspoon garlic powder
¼ teaspoon ground black pepper
½ teaspoon ground red pepper
2 (8-ounce) catfish fillets

• **Combine** first 4 ingredients; sprinkle over catfish.
• **Cook** catfish in a hot, lightly greased 10-inch cast-iron skillet over medium-high heat 3 to 4 minutes on each side or until fish flakes with a fork. **Yield:** 2 servings.

Judith Furelia
Wells Point, Texas

BAKED FISH WITH PARMESAN-SOUR CREAM SAUCE

Pair this delicate fish with herbed rice and roasted carrots. Tilapia, flounder, or any other white fish works in place of orange roughy.

Prep: 10 minutes
Bake: 25 minutes

1½ pounds orange roughy fillets
1 (8-ounce) container sour cream
¼ cup shredded Parmesan cheese
½ teaspoon paprika
½ teaspoon salt
¼ teaspoon pepper
2 tablespoons Italian-seasoned breadcrumbs
2 tablespoons butter or margarine, melted

• **Place** fillets in a single layer in a lightly greased 13- x 9-inch pan.
• **Stir** together sour cream and next 4 ingredients; spread mixture evenly over fillets. Sprinkle with breadcrumbs, and drizzle with butter.
• **Bake** at 350° for 20 to 25 minutes or until fish flakes with a fork. **Yield:** 4 to 6 servings.

Demetra Economos Anas
Potomac, Maryland

GRILLED SALMON WITH MUSTARD-MOLASSES GLAZE

Prep: 10 minutes
Grill: 10 minutes

½ cup coarse-grained mustard
½ cup molasses
¼ cup red wine vinegar
6 (4- to 5-ounce) salmon fillets
⅛ teaspoon salt
⅛ teaspoon pepper

• **Whisk** together first 3 ingredients in a medium bowl.
• **Sprinkle** fillets with salt and pepper. Brush with half of mustard mixture.
• **Grill,** covered with grill lid, over high heat (400° to 500°) 4 to 5 minutes on each side or until fish flakes with a fork. Baste with remaining mustard mixture. **Yield:** 6 servings.

Jan Birnbaum
Catahoula Restaurant
Calistoga, California

FISH FACTS

■ Prepare fish that has a fresh odor (not a strong one) and a moist appearance.

■ Use fresh or thawed frozen fish within a day or two.

■ Thaw frozen fish by rinsing with cold water 3 to 4 minutes.

■ Dense, sturdy fish, such as salmon or tuna, can be prepared using any cooking method. Softer textured fish, such as orange roughy, tilapia, or snapper, should be baked or sautéed because it may fall apart when grilled or steamed.

What's for Supper?

Meat loaf, a familiar favorite, takes on a different look.

The rich, savory aroma of a meat loaf holds the promise of a delicious meal. This favorite brings back pleasant childhood memories. Its flavor is limited only by one's imagination. If you're looking for a recipe with spunk, try our sweet and saucy version.

MEAT LOAF SANDWICH

Enjoy this hearty sandwich fresh from the oven—no need to wait for leftovers.

Prep: 20 minutes
Bake: 1 hour, 15 minutes

1 (16-ounce) Italian or sourdough bread loaf
2½ tablespoons butter or margarine, divided
1 small onion, chopped
½ (8-ounce) package sliced fresh mushrooms
1 large egg
6 to 7 tablespoons ketchup, divided
1½ cups (6 ounces) shredded Cheddar cheese, divided
1 pound lean ground beef
½ cup dry red wine or beef broth
1 teaspoon garlic salt
¼ teaspoon dried thyme
2 to 3 tablespoons mayonnaise

• **Cut** bread loaf in half lengthwise. Scoop out bread, leaving ¼-inch-thick shells. Tear reserved bread into pieces, and measure 1½ cups, reserving remaining bread pieces for other use. Set bread shells and 1½ cups breadcrumbs aside.
• **Melt** 1½ tablespoons butter in a large skillet over medium heat; add chopped onion and mushrooms, and sauté 8 minutes or until tender.
• **Stir** together egg and 2 tablespoons ketchup in a large bowl. Add onion mixture, 1½ cups breadcrumbs, ½ cup cheese, ground beef, and next 3 ingredients, blending well. Shape mixture into a 6- to 7-inch loaf. Place on a lightly greased rack in a roasting pan.
• **Bake** at 350° for 1 hour or until done.
• **Spread** bottom bread shell with mayonnaise; top with meat loaf. Top with remaining ketchup; sprinkle with remaining 1 cup cheese. Top with remaining bread half. Melt remaining 1 tablespoon butter; brush over bread top. Wrap in aluminum foil.
• **Bake** at 350° for 10 to 15 minutes or until heated. **Yield:** 4 servings.

Mildred Bickley
Bristol, Virginia

SWEET 'N' SAUCY MEAT LOAF

Prep: 30 minutes
Bake: 1 hour, 15 minutes

1 pound lean ground beef
1 pound lean ground pork sausage
1 cup fine, dry breadcrumbs
1 large egg, lightly beaten
1 medium onion, diced
½ cup milk
2 garlic cloves, chopped
1 tablespoon chopped fresh parsley
1 tablespoon curry powder
1 teaspoon salt
½ teaspoon pepper
Sweet 'n' Saucy Sauce

• **Combine** first 11 ingredients. Shape into a loaf, and place in a lightly greased 9- x 5-inch loafpan.
• **Bake** at 375° for 30 minutes. Pour half of Sweet 'n' Saucy Sauce over meat loaf; bake 45 more minutes. Remove from pan; serve with remaining sauce. **Yield:** 6 servings.

Sweet 'n' Saucy Sauce

Prep: 10 minutes
Cook: 20 minutes

2 tablespoons butter or margarine
1 small onion, diced
½ cup ketchup
¼ cup firmly packed brown sugar
¼ cup water
¼ cup beef broth
¼ cup Worcestershire sauce
1 tablespoon instant coffee granules
2 tablespoons rice vinegar
2 teaspoons lemon juice

• **Melt** butter in a large skillet over medium-high heat; add onion, and sauté 5 minutes or until tender. Stir in ½ cup ketchup and remaining ingredients. Bring to a boil, stirring constantly; reduce heat, and simmer 10 minutes. **Yield:** 1½ cups.

Marion Hall
Knoxville, Tennessee

MAKING MEAT LOAF

■ Bake meat loaf on a rack in a roasting pan to keep it out of the fatty drippings.

■ Prevent meat loaf from sticking and speed cleanup by spraying pan with vegetable cooking spray.

■ Use a meat thermometer to be sure your meat loaf is done. It should register 160°, the meat should have no pinkness, and the juices should run clear.

■ Make two meat loaves, and freeze one for later use.

Turnip Greens

Freshly baked cornbread and pepper sauce are essential accompaniments to turnip greens and pot liquor.

Some folks have been cooking turnip greens most of their lives. Many add personal touches such as onion, garlic, ham, salt pork, bacon, or peeled, cubed turnip roots. Whatever your choice, don't pass up the cooking liquid called pot liquor or potlikker—it's almost as good as the greens. Have handy a bottle of pepper sauce (hot peppers in vinegar, not to be confused with hot sauce) to drizzle on your serving.

When choosing fresh turnip greens, avoid those with leaves that are wilted, yellowing, or have dark patches of slime on them. After removing stems and heavy ribs, place the leaves in cold water in the sink or a very large pot. Let stand a few minutes to loosen grit and sand. Lift greens from the water. Rinse sink or pot; repeat procedure several times, depending on how gritty the leaves are. Then try one of our methods for cooking turnip greens.

TURNIP GREENS WITH TURNIPS

Prep: 30 minutes
Cook: 2 hours

2 (1-pound) packages prewashed fresh turnip greens
2 turnips
¼ pound salt pork (streak of lean) or smoked pork shoulder
1 quart water
1 tablespoon bacon drippings
½ teaspoon sugar
Pepper Sauce (optional)

• **Remove** and discard stems and discolored spots from greens. Peel and coarsely chop turnips; set aside. Wash greens thoroughly; drain and tear into 2-inch pieces.

• **Bring** salt pork and 1 quart water to a boil in a Dutch oven. Cover, reduce heat, and cook 45 minutes to 1 hour or until liquid is reduced by half and meat is tender. Add greens, bacon drippings, and sugar; cook, without stirring, 30 minutes or until greens are tender.
• **Add** turnips; cover, reduce heat, and simmer 30 minutes or until turnips are tender. Serve with Pepper Sauce, if desired. **Yield:** 4 to 6 servings.

SUPER-CHARGED GREENS
(pictured on page 225)

Prep: 30 minutes
Cook: 40 minutes

2 (1-pound) packages prewashed fresh turnip greens
3 bok choy stalks, halved lengthwise and cut into ¾-inch pieces
1 medium onion, diced
1 red bell pepper, chopped
2 garlic cloves, thinly sliced
8 thinly sliced fresh ginger strips (about 1½ inches long) (optional)
2 to 3 tablespoons vegetable oil
1½ teaspoons seasoned salt
½ teaspoon pepper

• **Remove** and discard stems and discolored spots from greens. Wash greens thoroughly; drain and tear greens into 1- to 2-inch pieces.
• **Sauté** bok choy, next 3 ingredients, and, if desired, ginger in hot oil in a Dutch oven over medium heat 3 minutes or until onion is tender. Add greens, salt, and pepper; cook, stirring often, 5 minutes or until greens wilt. Cover; simmer 30 minutes. **Yield:** 6 to 8 servings.

Iris L. Spira
Plano, Texas

SIMPLE TURNIP GREENS

Sugar can be added during cooking to eliminate a bitter taste—although this technique is sometimes debated.

Prep: 30 minutes
Cook: 1 hour, 35 minutes

1 bunch fresh turnip greens (about 4½ pounds)
1 pound salt pork (streak of lean) or smoked pork shoulder
3 quarts water
¼ teaspoon freshly ground pepper
2 teaspoons sugar (optional)

• **Remove** and discard stems and discolored spots from greens. Wash greens thoroughly; drain and tear greens into pieces. Set aside.
• **Slice** salt pork at ¼-inch intervals, cutting to, but not through, the skin.
• **Combine** salt pork, 3 quarts water, pepper, and, if desired, sugar in a Dutch oven; bring mixture to a boil. Cover, reduce heat, and simmer 1 hour.
• **Add** greens, and cook, uncovered, 30 to 35 minutes or until tender. Serve with a slotted spoon. **Yield:** 4 to 6 servings.

PEPPER SAUCE

You can find bottles of this fiery condiment alongside hot sauce at the grocery store.

Prep: 20 minutes

¾ cup cider or white wine vinegar
10 long fresh green chile peppers, washed and trimmed *

• **Bring** vinegar to a boil in a saucepan.
• **Pack** peppers tightly into a hot 12-ounce jar. Cover with boiling vinegar. Cover at once with metal lid, and screw on band. Store at room temperature up to 2 weeks. **Yield:** 1 (12-ounce) jar.

*Substitute banana peppers, jalapeño, or other hot peppers, if desired.

Note: For an 8-ounce jar, use 6 peppers and ½ cup vinegar.

Top-Rated Menu

Bring back the classic meat and three

with our easy, everyday menu.

Family Favorites
Serves 4

Buttermilk Baked Chicken

Whipped Celery Potatoes

Apricot-Glazed Carrots   Steamed green beans

Applesauce Pie

Iced tea   Coffee

Sometimes the simplest food is the absolute best. Our menu for four offers humble but delicious dishes that are sure to satisfy all your cravings for hearty eating. Perfect for a weekday or even a Sunday supper, this meal is on the table in one hour flat. Don't forget to save some room for our favorite Applesauce Pie or the dessert of your choice.

BUTTERMILK BAKED CHICKEN

2000 Recipe Hall of Fame

Prep: 10 minutes
Bake: 45 minutes

¼ **cup butter or margarine**
4 **bone-in chicken breast**
    halves *
½ **teaspoon salt**
½ **teaspoon pepper**
1½ **cups buttermilk, divided**
¾ **cup all-purpose flour**
1 **(10¾-ounce) can cream of**
    mushroom soup, undiluted
Garnish: chopped fresh parsley

• **Melt** butter in a lightly greased 13- x 9-inch baking dish in a 425° oven.
• **Sprinkle** chicken with salt and pepper. Dip chicken in ½ cup buttermilk, and dredge in flour.
• **Arrange** chicken, breast side down, in baking dish.
• **Bake** at 425° for 25 minutes. Turn chicken, and bake 10 more minutes.
• **Stir** together remaining 1 cup buttermilk and cream of mushroom soup; pour over chicken, and bake 10 more minutes, shielding chicken with aluminum foil to prevent excessive browning, if necessary. Drizzle gravy over chicken and Whipped Celery Potatoes. Garnish, if desired. **Yield:** 4 servings.

* Substitute 4 skinned and boned chicken breast halves, if desired. Bake at 425° for 15 minutes. Turn, and bake 10 minutes.

Note: Substitute light butter; nonfat buttermilk; and reduced-sodium, reduced-fat cream of mushroom soup, if desired.

WHIPPED CELERY POTATOES

Enhance this rich, creamy side dish with an extra ladle of the golden gravy from Buttermilk Baked Chicken.

1994 Recipe Hall of Fame

Prep: 20 minutes
Cook: 30 minutes

1¾ **pounds Yukon gold or red**
      potatoes, peeled and cubed
3½ **cups water**
1½ **teaspoons salt**
½ **cup butter or margarine,**
      divided
3 **celery ribs, diced**
½ **small onion, diced**
⅓ **cup milk**
¾ **teaspoon salt**
¾ **teaspoon pepper**

• **Bring** first 3 ingredients to a boil in a large saucepan; cover, reduce heat, and simmer 30 minutes or until tender. Drain and transfer to a mixing bowl.
• **Melt** 2 tablespoons butter in saucepan; add celery and onion, and sauté 3 to 4 minutes or until tender.
• **Add** celery mixture to potatoes; beat at low speed with an electric mixer until potatoes are mashed. Add remaining butter, milk, salt, and pepper; beat at high speed until whipped. Serve immediately. **Yield:** 4 to 6 servings.

APRICOT-GLAZED CARROTS

Apricot preserves, nutmeg, and citrus embellish sweet baby carrots.

1998 Recipe Hall of Fame

Prep: 10 minutes
Cook: 25 minutes

1 **pound baby carrots**
1¼ **teaspoons salt, divided**
3 **tablespoons butter or margarine**
⅓ **cup apricot preserves**
¼ **teaspoon ground nutmeg**
1 **teaspoon grated orange rind**
2 **tablespoons fresh orange juice**

- **Cook** baby carrots and 1 teaspoon salt in boiling water to cover in a large saucepan 15 to 20 minutes or until carrots are tender; drain.
- **Melt** butter in saucepan, and stir in preserves until blended.
- **Stir** in remaining ¼ teaspoon salt, nutmeg, orange rind, and orange juice; cook 5 minutes.
- **Add** carrots; gently toss to coat. **Yield**: 4 servings.

APPLESAUCE PIE
(pictured on page 228)

A subtle lemon flavor infuses this homestyle pie, balancing its sweetness. A dollop of whipped cream completes the dessert.

1998 Recipe Hall of Fame

Prep: 45 minutes
Cook: 40 minutes
Bake: 35 minutes

10 large Granny Smith apples, peeled and chopped
1 large lemon, sliced and seeded
2½ cups sugar
3 tablespoons butter or margarine
1 teaspoon vanilla extract
1 (15-ounce) package refrigerated piecrusts
Whipped cream (optional)

- **Cook** first 3 ingredients in a Dutch oven over medium heat, stirring often, 35 minutes or until thickened. Remove from heat, and discard lemon slices. Add butter and vanilla; cool.
- **Fit** 1 piecrust into a 9-inch pieplate according to package directions. Pour applesauce mixture into crust.
- **Roll** remaining piecrust to press out fold lines, and cut into ½-inch strips. Arrange strips in a lattice design over filling; fold edges under, and crimp.
- **Bake** on lowest oven rack at 425° for 30 to 35 minutes or until golden, shielding pie with aluminum foil to prevent excessive browning, if necessary. Serve with whipped cream, if desired. **Yield:** 1 (9-inch) pie.

Warm Veggie Sides

Choose one of these vegetable sides to round out any entrée.

Selecting a side dish to serve with a meal can be frustrating. Don't let it be. Using a variety of fresh and frozen vegetables, we offer recipes to satisfy your palate and solve that dinnertime dilemma. So avoid the headache. Choose one of these delicious sides, and your menu is a done deal.

MIXED-UP MUSHROOMS

An assortment of fresh mushrooms makes this dish interesting and flavorful.

Prep: 10 minutes
Cook: 15 minutes

3 tablespoons butter or margarine
1 pound assorted fresh mushrooms, chopped
1½ tablespoons all-purpose flour
1 (8-ounce) container sour cream
½ (8-ounce) jar water chestnuts, chopped
1 teaspoon celery salt
1 teaspoon lemon juice
¼ teaspoon salt
1 tablespoon minced fresh cilantro

- **Melt** butter in a large nonstick skillet over medium heat; add mushrooms, and sauté 10 minutes. Sprinkle with flour, and cook, stirring constantly, 1 minute.
- **Add** sour cream and next 4 ingredients, and cook, stirring constantly, 3 to 5 minutes or until thoroughly heated. Stir in minced cilantro. Serve immediately. **Yield:** 4 to 6 servings.

Note: For testing purposes only, we used ¼ pound each of button, cremini, shiitake, and oyster mushrooms.

Tom Davis
Waynesboro, Mississippi

RUTABAGA SOUFFLÉ

Prep: 20 minutes
Cook: 50 minutes
Bake: 40 minutes

1 large rutabaga, peeled and sliced ✻
1½ teaspoons salt, divided
½ teaspoon sugar
½ cup butter or margarine
2 tablespoons all-purpose flour
⅔ cup milk
4 large eggs, separated
3 bacon slices, cooked and crumbled

- **Cook** rutabaga slices, ½ teaspoon salt, and sugar in boiling water to cover in a Dutch oven over medium heat 45 minutes or until tender. Drain rutabaga well, and place in a large bowl. Beat at low speed with an electric mixer until mashed.
- **Melt** butter in Dutch oven over medium heat. Whisk in flour and remaining 1 teaspoon salt until smooth, and cook, whisking constantly, 1 minute. Gradually add milk, whisking constantly. Cook, whisking constantly, 2 minutes.
- **Beat** egg yolks until blended; gradually stir ½ cup hot milk mixture into yolks. Stir into remaining hot milk mixture, and cook 1 minute. Stir in mashed rutabaga, and remove from heat.
- **Beat** egg whites at medium speed with an electric mixer until stiff peaks form. Fold into rutabaga mixture, and spoon into a lightly greased 11- x 7-inch baking dish. Sprinkle with bacon.
- **Bake** at 350° for 40 minutes or until golden brown. **Yield:** 6 to 8 servings.

✻Substitute 6 medium turnips, peeled and sliced, for rutabaga, if desired.

Ellie Wells
Lakeland, Florida

FIELD PEAS, OKRA, AND CORN COMBO

Enjoy this colorful combo as a side dish or as a one-dish meal.

Prep: 10 minutes
Cook: 1 hour

2 celery ribs, sliced
1 large onion, halved and sliced
½ large green bell pepper, diced
1 garlic clove, minced
1 tablespoon olive oil
1 tablespoon Worcestershire sauce
2 teaspoons Creole seasoning
1 teaspoon freshly ground pepper
1 teaspoon hot sauce
½ teaspoon salt
1 (14½-ounce) can chicken broth
½ cup dry white wine or chicken broth
1 (16-ounce) package frozen field peas with snaps, unthawed
1 (16-ounce) package frozen sliced okra, unthawed
1 (16-ounce) package frozen whole kernel corn, unthawed
Hot cooked rice
Garnishes: chopped tomato, sliced green onions

• **Sauté** first 4 ingredients in hot oil in a Dutch oven over medium heat 8 minutes or until onion is lightly browned. Add Worcestershire sauce and next 4 ingredients, and cook, stirring constantly, 3 minutes.
• **Stir** in chicken broth and wine, and bring to a boil. Stir in field peas; return to a boil. Cover, reduce heat, and simmer 25 minutes.
• **Stir** in okra, corn, and, if needed, up to ½ cup water; bring to a boil. Cover, reduce heat, and simmer 10 minutes or until vegetables are tender. Serve over rice. Garnish, if desired. **Yield:** 6 to 8 servings.

Martha B. Gilbert
Charlotte, North Carolina

Fall Cobblers

These traditional deep-dish pies are made to satisfy.

Cobblers are old-fashioned Southern treasures—easy-to-prepare, mouth-watering treats. Soft doughs and crumbly drop biscuits add richness atop both sweet and savory fillings. Use a light touch to prepare the delicate toppings, being careful not to overknead the dough or add an extra stir or two. Cobblers may be long on ingredients, but they assemble quickly.

SWEET POTATO COBBLER

Prep: 20 minutes
Bake: 45 minutes

½ cup butter or margarine
2 tablespoons whipping cream
1 cup granulated sugar
¼ cup firmly packed light brown sugar
1 teaspoon ground cinnamon
¼ teaspoon ground nutmeg
¼ teaspoon salt
2 large sweet potatoes, peeled and thinly sliced (about 1½ pounds)
⅓ cup butter or margarine
1⅔ cups self-rising flour
½ cup buttermilk
Streusel Topping

• **Melt** ½ cup butter in a 10½-inch cast-iron skillet over medium heat. Whisk in whipping cream and next 5 ingredients. Remove from heat.
• **Layer** sweet potato slices evenly in cream mixture. Cover with aluminum foil, and place on a baking sheet.
• **Bake** at 350° for 20 minutes. Uncover.
• **Cut** ⅓ cup butter into flour with a fork or pastry blender until crumbly; stir in buttermilk until moistened. Turn dough out onto a lightly floured surface; knead 3 or 4 times. Pat or roll into a 10½-inch circle; place over cobbler. Sprinkle with Streusel Topping.
• **Bake,** uncovered, at 350° for 25 minutes or until golden. **Yield:** 6 servings.

Streusel Topping

Prep: 10 minutes

⅓ cup uncooked regular oats
⅓ cup all-purpose flour
⅓ cup firmly packed light brown sugar
3 tablespoons butter or margarine, cut up
⅓ cup chopped pecans

• **Combine** first 3 ingredients; cut in butter with a fork or pastry blender until crumbly. Stir in chopped pecans. **Yield:** 1⅓ cups.

PEAR-GINGER COBBLER

Ground ginger and toasted almonds mingle in the golden topping and accent the sweet, juicy pears.

Prep: 20 minutes
Bake: 50 minutes

8 large red or green Anjou pears, sliced
2 tablespoons lemon juice
½ cup apple cider
½ cup maple syrup
¼ cup firmly packed brown sugar
2 tablespoons all-purpose flour
1 teaspoon ground cinnamon
¼ teaspoon ground nutmeg
3 tablespoons butter or margarine, cut up
Ginger-Almond Topping
2 tablespoons granulated sugar
Whipped cream
Crystallized ginger (optional)

• **Toss** together pears and lemon juice.
• **Whisk** together apple cider and next 5 ingredients in a large bowl; add pears,

tossing to coat. Pour mixture into a 2-quart baking dish; dot with butter.

• **Spread** Ginger-Almond Topping over mixture; sprinkle with granulated sugar.

• **Bake** at 350° for 45 to 50 minutes or until golden. Serve with whipped cream; sprinkle with crystallized ginger, if desired. **Yield:** 6 to 8 servings.

Ginger-Almond Topping

Prep: 10 minutes

1½ cups all-purpose flour
1 tablespoon sugar
2 teaspoons baking powder
½ teaspoon salt
⅓ cup shortening
1 to 2 teaspoons ground ginger
½ cup chopped almonds, toasted
1 to 1¼ cups milk

• **Combine** first 4 ingredients; cut in shortening with a fork or pastry blender until crumbly. Stir in ground ginger, toasted almonds, and enough milk to make a soft dough. **Yield:** enough topping for 2-quart dish.

APPLE-VINEGAR BISCUIT COBBLER
(pictured on page 228)

A scoop of ice cream complements the vinegar flavor in this sweet-tart dessert.

Prep: 25 minutes
Cook: 20 minutes
Bake: 20 minutes

8 Granny Smith apples, peeled and cut into wedges
2 cups sugar
1 (3-ounce) package cream cheese
⅓ cup butter or margarine, cut up
2½ cups self-rising flour
1 cup milk
¼ cup butter or margarine
⅓ cup cider vinegar
1 teaspoon grated lemon rind
1 teaspoon ground cinnamon
1 teaspoon ground allspice
¼ teaspoon ground cloves
Vanilla ice cream (optional)

• **Combine** apple and sugar; set aside.

• **Cut** cream cheese and ⅓ cup butter into flour with a fork or pastry blender until crumbly; stir in milk.

• **Turn** dough out onto a lightly floured surface; knead 3 or 4 times. Pat or roll dough to ½-inch thickness. Cut with a 2½-inch round cutter; set aside.

• **Melt** ¼ cup butter in a large skillet over medium-high heat; add apple mixture. Cook, stirring often, 20 minutes or until apple is tender and syrup thickens slightly. Stir in vinegar and next 4 ingredients. Pour into a lightly greased 11- x 7-inch baking dish; place dish on a foil-lined baking sheet. Arrange 12 biscuits over hot mixture. Place remaining biscuits on a baking sheet.

• **Bake** cobbler at 425° for 20 minutes or until biscuits are golden. Bake biscuits at 425° for 12 to 15 minutes. Serve cobbler with ice cream, if desired. **Yield:** 6 to 8 servings.

AUTUMN VEGETABLE COBBLER

Crumbly cornbread rounds crown this savory, satisfying dish. Offer it as a side dish or as a meatless entrée.

Prep: 25 minutes
Bake: 30 minutes

1 small onion, sliced
2 teaspoons olive oil
4 small red potatoes, cubed
2 carrots, chopped
¼ cup water
2 medium leeks, halved lengthwise and cut into slices
2 cups chopped fresh spinach *
1 cup vegetable broth
2 teaspoons all-purpose flour
3 tablespoons minced fresh parsley
1 tablespoon soy sauce
½ teaspoon salt
Cornbread Topping

• **Sauté** sliced onion in hot oil in a large saucepan over medium-high heat until tender. Add potato, carrot, and ¼ cup water; cook, stirring constantly, 2 minutes. Add leeks and spinach, and cook 3 minutes or until spinach wilts.

• **Whisk** together vegetable broth and flour until smooth. Stir broth mixture, minced parsley, soy sauce, and salt into spinach mixture. Bring to a boil; cook, stirring constantly, 1 minute. Reduce heat to low; cook, stirring often, 5 minutes or until thickened.

• **Spoon** vegetable mixture into a lightly greased 8-inch square baking dish. Drop Cornbread Topping by heaping tablespoonfuls onto hot vegetable mixture.

• **Bake** at 400° for 30 minutes or until golden. **Yield:** 4 servings.

✳ Substitute chopped kale, collard greens, or turnip greens, if desired.

Cornbread Topping

Prep: 10 minutes

1 cup all-purpose flour
½ cup cornbread mix
1 teaspoon baking powder
½ teaspoon salt
¼ teaspoon baking soda
2 tablespoons butter or margarine, softened
¾ cup buttermilk
2 teaspoons honey

• **Combine** first 5 ingredients; cut in butter with a fork or pastry blender until crumbly. Stir together buttermilk and honey; stir into flour mixture. **Yield:** 6 cornbread rounds.

Lilann Hunter Taylor
Savannah, Georgia

Living Light

You'll be the envy of your co-workers with these flavorful lunch selections.

Say goodbye to dull midday fare. These recipes are simple to prepare and even worthy of a little lunchtime envy. Combine them with recommended sides (see "Smart Bites" on facing page) to balance your meal and avoid the afternoon slump.

TUNA-VEGGIE STUFFED PITA

Prep: 20 minutes

1 (6-ounce) can albacore tuna in water, drained
2 tablespoons chopped onion
1 celery rib, chopped
¼ red or green bell pepper, chopped
½ cup shredded carrot
3 tablespoons light mayonnaise
2 teaspoons lemon juice
½ teaspoon grated lemon rind
¼ teaspoon salt
¼ teaspoon pepper
4 (6½-inch) whole wheat pita rounds
Lettuce leaves
Toppings: shredded carrot, tomato slices (optional)

• **Stir** together first 10 ingredients.
• **Cut** a pocket into each pita round. Line with lettuce. Spoon ½ cup tuna mixture into pitas. Top with shredded carrot and tomato slices, if desired. **Yield:** 4 servings.

Laura Fillmore
Harrison, Ohio

♥ Per serving: Calories 255 (18% from fat)
Fat 5g (sat 0.9g, mono 0.5g, poly 1g)
Protein 15g Carb 40g Fiber 6g
Chol 16mg Iron 2.7mg
Sodium 686mg Calc 33mg

SOUTHWESTERN TABBOULEH SALAD

This nutrient-packed salad has both wonderful flavor and texture.

Prep: 40 minutes
Chill: 8 hours

1 cup uncooked bulghur wheat
1 cup boiling water
2 tomatoes, chopped
4 green onions, chopped
1 (15½-ounce) can black beans, rinsed and drained
¼ cup chopped fresh cilantro
½ teaspoon grated lime rind
¼ cup fresh lime juice
2 tablespoons olive oil
½ teaspoon ground cumin
½ teaspoon ground red pepper
1 (8¾-ounce) can no-salt-added corn kernels, drained
¼ teaspoon salt

• **Place** bulghur in a large bowl, and add 1 cup boiling water. Cover and let stand 30 minutes.
• **Add** chopped tomato and remaining ingredients to bulghur. Toss gently. Chill up to 8 hours. **Yield:** 8 cups.

♥ Per cup: Calories 157 (24% from fat)
Fat 4g (sat 0.6g, mono 2.8g, poly 0.6g)
Protein 4g Carb 28g Fiber 6.7g
Chol 0mg Iron 1.3mg
Sodium 226mg Calc 24mg

CREAMY SHELLS AND CHEESE

Redefine the brown bag lunch with this comforting midday meal.

Prep: 20 minutes
Bake: 30 minutes

1½ cups small shell pasta, uncooked
5 green onions, chopped
2 garlic cloves, minced
2 teaspoons vegetable oil
2 tablespoons all-purpose flour
½ teaspoon dried basil
1¾ cups fat-free milk
½ (8-ounce) package reduced-fat cream cheese
1 cup (4 ounces) shredded reduced-fat sharp Cheddar cheese
¼ teaspoon hot sauce
½ teaspoon salt
Vegetable cooking spray
8 stone-ground wheat crackers, crushed

• **Cook** pasta according to package directions, omitting salt and fat. Drain pasta, and set aside.
• **Cook** chopped green onions and garlic in hot oil in a large skillet over medium-high heat 8 to 10 minutes or until onions are tender.
• **Add** flour, basil, and milk, whisking constantly until mixture is smooth. Add cream cheese, and cook over medium heat, whisking constantly, 8 minutes or until mixture thickens. Add Cheddar cheese, hot sauce, and salt, stirring until cheese is melted.
• **Spoon** pasta into a 1-quart baking dish coated with cooking spray. Add cheese mixture, stirring well. Sprinkle with cracker crumbs.
• **Bake,** covered, at 350° for 30 minutes or until lightly browned. **Yield:** 4½ cups.

Alma Joyce Hahn
Benton, Arkansas

♥ Per cup: Calories 331 (27% from fat)
Fat 10g (sat 4g, mono 3.7g, poly 1.3g)
Protein 18g Carb 41g Fiber 2g
Chol 21mg Iron 2.2mg
Sodium 584mg Calc 252mg

SMART BITES

■ Hot Ham-and-Cheese Rollup goes great with a mixed green salad splashed with balsamic vinaigrette; finish with a cup of fresh pineapple chunks.

■ Southwestern Tabbouleh Salad, a 1-ounce serving of fat-free pita chips or 1 matzo cracker, and fresh orange sections make a completely delicious and healthy lunch.

■ Complete Creamy Shells and Cheese with a cup of baby carrots and broccoli florets. Crisp apple slices dipped in fat-free vanilla yogurt offer a sweet finale.

■ Sesame melba toasts or crispbread rye crackers complement Wild Rice Salad With Spicy Lime Vinaigrette. Satisfy your sweet tooth with a 4-ounce container of fat-free chocolate pudding.

■ Serve Tuna-Veggie Stuffed Pita with a 4-ounce mixed fruit cup and 1 ounce of baked potato crisps.

WILD RICE SALAD WITH SPICY LIME VINAIGRETTE

Prep: 15 minutes
Cook: 20 minutes

½ cup uncooked wild rice
½ teaspoon salt
2 green onions, chopped
1 orange, peeled and sectioned
1 cup angel hair slaw mix
4 pecan halves, chopped and toasted
¼ cup (1 ounce) shredded smoked
    mozzarella or smoked Cheddar
    cheese
1 tablespoon chopped fresh or
    1 teaspoon dried mint
Spicy Lime Vinaigrette

• **Cook** rice with salt according to package directions, omitting fat. Cool.
• **Combine** rice, green onions, and next 5 ingredients. Add 4 tablespoons vinaigrette; toss gently to coat. **Yield:** 2 cups.

Note: Recipe may be prepared a day in advance.

♥ Per cup: Calories 361 (44% from fat)
Fat 18g (sat 3.4g, mono 11g, poly 3g)
Protein 11g Carb 42g Fiber 5g
Chol 7.7mg Iron 1.4mg
Sodium 830mg Calc 151mg

Spicy Lime Vinaigrette

Enjoy remaining vinaigrette over salad greens or drizzled over fish.

Prep: 5 minutes

3 tablespoons fresh lime juice
2 tablespoons honey
3 tablespoons rice wine vinegar
1 teaspoon Dijon mustard
⅓ cup olive oil
½ teaspoon salt
1 teaspoon chipotle in adobo sauce
    (optional)

• **Process** first 6 ingredients and chipotle in adobo sauce, if desired, in a blender until blended. **Yield:** 1 cup.

Devon Delaney
Princeton, New Jersey

♥ Per 2 tablespoons: Calories 101 (81% from fat)
Fat 9g (sat 1.2g, mono 6.7g, poly 0.8g)
Protein 0.1g Carb 6g Fiber 0g
Chol 0mg Iron 0.1mg
Sodium 162mg Calc 1.9mg

HOT HAM-AND-CHEESE ROLLUP

To enjoy for lunch, reheat rollup in microwave at HIGH 1 minute or until thoroughly heated.

Prep: 20 minutes
Bake: 25 minutes

1 (12-ounce) refrigerated pizza crust
2 tablespoons chopped fresh or
    2 teaspoons dried basil
6 ounces thinly sliced
    maple-glazed ham
1 cup (4 ounces) shredded part-skim
    mozzarella cheese
Vegetable cooking spray
Pasta sauce or mustard (optional)

• **Roll** out dough into a 12-inch square. Sprinkle with basil to ½ inch from edges. Top with ham slices, and sprinkle with cheese to ½ inch from edges.
• **Roll up** dough, beginning at 1 end, and place, seam side down, on an aluminum foil-lined baking sheet coated with cooking spray.
• **Bake** at 400° for 20 to 25 minutes or until golden brown. Cool 5 minutes. Cut into 1½-inch slices. Serve rollups with pasta sauce or mustard, if desired. **Yield:** 4 servings.

Adelyn Smith
Dunnville, Kentucky

♥ Per serving: Calories 381 (29% from fat)
Fat 12g (sat 6g, mono 3.3g, poly 0.2g)
Protein 27g Carb 39g Fiber 1g
Chol 43mg Iron 2.3mg
Sodium 1,382mg Calc 324mg

Chock-full of Chips

Capture the sweet sensation of chocolate with these delightful morsels.

Chocolate chips have long been the darling of bakers and chocoholics alike. These tiny morsels are irresistible, often luring us to take just one more bite of dessert or to sneak a few right out of the bag. Their smooth, intense flavor stands out in all-American chocolate-chip cookies, but they also work well in a variety of sweets. Indulge with some of our favorites.

HEAVENLY CHOCOLATE-CHIP MERINGUE COOKIES

Store these light, airy cookies in an airtight container to keep them crisp.

Prep: 15 minutes
Cook: 8 hours

2 egg whites
¼ teaspoon cream of tartar
⅔ cup sugar
½ cup (3 ounces) semisweet chocolate mini morsels

• **Beat** egg whites and cream of tartar at high speed with an electric mixer 1 minute or until soft peaks form. Gradually add sugar to egg white mixture, beating 2½ minutes or until stiff peaks form and sugar dissolves. Gently fold in chocolate morsels.
• **Drop** mixture by teaspoonfuls onto 2 lightly greased parchment paper-lined baking sheets.
• **Place** in 400° oven, and turn oven off. Leave in oven overnight or 8 hours. **Yield:** 31 cookies.

Christine Testani
Atlanta, Georgia

TOFFEE

Milk chocolate morsels add an extra layer of richness to this buttery, crunchy confection.

Prep: 30 minutes
Cook: 20 minutes

1 cup slivered almonds
1 cup butter
1 cup sugar
⅓ cup water
½ teaspoon vanilla extract
¼ teaspoon salt
2 cups (12 ounces) milk chocolate morsels
1 cup finely ground walnuts

• **Place** almonds in a single layer on an aluminum foil-lined baking sheet coated with cooking spray.
• **Cook** butter and next 4 ingredients in a heavy saucepan over high heat, stirring mixture constantly, 15 to 18 minutes or until a candy thermometer registers 310° (hard crack stage). Remove from heat, and immediately pour over almonds (do not scrape the pan).
• **Sprinkle** immediately with chocolate morsels, and spread evenly to ½ inch from sides. Sprinkle with ground walnuts, and let stand until firm. Break into small pieces, and store in an airtight container. **Yield:** 1¾ pounds.

Elsa Vester
Florence, Alabama

CHOCOLATE-CHIP SUPREME COOKIES

Set out a plate of these fresh-from-the-oven cookies, and watch how fast they disappear.

Prep: 15 minutes
Bake: 12 minutes per batch

½ cup shortening
½ cup butter or margarine, softened
¾ cup firmly packed dark brown sugar
¾ cup sugar
2 large eggs
1 (3.4-ounce) package vanilla instant pudding mix
1 tablespoon vanilla extract
2¼ cups all-purpose flour
1 tablespoon baking soda
1 teaspoon ground cinnamon
½ teaspoon ground nutmeg
½ teaspoon salt
2 cups (12 ounces) semisweet chocolate morsels
1½ cups chopped pecans
1 cup uncooked quick-cooking oats

• **Beat** shortening and butter at medium speed with an electric mixer until mixture is creamy; gradually add sugars, beating well. Add eggs, beating until blended. Add pudding mix and vanilla; beat until blended.
• **Combine** flour and next 4 ingredients. Gradually add to butter mixture, beating until blended. Stir in morsels, pecans, and oats.
• **Shape** dough into 1½-inch balls; place on lightly greased baking sheets, and press to 1-inch thickness.
• **Bake** at 375° for 10 to 12 minutes. Remove cookies to wire racks to cool. **Yield:** 3 dozen.

Angie Sinclair
Birmingham, Alabama

Taste of the South

You may dispute the origin of Brunswick Stew,

but there's no arguing about its great flavor.

Brunswick stew is a sturdy, long-cooking concoction made of meat, tomatoes, and vegetables. Its origin is the cause of much heated discussion. Depending on which version of the story you accept, the dish was created either in Brunswick County, Virginia, in 1828, or on St. Simons Island, Georgia, in 1898. Supporters on both sides hotly dispute which state possesses bragging rights and which version tastes best.

In Virginia, skilled "stewmasters" do most of the cooking, and they do it in large quantities. It's a male-dominated ritual, usually performed to benefit the community.

The flavors differ from one stewmaster to the next, says John Drew Clary of Lawrenceville, but the basic ingredients are the same—boiled chicken, potatoes, onions, butterbeans, corn, and tomatoes. The mixture is cooked and stirred for hours, resulting in a thick stew that can be (and is) eaten with a fork. Virginians serve their Brunswick Stew as a main dish with bread on the side.

John Drew has been cooking up stews since 1973, but he says business picked up considerably in 1988, when the Virginia General Assembly issued a decree naming Brunswick County, Virginia, the home of Brunswick Stew. Now, he says, "We generally cook one Saturday a month between September and May. We cook 500 quarts at once and we sell it all ahead of time. The money we make goes for all kinds of community causes."

Georgians cook in smaller batches, and unless you have the good fortune to know someone who cooks stew at home, cafes are the place to taste this delicacy. "Ours has a different consistency—you can see what's in there," says Brad Brown, mayor of Brunswick, Georgia.

It's true that some Virginia stewmasters gauge doneness by whether a stirring paddle will stand up in the middle of the pot. But the consistency varies, and aficionados have their favorites.

As to the ownership of the original Brunswick Stew, we'd rather not muddy the broth. We'll leave the deciding (and the bickering) to the folks of Virginia and Georgia. After all, the important thing to most of us is not where this fine traditional dish originated, but that it tastes wonderful.

MORE ABOUT STEW

■ The Virginia stewmasters have a Web site with more information. Check it out at www.brunswickstew.cc.

■ Two great places to try Georgia-style stew, according to Mayor Brad Brown, are Spanky's Marsh Side Restaurant and Twin Oaks Barbecue, both in Brunswick.

■ For the whole story, check out Stan Woodward's video, *Brunswick Stew: A Virginia Treasure.* It's available for sale on the Virginia stewmasters Web site.

■ Richmond's annual Brunswick Stew Festival will be held this year on November 3 from 11 a.m. to 4 p.m. For more information call (804) 780-8597 or see the calendar of events on the Richmond Farmers Market Web site at www. 17thstreetfarmersmarket.com.

BRUNSWICK STEW

This recipe came to us from Tim Smith, who got it from his late father, Zack. To make it thicker, cook it longer, being sure to stir it often.

Prep: 2 hours
Smoke: 6 hours
Cook: 3 hours

Hickory wood chips
2 (2½-pound) whole chickens★
1 (3-pound) Boston butt pork roast★
3 (14½-ounce) cans diced tomatoes
2 (16-ounce) packages frozen whole kernel yellow corn, thawed
2 (16-ounce) packages frozen butterbeans, thawed
2 medium onions, chopped
1 (32-ounce) container chicken broth
1 (24-ounce) bottle ketchup
½ cup white vinegar
½ cup Worcestershire sauce
¼ cup firmly packed brown sugar
1 tablespoon salt
1 tablespoon pepper
2 tablespoons hot sauce

● **Soak** wood chips in water for at least 30 minutes. Prepare charcoal fire in smoker; let burn 15 to 20 minutes.
● **Drain** wood chips, and place on coals. Place water pan in smoker; add water to depth of fill line.
● **Remove** and discard giblets from chicken. Tuck wings under; tie with string, if desired. Place chicken and pork on lower food rack; cover with smoker lid.
● **Cook** chicken 2½ hours; cook pork 6 hours or until a meat thermometer inserted into thickest portion registers 165°. Let cool.
● **Remove** chicken from bone. Chop chicken and pork.
● **Stir** together chicken, pork, diced tomatoes, and remaining ingredients in a 6-quart Dutch oven. Cover and simmer over low heat, stirring occasionally, 2½ to 3 hours. **Yield:** 28 cups.

★Substitute 2 pounds smoked, cooked chicken and 2½ pounds smoked, cooked pork, if desired.

Tim Smith
Birmingham, Alabama

From Our Kitchen

Have Food, Will Travel

When transporting food, the challenge is to have it all arrive safely. Foods Editor Andria Scott Hurst packs frozen foods with dry ice for overnight delivery. For road trips, she keeps two ice chests and a stack of newspaper in her car at all times.

Produce wrapped in newspaper and packed in an ice chest stays cool for four to five hours. Andria uses frozen bottles of water as cooling agents that won't get foods or the newspapers soggy. When they melt, the cold water is ready to drink.

Wrap hot casseroles, pots, and pans in newspaper. Secure the dishes in a box to prevent accidental spills. Unwrap and serve these foods right away. When transporting cooked food a long distance, the safest method is to chill it thoroughly, wrap it well, and reheat at the destination.

What Does It Mean?

The listings on the board at the fish market can sometimes have you guessing. These clues will help you.

Whole fish: just as it's caught, needs to be cleaned completely
Drawn fish: entrails removed, but still needs to be scaled or skinned
Dressed fish: completely cleaned and ready to cook
Fish steaks: thick slices cut crosswise through the whole fish
Fish fillets: boneless pieces cut from the sides
Cold-smoked: cured and partially dried
Smoked: cooked over heat

When buying from the freezer case, be sure your selection has no fishy odor. The fish should be solidly frozen with no discoloration and no ice crystals inside the package. It should be wrapped securely— no air between the fish and wrapping. (Air promotes freezer burn.)

SEAFOOD CELEBRATION

October is National Fish and Seafood Month. Use these tips to keep seafood at its best.

Fish and some shellfish benefit from being stored on ice in the refrigerator. Put fillets in a plastic bag so the ice won't dilute the flavor. Mussels, clams, crabs, and oysters fare well when stored in the crisper covered with wet paper towels or newspaper.

Only cook live shellfish. If bivalves are open, tap on the shell to see if they close. Still not sure? Leave shellfish at room temperature for about 15 minutes, and then tap the shell again. Crabs often appear dead when they are cool. To check, gently pull on a claw with a pair of tongs; if it pulls back slightly, the crab is still alive.

Get to the Bottom of It

Associate Foods Editor Peggy Smith demonstrates the earthy flavor of fresh turnip greens on page 211. But Foods Editor Andria Scott Hurst's mom, Mattie Scott, buys bunches of turnip greens as much for the roots as for the leaves. When bunches don't yield enough beautiful "bottoms," as she calls them, she buys extras. She drops small, peeled whole turnips into the pot when the greens are almost done, or she peels, cooks, and mashes turnips with cream and butter. She serves them sliced thin and fried like chips, and her cheesy turnips au gratin is fantastic. So take a second look at those bulblike roots on turnip greens. According to Andria's mom, they're the prize.

Tips and Tidbits

■ As you choose or purchase new equipment, we recommend silver (light gray) baking pans and baking sheets. Dark and/or black baking pans yield dark baked goods that may appear burned. Some brightly colored tube and Bundt pans with glazed white linings can also produce darker cakes with dry edges.
■ Chicken and rice is an all-time family favorite. If you want to change the character of the dish, use different rice varieties such as brown, wild, or flavored rice mixes. For a nutty flavor and texture, toast the rice in a skillet with a little oil and butter before cooking it. Short-grain rice makes a creamy dish; long-grain rice produces a fluffy result.
■ When you're baking and discover an ingredient is missing, a solution may be in your pantry. Try these in a pinch.
   •Substitute 1 cup sugar + 1 tablespoon cornstarch (processed in food processor) for 1 cup powdered sugar
   •1¼ cups sugar + ¼ cup water for 1 cup honey
   •1 cup regular oats, toasted, for 1 cup chopped pecans
   •1 cup sugar + ¼ cup water for 1 cup light corn syrup
■ To introduce pumpkin as a vegetable side dish, mash it with an equal amount of baked sweet potatoes. The pumpkin flavor will come through, and the sweet potatoes add a rich, smooth texture. Even those finicky eaters who don't like the taste of pumpkin will favor this combination.
■ Beat the rush and stock your pantry now for holiday baking. Store chocolate morsels in a cool, dry place. If stored at too warm a temperature, they will appear ashy gray. We don't recommend freezing them, because chocolate that's exposed to too much humidity may develop a slightly grainy texture. Neither of these instances is cause for alarm; the chocolate will still work when incorporated in your recipes.
■ If you get stuck with too much candy after Halloween, use it in upcoming holiday desserts. Add chopped chocolate bars to brownie or cheesecake batter, and stir crushed hard candies into ice cream.

November

Creole Celebration

Renowned chef Leah Chase shares her Louisiana recipes guaranteed to please a crowd.

Leah Chase reigns as the queen of Creole cooking. In New Orleans, her restaurant, Dooky Chase's, is a bona fide landmark, and her road to the city's culinary throne is no secret. A few years after her marriage to Dooky Jr., Leah began to work in his parents' small neighborhood sandwich shop. Anxious to enhance the menu, she cooked and served some of her favorite dishes. Her wonderful food was immediately in great demand. As the small shop expanded she and Dooky took over the family business. That was all more than 50 years ago, and she's still cooking—and loving it.

"People always ask if I serve soul food," says Leah. "I remind them that all food is soul food, it just depends on where your soul resides. I do good, simple cooking from my Creole background. But if you tell me what your soul likes," she adds with a smile, "I'll cook it for you."

For a taste of what's dear to Leah's soul, sample her holiday dinner menu.

ROAST PORK LOIN
(pictured on page 264)

Prep: 20 minutes
Bake: 1 hour
Stand: 10 minutes

2 (4-pound) center-cut boneless pork loins
1 teaspoon salt
1 teaspoon pepper
⅓ cup all-purpose flour
2 tablespoons olive oil
4 large sweet potatoes, peeled and cut into ½-inch slices
1 (12-ounce) package medium-size pitted prunes
2 (6-ounce) packages dried apricots
2 cups chicken broth
1 cup Madeira wine

• **Rub** pork loins evenly with salt and pepper; dredge in flour.
• **Brown** pork loins on all sides, 1 at a time, in hot oil in a large skillet over medium heat. Place in a large lightly greased roasting pan. Arrange sweet potatoes and prunes around pork.
• **Combine** apricots, broth, and wine in a large saucepan; bring to a boil, and cook 5 minutes. Pour apricot mixture over pork, sweet potato slices, and prunes.
• **Bake** at 375° for 1 hour or until a meat thermometer inserted into thickest portion of pork registers 160°, basting every 15 minutes. Let stand 10 minutes before serving. **Yield:** 12 to 16 servings.

RICE DRESSING
(pictured on page 264)

Try this hearty rice dish seasoned with sausage and herbs for a change of pace from typical cornbread dressing.

Prep: 20 minutes
Cook: 45 minutes
Bake: 12 minutes

6 cups chicken broth
3 cups uncooked long-grain rice
1 cup chicken giblets
½ cup water
1½ pounds ground pork sausage
3 garlic cloves, chopped
2 celery ribs, chopped
1 large onion, chopped
1 red bell pepper, chopped
1½ teaspoons salt
1 teaspoon dried thyme
1 teaspoon dried sage
1 teaspoon hot sauce
½ teaspoon pepper

• **Cook** chicken broth and rice in a saucepan over medium heat 30 minutes or until broth is absorbed and rice is tender. Set aside.
• **Combine** giblets and ½ cup water in a saucepan; bring to a boil, and cook 3 to 4 minutes. Drain and chop.
• **Cook** sausage in a large skillet over medium-high heat, stirring until it crumbles and is no longer pink. Remove sausage, and drain, reserving 2 tablespoons drippings in skillet. Set sausage aside.

- **Sauté** chopped garlic and next 3 ingredients in hot drippings 7 minutes or until tender.
- **Stir** together rice, giblets, sausage, vegetables, salt, and remaining ingredients. Spoon mixture into a greased 2-quart baking dish.
- **Bake** dressing at 375° for 10 to 12 minutes. **Yield:** 12 servings.

GREEN BEANS WITH HAM AND POTATOES

(pictured on page 264)

Smoky ham, sweet onions, and new potatoes transform frozen green beans into a side dish worthy of its starring role on the holiday table.

Prep: 10 minutes
Cook: 30 minutes

½ cup butter or margarine
2½ cups diced smoked ham
2 large sweet onions, diced
3 (1-pound) packages frozen cut green beans, thawed
2 cups chicken broth
1 pound small new potatoes, halved
1 teaspoon freshly ground black pepper
¼ teaspoon ground red pepper
1 small red bell pepper, diced

- **Melt** butter in a large Dutch oven over medium-high heat; add ham, and sauté 5 minutes.
- **Add** onion, and sauté 5 minutes. Add green beans and next 4 ingredients; bring to a boil.
- **Reduce** heat to low, cover, and cook 15 to 20 minutes or until potatoes are tender, stirring in bell pepper during the last 2 to 3 minutes. **Yield:** 12 to 16 servings.

STUFFED SQUASH

(pictured on page 264)

Prep: 45 minutes
Cook: 30 minutes
Bake: 15 minutes

6 large yellow squash, halved and seeded *
1 pound unpeeled, medium-size fresh shrimp
½ cup butter or margarine
½ pound smoked ham, minced
1 onion, chopped
4 green onions, chopped
2 garlic cloves, minced
1 tablespoon chopped fresh parsley
1 teaspoon salt
1 teaspoon ground white pepper
1¼ cups fine, dry breadcrumbs, divided
¼ teaspoon paprika

- **Combine** squash and water to cover in a Dutch oven; bring to a boil, and cook 15 minutes or until tender. Drain and let cool. Scoop out pulp, keeping shells intact; reserve pulp.
- **Peel** shrimp, and devein, if desired; chop shrimp.
- **Melt** butter in Dutch oven over medium heat; add ham and 1 onion, and cook 3 to 4 minutes or until onion is tender. Stir in shrimp and squash pulp. Add green onions and next 4 ingredients; cook 20 to 30 minutes. Stir in 1 cup breadcrumbs. Spoon mixture into shells.
- **Stir** together remaining ¼ cup breadcrumbs and paprika; sprinkle over shells. Bake at 375° for 15 minutes. **Yield:** 12 servings.

*Substitute 6 large mirlitons, if desired.

OLD-FASHIONED BREAD PUDDING

(pictured on page 265)

One spoonful will tell you why this received our highest rating. You'll need to bake two to serve 12.

Prep: 15 minutes
Bake: 45 minutes

1 (16-ounce) day-old French bread loaf, cubed
2 (12-ounce) cans evaporated milk
1 cup water
6 large eggs, lightly beaten
1 (8-ounce) can crushed pineapple, drained
1 large Red Delicious apple, grated
1 cup raisins
1½ cups sugar
5 tablespoons vanilla extract
¼ cup butter or margarine, cut up and softened
Bourbon Sauce

- **Combine** first 3 ingredients; stir in eggs, blending well. Stir in pineapple and next 4 ingredients. Stir in butter, blending well. Pour mixture into a greased 13- x 9-inch baking dish.
- **Bake** at 350° for 35 to 45 minutes or until set. Serve with Bourbon Sauce. **Yield:** 8 servings.

Bourbon Sauce

Prep: 15 minutes

3 tablespoons butter or margarine
1 tablespoon all-purpose flour
½ cup sugar
1 cup whipping cream
2 tablespoons bourbon
1 tablespoon vanilla extract
1 teaspoon ground nutmeg

- **Melt** butter in a small saucepan; whisk in flour, and cook 5 minutes. Stir in sugar and whipping cream; cook 3 minutes. Stir in bourbon, vanilla, and nutmeg, and simmer 5 minutes. **Yield:** 1½ cups.

A Visit With Jan Karon

The best-selling author of the Mitford series talks about her career, her new Virginia home, and her favorite comfort foods.

Jan Karon, best-selling author of the Mitford book series, lives on a farm in Virginia. Her home in Blowing Rock, North Carolina, remains close to her heart, but she wanted to live on a farm. Jan finally found what she was looking for in Virginia. "The farm offers me the opportunity to grow, replenish, and nourish my soul while restoring the land," she says. She has a farm manager, but Jan is very much a hands-on landowner.

"I looked for two years for this place," Jan says, "I have room to breathe here." Indeed she does have room—several hundred acres of gorgeous countryside.

The huge circa-1816 main house is a majestic structure on a hill. "I'm a romantic, and I know this old house needs me. This is a wonderful, complex, layered journey of faith," Jan admits. She's working on a book about the farm (tentatively titled *A Larger Life*), which chronicles the process of restoring this nationally registered historic property.

Explains Jan, "I'm working closely with the senior architectural historian of the Commonwealth to restore as much of the original fabric of the structures as possible." A newly finished guest cottage demonstrates her commitment to preservation. She had an artist develop a special paint for the new walls of the old smokehouse. The original interior walls were cleaned to reveal beautiful old brick and random masses of plaster. The blackened ceiling beams wear a light coating of wax and provide a perfect contrast to the antique heart-pine floor.

The small kitchen features every convenience. "My dad used to say nothing is more comforting than a woman in an apron," Jan says as she ties a white one at her waist. "I love to cook, and cooking for one can be fun. I make things I like, and I keep them simple." When she wants fancy food, she dines out and is also quick to confide (with a wink), "Hot, crisp fried chicken is just down the road at the gas station/corner store." But Jan prepares divine roasted chicken and potatoes for Foods Editor Andria Scott Hurst. Near day's end she takes Andria for a ride on the "Gator" (an army-green all-terrain vehicle) to share ideas for other parts of the farm.

The next morning she greets Andria with a breakfast of homemade apple pie and coffee. Afterward they walk and talk about Mitford. Where is it, really? "Mitford is small-town universal," Jan answers. "We know these people. They read *Southern Living* and lead rich, ordinary lives."

MORE OF MITFORD

Patches of Godlight: Father Tim's Favorite Quotes and *The Mitford Snowmen,* a stocking stuffer treat, are currently available in stores. And fans of Mitford can visit the little town with the big heart anytime at the Web site www.penguinputnam.com/mitford.

JAN'S ROASTED CHICKEN

Prep: 15 minutes
Bake: 1 hour, 30 minutes

- **1** (3- to 4-pound) whole chicken
- **3** tablespoons olive oil, divided
- **3** garlic cloves
- **1** teaspoon salt
- **1** tablespoon coarsely ground pepper
- **3** sprigs fresh rosemary
- **1** lemon, quartered

- **Rub** chicken and cavities with 2 tablespoons olive oil, garlic cloves, salt, and pepper.
- **Tuck** chicken wings under; tie legs together with string, if desired. Pour remaining 1 tablespoon oil into a large cast-iron skillet; place chicken, breast side up, in skillet.
- **Place** 1 rosemary sprig and 2 lemon quarters into neck cavity of chicken; repeat in lower cavity. Place remaining rosemary sprig underneath skin.
- **Bake** at 450° for 30 minutes; reduce heat to 350°, and bake 1 more hour. Serve with Jan's Roasted Potatoes. **Yield:** 4 servings.

JAN'S ROASTED POTATOES

Prep: 5 minutes
Bake: 1 hour

- **8** medium-size new potatoes, halved
- **3** tablespoons butter or margarine, melted
- **1** teaspoon salt
- **1** teaspoon pepper

- **Place** potatoes on a baking sheet. Drizzle with butter; sprinkle with salt and pepper.
- **Bake** potatoes at 350° for 1 hour, turning every 20 minutes. **Yield:** 4 servings.

Super-Charged Greens with cornbread, page 211

Spicy Pecans, page 206

Pecan-Pie Muffins, page 206

Orange-Pecan Biscotti, page 207

Pecan-Pie Muffins,
page 206

Spicy Pecans, page 206

Cornish Hens With Spicy Pecan-Cornbread Stuffing, page 206

Apple-Vinegar Biscuit Cobbler, page 215

Applesauce Pie, page 213

Savory Cinnamon

Teach your palate a new way to enjoy this spice.

We'll bet when you think of cinnamon, you envision a bowl of creamy oatmeal or ooey-gooey breakfast rolls. But cinnamon has long been complementing meats, stews, curries, and rice dishes. The dried inner bark of a tropical evergreen tree, it comes in two varieties—cassia and Ceylon. Cassia, the most widely available in the United States, is a reddish brown color and bolder in flavor. Ceylon, pale tan in color, imparts a mild, more subtle flavor. Either works great in our recipes.

Ground cinnamon loses flavor and aroma quickly. Store it in an airtight container in a cool, dry place, and use it within a year of purchase. Sprinkle cinnamon into beef stews, spaghetti sauces, casseroles, or bean soups. It also rounds out the flavor of roasted beets, baked winter squash, and meat rubs or marinades. Start with a pinch or a dash—a little goes a long way. Your family may not know what's different; they'll just know it tastes divine. If you can't imagine adding cinnamon to your savory recipes, try our sampling.

CINNAMON RICE PILAF

Prep: 20 minutes
Bake: 25 minutes

3 tablespoons butter or
　　margarine
2 medium shallots, minced
1 cup uncooked basmati rice
2 ounces uncooked vermicelli,
　　broken into ½-inch pieces
1 (14½-ounce) can chicken broth
½ teaspoon salt
¾ teaspoon ground cinnamon

• **Melt** butter in an ovenproof skillet over medium heat. Add shallots, and cook, stirring constantly, 2 minutes.

Add rice and pasta; cook, stirring constantly, 1 minute. Stir in broth, salt, and cinnamon.
• **Bake,** covered, at 350° for 25 minutes or until liquid is absorbed. **Yield:** 4 servings.

PORK-STUFFED POBLANOS WITH WALNUT CREAM SAUCE

Fluffy Cinnamon Rice Pilaf (at left) pairs perfectly with this subtly spiced dish.

Prep: 25 minutes
Cook: 25 minutes
Bake: 30 minutes

8 large poblano chile peppers
1 pound ground pork
1 tablespoon olive oil
1 medium onion, chopped
1 large garlic clove, minced
1 teaspoon ground cumin
¾ teaspoon ground cinnamon
¼ teaspoon ground red pepper
2 large tomatoes, chopped
1 small apple, chopped
⅓ cup raisins
⅓ cup diced almonds, toasted
1 tablespoon cider vinegar
1 teaspoon salt
1 cup tomato sauce
1 teaspoon sugar
¼ teaspoon salt
¼ teaspoon dried crushed red
　　pepper
Walnut Cream Sauce
Garnish: cinnamon sticks

• **Broil** chile peppers on an aluminum foil-lined baking sheet 5 inches from heat about 5 minutes on each side or until peppers look blistered.
• **Place** chile peppers in a heavy-duty zip-top plastic bag; seal and let stand 10 minutes to loosen skins. Peel peppers. Gently split chile peppers open lengthwise, keeping stems intact; remove and discard seeds. Set peppers aside.
• **Cook** pork in hot oil in a large skillet over medium-high heat until it crumbles and is no longer pink; drain. Add chopped onion and next 4 ingredients; cook, stirring often, 7 minutes or until onion is tender.
• **Stir** in tomato and next 4 ingredients. Cover, reduce heat, and simmer 5 minutes. Stir in 1 teaspoon salt.
• **Stir** together tomato sauce and next 3 ingredients in a small saucepan over low heat 5 minutes.
• **Spoon** about ½ cup pork mixture into each pepper, and place in a lightly greased 13- x 9-inch baking dish. Pour tomato sauce mixture over peppers.
• **Bake,** covered, at 350° for 30 minutes. Top with Walnut Cream Sauce. Garnish, if desired, and serve over Cinnamon Rice Pilaf (recipe at left). **Yield:** 8 servings.

Note: Small green bell peppers may be substituted for poblanos. (Do not roast.) Proceed as directed. Bake 45 minutes or until peppers are tender.

Walnut Cream Sauce

Prep: 10 minutes

1 (3-ounce) package cream cheese,
　　softened
½ cup walnuts, toasted
½ cup sour cream
¼ cup milk
1 teaspoon ground cinnamon
½ teaspoon ground red pepper
½ teaspoon sugar
¼ teaspoon salt

• **Process** all ingredients in a food processor or blender until smooth, stopping to scrape down sides. **Yield:** 1½ cups.

Moroccan Spiced Pork Chops

Prep: 15 minutes
Cook: 25 minutes

1¾ teaspoons Moroccan Spice
    Mixture, divided
½ teaspoon salt, divided
4 (6-ounce) boneless pork loin chops
1 tablespoon butter or margarine
1 tablespoon vegetable oil
½ small onion, diced
2 apples, peeled and chopped
2 ripe pears, peeled and chopped
1 cup chicken broth

• **Rub** 1 teaspoon Moroccan Spice Mixture and ¼ teaspoon salt evenly on both sides of pork chops.
• **Melt** butter with oil in a large skillet over medium-high heat. Cook pork chops 4 minutes on each side or until done. Remove pork chops from skillet, and keep warm.
• **Add** onion to drippings in skillet; cook over medium-high heat, stirring occasionally, 5 minutes. Stir in apple, pear, and broth. Cover, reduce heat, and cook 5 minutes or until fruit is tender. Stir in remaining ¾ teaspoon Moroccan Spice Mixture and ¼ teaspoon salt; cook over medium-high heat 5 minutes. Serve over pork chops. **Yield:** 4 servings.

Moroccan Spice Mixture

1 tablespoon cumin seeds
1 tablespoon coriander seeds
1 tablespoon paprika
3 whole cloves
½ teaspoon ground cinnamon
¼ teaspoon ground red pepper

• **Heat** a nonstick skillet over medium-high heat. Remove skillet from heat; add cumin and coriander seeds. Toast, stirring often, 2 minutes or until spices are fragrant (do not brown). Cool.
• **Process** seeds, paprika, and remaining ingredients in a spice mill or coffee grinder until finely ground. Store spice mixture in an airtight container up to 1 month. **Yield:** ¼ cup.

Savory Beef Pies

Enjoy these alone or dipped in your favorite chutney.

Prep: 35 minutes
Bake: 15 minutes

1 medium onion, diced
3 tablespoons olive oil
1 garlic clove, minced
1 pound ground round
2 tablespoons instant mashed
    potato flakes
¼ cup hot water
½ teaspoon ground cinnamon
¼ teaspoon ground cloves
1 teaspoon salt
1 teaspoon freshly ground pepper
2 (15-ounce) packages refrigerated
    piecrusts
Tomato chutney (optional)

• **Sauté** onion in hot oil in a large skillet over medium-high heat 5 minutes. Add garlic, and cook 1 minute. Add beef; cook, stirring often, until meat crumbles and is no longer pink. Drain, cool, and set aside.
• **Stir** together potato flakes and ¼ cup hot water until smooth.
• **Add** potato, cinnamon, and next 3 ingredients to beef mixture, stirring until blended.
• **Roll** piecrusts into 12-inch circles; cut each crust into 6 (4-inch) circles. Roll out enough remaining crust to make 2 more (4-inch) circles.
• **Spoon** 1 rounded tablespoonful of beef mixture onto half of each pastry circle. Moisten edges with water; fold pastry over filling, pressing edges with a fork to seal. Place pies on ungreased baking sheets.
• **Bake** at 400° for 15 minutes or until lightly browned. Serve warm with chutney, if desired. **Yield:** 26 pies.

Note: Meat mixture may be frozen up to 3 months. Thaw in refrigerator and prepare pies as directed.

Scoring Big With Turkey Leftovers

In bowling, three successive strikes is referred to as a turkey. Score big with this turkey salad instead of a sandwich.

Honey-Mustard Turkey Salad

Prep: 15 minutes
Cook: 5 minutes

1 (3-ounce) package Japanese curly
    noodles, uncooked
2 cups cubed turkey
½ pound bacon, cooked and crumbled
4 button mushrooms, sliced
¼ cup red bell pepper strips
3 green onions, chopped
½ cup lightly salted cashews
Honey-Mustard Dressing
1 (10-ounce) package spinach leaves,
    shredded

• **Prepare** noodles according to package directions; drain and chill.
• **Combine** turkey and next 5 ingredients in a bowl. Stir in Honey-Mustard Dressing. Serve salad on spinach, and sprinkle with noodles. **Yield:** 6 servings.

Honey-Mustard Dressing

Prep: 5 minutes

⅔ cup mayonnaise ✱
2 tablespoons Dijon mustard
3 tablespoons honey
1 teaspoon soy sauce
1 teaspoon lemon juice

• **Stir** together all ingredients until well blended. Chill, if desired. **Yield:** 6 cups.

✱ Substitute low-fat mayonnaise for regular, if desired.

Laurie McIntyre
Houston, Texas

Taste of the South

Southerners are both passionate and opinionated about the various recipes for chicken and dumplings. The dumplings must be rolled—or they must be dropped. Celery is either the salvation or the ruination of the broth. And don't even think about asking if you could use a package of chicken breasts instead of the whole bird.

We tried Test Kitchen staffer Lyda Jones's variation on a recipe from a beloved family friend. Here's what we learned.

• Skimming fat off warm broth can be tricky. If you boil the chicken the night before and refrigerate the broth, all the fat will collect on the surface, making it easy to remove. Plus, the chicken will be cool when you're ready to pull it off the bone.
• The even distribution of ingredients is key to dumpling success. Break shortening into small pieces, and use solidified bacon drippings.
• The more you handle the dough, the tougher your dumplings are likely to be. So as soon as you have a moist ball of dough, resist the urge to keep working it.

CHICKEN AND DUMPLINGS

Prep: 30 minutes
Cook: 1 hour, 30 minutes

1 (2½-pound) whole chicken, cut up
2½ teaspoons salt, divided
¾ teaspoon pepper, divided
½ teaspoon garlic powder
½ teaspoon dried thyme
¼ teaspoon ground red pepper
1 teaspoon chicken bouillon granules
3 cups self-rising flour
½ teaspoon poultry seasoning
⅓ cup shortening
2 teaspoons bacon drippings
1 cup milk

• **Cover** chicken with water, and bring to a boil in a large Dutch oven. Add 1½ teaspoons salt, ½ teaspoon pepper, and

next 3 ingredients; cover, reduce heat, and simmer 1 hour. Remove chicken, reserving broth in Dutch oven; cool chicken. Skim fat from broth; bring to a simmer.
• **Skin,** bone, and coarsely chop chicken. Add chopped chicken, bouillon, and remaining salt and pepper to broth. Return to simmer.
• **Combine** flour and poultry seasoning in a bowl. Cut in shortening and bacon drippings with a pastry blender until mixture is crumbly. Add milk, stirring until dry ingredients are moistened.
• **Turn** dough out onto a lightly floured surface. Roll out to ⅛-inch thickness; cut into 1-inch pieces.
• **Bring** broth mixture to a boil. Drop dumplings, a few at a time, into boiling broth, stirring gently. Reduce heat, cover, and simmer, stirring often, for 25 minutes. **Yield:** 8 servings.

Kid-Friendly Snacks

If you don't eat the holiday meal until late afternoon, the children may need snacks to tide them over. Tempting munchies help deter the hunger pangs, so let the kids choose a recipe and lend a helping hand in the kitchen. Who knows? You might even find an adult sneaking a bite or two.

PIZZA SNACKS

Prep: 10 minutes
Bake: 12 minutes

1 (8-ounce) can crescent rolls
1 (6-ounce) package pepperoni slices
2 (1-ounce) mozzarella cheese sticks, cut into fourths
1 teaspoon Italian seasoning
¼ teaspoon garlic salt

• **Separate** rolls into 8 triangles, and place on a baking sheet. Place 2 pepperoni slices on each triangle; place 1 piece

cheese at wide end of triangle. Sprinkle with Italian seasoning. Roll up, starting at wide end. Sprinkle with garlic salt.
• **Bake** at 375° for 10 to 12 minutes or until golden. **Yield:** 8 snacks.

Mark Kohlhoff
Houston, Texas

CHEESE COOKIE SNACKS

Prep: 10 minutes
Bake: 18 minutes

1 cup (4 ounces) shredded Cheddar cheese
½ cup butter or margarine, softened
1 cup all-purpose flour
¼ teaspoon salt
1 cup crisp rice cereal

• **Stir** together cheese and butter until blended. Stir in flour and salt; blend well. Stir in cereal. (Dough will be stiff.)
• **Shape** dough into 1-inch balls; place on an ungreased baking sheet 2 inches apart. Flatten cookies to ¼-inch thickness with a fork, making a crisscross.
• **Bake** at 350° for 15 to 18 minutes. Remove to a wire rack to cool. Store in an airtight container. **Yield:** 2 dozen.

YUMMY BANANA POPS

Prep: 5 minutes
Freeze: 3 hours

4 small bananas, mashed
1 cup orange juice
2 tablespoons sugar
2 tablespoons water
1 teaspoon lemon juice
6 wooden craft sticks

• **Combine** all ingredients. Place 6 (4-ounce) paper cups in a muffin pan. Spoon mixture into cups. Freeze 1 hour or until slightly firm; insert a stick into the center of each. Freeze 2 hours or until firm. Peel off cups, and serve. **Yield:** 6 servings.

Suzan L. Wiener
Spring Hill, Florida

Holiday Dinners®

Be our guest as we celebrate this joyous season with a Southwest-inspired Thanksgiving menu from our staff, a bounty of down-home desserts, a visit to a family reunion, and much more.

Southwestern-Style Dinner

> ### A Southwestern Thanksgiving
> *Serves 10 to 12*
>
> Southwestern Cheese Appetizer   Assorted crackers
>
> Smoked Pork
>
> Southwestern Cornbread Dressing Cakes
>
> Cranberry-Jalapeño Salsa
>
> Roasted Sweet Potatoes and Onions
>
> Bean Bundles   Cheese Biscuits With Chipotle Butter
>
> Chocolate-Praline Cake
>
> Pineapple Limeade

We like to offer our readers an extra-special menu for the holidays each year. This time, in response to many requests, we created a feast with Southwestern flavors. Three members of our Test Kitchens staff—Vanessa McNeil, Jan Moon, and Mary Allen Perry—worked to develop dishes that deliver bold flavors but keep the spirit of the season in mind.

"We took some of our favorite traditional dishes and gave them a twist," says Mary Allen. "The colors and flavors are perfect for the holidays," says Jan.

The menu is one of our best, and most of the recipes can be made ahead. "It's different, but it's familiar enough that you won't feel like you missed out on a tradition," Mary Allen says.

SOUTHWESTERN CHEESE APPETIZER
(pictured on page 263)

Prep: 30 minutes
Chill: 8 hours

½   cup olive oil
½   cup white wine vinegar
¼   cup fresh lime juice
½   (7.5-ounce) jar roasted sweet red peppers, drained and diced
3   green onions, minced
3   tablespoons chopped fresh parsley
3   tablespoons chopped fresh cilantro
1   teaspoon sugar
½   teaspoon salt
½   teaspoon freshly ground pepper
1   (8-ounce) block sharp Cheddar cheese, chilled
1   (8-ounce) block Monterey Jack cheese with peppers, chilled
1   (8-ounce) package cream cheese, chilled

● **Whisk** together first 3 ingredients until mixture is blended; stir in diced red peppers and next 6 ingredients. Set marinade aside.

● **Cut** block of Cheddar cheese in half lengthwise. Cut halves crosswise into ¼-inch-thick slices. Repeat procedure with Monterey Jack cheese and cream cheese.

● **Arrange** cheese slices alternately in a shallow dish, standing slices on edge.

Pour marinade over cheeses. Cover and chill at least 8 hours. Transfer cheese to a serving plate; spoon remaining marinade over top. Serve with crackers. **Yield:** 16 appetizer servings.

SMOKED PORK
(pictured on page 262)

Ask the butcher to remove the chine bone for easier cutting.

Prep: 30 minutes
Marinate: 8 hours
Cook: 5 hours

1 (7-pound) pork loin rib roast
    (10 ribs), chine bone removed *
1 cup Cajun butter injector sauce
2 teaspoons salt
1 tablespoon pepper
2 tablespoons dried cilantro
Mesquite chips

• **Trim** fat from roast. Inject butter sauce evenly into pork. Combine salt, pepper, and cilantro, and rub mixture over pork. Cover pork; chill 8 hours.
• **Soak** mesquite chips in water at least 30 minutes.
• **Prepare** charcoal fire in smoker, and let burn 15 to 20 minutes. Drain chips, and place on coals. Place water pan in smoker; add water to depth of fill line. Place pork on lower food rack; cover with smoker lid.
• **Cook** pork roast 4 to 5 hours or until a meat thermometer inserted into thickest portion of roast registers 160°. **Yield:** 10 servings.

* Substitute 1 (7-pound) boneless pork loin roast, if desired.

Note: For testing purposes only, we used Original Cajun Marinade Injector for Cajun butter sauce.

Roasted Pork: Place pork in a roasting pan, and bake at 425° for 45 minutes; reduce oven temperature to 350°, and bake 20 more minutes or until meat thermometer registers 160°.

SOUTHWESTERN CORNBREAD DRESSING CAKES
(pictured on page 262)

Prep: 20 minutes
Cook: 28 minutes

1 recipe Cornbread (recipe on
    following page), crumbled
1 cup soft white breadcrumbs
    (homemade)
4 ears fresh corn
2 tablespoons butter or margarine
2 medium-size sweet onions, diced
2 (4.5-ounce) cans chopped green
    chiles, drained
½ cup chopped fresh cilantro
2 teaspoons seasoned pepper
1 teaspoon garlic salt
3 large eggs, lightly beaten
1 cup mayonnaise
1 teaspoon ground red pepper
    (optional)
4½ tablespoons vegetable oil
Garnish: fresh cilantro sprigs

• **Combine** crumbled cornbread and breadcrumbs in a large bowl, and set mixture aside.
• **Cut** corn kernels from cob.
• **Melt** 2 tablespoons butter in a large nonstick skillet over medium-high heat; add diced onion, and sauté for 5 minutes or until tender. Add corn, and sauté 5 minutes.
• **Stir** together onion mixture, cornbread mixture, green chiles, next 5 ingredients, and, if desired, red pepper. Shape mixture into 20 (3-inch) patties. Chill, if desired.
• **Cook** one-third of patties in 1½ tablespoons hot oil in a large nonstick skillet over medium heat 2 to 3 minutes on each side or until patties are golden brown, turning gently once. Repeat procedure twice with remaining patties and oil. Serve immediately, or remove to a wire rack to cool. Cover and chill 8 hours, if desired. To reheat, bake in a single layer on a baking sheet at 400° for 8 to 10 minutes. Garnish, if desired. **Yield:** 20 patties.

COOK'S NOTES

3 Days Ahead:
■ Prepare Chocolate-Praline Cake, and freeze.
■ Prepare Southwestern Cornbread Dressing Cakes, and freeze.
■ Prepare Cheese Biscuits, and freeze.

2 Days Ahead:
■ Prepare Pineapple Limeade (except for adding sparkling water), and freeze.
■ Prepare Chipotle Butter, and chill.

1 Day Ahead:
■ Marinate Smoked Pork, and chill.
■ Thaw Southwestern Cornbread Dressing Cakes and Cheese Biscuits in the refrigerator.
■ Prepare Cranberry-Jalapeño Salsa, and chill.
■ Prepare Southwestern Cheese Appetizer; chill at least 8 hours.
■ Prepare veggies for Bean Bundles; cover and chill 8 hours.

The Day of the Dinner:
■ Prepare charcoal fire.
■ Place pork on grill.
■ Thaw cake at room temperature 4 to 6 hours.
■ Thaw Pineapple Limeade slightly; add sparkling water.
■ Cut up sweet potatoes and onions while limeade thaws, and toss potato and onion with seasonings.
■ Roast sweet potato and onion at 450° for 30 minutes. Bake Bean Bundles 25 minutes.
■ Warm Southwestern Cornbread Dressing Cakes at 400° for 8 to 10 minutes or until hot, and warm Cheese Biscuits at 400° for 5 minutes or until hot.

Holiday Dinners

Cornbread

Prep: 10 minutes
Bake: 30 minutes

½ cup butter
2 cups white cornmeal mix
1 cup all-purpose flour
2 tablespoons sugar
2 large eggs
2 cups buttermilk

• **Melt** butter in a 13- x 9-inch pan in a 425° oven for 5 minutes.
• **Stir** together white cornmeal mix and remaining 4 ingredients in a large bowl.
• **Tilt** pan to coat with butter; pour butter into cornmeal mixture, stirring well. Pour cornmeal mixture into hot pan.
• **Bake** at 425° for 30 minutes or until golden brown. **Yield:** 1 (13- x 9-inch) pan cornbread.

CRANBERRY-JALAPEÑO SALSA
(pictured on page 262)

Prep: 10 minutes

1 (12-ounce) package fresh cranberries
1 medium navel orange, unpeeled and coarsely chopped
3 tablespoons crystallized ginger
2 jalapeño peppers, seeded and coarsely chopped
¼ cup fresh mint leaves
1 cup sugar
Garnishes: fresh mint sprigs, orange wedges

• **Pulse** fresh cranberries in a food processor until minced. Transfer minced cranberries to a small bowl.
• **Pulse** orange and next 4 ingredients in food processor 3 to 5 times or until mixture is finely chopped. Stir into cranberries; cover and chill, if desired. Garnish, if desired. **Yield:** 2 cups.

ROASTED SWEET POTATOES AND ONIONS
(pictured on page 262)

Prep: 15 minutes
Bake: 30 minutes

4 to 5 sweet potatoes, peeled and cut into 1-inch cubes
2 large sweet onions, cut into wedges
3 tablespoons olive oil
2 tablespoons fajita seasoning

• **Toss** together all ingredients; place on an aluminum foil-lined baking pan.
• **Bake** at 450° for 30 minutes or until tender, stirring occasionally. **Yield:** 8 servings.

BEAN BUNDLES
(pictured on page 1)

Cook fresh green beans with carrot and red bell pepper strips in boiling water to cover until crisp-tender. Plunge into ice water to stop the cooking process; drain and set aside. Cook yellow squash in boiling water to cover until crisp-tender. Plunge into ice water to stop the cooking process, and drain. Cut squash into ½-inch-thick slices, and remove pulp from center of each slice with a round cutter or knife. Secure vegetables in bundles with squash rings, and place in a lightly greased 13- x 9-inch baking dish. Cover and chill 8 hours, if desired. Drizzle bean bundles with melted butter, and bake, covered, at 350° for 20 to 25 minutes or until thoroughly heated.

CHEESE BISCUITS WITH CHIPOTLE BUTTER
(pictured on page 262)

Smoky Chipotle Butter adds a burst of flavor to these warm, rich biscuits.

Prep: 10 minutes
Bake: 12 minutes

1 (6.25-ounce) package biscuit mix
1 (6-ounce) package cornbread mix
1 (8-ounce) container sour cream
⅓ cup buttermilk
1 cup (4 ounces) shredded Cheddar cheese
1 teaspoon fajita seasoning (optional)
Chipotle Butter
Garnish: fresh cilantro sprig

• **Stir** together first 5 ingredients, and, if desired, fajita seasoning. Turn dough out onto a lightly floured surface; pat or roll dough to ½-inch thickness. Cut dough with a 2-inch round cutter, and place rounds on a lightly greased baking sheet.
• **Bake** at 400° for 10 to 12 minutes. Serve with Chipotle Butter. Garnish, if desired. **Yield:** 2 dozen.

Chipotle Butter

Prep: 5 minutes

½ cup butter, softened
2 teaspoons chopped fresh parsley
1 chipotle pepper in adobo sauce, diced
2 teaspoons adobo sauce

• **Stir** together all ingredients in a bowl. **Yield:** ½ cup.

Holiday Dinners

CHOCOLATE-PRALINE CAKE
(pictured on page 263)

Prep: 30 minutes
Bake: 22 minutes

1 cup butter or margarine
¼ cup cocoa
1 cup water
½ cup buttermilk
2 large eggs
1 teaspoon baking soda
1 teaspoon vanilla extract
2 cups sugar
2 cups all-purpose flour
½ teaspoon salt
Chocolate Ganache
Praline Frosting
Garnish: pecan halves

• **Cook** first 3 ingredients in a saucepan over low heat, stirring constantly, until butter melts and mixture is smooth; remove butter mixture from heat.
• **Beat** buttermilk, 2 eggs, baking soda, and vanilla at medium speed with an electric mixer until smooth. Add butter mixture to buttermilk mixture, beating until well blended. Combine sugar, flour, and salt; gradually add to buttermilk mixture, beating until blended.
• **Coat** 3 (9-inch) round cakepans with cooking spray; line with wax paper. Pour batter evenly into pans. Bake at 350° for 18 to 22 minutes or until set. Cool in pans on wire racks 10 minutes. Remove from pans; cool completely.
• **Spread** about ½ cup ganache between cake layers; spread remaining on sides of cake. Pour frosting slowly over center of cake, spreading to edges, allowing some frosting to run over sides. Freeze, if desired; thaw at room temperature 4 to 6 hours. Garnish, if desired. **Yield:** 1 (9-inch) layer cake.

Chocolate Ganache

Prep: 20 minutes

2 cups (12 ounces) semisweet chocolate morsels
⅓ cup whipping cream
¼ cup butter or margarine, cut into pieces

• **Microwave** chocolate morsels and whipping cream in a glass bowl at MEDIUM (50% power) 2 to 3 minutes or until morsels are melted. Whisk until smooth. Gradually add butter, whisking until smooth. Cool, whisking often, 15 minutes or until spreading consistency. **Yield:** about 2 cups.

Praline Frosting

Do not prepare this frosting ahead because it'll harden very quickly.

Prep: 10 minutes
Cook: 5 minutes

¼ cup butter or margarine
1 cup firmly packed brown sugar
⅓ cup whipping cream
1 cup powdered sugar
1 teaspoon vanilla extract
1 cup chopped pecans, toasted

• **Bring** first 3 ingredients to a boil in a 2-quart saucepan over medium heat, stirring often; boil 1 minute. Remove from heat, and whisk in 1 cup powdered sugar and vanilla until smooth. Stir in toasted pecans, stirring gently 3 to 5 minutes or until mixture begins to cool and thicken slightly. Pour immediately over cake. **Yield:** about 1¾ cups.

PINEAPPLE LIMEADE

Prep: 10 minutes
Freeze: 8 hours

4 cups pineapple juice
⅔ cup fresh lime juice (about 4 limes)
¾ cup sugar
½ cup tequila (optional)
1 (32-ounce) bottle lime-flavored sparkling water

• **Stir** together first 3 ingredients and, if desired, tequila. Cover and freeze 8 hours. Stir in sparkling water just before serving. **Yield:** about 10 cups.

Note: Thaw slightly before adding sparkling water, if omitting tequila.

The Perfect Match

Entertaining can be easy when you offer our best-of-the-best appetizers paired with a complementary varietal. See the box below for suggestions from Assistant Foods Editor Scott Jones.

BLUE CHEESE CRISPS
(pictured on page 261)

1998 Recipe Hall of Fame

Prep: 8 minutes
Bake: 10 minutes

½ cup butter or margarine, softened
1 (4-ounce) package crumbled blue cheese, softened
½ cup finely chopped pecans or walnuts
1 French baguette, sliced

• **Stir** together butter and cheese until blended; stir in nuts. Set mixture aside.
• **Place** baguette slices in a single layer on baking sheets.
• **Bake** at 350° for 3 to 5 minutes. Turn slices, and spread with blue cheese mixture. Bake 5 more minutes. Serve immediately. **Yield:** 32 appetizers.

SCOTT'S PICKS

■ **Sangiovese:** Antinori, Santa Cristina, Renaissance, Shenandoah

■ **Cabernet Sauvignon:** Liberty School, Beringer, Peter Lehmann

■ **Sauvignon Blanc:** Villa Maria, Callaway, Cloudy Bay, Baron Philippe de Rothschild

---

BLUE CHEESE-AND-BACON PUFFS
(pictured on page 261)

1997 Recipe Hall of Fame

Prep: 20 minutes
Bake: 25 minutes

1½ cups water
½ cup butter or margarine
1½ cups all-purpose flour
½ teaspoon salt
¼ teaspoon ground black pepper
¼ teaspoon ground red pepper
6 large eggs
8 ounces crumbled blue cheese
8 bacon slices, cooked and crumbled
4 green onions, finely chopped

• **Bring** 1½ cups water and butter to a boil in a heavy saucepan over medium heat. Add flour and next 3 ingredients; cook, beating with a wooden spoon, until mixture leaves sides of pan and forms a smooth ball of dough. Remove from heat, and cool 5 minutes.
• **Add** eggs, 1 at a time, beating well with spoon after each addition. Beat in cheese, bacon, and chopped green onions.
• **Drop** dough by rounded teaspoonfuls 2 inches apart onto lightly greased baking sheets.
• **Bake** at 400° for 20 to 25 minutes or until golden. (Puffs will be moist in center.) Serve puffs warm or at room temperature. **Yield:** 6 dozen.

Note: Puffs may be frozen up to 3 months. Thaw in refrigerator overnight, and reheat at 350° for 5 minutes or until thoroughly heated.

A Texas Thanksgiving With a Twist

Tradition With a Twist
Serves 6 to 8

Shanghai Spring Rolls With Sweet Chili Sauce
Roasted Pork
Chicken Vermicelli   Asian Green Beans
Caramel Custard

Larry Perdido makes no apologies for the food he and his brothers enjoyed as children. "Growing up, there was nothing we liked more than hamburgers and pizza," he remembers. Although his parents were born in the Philippines and his mother, Melva, regularly cooked Filipino dishes, Larry was just another kid in suburban Texas. "Mom always cooked," he says, "but she wasn't good at making what we liked. She was more into ethnic foods."

However, Larry's tune quickly changed once he left for college. Now the chef-owner of Saba Blue Water Café in Austin and Houston, Larry still looks forward to his mother's cooking, particularly when his family gets together for Thanksgiving.

SHANGHAI SPRING ROLLS WITH SWEET CHILI SAUCE

Prep: 30 minutes
Cook: 15 minutes

½ pound unpeeled fresh shrimp
2 large eggs, lightly beaten
½ pound ground pork
1 (8-ounce) can water chestnuts, drained and minced
1 (8-ounce) can bamboo shoots, drained and minced
3 garlic cloves, minced
2 green onions, diced
2 tablespoons minced fresh ginger
1 tablespoon soy sauce
⅛ teaspoon salt
⅛ teaspoon pepper
1 (12-ounce) package spring roll wrappers
Vegetable oil
Sweet Chili Sauce
Lettuce leaves (optional)

• **Peel** shrimp, and devein, if desired; finely chop.

Holiday Dinners

• **Stir** together shrimp, 1 egg, pork, and next 8 ingredients. Spoon 1 tablespoon mixture in center of each spring roll wrapper. Fold top corner of each wrapper over filling, tucking tip of corner under filling, and fold left and right corners over filling. Lightly brush remaining corner with remaining egg; tightly roll filled end toward remaining corner, and gently press to seal.

• **Pour** oil to a depth of 2 inches into a medium saucepan, and heat to 350°. Fry spring rolls, a few at a time, 6 minutes or until golden. Drain on paper towels. Serve with Sweet Chili Sauce and over lettuce leaves, if desired. **Yield:** 15 spring rolls.

Sweet Chili Sauce

Prep: 10 minutes

1 (7-ounce) bottle hot chili sauce
    with garlic
½ cup water
½ cup rice wine vinegar
¼ cup sugar
¼ cup lemon juice
2 tablespoons chili paste

• **Stir** together all ingredients. Cover; chill until ready to serve. **Yield:** 2 cups.

Roasted Pork

Prep: 5 minutes
Chill: 8 hours
Bake: 4 hours

1 (5-pound) Boston butt pork roast
6 garlic cloves, minced
1 tablespoon salt
1 tablespoon pepper

• **Rub** pork with garlic, salt, and pepper. Wrap tightly with plastic wrap; chill at least 8 hours or up to 24 hours. Unwrap pork; place on a rack in a roasting pan.

• **Bake** at 325° for 4 hours or until a meat thermometer inserted into thickest portion registers 160°, basting occasionally with drippings in pan. Let stand 10 minutes. **Yield:** 10 servings.

Chicken Vermicelli

Prep: 25 minutes
Cook: 23 minutes

1 (8-ounce) package vermicelli rice
    noodles
1 onion, diced
2 tablespoons sesame oil
4 carrots, shredded
3 medium celery ribs, diced
2 cups shredded cooked chicken
2 garlic cloves, minced
1 small napa cabbage, finely chopped
1 cup reduced-sodium chicken broth
1 tablespoon cornstarch
¼ cup soy sauce
1 tablespoon oyster sauce
Garnishes: chopped green onions,
    lemon slices

• **Soak** noodles in hot water 10 minutes; drain and set aside.

• **Sauté** diced onion in hot oil in a large skillet over medium-high heat 5 minutes or until tender. Add carrot and next 4 ingredients; cook, stirring occasionally, 2 minutes.

• **Stir** together broth and cornstarch until smooth; add to chicken mixture. Add soy sauce and oyster sauce; bring to a boil, and cook 1 minute. Remove from heat; serve over noodles. Garnish, if desired. **Yield:** 6 to 8 servings.

Asian Green Beans

Prep: 25 minutes
Cook: 10 minutes

1 pound fresh green beans, trimmed
2 green onions, diced
2 garlic cloves, minced
2 to 3 teaspoons minced fresh ginger
2 tablespoons sesame oil
½ cup roasted sweet red bell pepper,
    thinly sliced
1 tablespoon oyster sauce
⅛ teaspoon pepper
¼ cup slivered almonds, toasted

• **Cook** green beans in boiling water 4 to 6 minutes or until crisp-tender; drain.

Plunge into ice water to stop the cooking process; drain.

• **Sauté** green onions, minced garlic, and ginger in hot sesame oil in a large nonstick skillet over medium heat 1 minute. Add green beans and bell pepper; cook 1 minute. Add oyster sauce and pepper, stirring until thoroughly heated. Sprinkle with almonds. **Yield:** 6 servings.

Caramel Custard

Finish off a wonderful meal with the simple pleasure of this creamy dessert.

Prep: 30 minutes
Bake: 1 hour, 10 minutes
Chill: 3 hours

1½ cups sugar, divided
½ cup water
3 large eggs
2 egg yolks
2½ cups warm milk
1 tablespoon vanilla extract

• **Combine** 1 cup sugar and ½ cup water in a heavy saucepan; cook over low heat 10 minutes or until sugar caramelizes, tipping pan to incorporate mixture. Pour evenly into 8 (4-ounce) custard cups.

• **Whisk** together eggs, egg yolks, and remaining ½ cup sugar until blended. Gradually add warm milk, whisking constantly; stir in vanilla. Pour mixture into prepared custard cups. Cover each with aluminum foil; place in a jellyroll pan. Add hot water to pan to a depth of ¼ to ½ inch.

• **Bake** at 325° for 1 hour and 10 minutes or until a knife inserted in center comes out clean. Remove custard cups from water; uncover. Cool in cups on a wire rack. Cover and chill 3 hours.

• **Run** a knife around edge of custard to loosen; invert each onto a dessert plate. **Yield:** 8 servings.

Note: Custard can also be made in a 9-inch cakepan. Caramelize sugar in cakepan instead of saucepan.

Elegant Entertaining

Elegant Holiday Buffet

Serves 8 to 10

Curry-Almond Cheese Spread   Assorted crackers
Spicy Holiday Meatballs
Holiday Beef Tenderloin   Escalloped Potatoes
Artichoke-Stuffed Mushrooms
Asparagus Rollups   Banana-Nut Bread

West Virginians Robin Jean Davis and Scott Segal decided on a whim to treat their friends to a Christmas party. That was eight years ago. The formal event was such a success, the couple has been holding the annual get-together in their Charleston home ever since. Here they share some of their family's favorite recipes enjoyed at the annual event.

CURRY-ALMOND CHEESE SPREAD

Prep: 20 minutes
Chill: 1 hour

2 (8-ounce) packages cream cheese, softened
1 (9-ounce) jar mango chutney
1 cup slivered almonds, toasted
1 tablespoon curry powder
½ teaspoon dry mustard
Toasted slivered almonds
Assorted crackers

• **Process** first 5 ingredients in a food processor until smooth, stopping to scrape down sides. Cover; chill 1 hour.
• **Shape** mixture into a round. Chill until ready to serve. Sprinkle with almonds. Serve with assorted crackers. **Yield:** 3 cups.

SPICY HOLIDAY MEATBALLS

Prep: 30 minutes
Cook: 1 hour
Bake: 25 minutes

2 small onions, finely chopped and divided
2 tablespoons olive oil
1 (10¾-ounce) can tomato puree
1 cup water
¼ cup red wine vinegar
2 to 3 tablespoons prepared mustard
1 tablespoon Worcestershire sauce
1 teaspoon brown sugar
½ teaspoon salt
½ teaspoon chili powder
¼ teaspoon garlic powder
1 pound ground beef
1 small jalapeño pepper, seeded and finely chopped
1 large egg, lightly beaten
½ cup cracker meal
½ cup ketchup
1 teaspoon salt
1 teaspoon pepper
½ teaspoon hot sauce
Garnish: chopped fresh sage

• **Sauté** 1 chopped onion in hot oil in a large skillet over medium-high heat 5 minutes or until tender.

• **Add** tomato puree and next 8 ingredients. Bring to a boil; reduce heat, and simmer, stirring occasionally, 1 hour.
• **Combine** ground beef, remaining 1 chopped onion, jalapeño pepper, and next 5 ingredients. Shape mixture into 40 (½-inch) balls. Place on a lightly greased rack in a roasting pan.
• **Bake** at 350° for 25 minutes or until no longer pink; add to sauce in skillet, stirring gently to coat. Stir in hot sauce just before serving. Garnish, if desired. **Yield:** 10 to 12 servings.

Note: Cooked or uncooked meatballs may be frozen up to 1 month. Reheat frozen cooked meatballs in a 350° oven 10 to 12 minutes or until thoroughly heated. Bake uncooked frozen meatballs in a 350° oven 25 minutes. Freeze sauce separately; thaw in refrigerator, and cook until thoroughly heated.

HOLIDAY BEEF TENDERLOIN

(pictured on page 1)

Prep: 10 minutes
Chill: 8 hours
Bake: 35 minutes

1 tablespoon salt
1½ teaspoons onion powder
1½ teaspoons garlic powder
1½ teaspoons pepper
1 teaspoon ground red pepper
½ teaspoon ground cumin
½ teaspoon ground nutmeg
1 (5-pound) beef tenderloin, trimmed
¼ cup olive oil
Garnishes: fresh rosemary sprigs, fresh sage sprigs

• **Combine** first 7 ingredients.
• **Rub** tenderloin with oil; coat with spice mixture. Place in a roasting pan; cover and chill 8 hours.
• **Bake** at 500° for 15 minutes or until lightly browned. Lower temperature to 375°; bake 20 more minutes or until desired degree of doneness. Let stand 10 minutes. Slice, and serve with horseradish mayonnaise. Garnish, if desired. **Yield:** 8 servings.

Holiday Dinners

ESCALLOPED POTATOES

Prep: 45 minutes
Cook: 30 minutes
Bake: 35 minutes

6 medium potatoes, peeled and thinly
    sliced (about 3 pounds)
6 to 8 bacon slices
1 large onion, thinly sliced
⅓ cup chopped fresh chives
2 cups (8 ounces) shredded sharp
    Cheddar cheese
1 teaspoon salt
¾ teaspoon pepper
¼ cup butter or margarine
¼ cup all-purpose flour
3 cups milk

• **Bring** potato and salted water to cover to a boil in a saucepan over medium heat; reduce heat, and cook 8 minutes or until tender. Drain and set aside.
• **Cook** bacon in a large skillet until crisp. Drain bacon on paper towels, reserving 2 tablespoons drippings in skillet. Crumble bacon, and set aside.
• **Sauté** onion in drippings in skillet over medium-high heat 15 minutes or until tender. Stir in bacon and chives.
• **Layer** a lightly greased 13- x 9-inch baking dish with one-third of potato slices, one-third of onion mixture, and ⅔ cup cheese, and sprinkle with ⅓ teaspoon salt and ¼ teaspoon pepper. Repeat twice.
• **Melt** butter in a heavy saucepan over low heat; whisk in flour until smooth. Cook, whisking constantly, 1 minute. Gradually whisk in milk until smooth. Pour over potato mixture. Bake at 400° for 35 minutes or until golden. Let stand 10 minutes. **Yield:** 8 to 10 servings.

ARTICHOKE-STUFFED MUSHROOMS

Prep: 25 minutes
Cook: 10 minutes
Bake: 15 minutes

1½ pounds large fresh mushrooms
¼ cup chopped onion
2 garlic cloves, chopped
1 tablespoon olive oil
¼ cup dry white wine
¼ cup soft breadcrumbs
1 (14-ounce) can artichoke hearts,
    drained and chopped
3 green onions, chopped
½ cup grated Parmesan cheese
½ cup mayonnaise
¼ teaspoon salt
¼ teaspoon pepper

• **Rinse** mushrooms; pat dry. Remove stems; chop. Reserve mushroom caps.
• **Sauté** mushroom stems, onion, and garlic in hot oil in a skillet over medium heat 5 minutes or until onion is tender.
• **Add** wine, and cook 2 minutes or until liquid evaporates. Stir in breadcrumbs. Remove from heat, and cool.
• **Combine** onion mixture, artichoke, and remaining 5 ingredients. Spoon 1 teaspoonful into each cap. Place on a lightly greased rack in a roasting pan.
• **Bake** at 350° for 12 to 15 minutes or until golden. **Yield:** 25 to 30 appetizer servings.

ASPARAGUS ROLLUPS

Prep: 25 minutes
Bake: 12 minutes

24 fresh asparagus spears
1 (8-ounce) package cream cheese,
    softened
1 (4-ounce) package crumbled blue
    cheese
2 tablespoons mayonnaise
1 tablespoon chopped fresh chives
12 bread slices, trimmed
12 thinly sliced deli ham slices
¼ cup butter or margarine, melted
Paprika

• **Snap** off tough ends of asparagus. Arrange asparagus in a steamer basket over boiling water. Cover and steam 4 to 6 minutes or until crisp-tender. Remove from steamer; cool.
• **Stir** together cream cheese and next 3 ingredients. Roll each bread slice with a rolling pin to flatten. Spread 1 side of each slice with 2 tablespoons cream cheese mixture; top with 1 ham slice.
• **Place** 2 asparagus spears, tips toward opposite ends, on 1 end of each bread slice; roll up, and place, seam side down, on a greased baking sheet. Brush with butter; sprinkle with paprika.
• **Bake** at 400° for 12 minutes or until golden. Serve immediately. **Yield:** 12 appetizer servings.

Note: Freeze unbaked rollups up to 1 month in an airtight container. Thaw in refrigerator, and bake as directed.

BANANA-NUT BREAD

Prep: 10 minutes
Bake: 1 hour
Cool: 30 minutes

1 cup sugar
½ cup shortening
2 large eggs
3 small bananas, mashed
1 teaspoon vanilla extract
2 cups all-purpose flour
1 teaspoon baking powder
½ teaspoon baking soda
1 teaspoon salt
½ cup chopped walnuts, toasted

• **Beat** sugar and shortening at medium speed with an electric mixer until creamy. Add eggs, banana, and vanilla, beating well. Combine flour and next 3 ingredients; add to banana mixture, beating until combined. Stir in walnuts.
• **Pour** into a greased and floured 8-inch loafpan. Bake at 350° for 1 hour or until a wooden pick inserted in center comes out clean. Cool on a wire rack 10 minutes; remove loaf from pan, and cool completely on wire rack. **Yield:** 1 loaf.

Festive Party Sippers

Toast the season

with an array of alcohol-free punches.

Think that nonalcoholic drinks are boring? Well, think again. These libations offer plenty of satisfaction. Teetotalers and imbibers alike will welcome these alternatives to plain sodas and juices. They're all the more spirited when garnished and served in decorative glasses. Cheers!

MULLED CRANBERRY TEA

Prep: 10 minutes
Cook: 15 minutes

4 to 6 (5-inch) cinnamon sticks
1 tablespoon whole cloves
2 cups sugar
2 quarts water
1 (32-ounce) bottle cranberry juice
¼ cup lemon juice
1 cup orange juice
Garnish: whole cranberries

• **Place** cinnamon sticks and cloves in a 4-inch square of cheesecloth, and tie with string.
• **Bring** spice bag and next 4 ingredients to a boil in a large saucepan. Reduce heat; simmer 10 minutes.
• **Remove** and discard spice bag, and stir in orange juice. Serve hot or cold. Garnish, if desired. **Yield:** 3¼ quarts.

Glenna Wilson
Florence, Alabama

PINEAPPLE WASSAIL

Prep: 5 minutes
Cook: 20 minutes

4 cups unsweetened pineapple juice
1 (12-ounce) can apricot nectar
2 cups apple cider
1 cup orange juice
1 teaspoon whole cloves
3 (6-inch) cinnamon sticks, broken

• **Bring** all ingredients to a boil in a Dutch oven; reduce heat, and simmer 20 minutes. Pour through a strainer; discard spices. Serve hot. **Yield:** 2 quarts.

Marilu Peck
Concord, North Carolina

CREAMY NOG PUNCH

Prep: 10 minutes

1 gallon vanilla ice cream
½ gallon eggnog
1 teaspoon ground nutmeg
½ teaspoon ground cinnamon
1 (16-ounce) container frozen whipped topping, thawed

• **Scoop** ice cream into a punch bowl. Pour eggnog over ice cream; sprinkle with nutmeg and cinnamon; stir in whipped topping. Serve immediately. Stir, as needed. **Yield:** 1½ gallons.

Paula Kay Wilson
Texarkana, Texas

CHRISTMAS FRUIT TEA

Prep: 5 minutes
Chill: 30 minutes

1 gallon unsweetened tea
1 (46-ounce) can unsweetened pineapple juice
½ gallon lemonade
½ gallon orange juice
½ gallon cranberry juice cocktail
½ gallon apple juice
2 cups sugar
1 (6-ounce) package mulling spices
1 (2-liter) bottle ginger ale

• **Stir** together first 8 ingredients in a large 5-gallon container. Chill 30 minutes. Stir in ginger ale just before serving. **Yield:** 5 gallons.

Marcia Mullins
Brentwood, Tennessee

SPICED MOCHA MELT

Prep: 10 minutes
Cook: 5 minutes

1 (4-ounce) sweet dark chocolate bar, chopped
¾ to 1 cup milk
1 teaspoon instant espresso granules
1 teaspoon vanilla extract
¼ teaspoon ground cinnamon
¼ teaspoon almond extract
4 cups coffee ice cream

• **Cook** first 6 ingredients in a saucepan over low heat, stirring until chocolate melts. Cool.
• **Process** coffee ice cream and chocolate mixture in a blender until smooth. Serve immediately in chilled glasses. **Yield:** 4 cups.

Appetizers Aplenty

Enjoy stress-free entertaining with make-ahead recipes.

Holiday Appetizer Buffet
Serves 12 to 15

Creole Roasted Pecans   Spinach Quiches
Rolled Olive Sandwiches
Pumpkin Pie Dip   Gingersnaps   Apple slices
Triple Chocolate Clusters   Pecan Sticks
Cranberry-Wine Punch

Lost touch with your friends and neighbors during the year? Now is the perfect time to invite them to your home.

Lisa Reid O'Rourke of Baton Rouge shares her secret—cook as much as you can in advance. Her philosophy works well for her big annual holiday gathering. "I invite all my friends," she says. "I start a couple of weeks before the occasion so I will have as few things as possible to do close to the party."

Follow Lisa's recipes so you, too, can enjoy your party as much as your guests.

CREOLE ROASTED PECANS

Prep: 5 minutes
Bake: 45 minutes

3 cups pecan halves
¼ cup butter, melted
1 tablespoon Worcestershire
   sauce
1 teaspoon Creole seasoning

● **Stir** together first 3 ingredients in a 15- x 10-inch jellyroll pan.

● **Bake** at 250° for 45 minutes, stirring every 15 minutes. Drain on paper towels. Sprinkle with Creole seasoning. Store in an airtight container 1 week, or freeze up to 2 months. **Yield:** 3 cups.

SPINACH QUICHES

Prep: 15 minutes
Cook: 10 minutes
Bake: 35 minutes

1 (15-ounce) package refrigerated
   piecrusts
2 tablespoons butter or margarine
1 small onion, chopped
2 green onions, chopped
¼ cup chopped fresh parsley
1 (10-ounce) package frozen chopped
   spinach, thawed and well drained
1 tablespoon Worcestershire sauce
1 teaspoon salt
½ teaspoon pepper
3 large eggs
¼ cup milk
1 cup (4 ounces) shredded Swiss
   cheese

● **Roll** each piecrust into a 12-inch square; cut each square into 24 pieces. Shape into balls, and press into lightly greased miniature muffin pans.

● **Melt** butter in a large skillet over medium heat. Add onions and parsley; sauté until onions are tender. Add spinach; cook 2 minutes. Stir in Worcestershire sauce, salt, and pepper. Remove from heat.

● **Whisk** together eggs and milk until blended; stir in cheese. Add egg mixture to spinach mixture; spoon evenly into prepared pans.

● **Bake** at 350° for 30 to 35 minutes. Remove immediately from pans, and cool on wire racks. Freeze quiches up to 2 months. **Yield:** 4 dozen.

Note: Thaw frozen quiches in refrigerator; bake at 300° for 10 minutes or until thoroughly heated.

ROLLED OLIVE SANDWICHES

Prep: 20 minutes
Chill: 4 hours

24 thin sandwich bread slices
1 (8-ounce) package cream cheese,
   softened
1 cup diced salad olives
½ cup chopped pecans, toasted
½ cup mayonnaise
¼ teaspoon pepper

● **Remove** crusts from bread; reserve crusts for another use. Flatten bread slices with a rolling pin.

● **Stir** together cream cheese and remaining 4 ingredients. Spread 2 tablespoons cream cheese mixture on 1 side of each bread slice. Roll up tightly; cover and chill at least 4 hours. To serve, cut each roll into 4 slices. **Yield:** 8 dozen.

PUMPKIN PIE DIP

Crisp apple slices and crunchy gingersnaps complement this smooth, spice-flavored dip.

Prep: 5 minutes
Chill: 8 hours

1 (8-ounce) package cream cheese, softened
2 cups powdered sugar
1 (15-ounce) can pumpkin pie filling
1 teaspoon ground cinnamon
½ teaspoon ground ginger
Garnishes: ground cinnamon, cinnamon sticks

• **Beat** cream cheese and sugar at medium speed with an electric mixer until smooth. Add pie filling, 1 teaspoon cinnamon, and ginger, beating well. Cover and chill 8 hours. Serve with gingersnaps and apple slices. Garnish, if desired. **Yield:** 3 cups.

TRIPLE CHOCOLATE CLUSTERS

Prep: 20 minutes

2 (4-ounce) white chocolate bars
1 cup milk chocolate morsels
1 cup (6 ounces) semisweet chocolate morsels
1½ cups chopped pecans
1½ cups broken pretzels

• **Melt** first 3 ingredients in a heavy saucepan over low heat, stirring constantly. Stir in pecans and pretzels. Drop by tablespoonfuls onto lightly greased wax paper. Cool until hardened. Store in an airtight container in refrigerator up to 1 month. **Yield:** about 6 dozen.

PECAN STICKS

Prep: 7 minutes
Bake: 25 minutes

1 cup butter or margarine, softened
1 cup sugar
1 large egg, separated
2 cups all-purpose flour
1 teaspoon ground cinnamon
1 teaspoon ground nutmeg
1 teaspoon vanilla extract
1¼ cups chopped pecans

• **Beat** butter and sugar at medium speed with an electric mixer until creamy; add egg yolk, flour, and next 3 ingredients, beating well. Press mixture evenly into a lightly greased 15- x 10-inch jellyroll pan.
• **Beat** egg white until soft peaks form; spread over dough in pan. Sprinkle with chopped pecans, gently pressing into dough.
• **Bake** at 325° for 25 minutes. Cut into 2- x 1-inch sticks while warm. Cool on wire racks. Store in an airtight container up to 2 weeks or freeze up to 3 months. **Yield:** about 5 dozen.

CRANBERRY-WINE PUNCH

Prep: 15 minutes
Freeze: 8 hours

1 (10-ounce) package frozen strawberries, thawed
½ cup sugar
½ cup brandy
1 (48-ounce) bottle cranberry juice cocktail, chilled
1 (750-milliliter) bottle sparkling white wine, chilled
1 (28-ounce) bottle club soda, chilled

• **Mash** strawberries with a potato masher or fork in a large bowl; stir in sugar, brandy, and cranberry juice. Cover and freeze 8 hours.
• **Transfer** to a punch bowl; add wine and club soda. **Yield:** about 14 cups.

Brunch With the Family

Christmas morning brunch is a 40-year tradition for Jeanne and Raymond Wilson. They started it so their parents could celebrate with children and grandchildren in the Norfolk, Virginia, area. Sample some of their favorite recipes.

CINNAMON ROLLS
(pictured on page 267)

Prep: 25 minutes
Rise: 2 hours, 40 minutes
Bake: 17 minutes

¼ cup warm water (100° to 110°)
1 (¼-ounce) envelope active dry yeast
¾ cup sugar, divided
2½ to 2⅔ cups all-purpose flour, divided
¾ cup warm milk (100° to 110°)
1 teaspoon salt
1 large egg, lightly beaten
¼ cup shortening
¼ cup butter or margarine, softened
2 teaspoons ground cinnamon
2 cups powdered sugar
3 to 4 tablespoons milk
¼ teaspoon vanilla extract

• **Stir** together ¼ cup warm water, yeast, and ¼ cup sugar, and let stand 5 minutes.
• **Combine** yeast mixture, 1¾ cups flour, milk, salt, egg, and shortening in a large mixing bowl. Beat at medium speed with an electric mixer until well blended. Gradually stir in enough remaining flour to make a soft dough.
• **Turn** dough out onto a well-floured surface; knead until smooth and elastic (about 5 minutes). Place in a well-greased bowl, turning to grease top.

Legacy of Sweets

Create holiday memories with these delicious,

down-home desserts.

• **Cover** and let rise in a warm place (85°), free from drafts, 1½ hours or until doubled in bulk.
• **Punch** dough down; cover and let rise in a warm place, free from drafts, 30 minutes or until doubled in bulk.
• **Turn** dough out onto a floured surface, and roll dough into a 15- x 9-inch rectangle. Spread with butter, and sprinkle with remaining ½ cup sugar and cinnamon.
• **Roll up,** jellyroll fashion, starting at a long edge. Cut dough into 1-inch slices. Arrange in a lightly greased 13- x 9-inch pan.
• **Cover** and let rise in a warm place, free from drafts, 30 to 40 minutes or until doubled in bulk.
• **Bake** at 375° for 17 minutes or until done. Stir together powdered sugar, 3 to 4 tablespoons milk, and vanilla until blended, and drizzle over rolls. **Yield:** 14 rolls.

BREAKFAST CASSEROLE

Prep: 15 minutes
Chill: 8 hours
Stand: 30 minutes
Bake: 50 minutes

1½ pounds ground pork sausage
3 to 4 bread slices, cubed
1½ cups (6 ounces) shredded
    Cheddar cheese
9 large eggs
3 cups milk
1½ teaspoons dry mustard
1 teaspoon salt
⅛ teaspoon pepper

• **Cook** sausage in a skillet, stirring until it crumbles and is no longer pink; drain well.
• **Arrange** bread cubes in bottom of a lightly greased 13- x 9-inch baking dish. Top with sausage and cheese.
• **Whisk** together eggs and next 4 ingredients; pour evenly over cheese. Cover and chill 8 hours.
• **Let** stand at room temperature 30 minutes. Bake at 350° for 45 to 50 minutes or until set. **Yield:** 8 to 10 servings.

Battling mall crowds to find the perfect gift is an annual rite for many folks, but for Yolanda Powers of Decatur, Alabama, the best gifts come from her heart—and her kitchen. When her four kids were young, she began baking cakes and pies for gifts and events, and now, throughout the year, she also shares them with friends.

Yolanda attributes her baking passion to growing up in a family of great cooks. She developed her culinary knack while watching her mother, father, and stepfather perfect their talents. And their lessons still inspire her.

One of her fondest memories is receiving an Easy Bake Oven when she was 10 years old and making all of the cake mixes in one day. Her desserts have come a long way since then, but she's never lost sight of the priceless family recipes passed down to her. "My mom was a great cook," she explains, "but I would always add something a little different to her recipes to make them my own." Yolanda takes pride in improvising, but when it comes to baked goods, she admits, "I always measure, even though I hate to."

Taste some of Yolanda's favorite desserts, and you will see why so many of her friends and family look forward to receiving a gift from her. Her philosophy is, "If you don't like cooking it, you just can't make it taste good," and this thought guides her hands in each treat she prepares. No matter which recipe you try, you'll find that love is the ingredient common to them all.

SWEET POTATO PIE
(pictured on page 267)

A warm slice of this pie adds a sweet finish to any holiday meal.

Prep: 10 minutes
Cook: 30 minutes
Bake: 50 minutes

2 pounds sweet potatoes, peeled and sliced
½ cup butter or margarine
3 large eggs
1 cup sugar
½ cup sweetened condensed milk
½ cup evaporated milk
1 teaspoon ground nutmeg
1 teaspoon vanilla extract
1 teaspoon lemon extract
1 (12-ounce) package frozen deep-dish piecrusts, thawed
Garnishes: whipped cream, grated nutmeg

• **Cook** sweet potato in boiling water to cover 30 minutes or until tender; drain.
• **Beat** sweet potato and butter at medium speed with an electric mixer until smooth. Add eggs and next 6 ingredients, beating well. Pour mixture evenly into each piecrust.
• **Bake** at 350° on lower oven rack for 45 to 50 minutes or until set. Garnish, if desired. **Yield:** 2 (9-inch) pies.

Holiday Dinners

RED VELVET CAKE

Prep: 15 minutes
Bake: 22 minutes

½ cup butter or margarine, softened
1½ cups sugar
1 tablespoon white vinegar
1 teaspoon vanilla extract
3 large eggs
1 (1-ounce) bottle liquid red food
    coloring
2½ cups all-purpose flour
2 tablespoons cocoa
1 teaspoon baking soda
½ teaspoon salt
1 cup buttermilk
Cream Cheese Frosting

• **Beat** butter at medium speed with an electric mixer until creamy; gradually add sugar, vinegar, and vanilla, beating well. Add eggs, 1 at a time, beating until blended after each addition. Add food coloring, beating until combined.
• **Combine** flour and next 3 ingredients; add to butter mixture alternately with buttermilk, beginning and ending with flour mixture. Beat at low speed until blended after each addition. Pour into 2 greased and floured 9-inch cakepans.
• **Bake** at 350° for 20 to 22 minutes or until a wooden pick inserted in center comes out clean. Cool in pans on wire racks 5 minutes; remove from pans, and cool on wire racks.
• **Spread** Cream Cheese Frosting between layers and on top and sides of cake. **Yield:** 1 (2-layer) cake.

Cream Cheese Frosting

Prep: 5 minutes

1 (8-ounce) package cream cheese,
    softened
½ cup butter or margarine, softened
1 (16-ounce) package powdered sugar
1½ teaspoons vanilla extract
1 cup chopped pecans

• **Beat** cream cheese and butter until creamy; gradually add sugar and vanilla, beating well. Stir in pecans. **Yield:** 3 cups.

PECAN PIE

Prep: 10 minutes
Bake: 30 minutes

½ (15-ounce) package refrigerated
    piecrusts
4 large eggs
¾ cup sugar
1 cup light corn syrup
½ cup butter or margarine, melted
¼ cup firmly packed light brown
    sugar
1 teaspoon vanilla extract
¼ teaspoon salt
1 cup pecans, coarsely chopped

• **Unfold** 1 piecrust, and roll to press out fold lines. Fit into a 9-inch pieplate according to package directions; fold edges under, and crimp.
• **Whisk** together eggs and next 6 ingredients in a saucepan over low heat until well blended. Pour into piecrust, and sprinkle with pecans.
• **Bake** at 350° on lower rack 30 minutes or until pie is set. **Yield:** 1 (9-inch) pie.

CREAM CHEESE POUND CAKE

This delicately crumbed cake received the highest possible recipe rating from our Test Kitchens Staff.

Prep: 15 minutes
Bake: 1 hour, 40 minutes

1½ cups butter or margarine,
    softened
1 (8-ounce) package cream cheese,
    softened
3 cups sugar
6 large eggs
3 cups all-purpose flour
⅛ teaspoon salt
1 tablespoon vanilla extract

• **Beat** butter and cream cheese at medium speed with an electric mixer until creamy; gradually add sugar, beating well. Add eggs, 1 at a time, beating until blended after each addition.

• **Combine** flour and salt; gradually add to butter mixture, beating at low speed just until blended. Stir in vanilla. Pour batter into a greased and floured 10-inch Bundt pan.
• **Bake** at 300° for 1 hour and 40 minutes or until a wooden pick inserted in center comes out clean. Cool in pan on a wire rack 10 to 15 minutes; remove from pan, and let cool completely on wire rack. **Yield:** 1 (10-inch) cake.

BUTTER COCONUT PIE

Prep: 15 minutes
Bake: 40 minutes

1 (9-inch) frozen piecrust
1 cup sugar
1 tablespoon all-purpose flour
3 large eggs, lightly beaten
1 (3.5-ounce) can sweetened flaked
    coconut
½ cup evaporated milk
⅓ cup butter or margarine, melted
1 teaspoon vanilla extract

• **Line** piecrust with parchment paper; fill with pie weights or dried beans.
• **Bake** at 400° for 10 minutes or until crust is lightly browned. Remove paper and weights.
• **Combine** sugar and flour in a large bowl; stir in eggs, blending well. Stir in coconut and remaining 3 ingredients, blending well. Pour filling into prepared piecrust.
• **Bake** at 325° for 35 to 40 minutes or until pie is set. **Yield:** 1 (9-inch) pie.

Holiday Dinners

A Santa Celebration

This Atlanta family shares a very special evening with friends.

Cindy and Bart McLean and their closest friends and family members know that every Christmas Eve they will be celebrating together at the McLeans' home in Atlanta.

"The party began in 1993," Cindy says. "Neither of our parents were able to visit for the holidays, and some of the neighbors had similar situations, so we started this party. Some of the children have attended every year since."

The party has also grown with time. More than 50 people now attend, ranging "from ages 4 to 84," Cindy says cheerily. The evening starts with appetizers for the adults and a visit from Santa for the kids. When Santa leaves to make his rounds, Cindy serves an elaborate buffet dinner, topped off by an assortment of lavish desserts. The children even have their own Sugar Plum Fairy table, covered with a colorful array of child-friendly sweets.

Enjoy this sampling of recipes from their annual gathering.

WARMED CRANBERRY BRIE

Prep: 10 minutes
Bake: 5 minutes

1 (16-ounce) round Brie
1 (16-ounce) can whole-berry cranberry sauce
¼ cup firmly packed brown sugar
2 tablespoons spiced rum★
½ teaspoon ground nutmeg
¼ cup chopped pecans, toasted

• **Trim** rind from top of Brie, leaving a ⅓-inch border. Place on a baking sheet.

• **Stir** together cranberry sauce and next 3 ingredients; spread mixture evenly over top of Brie. Sprinkle with pecans.
• **Bake** Brie at 500° for 5 minutes. Serve with crackers and apple and pear slices. **Yield:** 8 appetizer servings.

★ Substitute 2 tablespoons orange juice for spiced rum, if desired.

CRAB CAKES

Prep: 15 minutes
Cook: 16 minutes

4 green onions, sliced
⅓ cup mayonnaise
1 large egg, lightly beaten
1 to 2 teaspoons capers
1 teaspoon Cajun seasoning
1 teaspoon Dijon mustard
1 pound fresh lump crabmeat, drained
1½ cups soft breadcrumbs (homemade)
1 tablespoon butter or margarine
1 tablespoon olive oil

• **Stir** together first 6 ingredients in a large bowl; gently fold in crabmeat and breadcrumbs.
• **Shape** mixture into 10 patties.
• **Heat** ½ tablespoon butter and ½ tablespoon oil in a large nonstick skillet over medium-high heat. Cook 5 crab cake patties 4 minutes on each side or until golden. Place crab cakes on paper towels to drain. Repeat procedure with remaining ½ tablespoon butter, remaining ½ tablespoon oil, and remaining crab cake patties. **Yield:** 10 servings.

Cindy McLean
Atlanta, Georgia

TANGY LEMON TART

Prep: 25 minutes
Bake: 30 minutes
Chill: 4 hours, 50 minutes

1¾ cups all-purpose flour
1 cup powdered sugar
¼ teaspoon salt
9 tablespoons cold butter or margarine, cut up
7 large eggs, divided
1½ tablespoons grated lemon rind
½ cup fresh lemon juice (about 4 large lemons)
1 cup sugar
6 tablespoons butter or margarine, softened
Whipped cream (optional)
Garnishes: fresh mint leaves, fresh raspberries

• **Pulse** first 3 ingredients in a food processor 3 or 4 times or until mixture is combined.
• **Add** 9 tablespoons butter; pulse 5 or 6 times or until crumbly. Add 1 egg, and process until dough forms a ball and leaves sides of bowl. Shape dough into a disc; wrap in plastic wrap, and chill 30 minutes.
• **Press** dough into bottom and up sides of a 10-inch tart pan. Prick bottom with a fork. Chill 20 minutes.
• **Line** dough with greased aluminum foil; fill with pie weights or dried beans.
• **Bake** at 350° for 15 minutes. Remove weights and foil; bake 15 more minutes or until lightly browned.
• **Whisk** together remaining 6 eggs, lemon rind, and lemon juice in a non-aluminum saucepan over low heat.
• **Add** sugar and 6 tablespoons butter, and cook, whisking constantly, 8 minutes or until lemon mixture is thickened and bubbly. Let cool 15 to 20 minutes. Pour filling into prepared crust; cover and chill 4 hours or until set. Serve with whipped cream, if desired. Garnish, if desired. **Yield:** 1 (10-inch) tart.

Marilyn Allegra
Atlanta, Georgia

CHOCOLATE-MARSHMALLOW BROWNIES

Although these brownies can be eaten just after they cool, we find them at their best if you let them stand overnight.

Prep: 25 minutes
Bake: 35 minutes
Stand: 8 hours

4 (1-ounce) unsweetened chocolate
    squares
1 cup butter or margarine
2 cups sugar
4 large eggs
1 cup all-purpose flour
⅛ teaspoon salt
2 teaspoons vanilla extract
2 cups (12 ounces) semisweet
    chocolate morsels
2 cups miniature marshmallows

• **Heat** chocolate squares and butter in a saucepan over medium-high heat, stirring constantly, until melted. Stir in sugar, and cook, stirring constantly, until sugar melts. Cool 15 minutes.
• **Add** eggs; stir until blended. Add flour, salt, and vanilla, stirring until blended. Stir in chocolate morsels and marshmallows, and pour into a greased 13- x 9-inch pan.
• **Bake** at 350° for 30 to 35 minutes, and cool in pan on a wire rack. Cover brownies, and let stand at room temperature 8 hours. **Yield:** 24 brownies.

Reuniting for the Holidays

The Pafford family welcomes Thanksgiving with an old-fashioned get-together.

Holiday Family Reunion
Serves 6

Crispy Chicken

Wild Rice Salad   Mexican Cornbread

Iced tea   Chocolate cake

On the third Sunday in November, the Pafford family gathers at Carl and Beverly Pafford's home in Nashville, Georgia. "This is the 24th year we've held the reunion at our place," recalls Beverly, "but it has been going on for more than 50 years." These recipes explain why.

CRISPY CHICKEN

Soak: 8 hours
Prep: 10 minutes
Bake: 1 hour, 10 minutes

1 (3½-pound) package chicken
    pieces, skinned
2 cups buttermilk
½ (16-ounce) package herb-seasoned
    stuffing mix (4 cups)
2 tablespoons grated Parmesan
    cheese
⅛ teaspoon salt
⅛ teaspoon ground red pepper
⅛ teaspoon ground black pepper
½ cup butter, melted

• **Soak** chicken in buttermilk 8 hours. Drain and discard buttermilk.
• **Process** stuffing mix and next 4 ingredients in a food processor or blender until it resembles fine crumbs.
• **Dip** chicken pieces into melted butter, and roll in stuffing mixture until well coated. Place chicken on a baking sheet.
• **Bake** at 350° for 1 hour and 10 minutes or until golden brown. **Yield:** 4 to 6 servings.

Note: For testing purposes only, we used Pepperidge Farm Stuffing.

Cheryl Pafford
Charlotte, North Carolina

Holiday Dinners

WILD RICE SALAD

Prep: 10 minutes
Cook: 10 minutes
Chill: 8 hours

1 (6-ounce) package quick-cooking long-grain and wild rice mix
2 cups chopped cooked chicken
½ cup dried cranberries
1 Granny Smith apple, peeled and diced
1 medium carrot, grated
⅓ cup white balsamic vinegar*
¼ cup olive oil
¼ teaspoon salt
¼ teaspoon pepper
2 green onions, chopped
1 (2.25-ounce) package sliced almonds, toasted

• **Cook** rice according to package directions; cool. Stir together chicken, next 8 ingredients, and rice. Cover; chill 8 hours. Sprinkle with almonds just before serving. **Yield:** 6 servings.

*Substitute red wine vinegar, if desired.

Note: For testing purposes only, we used Uncle Ben's Quick Cooking Long-Grain and Wild Rice Mix.

Brenda Pafford
Nashville, Georgia

MEXICAN CORNBREAD

Prep: 15 minutes
Bake: 40 minutes

½ cup vegetable oil, divided
1 medium onion, chopped
1 garlic clove, minced
1 red bell pepper, finely chopped
1 jalapeño pepper, seeded and finely chopped
1 (15¼-ounce) can whole kernel corn, drained
1½ cups cornmeal mix
1 teaspoon sugar
¼ teaspoon cumin (optional)
¾ cup grated Monterey Jack cheese
2 large eggs
1 cup buttermilk

• **Heat** 2 tablespoons oil in a nonstick skillet over medium heat; add onion and next 4 ingredients. Sauté 10 minutes or until tender. Remove from heat; cool.
• **Stir** together cornmeal mix, next 5 ingredients, and ¼ cup oil until blended. Stir in onion mixture.
• **Heat** remaining 2 tablespoons oil in a 9-inch cast-iron skillet in a 400° oven 10 minutes. Pour cornmeal mixture into skillet.
• **Bake** at 400° for 30 minutes or until done. **Yield:** 8 servings.

Sherry Collins Crews
Nashville, Georgia

Quick Gift Solutions

Planning ahead makes the holidays less hectic, but sometimes even the best laid plans can go awry. A quick-to-fix homemade present from your kitchen will make the season merrier for anyone.

Package these treats in decorative jars, bottles, boxes, or bags, and add a unique or helpful gadget for a special touch. You'll be amazed at how easy such last-minute gifts are to make.

TEX-MEX SPICE MIX

Prep: 10 minutes

3 tablespoons chili powder
2 tablespoons ground cumin
1 tablespoon ground black pepper
1 tablespoon salt
1 tablespoon garlic powder
1½ teaspoons ground red pepper

• **Stir** together all ingredients, and store in an airtight container up to 6 months. Sprinkle on chicken, beef, potatoes, corn, and popped popcorn. **Yield:** ½ cup.

BLOND BROWNIE MIX

Prep: 15 minutes
Bake: 45 minutes

1 (16-ounce) package light brown sugar
2 cups self-rising flour
1½ cups chopped pecans
1½ cups sweetened flaked coconut
1 cup golden raisins

• **Layer** ingredients in order in an airtight 2-quart glass container. Store in a cool, dry place up to 2 months. **Yield:** about 8⅓ cups.
Directions for gift card: Beat 3 large eggs; ½ cup butter, softened; and 1 tablespoon vanilla extract at medium speed with an electric mixer until blended; gradually add Blond Brownie Mix, beating until blended. Spoon into a greased and floured 13- x 9-inch pan. Bake at 350° for 20 minutes; reduce temperature to 325°, and bake 25 more minutes. Cool in pan on a wire rack. Cut into squares. **Yield:** 16 brownies.

Mary Lynn Enfinger
Midland City, Alabama

EASY SWEET-TANGY MUSTARD

Prep: 5 minutes

1 (14-ounce) can sweetened condensed milk
1 (8-ounce) bottle prepared mustard
2 tablespoons prepared horseradish
2 tablespoons Worcestershire sauce

• **Stir** together all ingredients until blended. Store in refrigerator up to 3 months. Serve with pretzels or egg rolls or as a sandwich spread. **Yield:** about 3 cups.

Deborah Pate Shepardson
New Holland, Pennsylvania

PEACH RIB SAUCE

Prep: 10 minutes

1 (6-ounce) jar peach baby food
½ cup firmly packed brown sugar
⅓ cup ketchup
⅓ cup white vinegar
2 tablespoons soy sauce
2 garlic cloves, minced *
1 teaspoon ground ginger

• **Stir** together all ingredients; place in an airtight 2-cup jar, and chill up to 2 weeks. Use as a grilling or basting sauce for pork chops, ribs, or chicken. **Yield:** 1½ cups.

*Substitute ⅛ teaspoon garlic powder for garlic cloves, if desired.

Sandy Isleib
Apex, North Carolina

SEASONED RICE MIX

Prep: 10 minutes
Cook: 20 minutes

3 cups uncooked long-grain rice
¼ cup dried parsley flakes
2 tablespoons chicken bouillon
   granules
2 teaspoons onion powder
½ teaspoon garlic powder
¼ teaspoon dried thyme

• **Stir** together all ingredients. Place 1 cup mixture into each of 3 airtight containers. Store in a cool, dry place. **Yield:** 3 cups.
Directions for gift card: Bring 2 cups water and 1 tablespoon butter or margarine to a boil in a saucepan; stir in rice mix. Cover, reduce heat, and simmer 20 minutes or until liquid is absorbed. **Yield:** 4 servings.

Hilda Marshall
Culpeper, Virginia

Preserving a Southern Christmas Tradition

A transplanted Southerner remembers a beloved friend and mentor and celebrates her heritage.

Southern-Style Christmas
Serves 4 to 6

Curried Butternut-Shrimp Bisque
Topless Oysters   Fresh Tomato Salsa
Roasted Quail With Cranberry-Orange-Pecan Stuffing
Hoppin' John Salad   Sweet Potato Biscuits
Ambrosia With Sprinkles   Key Lime Curd Tartlets

Caroline Stuart, a third generation Floridian, comes from a long line of cooks. Continuing her family's appreciation of food, Caroline moved to New York City after finishing her degree at the University of Alabama. Once in the Big Apple, she became friends with the late James Beard, considered by many to be the father of American cooking.

After Beard's death in 1985, Caroline helped establish the James Beard Foundation, which promotes the culinary profession and offers more than $400,000 a year in culinary scholarships.

Although Caroline and her husband, artist John Brainard, reside north of the Mason-Dixon line, she continues to embrace all things Southern. We're sure you, too, will enjoy sharing these recipes with your family.

CURRIED BUTTERNUT-SHRIMP BISQUE

Prep: 25 minutes
Cook: 30 minutes

1 pound unpeeled, medium-size
   fresh shrimp
3 tablespoons unsalted butter
1 large yellow onion, chopped
1 (3-pound) butternut squash, peeled,
   seeded, and cut into ½-inch cubes
3 (14.5-ounce) cans chicken broth,
   divided
2 teaspoons curry powder
1 teaspoon dried thyme
1 cup whipping cream
¼ teaspoon salt
¼ teaspoon ground red pepper
Garnishes: whipping cream, paprika

Holiday Dinners

• **Peel** shrimp, and devein, if desired. Set aside.

• **Melt** butter in a 4-quart heavy saucepan over medium-high heat; add onion, and sauté 7 to 8 minutes or until tender. Reduce heat to medium; add squash, and cook, stirring occasionally, 15 minutes or until tender.

• **Add** 1 can broth, shrimp, curry, and thyme, and cook 2 to 3 minutes or just until shrimp turn pink. Let cool slightly.

• **Process** mixture in a blender or food processor until smooth, stopping to scrape down sides.

• **Return** mixture to saucepan; add remaining broth, and bring to a boil. Stir in 1 cup cream, salt, and pepper; reduce heat to low, and simmer 5 minutes. Garnish, if desired. **Yield:** 9½ cups.

TOPLESS OYSTERS

Choose from a trio of sauces to dress up oysters on the half shell.

Prep: 55 minutes

2½ cups water
2 fresh kumquats
¼ cup fresh lime juice
1 teaspoon grated fresh ginger
¼ cup rice vinegar
1½ teaspoons lite soy sauce
1 shallot, minced
2 dozen fresh oysters (in the shell)
Fresh Tomato Salsa
Lemon wedges

• **Bring** 2½ cups water to a boil in a small saucepan. Reduce heat, and add kumquats; simmer 1 minute or until tender. Drain; let cool. Remove seeds, and cut kumquats into thin slices.

• **Combine** kumquats, lime juice, and ginger, tossing gently to coat. Set aside.

• **Stir** together vinegar, soy sauce, and shallot.

• **Scrub** oyster shells; open, discarding tops. Arrange shell bottoms (containing oysters) over crushed ice on a serving platter. Serve with kumquat sauce, vinegar sauce, Fresh Tomato Salsa, and lemon wedges. **Yield:** 4 to 6 servings.

Fresh Tomato Salsa

Prep: 10 minutes

3 plum tomatoes, peeled, seeded, and diced
2 tablespoons chopped fresh cilantro
1 tablespoon minced onion
1 to 2 teaspoons minced jalapeño pepper
1 teaspoon fresh lime juice
⅛ teaspoon salt

• **Combine** all ingredients in a small bowl. **Yield:** 1½ cups.

ROASTED QUAIL WITH CRANBERRY-ORANGE-PECAN STUFFING

Prep: 1 hour, 30 minutes
Cook: 27 minutes
Bake: 1 hour
Broil: 4 minutes

1½ cups cranberry juice
1¼ cups sugar
1½ cups fresh or frozen cranberries
1½ teaspoons grated orange rind
½ cup orange juice
¼ cup butter or margarine, melted
Cranberry-Orange-Pecan Stuffing
8 quail, dressed
½ teaspoon salt
½ teaspoon pepper
Garnish: orange rind strips

• **Cook** cranberry juice and sugar in a saucepan over medium heat, stirring constantly, 25 minutes or until sugar dissolves and mixture thickens. Add cranberries and orange rind, and cook, stirring constantly, 2 minutes or until cranberries pop. Remove cranberry glaze from heat; let cool.

• **Stir** together orange juice and melted butter.

• **Spoon** about ¼ cup Cranberry-Orange-Pecan Stuffing into each quail, and tie legs together with string. Sprinkle with salt and pepper; place in a

shallow roasting pan. Brush with orange juice mixture.

• **Bake** at 325° for 1 hour, basting quail with orange juice mixture every 15 minutes. Broil 5½ inches from heat 3 to 4 minutes or until golden, if necessary. Serve with cranberry glaze. Garnish, if desired. **Yield:** 4 servings.

Cranberry-Orange-Pecan Stuffing

Prep: 30 minutes

2 tablespoons butter or margarine
½ medium onion, diced
2 celery ribs, diced
¾ cup chopped pecans, toasted
⅓ cup chopped orange sections
⅓ cup chopped cranberries
1 tablespoon sugar
2 white bread slices, toasted and cut into ½-inch pieces
½ teaspoon salt
½ teaspoon dried thyme
½ teaspoon rubbed sage
1 large egg, lightly beaten
2 tablespoons orange juice

• **Melt** butter in a large saucepan over medium heat; add onion and celery, and sauté until onion is tender. Stir in pecans and next 3 ingredients; remove from heat.

• **Combine** bread pieces and next 3 ingredients in a bowl, and add to cranberry mixture, stirring until mixture is combined. Stir in egg and orange juice. **Yield:** 2 cups.

Holiday Dinners

HOPPIN' JOHN SALAD

Prep: 20 minutes
Chill: 4 hours

2 celery ribs
1 yellow bell pepper
1 red bell pepper
½ medium onion
4 (15-ounce) cans black-eyed peas,
    rinsed and drained
2 jalapeño peppers, seeded and diced
2 tablespoons chopped fresh parsley
1 garlic clove, minced
1 teaspoon salt
1 teaspoon freshly ground pepper
½ teaspoon ground cumin
½ cup red wine vinegar
2 tablespoons balsamic vinegar
¼ cup olive oil
4 bacon slices, cooked and crumbled
Garnish: chopped fresh parsley

• **Dice** first 4 ingredients. Combine diced vegetables, peas, and next 6 ingredients in a large bowl.
• **Combine** vinegars in a small bowl, and whisk in oil in a slow, steady stream, blending well. Add to vegetable mixture, tossing gently to coat. Cover and chill 3 to 4 hours.
• **Stir** in bacon. Garnish, if desired. **Yield:** 7 cups.

SWEET POTATO BISCUITS

(pictured on page 1)

Prep: 25 minutes
Rise: 4 hours, 30 minutes
Bake: 12 minutes

1 (¼-ounce) envelope active dry yeast
¼ cup warm water (100° to 110°)
1 (15-ounce) can sweet potatoes
    in syrup, drained and mashed
½ cup butter or margarine, softened
½ cup sugar
1 teaspoon salt
2½ cups all-purpose flour
1 teaspoon baking powder
Melted butter

• **Combine** yeast and ¼ cup warm water in a glass measuring cup; let stand 5 minutes.
• **Stir** together sweet potato and butter, blending well. Stir in sugar and salt; add yeast mixture, stirring until smooth.
• **Combine** flour and baking powder; gradually stir into potato mixture until well blended. Lightly knead until dough holds together.
• **Shape** dough into a ball; place in a greased mixing bowl. Brush top with melted butter. Cover and let rise in a warm place (85°), free from drafts, 2½ hours or until doubled in bulk.
• **Punch** dough down, and turn out onto a floured surface. Roll dough to ½-inch thickness; cut with a 2-inch round cutter, and place on greased baking sheets. Cover and let rise in a warm place, free from drafts, 2 hours or until doubled in bulk.
• **Bake** at 400° for 12 minutes or until golden. **Yield:** 34 biscuits.

AMBROSIA WITH SPRINKLES

Add the sparkle of seasonal citrus to your dinner table with this colorful dish.

Prep: 20 minutes
Chill: 8 hours

7 to 8 navel oranges, peeled, seeded,
    and sectioned
½ pineapple, peeled and cut into chunks
¾ cup orange juice
2 bananas, sliced
2 tablespoons lemon juice
Sugar (optional)
1½ cups pecan halves, toasted
1¼ cups sweetened flaked coconut,
    toasted

• **Combine** first 3 ingredients in a large bowl, gently tossing to coat. Cover and chill 8 hours.
• **Toss** together banana and lemon juice, and add to orange mixture. Sprinkle fruit mixture with sugar, if desired. Sprinkle each serving evenly with toasted pecans and coconut. **Yield:** 8 servings.

KEY LIME CURD TARTLETS

This refreshing, lip-puckering dessert makes an ideal ending to your Christmas meal.

Prep: 45 minutes
Chill: 8 hours
Bake: 13 minutes

4 large eggs
⅔ cup fresh Key lime juice
¾ cup sugar
6 tablespoons unsalted butter
2 teaspoons grated Key lime rind
1¼ cups all-purpose flour
¾ cup sifted cake flour
1½ tablespoons sugar
¾ teaspoon salt
¼ teaspoon baking powder
1 cup butter or margarine,
    cut up
¼ cup shortening
6 tablespoons cold water
1 pint fresh strawberries,
    sliced

• **Whisk** together first 4 ingredients in a saucepan, and cook over medium-low heat, whisking constantly, 12 minutes or until mixture is thickened. Stir in lime rind. Pour carefully through a wire-mesh strainer into a bowl. Cover mixture, and refrigerate 4 to 6 hours.
• **Pulse** flours, sugar, salt, and baking powder in a food processor until combined. Add 1 cup butter and shortening, and pulse until mixture is crumbly. Add cold water, 1 tablespoon at a time, pulsing after each addition. Remove dough, and wrap in plastic wrap; chill at least 2 hours.
• **Shape** dough into 34 (1-inch) balls, and press balls into lightly greased miniature tart pans. Prick with a fork.
• **Bake** at 375° for 13 minutes or until golden. Remove from pans, and let cool on wire racks.
• **Spoon** 1 to 2 teaspoons lime curd into each tart shell; top with strawberry slices. **Yield:** 34 tartlets.

Note: Substitute miniature muffin pans for the miniature tart pans, if desired.

Wrapped for the Holidays

Need an updated look for traditional holiday meats? Wrap them in delicate phyllo dough or rich puff pastry to make a lasting impression on your guests. Careful, unhurried preparation and a few pointers simplify the process. See "It's A Wrap" at right.

CHEESE-STUFFED CHICKEN IN PHYLLO

Prep: 25 minutes
Cook: 7 minutes
Bake: 40 minutes

8 skinned and boned chicken breast halves
1 teaspoon salt
½ teaspoon pepper
4 cups chopped fresh spinach
1 medium onion, chopped
2 tablespoons olive or vegetable oil
½ (8-ounce) package cream cheese, softened and cut up
1 cup (4 ounces) shredded mozzarella cheese
½ cup (2 ounces) crumbled feta cheese
½ cup (2 ounces) shredded Cheddar cheese
1 egg yolk, lightly beaten
1 tablespoon all-purpose flour
½ teaspoon ground nutmeg
½ teaspoon ground cumin
16 frozen phyllo pastry sheets, thawed
Melted butter or margarine

• **Place** chicken between 2 sheets of heavy-duty plastic wrap, and flatten to ⅛-inch thickness, using a meat mallet or rolling pin. Sprinkle evenly with salt and pepper, and set aside.
• **Sauté** spinach and onion in hot oil in a large skillet over medium-high heat 3 to

4 minutes or until onion is tender. Remove from heat, and stir in cream cheese until blended. Stir in mozzarella and next 6 ingredients. Spoon ¼ cup spinach mixture on each chicken breast half; roll up, jellyroll fashion.
• **Unfold** phyllo on a lightly floured surface. Stack 2 sheets, brushing with butter between sheets. (Keep remaining sheets covered with plastic wrap.) Place 1 chicken roll on short side of phyllo stack; gently roll up, folding in long side. Repeat procedure with remaining pastry, butter, and chicken. Place rolls in a shallow pan; brush with butter.
• **Bake** at 350° for 35 to 40 minutes or until done. **Yield:** 8 servings.

Betty Rabe
Plano, Texas

HOLIDAY CHICKEN PRESENTS

Prep: 1 hour, 15 minutes
Cook: 20 minutes
Bake: 35 minutes

1 pound skinned and boned chicken breast halves
¾ teaspoon garlic salt
2 tablespoons butter or margarine
2 shallots, chopped
½ small onion, minced
2 cups fresh mushrooms, sliced
½ (8-ounce) package cream cheese, softened
2 tablespoons milk
2 tablespoons sherry
1 teaspoon grated Parmesan cheese
⅛ teaspoon salt
⅛ teaspoon pepper
2 (17¼-ounce) packages frozen puff pastry sheets, thawed
12 (1-ounce) Swiss cheese slices
12 (1-ounce) country ham slices
1 egg white, lightly beaten
½ cup butter or margarine, melted
¼ cup Dijon mustard
1 teaspoon poppy seeds
1 teaspoon lemon juice

• **Sprinkle** chicken with garlic salt.
• **Cook** chicken in a lightly greased nonstick skillet over medium-high heat

7 to 8 minutes on each side or until lightly browned. Remove from skillet; chop chicken, and set aside.
• **Melt** 2 tablespoons butter in skillet over medium heat; add shallots and onion, and sauté 3 minutes. Add mushrooms; sauté 5 minutes. Reduce heat to low; add cream cheese and milk, stirring until blended. Remove from heat, and add chopped chicken. Stir in sherry and next 3 ingredients.
• **Unfold** 3 pastry sheets on a lightly floured surface; cut into fourths. Roll into 10-inch squares. Place 1 cheese slice and 1 ham slice in center of each puff pastry square; top with ¼ cup chicken mixture. Bring corners together over filling, gently pressing to seal.
• **Cut** remaining pastry sheet into thin strips; tie each bundle with pastry ribbon. Place on a baking sheet; brush with egg white.
• **Bake** at 400° for 35 minutes or until golden. Whisk together melted butter and remaining 3 ingredients. Serve over pastry bundles. **Yield:** 12 servings.

Rollin McLennan
Atlanta, Georgia

IT'S A WRAP

■ Thaw frozen phyllo in refrigerator to avoid sticky dough.

■ Cover phyllo with plastic wrap and a damp towel until ready to use to prevent drying out.

■ Instead of brushing phyllo with butter, use butter-flavored cooking spray to save calories.

■ Thaw frozen puff pastry (20 minutes at room temperature) before using, but keep refrigerated until ready to use.

■ Dust flat surfaces lightly with flour when using either pastry.

Irresistible Desserts

The season calls for a fantastic finale
to celebrate special meals.

MINI BEEF WELLINGTONS

Prep: 35 minutes
Bake: 30 minutes
Cook: 25 minutes

- 6½ tablespoons butter or margarine, divided
- 8 (3-ounce) beef tenderloin fillets, 1 inch thick
- ¼ teaspoon salt
- ¼ teaspoon pepper
- 3 large fresh mushrooms, chopped
- 1 (8-ounce) package fresh mushrooms, chopped
- 2 tablespoons dry sherry or beef broth
- 1 (17¼-ounce) package frozen puff pastry sheets, thawed
- 1 egg white, lightly beaten
- 1½ tablespoons all-purpose flour
- 1 tablespoon tomato paste
- 2 (14½-ounce) cans beef broth
- 1 bay leaf, crushed

• **Melt** 3 tablespoons butter in a large skillet over medium heat; add beef, and cook 3 minutes on each side or until browned. Remove from skillet; sprinkle with salt and pepper, and let cool.

• **Melt** 2 tablespoons butter in skillet; add mushrooms, and sauté 5 minutes. Stir in sherry.

• **Unfold** pastry sheets on a lightly floured surface; roll to ⅛-inch thickness, and cut into fourths. Place 1 fillet in center of each square; top with mushroom mixture. Bring opposite corners of squares together over beef, gently pressing to seal. Place on a baking sheet; brush with egg white.

• **Bake** at 425° on the lowest oven rack for 25 to 30 minutes or until golden.

• **Melt** remaining 1½ tablespoons butter in skillet; whisk in flour. Cook, whisking constantly, 2 to 3 minutes or until lightly browned. Add tomato paste; cook, stirring constantly, 1 to 2 minutes. Gradually whisk in broth. Add bay leaf; simmer 20 minutes. Pour through a wire-mesh strainer into a bowl. Serve sauce with Beef Wellingtons. **Yield:** 8 servings.

Sue Siegel
Seminole, Florida

The happy ending to the meal should complement the rest of your menu. If you serve a heavy dinner, follow it with a simple treat, such as Pecan Pound Cake. A richer dessert is more appropriate with a lighter meal. Of course, during the holidays, all rules may be bent or broken.

If time is a factor, try a sweet that can be prepared in advance. Regardless of which of these creations you choose, all can be served with pride and eaten with pleasure.

CHOCOLATE-VANILLA HOLIDAY TORTE
(pictured on page 268)

Wrap up your holiday meal with this elegant dessert.

Prep: 40 minutes
Bake: 2 hours
Chill: 8 hours

- 2 (8-ounce) packages semisweet chocolate squares, chopped
- 1 cup butter or margarine, cut into pieces
- 3 cups sugar, divided
- 11 large eggs, divided
- 3 (8-ounce) packages cream cheese, softened
- 3 tablespoons all-purpose flour
- 1 (8-ounce) container sour cream
- 4 (1-ounce) white chocolate squares, grated
- 1 tablespoon vanilla extract
- White Chocolate Ganache
- Burgundy food paste color
- White Chocolate Ribbons and Bow
- Garnish: silver ornaments

• **Line** 2 (9-inch) square cakepans with aluminum foil; grease foil.

• **Cook** semisweet chocolate and butter in a small saucepan over low heat, stirring until blended. Cool.

• **Beat** 2 cups sugar and 8 eggs at medium speed with an electric mixer 3 minutes or until foamy. Gradually add chocolate mixture, beating at low speed until blended. Pour into 1 prepared pan.

• **Bake** at 325° for 1 hour or until set. Cool on a wire rack. Cover and chill 8 hours. Remove from pan, discarding foil. Trim edges, if necessary.

• **Beat** cream cheese at medium speed with an electric mixer until creamy. Add remaining 1 cup sugar and flour, beating well. Add remaining 3 eggs, 1 at a time, beating just until blended after each addition. Stir in sour cream, white chocolate, and vanilla. Pour into remaining prepared pan.

• **Bake** at 325° for 1 hour. Turn oven off. Leave cake layer in oven, with oven door partially opened, 30 minutes. Remove cake from oven; cool in pan on a wire rack. Cover cake; chill 8 hours. Remove from pan, discarding foil.

• **Reserve** 1 cup White Chocolate Ganache.

• **Place** chocolate layer, bottom side up, on a serving plate. Spread with ½ cup White Chocolate Ganache, and top with white chocolate layer, bottom side up. Spread top and sides of cake with remaining ganache.

• **Stir** desired amount of food paste into reserved 1 cup ganache.

• **Insert** metal tip No. 2 into a large decorating bag; fill with ganache. Pipe lace design (continuous string of frosting without touching) on top and sides of cake.

• **Arrange** 2 (17- x 2½-inch) White Chocolate Ribbons on cake. Form bow with 1 (13- x 2½-inch) strip; arrange 2 (4- x 2½-inch) strips and 2 (3- x 2½-inch) strips for bow ends. Place 1 (2½- x 1-inch) strip in center of bow for knot.

• **Store** cake in refrigerator. Remove from refrigerator; let stand at room temperature 1 hour before serving. Garnish, if desired. **Yield:** 1 (2-layer) torte.

White Chocolate Ganache

Prep: 5 minutes
Chill: 45 minutes

2 (12-ounce) packages white
    chocolate morsels
1 cup whipping cream

• **Cook** chocolate morsels and cream in a heavy saucepan over low heat, stirring often, until chocolate melts. Chill 45 minutes or until thickened. Beat at medium speed with an electric mixer until spreading consistency. **Yield:** 5 cups.

White Chocolate Ribbons and Bow

Prep: 1 hour

6 ounces vanilla bark coating
3½ tablespoons light corn syrup
Burgundy food paste color

• **Melt** coating in a small saucepan over low heat. Remove from heat; stir in corn syrup and desired amount of food paste. Cover; chill 1 hour.

• **Knead** mixture until the consistency of dough. (Kneading with warm hands keeps mixture soft; letting it stand on a cool surface hardens it.)

• **Roll** bark coating mixture out onto a cool surface to ⅛-inch thickness. Using a fluted pastry wheel, cut into 2 (17- x 2½-inch) ribbons. Cut remaining mixture into 1 (13- x 2½-inch) strip, 2 (4- x 2½-inch) strips, 2 (3- x 2½-inch) strips, and 1 (2½- x 1-inch) strip. **Yield:** enough for 2 ribbons and 1 bow.

ALMOND-APPLE TART

Prep: 30 minutes
Bake: 40 minutes

1 (15-ounce) package refrigerated
    piecrusts
6½ tablespoons butter or margarine,
    softened and divided
4 ounces almond paste, crumbled
5 tablespoons sugar, divided
¼ cup brandy, divided
⅓ cup plus 2 tablespoons all-purpose
    flour, divided
1 large egg
1 teaspoon vanilla extract
¼ teaspoon almond extract
2 medium Granny Smith apples, peeled
    and thinly sliced
½ cup apricot preserves
1 tablespoon whipping cream

• **Unfold** piecrusts; stack on a lightly floured surface. Roll into a 12-inch circle. Fit into a 10-inch tart pan with removable bottom; trim excess pastry.

• **Beat** 4 tablespoons butter, almond paste, 1 tablespoon sugar, 2 tablespoons brandy, ⅓ cup flour, and next 3 ingredients at medium speed with an electric mixer until blended; spread in crust.

• **Toss** together 2 tablespoons sugar and apple; arrange in circles, overlapping slices, on top of filling.

• **Cook** preserves in a saucepan over low heat until melted. Pour through a fine wire-mesh strainer, discarding solids. Stir in 1 tablespoon butter, remaining 2 tablespoons brandy, and cream; drizzle over apple.

• **Combine** remaining 2 tablespoons sugar and remaining 2 tablespoons flour, and cut in remaining 1½ tablespoons butter with a fork until crumbly. Sprinkle evenly over apple.

• **Bake** at 400° on bottom rack 40 minutes. Cool in pan on a wire rack 15 minutes. **Yield:** 1 (10-inch) tart.

Almond-Pear Tart: Substitute 2 red pears, unpeeled and thinly sliced, for Granny Smith apples.

Patricia A. Davy
Oak Ridge, Tennessee

PECAN POUND CAKE

Prep: 15 minutes
Bake: 1 hour, 30 minutes

1½ cups butter or margarine, softened
1 (8-ounce) package cream cheese,
    softened
3 cups sugar
6 large eggs
3 cups all-purpose flour
½ teaspoon salt
¼ cup bourbon or milk
1½ teaspoons vanilla extract
1½ cups chopped pecans, toasted

• **Beat** butter and cream cheese at medium speed with an electric mixer about 2 minutes or until creamy. Gradually add sugar, beating 5 minutes. Add eggs, 1 at a time, beating just until yellow disappears.

• **Combine** flour and salt, and add to butter mixture alternately with bourbon, beginning and ending with flour mixture. Beat at low speed just until blended after each addition. Stir in vanilla and chopped pecans. Pour into a greased and floured 10-inch tube pan.

• **Bake** at 325° for 1 hour and 30 minutes or until a long wooden pick inserted in center comes out clean. Cool in pan on a wire rack 10 to 15 minutes. Remove from pan, and cool completely on wire rack. **Yield:** 1 (10-inch) cake.

Wiley R. Beales
Elizabeth City, North Carolina

Living Light

A Trim Thanksgiving Menu
Serves 10

Tomato-Basil Toasts*

Citrus-and-Herb Turkey   Cranberry Salsa*

Rosemary Roasted Root Vegetables*

Parmesan Corn Muffins   Cinnamon Swirl Cake

* Double recipes to serve 10.

TOMATO-BASIL TOASTS

Prep: 20 minutes
Chill: 1 hour
Bake: 9 minutes

8 plum tomatoes, seeded and chopped
2 green onions, chopped
1 garlic clove, minced
¼ cup balsamic vinegar
2 tablespoons chopped fresh or
    2 teaspoons dried basil
2 teaspoons olive oil
½ teaspoon salt
½ teaspoon freshly ground pepper
1 (8-ounce) French baguette, cut into
    ½-inch-thick slices
Vegetable cooking spray

• **Stir** together first 8 ingredients; cover and chill at least 1 hour.
• **Arrange** bread slices on a baking sheet; lightly coat with cooking spray.
• **Bake** at 425° for 7 to 9 minutes or until lightly browned.
• **Spoon** tomato mixture over baguette slices. Serve immediately. **Yield:** 6 servings.

Lisa M. Burtch
Orland Park, Illinois

❤ Per serving: Calories 144 (18% from fat)
Fat 2.9g (sat 0.5g, mono 1.6g, poly 0.5g)
Protein 4g   Carb 26g   Fiber 2.3g
Chol 0mg   Iron 1.5mg
Sodium 435mg   Calc 39mg

CITRUS-AND-HERB TURKEY

Serve this juicy and flavorful bird for any special occasion.

Prep: 20 minutes
Bake: 2 hours, 15 minutes

1 (7½-pound) bone-in turkey
    breast
1 teaspoon salt
1 teaspoon freshly ground pepper
1 tablespoon butter or margarine,
    softened
3 tablespoons chopped fresh
    rosemary
3 tablespoons chopped fresh
    sage
2 oranges, thinly sliced
2 lemons, thinly sliced
Vegetable cooking spray
1 large onion, quartered
3 cups Riesling
Cranberry Salsa (recipe at right)

• **Sprinkle** turkey breast evenly with salt and pepper.
• **Stir** together butter, rosemary, and sage. Loosen skin from turkey without detaching it; spread butter mixture under skin. Arrange one-fourth of orange and lemon slices over butter mixture. Gently pull skin over fruit. Coat skin with cooking spray. Place turkey in an aluminum foil-lined baking pan coated with cooking spray. Place onion and remaining orange slices and lemon slices in pan. Drizzle with wine.
• **Bake** turkey at 325° for 2 hours and 15 minutes or until a meat thermometer inserted into thickest portion registers 170°, basting every 30 minutes. Cover loosely with aluminum foil coated with cooking spray to prevent excessive browning after 1 hour and 30 minutes, if necessary. Serve with Cranberry Salsa. **Yield:** 18 servings.

Brenda Tollett
Dalhart, Texas

❤ Per 4-ounce serving with skin:
Calories 237 (38% from fat)
Fat 10g (sat 3g, mono 3.3g, poly 2.3g)
Protein 36g   Carb 6.7g   Fiber 0.9g
Chol 94mg   Iron 1.9mg
Sodium 217mg   Calc 45mg

CRANBERRY SALSA

Prep: 10 minutes
Chill: 8 hours

1½ cups fresh cranberries
1 teaspoon grated orange rind
1 orange, peeled and chopped
½ yellow bell pepper, diced
⅓ cup sugar
2 tablespoons fresh orange juice
¼ to ½ teaspoon ground allspice
¼ teaspoon salt
2 teaspoons olive oil

• **Pulse** cranberries in a blender or food processor 5 or 6 times until coarsely chopped, and place in a bowl. Stir in orange rind and remaining ingredients. Cover and chill 8 hours. **Yield:** 1¾ cups.

Stuart Byford
Waldron, Arkansas

❤ Per ¼-cup serving: Calories 62 (20% from fat)
Fat 1.4g (sat 0g, mono 1g, poly 0g)
Protein 0.4g   Carb 16g   Fiber 1.7g
Chol 0mg   Iron 0mg
Sodium 84mg   Calc 15mg

COUNTDOWN TO DINNER

1 day ahead:
■ Toast pecans for Cinnamon Swirl Cake; place in a zip-top plastic bag, and set aside.
■ Chop fresh herbs, and slice citrus for Citrus-and-Herb Turkey. Chill herbs and citrus in separate bags.
■ Prepare Cranberry Salsa; cover, and chill.

Thanksgiving morning:
■ Bake Cinnamon Swirl Cake. Cool completely; cover until time to serve.
■ Prepare tomato mixture for Tomato-Basil Toasts. Cover; chill.

3 hours, 15 minutes before dinner:
■ Prepare turkey; place in 325° oven.
■ Prepare Rosemary Roasted Root Vegetables; cover and chill until time to add to roasting pan.

2 hours, 15 minutes before dinner:
■ Spoon uncooked root vegetables around turkey. (Stir every 20 minutes.) Continue baking turkey another 1 hour and 15 minutes or until it reaches 170°. Remove turkey, and cook vegetables 30 more minutes or until tender.
■ Prepare Parmesan Corn Muffins mixture; set pans aside.

30 minutes before dinner:
■ Bake muffins 6 minutes at 425°.
■ Add toasts for Tomato-Basil Toasts to oven, and bake 9 minutes. Remove muffins and toasts from oven.

15 minutes before dinner:
■ Assemble Tomato-Basil Toasts.
■ Slice turkey.

ROSEMARY ROASTED ROOT VEGETABLES

Prep: 30 minutes
Bake: 1 hour

4 small red potatoes
2 medium turnips, peeled
2 medium parsnips, peeled
1 small rutabaga, peeled
8 shallots, peeled and halved
2 garlic cloves, minced
1 to 2 tablespoons chopped fresh or
    1 teaspoon dried rosemary
1½ tablespoons olive oil
1 teaspoon salt
½ teaspoon freshly ground pepper
Vegetable cooking spray

• **Cut** potatoes and next 3 ingredients into ½-inch cubes.
• **Combine** cubed vegetables, shallots, and next 5 ingredients in a large bowl, tossing to coat.
• **Place** vegetable mixture on an aluminum foil-lined jellyroll pan coated with cooking spray. Bake at 425° for 1 hour or until browned, stirring every 20 minutes. **Yield:** 4½ cups.

Note: To roast vegetables with the Citrus-and-Herb Turkey, place vegetables around turkey, and bake at 325° for 1 hour and 45 minutes or until browned, stirring every 20 minutes.

Beth Shroat
Atlanta, Georgia

♥ Per ¾-cup serving: Calories 102 (4% from fat)
Fat 0.4g Protein 3.2g Carb 24g
Fiber 4.4g Chol 0mg Iron 1.2mg
Sodium 435mg Calc 70mg

PARMESAN CORN MUFFINS

Prep: 10 minutes
Bake: 15 minutes

2 cups white cornmeal mix
¾ cup all-purpose flour
½ cup grated Parmesan cheese
¼ teaspoon ground red pepper
2½ cups fat-free buttermilk
½ cup egg substitute
2 tablespoons vegetable oil
Vegetable cooking spray

• **Combine** first 4 ingredients in a large bowl; make a well in center of mixture.
• **Stir** together buttermilk, egg substitute, and oil; add to dry ingredients, stirring just until moistened. Spoon into muffin pans coated with cooking spray, filling two-thirds full.
• **Bake** at 425° for 15 minutes or until golden. Remove from pans immediately, and cool on wire racks. **Yield:** 17 muffins.

♥ Per muffin: Calories 118 (29% from fat)
Fat 3.7g (sat 1g, mono 1.5g, poly 0.9g)
Protein 5g Carb 16g Fiber 1g
Chol 4.6mg Iron 1.2mg
Sodium 284mg Calc 138mg

CINNAMON SWIRL CAKE
(pictured on page 266)

Prep: 15 minutes
Bake: 45 minutes

½ cup firmly packed light brown sugar
½ cup chopped pecans, toasted
2 teaspoons ground cinnamon
1 (18.25-ounce) package white cake mix
1⅓ cups fat-free buttermilk
¾ cup egg substitute
⅓ cup sugar
1 teaspoon vanilla extract
Garnish: cinnamon sticks

• **Combine** first 3 ingredients; set aside.
• **Beat** cake mix and next 4 ingredients at medium speed with an electric mixer 2 minutes or until blended. Pour one-third of cake batter into a greased and floured 12-cup Bundt pan. Sprinkle with half of brown sugar mixture. Repeat layers twice, ending with batter.
• **Bake** at 325° for 45 minutes or until a wooden pick inserted in center comes out clean. Cool in pan on a wire rack 10 minutes. Remove from pan, and cool completely on wire rack. Garnish, if desired. **Yield:** 16 servings.

♥ Per serving: Calories 231 (27% from fat)
Fat 7g (sat 2g, mono 2.6g, poly 1g)
Protein 4g Carb 39g Fiber 0.5g
Chol 3.3mg Iron 1mg
Sodium 270mg Calc 76mg

Dressed-Up Casseroles

Some clever ideas make these suppertime classics look special enough for company.

The holidays are a prime time to surprise your family and guests with sinfully delicious and attractive recipes. The only glitch is that the season's nonstop activities often leave us short on time. These casseroles are prepared with simple ingredients or call for timesaving products that shorten prep time.

CARAMELIZED ONION-AND-GORGONZOLA MASHED POTATOES

Prep: 30 minutes
Cook: 25 minutes
Broil: 5 minutes

3 pounds Yukon gold potatoes, peeled and quartered
1¾ teaspoons salt, divided
2 tablespoons butter or margarine
1 tablespoon olive oil
2 medium onions, diced
4 garlic cloves, minced
2 teaspoons chopped fresh or ½ teaspoon dried rosemary
½ cup butter or margarine
¾ cup half-and-half
¾ cup crumbled Gorgonzola or blue cheese
¾ teaspoon pepper
Garnish: fresh rosemary sprigs

• **Bring** potato, 1 teaspoon salt, and water to cover to a boil in a Dutch oven; cook 20 to 25 minutes or until tender. Drain and keep warm.
• **Melt** 2 tablespoons butter with olive oil in a skillet over medium heat; add onion, and cook, stirring often, 12 to 17 minutes or until tender. Add minced garlic, and cook 3 minutes. Stir in rosemary, and remove from heat.
• **Mash** potato with a potato masher; stir in ½ cup butter, half-and-half, and cheese until blended. Stir in onion mixture, remaining ¾ teaspoon salt, and pepper. Spoon enough mixture into a decorative ovenproof dish or 13- x 9-inch baking dish to fill bottom; pipe or dollop remaining mixture over top.
• **Broil** 3 inches from heat 5 minutes or until top is lightly browned. Garnish, if desired. **Yield:** 6 servings.

Edwina Gadsby
Great Falls, Montana

CHEESY BACON-AND-HAM CASSEROLE

Prep: 15 minutes
Cook: 20 minutes
Bake: 45 minutes

½ pound bacon
½ pound chopped cooked ham
¾ cup quick-cooking grits
1 (16-ounce) loaf pasteurized prepared cheese product, cubed
¼ cup butter or margarine
6 large eggs, lightly beaten
½ cup milk
2 teaspoons baking powder
½ teaspoon freshly ground pepper

• **Cook** bacon in a skillet until crisp; remove bacon, and drain on paper towels, reserving 1 tablespoon drippings in skillet. Crumble bacon; set aside.
• **Cook** ham in reserved drippings in skillet over medium heat until browned.
• **Cook** grits according to package directions. Remove from heat, and stir in cheese and butter until melted. Stir in bacon, ham, eggs, and remaining ingredients. Pour into a lightly greased 13- x 9-inch baking dish.
• **Bake** at 350° for 45 minutes or until set. **Yield:** 8 servings.

Note: Casserole may be prepared a day ahead; cover and chill. Remove from refrigerator the following day, and let stand at room temperature 30 minutes. Bake as directed.

Lynette S. Granade
Mobile, Alabama

CREAMY SHRIMP-AND-SCALLOPS CASSEROLE

Phyllo dough twists top this dish to create an elegant entrée.

Prep: 25 minutes
Cook: 15 minutes
Bake: 19 minutes
Stand: 10 minutes

16 frozen phyllo pastry sheets, thawed
2½ pounds unpeeled, medium-size fresh shrimp
2 (10-ounce) packages frozen chopped spinach, thawed
5 tablespoons butter, divided
2 garlic cloves, minced
1 pound fresh bay scallops
1 (8-ounce) package cream cheese, softened
1 (8-ounce) container sour cream
⅓ cup shredded Parmesan cheese
1 teaspoon salt
½ teaspoon ground red pepper
¼ cup all-purpose flour
2 cups half-and-half

• **Cut** phyllo sheets into 13- x 9-inch rectangles; reserve half of phyllo sheets, keeping covered with a damp towel to prevent drying out. Stack remaining 8 sheets in a lightly greased 13- x 9-inch baking dish, lightly coating each sheet with vegetable cooking spray.

- **Bake** on lowest oven rack at 400° for 5 minutes or until lightly browned, and set aside.
- **Peel** shrimp, and devein, if desired.
- **Drain** spinach well, pressing between paper towels.
- **Melt** 1 tablespoon butter in a large skillet over medium heat; add garlic, and sauté 2 minutes. Add shrimp and scallops; cook 5 minutes or just until shrimp turn pink. Stir in cream cheese and next 4 ingredients until blended; remove from heat. Stir in spinach.
- **Melt** remaining 1/4 cup butter in a saucepan over medium heat. Add flour, whisking constantly; cook, whisking constantly, 1 minute. Gradually add half-and-half; cook, whisking constantly, 3 minutes or until mixture is thickened. Stir flour mixture into shrimp mixture. Spoon into prepared baking dish.
- **Stack** reserved phyllo sheets, coating each sheet with cooking spray. Roll up, jellyroll fashion, starting at long end, and cut into 1/4-inch slices. Unroll each piece, and gently twist; arrange twists in a diamond pattern over casserole.
- **Bake** at 400° for 14 minutes or until golden. Let stand 10 minutes. **Yield:** 8 servings.

Jeanette Brewer
Marietta, Georgia

Quick & Easy

To speed up meal preparation, take a look at all the shortcuts available at your grocery store. You'll find everything from prepared sauces and soup mixes to large, deveined frozen shrimp.

Here we've put together a collection of recipes—from appetizer to main dish to breakfast offerings—that take advantage of these timesaving products. Chopping fresh vegetables increases the recipe prep time—and boosts the flavor—of Texas Caviar. But if you're in a hurry, try frozen chopped onion or bell pepper for satisfactory substitutes.

TEXAS CAVIAR

Prep: 20 minutes

2 (15.5-ounce) cans black-eyed peas with jalapeño peppers, rinsed and drained
1 (10-ounce) can diced tomato and green chiles
2 avocados, diced
1 small green bell pepper, diced
1/2 purple onion, diced
3/4 cup zesty Italian salad dressing
1 tablespoon fresh lime juice
1/4 teaspoon salt

- **Stir** together all ingredients. Cover and chill, if desired. Serve with corn chips. **Yield:** 6 cups.

Lori Cook
Wichita Falls, Texas

FETTUCCINE WITH SHRIMP-AND-CREAMY HERB SAUCE

Prep: 10 minutes
Cook: 15 minutes

1 (1-ounce) envelope garlic-herb soup mix
1¾ cups milk
8 ounces peeled frozen shrimp, partially thawed
1/2 cup frozen sweet green peas, partially thawed
6 ounces fettuccine, cooked
1/4 cup grated Parmesan cheese

- **Whisk** together soup mix and milk in a 2-quart saucepan; bring to a boil, stirring constantly.
- **Add** shrimp and peas; reduce heat, and simmer 3 minutes or until shrimp turn pink. Toss with fettuccine, and sprinkle with Parmesan cheese. **Yield:** 2 servings.

Fettuccine With Chicken-and-Creamy Herb Sauce: Substitute 1 cup chopped cooked chicken for shrimp and sugar snap peas for sweet peas. Complete as directed.

Mary Pappas
Richmond, Virginia

LIMEADE CHICKEN

Prep: 10 minutes
Cook: 25 minutes

8 skinned and boned chicken breast halves
1/4 teaspoon salt
1/8 teaspoon pepper
1 (6-ounce) can frozen limeade concentrate, thawed and undiluted
3 tablespoons brown sugar
3 tablespoons ketchup

- **Sprinkle** chicken evenly with salt and pepper.
- **Brown** chicken in a lightly greased nonstick skillet over medium-high heat 4 minutes on each side, and remove from skillet.
- **Add** limeade concentrate, brown sugar, and ketchup to skillet; bring to a boil. Cook, stirring constantly, 5 minutes or until thickened. Return chicken to skillet; cover and cook 10 minutes or until done. **Yield:** 8 servings.

Anne Powers
Munford, Alabama

ORANGE ROLLS

Prep: 15 minutes
Bake: 25 minutes

1/2 cup sugar
1½ teaspoons grated orange rind
1/2 teaspoon ground cinnamon
1 (12-ounce) can refrigerated biscuits
3 tablespoons fresh orange juice

- **Combine** first 3 ingredients.
- **Dip** each biscuit in orange juice, and dredge in sugar mixture.
- **Arrange** biscuits in a lightly greased 9-inch round baking dish or cakepan.
- **Sprinkle** biscuits with remaining sugar mixture, and drizzle with remaining orange juice.
- **Bake** at 350° for 25 minutes or until golden. Serve warm. **Yield:** 10 rolls.

Marne Wood
Jenkintown, Pennsylvania

Fresh From Your Freezer

Convenient and versatile, frozen shrimp offer great flavor at a nice price.

In search of ideas for an effortless weeknight supper? Look no further than frozen shrimp. Easy to use and economical, they're perfect for everything from a quick stir-fry to an almost instant appetizer.

Frozen shrimp come cooked or raw, unpeeled, tail on, or fully peeled. No matter which brand you prefer, be sure to shop for them at stores with high product turnover. We found that Celine brand consistently offered the best taste and texture. Avoid bags with excess ice, particularly in clumps, which is a telltale sign the shrimp has thawed and refrozen.

SHRIMP-AND-SPINACH PASTA

Prep: 15 minutes
Cook: 17 minutes

1 pound frozen, peeled and deveined medium shrimp
1 (10-ounce) package frozen chopped spinach, thawed
½ medium onion, diced
1 tablespoon olive oil
1 (14½-ounce) can diced tomatoes
1 (14½-ounce) can chicken broth
1 teaspoon Greek seasoning
1 (8-ounce) package angel hair pasta, cooked
½ (4-ounce) package crumbled feta cheese

• **Thaw** shrimp according to package directions.
• **Drain** spinach well, pressing between paper towels, and set aside.

• **Sauté** onion in hot oil in a large skillet over medium-high heat 5 minutes or until tender. Stir in tomatoes, broth, and Greek seasoning; bring to a boil, and cook, stirring occasionally, 10 minutes.
• **Add** shrimp; cook 2 minutes. Stir in spinach. Spoon over pasta; sprinkle with cheese, and serve immediately. **Yield:** 4 servings.

Virginia Anthony
Jacksonville, Florida

SHRIMP STIR-FRY

Prep: 20 minutes
Cook: 13 minutes

1 pound frozen, peeled and deveined medium shrimp
1 (14½-ounce) can low-sodium, fat-free chicken broth
½ cup lite soy sauce
2 tablespoons cornstarch
2 tablespoons sesame oil
4 garlic cloves, minced
½ teaspoon ground ginger
1½ cups chopped fresh broccoli
5 large mushrooms, thinly sliced
1 large sweet onion, chopped
1 small green bell pepper, chopped
Hot cooked rice

• **Thaw** shrimp according to package directions.
• **Stir** together chicken broth, soy sauce, and cornstarch; set aside.

• **Heat** oil in a large skillet over medium-high heat 2 minutes. Add garlic and ginger, and stir-fry 1 minute. Add broccoli and next 3 ingredients; stir-fry 4 minutes or until crisp-tender. Remove from skillet.
• **Add** shrimp to skillet, and stir-fry 3 minutes; stir in vegetables and chicken broth mixture. Bring to a boil, and stir-fry 2 to 3 minutes or until sauce thickens. Serve shrimp mixture over rice. **Yield:** 4 to 6 servings.

Stephanie Leatherman
Columbia, South Carolina

SHRIMP AND GRITS

Prep: 15 minutes
Cook: 10 minutes

2 pounds frozen, peeled and deveined large shrimp
2 teaspoons Cajun seasoning
1 teaspoon dried Italian seasoning
1 teaspoon paprika
¼ cup butter or margarine
2 garlic cloves, pressed
1 cup chicken broth, divided
2 teaspoons Worcestershire sauce
1 teaspoon hot sauce
2 teaspoons all-purpose flour
Hot cooked grits

• **Thaw** shrimp according to package directions.
• **Combine** Cajun seasoning, Italian seasoning, and paprika; toss together seasoning mixture and shrimp.
• **Melt** butter in a large skillet over medium heat; add garlic, and sauté 1 minute. Add shrimp, ¾ cup broth, Worcestershire sauce, and hot sauce; cook 5 minutes or just until shrimp turn pink. Remove shrimp with a slotted spoon, reserving broth mixture in skillet.
• **Whisk** together remaining ¼ cup chicken broth and flour until blended; whisk flour mixture into broth mixture in skillet, and cook, whisking constantly, 2 to 3 minutes or until thickened. Add shrimp, and cook 1 minute. Serve immediately over grits. **Yield:** 4 servings.

What's for Supper?

Plan ahead to have dinner on the table fast.

OVEN BARBECUE BRISKET

*Prep: 10 minutes
Cook: 3 hours
Chill: 8 hours
Bake: 3 hours*

1 (4-pound) beef brisket
2 gallons water
3 tablespoons pickling spice
1 cup ketchup
1 cup cola soft drink
½ cup firmly packed light brown
   sugar
2 tablespoons prepared mustard

● **Bring** brisket, 2 gallons water, and pickling spice to a boil in a stockpot; reduce heat, and simmer 2½ hours.
● **Drain;** cover and chill 8 hours.
● **Place** brisket in a lightly greased shallow roasting pan.
● **Stir** together 1 cup ketchup and remaining 3 ingredients. Drizzle one-third of sauce over brisket.
● **Bake** brisket at 350° for 3 hours, basting every hour with remaining sauce. **Yield:** 12 servings.

*Diane B. Hester
Lumberton, North Carolina*

HEARTY BAKED BEANS

*Prep: 30 minutes
Cook: 3 hours (on HIGH) or
6 hours (on LOW)*

3 bacon slices, chopped
1 large onion, chopped
2 garlic cloves, minced
3 (16-ounce) cans pinto beans, drained
⅓ cup firmly packed brown sugar
⅓ cup molasses
⅓ cup ketchup
2½ tablespoons prepared mustard
½ medium-size green bell pepper,
   chopped

● **Cook** chopped bacon in a skillet until crisp; remove bacon, reserving drippings in pan.
● **Sauté** onion and garlic in reserved drippings until tender. Combine bacon, onion mixture, beans, and remaining ingredients in a slow cooker.
● **Cover** and cook on HIGH 2½ to 3 hours or on LOW 5 to 6 hours. **Yield:** 6 to 8 servings.

RAINBOW SLAW

A food processor makes quick work of shredding cabbage; substituting packaged shredded cabbage is even faster.

*Prep: 35 minutes
Chill: 4 hours*

2 cups finely shredded green
   cabbage
2 cups finely shredded red cabbage
½ medium jícama, peeled and cut
   into thin strips
½ medium onion, chopped
½ medium-size green bell pepper,
   chopped
1 jalapeño pepper, seeded and
   chopped
¼ cup chopped fresh cilantro
⅓ cup vegetable oil
⅓ cup fresh lime juice
1¼ teaspoons salt
⅛ teaspoon pepper

● **Combine** first 7 ingredients in a large bowl.
● **Whisk** together oil and remaining 3 ingredients. Drizzle over cabbage mixture, tossing to coat. Cover and chill 4 hours. **Yield:** 6 servings.

*Linda Morten
Katy, Texas*

COOK'S NOTES

■ Prepare Oven Barbecue Brisket; divide in half. Place one portion in an airtight freezer container; freeze up to 3 months. Thaw in refrigerator overnight for other uses. Serve remaining portion for this menu.

■ Prepare Hearty Baked Beans in a slow cooker or assemble Simple Seasoned Potatoes for the oven in only 8 minutes. Linda Kirkpatrick of Westminster, Maryland, shared this recipe.

Simple Seasoned Potatoes: Peel and cut 3 pounds potatoes into 1-inch pieces. Place in a heavy-duty zip-top plastic bag; add ¼ cup vegetable oil. Seal; shake to coat. Add 3 tablespoons Old Bay seasoning; seal and shake. Place in a greased 13- x 9-inch pan. Bake at 350° for 45 minutes. **Yield:** 6 servings.

From Our Kitchen

Ways With Turkey

In the South, turkey is part of the treasured holiday tradition. But if you don't want to prepare the whole bird, there are plenty of delicious options. Check these out at your market to find the one that suits your needs.

■ **Turkey breast:** It comes fresh or frozen and is all white meat that you can carve at the table.

■ **Turkey mignons:** Poultry's version of the beef specialty, these tender pieces of breast meat are wrapped in bacon. They're perfect single servings.

■ **Turkey cutlets:** These thin slices of breast may be baked or breaded and pan-fried. You can get cutlets to the table in a hurry, and they're just the right size for hot sandwiches.

■ **Turkey roll:** This boneless roast of combined white and dark meat is found in the frozen foods section of the market.

If you're roasting the whole bird and want some additional advice, contact the Butterball Turkey Talk-Line at 1-800-288-8372 (1-800-BUTTERBALL), or visit the Web site at www.butterball.com.

Play It Safe

Pay as much attention to the food after the feast as you did in preparation. Refrigerate leftovers in airtight containers immediately following the meal. Don't leave out turkey, stuffing, and gravy for more than 45 minutes.

Remember to keep containers tightly closed, and plan to use within two days. If you need to store the food longer, it should be packaged, labeled, and frozen.

EXPRESS YOURSELF

Here are some little things that make holiday meals extra special.

■ Serve smooth soups in small china cups instead of bowls.

■ Have guests create novelty napkin folds.

■ Serve creamy desserts in stemmed glasses.

■ Keep bread warm at the table by placing aluminum foil between the bread basket and the basket liner.

■ Make ice cubes of tea and/or fruit juice for serving iced beverages without diluting the flavor.

■ Don't limit sage to the stuffing. Fresh or dried, it's terrific with veal, pork, lima beans, and some corn dishes.

Tips and Tidbits

Walter Taliaferro of Winston-Salem, North Carolina, has a solution for recipes in small print. He recommends gluing your favorites onto index cards and enlarging them on a copier.

He also offers help for badly soiled oven racks. Put stainless steel racks in a large plastic leaf bag. Pour 4 cups of ammonia into the bag, and secure the top. (To keep the fumes out of the house, do this on a back porch or patio.) Leave 3 to 4 hours or overnight. Remove oven racks from bag, and brush off burned-on grease with warm soapy water and very little effort.

Chop, Chop

No matter what you call it, stuffing or dressing, most recipes for this holiday staple include onion, green bell pepper, and celery as vital ingredients. To get a jump start on the preparations, chop and freeze the trio of vegetables in heavy-duty zip-top freezer bags. When you need them, add them directly from the freezer to any recipe. Store remaining vegetables for soup, meat loaf, or casserole recipes.

Make cornbread for dressing a day or two ahead. Cool, crumble, and refrigerate in a zip-top plastic bag. The day before the feast, stir together all dry ingredients for dressing, and refrigerate overnight for flavors to blend.

Equipment Checkup

■ You'll be chopping, carving, and dicing, so have your knives sharpened.

■ Buy one or two heavy foil roasting pans; they're great for sharing, freezing, and transporting foods.

■ Make room in the refrigerator and freezer for the additional loads they'll carry during the holiday season.

■ Check the placement of your oven racks for baking.

Stuffed Mirlitons (Chayote Squash)

Get a taste of Leah Chase's incredible Creole cooking on page 222. Her Stuffed Squash recipe is featured in the holiday menu she shared with us. Leah uses yellow squash and mirlitons when she prepares the dish. When using mirlitons, cut the pale-green squash in half, remove the large flat seed, and then proceed as directed in the recipe. You'll find many ways to use mirlitons: steamed and stuffed; peeled, sliced, and sautéed in butter; or peeled, thinly sliced, and tossed into salads. If you can't find mirlitons, yellow squash is a good substitute.

Blue Cheese-and-Bacon Puffs, page 236

Blue Cheese Crisps, page 235

Smoked Pork, Southwestern Cornbread Dressing Cakes, Roasted Sweet Potatoes and Onions, Cranberry-Jalapeño Salsa , Cheese Biscuits With Chipotle Butter, pages 233-234

Southwestern Cheese Appetizer, page 232

*Chocolate-Praline Cake,
page 235*

Roast Pork Loin, page 222;
Stuffed Squash, page 223;
Green Beans With Ham and
Potatoes, page 223;
Rice Dressing, page 222

Old-Fashioned Bread Pudding,
page 223

Cinnamon Swirl Cake,
page 255

Cinnamon Rolls, page 242

Sweet Potato Pie, page 243

*Chocolate-Vanilla
Holiday Torte,
page 252*

December

Simple, Classic Cakes

One simple layer cake that starts with a mix builds three oh-so-Southern desserts.

Anyone who has ever tasted divinity understands the traits that set this Southern favorite apart. The candy's meltingly sweet flavor offers a heavenly contrast to its airy texture and cloudlike appearance. In fact, the pecan halves on top seem to be the only earthly anchor for each sugary piece. These qualities, we reasoned, could make an inspired cake frosting—with a little tweaking, of course. It would be the perfect contrast to tender layers of sour cream cake.

While developing a foolproof version of the frosting, Mary Allen Perry of our Test Kitchens found inspiration from reader Ethelwyn Langston's Praline Cake and another Southern favorite, ambrosia. The recipes she developed are bound to become classics. Each of these cakes starts with the same easy layers, which can be made ahead and frozen. In fact, you can make the praline and ambrosia cakes start-to-finish and then freeze them up to one month.

Whether you make them the day you serve them, or freeze them for a holiday gathering, we have no doubt that you'll turn to these recipes again and again. Happy holidays.

SOUR CREAM CAKE LAYERS

It's easier to spread frosting on frozen or partially frozen cake layers.

Prep: 10 minutes
Bake: 17 minutes

1 (18.25-ounce) package white
   cake mix ✱
2 large eggs
1 (8-ounce) container sour cream
½ cup water
⅓ cup vegetable oil

• **Beat** all ingredients at low speed with an electric mixer 30 seconds or just until moistened; beat at medium speed 2 minutes. Pour batter evenly into 4 greased and floured 8-inch round cakepans.
• **Bake** at 350° for 15 to 17 minutes or until a wooden pick inserted in center comes out clean. Cool in pans on wire racks 10 minutes. Remove from pans, and cool completely on wire racks. Wrap layers in plastic wrap, and freeze 2 hours or up to 1 month, if desired. **Yield:** 4 (8-inch) layers.

✱ Substitute spice, chocolate, or your favorite flavor cake mix, if desired.

Note: To prepare 9-inch round Sour Cream Cake Layers, use 4 greased and floured 9-inch round cakepans. Bake at 350° for 12 to 14 minutes or until a wooden pick inserted in center comes out clean. Cool in pans on wire racks 10 minutes. Remove from pans, and cool completely on wire racks.

DIVINITY CAKE
(pictured on cover)

Enjoy this cake the day you assemble it; the Divinity Frosting won't hold up for longer storage.

Prep: 45 minutes

Divinity Frosting
Sour Cream Cake Layers (see recipe at
   left using 8-inch round cakepans)
Toasted pecan halves (optional)
Divinity Candy (optional)
Sugared Maraschino Cherries and
   Mint Sprigs (optional)
Small candy canes (optional)

• **Spread** about ½ cup Divinity Frosting between each cake layer; spread remaining Divinity Frosting on top and sides of cake.
• **Arrange** pecan halves and Divinity Candy on top of cake, if desired. Arrange Sugared Maraschino Cherries and Mint Sprigs and candy canes around bottom edge of cake, if desired. Store cake at room temperature. **Yield:** 1 (4-layer) cake.

Divinity Frosting

Prep: 10 minutes

1 (7.2-ounce) package home-style
   fluffy white frosting mix
½ cup boiling water
⅓ cup light corn syrup
2 teaspoons vanilla extract
1 (16-ounce) package powdered
   sugar
1½ cups chopped pecans,
   toasted

• **Place** first 4 ingredients in a 4-quart mixing bowl. Beat at low speed with a heavy-duty electric mixer 1 minute or until blended. Beat at high speed 3 to 5 minutes or until stiff peaks form. Gradually add powdered sugar, beating at low speed until blended. Stir in pecans. Spread frosting immediately on cake. **Yield:** about 4½ cups.

Note: For testing purposes only, we used Betty Crocker Home Style Fluffy White Frosting Mix.

Divinity Candy

Prep: 30 minutes
Stand: 16 hours

1 (7.2-ounce) package home-style
 fluffy white frosting mix
½ cup boiling water
⅓ cup light corn syrup
2 teaspoons vanilla extract
1 (16-ounce) package powdered sugar
1½ cups chopped pecans, toasted
Toasted pecan halves

• **Place** first 4 ingredients in a 4-quart mixing bowl. Beat at low speed with a heavy-duty electric mixer 1 minute or until blended. Beat at high speed 3 to 5 minutes or until stiff peaks form. Gradually add sugar, beating at low speed until blended. Stir in chopped pecans.
• **Drop** by rounded tablespoonfuls onto wax paper. Garnish with toasted pecan halves. Let stand 8 hours; remove to wire racks, and let stand 8 more hours or until bottom of candy is firm. Store in airtight containers. **Yield:** 5 dozen.

Divinity Candy With Sugared Maraschino Cherries: Substitute Sugared Maraschino Cherries for toasted pecan halves. Drop by rounded tablespoonfuls onto wax paper. Press tip of a lightly greased wooden spoon handle into center of each piece, making an indentation. Let stand as directed. Place 1 Sugared Maraschino Cherry in each indentation just before serving.

Sugared Maraschino Cherries and Mint Sprigs

Prep: 45 minutes
Stand: 3 hours

16 to 20 maraschino cherries with
 stems, rinsed and well drained
12 to 16 fresh mint sprigs, rinsed
1⅓ cups powdered sugar
⅓ cup water
1 tablespoon meringue powder
½ cup sugar

• **Place** cherries and mint on paper towels; let stand until completely dry.

• **Beat** powdered sugar, ⅓ cup water, and meringue powder at medium speed with an electric mixer 2 to 3 minutes or until smooth and creamy.
• **Brush** cherries and mint with meringue mixture, using a small paintbrush; sprinkle with sugar, and place on a wire rack. Let stand 2 to 3 hours or until dry. **Yield:** 20 cherries and 16 mint sprigs.

CRANBERRY-AMBROSIA CAKE

Prep: 30 minutes

Cranberry-Ambrosia Filling
Sour Cream Cake Layers (see recipe on
 opposite page using 9-inch round
 cakepans)
Cream Cheese Frosting
1½ cups Sugared Pecans (see recipe
 at right)
½ cup sweetened flaked coconut
Garnishes: mint sprigs, cranberries,
 orange rind strips

• **Spread** Cranberry-Ambrosia Filling between layers and on top of cake. Reserve 1½ cups Cream Cheese Frosting, and set aside. Spread remaining Cream Cheese Frosting on sides of cake.
• **Combine** Sugared Pecans and coconut, and press into sides of cake.
• **Spoon** remaining 1½ cups frosting into a decorating bag fitted with a star tip. Pipe a border around top and bottom edges of cake. Store in refrigerator, or freeze, if desired. Garnish, if desired. **Yield:** 1 (4-layer) cake.

Cranberry-Ambrosia Filling

Prep: 5 minutes
Cook: 10 minutes
Chill: 8 hours

1½ cups sugar
½ cup all-purpose flour
1 cup frozen cranberry juice
 concentrate, thawed
1 (8¼-ounce) can crushed pineapple
 in syrup
1 (12-ounce) container cranberry-
 orange relish
2 tablespoons butter or margarine
2 teaspoons grated orange rind

• **Stir** together 1½ cups sugar and flour in a 3-quart saucepan; stir in cranberry juice concentrate, pineapple, and relish. Bring to a boil (5 to 6 minutes) over medium heat, stirring constantly. Cook, stirring constantly, 3 minutes or until puddinglike thickness. Remove from heat, and stir in butter and orange rind. Cover, placing plastic wrap directly on filling, and chill 8 hours. **Yield:** about 4 cups.

Cream Cheese Frosting

Prep: 5 minutes

1 (8-ounce) package cream cheese,
 softened
¼ cup butter or margarine, softened
1 (16-ounce) package powdered sugar
1 teaspoon vanilla extract
½ teaspoon almond extract

• **Beat** cream cheese and butter at medium speed with an electric mixer until smooth. Gradually add powdered sugar, beating until light and fluffy. Stir in extracts. **Yield:** about 3 cups.

SUGARED PECANS

Prep: 5 minutes
Bake: 20 minutes

1 large egg white
2 cups chopped pecans *
1 cup sugar

• **Whisk** egg white until foamy; stir in pecans, coating well. Stir in sugar; coat well. Spread pecan mixture evenly in a lightly greased 15- x 10-inch aluminum foil-lined jellyroll pan.
• **Bake** at 350° for 10 minutes. Stir gently with a wooden spoon; bake 8 to 10 more minutes or until sugar is light golden brown. Remove from oven, and cool completely in pan. Store in an airtight container; freeze, if desired. **Yield:** about 2 cups.

Sugared Pecan Halves: Substitute 4 cups pecan halves for chopped pecans.

Praline Cream Cake

Prep: 20 minutes

Praline Cream
Sour Cream Cake Layers (see recipe on page 270 using 8-inch round cakepans)
2 cups chopped pecans, toasted
Garnish: Sugared Pecan Halves (recipe on page 271)

• **Spread** about ⅔ cup Praline Cream between layers and about 1 cup on top of Sour Cream Cake Layers. Spread a thin coat of Praline Cream (about 1 cup) on sides of cake. Press pecans on sides of cake. Garnish, if desired. Cover with plastic wrap; chill until ready to serve, or freeze, if desired. **Yield:** 1 (4-layer) cake.

Praline Cream

Prep: 5 minutes
Cook: 20 minutes
Chill: 8 hours

2 cups sugar, divided
1 tablespoon lemon juice
½ cup butter or margarine
4 egg yolks
2 cups milk
6 tablespoons all-purpose flour
1 cup chopped pecans, toasted

• **Stir** together 1 cup sugar and lemon juice in a 1½-quart saucepan over medium heat, and cook, tilting pan to melt sugar evenly and stirring occasionally, until sugar melts and turns a light golden color. Stir in butter.
• **Whisk** together remaining 1 cup sugar, egg yolks, milk, and flour in a heavy saucepan; bring just to a simmer over medium heat, whisking constantly.
• **Add** sugar mixture to milk mixture immediately, and cook, whisking constantly, 5 to 7 minutes or until pudding-like thickness. Stir in pecans. Cover, placing plastic wrap directly on filling, and chill 8 hours. **Yield:** 4 cups.

Ethelwyn Langston
Winfield, Alabama

Feliz Navidad

Try the Duran family recipe for a great gathering of friends and neighbors.

Tex-Mex Holiday Gathering
Serves 4

Brisket
Salsa   Flour tortillas
Mexican Rice
Lynda's Mex-Tex Cornbread
Margaritas   Iced tea

When the Southern sun sets in the west, the last rays of the day fall on El Paso. In this border town, Christmas takes its cue from two diverse cultures—Texas and Mexico. This rich blend of people and food is a hallmark of Lynda and Leonard Duran's annual holiday gathering.

Lynda hails from East Texas, where celebrating the season embraces traditional Southern style. Leonard's family, only two generations removed from Mexico, preserved many of that country's customs while living in Arizona. Leonard's Army career took them to El Paso in 1988, where he is now in private medical practice.

"When we first moved here, we had three young children, but no other family nearby," Lynda says. "The party was a way to celebrate Christmas and develop our own traditions with neighbors and friends."

The get-together spans generations as easily as it bridges cultures. "Our family custom of making tamales soon after Thanksgiving became the calling card of our party," Lynda says. "We make so many of them; it takes all of us working together to make enough for our guests." Adults and children eagerly anticipate the event, which now includes a new generation of grandchildren.

In addition to the beloved tamales, Lynda keeps the menu simple with a brisket, fresh salsa, tortillas, Mexican rice, and her special cornbread.

The Durans' holiday decor, not surprisingly, is also a Tex-Mex blend. On the mantel, nutcrackers stand sentinel over the den with chile pepper lights at their feet. "Each time we've lived in a different city or I saw a nutcracker that pertained to our family, I've added it to our collection," Lynda says. "The entire mantel is symbolic of how our family has evolved."

The party becomes more meaningful as time goes by, Lynda says. "It makes me realize what good friends we've made since we moved here all those years ago."

BRISKET

Prep: 15 minutes
Bake: 5 hours

1 (5- to 5½-pound) beef brisket
1 (1-ounce) envelope dry onion
    soup mix

• **Place** brisket on a large piece of heavy-duty aluminum foil; sprinkle both sides evenly with soup mix. Tightly fold foil to seal; place brisket in a large roasting pan.
• **Bake** at 350° for 4 to 5 hours. Remove brisket from foil, reserving pan drippings. Let brisket cool slightly.
• **Spoon** strained pan drippings over brisket; cut brisket diagonally across the grain into thin slices. Serve brisket with flour tortillas and salsa. **Yield:** 6 to 8 servings.

SALSA

Lynda serves this salsa with sliced brisket and soft flour tortillas, but it's great as a dip for chips, too.

Prep: 20 minutes
Chill: 4 hours

1 (15½-ounce) can whole
    tomatoes
3 garlic cloves, chopped
3 jalapeño peppers, seeded and
    coarsely chopped
2 (4.5-ounce) cans chopped green
    chiles, drained
6 to 7 green onions, chopped
½ teaspoon salt

• **Drain** tomatoes, reserving juice in a blender. Add garlic and jalapeño, and process until smooth, stopping to scrape down sides. Add tomatoes, and process until coarsely chopped.
• **Stir** together tomato mixture, green chiles, green onions, and salt. Cover and chill 4 hours. **Yield:** 4 cups.

MEXICAN RICE

Prep: 20 minutes
Cook: 25 minutes

1 cup uncooked long-grain rice
1 tablespoon vegetable oil
¼ cup chopped onion
2 garlic cloves, minced
1 (14½-ounce) can chicken broth
2 plum tomatoes, seeded and chopped
1 (8-ounce) can tomato sauce
½ teaspoon salt
¼ teaspoon pepper

• **Sauté** rice in hot oil in a skillet over medium-high heat 3 minutes or until lightly browned. Add onion and garlic, and sauté 2 minutes.
• **Stir** in broth and next 4 ingredients. Cover, reduce heat, and cook 15 to 20 minutes. Remove from heat, and let stand 5 minutes. Fluff rice with a fork. **Yield:** 4 servings.

LYNDA'S MEX-TEX CORNBREAD

Prep: 10 minutes
Bake: 25 minutes

2 (4.5-ounce) cans chopped
    green chiles
1 (8½-ounce) can cream-style corn
1 cup yellow cornmeal
½ cup (2 ounces) shredded colby-Jack
    cheese
1 large egg
¼ cup milk
1 tablespoon all-purpose flour
2 teaspoons baking powder
1 teaspoon salt
1 teaspoon sugar
2 teaspoons chopped jalapeño pepper
    (optional)
2 tablespoons bacon drippings

• **Stir** together first 10 ingredients in a bowl; stir in jalapeño pepper, if desired.
• **Coat** bottom and sides of a 9-inch cast-iron skillet with bacon drippings. Heat in a 450° oven 5 minutes. Pour cornbread batter into hot skillet.
• **Bake** at 450° for 20 to 25 minutes or until lightly browned. **Yield:** 4 servings.

TAMALE TIME

Making tamales as the Durans do each year is a labor of love. The family fills corn husks with masa and other ingredients, then rolls them into small bundles for steaming, a job that requires time and patience. Fortunately, there are companies that sell tamales by mail. Here are a few we've tried.

Pedro's in Lubbock offers traditional tamales in beef, pork, and chicken, as well as salsa, seasonings, and chili. To order, call 1-800-522-9531 or visit them at www.pedrostamales.com.

Hot Damn, Tamales! is Fort Worth's vegetarian choice—the tamales contain no meat or meat products, but are wonderfully flavorful. Choose from Black Bean and Oaxaca Cheese, Wild Mushroom and Texas Goat Cheese, Fresh Corn and Roasted Poblano, and Spring Tamales. To order, call 1-888-385-0125 or visit www.hotdamntamales.com.

Flavors of Hanukkah

Kentucky food enthusiast Julie Benson shares her special seasonal menu.

Hanukkah Holiday Meal

Serves 6

Potato Blini With Sour Cream and Caviar

Caramelized Maple-and-Garlic-Glazed Salmon

Sweet Potato Latkes

Asparagus Sauté

Hanukkah Doughnuts With Strawberry Preserves

The Benson family's Louisville, Kentucky, kitchen is filled with the sizzling sound of doughnuts frying. For Julie, her husband David, and their three strapping boys, Cooper, 17, Martin, 15, and Harris, 11, Hanukkah is a holiday for family and food.

Harris fidgets as he waits for his mom to dust warm, puffy doughnuts with powdered sugar. He pops one in his mouth, and his bright brown eyes gleam with pleasure. He flashes a mischievous smile, and every person in the room anticipates his or her own bite of heaven.

Julie Benson is an avid foodie. She's the founding president of the Louisville chapter of the Chaîne des Rotisseurs, the oldest and largest gastronomic society, based in Paris, France. A part-time cooking teacher, Julie says food has always been significant in her life. "I can remember sitting in booster chairs at Antoine's, Galatoire's, and Brennan's as a little girl."

These New Orleans icons of fine dining inspired Julie to cook with the freshest ingredients and to pay special attention to complementary flavors. She plans her Hanukkah menu with an eye on the same components, often pairing fresh salmon with asparagus.

The symbolism of Hanukkah takes its rightful place on the table too. Julie's homemade fried treats remind diners of the symbolism of the oil, which miraculously burned for eight days when only enough for one day remained (see "Hanukkah Facts" on opposite page). The menorah, a nine-branched candleholder also reminds Jews of those same miraculous eight days. The ninth candle, in the middle, serves to light the eight others. The Bensons light a family menorah, as well as individual ones.

While other holidays are holier on the Jewish calendar, the Christian festivities around this time of year give Julie and her family the perfect excuse to take time off to eat, celebrate, and spend time with each other.

POTATO BLINI WITH SOUR CREAM AND CAVIAR

These tiny potato pancakes marry perfectly with rich sour cream and indulgent caviar.

Prep: 20 minutes
Cook: 4 minutes per batch

2 large eggs, separated
1 large potato, finely grated
9 tablespoons all-purpose flour
2 tablespoons whipping cream
1 teaspoon salt
½ teaspoon pepper
Vegetable oil
Sour cream
Caviar

• **Beat** egg whites in a bowl at medium speed with an electric mixer until stiff peaks form.

• **Whisk** egg yolks until thickened. Stir in potato and next 4 ingredients. Fold in egg whites.

• **Pour** oil to a depth of ½ inch into a large heavy skillet; heat to 350°.

• **Drop** potato mixture by teaspoonfuls into hot oil; fry, in batches, 1 to 2 minutes on each side or until golden.

• **Drain** on paper towels. Serve immediately with sour cream and caviar. **Yield:** 6 appetizer servings.

CARAMELIZED MAPLE-AND-GARLIC-GLAZED SALMON

Broiling caramelizes the maple glaze atop these salmon fillets to a gorgeous finish.

Prep: 10 minutes
Cook: 9 minutes

1 (2½-pound) salmon fillet, cut into 6 pieces
1 teaspoon salt
2 tablespoons butter or margarine
⅓ cup maple syrup, divided
1 teaspoon granulated garlic
1 tablespoon chopped fresh chives

• **Sprinkle** salmon evenly with salt.
• **Melt** butter in a large skillet over medium heat. Add salmon, skin side up; cook 2 minutes.
• **Place** salmon, skin side down, on a lightly greased rack in a broiler pan. Brush salmon with half of syrup.
• **Broil** 5 inches from heat 5 to 7 minutes or until syrup caramelizes. Brush with remaining syrup; sprinkle with garlic and chives. **Yield:** 6 servings.

SWEET POTATO LATKES

Prep: 15 minutes
Cook: 8 minutes per batch

2½ pounds sweet potatoes, peeled and grated
6 tablespoons all-purpose flour
4 large eggs, lightly beaten
4 green onions, sliced
½ teaspoon salt
Vegetable oil

• **Stir** together potato and flour. Stir in eggs, green onions, and salt; blend well.
• **Pour** oil to a depth of ½ inch into a large heavy skillet. Heat to 350°.
• **Drop** potato mixture by tablespoonfuls into hot oil; gently flatten latkes with back of a spoon.
• **Fry,** in batches, 3 to 4 minutes on each side or until golden. Drain on paper towels. Serve immediately. **Yield:** 8 servings.

ASPARAGUS SAUTÉ

Save this quick sauté to cook at the last minute to maximize its pretty color and crisp-tender texture.

Prep: 15 minutes
Cook: 5 minutes

2 pounds fresh asparagus
¼ cup butter or margarine
1 large red bell pepper, diced
½ teaspoon salt
½ teaspoon pepper

• **Snap** off tough ends of asparagus.
• **Melt** butter in a large skillet over medium heat.
• **Add** asparagus and remaining ingredients; sauté 4 to 5 minutes or until crisp-tender. Serve immediately. **Yield:** 6 servings.

HANUKKAH DOUGHNUTS WITH STRAWBERRY PRESERVES

Crème Fraîche adds a rich finishing touch to these puffy sweets.

Prep: 20 minutes
Cook: 8 minutes per batch

1 cup water
½ cup butter or margarine
1 tablespoon sugar
1 cup all-purpose flour
2 large eggs
Vegetable oil
Powdered sugar
Strawberry preserves
Crème Fraîche

• **Bring** first 3 ingredients to a boil in a heavy saucepan. Add flour, and cook, whisking constantly, 3 to 4 minutes or until mixture thickens. Remove from heat; cool.
• **Spoon** mixture into a mixing bowl. Beat in eggs, 1 at a time, at medium speed with an electric mixer, beating well after each addition.
• **Turn** dough out onto a lightly floured surface.

• **Pat** or roll dough to ⅛-inch thickness, and cut with star- or dreidel-shaped cookie cutters.
• **Pour** oil to a depth of ½ inch; heat to 375°. Fry doughnuts, in batches, 3 to 4 minutes on each side or until golden. Drain on paper towels. Sprinkle with powdered sugar.
• **Microwave** preserves in a glass bowl at HIGH 1 to 2 minutes or until thoroughly heated, stirring once. Serve doughnuts with preserves and Crème Fraîche. **Yield:** 8 servings.

Crème Fraîche

Prep: 10 minutes
Stand: 8 hours

1 cup whipping cream
1 teaspoon buttermilk

• **Heat** cream and buttermilk in a small saucepan over low heat until lukewarm. Pour mixture into a glass jar, and loosely cover with lid. Let stand, free from drafts, 8 hours or until thickened. Store, tightly covered, in refrigerator up to 10 days. **Yield:** 8 servings.

HANUKKAH FACTS

Hanukkah, also known as the festival of lights, commemorates the miracle that happened during the rededication of the Hebrew temple in Israel in 165 B.C., when a one-day supply of oil burned for eight days. That long-burning light is remembered today with the lighting of the candles on the menorah every sunset for eight days.

You Can Go Home Again

A young family returns to their Mississippi home place, where they enjoy simple, time-honored Christmas traditions.

Christmas Dinner Menu
Serves 8 to 10

Festive Pork Roast
Spinach Loaf With Mushroom Sauce
Roasted Glazed Vegetables
Green beans
Bakery rolls
Macadamia-Fudge Cake (recipe on page 278)
Red wine   Iced tea   Coffee

If you've ever been away from the South for an extended period, then you know of its powerful call home, especially for those with deep family roots. This was certainly the case for Mary Frances and Moak Griffin, a young couple who recently returned to their picturesque hometown of Columbus, Mississippi, after spending several years in Chicago.

The couple has an appreciation for life in this small town and felt it would be the perfect place to raise children. "It's so nice to run into people you know in the grocery," explains Mary Frances. "That doesn't happen much in Chicago."

Now that she, Moak, and their new addition, Baby Moak, have returned home, they have reacquainted themselves with old friends and have the good fortune of seeing family members almost every day. They've even refurbished an old family home belonging to Mary Frances's great-aunt Mildred. It's a house they have put their hearts into, and they eagerly share it again with family during the holidays, much like her father, Bobby Caldwell, did when he was growing up. Aunt Mildred, still active, even in her nineties, enjoys visits to see the newest member of the family. "Baby Moak is the fifth generation Caldwell to live here," says Mary Frances, "and I'm glad his first Christmas was here."

One of the Griffins' main holiday objectives was to preserve the tradition of a family Christmas dinner. Brimming with memories of past generations, their home is the perfect place to establish their own traditions.

For some people, going home may seem like a return to the past. But for this young family, being back in Columbus is a way of making a new beginning, one they can share with those they love.

FESTIVE PORK ROAST

The robust marinade infuses the roast with intense flavor.

Prep: 30 minutes
Chill: 8 hours
Bake: 2 hours, 30 minutes

1½ cups dry red wine
⅔ cup firmly packed brown sugar
½ cup ketchup
½ cup water
¼ cup vegetable oil
4 garlic cloves, minced
3 tablespoons soy sauce
2 teaspoons curry powder
1 teaspoon ground ginger
½ teaspoon pepper
1 (5-pound) boneless rolled pork roast
4 teaspoons cornstarch

• **Combine** first 10 ingredients in a large shallow dish or heavy-duty zip-top bag; add pork. Cover or seal, and chill 8 hours, turning occasionally.
• **Remove** pork from marinade, reserving 2½ cups marinade. Bring reserved marinade to a boil in a saucepan; whisk in cornstarch, and cook, stirring constantly, 2 to 3 minutes or until thickened. Cool.
• **Pat** pork dry, and place on a rack in a shallow roasting pan.
• **Bake** pork at 325° for 2½ hours or until meat thermometer inserted into thickest portion registers 170°, basting with ¼ cup reserved sauce the last 15 minutes. Allow roast to stand 10 minutes before slicing. Serve with reserved sauce. **Yield:** 8 to 10 servings.

SPINACH LOAF WITH MUSHROOM SAUCE

An updated presentation adds an elegant touch to an everyday vegetable.

Prep: 20 minutes
Bake: 1 hour

2 pounds fresh spinach, stemmed
1 cup water
6 tablespoons butter or margarine, divided
3 to 4 green onions, chopped
4 large eggs
2 cups half-and-half, divided
1½ teaspoons salt, divided
¼ teaspoon pepper, divided
¼ teaspoon ground nutmeg
⅔ cup fine, dry breadcrumbs
½ cup grated Parmesan cheese
1 (8-ounce) package sliced fresh mushrooms
3 tablespoons all-purpose flour
3 tablespoons white wine

• **Cook** spinach and 1 cup water in a saucepan over high heat 4 minutes or until spinach wilts. Drain; rinse with cold water. Drain well, pressing between paper towels. Chop spinach, and set aside.
• **Melt** 2 tablespoons butter in a large skillet over medium heat; add green onions, and sauté 2 minutes.
• **Whisk** together eggs, 1 cup half-and-half, 1 teaspoon salt, ⅛ teaspoon pepper, and nutmeg. Stir in spinach, green onions, breadcrumbs, and cheese. Spoon mixture into a greased 9- x 5-inch loafpan. Place loafpan in a baking dish; fill baking dish with 2 inches hot water.
• **Bake** at 350° for 1 hour or until set. Let stand 10 minutes before unmolding.
• **Melt** remaining 4 tablespoons butter in skillet over medium heat; add mushrooms, and sauté 3 to 4 minutes or until tender. Whisk in flour, wine, remaining ½ teaspoon salt, and ⅛ teaspoon pepper. Cook, whisking constantly, 2 minutes; gradually add remaining half-and-half, stirring until mixture thickens. Serve over spinach loaf. **Yield:** 8 to 10 servings.

SIMPLIFY FOR THE SEASON

As a young family, Mary Frances and Moak Griffin wanted to spend more time with the baby than with elaborate decorations for their tree. Plus, in any new house, it's more fun to spend money on a new piece of furniture than on boxes of ornaments. Here are a few easy and inexpensive ideas that they used to decorate for the season.

■ Colorful ball ornaments are pretty off the tree. Scatter them along the table with candles, or pile them in a pretty bowl.

■ Decorate a tree with only lights and a tree topper, and use the gifts as ornaments. The tree will be festive and unique.

■ Make colorful paper-chain garlands with neighborhood friends and their children. In an afternoon, you can have enough decorations for several trees.

■ Plain fresh wreaths with a simple knot of ribbon add a festive touch. Tie jingle bells to those for the door to enjoy the cheerful holiday sound.

■ Wrap empty boxes to use as decorations. Placed in bowls, stacked on furniture, or scattered on a table, they add color and holiday flair.

ROASTED GLAZED VEGETABLES

Tender root vegetables spiced with cinnamon and nutmeg are sure to get the family around the table.

Prep: 20 minutes
Bake: 50 minutes

¼ cup butter or margarine, melted
¼ cup firmly packed brown sugar
¼ teaspoon ground nutmeg
½ teaspoon ground cinnamon
½ teaspoon pepper
4 medium parsnips, peeled and cut into 1-inch cubes
4 medium carrots, peeled and cut into 1-inch cubes
2 medium-size sweet potatoes, peeled and cut into 1-inch cubes
½ medium rutabaga, peeled and cut into 1-inch cubes

• **Heat** a roasting pan in a 325° oven for 10 minutes.
• **Stir** together first 5 ingredients in a large bowl; add vegetables, tossing to coat. Arrange vegetables in a single layer in hot roasting pan.
• **Bake** at 325° for 45 to 50 minutes or until vegetables are tender. **Yield:** 8 to 10 servings.

MACADAMIA-FUDGE CAKE

Prep: 15 minutes
Bake: 30 minutes

½ cup butter or margarine,
    softened
¾ cup sugar
1 large egg
¾ cup sour cream
½ teaspoon vanilla extract
1 cup all-purpose flour
3 tablespoons unsweetened cocoa
1 teaspoon instant coffee granules
½ teaspoon baking soda
½ teaspoon baking powder
¼ teaspoon salt
Macadamia-Fudge Topping
Garnish: toasted macadamia nuts

• **Beat** butter at medium speed with an electric mixer until creamy; gradually add sugar, beating until blended. Add egg, sour cream, and vanilla; beat well.
• **Combine** flour and next 5 ingredients; gradually add to butter mixture, beating until blended. Pour batter into a greased, wax paper-lined 9-inch pan.
• **Bake** at 350° for 25 to 30 minutes or until a wooden pick inserted in center comes out clean. Cool in pan 10 minutes. Remove from pan, and cool on a wire rack 10 minutes. Pour Macadamia-Fudge Topping over cake. Chill until ready to serve. Garnish, if desired. **Yield:** 1 (9-inch) cake.

Macadamia-Fudge Topping

Prep: 10 minutes

4 (1-ounce) semisweet chocolate
    squares
1 (7-ounce) jar macadamia nuts,
    toasted and coarsely chopped
1 cup whipping cream
¾ cup sugar
2 tablespoons butter or margarine
1 tablespoon corn syrup
1 teaspoon vanilla extract

• **Cook** first 6 ingredients in a saucepan over medium heat 5 minutes or until blended, stirring constantly. Remove from heat, and stir in vanilla. Let cool 10 minutes. **Yield:** 1¼ cups.

Chicken Plus Rice

Combine chicken with rice for flavorful, economical one-dish meals your family will ask for again and again.

Readers share their chicken and rice recipes with us from every corner of the South. Like most dishes, these recipes vary widely from cook to cook and region to region.

This one-dish meal is a favorite in many cultures—each with its own flavors. Arroz Con Pollo, made with yellow rice, chicken, vegetables, and seasonings, reflects Spanish flavors. Jambalaya, cousin to paella, reflects its Creole heritage, which uses a lot of green bell pepper, onion, and celery.

Cooking rice with chicken adds extra flavor. It's economical too. If you wish to substitute bone-in chicken breasts for chicken pieces, they'll be a little more expensive, but cook in about the same amount of time. Remove the skin from the chicken, if desired.

CHICKEN-AND-SAUSAGE JAMBALAYA

Smoked sausage and chopped cooked chicken update this jambalaya, while keeping it as Southern and equally satisfying as the original version that used ham.

Prep: 10 minutes
Cook: 40 minutes

2 tablespoons butter or margarine
2 celery ribs, chopped
1 medium onion, chopped
1 medium-size green bell pepper,
    chopped
1 pound smoked sausage, cut into
    ½-inch-thick pieces
4 cups chopped cooked chicken
2 cups uncooked long-grain rice
2 (10½-ounce) cans beef broth
½ teaspoon salt
¼ teaspoon pepper

• **Melt** butter in a large Dutch oven over medium heat; add celery, onion, and bell pepper, and sauté 5 minutes or until vegetables are tender. Add sausage, and sauté 5 minutes.
• **Stir** in chicken and remaining ingredients; bring to a boil. Cover, reduce heat to low, and simmer 30 minutes. **Yield:** 6 to 8 servings.

Judy Grimes
Brandon, Mississippi

ARROZ CON POLLO

If yellow rice seasoning mix isn't available, substitute yellow rice dinner for long-grain rice.

Prep: 15 minutes
Cook: 1 hour, 30 minutes

1 (3½-pound) package chicken
   pieces
3 tablespoons olive oil
2 large onions, diced
1 large green bell pepper, chopped
4 garlic cloves, minced
1 medium tomato, chopped
1 (0.28-ounce) package yellow
   rice seasoning mix
2 bay leaves
1 teaspoon dried oregano
⅛ teaspoon ground cloves
2 (14½-ounce) cans chicken
   broth
2 cups uncooked long-grain rice
1 teaspoon salt
½ teaspoon pepper

• **Brown** chicken in 2 batches in hot oil in a Dutch oven over medium-high heat 5 minutes. Remove chicken, and drain on paper towels.
• **Sauté** onion, bell pepper, and garlic in Dutch oven over medium heat 4 minutes or until tender. Add tomato and next 4 ingredients, and cook, stirring often, 15 minutes.
• **Add** chicken and broth; bring to a boil. Reduce heat, and simmer 15 minutes. Stir in rice, salt, and pepper; bring to a boil. Cover, reduce heat to low, and simmer 40 minutes or until rice is tender. **Yield**: 8 servings.

Note: For testing purposes only, we used Vigo Yellow Rice Seasoning Mix. It can be found with rice mixes at your local grocery.

Elisabeth Thompson
Louisville, Georgia

CHICKEN AND WILD RICE

Prep: 20 minutes
Cook: 45 minutes
Bake: 20 minutes

1 (2½- to 3-pound) chicken,
   cut-up
1 quart water
1¼ teaspoons salt, divided
1 (6-ounce) package long-grain
   and wild rice mix
¼ cup butter or margarine
⅓ cup minced green bell pepper
¼ cup all-purpose flour
1 (12-ounce) can evaporated
   milk
¼ teaspoon pepper
¾ cup shredded Parmesan cheese
1 (4.5-ounce) jar sliced
   mushrooms, drained

• **Bring** chicken, 1 quart water, and 1 teaspoon salt to a boil in a Dutch oven; reduce heat, and simmer 45 minutes or until done. Remove chicken, and cool slightly, reserving broth. Skin and bone chicken, and cut into bite-size pieces. Set chicken aside.
• **Cook** rice mix according to package directions, substituting 1½ cups reserved broth for water. Set remaining broth aside.
• **Melt** butter in a large skillet; add bell pepper, and sauté until tender. Whisk in flour, and cook, whisking constantly, 1 minute. Gradually whisk in evaporated milk until smooth. Cook over medium-high heat, whisking constantly, until thickened and bubbly.
• **Stir** in chicken, rice, remaining ¼ teaspoon salt, pepper, Parmesan cheese, and mushrooms. Pour into a lightly greased 13- x 9-inch baking dish.
• **Bake** at 350° for 20 minutes. **Yield**: 4 to 6 servings.

Gayle Millican
Rowlett, Texas

ONE-DISH CHICKEN AND RICE

This tasty entrée is easy on the budget and the cook.

Prep: 12 minutes
Cook: 1 hour

1 (16-ounce) package yellow rice
   dinner
1 (3½-pound) package chicken
   pieces
3 tablespoons vegetable oil
1 large onion, diced
½ green bell pepper, diced
1 plum tomato, diced
1 (14½-ounce) can chicken broth
½ teaspoon salt
¼ teaspoon pepper
¼ teaspoon garlic powder
⅛ teaspoon ground red pepper
1 (8½-ounce) can sweet green peas,
   drained

• **Cook** rice according to package directions; set aside.
• **Brown** chicken in 2 batches in hot oil in a Dutch oven over medium-high heat 5 minutes. Remove chicken, and drain on paper towels.
• **Sauté** onion, bell pepper, and tomato in Dutch oven 10 minutes.
• **Add** chicken pieces, chicken broth, and next 4 ingredients; cover, reduce heat, and simmer 30 minutes. Stir in rice and peas; cover, reduce heat to low, and simmer 20 minutes. **Yield:** 6 to 8 servings.

Note: For testing purposes only, we used Pick-of-the Chick for chicken pieces.

Pat Benigno
Vicksburg, Mississippi

Holiday Recipe Contest Winners

These reader recipes were, in our opinion, simply the best.

It seemed like Christmas in July. While the searing Alabama sun wilted plants and people outside, the *Southern Living* Foods staff sorted, tasted, rated, and photographed holiday dishes inside. Christmas music wafted through the Test Kitchens, holiday china set the tone, and red and green became the colors of the day. The annual Holiday Recipe Contest was in full swing.

This year, we selected our winners from a field of more than 3,800 entries. Grand Prize Winners received $1,000, Runners-Up won $500. It was a daunting task, but the end result is 15 wonderful recipes to share with you. We hope you enjoy them as much as we did.

WINNING WAYS

Southern Living will offer a new recipe contest in 2002, featuring a Grand Prize of $100,000. Look for details in "Our Year at *Southern Living*" on page 10.

Fabulous Entrées

PEPPER-SEARED BEEF TENDERLOIN WITH HORSERADISH CREAM SAUCE

GRAND PRIZEWINNER

Angela Kotowicz and her husband, Chris, serve their winning recipe on Christmas Eve and other special occasions. "Every time we have made it, we have adapted the sauce to our liking, adding and changing things," Angela says. Horseradish, she notes, is Chris's favorite condiment.

Prep: 5 minutes
Cook: 8 minutes

4 (6-ounce) beef tenderloin fillets
¾ teaspoon salt, divided
1 tablespoon cracked pepper
½ cup butter or margarine, divided
2 teaspoons all-purpose flour
¼ teaspoon ground pepper
⅔ cup whipping cream
2 tablespoons prepared horseradish
1 teaspoon Dijon mustard

• **Sprinkle** fillets evenly with ½ teaspoon salt; press cracked pepper into all sides of fillets.
• **Melt** ¼ cup butter in a large heavy skillet over medium-high heat; add beef, and cook 3 to 4 minutes on each side or until desired degree of doneness.
• **Melt** remaining ¼ cup butter in a saucepan over medium heat. Whisk in flour, remaining ¼ teaspoon salt, and ground pepper until blended; cook, whisking constantly, 1 minute. Add cream, and cook, whisking constantly, 1 minute or until thickened and bubbly. Stir in horseradish and mustard. Drizzle over fillets. **Yield:** 4 servings.

Angela M. Kotowicz
St. Louis, Missouri

SPIKED PORK TENDERLOIN WITH SUNNY PEAR CHUTNEY

RUNNER-UP

Rosemary Johnson says this dish began with a cheesecake. "I had loads of tequila left over, so I decided to use it with a tenderloin. And I love all kinds of chutneys, so I thought it would be fun to make one for this dish."

Prep: 15 minutes
Chill: 30 minutes
Bake: 35 minutes
Stand: 10 minutes

½ cup tequila
1 tablespoon brown sugar
2 tablespoons walnut oil
1 teaspoon dried rosemary
1 teaspoon dried thyme
1 teaspoon paprika
½ teaspoon kosher salt
1 (2.8-pound) package pork tenderloins
Sunny Pear Chutney

- **Combine** first 7 ingredients in a large shallow dish; add pork. Cover and chill 30 minutes, turning occasionally.
- **Remove** pork from marinade, reserving marinade. Bring marinade to a boil in a saucepan; keep warm.
- **Place** pork on a lightly greased rack in a roasting pan.
- **Bake** at 375° for 30 to 35 minutes or until a meat thermometer inserted into thickest portion registers 160°, basting often with reserved marinade. Let tenderloins stand 10 minutes before slicing. Serve with Sunny Pear Chutney. **Yield:** 6 servings.

Sunny Pear Chutney

Prep: 15 minutes
Cook: 30 minutes

2 tangerines, sectioned and chopped*
2 Bosc pears, chopped
2 tablespoons grated fresh ginger
½ cup raspberry vinegar
¼ cup firmly packed brown sugar
1 (3-inch) cinnamon stick
¼ teaspoon ground allspice
¼ cup chopped walnuts
¼ cup lime juice
¼ teaspoon ground red pepper

- **Cook** first 7 ingredients in a large saucepan over medium heat 20 minutes. Stir in walnuts, lime juice, and red pepper; cook 10 minutes. Cool slightly. Remove and discard cinnamon stick before serving. **Yield:** 2 cups.

*Substitute 1 (11-ounce) can mandarin oranges, if desired.

Rosemary Johnson
Irondale, Alabama

COASTAL BEND REDFISH WITH SHRIMP AND CRAB

RUNNER-UP

Peter and Diane Halferty live right on the water in Corpus Christi and love to fish. Peter, a former tugboat captain, says he began cooking because "You can only paint the kitchen so many times!"

Prep: 35 minutes
Broil: 4 minutes

½ pound unpeeled, large fresh shrimp
1 cup Beurre Blanc
⅓ cup tomato puree
1 teaspoon sugar
1 teaspoon garlic salt
2 shallots, minced
1 small jalapeño pepper, seeded and minced
¼ cup olive oil, divided
2 plum tomatoes, peeled, seeded, and diced
½ pound fresh jumbo lump crabmeat
4 (6- to 8-ounce) redfish or red snapper fillets, skinned
1 teaspoon salt
1 teaspoon pepper
12 asparagus spears, cooked
8 small carrots, sliced and cooked
2 zucchini, cooked and sliced
2 large plum tomatoes, seeded and chopped
½ cup grated fontina cheese
Garnish: fresh chopped cilantro

- **Peel** shrimp, and devein, if desired; chop, and set aside.
- **Whisk** together Beurre Blanc and next 3 ingredients.
- **Sauté** shallots and jalapeño in 2 tablespoons hot oil in a large skillet over medium heat 1 minute. Add shrimp, and cook 1 minute or just until shrimp turn pink. Add diced tomato; sauté 30 seconds. Stir in crabmeat and Beurre Blanc mixture; keep warm.
- **Brush** fillets with remaining 2 tablespoons olive oil; sprinkle with salt and pepper. Place on a rack in a broiler pan.
- **Broil** 4 inches from heat 2 minutes on each side or until fish flakes with a fork.

Remove to a serving platter. Arrange asparagus and next 3 ingredients around fillets; sprinkle with cheese. Serve with shrimp mixture; garnish, if desired. **Yield:** 4 servings.

Beurre Blanc

Prep: 15 minutes
Cook: 30 minutes

¾ cup dry white vermouth
2 shallots, minced
2 tablespoons white wine vinegar
¾ cup whipping cream
½ cup butter or margarine, cut up
1 tablespoon fresh lemon juice
½ teaspoon salt
⅛ teaspoon ground white pepper

- **Bring** first 3 ingredients to a boil in a small saucepan; cook 15 minutes or until liquid is reduced to ¼ cup. Stir in cream, and cook 10 minutes or until reduced to ⅓ cup.
- **Reduce** heat, and whisk in butter, 1 tablespoon at a time; cook, whisking constantly, 5 minutes or until sauce thickens. Stir in lemon juice, salt, and pepper. **Yield:** 2 cups.

Peter Halferty
Corpus Christi, Texas

THE SCENT OF THE HOLIDAYS

You don't have to be a cook to create an inviting aroma in the kitchen. Along with the hint of pine from your wreaths, offer guests the subtle scent of holiday spices.

Simply simmer a few cinnamon sticks and whole cloves in 2 cups of water. (Tip: Set a timer to remind yourself to add water to the saucepan or to turn off the stove.)

CHICKEN POT PIE

GRAND PRIZEWINNER

Mary Cale's daughter-in-law was so convinced this recipe would win that she submitted it for her mother-in-law. Mary says, "It's just an old country recipe I've been making for a few years, and it's one of our family's favorites. It's also a good dish to give to people in the church or take to a party."

Prep: 45 minutes
Cook: 1 hour, 50 minutes
Bake: 25 minutes

1 (3½-pound) whole chicken
5 cups water
2 celery rib tops with leaves
1¼ teaspoons salt
¼ teaspoon pepper
3 to 4 bacon slices
3 green onions, sliced
2 large celery ribs, chopped
½ cup all-purpose flour
3 hard-cooked eggs, sliced
3 carrots, cooked and diced
1 (8.5-ounce) can sweet green peas, drained
1 teaspoon salt
¼ teaspoon pepper
⅛ teaspoon dried thyme
½ (15-ounce) package refrigerated piecrusts
Cranberry sauce

• **Bring** first 5 ingredients to a boil in a large Dutch oven; reduce heat, and simmer 1½ hours or until chicken is done.
• **Remove** chicken, reserving 3½ cups broth in Dutch oven; discard celery tops. Let chicken cool; skin, bone, and cut into bite-size pieces.
• **Cook** bacon in a skillet until crisp; remove bacon, and drain on paper towels, reserving 3 tablespoons drippings in skillet. Crumble bacon, and set aside.
• **Sauté** green onions and chopped celery in hot drippings in skillet over medium heat 5 minutes or until tender. Gradually whisk in ½ cup flour until blended. Gradually add reserved broth; cook, whisking constantly, 3 minutes or

until thickened and bubbly. Stir in chicken, bacon, eggs, and next 5 ingredients. Spoon mixture into a 3-quart baking dish; top with piecrust.
• **Bake** at 450° for 25 minutes or until golden and bubbly. Serve with cranberry sauce. **Yield:** 6 to 8 servings.

Mary Cale
Birmingham, Alabama

STROLLING-THROUGH-THE-HOLIDAYS STROGANOFF

RUNNER-UP

This dish is just one of the simple meals Clairiece Humphrey makes for her family. "It is wonderful comfort food," she says.

Prep: 30 minutes
Cook: 26 minutes

2 pounds unpeeled, large fresh shrimp
½ cup butter or margarine, divided
2 cups chopped cooked chicken
½ pound smoked Polish sausage, cut into ½-inch slices
1 (8-ounce) package sliced fresh mushrooms
½ small onion, diced
1 garlic clove, minced
¼ cup all-purpose flour
1 cup chicken broth
½ cup milk
½ cup white wine
1 teaspoon ketchup
½ teaspoon Worcestershire sauce
1 (8-ounce) container sour cream
1 tablespoon chopped fresh dillweed
Hot cooked rice

• **Peel** shrimp, and devein, if desired.
• **Melt** ¼ cup butter in a Dutch oven over medium-high heat; add shrimp, and cook 3 to 5 minutes or just until shrimp turn pink. Remove shrimp, and set aside. Add chicken and sausage to pan; cook 5 minutes or until thoroughly heated. Remove from pan; keep warm.
• **Melt** remaining ¼ cup butter in Dutch oven over medium-high heat; add mushrooms, and sauté 5 minutes. Add onion and garlic; sauté 5 minutes or until tender. Whisk in flour, and cook,

whisking constantly, 1 minute. Add broth, milk, and wine; cook, whisking constantly, 5 minutes or until thickened.
• **Stir** in ketchup, Worcestershire sauce, and shrimp.
• **Remove** from heat, and stir in sour cream and dillweed. Stir in chicken mixture; serve over rice. **Yield:** 6 to 8 servings.

Clairiece Gilbert Humphrey
Charlottesville, Virginia

MEXICAN LASAGNA

RUNNER-UP

"I'm a casserole person," declares Christina Valenta. "I came up with this dish in a New York minute, from leftovers."

Prep: 30 minutes
Bake: 30 minutes

½ pound ground mild pork sausage
½ pound ground beef
1 (15-ounce) can jalapeño Ranch-style pinto beans, drained
⅔ cup canned diced tomatoes and green chiles
1 teaspoon garlic powder
1 teaspoon ground cumin
½ teaspoon salt
½ teaspoon pepper
1 (10¾-ounce) can cream of celery soup
1 (10¾-ounce) can cream of mushroom soup
1 (10-ounce) can enchilada sauce
9 (6-inch) corn tortillas
2 cups (8 ounces) shredded Cheddar cheese
1 cup (4 ounces) shredded Monterey Jack cheese
1 medium tomato, seeded and diced
4 green onions, chopped
¼ cup chopped fresh cilantro
1 medium avocado, chopped

• **Cook** sausage and ground beef in a large skillet over medium-high heat, stirring until meat crumbles and is no longer pink. Drain. Stir in beans and next 5 ingredients; cook until thoroughly heated.

- **Stir** together soups and enchilada sauce in a saucepan; cook until heated.
- **Spoon** one-third of sauce into a lightly greased 13- x 9-inch baking dish; top with 3 tortillas. Spoon half of beef mixture and one-third of sauce over tortillas; sprinkle with half of Cheddar cheese. Top with 3 tortillas; repeat layers of beef, sauce, Cheddar cheese, and tortillas, ending with tortillas. Sprinkle with Monterey Jack cheese and next 3 ingredients.
- **Bake** at 350° for 30 minutes. Top with avocado. **Yield:** 6 to 8 servings.

Christina Valenta
Friendswood, Texas

Make-Ahead Appetizers

MINI PRIME RIBS AND YORKSHIRE PUDDINGS

GRAND PRIZEWINNER

Every year, Terri Kurlan holds a Christmas party for about 100 folks. "I always try to come up with something different," she says. "These are great because you can make them ahead. I made 500 of them last year, and within an hour they were all gone!"

Prep: 45 minutes
Chill: 8 hours
Stand: 15 minutes
Bake: 1 hour, 46 minutes

3 large eggs, lightly beaten
1 cup all-purpose flour
1 cup milk
1 (4- to 6-pound) bone-in prime rib roast
1 teaspoon salt
1 teaspoon pepper
Horseradish sauce or prepared horseradish *

- **Stir** together eggs, flour, and milk; cover and chill batter 8 hours.
- **Sprinkle** roast with salt and pepper, and place on a rack in an aluminum foil-lined roasting pan.
- **Bake** at 500° for 30 minutes. Reduce temperature to 350°, and bake 30

minutes. Increase temperature to 450°; bake 35 more minutes or to desired degree of doneness. Remove roast, and let stand 15 minutes before slicing, reserving about ½ cup drippings in pan.
- **Spoon** drippings into miniature muffin pan cups, filling one-fourth full.
- **Bake** at 450° for 2 minutes or until thoroughly heated.
- **Stir** chilled batter; spoon into miniature muffin pans, filling half full.
- **Bake** at 450° for 9 minutes or until puffy and golden. Remove from oven; make a well in center of pudding. Arrange prime rib slices in centers; top with horseradish sauce or horseradish. Serve warm. **Yield:** 64 appetizers.

*Substitute ½ cup sour cream, 1 tablespoon prepared horseradish, 2 tablespoons lemon juice, and ¼ teaspoon salt combined for horseradish sauce, if desired. Makes about ⅔ cup sauce.

Note: Freeze Yorkshire Puddings, if desired. Let thaw at room temperature 30 minutes; reheat at 400° for 5 to 7 minutes. Assemble as directed.

Terri Kurlan
McKinney, Texas

SPINACH CROSTINI

RUNNER-UP

"I first tasted this recipe at a New Year's Eve party," says Pam Binkowski, "and I changed things around until it became what it is." She occasionally serves it as a light meal for herself and her husband.

Prep: 25 minutes
Bake: 18 minutes

1 (10-ounce) package frozen chopped spinach, thawed and drained
2 plum tomatoes, diced
1 small onion, diced
1 garlic clove, minced
½ cup crumbled feta cheese
¼ cup mayonnaise
¼ cup sour cream
¼ teaspoon pepper
1 (16-ounce) French bread loaf, cut into ½-inch slices

- **Combine** first 8 ingredients; spread on 1 side of each bread slice. Place on a baking sheet.
- **Bake** at 350° for 18 minutes or until golden. **Yield:** 8 appetizer servings.

Pam Binkowski
Cullman, Alabama

SPICY CRAB-AND-GINGER SALSA WITH SESAME WONTONS

RUNNER-UP

Edwina Gadsby added crab to her favorite Thai cucumber salsa with delicious results. "The ginger and lime seem to enhance the crab," she says.

Prep: 25 minutes
Cook: 1 minute per batch

3 tablespoons rice wine vinegar
2 tablespoons vegetable oil
1 tablespoon lime juice
1 to 2 teaspoons Thai chili-garlic sauce
1 teaspoon sesame oil
½ teaspoon salt
12 ounces lump crabmeat, drained and coarsely chopped
1 cucumber, peeled, seeded, and diced
2 green onions, sliced
2 tablespoons chopped pickled ginger
Peanut oil
24 wontons
2 tablespoons sesame seeds, toasted

- **Whisk** together first 6 ingredients. Stir in crabmeat and next 3 ingredients. Cover and chill until ready to serve.
- **Pour** peanut oil to a depth of ½ inch into a large skillet. Fry wontons, in batches, in hot oil over medium-high heat 30 seconds on each side or until golden. Drain on paper towels; sprinkle with sesame seeds. Serve with salsa. **Yield:** 8 appetizer servings.

Note: Look for chili-garlic sauce or paste in the Asian section of the supermarket or in gourmet stores.

Edwina Gadsby
Great Falls, Montana

CAJUN CORN
MAQUE CHOUX

GRAND PRIZEWINNER

Maque choux (or mock cabbage) is a dish Georgette Dugas grew up making and eating in South Louisiana. She added her own touches, including andouille sausage. "It's not exactly the way my mother made it," she says, "but I thank her for the basics."

Prep: 10 minutes
Cook: 28 minutes

1 small onion, chopped
¼ cup chopped green bell pepper
1 to 2 tablespoons olive oil
3 cups frozen shoepeg corn, thawed
2 plum tomatoes, diced
¼ pound andouille sausage, cooked and diced
¼ cup chopped green onion tops
¼ teaspoon salt
¼ teaspoon pepper

• **Sauté** onion and bell pepper in hot oil in a large skillet over medium heat 8 minutes or until tender.
• **Add** corn, tomato, and sausage, and cook, stirring often, 15 minutes. Stir in green onions, salt, and pepper; cook 5 minutes. **Yield:** 6 servings.

Georgette M. Dugas
Crowley, Louisiana

CARROT
SOUFFLÉ

RUNNER-UP

"I love carrots," says Trish Conroy. "They're great as a side dish." This old-fashioned bake, she says, has become a family favorite.

Prep: 10 minutes
Cook: 45 minutes
Bake: 45 minutes

1 pound carrots, peeled and chopped
3 large eggs, lightly beaten
½ cup sugar
½ cup butter or margarine, melted
3 tablespoons all-purpose flour
1 teaspoon baking powder
1 teaspoon vanilla extract

• **Bring** carrots and water to cover to a boil in a medium saucepan; cook 45 minutes or until very tender. Drain.
• **Process** carrots in a food processor until smooth.
• **Stir** together carrot puree, eggs, and remaining ingredients. Spoon into a lightly greased 1-quart baking dish.
• **Bake** at 350° for 45 minutes or until set. **Yield:** 8 servings.

Trish Conroy
Lynchburg, Virginia

SPINACH-PECAN
SALAD

RUNNER-UP

Kathy Moss's family challenged each other to bring some new dishes to Thanksgiving one year, and this salad was her contribution. It was a big hit, as she recalls. "No one in the family had ever thought of spinach for Thanksgiving!"

Prep: 10 minutes
Cook: 3 minutes

1 tablespoon butter or margarine
½ cup pecan halves
1 tablespoon brown sugar
1 (6-ounce) package fresh baby spinach
1 large Granny Smith apple, thinly sliced
½ cup crumbled blue cheese
2 tablespoons olive oil
2 tablespoons white vinegar

• **Melt** butter in a small skillet over low heat; add pecans and brown sugar. Cook, stirring constantly, 2 to 3 minutes or until caramelized. Cool pecans on wax paper.
• **Place** spinach in a large serving bowl. Toss in pecans, apple, and blue cheese. Add oil and vinegar, tossing gently to coat. **Yield:** 4 servings.

Kathy Moss
Siloam Springs, Arkansas

Gracious Southern Desserts

There was such enthusiastic discussion in this category that Editor John Floyd suggested we select two Grand Prizewinners.

PRALINE-PUMPKIN TORTE

GRAND PRIZEWINNER

Mila Bryning gets rave reviews on this cake she adapted from her sister's recipe. "I've taken this cake all over," she says, "to church gatherings and family reunions, and I've given the recipe to everyone."

Prep: 15 minutes
Bake: 35 minutes

¾ cup firmly packed brown sugar
⅓ cup butter or margarine
3 tablespoons whipping cream
¾ cup chopped pecans
4 large eggs
1⅔ cups sugar
1 cup vegetable oil
1 (15-ounce) can pumpkin
¼ teaspoon vanilla extract
2 cups all-purpose flour
2 teaspoons baking powder
2 teaspoons pumpkin pie spice
1 teaspoon baking soda
1 teaspoon salt
Whipped Cream Topping
Chopped pecans

• **Cook** first 3 ingredients in a saucepan over low heat, stirring until sugar dissolves. Pour into 2 greased 9-inch round cakepans; sprinkle evenly with ¾ cup pecans. Cool.
• **Beat** eggs, sugar, and oil at medium speed with an electric mixer. Add pumpkin and vanilla; beat well.
• **Combine** flour and next 4 ingredients; add to pumpkin mixture, beating until blended. Spoon batter evenly into prepared cakepans.
• **Bake** at 350° for 30 to 35 minutes or until a wooden pick inserted in center comes out clean. Cool in pans on wire racks 5 minutes; remove from pans, and cool on wire racks.

• **Place** cake layer on a serving plate, praline side up; spread evenly with half of Whipped Cream Topping. Top with remaining layer, praline side up, and spread remaining Whipped Cream Topping over top of cake. Sprinkle with pecans. Store in refrigerator. **Yield:** 1 (9-inch) layer cake.

Whipped Cream Topping

Prep: 5 minutes

1¾ cups whipping cream
¼ cup powdered sugar
¼ teaspoon vanilla extract

• **Beat** cream until soft peaks form. Add sugar and vanilla, beating until blended. **Yield:** 3½ cups.

Mila Bryning
Alexandria, Virginia

ORANGE DATE-NUT CAKE

GRAND PRIZEWINNER

"I've had this recipe for over 50 years," Betty Skinner says. "I got it from a 90-year-old woman. It's such a rich cake that you don't need but a small slice." Still, she admits to adding a dab of whipped cream to dress it up.

Prep: 25 minutes
Bake: 1 hour, 10 minutes

1 cup butter or margarine, softened
4 cups sugar, divided
4 large eggs
4 cups all-purpose flour
1 teaspoon baking soda
1½ cups buttermilk
1 (8-ounce) package chopped sugared dates
1 cup chopped pecans, toasted
4 teaspoons grated orange rind, divided
1 cup orange juice

• **Beat** butter at medium speed with an electric mixer until creamy. Gradually add 2 cups sugar, beating well. Add eggs, 1 at a time, beating until blended after each addition.

• **Combine** flour and baking soda; add to butter mixture alternately with buttermilk, beginning and ending with flour mixture. Beat at low speed until blended after each addition. Stir in dates, pecans, and 2 teaspoons orange rind. Pour batter into a greased and floured 10-inch tube pan.
• **Bake** at 350° for 1 hour and 10 minutes or until a wooden pick inserted in center comes out clean.
• **Bring** orange juice, remaining 2 cups sugar, and remaining 2 teaspoons orange rind to a boil in a saucepan; cook, stirring constantly, 1 minute.
• **Run** a knife around edge of cake gently; punch holes in cake with a wooden pick. Drizzle glaze over warm cake. Cool cake in pan on a wire rack. **Yield:** 1 (10-inch) cake.

Betty W. Skinner
Blacksburg, Virginia

DECK THE KITCHEN HALLS

Create a holiday atmosphere in your kitchen by paying attention to details.

Household traffic never fails to end up in the kitchen. Whether guests are lured there by tasty treats or enticing scents from the oven, this room usually becomes the center of activity in most homes. Be prepared for kitchen gatherings, and have a few surprises waiting there to greet friends and family members. With some quick decorative touches, you can make this space ready for a round of holiday visitors.

■ When hanging boughs of holly, don't forget the kitchen. Greenery is a quick way to add seasonality. To adorn bare windows, hang wreaths with clear filament line. Conceal filament by taping one straight piece of decorative ribbon over the wire. Attach a bow to the top of the wreath to give the appearance that the ribbon is one continuous piece. Live wreaths—such as eucalyptus, pine, or fir—offer familiar and pleasant scents.

■ Clip several pieces of greenery from the yard—all readily available outside your door—to include in tabletop displays.

■ Decorate cabinet knobs or door handles by hanging Christmas ornaments from ribbon. When hanging them in high places or in well-used spots, be sure to select unbreakable ornaments— soft or beaded ones—or bells. A fall or accident could break fragile treasures.

FESTIVE PIÑA COLADA CHEESECAKE

RUNNER-UP

Marie Rizzio declares that she hasn't found a single person who doesn't like this dessert. "And," she adds, "who won't fight over the last bite on the plate!"

Prep: 15 minutes
Bake: 1 hour, 15 minutes
Chill: 8 hours

6 tablespoons unsalted butter, melted
1¾ cups graham cracker crumbs
¾ cup chopped pecans, toasted
1 tablespoon sugar
3 (8-ounce) packages cream cheese, softened
½ cup sugar
5 large eggs
1 (8-ounce) can crushed pineapple, drained
1 cup cream of coconut
1 cup sour cream
⅓ cup light rum
4 teaspoons coconut extract
Glaze
Garnishes: whipped cream, toasted coconut

• **Stir** together first 4 ingredients, and press into bottom and 1½ inches up sides of a lightly greased 10-inch springform pan.
• **Beat** cream cheese and ½ cup sugar at medium speed with an electric mixer 3 minutes or until fluffy.
• **Add** eggs, 1 at a time, beating well after each addition.
• **Add** pineapple and next 4 ingredients, beating until blended. Pour pineapple mixture into prepared crust.
• **Bake** at 325° for 1 hour and 15 minutes or until center of cheesecake is almost set.
• **Cool** on a wire rack. Spread Glaze over top of cheesecake.
• **Cover** and chill cheesecake at least 8 hours. Garnish, if desired. **Yield:** 1 (10-inch) cheesecake.

Glaze

Prep: 5 minutes
Cook: 5 minutes

1 tablespoon cornstarch
1 tablespoon water
1 (8-ounce) can crushed pineapple
¼ cup sugar
2 tablespoons lemon juice

• **Stir** together cornstarch and 1 tablespoon water until smooth. Combine cornstarch mixture, pineapple, sugar, and lemon juice in a saucepan over medium heat; cook, stirring constantly, 5 minutes or until thickened and bubbly. Remove from heat; cool completely. **Yield:** 1 cup.

Marie Rizzio
Traverse City, Michigan

Taste of the South

*Eggnog is a beloved Southern tradition—
with or without the bourbon. Savor a sip of
of this rich, creamy beverage as you celebrate the
holidays with family and friends.*

Nothing brings the glad tidings of Christmas like a cup of cold sweet, creamy eggnog. We traditionally toast guests' health and happiness with this milk-punch beverage that originated in England. Settlers brought the custom to America, where dairy farms offered a plentiful supply of milk, cream, and eggs. Inventive Southerners replaced expensive rum and brandy with the more readily available favorite, bourbon. Thus, eggnog evolved into the beverage of spirit and spice we love so much today.

Test Kitchens staffer Jan Moon's Aunt Kat has a secret family recipe that Jan's divulging today—please don't tell Aunt Kat. The family has served it proudly every Christmas since Aunt Kat was a little girl. Her mother, Jan's Grandmother Lillie, made it in generous amounts for all the friends and relatives that would always drop in during the holidays. As a younger woman, though, Grandmother Lillie found that same eggnog to be a sinful potion.

Aunt Kat loves to tell the story of the first Christmas Lillie spent with her husband's family. Lillie came from a long line of Baptist ministers who preached against the evils of alcohol. She was shocked when her father-in-law pulled a shiny white jug of bourbon from the large mahogany sideboard in the dining room. When he proceeded to pour the whiskey into the enormous cut-glass punch bowl of eggnog, Lillie fainted with fear. When she came to, she was lovingly presented a small cup of the very same eggnog.

Aunt Kat laughs and says, "After that, Mother never did serve eggnog without the bourbon. And you can be sure if Christmas was at Aunt Oma's it would always have an extra-generous portion of whiskey, which just added to our Christmas cheer!"

Assistant Foods Editor Cindy Briscoe, a bourbon connoisseur, wholeheartedly argues there is no substitute for the bourbon in eggnog. But if your principles prompt you to abstain, just replace it with milk or cream.

Aunt Kat recalls her mother being very particular about where she bought her cream and eggs. She would carefully heat the milk and sugar and ever so slowly add the fresh eggs so they would not cook in the hot milk. She would let each child have his turn at stirring the pot with her big wooden spoon until the mixture became a thick, satiny liquid. She then gently poured this into a large crock to cool until she could fold in the whipped cream. This process was repeated several times over the holidays as company came and went.

Even today Jan's family looks forward with anticipation to that first batch of eggnog. This wonderfully rich cup of Christmas will bring a soft sigh to the weary people on your guest list. The *Southern Living* Foods staff liked it so much, we gave it our highest rating. We hope you will give Aunt Kat's eggnog a try—she would be so proud.

AUNT KAT'S CREAMY EGGNOG

Prep: 10 minutes
Cook: 30 minutes

1 quart milk
12 large eggs
¼ teaspoon salt
1½ cups sugar
¾ cup to 1½ cups bourbon ∗
1 tablespoon vanilla extract
½ teaspoon ground nutmeg, divided
1 quart whipping cream

• **Heat** milk in a large saucepan over medium heat. (Do not boil.)
• **Beat** eggs and salt at medium speed with an electric mixer until thick and pale; gradually add sugar, beating well. Gradually stir about one-fourth of hot milk into egg mixture; add to remaining hot milk, stirring constantly.
• **Cook** over medium-low heat, stirring constantly, 25 to 30 minutes or until mixture thickens and reaches 160°.
• **Stir** in bourbon, vanilla, and ¼ teaspoon nutmeg. Remove from heat; cool. Cover and chill up to 2 days.
• **Beat** whipping cream at medium speed with an electric mixer until soft peaks form. Fold whipped cream into egg mixture. Sprinkle with remaining ¼ teaspoon nutmeg before serving. **Yield:** 3 quarts.

∗ Substitute 1½ to 2 cups milk for bourbon, if desired.

Living Light

*Choose from three menus or combine them
for a dazzling brunch.*

All the Fixins' Menu

Pineapple-Glazed Ham
Veggie Scramble   Whole-grain toast
Baked Cheese Grits
Champagne-Poached Pears
Green Onion-and-Cream Cheese Muffins
Fresh fruit such as grapes, strawberries, and kiwi (optional)

♥ Per person: 973 calories,
41g fat (38% calories from fat)

Hosting a brunch for friends can be fun and relaxing if you plan ahead and keep your menu simple. We've created two menus, plus a mixed menu, to serve as your guide. If you're looking for a "stick-to-your-ribs" meal, select the Down-Home Menu. For a lighter, quick-to-fix option, try the Continental Menu. If a hearty menu with more variety is what you're after, choose the All the Fixins' Menu. Whichever you choose, these options will be a hit with your midday guests.

PINEAPPLE-GLAZED HAM

To lower sodium, buy a reduced-sodium ham, and omit salt.

Prep: 20 minutes
Chill: 8 hours
Bake: 2 hours

1 (10-pound) smoked ham
3 tablespoons whole cloves
1 (20-ounce) can crushed pineapple, undrained
2 cups pineapple juice
1½ cups firmly packed dark brown sugar
1 cup bourbon
½ teaspoon salt

• **Remove** skin and excess fat from ham. Score ham in a diamond design, and insert cloves at 1-inch intervals. Place ham in an aluminum foil-lined roasting pan.

• **Stir** together pineapple and remaining 4 ingredients; pour over ham. Cover and chill 8 hours.
• **Bake** at 350° for 2 hours, basting every 30 minutes. **Yield:** about 25 (3½-ounce) servings.

Patsy Butts
Jacksonville Beach, Florida

♥ Per 3½ ounces: Calories 223 (56% from fat)
Fat 14g (sat 5g, mono 6.5g, poly 1.5g)
Protein 18g Carb 4.7g Fiber 0g
Chol 51mg Iron 0.8mg
Sodium 996mg Calc 9.5mg

VEGGIE SCRAMBLE

Prep: 10 minutes
Cook: 10 minutes

½ small red bell pepper
½ small green bell pepper
¼ small sweet onion
Vegetable cooking spray
8 large eggs, lightly beaten
¼ teaspoon salt
½ teaspoon freshly ground pepper
½ cup (2 ounces) shredded reduced-fat sharp Cheddar cheese

• **Chop** bell peppers and onion. Cook in a large skillet coated with cooking spray over medium-high heat 5 minutes or until vegetables are tender.
• **Whisk** together eggs, salt, and pepper. Add mixture to skillet; cook, without stirring, until eggs begin to set on bottom. Draw a spatula across bottom of skillet to form large curds. Sprinkle with cheese; continue cooking until eggs are thickened but still moist. (Do not stir constantly.) Remove from heat. Serve immediately with whole-grain toast. **Yield:** 4 servings.

Mary Pappas
Richmond, Virginia

♥ Per serving: Calories 187 (56% from fat)
Fat 11.7g (sat 3.9g, mono 4.4g, poly 1.5g)
Protein 16g Carb 3g Fiber 0.5g
Chol 427mg Iron 1.4mg
Sodium 356mg Calc 113mg

BAKED CHEESE GRITS

Prep: 15 minutes
Bake: 40 minutes

2⅔ cups water
⅔ cup quick-cooking grits
2 tablespoons light margarine
2 large eggs, lightly beaten
½ (8-ounce) loaf light pasteurized
     prepared cheese product, cut into
     ½-inch pieces
¼ teaspoon salt
¼ teaspoon ground red pepper
Vegetable cooking spray

• **Bring** 2⅔ cups water to a boil; add grits, and cook, stirring often, 5 minutes or until thickened. Remove from heat. Add margarine and next 4 ingredients; stir until blended. Spoon into a 2-quart baking dish coated with cooking spray.
• **Bake** at 350° for 40 minutes or until lightly browned. **Yield:** 3½ cups.

Note: Casserole may be chilled up to 8 hours. Let stand at room temperature 30 minutes; bake as directed.

Howard Wiener
Spring Hill, Florida

❤ Per ½ cup: Calories 131 (36% from fat)
Fat 5g (sat 1.9g, mono 1.3g, poly 1g)
Protein 6.3g Carb 14g Fiber 0.3g
Chol 67mg Iron 0.3mg
Sodium 389mg Calc 101mg

CHAMPAGNE-POACHED PEARS

For an elegant presentation, serve individually in tea cups.

Prep: 20 minutes
Cook: 15 minutes

8 Bosc or Bartlett pears
1 (750-milliliter) bottle champagne or
     sparkling wine
½ gallon orange juice
1 (3-inch) cinnamon stick
5 whole cloves
Garnishes: orange and lemon rind
     strips

• **Peel** and core pears, leaving stems intact. Cut a thin slice from bottom of each pear, forming a base for pears to stand on.
• **Place** pears upright in a Dutch oven; pour champagne and orange juice over pears. Add cinnamon stick and cloves. Bring to a boil; reduce heat, and simmer 15 minutes or until pears are tender. Serve warm. Garnish, if desired. **Yield:** 8 servings.

Becki Connally
Mobile, Alabama

❤ Per serving: Calories 170 (5% from fat)
Fat 1g Protein 1.5g Carb 38g
Fiber 4g Chol 0mg Iron 0.7mg
Sodium 2mg Calc 34mg

GREEN ONION-AND-CREAM CHEESE MUFFINS

Prep: 10 minutes
Bake: 27 minutes

½ (8-ounce) package reduced-fat
     cream cheese, softened
1¾ cups reduced-fat biscuit mix
1¼ cups fat-free milk
3 green onions, chopped
¼ cup egg substitute
⅓ cup vegetable oil
1 tablespoon sugar
Vegetable cooking spray

• **Beat** cream cheese at low speed with an electric mixer until smooth; add biscuit mix alternately with milk, beginning and ending with biscuit mix. Stir in chopped green onions and next 3 ingredients.
• **Spoon** batter into 3-inch muffin cups coated with cooking spray.
• **Bake** at 400° for 25 to 27 minutes or until a wooden pick inserted in center comes out clean. Cool on wire racks. **Yield:** 1 dozen.

Charlotte Pierce-Bryant
Greensburg, Kentucky

❤ Per muffin: Calories 142 (57% from fat)
Fat 9g (sat 1.7g, mono 4g, poly 2g)
Protein 4g Carb 15g Fiber 0.2g
Chol 6mg Iron 0.7mg
Sodium 253mg Calc 51mg

MENU MAGIC

If you prefer a simpler menu, choose from these two delicious options.

Continental Menu

Veggie Scramble
Green Onion-and-Cream
Cheese Muffins
Mixed Fruit Granola
(recipe on page 290)
Vanilla yogurt, strawberries (optional)
❤ Per person: 639 calories,
26g fat (37% calories from fat)

Down-Home Menu

Pineapple-Glazed Ham
Baked Cheese Grits
Champagne-Poached Pears
Reduced-fat biscuits and jam
(optional)
❤ Per person: 762 calories,
27g fat (32% calories from fat)

MIXED FRUIT GRANOLA

Serve with nonfat vanilla yogurt for a creamy-chewy treat.

Prep: 10 minutes
Bake: 30 minutes

6 cups uncooked regular oats
½ cup wheat germ
½ cup sunflower kernels
½ cup chopped pecans
¼ cup sesame seeds
½ cup honey
2 tablespoons vegetable oil
½ tablespoon ground cinnamon
1½ teaspoons vanilla extract
Vegetable cooking spray
1½ cups chopped mixed dried
    fruit

• **Combine** first 9 ingredients; spread on 2 pans coated with cooking spray.
• **Bake** at 350° for 25 to 30 minutes, stirring 3 times. Cool. Stir in dried fruit. **Yield:** 7½ cups.

Note: Store in an airtight container up to 2 weeks.

Susan Cearley
Pipe Creek, Texas

♥ Per ¼ cup: Calories 145 (33% from fat)
Fat 5.3g (sat 0.6g, mono 2.1g, poly 2.2g)
Protein 4g   Carb 22g   Fiber 3g
Chol 0mg   Iron 1.4mg
Sodium 2.4mg   Calc 28mg

Top-Rated Menu

Simplify dinnertime this season with an easy but satisfying meal.

Soup for Supper Menu
Serves 6

Pot Liquor Soup
Skillet Cornbread
Praline Coffee   Shortbread cookies

If the holidays seem to pass you by in a blur, take time to savor a simple, wholesome supper with family and friends. Our casual menu offers a welcome departure from the usual indulgent foods of the season, and see "Buffet Bonus" on the opposite page to make serving the meal almost effortless.

This one-pot meal is simple to prepare and just right for the season's busy weeknights. Add a slice of hot, buttered cornbread to a steaming bowl of soup, and you've got a wonderfully warming meal.

Pot Liquor Soup is a meal in itself, and it also freezes well if you want to make it ahead. If you'd like to forgo rich sweet offerings, serve a delicious dessert coffee and cookies purchased from your local bakery.

We can't eliminate shopping for you, but navigating crowded supermarkets will be much easier with our grocery list in hand. Enjoy the menu, but most of all, treasure the company of your loved ones.

POT LIQUOR SOUP

1998 Recipe Hall of Fame

Prep: 1 hour
Cook: 55 minutes

2 pounds fresh collard greens
¾ pound smoked ham hocks
1 (1½-pound) ham steak, chopped
2 tablespoons hot sauce
3 tablespoons olive oil
3 medium onions, chopped
1 garlic clove, minced
6 red potatoes, diced
3 (14½-ounce) cans chicken broth
2 (15.8-ounce) cans field peas with
    snaps, rinsed and drained
2 (15.8-ounce) cans crowder peas,
    rinsed and drained
2 cups water
½ cup vermouth
1 tablespoon white vinegar
1 teaspoon salt

• **Remove** and discard stems and discolored spots from collards; rinse with cold water. Drain, and tear collards into 1-inch pieces.

- **Bring** collards, ham hocks, and water to cover to a boil in a large Dutch oven. Remove from heat; drain. Repeat procedure once.
- **Toss** together chopped ham and hot sauce; cook in hot oil in Dutch oven over medium-high heat 6 to 8 minutes or until browned.
- **Add** onion and garlic; sauté until tender. Stir in collards, hocks, potato, and remaining ingredients. Bring to a boil; reduce heat, and simmer, stirring occasionally, 45 minutes.
- **Remove** meat from hocks; discard hocks. Return meat to soup. **Yield:** 2½ quarts.

SKILLET CORNBREAD

2000 Recipe Hall of Fame

Prep: 10 minutes
Bake: 15 minutes

2 to 3 teaspoons bacon drippings or
   vegetable oil
2 cups buttermilk
1 large egg
1¾ cups white cornmeal
1 teaspoon baking powder
1 teaspoon baking soda
1 teaspoon salt
Butter

- **Coat** bottom and sides of a 10-inch cast-iron skillet with bacon drippings; heat in a 450° oven 10 minutes.
- **Whisk** together buttermilk and egg. Add cornmeal, stirring well.
- **Stir** in baking powder, soda, and salt. Pour batter into hot skillet.
- **Bake** at 450° for 15 minutes or until lightly browned. Serve with butter. **Yield:** 6 servings.

Note: This recipe is adapted from *Hoppin' John's Lowcountry Cooking* by John Martin Taylor.

PRALINE COFFEE

1997 Recipe Hall of Fame

Linger over this rich, creamy coffee, and enjoy your favorite shortbread cookie for an after-dinner treat.

Prep: 5 minutes
Cook: 5 minutes

3 cups hot brewed coffee
⅔ to ¾ cup firmly packed light
   brown sugar
¾ cup half-and-half
¾ cup praline liqueur
Sweetened whipped cream

- **Cook** first 3 ingredients in a saucepan over medium heat, stirring constantly, until thoroughly heated. (Do not boil.) Stir in liqueur, and serve coffee with dollops of sweetened whipped cream. **Yield:** 5 cups.

BUFFET BONUS

The perfect way to host a casual get-together during the holiday season is to serve the food buffet style. Guests and family members will enjoy the ease and freedom to serve themselves and mingle in an atmosphere of festive hospitality. Plus, a buffet allows you to focus on friends and family rather than on the food.

SHOPPING LIST

Staples on Hand
White vinegar (1 tablespoon)
Baking powder (1 teaspoon)
Baking soda (1 teaspoon)
Bacon drippings or vegetable oil
   (1 tablespoon)
Olive oil (3 tablespoons)
White cornmeal (1¾ cups)
Light brown sugar (⅔ to ¾ cup)
Coffee (3 cups hot brewed)
Salt

General
Hot sauce (2 tablespoons)
3 (14½-ounce) cans chicken
   broth
2 (15.8-ounce) cans field peas
   with snaps
2 (15.8-ounce) cans crowder peas
Vermouth (½ cup)
Praline liqueur (¾ cup)
Shortbread cookies

Produce
2 pounds fresh collard greens
3 medium onions
1 garlic clove
6 red potatoes

Dairy
2 cups buttermilk
1 large egg
¾ cup half-and-half
Butter
Whipped cream

Meat
¾ pound smoked ham hocks
1 (1½-pound) ham steak

Merging Cultures

*This Kwanzaa feast blends
both Southern and Jamaican family favorites.*

Sharon and Darrell Green's holiday feast blends both Southern and Jamaican family favorites. A buffet of fruit and vegetable dishes acts as the main event for the Atlanta couple, while Black Cake is always the star dessert. It's a fabulously rich confection, a part of Sharon's Jamaican heritage, and one of the best fruitcakes you'll ever taste.

The fruits are soaked in rum and pureed before they're added to the batter. Burnt sugar syrup adds to the distinct flavor, while prunes, raisins, currants, and dark brown sugar give the cake its deep, almost black color. Port is poured over the cake—made weeks in advance—so flavors mellow as the wine is absorbed.

"I enjoy sharing the flavors of my childhood. Black Cake is easy to make," Sharon says. "The key is soaking the fruit. The longer you soak it, the better the flavor and texture of the cake. Some of my family start soaking the fruit several months ahead."

In addition to adoring the fruitcake, Sharon and Darrell's sons, Khalfani and Azikiwea, love the sweet, pungent flavor of a beverage Sharon makes from fresh ginger. They call it Ginger Beer. The drink tastes like ginger ale without the fizz. "It's easy to keep some on hand to serve—hot or cold—when friends visit," says Sharon.

The Greens enjoy the season in many ways and places—from spending Christmas in South Carolina or Jamaica to observing Kwanzaa at home in Atlanta. No matter how you celebrate, Black Cake and Ginger Beer are delicious additions to your holiday menus.

BLACK CAKE (A KWANZAA FRUITCAKE)

*Serve this moist, flavorful cake
in small slices.*

*Prep: 30 minutes
Chill: 8 hours
Bake: 1 hour, 40 minutes*

1¾ cups currants
1½ cups raisins
1½ cups pitted prunes
1 (8-ounce) package candied cherries
½ (7-ounce) package mixed dried fruit
2 cups dark rum
6 large eggs
⅛ teaspoon ground cinnamon
⅛ teaspoon ground nutmeg
½ pound butter
½ pound dark brown sugar
2 cups all-purpose flour
1½ teaspoons baking powder
¼ cup burnt sugar syrup
2 cups tawny port wine
Whipped cream

• **Combine** first 6 ingredients in a bowl; cover and chill 8 hours or up to 1 week.
• **Process** fruit mixture, in batches, in a food processor until smooth, stopping to scrape down sides; set aside.
• **Whisk** together eggs, cinnamon, and nutmeg until foamy.
• **Beat** butter and sugar at medium speed with an electric mixer until creamy. Add egg mixture, beating until blended. Add fruit puree; blend well.
• **Combine** flour and baking powder; stir into fruit mixture. Stir in burnt sugar syrup. Spoon into a greased and floured 10-inch springform pan.
• **Bake** at 300° for 1 hour and 40 minutes or until a wooden pick inserted in center comes out clean. Cool in pan on a wire rack 1 hour; remove from pan, and cool completely on wire rack.
• **Pour** 1 cup port wine evenly over top of cake; let stand 10 minutes. Pour remaining wine over cake. Wrap cake with cheesecloth; place in a covered container. Let stand 2 to 3 days. (Do not refrigerate.) Serve with whipped cream, if desired. **Yield:** 1 (10-inch) fruitcake.

Note: Burnt sugar syrup is available by mail order from Eve Sales Corporation. Contact the company at 945 Close Avenue, Bronx, NY 10473; or call (718) 589-6800. The syrup costs $1.75 plus shipping and handling.

*Margarite Reed
Atlanta, Georgia*

GINGER BEER

*Prep: 10 minutes
Chill: 4 hours*

1 quart water
1 cup sugar
⅓ cup grated fresh ginger
1½ teaspoons grated lime rind
2 tablespoons fresh lime juice

• **Combine** all ingredients, stirring until sugar dissolves. Cover; chill 4 hours.
• **Pour** through a wire-mesh strainer into a large pitcher, discarding solids. Serve over crushed ice. **Yield:** 5 cups.

A LOOK AT KWANZAA

This 7-day celebration, more than a mere holiday, is a way of thinking and living. Kwanzaa, which means "first fruits," focuses on the strength and unity of the African-American family through principles, rituals, and symbols. For more information, visit www.geocities.com/ninure/kwaanza.html.

Hard-Shell Winter Squash

Winter squashes should be enjoyed now during this peak season. Their delicate flavors and tender flesh complement a variety of dishes. Baking is the most common method of cooking these sturdy vegetables. To bake, place the squash upside down in a baking dish, and fill with water to a depth of 1 inch. This provides moisture and even heat distribution. Then prepare them for your table with these delectable recipes.

ACORN SQUASH WITH PEAR STUFFING

Pears, bourbon, and ginger flavor this seasonal side dish.

Prep: 10 minutes
Cook: 35 minutes
Bake: 1 hour, 5 minutes

2 acorn squash
2 tablespoons butter or margarine
1 small onion, chopped
2 medium pears, peeled and chopped
2 tablespoons light brown sugar
2 tablespoons bourbon
1 teaspoon salt
½ teaspoon ground ginger
½ teaspoon ground nutmeg
1½ cups orange juice
¾ cup sugar

• **Cut** each squash in half lengthwise; remove and discard seeds and membranes. Place squash halves, cut side down, in a 13- x 9-inch baking dish. Add water to a depth of 1 inch.
• **Bake,** covered, at 400° for 45 minutes. Drain. Return squash halves to dish, cut side up. Set aside.
• **Melt** butter in a large skillet over medium heat; add onion, and cook, stirring occasionally, 20 minutes. Add pear and next 5 ingredients; cook, stirring occasionally, 5 minutes. Spoon mixture into squash halves.
• **Bake** at 350° for 15 to 20 minutes.
• **Bring** orange juice to a boil in a small saucepan. Stir in sugar, and boil 10 minutes. Serve over squash. **Yield:** 4 servings.

SQUASH PUFF

Prep: 45 minutes
Bake: 1 hour, 35 minutes

1 medium butternut squash (about 1½ pounds)
3 large eggs, separated
1¼ cups whipping cream
¼ cup butter or margarine, melted
¼ cup maple syrup
3 tablespoons cornstarch
2 tablespoons brown sugar
1 teaspoon salt
3 tablespoons slivered almonds

• **Cut** squash in half lengthwise; remove and discard seeds and membranes. Place squash halves, cut side down, in a 13- x 9-inch baking dish. Add water to a depth of 1 inch.
• **Bake,** covered, at 375° for 30 to 40 minutes. Let squash cool; scoop out pulp, and mash.
• **Beat** pulp, egg yolks, whipping cream, and next 5 ingredients at medium speed with an electric mixer until blended. Set mixture aside.
• **Beat** egg whites at high speed until stiff peaks form, and gently fold into squash mixture. Spoon mixture into a lightly greased 2-quart soufflé dish. Sprinkle with almonds.
• **Bake** at 350° for 55 minutes or until puffed and golden. Serve immediately. **Yield:** 4 to 6 servings.

Lisa Goldstein
Brentwood, Tennessee

BUTTERNUT SQUASH CASSEROLE

Prep: 10 minutes
Cook: 35 minutes
Bake: 1 hour, 15 minutes

1 butternut squash, peeled, seeded, and cut into 2-inch cubes (about 1¾ pounds)
1 tablespoon butter or margarine
1 small onion, minced
1 garlic clove, minced
3 tablespoons butter, melted and divided
2 large eggs, lightly beaten
1 tablespoon sugar
1 teaspoon salt
¼ teaspoon pepper
¼ cup fresh cranberries, chopped
1 cup soft breadcrumbs (homemade)

• **Bring** squash and water to cover to a boil; cook 30 minutes or until tender. Remove from heat; drain. Mash until smooth.
• **Melt** 1 tablespoon butter in a skillet. Add onion and garlic; sauté 5 minutes or until tender.
• **Remove** from heat; stir in squash, 2 tablespoons melted butter, eggs, and next 3 ingredients. Fold in cranberries. Spoon into a lightly greased 1-quart baking dish.
• **Combine** breadcrumbs and remaining 1 tablespoon melted butter. Sprinkle over casserole.
• **Bake** at 375° for 1 hour and 15 minutes or until set and golden. **Yield:** 4 to 6 servings.

Mary Ann Lee
Marco Island, Florida

Cookie Kings and Queens

Readers nominated their own candidates for cookie royalty.

Last November we celebrated the holiday cookie-baking efforts of former Associate Foods Editor Patty Vann in a story called "The Cookie Queen." Apparently Patty isn't the only cookie queen (or king, for that matter) out there.

After reviewing the copious stacks of correspondence, three folks in particular caught our attention. We're sure you'll have as much fun as we did reading their stories and preparing their cookies.

Dick Jack
Galena, Missouri

Dick's son Craig gave us the heads-up on his father in a letter that opened, "I think you need an article about 'The Cookie King.' My dad makes about 330 dozen cookies every holiday season. (Last year that total came to 541 dozen!) I can attest to his cookies, and there's nothing better."

Dick credits his zeal for baking to a former coworker who used to bring a variety of Italian cookies to work every Christmas. Once Dick caught the cookie-baking bug, he never looked back. "It's so much fun. I have flour strewn from one end of the house to the other. But the fun really kicks in when my friends help out," he says.

CRUNCHY LACE COOKIES

Prep: 10 minutes
Bake: 8 minutes per batch

2 tablespoons hot water
1½ teaspoons baking soda
¾ cup butter or margarine, melted
1 tablespoon light corn syrup
1½ cups uncooked regular oats
1½ cups firmly packed light brown sugar
1½ cups all-purpose flour
1½ cups sweetened flaked coconut

• **Stir** together 2 tablespoons hot water and baking soda in a large bowl until baking soda is dissolved. Add butter and syrup, stirring until blended.
• **Combine** oats and remaining 3 ingredients; stir into butter mixture, stirring until blended.
• **Shape** cookie dough into ¾-inch balls, and place 3 inches apart onto lightly greased baking sheets. Slightly flatten balls.
• **Bake** at 350° for 7 to 8 minutes or until golden brown. Remove cookies to wire racks to cool completely. **Yield:** 2 dozen.

Richard Jack
Galena, Missouri

DATE MOONS

Prep: 20 minutes
Chill: 1 hour
Bake: 15 minutes per batch

½ cup butter or margarine, softened
1 (3-ounce) package cream cheese, softened
1 cup all-purpose flour
⅛ teaspoon salt
1 cup chopped dates
¼ cup sugar
¼ cup water
½ cup chopped walnuts
1 teaspoon grated orange rind
½ cup powdered sugar

• **Beat** butter and cream cheese at medium speed with an electric mixer until smooth. Add flour and salt; beat until blended.
• **Shape** dough into a ball; cover with wax paper, and chill 1 hour.
• **Stir** together dates, sugar, and ¼ cup water in a saucepan over medium heat 3 to 5 minutes or until thickened. Remove from heat; stir in walnuts and orange rind, and let cool.
• **Divide** dough in half. Place 1 portion on a lightly floured surface, and roll to ⅛-inch thickness. Cut dough with a 2½-inch round cutter, and place on a lightly greased baking sheet. Spoon ½ teaspoon date mixture into center of each cookie. Repeat procedure with remaining dough.
• **Fold** dough over filling, pressing edges to seal with tines of a fork.
• **Bake** at 375° for 15 minutes or until lightly browned. Sprinkle with powdered sugar. **Yield:** 3 dozen.

Richard Jack
Galena, Missouri

ENGLISH ROCKS

Prep: 20 minutes
Bake: 20 minutes per batch

¾ cup firmly packed light
   brown sugar
½ cup butter or margarine, softened
2 large eggs
1½ cups all-purpose flour
1 teaspoon ground cinnamon
½ teaspoon baking soda
¼ teaspoon salt
¼ teaspoon ground cloves
¼ teaspoon ground allspice
¼ cup brandy *
2 cups chopped pecans
½ pound candied cherries, halved
½ pound candied pineapple, chopped
1 cup pitted dates, chopped
1 cup raisins

• **Beat** sugar and butter at medium speed with an electric mixer until smooth. Add eggs, beating until blended.
• **Combine** flour and next 5 ingredients; gradually add to butter mixture, beating until blended. Add brandy, beating until blended. Combine pecans and next 4 ingredients in a bowl. Pour over pecan mixture; stir until blended.
• **Drop** dough by rounded teaspoonfuls 2 inches apart onto lightly greased baking sheets.
• **Bake** at 325° for 20 minutes or until lightly browned. Cool on baking sheets 2 to 3 minutes. Remove to wire racks to cool completely. **Yield:** 4 dozen.

✱ Substitute ¼ cup apple juice for brandy, if desired.

Jeanne Wood
New Orleans, Louisiana

GREAT GIVING

When you make gifts to give from your kitchen, you'll want them to look as nice as they taste. Here are simple ideas.

Thoughtfulness takes on a special meaning during the holidays. In the hustle and bustle of busy times, taking a moment to deliver handmade treats brightens the season. Here are a few tips and gift-giving ideas.

■ Purchase a selection of different-shaped jars and decorative tins at grocery and larger variety stores.

■ Decorate jar lids with fabric scraps, colored or textured tissue papers, or linen napkins. Cut with decorative scissors to fit, if desired.

■ Shop crafts stores for small tie-on kitchen utensils and decorations.

■ Generate recipe cards on the computer using colored paper stock and designs.

■ Wash a potato chip can. Cut a piece of fabric large enough to wrap the can, allowing enough fabric to fold over the top. Turn under the raw edge of the fabric at the seam; glue the fabric in place along the seam and on the inside of the can at the top. Glue ribbon or fabric trim along the bottom to hide the raw edge of the fabric.
   Spray paint the plastic top gold; let dry. Punch a hole in the center of the top, and thread cording or tassels through the hole, knotting the cording on the back side of the lid to hold it in place.

Jeanne Wood
New Orleans, Louisiana

"I love to bake cookies during the holidays, so when I read the article about Patty, I wondered if the story could be about me," says Jeanne. Known around her neighborhood as the 'Cookie Queen,' Jeanne was first encouraged by her daughter-in-law, Sonia, to bake cookies each holiday season. "Now my friends have really come to expect a box each year, and I keep telling them they're going to bake me into my grave," jokes Jeanne. To celebrate the holidays, and the arrival of Jeanne's cookies, her friends come over to sample the wonderful baked goods and sip mugs of warm café brûlot.

Her secret is to get all the cookies (12 different kinds) baked and in the freezer by Thanksgiving. Otherwise, Jeanne says, the family's busy holiday schedule takes over and she simply runs out of time.

Susan Spray
Little Rock, Arkansas

Nominated by her periodontist's office staff, Susan came with a glowing recommendation. "You need to know about the real 'Cookie Queen' in Little Rock. Susan makes boxes of the most delicious and elegant holiday cookies we've ever seen," exclaims La Donna Straley, office assistant to Dr. Frederick Church Jr.

"My love for Christmas cookies was sparked when I was 10 years old," remembers Susan. "We received this amazing tin of assorted cookies from family members. By the time I was 18, I had collected quite a few cookie recipes and was really baking a lot. I couldn't decide on one specific cookie, so I decided to bake a wide variety, 20 different kinds with a double batch of each. I've been doing it ever since—almost 30 years."

One person who can't wait to receive one of Susan's tins is her daughter, Ella, who lives in Germany. "I really had to master the art of packing for Ella's cookies," she reveals. "In fact, I even use cookies to pack the tin. I use a sturdy round cookie with lots of almond paste between the more delicate cookies packaged in paper baking cups. A few of the 'packing' cookies in the tin get broken, but most of the cookies stay intact," she says with a smile.

SWEDISH HOLIDAY COOKIES

Prep: 20 minutes
Chill: 8 hours
Bake: 8 minutes per batch

1 cup butter or margarine, softened
¾ cup sugar
1½ tablespoons dark molasses
2 teaspoons ground cinnamon
½ teaspoon ground cardamom
1 tablespoon water
1 teaspoon baking powder
2½ cups all-purpose flour
2 egg whites, lightly beaten
Sugar

• **Beat** butter at medium speed with an electric mixer until creamy. Add ¾ cup sugar, beating until smooth. Add molasses, cinnamon, and cardamom, beating until blended.
• **Stir** together 1 tablespoon water and baking powder until baking powder is dissolved; add to butter mixture. Gradually add flour to butter mixture, beating until blended. Cover and chill 8 hours.
• **Turn** dough out onto a lightly floured surface; roll to ¼-inch thickness. Cut with a 2-inch round or other desired shape cutter. Place 2 inches apart on lightly greased baking sheets; brush evenly with egg whites, and sprinkle with sugar.
• **Bake** at 375° for 8 minutes or until lightly browned. Cool on baking sheets 5 to 6 minutes. Remove to wire racks to cool completely. **Yield:** about 5 dozen.

Susan Spray
Little Rock, Arkansas

PLAN A COOKIE SWAP

You may be inspired to host a cookie swap after reading these wonderful recipes. This unique event will add a luscious assortment of homemade goodies to your holidays. Here are some hints.

■ Have every guest bake a dozen or half-dozen cookies for each person attending. (The more people you invite, the more each person will have to bake; but this also means having a greater variety of cookies.)

■ Ask participants to bring extra cookies for sampling. The only refreshment you'll have to prepare, besides your cookies, is a beverage.

■ Tell everyone how to bring their cookies to trade. They can package them for guests by the dozen or half-dozen; or have them bring the whole batch in one container, plus a container for collecting their share of cookies from other bakers.

■ Have guests bring copies of their cookie recipes to share with others.

What's for Supper?

*Eliminate the dinnertime dilemma
with easy-on-the-budget, classic meat pies.*

Running out of imaginative dinner ideas? Then return to the basics. Try a hearty meat pie. Mom's chunky chicken pot pie may come to mind, but we offer a variety of flavors to suit diverse tastes. Both kids and grown-ups will find it hard to resist the down-home comfort of these entrées.

You'll love them even more because they're so quick. There's no need to worry about making pastry from scratch. In these recipes, prepared piecrusts make it easy to produce the golden shells that hold the savory fillings, and a quick cornbread crust caps Beef-and-Onion Cornbread Pie.

While the pies bake, put together a fresh salad with ready-to-serve greens; then toss with a flavorful vinaigrette. Your favorite beverage and ice cream for dessert complete the meal.

Hang on to these recipes for your favorites file; we promise you'll return to them time and again.

ITALIAN MEAT PIE

Prep: 20 minutes
Bake: 25 minutes

1   pound lean ground beef
⅓   cup chopped green bell pepper
¾   cup water
1   (6-ounce) can tomato paste
1   (1½-ounce) package spaghetti sauce mix
⅓   cup shredded Parmesan cheese, divided
1   (9-inch) frozen deep-dish pastry shell
1½   cups (6 ounces) shredded mozzarella cheese, divided

• **Cook** beef and bell pepper in a large skillet over medium-high heat, stirring until beef crumbles and is no longer pink; drain. Stir in water, tomato paste, and sauce mix. Cover, reduce heat to low, and simmer 10 minutes.
• **Sprinkle** half of Parmesan cheese onto frozen pastry shell; top with half of meat mixture, and sprinkle with 1 cup mozzarella cheese. Top with remaining meat mixture and Parmesan cheese. Place shell on a baking sheet.
• **Bake** on lowest oven rack at 400° for 20 minutes. Sprinkle with remaining mozzarella cheese; bake 5 more minutes or until cheese melts. **Yield:** 4 to 6 servings.

Mildred Sherrer
Bay City, Texas

TURKEY-SAUSAGE PIE

Prep: 20 minutes
Bake: 20 minutes

1   (15-ounce) package refrigerated piecrusts
2   tablespoons butter or margarine
½   pound smoked sausage or kielbasa, diced
½   small sweet onion, diced
2   tablespoons all-purpose flour
1   cup milk
3   cups frozen mixed vegetables, thawed
2   cups diced cooked turkey
¼   to ½ teaspoon salt
½   teaspoon seasoned pepper
¼   teaspoon dried thyme (optional)

• **Fit** 1 piecrust in bottom and up sides of a 2-quart baking dish.
• **Bake** at 400° for 9 minutes or until lightly browned.
• **Melt** butter in a large saucepan over medium-high heat; add sausage, onion, and flour, and sauté 5 minutes. Whisk in milk; cook, whisking constantly, 5 minutes or until thickened.
• **Remove** from heat; stir in vegetables, next 3 ingredients, and, if desired, thyme. Pour into prepared piecrust.
• **Unfold** remaining piecrust, and roll to press out fold lines; place piecrust over turkey mixture, trimming to fit. Crimp and cut slits on top for steam to escape.
• **Bake** at 400° for 20 minutes or until golden. **Yield:** 4 to 6 servings.

Note: For testing purposes only, we used McKenzie's Vegetable Gumbo Mixture.

Teri Walle
Charlotte, North Carolina

BEEF-AND-ONION CORNBREAD PIE

This Southwestern-style main dish will score a home run with your family.

Prep: 25 minutes
Bake: 20 minutes

1 pound ground beef
1 large onion, chopped
½ green bell pepper, chopped
1 (11-ounce) can whole kernel corn, drained
1 (10¾-ounce) can tomato soup
1 cup water
1 tablespoon chili powder
1 teaspoon salt
¾ teaspoon pepper
Cornbread Topping
Garnishes: shredded Cheddar cheese, sour cream, cilantro sprigs

● **Cook** first 3 ingredients in a large skillet over medium-high heat, stirring until beef crumbles and is no longer pink; drain. Stir in corn and next 5 ingredients. Reduce heat, and simmer 15 minutes.
● **Pour** beef mixture into a lightly greased 2-quart baking dish. Spread Cornbread Topping over beef mixture.
● **Bake** at 425° for 18 to 20 minutes or until golden. Garnish, if desired. **Yield:** 4 to 6 servings.

Cornbread Topping

Prep: 5 minutes

¾ cup cornmeal
1 tablespoon all-purpose flour
1½ teaspoons baking powder
½ teaspoon salt
1 large egg
½ cup milk
1 tablespoon vegetable oil

● **Stir** together first 4 ingredients. Add egg, milk, and oil, stirring well. **Yield:** about 1 cup.

Nicole Kandill
Stafford, Virginia

Fall's Best Harvest

Robust fall vegetables have never tasted so good.

Not to brag, but we think we've hit the jackpot this month. Vegetable recipes don't always inspire oohs and aahs from our Foods staff, but these two sure did.

Many of us aren't quite sure how to fix cauliflower other than to dip it in Ranch dressing or boil it beyond recognition and smother it with cheese sauce. But the possibilities, we've learned, are endless for this and other fall vegetables.

Cabbage and brussels sprouts are at their peak this time of year and are incredibly versatile. Add a few ingredients and you've got a table filled with flavorful side dishes. Thanks to our creative contributors, these recipes will become family favorites at your house for years to come.

ROASTED VEGETABLE MEDLEY

Prep: 25 minutes
Bake: 45 minutes

4 garlic cloves, minced
3 tablespoons white balsamic vinegar
1 teaspoon sugar
1 teaspoon salt
½ teaspoon freshly ground pepper
⅓ cup olive oil
1 pound brussels sprouts, quartered
2 cups baby carrots
2 parsnips, cut into ½-inch slices
½ head cauliflower, cut into florets

● **Combine** first 5 ingredients; whisk in oil in a slow, steady stream.

● **Place** brussels sprouts and remaining 3 ingredients in a lightly greased aluminum foil-lined 15- x 10-inch jelly-roll pan. Drizzle with vinegar mixture, tossing vegetables to coat.
● **Bake** at 400° for 45 minutes or until vegetables are crisp-tender and lightly browned, stirring every 15 minutes. **Yield:** 4 to 6 servings.

BRAISED RED CABBAGE AND PEARS

Prep: 15 minutes
Cook: 23 minutes

2 pears, peeled and coarsely chopped
2 tablespoons bacon drippings or vegetable oil
2 cups apple juice
½ head red cabbage, chopped
1 teaspoon salt
½ teaspoon ground ginger
½ teaspoon pepper
1 tablespoon butter or margarine

● **Cook** pears in drippings in a medium skillet over medium heat 3 minutes or until lightly browned.
● **Add** apple juice and next 4 ingredients, and bring to a boil. Cover; reduce heat, and simmer 20 minutes. Stir in butter until melted. **Yield:** 4 servings.

David Druda
Largo, Florida

Quick & Easy

Trim the tree, and enjoy this make-ahead supper menu.

Make-Ahead Menu
Serves 8

Ham-and-Cheese Sandwiches
Deviled Eggs
Vegetable platter with dip
Cupcake Surprises

Invite your friends over to trim the tree, then satisfy the hungry decorating crew with this make-ahead supper. Assemble and freeze sandwiches up to a week in advance. Make Cupcake Surprises up to two days ahead. Tangy Deviled Eggs can be made a day before eating them.

On decoration day, set a buffet table, assign the tasks, and let the fun begin. One hour before the supper break, put the foil-wrapped, frozen sandwiches in the oven. Enjoy the meal while you admire everyone's handiwork.

HAM-AND-CHEESE SANDWICHES

Prep: 8 minutes
Bake: 1 hour

¼ cup butter or margarine, softened
¼ cup mayonnaise
3 tablespoons Creole mustard
1 tablespoon grated onion
2 teaspoons poppy seeds
8 hamburger buns, split
1 (6-ounce) package Swiss cheese slices
1 pound thinly sliced ham

• **Combine** first 5 ingredients; spread evenly on each bun half. Layer 8 bun halves evenly with cheese and ham; top with remaining halves. Wrap in aluminum foil; freeze.
• **Bake** frozen in foil at 350° for 1 hour or until thoroughly heated. **Yield:** 8 servings.

Beverly Martinez
San Antonio, Texas

DEVILED EGGS

Prep: 5 minutes

5 hard-cooked eggs, peeled
1½ tablespoons Dijon mustard
1½ tablespoons mayonnaise
5 pimiento-stuffed green olives, halved
1 teaspoon Cajun seasoning

• **Cut** eggs in half lengthwise; carefully remove yolks.
• **Mash** yolks, and stir in mustard and mayonnaise; blend well.
• **Spoon** yolk mixture evenly into egg whites.
• **Place** an olive half in the center of each; sprinkle with Cajun seasoning. **Yield:** 10 eggs.

Audrey Rinker
New Port Richey, Florida

CUPCAKE SURPRISES

Prep: 20 minutes
Bake: 22 minutes

1 (18.25-ounce) package Swiss chocolate cake mix
2 (3-ounce) packages cream cheese, softened
½ cup sugar
1 large egg, lightly beaten
1 cup (6 ounces) milk chocolate morsels
¼ cup sweetened flaked coconut

• **Prepare** cake batter according to package directions; set batter aside.
• **Stir** together cream cheese, sugar, and egg. Stir in milk chocolate morsels and coconut.
• **Spoon** cake batter evenly into 24 paper-lined muffin cups, filling each half full. Drop cream cheese mixture by rounded teaspoonfuls evenly into center of cupcakes.
• **Bake** at 350° for 19 to 22 minutes or until a wooden pick inserted in center comes out clean. Cool in pans on a wire rack 15 minutes; remove from pans, and cool on a wire rack. **Yield:** 2 dozen.

Thyra Lynn Hess
Tunica, Mississippi

PEPPERMINT STICK VOTIVES

Peppermint stick candles shed cheery light on a festive tablescape. Place a small dab of hot glue on a peppermint stick, and press it to a pillar candle until it adheres. Repeat the process until the candle is surrounded with peppermint sticks, and wrap the bundle in a piece of pretty ribbon. A decorative bow will tie up this package perfectly.

After the party, consider using this colorful collection on a mantel or coffee table.

From Our Kitchen

Gifts for Cooks

For the cook who has everything, Brookstone introduces "Tools That Think." The Barbecue Collection includes a chef's fork with thermometer, a "smart" spatula, and retractable tongs. Select the type of meat you're cooking, and these tools help you serve it perfectly every time. The grilling enthusiast on your list will love it.

Other tools include a Pastasmart Pasta Fork with timer, which automatically calculates the perfect cooking time—from al dente to fully done. The Fish Smart Turner, with a head designed for turning fillets, reads the cooking temperature of fish and tells you when it's ready. Order Tools That Think—from $25 to $70—online at www.brookstone.com, or call 1-800-351-7222.

Give the gift of flavor from the Spice Kit Company. It's a wonderful way to introduce new cooks to regional and ethnic flavors. Company owner Sherrill Kelley created five spice kits: Basic, Cajun, Mexican, Indian, and Mediterranean Pantries. Each $39.95 kit contains 16 herbs and spices and a recipe book in a heavy vinyl container that stores neatly on a kitchen bookshelf. For your nearest local retail shop, call 1-888-510-0055, or visit www.spicekit.com.

CHEERS!

The holidays are filled with an enormous variety of flavors, which makes picking one definitive wine an almost impossible task. This year, instead of wasting time pacing up and down the wine aisle, embrace the seasonal diversity in food with this selection of wines (all under $14). They pair well with all sorts of holiday favorites, particularly those recipes in this chapter.

Red:
■ 1999 Pinot Noir, Beringer Founders' Estate, California ("You Can Go Home Again," page 276).

■ 1999 Shiraz-Mourvedre, Penfolds, Bin 2, South Eastern Australia ("What's for Supper?" page 297).

White:
■ 1997 Chardonnay, Yarden, Galil, Israel. In addition to being a terrific wine, it's also kosher, so it's perfect for Hanukkah. Yarden also makes a tasty Cabernet Sauvignon ("Flavors of Hanukkah," page 274).
■ 2000 Sauvignon Blanc, Villa Maria, Private Bin, Marlborough, New Zealand ("Living Light," page 288).

Dial-a-Chef

Once again the Dial-A-Chef Holiday Hotline is ready with menu ideas and recipes. Now through January 1, 2002, Shady Brook Farms brings the expertise of some of the country's most prominent chefs to our fingertips. This year's Dial-A-Chef Holiday Hotline chefs are Ris Lacoste of 1798 in Washington, D.C.; Mark Salter of The Inn at Perry Cabin in St. Michaels, Maryland; and Todd English of Olives in Charlestown, Massachusetts and New York City. They share recipes for turkey and complementary side dishes, along with tips for entertaining. The toll-free hotline is open 24 hours a day. Call 1-888-723-4468, or visit www.dialachef.com.

Tips and Tidbits

■ Keep a soft, toothbrush handy for easy cleaning of spice grinders and graters.

■ Keep cakes and soft cookies moist by placing a piece of cut apple in the airtight container.

■ Caught with too much candied fruit after the holidays? Freeze any leftovers in an airtight container up to 6 months. Thaw and then add a few tablespoons of the finely chopped fruit to fresh apple cobbler.

■ Large cuts of meat make beautiful table presentations, but they take up too much refrigerator space when the party's over. Thinly slice, label, and store leftover meat in airtight containers in the refrigerator or freezer. This makes it easy to reheat small meal portions, and you'll have sandwich fixings ready.

Recipe Index Available Online

Access an online index of each month's recipes at southernliving.com. Click on "Foods" in the top right corner of the home page. Scroll down below "Top-Rated Recipes," and click on "Magazine Recipe Index."

The current month's index will pop up immediately, including information that may run only in certain states. Below that listing, you'll find a place to explore indexes that go as far back as 1996. Your search for that perfect recipe has just been made easier.

Praline-Mustard Glazed Ham,
page 306

Spinach salad with Apple-Cider
Vinaigrette, page 306

Pork-Pepper Skillet, page 309

Grilled Vegetable Sandwich, page 310

*Caramelized Onion Soup With
Goat Cheese-and-Chive Croutons, page 312*

Chocolate-Raspberry Cake, page 319

Southern Living Cooking School

Bonus Section

Four Easy Meals

Simplify your busy fall schedule by following one of our four-day menu plans (see box at right). Pick the plan your family will enjoy most.

We know that family menu planning can be a hassle, so we've done it for you. Here we offer two variations on four days of menus, so the only decision to make is which meal plan will bring the most dinnertime smiles around your table. Then, at the end of the week, you'll have a satisfied family, plus one bonus dish that will get you started for the next week.

PECAN PIE WITH HOT FUDGE SAUCE

Prepare this simple pie on Monday, and serve it for dessert throughout the week.

Prep: 5 minutes
Thaw: 2 hours
Cook: 6 minutes

1 (2-pound 4-ounce) package frozen MRS. SMITH'S Special Recipe Southern Pecan Pie
2 (14-ounce) cans sweetened condensed milk
1 cup semisweet chocolate morsels
2 teaspoons vanilla extract
Dash of salt

• **Remove** and discard paper circle from pecan pie.
• **Thaw** pecan pie at room temperature 2 hours.
• **Cook** condensed milk and remaining ingredients in a heavy saucepan over medium-low heat, stirring constantly, 4 to 6 minutes or until smooth. Serve warm over pie. **Yield:** 6 to 8 servings.

PRALINE-MUSTARD GLAZED HAM
(pictured on page 301)

Maple syrup and Dijon mustard complement the smoky, salty ham.

Prep: 5 minutes
Bake: 2 hours, 30 minutes
Stand: 10 minutes

1 (7- to 8-pound) bone-in smoked spiral-cut ham half
1 cup maple syrup
¾ cup firmly packed DOMINO Light Brown Sugar
¾ cup Dijon mustard
⅓ cup apple juice
¼ cup raisins
1 cooking apple, thinly sliced

• **Remove** skin and excess fat from smoked ham; place ham in a lightly greased 13- x 9-inch pan.
• **Stir** together maple syrup and next 3 ingredients. Pour mixture over ham.
• **Bake** at 350° on lower oven rack 2 hours and 30 minutes or until a meat thermometer inserted into thickest portion registers 140°, basting every 20 minutes with glaze. Let ham stand 10 minutes. Remove from pan, reserving drippings. If desired, cool, cover, and chill ham.
• **Remove** fat from drippings with a fat separator, and discard. Cover and chill drippings, if desired. Cook drippings, raisins, and apple slices in a saucepan over low heat 5 minutes. Serve warm sauce with ham. **Yield:** 12 servings.

APPLE CIDER VINAIGRETTE
(pictured on page 301)

Prep: 10 minutes

¾ cup vegetable oil
⅓ cup cider vinegar
⅓ cup firmly packed DOMINO Light Brown Sugar
1 teaspoon celery salt
¾ teaspoon dry mustard
1 tablespoon grated onion

• **Process** all ingredients in a blender or food processor until smooth. Cover and chill, if desired.
• **Stir** well before drizzling over spinach salad or fresh fruit. **Yield:** 1 cup.

SAUCY CHEESE-VEGETABLE LASAGNA

Prep: 30 minutes
Bake: 45 minutes
Stand: 15 minutes

2 (10-ounce) packages frozen chopped spinach, thawed
1½ cups (6 ounces) shredded mozzarella CHEESE, divided
2 (15-ounce) containers ricotta CHEESE
1 (8-ounce) container chive-and-onion-flavored soft cream CHEESE
4 ounces provolone CHEESE, shredded
1 teaspoon pepper
2 large eggs, lightly beaten
2 (10-ounce) containers refrigerated Alfredo sauce, divided
2 (14-ounce) cans artichoke hearts, drained and coarsely chopped
2 (3-ounce) packages shredded Parmesan CHEESE
¼ cup mayonnaise
6 green onions, sliced
12 lasagna noodles, cooked

• **Drain** spinach, and press between layers of paper towels to remove excess moisture.
• **Stir** together spinach, 1 cup mozzarella cheese, and next 5 ingredients.
• **Stir** together 1 container of Alfredo sauce and next 4 ingredients.

BONUS SECTION

MEAL PLAN 1

Monday
Praline-Mustard Glazed Ham
Baked sweet potatoes
Spinach salad with Apple Cider
   Vinaigrette
Pecan Pie With Hot Fudge Sauce
Tuesday
Saucy Cheese-Vegetable
   Lasagna
Rosemary-Red Pepper Focaccia
Wednesday
Ham-and-Asparagus
   Sandwiches
Fruit salad with Apple Cider
   Vinaigrette
Thursday
Shrimp-Herb Fettuccine
Steamed broccoli
Crispy Parmesan Toasts

MEAL PLAN 2

Monday
Praline-Mustard Glazed Ham
Baked sweet potatoes
Spinach salad with Apple Cider
   Vinaigrette
Cinnamon Chip Icebox Cookies
Tuesday
Saucy Cheese-Vegetable Lasagna
Rosemary-Red Pepper Focaccia
Wednesday
Savory Ham-and-Swiss Casserole
Fruit salad with Apple Cider
   Vinaigrette
Cinnamon-Pecan Biscuits With
   Cinnamon Butter
Thursday
Chicken Noodle Casserole
Steamed broccoli
Crispy Parmesan Toasts

HAM-AND-ASPARAGUS SANDWICHES

Pair leftover ham with asparagus for these scrumptious sandwiches.

Prep: 10 minutes
Broil: 1 minute

3 tablespoons butter or margarine,
   softened
2 small garlic cloves, minced
1 (16-ounce) round bread loaf, split
¼ cup mayonnaise
16 Praline-Mustard Glazed Ham slices
1 (10-ounce) package frozen
   asparagus spears, thawed
1 (6-ounce) package Muenster
   CHEESE slices
1 (6-ounce) package Swiss CHEESE
   slices

• **Stir** together butter and garlic.
• **Spread** butter mixture evenly over bottom half of bread. Spread mayonnaise evenly over top half of bread. Layer bottom half evenly with ham slices, asparagus, and cheese slices; place on a baking sheet.
• **Broil** 2 inches from heat 1 minute or just until cheese melts. Top with remaining bread half. **Yield:** 4 servings.

• **Spread** remaining container of Alfredo sauce evenly into 2 lightly greased 8-inch square baking dishes. Top each with 2 lasagna noodles and one-fourth of spinach mixture. Repeat procedure with 4 noodles and remaining spinach mixture. Top evenly with remaining 4 noodles, and spread with artichoke mixture.
• **Bake** both casseroles at 350° for 40 minutes or just until set and lightly browned. Sprinkle evenly with remaining ½ cup mozzarella cheese, and bake 5 more minutes. Let stand 15 minutes.
• **Cool** 1 casserole. Wrap in heavy-duty aluminum foil, and freeze up to 1 month. **Yield:** 4 to 6 servings per casserole.

Note: Thaw frozen casserole in refrigerator overnight. Bake, covered, at 350° for 45 to 50 minutes.

ROSEMARY-RED PEPPER FOCACCIA

Prep: 10 minutes
Bake: 25 minutes

4½ cups BISQUICK Original
   All-Purpose Baking Mix
½ teaspoon salt
2 teaspoons dried rosemary
2 garlic cloves, minced
⅔ cup buttermilk
⅓ cup olive oil
1 (12-ounce) jar roasted red bell
   peppers, drained and chopped

• **Combine** first 4 ingredients in a large bowl. Whisk together buttermilk and oil, and stir into baking mix mixture until blended. Stir in bell pepper.
• **Turn** dough out onto a lightly floured surface; knead 1 to 2 minutes. Press dough into an 11- x 7-inch rectangle on a lightly greased baking sheet.
• **Bake** at 400° for 20 to 25 minutes or until golden. Cool slightly. Invert onto a cutting board, and cut. **Yield:** 8 servings.

CRISPY PARMESAN TOASTS

Prep: 10 minutes
Bake: 15 minutes

4 pita bread rounds
1 cup finely shredded Parmesan
   CHEESE
½ cup mayonnaise
2 teaspoons dried Italian seasoning
1 teaspoon fresh lemon juice

• **Cut** each bread round into 6 triangles; place on a baking sheet.
• **Whisk** together Parmesan and remaining ingredients. Spread on triangles.
• **Bake** at 350° for 12 to 15 minutes or until golden. Serve toasts immediately. **Yield:** 2 dozen.

Bonus Section

Shrimp-Herb Fettuccine

Prep: 15 minutes
Cook: 20 minutes

2 pounds unpeeled, medium-size
   fresh shrimp
½ cup butter or margarine, divided
3 garlic cloves, minced
½ cup FETZER Sundial Chardonnay
1 cup whipping cream
1 cup finely shredded Parmesan
   cheese
¼ cup chopped fresh parsley
¼ cup chopped fresh basil
¼ cup chopped fresh chives
8 ounces fettuccine, cooked

• **Peel** shrimp, and devein, if desired.
• **Melt** 3 tablespoons butter in a large skillet over medium-high heat; add shrimp, and sauté 3 to 4 minutes. Remove shrimp with a slotted spoon.
• **Melt** remaining butter in skillet over medium-high heat; add garlic, and sauté 1 minute. Add wine, and cook 4 minutes or until mixture is reduced by half. Stir in whipping cream, and cook, stirring occasionally, 4 to 5 minutes or until slightly thickened. Add shrimp, cheese, and herbs; cook, stirring occasionally, just until cheese melts. Serve over fettuccine. **Yield:** 4 to 6 servings.

Chicken Noodle Casserole

Prep: 10 minutes
Bake: 25 minutes

1 (40-ounce) package STOUFFER'S
   Family Style Favorites Escalloped
   Chicken and Noodles
1½ teaspoons butter or margarine
1 small onion, chopped
1 small green bell pepper, chopped
   (optional)
2 cups (8 ounces) shredded Cheddar
   cheese
½ (2-ounce) jar diced pimiento,
   drained
¼ teaspoon pepper
2 tablespoons fine, dry breadcrumbs

• **Thaw** escalloped chicken and noodles in refrigerator overnight.
• **Melt** butter in a large skillet over medium-high heat. Add onion and bell pepper, if desired; sauté until tender. Add cheese, and cook, stirring constantly, until cheese melts. Stir in escalloped chicken and noodles, diced pimiento, and pepper. Spoon into a lightly greased 9-inch square baking dish. Sprinkle with breadcrumbs.
• **Bake** at 350° for 25 minutes. **Yield:** 4 servings.

Savory Ham-and-Swiss Casserole

Prep: 30 minutes
Bake: 55 minutes
Stand: 10 minutes

1⅔ cups water
1 cup whipping cream
2 tablespoons butter or margarine
1 teaspoon salt
¼ teaspoon pepper
⅔ cup uncooked quick-cooking
   grits
2 cups (8 ounces) shredded Swiss
   cheese, divided
4 garlic cloves, pressed
8 large eggs, divided
2 cups chopped Praline-Mustard
   Glazed Ham (recipe on page 306)
6 green onions, chopped
2 cups milk, divided
3 cups BISQUICK Original All-Purpose
   Baking Mix

• **Bring** first 5 ingredients to a boil in a medium saucepan; gradually stir in grits. Cover, reduce heat, and simmer, stirring occasionally, 5 to 7 minutes. Add ½ cup cheese and garlic, stirring until cheese melts; let mixture cool 10 to 15 minutes. Stir in 2 eggs, and pour into a lightly greased 13- x 9-inch baking dish.
• **Bake** at 350° for 20 minutes; remove from oven. Increase oven temperature to 400°.
• **Sprinkle** remaining 1½ cups cheese, ham, and green onions evenly over grits crust. Whisk together remaining 6 eggs and ½ cup milk; pour into crust.
• **Stir** together remaining 1½ cups milk and baking mix; pour over egg mixture, spreading to edge of dish with back of spoon.
• **Bake** at 400° for 35 minutes. Let stand 10 minutes, and cut into squares. **Yield:** 8 servings.

Cinnamon Chip Icebox Cookies

These cookies are a delicious departure from chocolate chip cookies.

Prep: 12 minutes
Chill: 8 hours
Bake: 15 minutes per batch

1 cup butter or margarine, softened
2 cups sugar
2 large eggs
2 teaspoons vanilla extract
4 cups all-purpose flour
1 (10-ounce) package HERSHEY'S
   Cinnamon Chips
1 cup chopped pecans, toasted

• **Beat** butter at medium speed with an electric mixer until creamy. Gradually add sugar, beating well. Add eggs and vanilla, beating until blended. Gradually add flour, beating at low speed just until blended. Stir in cinnamon chips and pecans.
• **Divide** dough into 3 (2-cup) portions; roll each into a 12-inch log. Wrap logs in wax paper. Chill 8 hours, or freeze in an airtight container up to 3 months.
• **Cut** each log into 24 (½-inch-thick) slices, and place slices on ungreased baking sheets.
• **Bake** at 350° for 13 to 15 minutes or until edges are lightly browned. Cool on baking sheets 5 minutes. Remove cookies to wire racks to cool completely. **Yield:** 6 dozen.

Note: Cookie dough may be dropped by rounded tablespoonfuls, 2 inches apart, onto ungreased baking sheets, and then baked.

CINNAMON-PECAN BISCUITS WITH CINNAMON BUTTER

Enhance these rich biscuits with a pat of sweet, creamy Cinnamon Butter.

Prep: 15 minutes
Bake: 20 minutes

4 cups biscuit mix
1 cup HERSHEY'S Cinnamon Chips
1 cup chopped pecans, toasted
¼ cup sugar
1 cup whipping cream
Cinnamon Butter

• **Stir** together first 4 ingredients in a large bowl; make a well in center, and add whipping cream, stirring just until dry ingredients are moistened.
• **Turn** biscuit dough out onto a sheet of wax paper, and pat dough into ¾-inch thickness; cut with a 2½-inch round cutter. Place biscuits in a 13- x 9-inch pan. Reshape remaining dough, and repeat procedure.
• **Bake** at 400° for 18 to 20 minutes or until lightly browned. Remove from pan immediately. Serve with Cinnamon Butter. **Yield:** 14 biscuits.

Cinnamon Butter

Prep: 5 minutes

½ cup butter or margarine, softened
⅔ cup HERSHEY'S Cinnamon Chips
2 tablespoons whipping cream

• **Beat** butter at medium speed with an electric mixer until creamy.
• **Microwave** cinnamon chips and whipping cream in a glass bowl at HIGH 1 minute, stirring once. Stir until blended; cool.
• **Stir** together butter and cinnamon mixture; cover and chill. Serve at room temperature. **Yield:** about 1 cup.

One-Dish Wonders

Receive smiles of approval from family or friends when you add a side dish to these easy meals.

The hustle and bustle of school schedules and meal planning returns after a not-as-stressful summer. Keeping in mind that we want to spend less time in the kitchen, here are some family-friendly recipes that will please any palate.

SHORTCUT PAELLA

Prep: 20 minutes
Cook: 1 hour

1½ pounds unpeeled, medium-size fresh shrimp
1 (16-ounce) package chorizo sausage, sliced *
1 (¾-pound) package chicken tenders
2 (10-ounce) cans ROTEL Mexican Festival Diced Tomatoes With Lime Juice & Cilantro
2 (14½-ounce) cans low-sodium fat-free chicken broth
½ teaspoon ground cumin
1 (10-ounce) package saffron rice
1 (9-ounce) package frozen sweet green peas

• **Peel** and devein shrimp, if desired; set shrimp aside.
• **Sauté** sausage and chicken tenders in a large, deep skillet over medium-high heat 10 minutes. Add tomatoes, chicken broth, and cumin.
• **Bring** to a boil. Stir in rice, and cook, uncovered, over medium heat 45 minutes or until liquid is almost absorbed, stirring occasionally. Stir in shrimp and peas, and cook 4 minutes or until shrimp turn pink. **Yield:** 6 servings.

*Substitute 1 (16-ounce) package smoked sausage, if desired.

PORK-PEPPER SKILLET
(pictured on page 302)

Prep: 20 minutes
Cook: 30 minutes

All Natural PAM Garlic Flavor Cooking and Seasoning Spray
1 green bell pepper, sliced
1 red bell pepper, sliced
1 bunch green onions, cut into 2-inch pieces
¾ pound breakfast pork chops, cut into thin strips
2 tablespoons cornstarch
1 (14½-ounce) can beef broth
1 tablespoon chili-garlic paste
Hot cooked soba noodles or rice
Sesame seeds (optional)
Garnish: green onion fan

• **Coat** a large skillet with cooking spray 2 seconds; heat over medium heat. Add sliced bell pepper and green onions, and sauté 3 to 4 minutes. Remove skillet from heat, and remove mixture from skillet; set mixture aside.
• **Coat** pork evenly with cooking spray 5 seconds; toss with cornstarch.
• **Coat** skillet with cooking spray 2 seconds; heat over medium heat. Add pork, in batches, and sauté 3 to 4 minutes or until browned. Add bell pepper mixture, broth, and chili-garlic paste. Bring to a boil; reduce heat, and simmer 8 to 10 minutes. Serve over noodles, and sprinkle with sesame seeds, if desired. Garnish, if desired. **Yield:** 4 servings.

AVOCADO-VEGETABLE LASAGNA

Prep: 25 minutes
Bake: 45 minutes
Stand: 15 minutes

2 (15-ounce) containers ricotta cheese
2 (6-ounce) packages shredded Italian cheese blend
3 large eggs
¼ cup chopped fresh basil
¼ teaspoon ground red pepper
1 teaspoon salt, divided
1 teaspoon freshly ground black pepper, divided
1 (6-ounce) jar oil-packed artichoke hearts
3 large GENUINE CALIFORNIA AVOCADOS, peeled and chopped
4 green onions, sliced
2 tablespoons butter or margarine
2 garlic cloves, minced
2 tablespoons all-purpose flour
2 cups whipping cream
1½ cups shredded Parmesan cheese, divided
12 lasagna noodles, cooked

• **Stir** together first 5 ingredients, ½ teaspoon salt, and ½ teaspoon pepper. Set aside.
• **Drain** artichoke hearts, reserving oil. Coarsely chop artichokes. Stir together artichoke, reserved oil, chopped avocado, green onions, and remaining ½ teaspoon salt and ½ teaspoon pepper. Set aside.
• **Melt** butter in a saucepan over medium-high heat; add garlic, and sauté 1 minute. Add flour, whisking until blended; cook, whisking constantly, 1 minute. Gradually whisk in whipping cream. Cook, whisking constantly, 3 to 4 minutes or until thickened and bubbly. Stir in 1 cup Parmesan cheese.
• **Layer** one-third of noodles, half of ricotta cheese mixture, ½ cup cream sauce, and half of avocado mixture into a lightly greased 13- x 9-inch baking dish.
• **Repeat** layers once, ending with remaining noodles and remaining cream

sauce. Sprinkle with remaining ½ cup Parmesan cheese.
• **Bake,** covered, at 400° for 40 minutes. Uncover and bake 5 more minutes or until lightly browned. Let stand 15 minutes. **Yield:** 8 servings.

EGGPLANT PARMIGIANA

Prep: 25 minutes
Bake: 20 minutes

2 medium eggplants (about 1½ pounds)
1 cup milk
1½ cups Italian-seasoned breadcrumbs
½ cup olive oil
2 (10-ounce) cans ROTEL Bold Italian Diced Tomatoes With Garlic, Basil, & Oregano
2 (10-ounce) cans ROTEL Original Diced Tomatoes & Green Chilies, drained
2 tablespoons chopped fresh basil, divided
¾ cup grated Parmesan cheese
2 cups (8 ounces) shredded mozzarella cheese

• **Peel** eggplants, and cut each into ½-inch-thick slices.
• **Dip** eggplant slices into milk, and dredge in breadcrumbs.
• **Fry** eggplant, in batches, in hot oil in a large skillet over medium-high heat 2 minutes on each side. Remove from skillet, and cool on a wire rack.
• **Process** Italian diced tomatoes in a blender until smooth. Stir in drained diced tomatoes and green chilies and 1 tablespoon chopped basil.
• **Spoon** half of tomato sauce into a lightly greased 13- x 9-inch baking dish. Top with half of eggplant; sprinkle with half each of Parmesan cheese and mozzarella cheese. Repeat procedure with remaining sauce and eggplant.
• **Bake** at 400° for 15 minutes. Sprinkle with remaining cheeses, and bake 5 more minutes. Sprinkle with remaining 1 tablespoon basil. **Yield:** 6 to 8 servings.

GRILLED VEGETABLE SANDWICHES
(pictured on page 303)

Prep: 10 minutes
Marinate: 1 hour
Grill: 16 minutes

2 zucchini
1 medium-size purple onion
2 red bell peppers
¼ cup KIKKOMAN Soy Sauce
¼ cup lemon juice
1 tablespoon honey
½ teaspoon ground red pepper
1 (11- x 9-inch) focaccia
Herbed Goat Cheese

• **Cut** zucchini diagonally into ½-inch-thick slices; cut onion into ¼-inch-thick slices. Cut bell peppers into strips.
• **Stir** together soy sauce and next 3 ingredients in a bowl; add vegetables, tossing to coat. Let stand at room temperature 1 hour, stirring occasionally.
• **Coat** food rack with cooking spray; place on grill over medium-high heat (350° to 400°). Arrange marinated vegetables on rack, and grill, without grill lid, 6 to 8 minutes on each side.
• **Trim** ½ inch from each end of focaccia, and cut bread into 4 equal squares. Slice each square horizontally in half. Toast bread on grill, if desired. Spread cut sides evenly with Herbed Goat Cheese; place grilled vegetables evenly on bottom halves of bread, and top with remaining bread. Serve immediately. **Yield:** 4 servings.

Herbed Goat Cheese

Prep: 10 minutes

3 ounces goat cheese, softened
1 (3-ounce) package cream cheese, softened
1 tablespoon KIKKOMAN Soy Sauce
1 teaspoon lemon juice
1 garlic clove, minced
1 tablespoon crushed fresh or dried rosemary

• **Stir** together all ingredients in a bowl. **Yield:** ¾ cup.

BONUS SECTION

SPICY BEEF-PASTA SALAD

Soy sauce, Dijon mustard, and Cajun seasoning make a zesty marinade for flank steak. Be sure to allow enough time for the flavors to permeate the meat.

Prep: 15 minutes
Chill: 8 hours
Cook: 20 minutes
Broil: 10 minutes

½ cup KIKKOMAN Soy Sauce
¼ cup Dijon mustard
2 tablespoons olive oil
2 to 3 teaspoons Cajun seasoning
¼ to ½ teaspoon dried crushed red pepper
1 (1-pound) package flank steak
1 (8-ounce) package bow tie pasta
1 green bell pepper, cut into 1-inch pieces
2 cups cherry tomatoes, halved

• **Stir** together first 5 ingredients. Pour half of soy sauce mixture into a shallow dish.
• **Add** steak to dish, turning to coat. Cover and chill steak 8 hours, turning occasionally. Cover and chill remaining soy sauce mixture 8 hours.
• **Cook** pasta according to package directions; drain and rinse with cold water. Drain and set aside.
• **Remove** flank steak from marinade, discarding marinade, and place on a lightly greased rack in a broiler pan.
• **Broil** steak 3 inches from heat 5 minutes on each side or to desired degree of doneness. Let stand 5 minutes, and cut steak diagonally across the grain into thin slices.
• **Combine** cooked pasta, steak slices, reserved soy sauce mixture, bell pepper, and tomato in a large bowl. Toss gently to coat. **Yield:** 6 servings.

EASY HERB CRUST CASSOULET

Smoked sausage, onion, garlic, and herbs pack this French-inspired dish with loads of flavor.

Prep: 30 minutes
Bake: 40 minutes

1 (16-ounce) package smoked sausage, sliced
1 small onion, chopped
1 carrot, sliced
3 garlic cloves, pressed
2 (15.5-ounce) cans great Northern beans, rinsed and drained
1 (14½-ounce) can chicken broth
2 tablespoons chopped fresh or 2 teaspoons dried thyme, divided
1¼ cups BISQUICK Original All-Purpose Baking Mix
½ cup plus 2 tablespoons milk
1 large egg, lightly beaten

• **Brown** sausage in a 10-inch deep-dish ovenproof skillet over medium-high heat, stirring occasionally, 4 to 6 minutes. Remove sausage, and drain on paper towels, reserving 2 tablespoons drippings in skillet. Add onion, carrot, and garlic; cook, stirring constantly, 2 to 3 minutes.
• **Stir** in sausage, beans, and chicken broth. Reduce heat, and simmer mixture 6 minutes. Stir in 1 tablespoon thyme, and remove from heat.
• **Stir** together baking mix, milk, egg, and remaining 1 tablespoon thyme with a fork until moistened.
• **Pour** dough evenly over top of sausage mixture in skillet.
• **Bake** at 400° for 40 minutes or until golden brown. **Yield:** 4 to 6 servings.

CREAM OF MUSHROOM-AND-LEEK SOUP

Prep: 8 minutes
Cook: 13 minutes

¼ cup butter or margarine
2¼ cups thinly sliced leeks (about 3)
2 (8-ounce) packages sliced fresh
     mushrooms
½ teaspoon salt
2 tablespoons brandy ✶
1 (2.64-ounce) package McCORMICK
     Original Country Gravy Mix
1 cup half-and-half
1 (14½-ounce) can chicken broth
½ teaspoon dried thyme

• **Melt** butter in a Dutch oven over medium-high heat. Add leeks, mushrooms, and salt; sauté 4 to 5 minutes or until tender. Add brandy, and cook, stirring often, 2 to 3 minutes.
• **Stir** in gravy mix and remaining ingredients, and cook 3 to 4 minutes or until slightly thickened. Serve soup immediately. **Yield:** about 4 cups.

✶ Substitute 2 tablespoons chicken broth for brandy, if desired.

Note: Soup will thicken upon standing. To thin soup, stir in ⅓ to ½ cup milk or until desired consistency.

CARAMELIZED ONION SOUP WITH GOAT CHEESE-AND-CHIVE CROUTONS
(pictured on page 303)

Prep: 15 minutes
Cook: 1 hour, 25 minutes

6 medium onions, sliced
½ cup MAZOLA Canola Oil
4 garlic cloves, pressed
8 cups water
3 tablespoons beef bouillon granules
1 teaspoon pepper
½ teaspoon dried thyme
2 tablespoons dry sherry (optional)
Goat Cheese-and-Chive Croutons
Garnish: fresh chives

• **Cook** onion in hot oil in a Dutch oven over medium-high heat, stirring occasionally, 45 minutes or until onion is caramel colored. Add garlic, and cook 1 minute. Stir in 8 cups water. Bring to a boil; stir in bouillon granules, pepper, thyme, and, if desired, sherry. Cover, reduce heat, and simmer, stirring occasionally, 20 minutes.
• **Ladle** soup into individual bowls; top with Goat Cheese-and-Chive Croutons. Garnish, if desired. **Yield:** 8 cups.

Goat Cheese-and-Chive Croutons

Prep: 5 minutes
Bake: 10 minutes

1 (8-ounce) French baguette
3 tablespoons MAZOLA Canola Oil
1 (3-ounce) log goat cheese
2 tablespoons chopped fresh chives
2 tablespoons mayonnaise

• **Cut** baguette diagonally into 8 slices; brush bread slices with oil.
• **Stir** together goat cheese, chopped chives, and mayonnaise. Spread mixture evenly on bread slices.
• **Bake** at 400° for 8 to 10 minutes. **Yield:** 8 croutons.

AUTUMN CHICKEN SALAD

Prep: 20 minutes

3 cups chopped cooked chicken
1 cup chopped seedless red grapes
3 celery ribs, chopped
1 medium-size Red Delicious apple,
     chopped
½ cup DIAMOND OF CALIFORNIA
     Shelled Pecan Halves, toasted
½ cup mayonnaise
¼ cup honey mustard
½ teaspoon salt
¼ teaspoon pepper
Lettuce leaves

• **Stir** together first 9 ingredients in a large bowl. Cover and chill. Serve on lettuce leaves. **Yield:** 6 servings.

GREEK EGGPLANT, TOMATO, AND FETA PIZZA

A baked pizza shell gets Mediterranean flair in this quick dish.

Prep: 30 minutes
Broil: 4 minutes
Bake: 10 minutes

1 pint grape tomatoes, halved ✶
½ cup shredded fresh basil
2 garlic cloves, pressed
2 tablespoons balsamic vinegar
¾ teaspoon salt
½ teaspoon pepper
1 pound eggplant
¼ cup MAZOLA Canola Oil
1 (16-ounce) package baked pizza
     shell ✶
4 ounces crumbled feta cheese

• **Stir** together first 6 ingredients, and set aside.
• **Cut** eggplant crosswise into ½-inch-thick slices. Brush both sides evenly with oil, and place on an aluminum foil-lined baking sheet.
• **Broil** 2 minutes on each side or until lightly browned.
• **Arrange** eggplant evenly on pizza crust; top with tomato mixture, and sprinkle with cheese.
• **Bake** at 450° for 8 to 10 minutes or until thoroughly heated. Serve immediately. **Yield:** 4 servings.

✶ Substitute 1 large tomato, seeded and chopped, for grape tomatoes, if desired; substitute 4 pita bread rounds or 1 French bread loaf for pizza shell, if desired.

Shortcut Desserts

These simple but creative desserts end any meal on a sweet note.

Why wait for a special occasion to serve dessert when you can make fabulous ones any day of the week? These easy sweets fit into even the busiest schedule. The secret to success is keeping your pantry and freezer well stocked with the quality convenience foods that inspired these imaginative takes on all-time favorites. Bake the desserts while dinner is cooking so they'll be ready when you finish. With these recipes in hand, there's no reason to skimp on everyone's favorite part of the meal. Besides, one bite will convince you that "made from scratch" desserts don't have to be time-consuming or complicated to be downright delicious.

CARAMEL-APPLE NAPOLEONS

These impressive dessert pastries make a dazzling finale.

Prep: 10 minutes
Cook: 30 minutes
Bake: 13 minutes

½ (17¼-ounce) package frozen puff pastry sheets, thawed
2 (12-ounce) packages STOUFFER'S Escalloped Apples
1 cup whipping cream
1 cup sugar
¼ cup water
1½ teaspoons lemon juice
¼ cup chopped pecans, toasted

• **Unfold** 1 pastry sheet, and cut into 9 (3⅓-inch) squares. Place on an ungreased baking sheet.

• **Bake** at 400° for 10 to 13 minutes; set aside.
• **Thaw** escalloped apples in microwave at MEDIUM (50% power) 6 to 7 minutes. Let stand 2 minutes. Set aside.
• **Heat** whipping cream in a saucepan over low heat; remove cream from heat.
• **Cook** sugar, ¼ cup water, and lemon juice over medium heat, stirring occasionally, about 15 minutes or until mixture turns an amber color. Gradually pour sugar mixture into whipping cream, stirring constantly. Cook over medium heat 5 to 7 minutes.
• **Split** each pastry square horizontally in half. Layer bottom halves evenly with 2 tablespoons escalloped apples. Spoon half of caramel sauce evenly over halves, and sprinkle evenly with half of pecans. Repeat procedure. Serve immediately. **Yield:** 9 servings.

CARAMEL SAUCE

Serve this delicious sauce over your favorite ice cream, pound cake, or warm pie.

Prep: 15 minutes
Chill: 1 hour

1 cup firmly packed DOMINO Light Brown Sugar
¼ cup butter
¼ cup whipping cream

• **Bring** all ingredients to a boil in a medium saucepan over medium heat, stirring constantly. Boil, stirring constantly, 1 minute. Remove from heat; cool. Chill 1 hour. **Yield:** 1 cup.

GINGERBREAD

Capture the essence of autumn in a warm slice of this sweetly spiced bread.

Prep: 20 minutes
Bake: 30 minutes

2 tablespoons butter or margarine, softened
½ cup granulated sugar
¼ cup applesauce
2 tablespoons molasses
1 cup all-purpose flour
½ teaspoon baking soda
⅛ teaspoon salt
1 tablespoon ground ginger
½ teaspoon pumpkin pie spice
½ cup nonfat buttermilk
2 egg whites
All Natural PAM Butter Flavor Cooking Spray
Garnishes: lemon curd, fresh mint sprigs

• **Beat** first 4 ingredients at medium speed with an electric mixer until blended.
• **Combine** flour and next 4 ingredients; add to butter mixture alternately with buttermilk, beginning and ending with flour mixture. Beat at low speed until blended after each addition. Add egg whites, and beat at medium speed 1 minute. Spray a 9-inch pieplate with cooking spray 5 seconds. Pour batter into pieplate.
• **Bake** at 350° for 25 to 30 minutes or until a wooden pick inserted in center comes out clean. Garnish, if desired. **Yield:** 6 servings.

Note: Spray measuring spoon with cooking spray 1 second before measuring molasses.

BONUS SECTION

MISSISSIPPI MUD DESSERT BROWNIES

Prep: 10 minutes
Bake: 46 minutes

1 cup all-purpose flour
1 teaspoon baking powder
¾ teaspoon salt
1¼ cups sugar
½ cup unsweetened cocoa
½ cup shortening
1 large egg
½ cup water
1 teaspoon vanilla extract
¾ cup caramel sauce
1 cup miniature marshmallows
¾ cup DIAMOND OF CALIFORNIA Shelled Pecan Halves, chopped and toasted
¾ cup semisweet chocolate morsels

• **Stir** together first 5 ingredients in a large bowl; cut in shortening with a pastry blender or fork until crumbly. Stir in egg, ½ cup water, and vanilla. Spread mixture into a lightly greased aluminum foil-lined 8-inch square pan.
• **Bake** at 350° for 35 to 38 minutes or until center is set. Remove from oven; spread with caramel sauce. Sprinkle with marshmallows and pecans, and bake 6 to 8 more minutes.
• **Microwave** chocolate morsels in a glass bowl at MEDIUM (50% power) 1 minute; stir until smooth. Drizzle over warm brownies. Cool and cut into squares. **Yield:** 16 brownies.

BLACKBERRY UPSIDE-DOWN CAKE

Prep: 12 minutes
Bake: 1 hour, 50 minutes

1 (2-pound) frozen MRS. SMITH'S Blackberry Cobbler
1 (18.25-ounce) package white cake mix
1¼ cups milk
2 large eggs
¼ cup butter or margarine, melted
½ cup all-purpose flour
⅓ cup sugar
⅓ cup firmly packed light brown sugar
½ teaspoon ground cinnamon
¼ teaspoon salt
¼ cup cold butter or margarine, cut into pieces
½ cup chopped walnuts, toasted

• **Remove** plastic overwrap from blackberry cobbler. Remove white cardboard cover from foil pan, and turn up edges of pan. Place cobbler on a baking sheet.
• **Bake** at 400° for 50 to 60 minutes or until golden brown. Cool cobbler on a wire rack.
• **Stir** together cake mix and next 3 ingredients. Spoon batter into a lightly greased 13- x 9-inch baking dish. Spread cobbler evenly over batter.
• **Combine** flour and next 4 ingredients; cut in cold butter with a pastry blender until crumbly; stir in walnuts. Sprinkle mixture evenly over cobbler.
• **Bake** at 350° for 45 to 50 minutes or until a wooden pick inserted in center comes out clean. **Yield:** 6 servings.

RUSTIC APPLE-CRANBERRY TART

Prep: 15 minutes
Bake: 30 minutes

2 (12-ounce) packages STOUFFER'S Escalloped Apples
½ cup sweetened dried cranberries
6 tablespoons brandy *
2 tablespoons water
¼ cup firmly packed light brown sugar
⅓ cup plus 3 tablespoons all-purpose flour, divided
⅓ cup firmly packed light brown sugar
¼ cup butter or margarine, softened
⅓ cup chopped walnuts
1 (15-ounce) package refrigerated piecrusts

• **Thaw** escalloped apples in microwave at MEDIUM (50% power) 6 to 7 minutes.
• **Microwave** cranberries, brandy, and 2 tablespoons water in a large glass bowl at HIGH 2½ minutes; stir in escalloped apples. Add ¼ cup brown sugar and 3 tablespoons flour, stirring to blend. Set aside.
• **Combine** remaining ⅓ cup flour and ⅓ cup brown sugar in a bowl; cut in butter with a pastry blender until crumbly. Stir in walnuts.
• **Unfold** piecrusts; stack on a lightly floured surface. Roll into a 15-inch circle. Place on a lightly greased baking sheet. Spoon apple mixture in center of pastry, leaving a 3-inch border. Sprinkle with walnut mixture. Lift pastry edges, and pull over apple mixture, leaving a 9-inch circle of fruit showing in center. Press folds gently to secure.
• **Bake** at 400° on lower oven rack for 30 minutes. **Yield:** 8 servings.

★ Substitute 6 tablespoons apple juice concentrate for brandy, if desired.

Note: For testing purposes only, we used Ocean Spray Craisins Sweetened Dried Cranberries.

Gingersnap Streusel Pumpkin Pie

Prep: 20 minutes
Bake: 1 hour, 30 minutes

1 (3-pound 1-ounce) package
    frozen MRS. SMITH'S Pumpkin
    Custard Pie
10 gingersnaps, coarsely crushed
⅓ cup honey-roasted almonds,
    chopped
2 tablespoons all-purpose flour
2 tablespoons light brown sugar
2 tablespoons butter or margarine,
    softened
¼ teaspoon ground cinnamon

• **Remove** and discard paper circle from pumpkin pie. Place frozen pie on a heavy baking sheet.
• **Bake** at 400° for 30 minutes. Remove from oven.
• **Stir** together crushed gingersnaps and remaining 5 ingredients until crumbly, and sprinkle evenly over pie.
• **Bake** at 400° for 1 hour, shielding top of pie with aluminum foil after 30 minutes. **Yield:** 6 servings.

Cinnamon-Raisin Bread Pudding

Prep: 15 minutes
Bake: 1 hour, 30 minutes

4 cups milk
5 large eggs
10 to 12 white bread slices, torn
    into pieces
3 cups NILLA Wafer crumbs (about
    55 wafers)
¾ cup sugar
½ teaspoon ground cinnamon
1¼ cups raisins

• **Whisk** together milk and eggs in a large bowl. Add bread and remaining ingredients, stirring until blended. Pour mixture into an aluminum foil-lined 11- x 7-inch baking dish; cover with foil, and place in a larger pan. Add water to larger pan to a depth of 1 to 1½ inches.

• **Bake** at 350° for 1 hour. Uncover and bake 20 to 30 more minutes. Serve with caramel sauce or softened ice cream, if desired. **Yield:** 10 servings.

Chocolate Cappuccino Cookies

Serve these irresistible cookies with a tall glass of cold milk or a warming latte.

Prep: 15 minutes
Bake: 10 minutes per batch

2 cups butter or margarine,
    softened
4 cups firmly packed light brown
    sugar
4 large eggs
5½ cups all-purpose flour
1 cup HERSHEY'S Cocoa
¼ cup instant coffee granules
1 teaspoon baking powder
1 teaspoon baking soda
1 teaspoon salt
1 (10-ounce) package HERSHEY'S
    Cinnamon Chips

• **Beat** butter at medium speed with an electric mixer until creamy. Gradually add brown sugar, beating well. Add eggs, beating until blended.
• **Combine** flour and next 5 ingredients. Gradually add to butter mixture, beating at low speed just until blended. Stir in cinnamon chips.
• **Drop** dough by rounded tablespoonfuls, 2 inches apart, onto lightly greased baking sheets.
• **Bake** at 350°, in batches, for 8 to 10 minutes. Cool on baking sheets 5 minutes. Remove to wire racks to cool completely. **Yield:** 8 dozen.

Peanut Butter-Banana Pie

Prep: 20 minutes
Chill: 2 hours

40 NILLA Wafers
⅓ cup honey-roasted peanuts
½ cup butter or margarine, melted
1⅓ cups firmly packed dark brown
    sugar, divided
1 (8-ounce) package cream cheese,
    softened
¾ cup creamy peanut butter
1 cup whipping cream, divided
1 teaspoon vanilla extract
2 bananas
Chopped honey-roasted peanuts
    (optional)

• **Process** first 3 ingredients and ⅓ cup brown sugar in a food processor until crumbly. Press mixture into bottom and up sides of a 10-inch deep-dish pieplate.
• **Bake** at 350° for 5 minutes. Set piecrust aside.
• **Beat** remaining 1 cup brown sugar, cream cheese, peanut butter, and 1 tablespoon whipping cream at medium speed with an electric mixer until mixture is light and fluffy. Set aside.
• **Beat** remaining whipping cream and vanilla until stiff peaks form. Fold one-third of whipped cream into peanut butter mixture; fold peanut butter mixture into remaining whipped cream.
• **Slice** bananas, and place on crust. Spread peanut butter mixture evenly over bananas. Sprinkle with chopped peanuts, if desired. Chill 2 hours. **Yield:** 1 (10-inch) pie.

All-Occasion Entrées

Discover these delicious main dishes
for any night of the week.

Wondering what to prepare for supper tonight? We've got the answer: sensational entrées that will fit any occasion or budget. Grilled, baked, or cooked on the cooktop, these recipes offer a diverse range of menu ideas to serve family or guests.

SWEET-AND-SPICY BARBECUED CHICKEN

Prep: 15 minutes
Grill: 30 minutes

1 cup white vinegar
½ cup SPLENDA Granular
½ cup ketchup
¼ cup lemon juice
1 teaspoon ground black pepper
½ teaspoon salt
½ teaspoon ground red pepper
2 (2½- to 3-pound) whole chickens, quartered

• **Bring** first 7 ingredients to a boil in a saucepan over medium-high heat, stirring often. Reduce heat, and simmer, stirring occasionally, 5 minutes.
• **Coat** food rack with cooking spray; place on grill over medium-high heat (350° to 400°). Arrange chicken quarters on rack, and grill, covered with grill lid, 10 to 15 minutes on each side or until done, basting often with barbecue sauce. (Discard any leftover barbecue sauce used for basting.) **Yield:** 8 servings.

Note: Decrease grilling time to 8 to 10 minutes on each side for skinned chicken quarters.

ROSEMARY-CRUSTED PORK CHOPS WITH PEARS

Prep: 10 minutes
Cook: 42 minutes

1 tablespoon finely chopped fresh or dried rosemary
2 garlic cloves, pressed
2 teaspoons pepper
1 teaspoon salt
All Natural PAM Olive Oil Flavor Cooking Spray
1 large purple onion, cut into eighths
6 boneless pork loin chops
½ cup dry white wine or apple juice
3 pears, peeled and quartered
2 tablespoons light brown sugar

• **Stir** together first 4 ingredients, and set aside.
• **Spray** a large skillet with cooking spray for 3 seconds; heat over medium-high heat. Add onion, and sauté 10 minutes or until lightly browned. Remove from pan.
• **Spray** pork chops on both sides with cooking spray 2 seconds, and press firmly with rosemary mixture. Spray each pork chop on both sides with cooking spray 1 more second, and place in skillet.
• **Cook** chops over medium-high heat 6 minutes on each side. Add wine; cook, covered, 10 minutes. Remove pork chops, reserving drippings in pan.
• **Add** onion, pear, and brown sugar to skillet; cook, stirring occasionally, 10 minutes. Serve over pork chops. **Yield:** 6 servings.

OVEN-BAKED CATFISH WITH TARTAR SAUCE

No one will ever guess
this catfish isn't fried.

Prep: 5 minutes
Chill: 2 hours
Bake: 18 minutes
Broil: 2 minutes

4 (4-ounce) catfish fillets
½ teaspoon salt
½ (2-ounce) bottle hot sauce
½ to ¾ cup cornmeal
Tartar Sauce

• **Sprinkle** fish fillets with salt, and place in a large shallow dish or heavy-duty zip-top plastic bag. Pour in hot sauce; cover or seal, and chill 2 hours, turning occasionally.
• **Remove** fish from marinade, discarding marinade. Dredge fish in cornmeal. Place fish on a lightly greased rack in a baking pan.
• **Bake** at 425° for 15 to 18 minutes or until fish flakes with a fork.
• **Broil** 3 inches from heat 2 minutes or until lightly browned. Serve with Tartar Sauce. **Yield:** 4 servings.

Tartar Sauce

Prep: 5 minutes
Chill: 1 hour

1 (8-ounce) jar MARZETTI Slaw Dressing
1½ tablespoons Dijon mustard
1 (3-ounce) jar green peppercorns, drained
2 garlic cloves, pressed
Garnish: flat-leaf parsley

• **Process** first 4 ingredients in a blender or food processor until smooth; chill sauce 1 hour. Garnish, if desired. **Yield:** 1¼ cups.

BEEF FILLETS WITH WINE SAUCE

Red wine adds depth and finesse to the rich pan sauce that accompanies these steaks.

Prep: 10 minutes
Cook: 35 minutes

6 (1½-inch-thick) beef tenderloin
   steaks
½ teaspoon salt
1 teaspoon freshly ground pepper
2 tablespoons olive oil
1 (10¾-ounce) can beef broth, undiluted
1 cup FETZER Eagle Peak Merlot
2 garlic cloves, pressed
3 tablespoons green peppercorns
¼ cup butter or margarine, cut into
   pieces

• **Sprinkle** steaks evenly with salt and pepper.
• **Brown** steaks in hot oil in a skillet over high heat. Remove from pan.
• **Add** broth, wine, and garlic to skillet; cook mixture over high heat 15 minutes. Return steaks to pan, and cook 5 to 6 minutes on each side or to desired degree of doneness. Remove pan from heat; remove steaks, reserving sauce in pan. Add peppercorns to sauce, and gradually whisk in butter. Serve sauce over steaks. **Yield:** 6 servings.

SEARED TUNA WITH OLIVE-ROSEMARY PESTO

A piquant pesto lends robust flavors to this meaty tuna.

Prep: 5 minutes
Cook: 14 minutes

4 (6-ounce) tuna fillets
¼ teaspoon salt
¼ teaspoon pepper
¼ cup butter or margarine
Olive-Rosemary Pesto

• **Sprinkle** tuna fillets evenly with salt and pepper.

• **Melt** butter in a large skillet over medium-high heat; add tuna, and cook 7 minutes on each side or to desired degree of doneness. Serve with Olive-Rosemary Pesto. **Yield:** 4 servings.

Olive-Rosemary Pesto

Prep: 5 minutes

1 cup kalamata olives, pitted
1 cup fresh parsley
¼ cup grated Romano cheese
¼ cup DIAMOND OF CALIFORNIA
   Shelled Pecan Halves
1 tablespoon fresh rosemary leaves
2 garlic cloves
3 tablespoons olive oil

• **Process** all ingredients in a blender or food processor until mixture is smooth, stopping to scrape down sides. **Yield:** about 1 cup.

BEEF TENDERLOIN WITH AVOCADO BÉARNAISE SAUCE

This company-worthy fare makes an elegant presentation.

Prep: 20 minutes
Chill: 2 hours
Bake: 50 minutes
Stand: 15 minutes

1 (4-pound) trimmed beef tenderloin
1½ teaspoons salt
¾ teaspoon freshly ground pepper
3 tablespoons butter or margarine,
   softened
3 garlic cloves, minced
¼ cup minced fresh parsley
1 tablespoon grated lemon rind
Avocado Béarnaise Sauce

• **Sprinkle** tenderloin evenly with salt and pepper. Stir together butter and next 3 ingredients, and rub mixture over tenderloin. Cover and chill 1 to 2 hours. Place in an aluminum foil-lined 15- x 10-inch jellyroll pan.
• **Bake** tenderloin at 400° for 50 minutes or until a meat thermometer

inserted into thickest portion registers 145° (medium rare). Remove from oven, and let stand 15 minutes. Serve with Avocado Béarnaise Sauce. **Yield:** 8 to 10 servings.

Avocado Béarnaise Sauce

Prep: 20 minutes
Cook: 10 minutes

4 large shallots, diced
¾ cup dry white wine
3 tablespoons white wine vinegar
2 teaspoons dried tarragon
4 small GENUINE CALIFORNIA
   AVOCADOS, peeled and
   chopped
½ cup mayonnaise
2 tablespoons lemon juice
½ teaspoon salt
½ teaspoon freshly ground
   pepper

• **Cook** first 4 ingredients in a small saucepan over medium-high heat 8 to 10 minutes or until liquid is reduced to about 2 tablespoons. Cool.
• **Process** reduced mixture, avocado, and remaining ingredients in a blender or food processor until smooth, stopping to scrape down sides. Chill up to 2 days, if desired. **Yield:** about 3 cups.

BONUS SECTION

GRILLED CHICKEN WITH CREAMY SAUCE

A jar of slaw dressing doubles as both the marinade and sauce for this tender, chargrilled chicken.

Prep: 5 minutes
Marinate: 8 hours
Grill: 1 hour

1 (16-ounce) jar **MARZETTI** Slaw Dressing
½ cup cider vinegar
2 tablespoons coarsely ground pepper
1 (2½- to 3-pound) package chicken pieces

• **Whisk** together first 3 ingredients. Reserve 1 cup sauce; cover and chill remaining sauce.
• **Arrange** chicken in a shallow dish. Pour reserved 1 cup sauce over chicken, turning to coat. Cover and chill 8 hours, turning chicken once.
• **Remove** chicken from marinade, discarding marinade.
• **Prepare** a hot fire by piling charcoal on one side of grill, leaving other side empty. (For gas grills, light only one side.) Place food rack on grill. Arrange chicken over empty side (unlit side of gas grill), and grill, covered with grill lid, 1 hour or until done, turning once.
• **Heat** remaining sauce, and serve with chicken. **Yield:** 4 servings.

CAJUN-STYLE COUNTRY-FRIED STEAK

Mashed potatoes make the perfect partner for these homestyle steaks; they welcome an extra ladle of the golden gravy.

Prep: 10 minutes
Cook: 22 minutes

½ cup all-purpose flour
¼ cup yellow cornmeal
1½ teaspoons Cajun seasoning
6 (4-ounce) cube steaks
Canola or vegetable oil
1 (2.64-ounce) package McCORMICK Original Country Gravy Mix
3 cups milk
¼ to ½ teaspoon ground red pepper

• **Combine** first 3 ingredients in a shallow dish; dredge steaks evenly in flour mixture.
• **Fry** steaks, in batches, in ¼ inch hot oil in a large nonstick skillet over medium-high heat 3 to 4 minutes on each side or until golden. Remove steaks, and keep warm. Carefully drain hot oil, reserving 2 tablespoons drippings in skillet.
• **Whisk** gravy mix, milk, and ground red pepper into reserved drippings in skillet; cook over medium-high heat, whisking constantly, 3 to 6 minutes or until thickened. Serve gravy with steaks. **Yield:** 6 servings.

Note: Gravy will thicken upon standing. To thin gravy, stir in ⅓ to ½ cup milk or enough to reach desired consistency.

HONEY-GARLIC PORK TENDERLOINS

The sweet and tangy sauce pairs nicely with the tender pork. Serve with mashed potatoes and green beans tossed with sautéed purple onion and crumbled feta cheese.

Prep: 15 minutes
Chill: 3 hours
Broil: 5 minutes
Bake: 30 minutes

1 cup Creole mustard, divided
¾ cup honey, divided
3 tablespoons lemon juice, divided
8 garlic cloves, minced
2 teaspoons salt
2½ teaspoons pepper, divided
2 pounds PORK Tenderloin
⅓ cup mayonnaise

• **Stir** together ½ cup mustard, ½ cup honey, 2 tablespoons lemon juice, garlic, salt, and 2 teaspoons pepper in a large shallow dish or heavy-duty zip-top plastic bag; add pork, turning to coat. Cover or seal, and chill 3 hours. Place pork on a lightly greased rack in an aluminum foil-lined roasting pan.
• **Broil** 6 inches from heat 5 minutes; reduce oven temperature to 425°, and bake 15 minutes. Cover loosely with foil, and bake 15 more minutes or until a meat thermometer inserted into thickest portion registers 160°.
• **Stir** together remaining ½ cup mustard, remaining ¼ cup honey, remaining 1 tablespoon lemon juice, remaining ½ teaspoon pepper, and mayonnaise. Serve mixture with pork. **Yield:** 6 servings.

Come to Sunday Dinner

Nourish relationships with good food and fellowship.

If Sunday is the only day of the week your family can enjoy a leisurely meal together, make it wonderful. Our high-flavor menu is sure to please, whether you serve the Chipotle Grilled Pork Ribs or the Black Bean-and-Corn Salsa Pork Chops. Plus you can choose between Chocolate-Raspberry Cake or Chocolate-Chip Chewies—both are easy-to-make sweet endings. Because Sunday afternoon is a good time to entertain, pull up another chair or two, and call your next-door neighbors—you'll all be glad you did.

BUTTERMILK CORN STICKS

Prep: 10 minutes
Bake: 12 minutes per batch

2 cups self-rising white cornmeal
¾ cup all-purpose flour
⅓ cup SPLENDA Granular
2 large eggs
2¼ cups nonfat buttermilk
⅓ cup butter or margarine, melted

• **Combine** first 3 ingredients; make a well in center of mixture.
• **Stir** together eggs, buttermilk, and melted butter. Add to cornmeal mixture, stirring just until dry ingredients are moistened.
• **Heat** cast-iron corn stick pans in oven heated to 425° for 5 minutes or until hot. Remove pans from oven, and coat evenly with cooking spray.
• **Spoon** batter into hot pans.
• **Bake** at 425° for 10 to 12 minutes or until lightly browned. Remove from pans immediately. **Yield:** 30 sticks.

CHIPOTLE GRILLED PORK RIBS

Chipotle peppers contribute their smoky essence to a cookout classic.

Prep: 40 minutes
Grill: 2 hours

¼ cup butter or margarine
1 medium-size sweet onion, chopped
1 garlic clove, minced
1 jalapeño pepper, seeded and chopped
1 cup ketchup
¼ cup red wine vinegar
¼ cup chipotle peppers in adobo sauce
1 tablespoon Worcestershire sauce
2½ to 3 pounds PORK Back Ribs
1½ teaspoons salt

• **Melt** butter in a saucepan over medium-high heat. Add onion, garlic, and jalapeño pepper, and sauté 2 to 3 minutes or until tender. Stir in ketchup and next 3 ingredients; bring to a boil. Reduce heat, and simmer 20 minutes. Reserve ½ cup sauce for dipping, if desired.
• **Cut** pork ribs into 2 sections, and sprinkle evenly with salt. Brush both sides of ribs with sauce.
• **Prepare** a hot fire by piling charcoal on one side of grill, leaving other side empty. (For gas grills, light only one side.) Coat food rack with cooking spray, and place on grill. Arrange food over empty side (unlit side of gas grill), and grill, covered with grill lid, 2 hours, turning and basting every 30 minutes. **Yield:** 4 to 6 servings.

CHOCOLATE-RASPBERRY CAKE
(pictured on page 304)

Prep: 15 minutes
Bake: 18 minutes
Cool: 30 minutes

1 (18.25-ounce) package Swiss chocolate cake mix without pudding
3 large eggs
½ cup vegetable oil
1⅓ cups water
1 (10-ounce) jar seedless raspberry jam
½ cup whipping cream
1 cup NESTLÉ TOLL HOUSE Semi-Sweet Chocolate Morsels
Garnishes: whipped cream, fresh mint sprigs

• **Beat** first 4 ingredients at medium speed with an electric mixer 2 minutes. Spoon batter into 3 greased and floured 8-inch round cakepans.
• **Bake** at 350° for 18 minutes or until a wooden pick inserted in center comes out clean. Cool cakes in pans on wire racks 10 minutes. Remove from pans, and cool completely on wire racks.
• **Spread** jam between layers.
• **Microwave** whipping cream at HIGH 1 minute; add chocolate morsels, stirring until melted. Pour mixture over top of cake, using a spatula to spread mixture around sides of cake. Chill. Garnish, if desired. **Yield:** 1 (3-layer) cake.

GRAPEFRUIT-WHITE WINE SPRITZERS

Prep: 5 minutes

4 cups pink grapefruit juice cocktail, chilled
1 (750-milliliter) bottle FETZER Sundial Chardonnay
⅔ cup sugar
1 pink grapefruit, thinly sliced
2 cups club soda, chilled

• **Stir** together first 3 ingredients until sugar dissolves; add grapefruit. Stir in club soda just before serving. Pour over ice, and serve immediately. **Yield:** 11 cups.

BLACK BEAN-AND-CORN SALSA PORK CHOPS

Prep: 10 minutes
Bake: 30 minutes

1 oven bag
1 tablespoon all-purpose flour
½ teaspoon garlic powder, divided
½ teaspoon salt, divided
½ teaspoon pepper, divided
2 (11-ounce) cans whole kernel corn with red and green peppers, drained
1 (15-ounce) can black beans, rinsed and drained
1 (10-ounce) can diced tomato and green chiles
4 (½-inch-thick) boneless center-cut PORK Chops, trimmed

• **Preheat** oven to 350°.
• **Place** oven bag in a 13- x 9-inch baking dish. Add flour, ¼ teaspoon garlic powder, ¼ teaspoon salt, and ¼ teaspoon pepper to oven bag. Twist end of bag, and shake to combine.
• **Add** corn, beans, and diced tomato to oven bag. Squeeze bag to blend ingredients. Sprinkle pork chops with remaining ¼ teaspoon garlic powder, ¼ teaspoon salt, and ¼ teaspoon pepper; arrange in an even layer over vegetables.
• **Close** oven bag with nylon tie; cut 6 (½-inch) slits in top of bag. Bake at 350° for 30 minutes. **Yield:** 4 servings.

CREAMY NEW POTATO GRATIN

Prep: 20 minutes
Bake: 30 minutes

2 pounds small new potatoes, cut into ¼-inch-thick slices
1 cup water
¼ cup butter or margarine, divided
1 sweet onion, chopped
2 cups milk
1 (2.64-ounce) package McCORMICK Original Country Gravy Mix
1 (8-ounce) package shredded Cheddar-American cheese blend
1 cup fine, dry breadcrumbs
2 teaspoons dried parsley flakes

• **Microwave** potato slices and 1 cup water in a shallow glass dish covered with plastic wrap at HIGH 10 minutes or until tender, stirring once after 5 minutes. Drain and set aside.
• **Melt** 2 tablespoons butter in a large saucepan over medium-high heat; add onion, and sauté 5 minutes or until tender. Add potato slices, and toss gently; remove mixture from saucepan.
• **Melt** remaining 2 tablespoons butter in saucepan over medium heat. Gradually whisk in milk and gravy mix; whisk until smooth. Add shredded cheese, whisking until cheese is melted. Remove from heat, and stir in potato mixture. Spoon into a lightly greased 2½-quart or 9-inch square baking dish. Combine breadcrumbs and dried parsley flakes; sprinkle over potato mixture.
• **Bake** at 400° for 25 to 30 minutes or until bubbly. **Yield:** 6 servings.

AVOCADO-CORN-POBLANO SALAD

Prep: 15 minutes
Grill: 10 minutes

6 small ears fresh corn
2 poblano peppers
Vegetable cooking spray
2 tablespoons extra-virgin olive oil
½ teaspoon grated lime rind
¼ cup fresh lime juice
½ teaspoon salt
¼ teaspoon coarsely ground pepper
¼ teaspoon ground cumin
4 small GENUINE CALIFORNIA AVOCADOS, peeled and coarsely chopped
½ medium-size purple onion, diced
3 tablespoons chopped fresh cilantro

• **Coat** corn and poblano peppers with cooking spray.
• **Grill** corn and peppers, covered with grill lid, over medium-high heat (350° to 400°) 10 minutes or until vegetables are lightly charred, turning occasionally. Cool slightly.
• **Cut** corn kernels from cobs. Remove stems and seeds from roasted peppers, and coarsely chop.
• **Stir** together olive oil and next 5 ingredients in a large bowl; add corn, chopped pepper, avocado, onion, and cilantro, tossing gently to coat. **Yield:** 6 to 8 servings.

CHOCOLATE-CHIP CHEWIES

Prep: 20 minutes
Bake: 22 minutes per batch

½ cup firmly packed light brown sugar
2 large eggs, divided
⅛ teaspoon salt
1 cup NESTLÉ TOLL HOUSE Semi-Sweet Chocolate Morsels
½ cup coarsely chopped walnuts
1 teaspoon vanilla extract, divided
½ cup butter or margarine, softened
⅓ cup sugar
⅓ cup firmly packed light brown sugar
1 cup all-purpose flour
½ teaspoon baking soda
½ teaspoon salt

• **Stir** together ½ cup brown sugar, 1 egg, and ⅛ teaspoon salt in a medium bowl; stir in chocolate morsels, walnuts, and ½ teaspoon vanilla. Set aside.
• **Beat** remaining ½ teaspoon vanilla, butter, ⅓ cup sugar, and ⅓ cup brown sugar at medium speed with an electric mixer until creamy. Add remaining egg, and beat until blended.
• **Combine** flour, baking soda, and ½ teaspoon salt; stir into butter mixture until blended.
• **Place** paper baking cups into miniature (1¾-inch) muffin pans, and coat with cooking spray; spoon 1½ teaspoons batter into each cup.
• **Bake** at 350° for 12 minutes. Spoon chocolate morsel mixture over cupcakes; bake 10 more minutes. **Yield:** about 3 dozen.

Fun and Food on the Road

Make these recipes, follow our packing guidelines, and hit the road for an adventure. Gather the gang, pack your cooler, and enjoy a splendid meal under the big blue sky.

Picnic Extravaganza
Serves 4 to 6

Crostini With Walnut-Blue Cheese or Tomato-Cheddar Spread
Chicken Poppers
Adobo Pork Sandwiches With Rosemary-Garlic Mayonnaise
Creamy Sweet Slaw
Buckeye Balls   Cranberry Tea Cooler

CROSTINI WITH WALNUT-BLUE CHEESE

Prep: 10 minutes
Bake: 10 minutes

¼ cup MAZOLA Canola Oil
2 garlic cloves, pressed
1 (8-ounce) French baguette, cut diagonally into ¼-inch-thick slices
1 (8-ounce) package cream cheese, softened
1 (4-ounce) package crumbled blue cheese *
2 tablespoons whipping cream or milk
1 cup chopped walnuts or almonds, toasted and divided
1 cup seedless red grapes, coarsely chopped

• **Stir** together oil and garlic; brush evenly on bread slices. Place bread on a baking sheet.
• **Bake** at 350° for 10 minutes or until lightly toasted.
• **Stir** together cream cheese, blue cheese, and whipping cream until blended. Stir in ½ cup walnuts; gently fold in grapes.
• **Shape** cheese mixture into 1 (9-inch) log. Roll in remaining ½ cup walnuts. Serve with crostini. **Yield:** 1 (9-inch) log.

*Substitute 4 ounces port wine cheese, crumbled, for blue cheese, if desired.

Note: To toast walnuts, spread on a baking sheet, and bake at 350°, stirring occasionally, 5 to 10 minutes.

TOMATO-CHEDDAR SPREAD

Prep: 25 minutes

1 (10-ounce) can ROTEL Original Diced Tomatoes & Green Chilies, drained
1 cup mayonnaise
1 teaspoon Worcestershire sauce
½ teaspoon salt
2 (8-ounce) blocks sharp Cheddar cheese, shredded
1 (4-ounce) jar chopped pimiento, drained

• **Stir** together first 4 ingredients in a large bowl. Stir in cheese and pimiento. Serve with crackers or on sandwiches. **Yield:** 2½ cups.

Note: Preshredded cheese is not recommended for this recipe.

CHICKEN POPPERS

Prep: 30 minutes
Cook: 24 minutes

20 NILLA Wafers, finely crushed
1½ teaspoons seasoned salt
¾ teaspoon ground red pepper
½ teaspoon pepper
1⅓ cups all-purpose flour, divided
¼ cup milk
1 large egg
6 skinned and boned chicken breast halves, cut into 1½-inch pieces
1 cup canola or vegetable oil
Ranch dressing
Garnish: sliced green onions

• **Stir** together first 4 ingredients and 1 cup flour. Stir together milk and egg.
• **Dredge** chicken pieces in remaining ⅓ cup flour; dip in egg mixture, and dredge in wafer mixture.
• **Pour** oil into a large skillet; heat to 375°. Fry chicken pieces, in 4 batches, 2 to 3 minutes on each side or until done. Drain chicken on paper towels, and serve with Ranch dressing. Garnish, if desired. **Yield:** 8 to 10 appetizer servings.

BONUS SECTION

ADOBO PORK SANDWICHES WITH ROSEMARY-GARLIC MAYONNAISE

Adobo sauce is a puree of chile peppers, herbs, and vinegar.

Prep: 20 minutes
Cook: 8 hours

2 cups drained canned chopped tomatoes
1 tablespoon brown sugar
1 tablespoon chili powder
3 tablespoons red wine vinegar
3 tablespoons adobo sauce
1 tablespoon honey
2 garlic cloves, chopped
4½ pounds PORK Shoulder
6 sandwich buns
Rosemary-Garlic Mayonnaise
Toppings: lettuce leaves, tomato slices

• **Process** first 7 ingredients in a blender or food processor until mixture is smooth.
• **Cut** pork in half, and place in a 5-quart slow cooker. Pour tomato mixture over pork. Cook at HIGH for 8 hours; remove from slow cooker. Cool slightly; shred and serve on buns with Rosemary-Garlic Mayonnaise and desired toppings. **Yield:** 6 servings.

Rosemary-Garlic Mayonnaise

Prep: 5 minutes

½ cup mayonnaise
2 garlic cloves, minced
1 tablespoon chopped fresh or dried rosemary
1 tablespoon lemon juice
⅛ teaspoon salt

• **Stir** together all ingredients. Chill. **Yield:** ½ cup.

CREAMY SWEET SLAW

Prep: 10 minutes
Chill: 2 hours

1 (10-ounce) package finely shredded cabbage
2 celery ribs, chopped
½ small green bell pepper, diced
1 (2-ounce) jar diced pimiento, drained
½ cup MARZETTI Slaw Dressing
1½ tablespoons white vinegar
2 tablespoons milk
½ teaspoon salt
¼ teaspoon pepper

• **Combine** first 4 ingredients in a large bowl. Stir together slaw dressing and remaining 4 ingredients; pour over cabbage mixture, tossing to coat. Cover and chill 2 hours. **Yield:** 4 servings.

BUCKEYE BALLS

Prep: 1 hour
Chill: 10 minutes

1 (16-ounce) jar creamy peanut butter
1 cup butter or margarine, softened
1½ (16-ounce) packages powdered sugar
1 (12-ounce) package NESTLÉ TOLL HOUSE Semi-Sweet Chocolate Morsels
2 tablespoons shortening

• **Beat** peanut butter and butter at medium speed with an electric mixer until blended. Gradually add powdered sugar, beating until blended.
• **Shape** into 1-inch balls, and chill 10 minutes or until firm.
• **Microwave** chocolate morsels and shortening in a 2-quart glass bowl at HIGH 1½ minutes or until melted, stirring twice.
• **Dip** each peanut butter ball into melted chocolate mixture until partially coated, and place on wax paper to harden. Store candy in an airtight container. **Yield:** 7 dozen.

CRANBERRY TEA COOLER

Prep: 20 minutes

2 family-size tea bags
2 (2½-inch) cinnamon sticks
1 teaspoon whole cloves
1 quart boiling water
1½ cups SPLENDA Granular
2 quarts water
2 cups cranberry juice cocktail
1 cup orange juice
¼ cup lemon juice

• **Stir** together first 4 ingredients; cover and steep 15 minutes.
• **Pour** mixture through a wire-mesh strainer into a container, discarding tea bags and spices. Stir in sweetener, 2 quarts water, and remaining ingredients. Serve over ice. **Yield:** about 4 quarts.

PICNIC GUIDE

■ Start the day before. Cook foods completely, and chill thoroughly in plastic containers or heavy-duty zip-top plastic bags.
■ Pack foods directly from the refrigerator or freezer into a cooler, putting ice or frozen gel packs between layers. Place coolest foods on the bottom.
■ One hour is the maximum time food should be left unrefrigerated if the outside temperature is above 85°.
■ Discard leftovers that sit out or stand in cold water for more than an hour.
■ Be sure to include plastic cups, trash bags, bottle openers, disposable utensils, paper towels, insect repellent, sunscreen, and hand sanitizer.
■ Pack a separate cooler for drinks—they'll stay colder, and you'll avoid opening the cooler containing perishables.

SOUTHERN LIVING FAVORITES

Specialties of the House

Members of our Southern Living *team share the recipes
they love to prepare for their family and friends.*

When it comes to cooking, we Foods editors like to think we're fairly capable in the kitchen. However, over the years, the *Southern Living* halls have been filled with tales of folks from other units of the magazine who have a real talent for cooking as well. (How dare they!)

After a bit of digging and some friendly coercing, several of these avid cooks agreed to share their favorite recipes—many of them tightly held. So the next time you leaf through our pages, remember, not only do these generous folks help produce our magazine each month, they're terrific cooks, too.

MAKE IT A MEAL

Here are some serving suggestions for these tried-and-true recipes.

Dana's Chicken-and Sausage Gumbo—green salad and French bread

Troy's Loaded Garlic Smashed Potatoes—grilled steak and sautéed mushrooms

Clay's Hush Puppies—fried catfish and coleslaw

Kathryn's Fried Okra and Green Tomatoes—corn on the cob and black-eyed peas

Dana Adkins Campbell, Foods/Travel Writer

When Dana moved from Cajun country to Birmingham, she had to learn a hard lesson. "Having never lived outside of Louisiana, I was shocked to learn that I couldn't get the sausage I had grown up on, an absolute key to this recipe," says Dana. To capture an authentic taste, she now orders sausage by phone and takes an ice chest with her every time she goes home.

CHICKEN-AND-SAUSAGE GUMBO

*Cajun flavors reign supreme in this
spicy, sans-seafood gumbo.*

*Prep: 55 minutes
Cook: 2 hours*

1 **pound Cajun-style smoked sausage, cut into ¼-inch-thick slices**
4 **skinned bone-in chicken breast halves**
Vegetable oil
¾ **cup all-purpose flour**
1 **medium onion, chopped**
½ **green bell pepper, chopped**
2 **celery ribs, sliced**
2 **quarts hot water**
3 **garlic cloves, minced**
2 **bay leaves**
2 **teaspoons Creole seasoning**
½ **teaspoon dried thyme**
1 **tablespoon Worcestershire sauce**
½ **to 1 teaspoon hot sauce**
4 **green onions, sliced**
Filé powder (optional)
Hot cooked rice

● **Cook** sausage, stirring constantly, in a Dutch oven over medium heat 5 minutes or until browned. Drain on paper towels, reserving drippings in Dutch oven. Set sausage aside.

● **Cook** chicken in reserved drippings in Dutch oven over medium heat 5 minutes or until browned. Remove to paper towels, reserving drippings in Dutch oven. Set chicken aside.

● **Add** enough oil to drippings in Dutch oven to measure ½ cup. Add flour, and cook over medium heat, stirring constantly, until roux is chocolate colored (about 20 to 25 minutes).

● **Stir** in onion, bell pepper, and celery, and cook, stirring often, 8 minutes or until tender. Gradually add 2 quarts hot water, and bring mixture to a boil; add chicken, garlic, and next 5 ingredients. Reduce heat to low, and simmer, stirring occasionally, 1 hour. Remove chicken; let cool.

● **Add** sausage to gumbo; cook 30 minutes. Stir in green onions, and cook 30 more minutes.

● **Bone** chicken, and cut into strips; return to gumbo, and simmer 5 minutes. Remove and discard bay leaves.

● **Remove** gumbo from heat. Sprinkle with filé powder, if desired. Serve over hot cooked rice. **Yield:** 4 to 6 servings.

Troy H. Black, Assistant Garden Design Editor

Troy is quick to point out that although his decadent "smashed" potatoes aren't the most heart-healthy recipe, they're well worth the splurge. In fact, Troy likes nothing more than to draw out his inner garlic-lover by pairing this chunky concoction with a perfectly grilled steak.

LOADED GARLIC SMASHED POTATOES

Savor every creamy bite of these extraordinary "smashed" potatoes, redolent of garlic and lavished with cheese.

Prep: 45 minutes
Bake: 40 minutes

2 medium garlic bulbs
1 tablespoon olive oil
6 bacon slices
1 bunch green onions, chopped
4 pounds red potatoes
1 (16-ounce) container sour cream
1½ cups (6 ounces) shredded Cheddar cheese, divided
⅓ cup butter or margarine, softened
¼ cup milk
½ teaspoon salt
¼ teaspoon pepper
Garnish: chopped fresh chives

• **Cut** off pointed end of garlic bulbs; place garlic on a piece of aluminum foil, and drizzle with oil. Fold foil to seal.
• **Bake** at 425° for 30 minutes; cool. Squeeze pulp from garlic; set aside.
• **Cook** bacon in a large skillet until crisp; remove bacon, and drain on paper towels, reserving 2 tablespoons drippings in skillet. Crumble bacon, and return to skillet; add green onions. Cook 1 minute or until green onions are tender. Set aside.
• **Peel** half of potatoes; cut into ¼-inch pieces. Cut remaining unpeeled potatoes into ¼-inch pieces.
• **Cook** potato in a Dutch oven in boiling salted water to cover 20 to 25 minutes or until tender; drain and place in a large bowl.

• **Add** roasted garlic pulp, bacon mixture, sour cream, 1 cup cheese, and next 4 ingredients; mash with a potato masher until blended. Spoon into a lightly greased 13- x 9-inch baking dish; top with remaining ½ cup cheese.
• **Bake** at 350° for 10 minutes or until cheese melts. Garnish, if desired.
Yield: 8 to 10 servings.

Clay Nordan, Managing Editor

Clay credits his late uncle Pat Wyatt for these light-as-a-feather gems. "Uncle Pat had a real gift for cooking for crowds, so he would multiply this recipe for what my mom called a 'log rolling,' where he would make more than a hundred of these at a time," says Clay.

HUSH PUPPIES

Pile a platter high with these crispy, melt-in-your-mouth morsels, and watch them disappear.

Prep: 15 minutes
Cook: 4 minutes per batch

1½ cups cornmeal
½ cup all-purpose flour
1 tablespoon baking powder
⅛ teaspoon baking soda
1 teaspoon salt
1 tablespoon sugar
½ medium-size onion, chopped
1 cup buttermilk
1 large egg
Vegetable oil

• **Combine** first 7 ingredients in a bowl; make a well in center of mixture.
• **Whisk** together buttermilk and egg; add to dry ingredients, stirring just until moistened.
• **Pour** oil to a depth of 3 inches into a Dutch oven; heat to 350°.
• **Drop** batter by rounded teaspoonfuls into hot oil. Fry, in batches, 1 to 2 minutes on each side or until golden. Drain on paper towels; serve immediately.
Yield: 3 dozen.

Kathryn Korotky, Production Assistant

Using only cornmeal, salt, and pepper to coat the okra and green tomatoes, Kathryn has developed a truly unique—and tasty—combination. Her best kitchen tip: Keep a wooden spoon nearby to slap the hands that try to eat the okra before it makes it to the table.

FRIED OKRA AND GREEN TOMATOES

When you crave some serious down-home Southern food, these golden nuggets are sure to satisfy.

Prep: 20 minutes
Cook: 8 minutes per batch

1 cup buttermilk
1 large egg
1½ cups cornmeal
⅛ teaspoon salt
¼ teaspoon pepper
1 pound fresh okra, sliced
2 or 3 green tomatoes, cut into
    ½-inch pieces *
Vegetable oil
Salt

• **Whisk** together buttermilk and egg. Combine cornmeal, ⅛ teaspoon salt, and pepper. Dip okra and tomato, in batches, into buttermilk mixture; coat in cornmeal mixture.
• **Pour** oil to a depth of 3 inches into a Dutch oven; heat to 375°.
• **Fry** okra and tomato, in batches, 4 minutes on each side or until golden. (Turning too soon will cause breading to fall off.) Drain on paper towels; sprinkle with salt. **Yield:** 8 servings.

* Substitute 2 or 3 firm red tomatoes for green tomatoes, if desired.

Lowcountry Flavors

Enjoy a taste of the Lowcountry in this sophisticated menu.

An Elegant Lowcountry Meal
Serves 8

Bourbon Sunrise

Shrimp Cakes With Watercress Rémoulade

Baked Garlic-and-Herb Grits

Benne Veggies

There's a saying in coastal South Carolina that once your toes touch the marsh mud—"pluff mud"—you'll always come back. Bring home the flavors of Charleston with this charming fare.

BOURBON SUNRISE

Prep: 15 minutes
Cook: 10 minutes

½ cup water
1 cup sugar
2 large navel oranges, sliced
1½ cups bourbon
1 quart orange juice
1 (10-ounce) jar maraschino cherries with stems, undrained

• **Combine** ½ cup water, sugar, and orange slices in a saucepan, squeezing slices to release juices. Bring to a boil; cook over medium-high heat, stirring often, 5 minutes. Cover; remove from heat. Cool.
• **Pour** syrup through a wire-mesh strainer into a pitcher, discarding orange slices; stir in bourbon and orange juice. Pour in cherry juice; add cherries. Serve over ice. **Yield:** 8 servings.

SHRIMP CAKES WITH WATERCRESS RÉMOULADE

Serve the cakes with lemon juice or tartar sauce, if desired. They also make great sandwiches.

Prep: 30 minutes
Chill: 2 hours
Cook: 20 minutes

⅓ cup butter or margarine
½ small sweet onion, minced
½ cup all-purpose flour
2 cups milk
1 tablespoon seafood seasoning
½ teaspoon ground red pepper
2 large eggs, lightly beaten
4 cups chopped cooked shrimp
1 cup saltine cracker crumbs
½ cup vegetable oil
Watercress Rémoulade
Garnish: whole cooked shrimp

• **Melt** butter in a large heavy saucepan over medium heat; add onion, and sauté 3 minutes or until onion is tender.
• **Whisk** in flour; cook, whisking constantly, about 1 minute. Gradually whisk in milk; cook, whisking constantly, until thickened. Remove from heat; stir in seasoning and red pepper. Cool.

• **Whisk** in beaten eggs, and stir in shrimp and cracker crumbs. Shape into 16 patties; cover and chill 2 hours.
• **Cook,** in 2 batches, in hot oil in a large skillet over medium-high heat 4 to 5 minutes on each side or until golden. Drain on paper towels. Serve shrimp cakes with Watercress Rémoulade. Garnish, if desired. **Yield:** 16 cakes.

Note: For testing purposes only, we used Chef Paul Prudhomme's Magic Seasoning Blends Seafood Magic for seafood seasoning.

Watercress Rémoulade

Prep: 15 minutes

1½ cups mayonnaise
2 tablespoons Dijon mustard
1 bunch watercress leaves, chopped
3 green onions, sliced
½ cup chopped fresh or frozen chives
1 garlic clove, minced
¼ teaspoon ground red pepper

• **Stir** together all ingredients in a large bowl. **Yield:** 2 cups.

BAKED GARLIC-AND-HERB GRITS

Prep: 50 minutes
Bake: 55 minutes

4 cups water
4 cups milk
1¼ teaspoons salt
2 cups uncooked regular grits
2 (6.5-ounce) containers garlic-and-herb-flavored spreadable cheese
1 teaspoon seasoned pepper
1 cup shredded Parmesan cheese
4 large eggs, lightly beaten
8 bacon slices, cooked and crumbled
¼ cup chopped fresh parsley

• **Bring** first 3 ingredients to a boil in a large saucepan over medium-high heat; gradually stir in grits.
• **Return** to a boil; reduce heat to low. Cook, covered, over low heat, stirring

often, 20 minutes or until done. Stir in spreadable cheese, pepper, and Parmesan cheese.

• **Stir** about one-fourth of grits mixture gradually into beaten eggs; add to remaining grits mixture, stirring constantly. Pour into a lightly greased 13- x 9-inch baking dish.

• **Bake** at 350° for 45 to 55 minutes or until golden and set. Sprinkle each serving with bacon and parsley. **Yield:** 8 to 10 servings.

Note: For testing purposes only, we used Alouette Garlic et Herbes Gourmet Spreadable Cheese.

BENNE VEGGIES

Raw sesame seeds flavor many Charleston dishes, most notably benne wafers. Purchase seeds in bulk from health food stores for the best price.

Prep: 20 minutes
Cook: 8 minutes

2 **pounds fresh asparagus**
2 **tablespoons butter or margarine**
2 **tablespoons dark sesame oil**
2 **shallots, chopped**
1 **tablespoon sugar**
2 **large yellow squash, cut into thin strips**
1 **large red bell pepper, cut into thin strips**
1 **tablespoon rice wine vinegar**
3 **tablespoons sesame seeds, toasted**
½ **teaspoon seasoned salt**
½ **teaspoon seasoned pepper**

• **Snap** off tough ends of asparagus. Cut asparagus in half lengthwise; cut each strip diagonally into 3-inch pieces.
• **Melt** butter with oil in a large skillet over medium-high heat; add shallots and sugar, and sauté 2 minutes or until shallots are tender. Add asparagus, squash, and bell pepper; sauté 5 minutes or until tender.
• **Stir** in vinegar and remaining ingredients; serve immediately. **Yield:** 6 to 8 servings.

Our Mutual Friends

Over and over some readers continue to share their great recipes with us.

Searching our extensive recipe files for the best dishes to publish can be a daunting task. There are thousands of recipes, neatly filed away, waiting for an opportunity to appear in *Southern Living*. As we sort through them, we begin to recognize certain readers' recipes by their appearances. One contributor's submissions are typed on sheets of embossed stationery; another's are written on yellow legal paper. After years of encountering their recipes, we greet these contributors as old friends. Each sends dozens of recipes annually, and all have appeared in the magazine numerous times. Allow us to introduce a few of them, as we share some of their best dishes.

GLAZED ROASTED CHICKEN

Prep: 20 minutes
Chill: 8 hours
Bake: 50 minutes

¼ **cup teriyaki sauce**
2 **tablespoons frozen orange juice concentrate, thawed and undiluted**
1½ **tablespoons dark sesame oil**
2 **garlic cloves, minced**
1 **(3-pound) whole chicken**
¼ **teaspoon freshly ground pepper**
Garnishes: mixed salad greens, green onion strips

• **Stir** together first 4 ingredients.
• **Sprinkle** chicken evenly with freshly ground pepper. Place in a large heavy-duty zip-top plastic bag, and pour half of teriyaki mixture over chicken. Set remaining teriyaki mixture aside. Seal bag, and chill 8 hours, turning chicken, if desired.

• **Remove** chicken from marinade, discarding marinade. Place chicken, breast side up, on an aluminum foil-lined 13- x 9-inch pan.
• **Bake** at 450° for 40 to 50 minutes or until a meat thermometer inserted into thigh registers 180°, shielding with foil after 30 minutes. Brush with reserved teriyaki mixture. Garnish, if desired. **Yield:** 4 servings.

William Cottrell
New Orleans, Louisiana

DILLED PEAS-AND-POTATOES VINAIGRETTE

Prep: 30 minutes
Chill: 2 hours

8 **small red potatoes**
1 **pound sugar snap peas**
6 **tablespoons white wine vinegar**
2 **tablespoons minced fresh dill**
½ **teaspoon salt**
½ **teaspoon freshly ground pepper**
½ **cup olive oil**
6 **green onions, chopped**

• **Cook** potatoes in a Dutch oven in boiling water to cover 25 to 30 minutes or until tender; drain. Thinly slice.
• **Cook** peas in boiling water to cover 2 minutes or until crisp-tender; drain. Plunge peas into ice water to stop the cooking process; drain.
• **Combine** vinegar and next 3 ingredients in a bowl; whisk in oil. Add potato slices, peas, and green onions, tossing gently to coat. Chill 2 hours, or serve immediately. **Yield:** 6 to 8 servings.

La Juan Coward
Jasper, Texas

SOUTHERN LIVING FAVORITES

JALAPEÑO-CHEESE GRITS

Prep: 20 minutes
Cook: 15 minutes
Bake: 45 minutes

1 (32-ounce) container chicken broth
1¾ cups uncooked quick-cooking grits
½ cup butter or margarine
1 medium onion, chopped
2 jalapeño peppers, seeded and diced
1 large red or green bell pepper, chopped
2 garlic cloves, pressed
2 cups (8 ounces) shredded sharp Cheddar cheese
2 cups (8 ounces) shredded Monterey Jack cheese
5 large eggs, lightly beaten
¼ teaspoon salt

• **Bring** broth to a boil in a large saucepan; stir in grits. Reduce heat, and simmer, stirring occasionally, 5 minutes. Cover.
• **Melt** butter in a large skillet; add chopped onion and next 3 ingredients, and sauté 5 minutes or until tender. Stir in grits, Cheddar cheese, and remaining ingredients. Pour into a lightly greased 13- x 9-inch baking dish.
• **Bake,** covered, at 350° for 45 minutes or until set; serve immediately.
Yield: 8 to 10 servings.

La Juan Coward
Jasper, Texas

LEMONGRASS-AND-PETITS POIS SOUP

A touch of exotic lemongrass enlivens green peas in this vibrant soup.

Prep: 30 minutes
Cook: 1 hour

2 lemongrass stalks
2½ cups chicken broth, divided
12 ounces frozen sweet peas, thawed
¼ cup butter or margarine
2 large potatoes, peeled and diced
1 large onion, diced
½ teaspoon salt
½ teaspoon pepper
½ cup half-and-half
3 tablespoons sour cream
2 teaspoons minced fresh mint
Garnishes: fresh mint sprigs, lemon slices

• **Crush** lemongrass bulbs.
• **Cook** lemongrass stalks and ¾ cup broth, covered, in a small saucepan over low heat 30 minutes. Remove from heat, and discard lemongrass. Add peas, and let stand, covered, 15 minutes. Set aside.
• **Melt** butter in a medium saucepan over medium heat. Add diced potato and onion, and sauté 5 minutes or until onion is tender.
• **Add** remaining 1¾ cups broth; bring to a boil. Reduce heat to low; cook mixture, covered, 30 minutes or until potato is tender. Cool. Stir in pea mixture, salt, and pepper.
• **Process** mixture in a blender or food processor until smooth, stopping to scrape down sides. Return to saucepan; stir in half-and-half. Cook over low heat until thoroughly heated.
• **Stir** together sour cream and minced mint; dollop over soup. Garnish, if desired. **Yield:** 6 cups.

Caroline Kennedy
Newborn, Georgia

TEX-MEX EGG ROLLS

Prep: 45 minutes
Cook: 35 minutes

1 bunch green onions, chopped
½ medium-size red bell pepper, finely chopped
3 tablespoons olive oil
6 cups shredded fresh spinach
1 (15-ounce) can black beans, rinsed and drained
1 cup frozen whole kernel corn, thawed
½ cup chopped fresh parsley
1½ teaspoons ground cumin
1 teaspoon salt
1 cup (4 ounces) shredded Monterey Jack cheese with peppers
10 egg roll wrappers
Peanut oil
¾ cup Ranch-style dressing
½ cup salsa
Garnish: finely chopped green onions

• **Sauté** green onions and bell pepper in hot olive oil in a large skillet over medium-high heat 5 minutes or until tender. Stir in spinach and next 5 ingredients; cook over low heat, stirring occasionally, 5 minutes or until spinach wilts. Remove from heat; let stand 15 minutes. Stir in cheese.
• **Spoon** 3 tablespoons mixture in center of each egg roll wrapper. Fold top corner over filling, tucking tip of corner under filling; fold left and right corners over filling. Lightly brush remaining corner with water; tightly roll filled end toward remaining corner, and gently press to seal.
• **Pour** peanut oil to depth of 1½ inches in a medium saucepan; heat to 350°. Fry egg rolls, in batches, 5 minutes or until golden; drain on paper towels.
• **Stir** together dressing and salsa; garnish, if desired, and serve with egg rolls. **Yield:** 10 egg rolls.

Judy Grigoraci
Charleston, West Virginia

328   SOUTHERN LIVING FAVORITES

WE SALUTE

William Cottrell first acquired a taste for international cuisines from his Dutch grandmother. When he went to school in Texas, he studied Czech, German, and Hispanic food.

La Juan Coward started cooking nearly 60 years ago, growing up on a farm near Dry Prong, Louisiana. "I was one of seven," she says, "so we had to learn to cook."

We can rely on **Caroline Kennedy** for dishes that are fresh and inventive. "I've been cooking since I was 8," she says. "My entire life has revolved around food and travel."

Judy Grigoraci writes a recipe-exchange column in West Virginia. She says, "My readers want shortcut recipes with a homemade feel—dishes that require few ingredients, yet are good and fast."

Patsy Bell Hobson is a "gardener first and a cook second." She uses her fresh herbs to flavor vinegars. When preparing a big meal, "I make something we can eat twice."

Janie Baur started cooking at age 10. "Now, I love having friends over for dinner. They love being guinea pigs because they know it's bound to be something good."

Charlotte Bryant works as a caregiver. "I get some of my best recipes from my patients," she says. She and her husband travel the South attending country music concerts.

Agnes Stone Mixon has been a contributor since 1979. She says, "I'm still learning about food all the time." She especially loves to make homemade bread and rolls.

Clairiece Gilbert Humphrey is the granddaughter and daughter of great cooks. "Treasured recipes keep us connected with other generations," she explains.

GRAPE TOMATOES WITH CAPERS

Prep: 15 minutes
Stand: 15 minutes

3 tablespoons drained small capers
3 tablespoons balsamic vinegar
2 tablespoons olive oil
½ teaspoon salt
½ teaspoon pepper
2 pints grape tomatoes
6 large fresh basil leaves, shredded
3 tablespoons shredded Parmesan
  cheese
Bibb lettuce leaves (optional)

• **Stir** together first 5 ingredients. Drizzle over tomatoes; toss to coat. Let stand at least 15 minutes or up to 1 hour. Sprinkle with basil and cheese. Serve over lettuce leaves, if desired. **Yield:** 6 servings.

Patsy Bell Hobson
Liberty, Missouri

PEAR, JÍCAMA, AND SNOW PEA SALAD

Prep: 25 minutes
Cook: 30 seconds

1 cup fresh snow pea pods
1 pear, peeled
1 small jícama, peeled
¾ teaspoon lemon juice
1 (6-ounce) package baby spinach,
  sliced
1 (2-ounce) package sliced almonds,
  toasted
Vinaigrette

• **Cook** snow peas in boiling salted water to cover 30 seconds or until crisp-tender; drain. Plunge into ice water to stop the cooking process; drain.
• **Cut** peas, pear, and jícama into thin strips; gently toss pear with lemon juice.
• **Layer** snow peas, pear, jícama, and spinach; sprinkle with almonds. Serve with Vinaigrette. **Yield:** 6 to 8 servings.

Vinaigrette

Prep: 10 minutes

¼ cup balsamic vinegar
1 teaspoon Dijon mustard
1 garlic clove
1 teaspoon sugar
¼ teaspoon coarsely ground
  pepper
¾ cup olive oil
2 green onions, chopped
2 tablespoons chopped fresh basil

• **Process** first 5 ingredients in a blender or food processor until smooth, stopping to scrape down sides. Gradually add olive oil in a slow, steady stream, and process mixture until well blended.
• **Stir** in green onions and basil. Serve with salad. **Yield:** ¾ cup.

Janie Baur
Spring, Texas

CHEESY ONION BISCUITS

Prep: 15 minutes
Bake: 15 minutes

2 cups all-purpose flour
3 tablespoons instant nonfat dry milk
    powder
4 teaspoons baking powder
¾ teaspoon salt
⅓ cup butter or margarine
½ cup grated Parmesan cheese
2 tablespoons finely chopped green
    onions
¾ cup water

• **Combine** first 4 ingredients in a large bowl; cut in butter with a pastry blender or fork until mixture is crumbly.
• **Stir** in Parmesan cheese and green onions. Add ¾ cup water, stirring mixture with a fork until dry ingredients are moistened.
• **Turn** dough out onto a lightly floured surface, and knead lightly 5 or 6 times.
• **Roll** dough to ½-inch thickness; cut with a 3-inch round cutter. Place on a lightly greased baking sheet.
• **Bake** at 400° for 15 minutes or until lightly browned. **Yield:** 8 biscuits.

Charlotte Bryant
Greensburg, Kentucky

LEMON ICE

Prep: 15 minutes
Freeze: 8 hours, 45 minutes

1 (12-ounce) can frozen lemonade
    concentrate, thawed
3 cups ice cubes
1 cup water
⅓ cup sugar
Garnish: lemon rind strips

• **Process** first 4 ingredients in a blender or food processor until smooth. Pour into a 13- x 9-inch pan; freeze 45 minutes.
• **Process** in blender or food processor until smooth. Return to pan; freeze 8 hours. Garnish, if desired. **Yield:** 4 cups.

Agnes Stone Mixon
Ocala, Florida

UNFORGETTABLE COCONUT CAKE

The Apricot Filling offers a tart contrast to the sweet cake layers and sugary frosting.

Prep: 2 hours
Bake: 20 minutes

2½ cups cake flour
2½ teaspoons baking powder
½ teaspoon salt
1 cup milk
¼ cup water
1½ teaspoons vanilla extract
4 egg whites
¼ cup sugar
½ cup shortening
¼ cup butter or margarine,
    softened
1¼ cups sugar
Apricot Filling
Fluffy White Frosting
1 (3-ounce) can sweetened flaked
    coconut

• **Combine** first 3 ingredients; set aside. Combine milk, ¼ cup water, and vanilla; set aside.
• **Beat** egg whites with an electric mixer until foamy. Gradually add ¼ cup sugar, 1 tablespoon at a time, beating until soft peaks form.
• **Combine** shortening, butter, and 1¼ cups sugar in a large mixing bowl; beat at medium speed 3 minutes. Add flour mixture alternately with milk mixture, beginning and ending with flour mixture. Mix well after each addition. Fold in beaten egg whites.
• **Pour** batter into 3 greased and floured 9- x 1¾-inch round cakepans.
• **Bake** at 350° for 15 to 20 minutes or until a wooden pick inserted in center comes out clean. Cool in pans 10 minutes; remove from pans, and cool completely on wire racks.
• **Spread** Apricot Filling between layers and Fluffy White Frosting on top and sides of cake. Sprinkle with coconut. **Yield:** 1 (3-layer) cake.

Note: For testing purposes only, we used Angel Flake sweetened coconut.

Apricot Filling

Prep: 10 minutes
Cook: 8 minutes
Chill: 1 hour

2 (6-ounce) packages dried apricots
⅔ cup sugar
1 tablespoon cornstarch
⅛ teaspoon salt
¾ cup water
1 tablespoon lemon rind
⅓ cup lemon juice
1 tablespoon butter or margarine
2 egg yolks, lightly beaten

• **Process** apricots and sugar in a blender or food processor until finely chopped.
• **Combine** apricot mixture, cornstarch, and next 5 ingredients in a heavy saucepan. Bring to a boil over medium heat, and cook, stirring constantly, 3 to 4 minutes or until thickened. Reduce heat, and cook, stirring constantly, 1 minute.
• **Gradually** stir about one-fourth of hot mixture into beaten egg yolks, and add to remaining hot mixture, stirring constantly.
• **Let** filling cool; cover and chill 1 hour. **Yield:** 2½ cups.

Fluffy White Frosting

Prep: 25 minutes

1 cup sugar
⅛ teaspoon cream of tartar
⅛ teaspoon salt
¼ cup cold water
2 egg whites
1½ teaspoons vanilla extract

• **Combine** first 5 ingredients in top of a double boiler. Beat at low speed with an electric mixer 30 seconds. Place over boiling water; beat at high speed 7 minutes or until stiff peaks form. Remove from heat. Add vanilla; beat 2 minutes or until thick enough to spread. **Yield:** 4¼ cups.

Clairiece Gilbert Humphrey
Charlottesville, Virginia

What's for Supper?

Tongs and spatulas are the weapons of choice

for this competition of dueling grills.

No-Fuss Cookout

Serves 6

Marinated Pork Loin
Corn on the Cob With
Garlic-Chive Butter
Roasted Vegetable Medley

Last-minute invitations for supper are the rule at Associate Foods Editor Peggy Smith's house. And grilling is her favorite way to entertain.

Morton, Peggy's husband, and Bill Garner, a friend, enjoy a grilling rivalry. Morton is a purist who prefers grilling with charcoal. Bill loves the convenience and heat control of a gas grill.

Of course, Carolyn, Bill's wife, and Peggy have no problem letting them duel it out. Everyone's a winner because the results are always great-tasting meals.

MARINATED PORK LOIN

Prep: 40 minutes
Chill: 2 hours
Grill: 50 minutes

2 **tablespoons granulated garlic**
2 **tablespoons salt**
2 **tablespoons pepper**
1½ **quarts white vinegar**
1 **(28-ounce) can tomato puree**
1 **large lemon, halved**
1 **(2- to 2½-pound) boneless pork loin roast**
Morton's Special Sauce

• **Combine** first 5 ingredients. Squeeze lemon juice into marinade; add lemon halves. Divide mixture in half; set aside.
• **Place** roast in a shallow dish or heavy-duty zip-top plastic bag; pour half of marinade over roast. Cover or seal, and chill 2 hours.
• **Prepare** a hot fire by piling charcoal on 1 side of grill, leaving other side empty. (For gas grills, light only 1 side.) Place food rack on grill. Remove roast from marinade, discarding marinade. Arrange roast over unlit side. Grill, covered with grill lid, 10 minutes.
• **Arrange** roast over lit side. Grill, covered with grill lid, over medium-high heat (350° to 400°) 40 minutes or until meat thermometer inserted into thickest portion registers 160°, turning occasionally and basting with reserved marinade the last 10 minutes. Serve with Morton's Special Sauce. **Yield:** 6 servings.

Morton's Special Sauce

Prep: 5 minutes
Cook: 30 minutes

Remaining marinade (about 2 cups)
¼ **cup firmly packed brown sugar**
3 **tablespoons molasses**

• **Stir** together all ingredients in a saucepan, and cook over low heat 30 minutes or until thoroughly heated. **Yield:** 3 cups.

CORN ON THE COB WITH GARLIC-CHIVE BUTTER

Prep: 30 minutes
Stand: 1 hour
Grill: 20 minutes

6 **ears fresh corn with husks**
½ **cup butter or margarine, softened**
2 **garlic cloves, minced**
¼ **cup finely chopped fresh chives ✳**

• **Pull** back corn husks; remove and discard silks. Pull husks over corn. Cover corn with water; let stand 1 hour (this keeps husks from burning). Drain.
• **Stir** together butter, garlic, and chives.
• **Grill** corn, without grill lid, over medium heat (300° to 350°) 20 minutes or until tender, turning often. Remove husks. Spread desired amount of butter mixture over corn. **Yield:** 6 servings.

✳ Substitute freeze-dried or frozen chives or garlic chives, if desired.

ROASTED VEGETABLE MEDLEY

Prep: 30 minutes
Bake: 40 minutes

2 **medium-size sweet onions, cut into small wedges**
1 **tablespoon olive oil**
3 **medium zucchini, cut into 1-inch slices**
2 **medium-size yellow squash, cut into 1-inch slices**
2 **medium-size red bell peppers, cubed**
3 **garlic cloves, pressed**
2 **tablespoons olive oil**
½ **teaspoon salt**
¼ **teaspoon freshly ground pepper**

• **Toss** onion with 1 tablespoon oil; arrange on an aluminum foil-lined jellyroll pan.
• **Bake** at 425° for 20 minutes or until tender, stirring once.
• **Combine** zucchini and next 6 ingredients; add to onion. Bake 20 more minutes, stirring twice. **Yield:** 6 servings.

Living Light

Try a deliciously cool drink and selection of appetizers for a perfect party on the porch.

Sharon Bradberry and Joy Zacharia have known each other since high school. Their paths crossed again seven years ago, and they've been cooking together ever since. Sharon, a Tallahassee native, loves anything Latin—especially food. She and Joy share a passion for creating dishes that burst with flavor and aroma. Joy's cousin Lisette Levy, of Mexico City, often serves as the official taster, a task Lisette deems supreme.

To be health conscious, these recipes are tweaked to lower saturated fat, cholesterol, and calories. Some things, however, are difficult to overhaul, so employ an alternate strategy—moderation, a way to enjoy most of the foods we all love.

These recipes fuse Sharon's Southern heritage with ingredients common to Latin cuisines. *Buen provecho* (enjoy).

SPICY CRAB BALL

Prep: 17 minutes
Chill: 2 hours

½ small sweet onion, chopped
1 teaspoon olive oil
1 (8-ounce) package reduced-fat cream cheese, softened
1 (6-ounce) can jumbo lump crabmeat, rinsed and drained
1 to 2 tablespoons adobo sauce (from canned chipotles)
10 smoked almonds, finely chopped

• **Sauté** onion in hot oil in a nonstick skillet over medium heat until tender.
• **Stir** together onion, cream cheese, crabmeat, and adobo sauce. Cover and chill 2 hours.

• **Shape** crab mixture into a ball; roll top in almonds. Cover; chill until ready to serve. Serve with fresh vegetables or low-fat crackers. **Yield:** 8 servings.

Sharon Bradberry
Tallahassee, Florida

♥ Per serving: Calories 107 (63% from fat)
Fat 7.5g (sat 3g, mono 0.5g, poly 0.3g)
Protein 6.8g Carb 3g Fiber 0.3g
Chol 29mg Iron 0.4mg
Sodium 232mg Calc 58mg

CANTALOUPE-LIME REFRESHER

Prep: 15 minutes

1 whole cantaloupe, peeled, seeded, and cut into chunks
1 cup water
½ teaspoon grated lime rind
½ cup sugar
¼ cup fresh lime juice
Garnish: small cantaloupe wedges

• **Process** first 3 ingredients in a blender until smooth, stopping to scrape down sides. Pour mixture through a wire-mesh strainer into a pitcher, pressing pulp with back of a spoon. Discard pulp.
• **Add** ½ cup sugar and lime juice, stirring until sugar dissolves. Serve over ice, and garnish, if desired. **Yield:** about 5 cups.

♥ Per cup: Calories: 118 (2% from fat)
Fat 0.3g (sat 0g, mono 0g, poly 0.6g)
Protein 1g Carb 30g Fiber 0.9g
Chol 0mg Iron 0.2mg
Sodium 10mg Calc 13mg

GRILLED JERK SHRIMP WITH CREAMY TOMATILLO SAUCE

Prep: 30 minutes
Chill: 1 hour
Grill: 4 minutes

1½ pounds unpeeled, large fresh shrimp
1 tablespoon jerk seasoning
1 (7-ounce) can tomatillo salsa
¼ cup reduced-fat mayonnaise
¼ cup reduced-fat sour cream
1 small jalapeño pepper, seeded and minced
¼ cup minced sweet onion
½ teaspoon ground cumin
Garnishes: fresh jalapeño pepper, fresh cilantro sprigs

• **Peel** shrimp; devein, if desired.
• **Place** shrimp in a heavy-duty zip-top plastic bag; add jerk seasoning. Seal and shake to coat. Chill 1 hour.
• **Thread** seasoned shrimp onto metal skewers.
• **Grill,** covered with grill lid, over medium-high heat (350° to 400°) 2 minutes on each side or just until shrimp turn pink.
• **Stir** together salsa and next 5 ingredients. Serve with shrimp. Garnish, if desired. **Yield:** 6 servings.

♥ Per serving: Calories 131 (36% from fat)
Fat 5.2g (sat 1g, mono 0.6g, poly 0.6g)
Protein 15.9g Carb 2.6g Fiber 0.2g
Chol 122mg Iron 2mg
Sodium 503mg Calc 53mg

POBLANO-AND-CORN QUESADILLAS

Serve with either Fiery Pickled Chiles Medley or Chunky Black-Eyed Pea Salsa.

Prep: 30 minutes
Cook: 24 minutes

3 cups fresh corn kernels *
3 poblano chile peppers
Vegetable cooking spray
3 tablespoons reduced-fat mayonnaise
2 tablespoons lime juice
½ teaspoon ground cumin
6 (8-inch) flour tortillas, halved
2 cups (8 ounces) shredded reduced-fat Monterey Jack cheese *

• **Broil** corn and peppers on an aluminum foil-lined baking sheet coated with cooking spray 5 inches from heat about 5 minutes on each side or until peppers look blistered. Set corn aside.
• **Place** peppers in a heavy-duty zip-top plastic bag; seal and let stand 10 minutes to loosen skins. Peel peppers; remove and discard seeds. Cut into thin strips.
• **Stir** together mayonnaise, lime juice, and cumin. Spread evenly over 1 side of each tortilla, and top evenly with corn, pepper strips, and cheese. Fold tortillas in half.
• **Cook** quesadillas, 1 at a time, in a large skillet coated with cooking spray over medium heat 30 seconds to 1 minute on each side or until browned. Cut each quesadilla in half. **Yield:** 12 servings.

*Substitute frozen whole kernel corn for fresh corn kernels, if desired. Substitute Asadero or Oaxaca cheese for Monterey Jack cheese, if desired.

❤ Per serving: Calories 149 (30% from fat)
Fat 4.9g (sat 2.1g, mono 0.1g, poly 0.2g)
Protein 8g Carb 20g Fiber 1.7g
Chol 14mg Iron 0.8mg
Sodium 312mg Calc 156mg

FIERY PICKLED CHILES MEDLEY

Prep: 45 minutes

2 pounds carrots, peeled
1 pound large sweet onions
1 pound jalapeño or serrano chile peppers
¼ pound cauliflower
2 garlic bulbs
1 cup vegetable oil
4 cups white vinegar
2 tablespoons salt
2 whole cloves
2 fresh thyme sprigs
½ cup water

• **Cut** carrots into thin slices; cut onions into eighths. Make a crosswise slit at the end of each pepper. Cut cauliflower into flowerets. Separate garlic bulbs into cloves.
• **Sauté** garlic in hot oil in a Dutch oven over medium-high heat 5 minutes or until golden. Add carrot, onion, peppers, and cauliflower; sauté 5 minutes.
• **Add** vinegar and remaining ingredients; bring to a boil, and cook 10 minutes or until vegetables are tender.
• **Pack** mixture into hot jars, and add liquid, filling to ½ inch from top. Remove air bubbles; wipe jar rims. Cover at once with metal lids, and screw on bands.
• **Process** in a boiling-water bath 10 minutes. Store in a cool, dark place up to 1 year. **Yield:** 8½ pints.

Note: After opening, store Fiery Pickled Chiles Medley in the refrigerator up to 3 months.

❤ Per ¼ cup: Calories 30 (51% from fat)
Fat 1.7g (sat 0.2g, mono 0.2g, poly 1.3g)
Protein 0.5g Carb 3.6g Fiber 0.7g
Chol 0mg Iron 0.2mg
Sodium 168mg Calc 10mg

CHUNKY BLACK-EYED PEA SALSA

Prep: 30 minutes

1 large poblano chile pepper
1 (15.8-ounce) can black-eyed peas, rinsed and drained
1 ripe mango, peeled and chopped (about ⅔ cup)
½ small sweet onion, chopped
½ small red bell pepper, chopped
¼ cup chopped fresh cilantro
½ teaspoon grated lime rind
3 tablespoons fresh lime juice
2 teaspoons olive oil
¼ to ½ teaspoon salt
¼ to ½ teaspoon ground pepper

• **Broil** poblano pepper on an aluminum foil-lined baking sheet 5 inches from heat about 5 minutes on each side or until pepper looks blistered.
• **Place** pepper in a heavy-duty zip-top plastic bag; seal and let stand 10 minutes to loosen skin. Peel pepper; remove and discard seeds. Chop pepper.
• **Stir** together pepper, peas, and remaining ingredients. Cover and chill. Serve with tortilla chips. **Yield:** 2 cups.

Sharon Bradberry
Tallahassee, Florida

❤ Per ¼ cup: Calories 70 (18% from fat)
Fat 1.4g (sat 0.2g, mono 0.9g, poly 0.2g)
Protein 3.5g Carb 12g Fiber 2g
Chol 0mg Iron 1.1mg
Sodium 244mg Calc 32mg

Quick & Easy

Whether you're entertaining at the lake, beach, park, or at home, you'll find this menu a savory success.

Family Picnic
Serves 10

Cajun Fried Chicken
Baked Beans
Creamy Potato Salad
Chewy Chocolate Cupcakes

CAJUN FRIED CHICKEN

Prep: 40 minutes
Cook: 36 minutes

3 (3-pound) whole chickens
3 tablespoons Cajun seasoning
1½ gallons peanut oil

• **Remove** giblets and necks, and rinse chickens with cold water. Drain cavities well; pat dry. Rub inside and outside of chickens with seasoning; set aside.
• **Pour** oil into a deep propane turkey fryer; heat to 350° according to manufacturer's instructions over medium-low flame. Place 1 chicken on fryer rod; carefully lower into hot oil. Fry 12 minutes or until a meat thermometer inserted into chicken breast registers 170°. (Keep oil temperature at 350°.)
• **Remove** from oil, and drain. Repeat procedure for 2 remaining chickens. Cool slightly before serving. **Yield:** 10 to 12 servings.

Note: To make ahead, fry chickens, and wrap in foil and then newspaper. Store in separate cooler from other cold items. For indoor preparation, fry chickens, 1 at a time, in 3 quarts oil in a Dutch oven.

BAKED BEANS

Prep: 15 minutes
Cook: 1 hour

3 bacon slices
1 small onion, finely chopped
3 (15-ounce) cans pork and beans
½ cup barbecue sauce
3 tablespoons brown sugar
2 tablespoons prepared mustard

• **Cook** bacon in a skillet until crisp; remove and drain on paper towels, reserving 2 tablespoons drippings in skillet. Crumble bacon; set aside.
• **Sauté** onion in hot drippings in skillet until tender. Stir together onion, beans, and next 3 ingredients in a lightly greased 2-quart baking dish. Sprinkle with bacon.
• **Bake** beans at 350° for 1 hour. **Yield:** 10 servings.

Note: To make ahead, bake beans without bacon the day before picnic, and store in zip-top plastic bags. Store cooked and crumbled bacon separately. Pour beans into microwave-safe dish or pan. Reheat in microwave or over propane cooker. Sprinkle with bacon.

CREAMY POTATO SALAD

Prep: 15 minutes
Cook: 30 minutes
Chill: 8 hours

4 pounds small red potatoes
1½ cups light mayonnaise
1½ cups light sour cream
1½ teaspoons prepared horseradish
1 teaspoon salt
½ teaspoon celery seeds
1 cup chopped fresh parsley
1 bunch green onions, finely chopped
4 bacon slices, cooked and crumbled (optional)

• **Cook** potatoes in boiling water to cover in a Dutch oven 30 minutes. Drain and cool. Thinly slice potatoes.
• **Stir** together mayonnaise and next 5 ingredients. Gently stir into potato.
• **Cover** and chill. Top with onions and, if desired, bacon. **Yield:** 10 servings.

CHEWY CHOCOLATE CUPCAKES

Prep: 15 minutes
Bake: 35 minutes

1 cup butter or margarine
4 (1-ounce) semisweet chocolate squares
1½ cups chopped pecans
1½ cups sugar
1 cup all-purpose flour
4 large eggs, lightly beaten
1 teaspoon vanilla extract

• **Melt** together butter and chocolate in a heavy saucepan over medium heat; stir in pecans. Remove from heat.
• **Combine** sugar and next 3 ingredients. (Do not beat.) Stir in chocolate mixture. Place baking cups in muffin pans; spoon batter into cups, filling three-fourths full.
• **Bake** at 325° for 35 minutes. (Do not overbake.) **Yield:** 16 cupcakes.

Note: To make ahead, prepare 1 or 2 days before; store in an airtight container.
Leigh Williams
Birmingham, Alabama

From Our Kitchen

Through the years our Foods staff has shared hundreds of kitchen tips and discoveries. This issue provides a perfect time to review some of our top tidbits for entertaining, cooking, food handling, and kitchen tips.

Entertaining

■ When you need a wonderful centerpiece for a dinner party, head to your grocer's produce section. Select colorful squash, baby pumpkins, shiny apples, or a citrus collection. Group them in assorted small baskets, or arrange them on a runner down the center of the table. When the party's over, use the centerpiece for next week's side dishes.

■ Forget ironing a tablecloth. Spread white butcher paper over the table, arm guests with crayons, and encourage them to doodle throughout the meal. For a reusable tablecloth, buy some cheap canvas fabric, and allow guests to autograph it with paint pens.

■ Use Oriental take-out cartons for eating in. (You can find a variety of colors and sizes at paper and party stores.) Bring individual servings in cartons to the table, and place them on charger plates.

■ For a hurry-up dessert, puree fresh berries or peaches in a blender with an equal amount of whipping cream or plain yogurt, and serve as a sauce over pound cake or ice cream.

■ The easiest recipes to double or triple are casseroles, sauces, cookies, muffins, soups, vegetables, and beverages. However, don't automatically double or triple the salt, pepper, herbs, and spices; taste and adjust seasonings carefully.

■ Ice will be clearer if you boil the water first, and then allow it to cool before you freeze it.

KITCHEN TIPS

■ For a tasty variation, cook rice in a flavorful liquid, such as chicken broth, beef broth, or fruit juice.

■ Keep finger sandwiches from drying out by placing them in a container lined with a damp towel and wax paper. Separate sandwich layers with wax paper, and cover with another layer of wax paper and a damp towel; refrigerate.

■ To loosen bacon slices before cooking them, roll the package of bacon into a tube before opening. This will relax the slices and keep them from sticking together.

■ If you accidentally grease more muffin cups than you need, fill the empty cups with water to keep the grease from baking on the cups.

■ To quickly separate eggs, break them into a small funnel. The whites will slip through, and the yolks won't.

■ When food boils over in the oven, sprinkle the burned surface with salt. This will stop smoke and odor from forming and make the spot easier to clean. Rubbing damp salt on dishes in which food has been baked will help remove brown spots.

Cooking

■ For savory pies and tarts, sprinkle Parmesan cheese or fresh cracked black pepper on your unbaked pastry. Lightly pass the rolling pin over it a few times. Place the pastry in a pieplate, and proceed as normal. This adds a subtle flavor surprise.

■ Lightly sprinkle beef and chicken strips with 1 or 2 tablespoons of cornstarch before stir-frying them. It helps the meat to brown beautifully and quickly. The velvety texture of the completed recipe is a bonus.

■ Cookie dough makes a great piecrust—and there's no rolling necessary. Simply press dough into pan, and refrigerate it before baking.

■ Potatoes that are cooked with the peel on and then cut hold their shape better and retain more nutrients than those that are peeled and cut before cooking.

■ Perk up the flavor of winter tomatoes with a sprinkle of fresh lemon juice, and serve them at room temperature.

■ Never add dry cornstarch to a hot mixture because it will become lumpy. Simply dilute the cornstarch in twice as much cold liquid, and stir until smooth. Then whisk gently into the hot mixture.

Food Handling

■ Keep disposable gloves in the kitchen to handle gooey meat loaf ingredients and cookie dough. When the deed is done, peel off the gloves into the garbage.

■ To perk up tired cauliflower and shriveled green beans, drop vegetables into a bowl of water with a few ice cubes. Thirty minutes will do the trick for most sliced or chopped produce, but overnight is best for sturdier broccoli and cauliflower.

■ When you need only a small amount of grated onion for a recipe, squeeze a piece of onion through a garlic press.

■ Don't throw away outdated yeast. It won't rise to lofty heights, but it will add flavor to pancake and waffle batter, muffin mixes, and biscuit dough.

■ Chop peppers, onions, and garlic, and freeze them separately in heavy-duty zip-top plastic bags or other small containers. They'll be ready to cook in any recipe.

■ Place peeled slices of fresh ginger in a jar, cover with a dry fortified wine such as sherry or Madeira, and refrigerate up to six months. Use this ginger-flavored wine in salad dressings or stir-fry recipes, and replace the used portion with additional wine to keep ginger immersed.

METRIC EQUIVALENTS

The recipes that appear in this cookbook use the standard United States method for measuring liquid and dry or solid ingredients (teaspoons, tablespoons, and cups). The information on this chart is provided to help cooks outside the U.S. successfully use these recipes. All equivalents are approximate.

METRIC EQUIVALENTS FOR DIFFERENT TYPES OF INGREDIENTS

A standard cup measure of a dry or solid ingredient will vary in weight depending on the type of ingredient. A standard cup of liquid is the same volume for any type of liquid. Use the following chart when converting standard cup measures to grams (weight) or milliliters (volume).

Standard Cup	Fine Powder	Grain	Granular	Liquid Solids	Liquid
	(ex. flour)	(ex. rice)	(ex. sugar)	(ex. butter)	(ex. milk)
1	140 g	150 g	190 g	200 g	240 ml
¾	105 g	113 g	143 g	150 g	180 ml
⅔	93 g	100 g	125 g	133 g	160 ml
½	70 g	75 g	95 g	100 g	120 ml
⅓	47 g	50 g	63 g	67 g	80 ml
¼	35 g	38 g	48 g	50 g	60 ml
⅛	18 g	19 g	24 g	25 g	30 ml

USEFUL EQUIVALENTS FOR DRY INGREDIENTS BY WEIGHT

(To convert ounces to grams, multiply the number of ounces by 30.)

1 oz	=	¹⁄₁₆ lb	=	30 g
4 oz	=	¼ lb	=	120 g
8 oz	=	½ lb	=	240 g
12 oz	=	¾ lb	=	360 g
16 oz	=	1 lb	=	480 g

USEFUL EQUIVALENTS FOR LENGTH

(To convert inches to centimeters, multiply the number of inches by 2.5.)

1 in				=	2.5 cm			
6 in	=	½ ft		=	15 cm			
12 in	=	1 ft		=	30 cm			
36 in	=	3 ft	=	1 yd	=	90 cm		
40 in				=	100 cm	=	1 m	

USEFUL EQUIVALENTS FOR LIQUID INGREDIENTS BY VOLUME

¼ tsp	=						1 ml
½ tsp	=						2 ml
1 tsp	=						5 ml
3 tsp	=	1 tbls		=	½ fl oz	=	15 ml
		2 tbls	=	⅛ cup	=	1 fl oz	=	30 ml
		4 tbls	=	¼ cup	=	2 fl oz	=	60 ml
		5⅓ tbls	=	⅓ cup	=	3 fl oz	=	80 ml
		8 tbls	=	½ cup	=	4 fl oz	=	120 ml
		10⅔ tbls	=	⅔ cup	=	5 fl oz	=	160 ml
		12 tbls	=	¾ cup	=	6 fl oz	=	180 ml
		16 tbls	=	1 cup	=	8 fl oz	=	240 ml
	1 pt	=	2 cups	=	16 fl oz	=	480 ml
	1 qt	=	4 cups	=	32 fl oz	=	960 ml
				33 fl oz	=	1000 ml	=	1 l

USEFUL EQUIVALENTS FOR COOKING/OVEN TEMPERATURES

	Fahrenheit	Celsius	Gas Mark
Freeze Water	32° F	0° C	
Room Temperature	68° F	20° C	
Boil Water	212° F	100° C	
Bake	325° F	160° C	3
	350° F	180° C	4
	375° F	190° C	5
	400° F	200° C	6
	425° F	220° C	7
	450° F	230° C	8
Broil			Grill

MENU INDEX

This index lists every menu by suggested occasion.
Recipes in bold type are provided with the menu.
Suggested accompaniments are in regular type. Top-rated
menus are accompanied by the symbol   (see page 13).

MENUS FOR SPECIAL OCCASIONS

Winter Brunch
Serves 10
page 42
Baked Ham With Bourbon Glaze
Almond-Citrus Salad
Sweet Potato Angel Biscuits

Spring Celebration
Serves 6 to 8
page 70
Tapenade
Fresh vegetables   Baguette slices
Lamb Chops With Mint Aioli
New Potato Gratin With Lima Beans and Egg
Steamed asparagus
Strawberry Tart

Mother's Day Menu
Serves 4
page 104
Citrus Salad With Sweet-and-Sour Dressing
Shrimp Enchiladas
Three-Ingredient Orange Sherbet

Salad Sampler
Serves 6
page 178
Chicken-and-Fruit Salad
Lemon-Basil Potato Salad
Warm Goat Cheese Salad
Breadsticks   Iced tea

Backyard Fiesta
Serves 8
page 186
Rio Grande Limeade
Roasted Poblano Chile Con Queso
Adobo Grilled Pork Tacos With Cucumber-Radish Salsa
Grilled Chicken Tortas   **Marinated Olives**
Margarita-Key Lime Pie With Gingersnap Crust

Spooktacular Halloween Party
Serves 8
page 204
Goblin Dip With Bone Crackers
Trash Mix   **Witches' Brew Chicken Soup**
Cheesy Witches' Brooms   **Candy Apples**

A Creole Menu
Serves 12
page 222
Roast Pork Loin
Rice Dressing
Green Beans With Ham and Potatoes
Stuffed Squash   Rolls
Old-Fashioned Bread Pudding
Iced tea   Coffee

A Southwestern Thanksgiving
Serves 10 to 12
page 232
Southwestern Cheese Appetizer   Assorted crackers
Smoked Pork
Southwestern Cornbread Dressing Cakes
Cranberry-Jalapeño Salsa
Roasted Sweet Potatoes and Onions
Bean Bundles   **Cheese Biscuits With Chipotle Butter**
Chocolate-Praline Cake   **Pineapple Limeade**

Menus for Special Occasions (continued)

Tradition With a Twist
Serves 6 to 8
page 236
Shanghai Spring Rolls With Sweet Chili Sauce
Roasted Pork
Chicken Vermicelli   Asian Green Beans
Caramel Custard

Southern-Style Christmas
Serves 4 to 6
page 248
Curried Butternut-Shrimp Bisque
Topless Oysters   Fresh Tomato Salsa
Roasted Quail With Cranberry-Orange-Pecan Stuffing
Hoppin' John Salad   Sweet Potato Biscuits
Ambrosia With Sprinkles   Key Lime Curd Tartlets

A Trim Thanksgiving Menu
Serves 10
page 254
Tomato-Basil Toasts*
Citrus-and-Herb Turkey   Cranberry Salsa*
Rosemary Roasted Root Vegetables*
Parmesan Corn Muffins
Cinnamon Swirl Cake

* Double recipes to serve 10.

Tex-Mex Holiday Gathering
Serves 4
page 272
Brisket
Salsa   Flour tortillas
Mexican Rice
Lynda's Mex-Tex Cornbread
Margaritas   Iced tea

Hanukkah Holiday Menu
Serves 6
page 274
Potato Blini With Sour Cream and Caviar
Caramelized Maple-and-Garlic-Glazed Salmon
Sweet Potato Latkes
Asparagus Sauté
Hanukkah Doughnuts With Strawberry Preserves

Christmas Dinner
Serves 8 to 10
page 276
Festive Pork Roast
Spinach Loaf With Mushroom Sauce
Roasted Glazed Vegetables
Green beans   Bakery rolls
Macadamia-Fudge Cake
Red wine   Iced tea   Coffee

All the Fixins' Brunch
page 288
Pineapple-Glazed Ham
Veggie Scramble   Whole-grain toast
Baked Cheese Grits   Champagne-Poached Pears
Green Onion-and-Cream Cheese Muffins
Fresh fruit such as grapes, strawberries, and kiwi (optional)

♥ Per person: 973 calories,
41g fat (38% calories from fat)

Continental Brunch
page 289
Veggie Scramble
Green Onion-and-Cream Cheese Muffins
Mixed Fruit Granola
Vanilla yogurt, fresh strawberries (optional)

♥ Per person: 639 calories,
26g fat (37% calories from fat)

Down-Home Breakfast
page 289
Pineapple-Glazed Ham
Baked Cheese Grits   Champagne-Poached Pears
Reduced-fat biscuits and jam (optional)

♥ Per person: 762 calories,
27g fat (32% calories from fat)

No-Fuss Cookout
Serves 6
page 331
Marinated Pork Loin
Corn on the Cob With Garlic-Chive Butter
Roasted Vegetable Medley

MENUS FOR THE FAMILY

Chinese Night
Serves 4
page 36
Shrimp Oriental   Lemon Rice Pilaf
Chinese Cabbage Slaw
Fortune cookies

Morning Menu
Serves 6
page 103
Cheesy Asparagus Pie
Easy Cheddar Biscuits or Blueberry muffins
Orange-Cranberry Cocktail

Casual Breakfast
Serves 6
page 130
Maple Coffee   Breakfast Casserole
Hot Tomato Grits   Grand Oranges
Blueberry-Streusel Muffins

Backyard Barbecue
Serves 6
page 147
Smoked Pork Shoulder
Cider Vinegar Barbecue Sauce   Peppery Vinegar Sauce
Brunswick Stew
Creamy Sweet Coleslaw
Hush Puppies

Picnic in the Park
Serves 8
page 163
Mom's Fried Chicken   Potato Salad
Broccoli-Grape Salad
Pink Lemonade

Grilling With Flair
Serves 6
page 195
Grilled Shrimp With Tropical Fruit Sauce
Crispy Asian Slaw
Grilled Pineapple With Vanilla-Cinnamon Ice Cream

Light Italian Fare
Serves 6 to 8
page 196
Cheesy Spinach Lasagna
Roasted Tomato-and-Pepper Salad
Parmesan Crisps
Two-Layered Ice-Cream Freeze

Family Favorites
Serves 4
page 212
Buttermilk Baked Chicken
Whipped Celery Potatoes
Apricot-Glazed Carrots   Steamed green beans
Applesauce Pie
Iced tea   Coffee

Holiday Family Reunion
Serves 6
page 246
Crispy Chicken
Wild Rice Salad   Mexican Cornbread
Chocolate cake   Iced tea

Make-Ahead Menu
Serves 6
page 259
Oven Barbecue Brisket
Hearty Baked Beans or **Simple Seasoned Potatoes**
Rainbow Slaw
Bakery brownies   Iced tea

Soup for Supper
Serves 6
page 290
Pot Liquor Soup   Skillet Cornbread
Shortbread cookies   **Praline Coffee**

Make-Ahead Lunch
Serves 4
page 299
Ham-and-Cheese Sandwiches
Deviled Eggs   Vegetable platter with dip
Cupcake Surprises

Picnic Extravaganza
Serves 4 to 6
page 321
Crostini With Walnut-Blue Cheese or
Tomato-Cheddar Spread   Chicken Poppers
Adobo Pork Sandwiches With Rosemary-Garlic Mayonnaise
Creamy Sweet Slaw
Buckeye Balls   Cranberry Tea Cooler

Family Picnic
Serves 10
page 334
Cajun Fried Chicken   Baked Beans
Creamy Potato Salad   Chewy Chocolate Cupcakes

WHEN COMPANY IS COMING

Top-Rated Menu
Serves 6
page 20
Baby Blue Salad
Beef Tenderloin With Henry Bain Sauce
Smoky Mashed Potato Bake
Tangy Green Beans With Pimiento
Homemade Butter Rolls
Pound cake with vanilla ice cream

Southern-Style Tapas Party
Serves 6 to 8
page 32
Black-Eyed Pea Cakes
White Bean Hummus   Crackers
Sliced cucumber   Olives
Dressed Mini Oyster Po'boys
Peppered Pork With Pecan Biscuits
Mexican beer

Spring Luncheon
Serves 8
page 72
Wild Rice-Chicken Salad
Cream of Pimiento Soup
Orange-Pecan Scones

Weekend Brunch
Serves 6
page 88
Quiche Lorraine
Spiced Mixed Fruit
Hot Cross Buns
Bellini

Garden Party
Serves 4
page 100
Garden Sangría
Basil-Cheese Torta   Toasted baguette slices
Garlic-and-Rosemary Shrimp

Supper With Style
Serves 6
page 110
Classic Trout Amandine
Grilled Asparagus Salad With Orange Vinaigrette
Steamed couscous   Bakery rolls
Rich Black-and-White Pudding

Dinner Party
Serves 6
page 144
Portobello Mushroom Burgers
Artichoke-Rice Salad
Chocolate Chubbies

Fresh Catch
Serves 6
page 157
Gazpacho
Grilled Snapper With Orange-Almond Sauce
Grilled Corn With Jalapeño-Lime Butter
Couscous With Peas and Feta   **Charred Tomato Salad**
Lemon icebox pie   White wine

Entertaining Menu
Serves 10
page 174
Fruit Spritzer
Fiery Salsa   Blue corn chips
Grilled Pork Tenderloins With Rosemary Pesto
Wild Rice-and-Kidney Bean Salad
Broccoli-and-Squash Casserole

Elegant Holiday Buffet
Serves 8 to 10
page 238
Curry-Almond Cheese Spread   Assorted crackers
Spicy Holiday Meatballs
Holiday Beef Tenderloin   **Escalloped Potatoes**
Artichoke-Stuffed Mushrooms
Asparagus Rollups   **Banana-Nut Bread**

Holiday Appetizer Buffet
Serves 12 to 15
page 241
Creole Roasted Pecans   **Spinach Quiches**
Rolled Olive Sandwiches
Pumpkin Pie Dip   Gingersnaps   Apple slices
Triple Chocolate Clusters   **Pecan Sticks**
Cranberry-Wine Punch

An Elegant Lowcountry Meal
Serves 8
page 326
Bourbon Sunrise
Shrimp Cakes With Watercress Rémoulade
Baked Garlic-and-Herb Grits   **Benne Veggies**

RECIPE TITLE INDEX

This index alphabetically lists every recipe by exact title.

All microwave recipe page numbers are preceded by an "M."

MONTH-BY-MONTH INDEX

This index alphabetically lists every food article and accompanying recipes by month. All microwave recipe page numbers are preceded by an "M."

December, *(continued)*

GENERAL RECIPE INDEX

This index lists every recipe by food category and/or major ingredient.

All microwave recipe page numbers are preceded by an "M."

Eggs *(continued)*

Deviled Eggs, 299
Scramble, Veggie, 288
ENCHILADAS
Enchiladas, Creamy Chicken, M94
Shrimp Enchiladas, 104

Fajitas

Tex-Mex Fajitas, 188
Turkey Fajitas, 108
FETTUCCINE
Chicken-and-Creamy Herb Sauce, Fettuccine
    With, 257
Shrimp-and-Creamy Herb Sauce, Fettuccine
    With, 257
Shrimp-Herb Fettuccine, 308
Spinach Alfredo Fettuccine, 164
FILLINGS
Savory
    Green Tomato Pie Filling, 141
Sweet
    Apricot Filling, 330
    Coffee Pastry Cream, 45
    Cranberry-Ambrosia Filling, 271
    Filling, 65
    Grand Marnier Pastry Cream, 45
    Peanut Butter Pastry Cream, 45
    Vanilla Pastry Cream, 45
FISH. *See also* **Clams, Crab, Crawfish,**
        Oysters, Salmon, Scallops, Seafood,
        Shrimp, Tuna.
    Baked Fish With Parmesan-Sour Cream
        Sauce, 209
    Catfish
        Fried Catfish, Classic, 135
        Oven-Baked Catfish With Tartar Sauce, 316
        Spicy Catfish, 209
    Redfish With Shrimp and Crab, Coastal
        Bend, 281
    Red Snapper With Lemon Sauce, 83
    Snapper With Orange-Almond Sauce,
        Grilled, 158
    Trout Amandine, Classic, 110
FRITTERS
    Apple Fritters With Lemon Sauce, 184
FROM OUR KITCHEN (FOK)
    Alcohol, substituting in recipes, 138
    Apples, storing, 202
    Asparagus, 118
        selecting, 118
        storing, 118
    Bacon, cooking, 335
    Beans, canned, 98
        baked, 166
    Beans, dried
        baked, 166
    Beef
        handling properly, 335
        stir-frying, 335
    Beverages
        ice cubes of tea and fruit juice, 260
        recipe, Chocolate Iced Coffee, 166
        recipe, Low-Fat Cappuccino Cooler, 166
    Blueberries
        freezing, 166
        storing, 166
    Breads
        refrigerated products, 202
        selecting fresh, 202
        serving warm, 260
    Cakes, storing, 300

Candies, using leftover in baking, 220
Casseroles, doubling, 335
Cauliflower, maintaining color of during
    cooking, 118
Celery, chopping, 202
Centerpieces, 335
Cheese
    browning, 50
    cooking with, 98
    melting, 50
    preshredded combinations, 138
    rinds of, 138
    waxed coverings of, 138
Chicken, preparing for stir frying, 335
Chocolate
    measuring, 118
    storing, 220
Coffee
    recipe, Chocolate Iced Coffee, 166
    recipe, Low-Fat Cappuccino Cooler, 166
Computer, index online, 300
Cookies
    storing, 300
    using dough as piecrust, 335
Cooking oils, 50, 118
    flavored, 50
Cooking torch, 50, 118
Cookware, selecting, 220
Cornstarch, adding to hot mixture, 335
Couscous, 50
Desserts
    glazing pastries, 50
    sauces, 335
Dressing/Stuffing
    preparing ahead, 260
Eggplant
    cooking, 166
    peeling, 166
    types of, 166
Eggs, separating, 335
Entertaining
    presenting food, 260
    table setting, 335
Fish
    buying, 220
    cooking, 220
    market forms of, 220
    storing, 220
Food processor, easy cleanup, 50
Freezer
    checking temperature of, 166
    cleaning out, 30
    foods that don't freeze well, 98
    foods that freeze well, 98
    storing nuts in, 50
Fruits, 30
    pureeing, 335
    storing, 98, 166, 300
Frying foods, 118
Garlic, freezing, 335
Gifts, nonfood, 300
Gingerroot, cooking with, 335
Grocery shopping
    making lists for, 98
    transporting cold and frozen items, 118
Grapefruit, 30
Handling food properly, 300
    transporting food, 220
Herbs
    as decoration, 118
    sage, 260
    substituting, 118

Holiday, hot lines, 300
Ice, freezing beverages as ice cubes, 260
Kitchen, gadgets, 50, 118, 138, 300
Knives, 260
Lamb
    buying, 98
    cooking, 98
    selecting, 98
    storing, 98
Leftovers
    freezing, 30
    of ham, 30
    storing, 30, 166
    of turkey, 30
Lemons, 98
Limes, 98
Measuring salt, 138
Meringue, browning, 50
Milk, as cooling agent to burning taste buds, 138
Mirlitons, 260
Muffin pans, greasing, 335
Mushrooms
    dried, 202
    preparing, 202
    storing, 202
    varieties of, 202
Nuts
    storing in freezer, 50
    toasting frozen, 50
Okra
    cooking, 166
    types of, 166
Olive oils, 50
Onions, grating, 335
Oranges, types of, 30
Ovens
    cleaning, 335
    checking oven temperature, 98
    racks, cleaning, 260
Pan sizes, 98
Peanut butter, storing, 202
Peas, black-eyed
    recipe, Marinated Black-Eyed Peas, 30
    recipe, Pickled Black-Eyed Peas, 30
Peppers
    cooking stuffed, 118
    dried chiles, 202
    handling hot peppers, 202
    selecting, 202
    types of, 166, 202
Piecrust
    flavor variations of, 335
    using cookie dough as, 335
Potatoes, preparing, 335
Pumpkins as a side dish, 220
Recipe preparation, 98
    cleaning up, 50, 166, 300
    doubling recipes, 335
    equipment, 260
    meal plans for recipes on pages 52-56, 67
    mistakes in, 50
    trying new recipes, 202
    utensils, 98
Recipes, enlarging copies of, 260
Refrigerator, 98
    checking temperature of, 166
    cleaning, 166
Rhubarb, freezing, 118
Rice
    cooking, 335
    flavoring, 335
    types of, 220

Grilled *(continued)*

Poultry
Chicken-and-Fruit Salad, 178
Chicken With Basting Sauce, Grilled, 146
Chicken With Creamy Sauce, Grilled, 318
Chicken With Grilled Green Onions, 94
Chicken With White Barbecue Sauce, 168
Clubs, Grilled Chicken-and-Pesto, 22
Tortas, Grilled Chicken, M187
Sauce, Peach Rib, 248
Vegetables
Asparagus Salad With Orange Vinaigrette, Grilled, 110
Corn on the Cob With Garlic-Chive Butter, 331
Corn, Smoked, 169
Corn With Jalapeño-Lime Butter, Grilled, 158
Kabobs, Vegetable, 132
Poblano Chile con Queso, Roasted, 186
Portobello Mushroom Burgers, 144
Salad, Avocado-Corn-Poblano, 320
Salad, Grilled Marinated Vegetable, 143
Sandwiches, Grilled Vegetable, 310
Sandwiches, Open-Faced Summer, 171
GRITS
Cheese
Baked Cheese Grits, 289
Chili-Cheese Grits, 86
Garlic-and-Herb Grits, Baked, 326
Jalapeño-Cheese Grits, 328
Squares, Chili-Cheese Grits, 86
Shrimp and Grits, 258
Tomato Grits, Hot, 131
GUMBOS. *See also* Chowders, Jambalaya, Soups, Stews.
Chicken-and-Sausage Gumbo, 324
Gumbo, 160
Mix, Okra Gumbo Freezer, 165
Okra Gumbo, 165

HAM. *See also* **Pork.**
Baked Ham With Bourbon Glaze, M42
Casseroles
Bacon-and-Ham Casserole, Cheesy, 256
Breakfast Casserole, Sausage-Ham, 54
Creamy Ham Casseroles, 55
Swiss Casserole, Savory Ham-and-, 308
Country Ham Hot-Water Cornbread, 29
Glazed
Baked Glazed Ham, 52
Pineapple-Glazed Ham, 288
Praline-Mustard Glazed Ham, 306
Green Beans With Ham and Potatoes, 223
Rollups, Asparagus, 239
Sandwiches
Asparagus Sandwiches, Ham-and-, 307
Cheese Sandwiches, Ham-and-, 299
Club Sandwich, Italian, 22
Monte Cristo Sandwiches, Open-Faced, 171
Panhandle Sandwiches, 56
Rollup, Hot Ham-and-Cheese, 217
Swiss-and-Asparagus Sandwiches, Ham-, 52
Wraps, Club, 23
HOMINY
Olé, Hominy, 17
HONEY
Dressing, Honey-Mustard, 230
Pork Chops, Honey-Pecan, 82
Pork Tenderloin, Honey-Garlic, 16

Pork Tenderloins, Honey-Garlic, 318
Turkey Salad, Honey-Mustard, 230
HUSH PUPPIES
Hush Puppies, 148, 325
Squash Puppies, 179

ICE CREAMS. *See also* **Sherbets.**
Beverages
Cappuccino Cooler, Low-Fat, 166
Mocha Melt, Spiced, 240
Pineapple-Buttermilk Shake, 173
Pineapple-Buttermilk Shake, Light, 173
Punch, Creamy Nog, 240
Strawberry-Banana Shake, Double, 173
Ice, Lemon, 330
Layered Ice-Cream Freeze, Two-, 197
Sundae, Ice Cream, 64
Vanilla-Cinnamon Ice Cream, 195

JAMBALAYA
Chicken-and-Sausage Jambalaya, 278
JAM AND MARMALADE
Green Tomato-Blueberry Jam, 140
Green Tomato Marmalade, 140
JÍCAMA
Salad, Pear, Jícama, and Snow Pea, 329
Salad With Jícama and Snow Peas, Pear, 56

KABOBS
Shrimp With Creamy Tomatillo Sauce, Grilled Jerk, 332
Vegetable Kabobs, 132

LAMB
Chops With Mint Aioli, Lamb, 70
Chops With Southwestern Butter, Broiled Lamb, 194
Leg of Lamb, Roast, 159
LASAGNA
Mexican Lasagna, 282
Vegetable
Avocado-Vegetable Lasagna, 310
Cheese-Vegetable Lasagna, Saucy, 306
Spinach Lasagna, Cheesy, 196
LEEKS
Soup, Cream of Mushroom-and-Leek, 312
LEMON
Beverages
Lemonade, Homemade, 143
Lemonade, Loaded, 93
Lemonade, Pink, 163
Desserts
Bars, Luscious Lemon, 161
Cake, Lemon Geranium Pound, 131
Cake, Lemon Sour Cream Pound, 117
Cookies, Lemon-Basil Butter, 117
Cookies, Lemon Butter, 90
Cupcakes, Lemon-Blueberry Ice-Cream, 172
Glaze, Lemon, 117
Ice, Lemon, 330
Pie, Lemon-Lime Chess, 23
Sauce, Blueberry-Lemon, 117
Sauce, Lemon, 184
Tart, Tangy Lemon, 245
Green Beans, Lemon-Dill, 181
Rice Pilaf, Lemon, 36
Salad, Lemon-Basil Potato, 178

Sauce, Potatoes and Green Beans With Lemon Dill-, 89
Sauce, Red Snapper With Lemon, 83
Spread, Lemon-Raisin, 48
Vinaigrette, Peppery Lemon, 122
LENTILS
Bean Pot Lentils, 35
LIME
Beverages
Limeade, 143
Limeade, Pineapple, 235
Limeade, Rio Grande, 186
Refresher, Cantaloupe-Lime, 332
Swamp Breeze, 146
Butter, Cilantro-Lime, 24
Butter, Grilled Corn With Jalapeño-Lime, 158
Chicken, Limeade, 257
Desserts
Pie, Lemon-Lime Chess, 23
Pie With Gingersnap Crust, Margarita-Key Lime, 187
Tartlets, Key Lime Curd, 250
Dressing, Lime-Peanut, 26
Vinaigrette, Spicy Lime, 217
LINGUINE
Baked Linguine With Meat Sauce, 41
Chicken Linguine, 128
LIVING LIGHT
Appetizers
Chiles Medley, Fiery Pickled, 333
Crab Ball, Spicy, 332
Dip, Apple-Berry, 109
Dip, Creamy Beef-and-Pasta Sauce, 108
Dip, Peanut Butter, 109
Dips, Fun Fruit, 109
Dip, Strawberry, 109
Nuts, Mexico, 27
Quesadillas, Poblano-and-Corn, 333
Salsa, Chunky Black-Eyed Pea, 333
Salsa With Cinnamon Crisps, Fruit, 108
Shrimp With Creamy Tomatillo Sauce, Grilled Jerk, 332
Breads
Muffins, Green Onion-and-Cream Cheese, 289
Muffins, Parmesan Corn, 255
Toasts, Tomato-Basil, 254
Crisps, Parmesan, 197
Desserts
Cake, Blue Ribbon Angel Food, 35
Cake, Cinnamon Swirl, 255
Cake, Lightened Hummingbird, 34
Cookies, Vanilla Meringue, 197
Frosting, Cream Cheese, 34
Ice-Cream Freeze, Two-Layered, 197
Salsa With Cinnamon Crisps, Fruit, 108
Drink, Yummy Breakfast, 133
Granola, Mixed Fruit, 290
Grits, Baked Cheese, 289
Lentils, Bean Pot, 35
Main Dishes
Chicken, Almond, 26
Fajitas, Turkey, 108
Ham, Pineapple-Glazed, 288
Lasagna, Cheesy Spinach, 196
Meat Loaf, Summer, 162
Pork, Cajun Pecan, 27
Pork Chops, An Apple-a-Day, 35
Scallops, Grilled Sweet-and-Sour, 92
Scramble, Veggie, 288
Stir-Fry, Curried Beef, 162
Tacos, Jerk Steak, 170

Chicken-and-Fruit Salad, 178
Goat Cheese Salad, Warm, 179
Potato Salad, Lemon-Basil, 178
Slaw, Crispy Asian, 195
Vinaigrette, Balsamic, 20
Vinaigrette, Orange-Raspberry, 178
Vinaigrette, Sesame, 195
Wild Rice-Chicken Salad, 72
Soup, Cream of Pimiento, 72
Vegetables
Carrots, Apricot-Glazed, 212
Green Beans With Pimiento, Tangy, 21
Potato Bake, Smoky Mashed, 21
Potatoes, Whipped Celery, 212
TORTILLAS. *See also* **Burritos, Enchiladas,
Fajitas, Quesadillas.**
Chimichangas, Bean-and-Cheese, 16
Crackers, Bone, 204
Crisps, Fruit Salsa With Cinnamon, 108
Philly Firecrackers, 142
Rollups, Parmesan-Turkey-Ranch, 177
Rollups, Southwestern, 135
Rollup, Veggie, 109
Tostadas, Chickpea-Chipotle, 54
Wraps, Chicken-Cranberry, 34
Wraps, Club, 23
Wraps, Smoked Turkey, 61
TUNA
Pita, Tuna-Veggie Stuffed, 216
Salad, White Bean-and-Tuna, 35
Seared Tuna With Olive-Rosemary Pesto, 317
TURKEY
Baked Turkey Tenders, 81
Citrus-and-Herb Turkey, 254
Cutlets, Parmesan Turkey, 81
Dijon With Garden Vegetables, Turkey, 102
Fajitas, Turkey, 108
Mignons, Sesame-Crusted Turkey, 81
Pie, Turkey-Sausage, 297
Salad, Honey-Mustard Turkey, 230
Salad, Old-Fashioned Layered, 96
Sandwiches
Clubs, Cobb, 22
Monte Cristo Sandwiches, Open-Faced, 171
Pineapple-Turkey Sandwich, 85
Rollups, Parmesan-Turkey-Ranch, 177
Wraps, Club, 23
Wraps, Smoked Turkey, 61
Sautéed Turkey Tenders, 81
Smoked Turkey Breast, 129
TURNIPS
Greens With Turnips, Turnip, 211

Vanilla
Cakes, Spring's Little, M91
Cookies, Vanilla Meringue, 197
Éclairs, Vanilla Cream-Filled, 45
Ice Cream, Vanilla-Cinnamon, 195
Pastry Cream, Vanilla, 45
S'mores, Indoor, 33
Torte, Chocolate-Vanilla Holiday, 252
VEGETABLES. *See also* specific types.
Appetizers
Caviar, Texas, 160, 257
Egg Rolls, Tex-Mex, 328
Rollup, Veggie, 109
Beef and Vegetables, 86
Benne Veggies, 327
Black-Eyed Peas, Marinated, 30
Bratwurst, Grilled, 159
Bread Bowl, Veggie, 132

Casseroles
Lasagna, Avocado-Vegetable, 310
Lasagna, Saucy Cheese-Vegetable, 306
Rotini, Baked, 185
Chicken, Beer-Smothered, 107
Clubs, Cobb, 22
Cobbler, Autumn Vegetable, 215
Fajitas, Tex-Mex, 188
Greens, Super-Charged, 211
Kabobs, Vegetable, 132
Mac-and-Cheese, Veggie, 111
Meat Loaf, Summer, 162
Pasta Italiano, 41
Pork Tenderloin With Vegetables, 122
Rice Jardin, 106
Roasted Glazed Vegetables, 277
Roasted Root Vegetables, Rosemary, 255
Roasted Vegetable Medley, 298, 331
Salads
Coleslaw With Garden Vegetables, 57
Grilled Marinated Vegetable Salad, 143
Hoppin' John Salad, 250
Layered Vegetable Salad With Parmesan
Dressing, 96
Marinated Veggies, 127
Radish-Vegetable Salad With Parmesan
Dressing, 101
Slaw, Rainbow, 259
Salsa With Citrus Dressing, Black Bean, 60
Sandwiches, Grilled Vegetable, 310
Sandwiches, Open-Faced Summer, 171
Sausage Supper, 28
Scramble, Veggie, 288
Soups
Chowder, Cheesy Vegetable, 18
Gazpacho, 157
Lemongrass-and-Petits Pois Soup, 328
Pot Liquor Soup, 290
Spanish Fiesta Soup, 66
Watercress Soup, 176
Stew, Brunswick, 148, 219
Stir-Fry, Chicken-Vegetable, 175
Stir-Fry, Shrimp, 258
Stuffing, Vegetable, 84
Tacos, Skillet Veggie, 170
Turkey Dijon With Garden Vegetables, 102

Waffles
Corn Waffles, 24
Waffles, 24
WALNUTS
Bread, Banana-Nut, 239
Cheese, Crostini With Walnut-Blue, 321
Chocolate Chubbies, 144
Date Moons, 295
Eggplant With Walnuts, Georgian, 87
Sauce, Walnut Cream, 229
Toffee, 218
WHAT'S FOR SUPPER?
Beans, Hearty Baked, 259
Grits, Chili-Cheese, 86
Grits Squares, Chili-Cheese, 86
Lemonade, Pink, 163
Mac-and-Cheese, Veggie, 111
Main Dishes
Beef and Vegetables, 86
Beef Patties, Marmalade-Glazed, 136
Brisket, Oven Barbecue, 259
Chicken, Cashew, 188
Chicken, Mom's Fried, 163
Chicken Oriental, 36

Fajitas, Tex-Mex, 188
Kielbasa With Beans, Easy Cheesy, 28
Meatballs, Marmalade-Glazed, 136
Meat Loaf, Sweet 'n' Saucy, 210
Noodles, Sesame, 188
Pie, Beef-and-Onion Cornbread, 298
Pie, Italian Meat, 297
Pie, Turkey-Sausage, 297
Pizza, Deep-Dish, 29
Pork Loin, Marinated, 331
Roast Beef, Mary's, 86
Roast Beef, Pressure Cooker, 86
Roast Beef, Slow Cooker, 86
Sausage and Cabbage, Skillet, 28
Sausage Supper, 28
Shrimp Oriental, 36
Rice Pilaf, Lemon, 36
Salads and Salad Dressings
Broccoli-Grape Salad, 163
Potato Salad, 163
Slaw, Chinese Cabbage, 36
Slaw, Rainbow, 259
Sandwiches
Beef Sandwiches, Barbecue, 136
Burgers, Garden Herb, 136
Crab Melts, Open-Faced, 171
Meat Loaf Sandwich, 210
Monte Cristo Sandwiches, Open-Faced, 171
Summer Sandwiches, Open-Faced, 171
Sauce, Morton's Special, 331
Sauce, Sweet 'n' Saucy, 210
Topping, Cornbread, 298
Vegetables
Corn on the Cob With Garlic-Chive
Butter, 331
Eggplant Italian Style, 111
Green Beans, Garlic, 111
Potatoes, Simple Seasoned, 259
Roasted Vegetable Medley, 331
WOK COOKING
Beef, Mongolian, 94
Beef Stir-Fry, Curried, 162
Chicken
Cashew Chicken, 188
Oriental, Chicken, 36
Vegetable Stir-Fry, Chicken-, 175
Pork and Cashews, Stir-Fry, 16
Shrimp Oriental, 36
Shrimp, Stir-Fry, 95
WONTONS
Sesame Wontons, Spicy Crab-and-Ginger Salsa
With, 283
Taco Teasers, 134

Yogurt
Malt, Chocolate-Yogurt, 173
Sauce, London Broil Sandwiches With Yogurt-
Cucumber, 162
Shake, Light Double Strawberry-Banana, 173
Shake, Three-Fruit Yogurt, 173

Zucchini
Muffins, Carrot-Zucchini, 200
Skillet, Zucchini-and-Corn, 137